$ /5 \frac{00}{c}

Tapestry of Terror

Tapestry of Terror

A Portrait of Middle East Terrorism, 1994–1999

Richard J. Chasdi

LEXINGTON BOOKS
Lanham • Boulder • New York • Oxford

LEXINGTON BOOKS

Published in the United States of America
by Lexington Books
An Imprint of the Rowman & Littlefield Publishing Group
4720 Boston Way, Lanham, Maryland 20706

PO Box 317
Oxford
OX2 9RU, UK

British Library Cataloguing in Publication Information Available

Library of Congress Cataloging-in-Publication Data

Chasdi, Richard J., 1958–
    Tapestry of terror : a portrait of Middle East terrorism, 1994–1999 / Richard J. Chasdi.
        p. cm.
    Includes bibliographical references and index.
    ISBN 0-7391-0354-7 (cloth : alk. paper) — ISBN 0-7391-0355-5 (pbk. : alk. paper)
        1. Terrorism—Middle East. I. Title.

HV6433.M5 C534 2002
303.6'25'095609049—dc21

                                                                2002066052

Printed in the United States of America

♾™ The paper used in this publication meets the minimum requirements of American
National Standard for Information Sciences—Permanence of Paper for Printed Library
Materials, ANSI/NISO Z39.48–1992.

For Sharon M. Applebaum and Neal A. Tolchin

Contents

Figures

Tables

Acknowledgments

First and foremost, I am indebted to my mentor, Professor Michael S. Stohl of Purdue University, who continues to teach me about the phenomenon of terrorism and provide me with his invaluable insight about political violence studies. I am also indebted to Professors Louis Rene Beres, James McCann, Robert Melson, Keith L. Shimko, and Michael Weinstein, all of the Department of Political Science at Purdue University. I am also deeply indebted to Professor Frederic S. Pearson, Director of the Center for Peace and Conflict Studies at Wayne State University, for his steadfast support, his insight into Middle East political affairs and political violence, and his helpful suggestions about the project. I am also very grateful to Professor John M. Strate of the Department of Political Science at Wayne State University for his help with the quantitative analysis, and Professor David Fasenfest, Director of the Center for Urban Studies at Wayne State University, for his kind support for this project. I am also very grateful for the exceptional diligence and expertise of Penelope Morris for layout, typesetting, and copy editing assistance, and to Della L. Barr for her excellent work on graphics. Special thanks is extended to Abdulahi Osman and Joseph Tenkorang of the Department of Political Science at Wayne State University for the several hours each devoted to the coder reliability testing process and to Jaclyn Cruz, Gary Gaub, and Carolyn Kapustij for proofreading. At a personal level, I would like to thank my uncle, Professor Richard A. Fey of the College of Staten Island-City University of New York, Herb, Kenneth, my mother, Professor Eleanor Hollenberg Chasdi of Wheelock College, and my brother David for their support. Also, I want to thank Reed and Frieda, John Franklin and Carolyn Keane, and Sam and Esther Tolchin for helping me to develop the skills and outlook I would need for the future. As always, I thank Sharon and Brendan Guy for helping me in all ways.

Foreword

The dramatic events of September 11, 2001, when the World Trade Center in New York City and the Pentagon in Washington, DC, were simultaneously attacked, had two different, but related, effects. First, it changed dramatically the international political system, ushering what Richard Chasdi calls "a ghost war world," an international environment that might be characterized by stealthy terrorist attacks, rather than by conventional frontal assaults. Al Queda has given would-be terrorists, as well as the intelligence services of all target states, a "clinic" on how to carry out a complex, large-scale terrorist strike in an almost pervasively efficient manner.

But "September 11"—possibly a new concept in contemporary international relations—did not only change our world but also the way in which we are likely to go about studying it. The Chasdi book is important in presenting a model for how such thinking can be done by posing for our consideration some of the most significant questions that we may want to focus on and by offering a systematic way of dealing with these questions.

It is reasonable and prudent to assume that future terrorist acts, including nonconventional assaults with chemical, biological, and even nuclear devices, will emanate from the most unstable regions of all, the Middle East. Therefore, Chasdi's focus on this particular area is so significant. His qualitative analysis and systematic effort to quantify the terrorist phenomenon is highly useful.

Richard Chasdi has already established himself as an important scholar in the field of international terrorism when he published his previous book, *Serenade of Suffering: A Portrait of Middle East Terrorism, 1968–1993* (1999). The current volume will enhance not only his reputation as an insightful scholar in the field but, more importantly, our knowledge of this increasingly important phenomenon.

ILAN PELEG, Charles A. Dana Professor
Department of Government and Law
Lafayette College
Easton, PA 18042-1780
February 7, 2002

Preface

From the Post Cold War World to the Ghost War World

As this book goes to press, the United States ruling elite is laying the ground-work for a set of stratagems to confront the perpetrators of the World Trade Center and Pentagon terrorist assaults of September 11, 2001. This set of terrorist assaults is so significant for the continuously evolving environment and structural shape of today's system of international politics that increased devotion to possible broader ramifications of those terrorist assaults, by means of this preface, informs us of possible change in world politics to come. It is probably no exaggeration to say that the terrorist assaults against the World Trade Center and the Pentagon carried out on September 11, 2001 marks a structural shift in our way of thinking about contemporary American national security interests. Seen from the vantage of a political scientist, what seems significant here is a set of challenges and opportunities for the United States, the hegemonic political power of our contemporary international political system, with the emergent reality of new alliances between state actors and between state and sub-national actors in a continuously evolving environment.

In the case of the former, the Russian Federation and the United States have national interests that closely parallel one another insofar as Islamic revivalist extremism is perceived to be inextricably bound up with the resistance in Chechnya and political instability and social unrest in areas of the "near abroad" such as in Tashkent, Uzbekistan. In the case of the latter, there seems to be a fledgling partnership between the Bush administration and the "Northern Alliance" with Burhanuddin Rabbani and General Muhammad Fahim at the helm. The "Northern Alliance" or United Front is a multi-group resistance movement in fierce competition with the Taliban over the political landscape of Afghanistan. Somewhat ironically, a set of interconnections between the Putin regime and the "Northern Alliance," that is comprised of many Afghani "mujahdeen" or "holy warriors" who once fought against the Soviets, is also evident within the context of the pursuit of Shaykh Osama bin Laden and his al-Qaida terrorist organization.[1]

In a broader sense, and seen from a slightly different angle, the terrorist assaults in Manhattan, New York, and Washington, D.C., showcase a broader array of challenges and opportunities that revolve around the central theme of more work on a task that both Henry Kissinger and Seyom Brown have described, namely the conceptualization of post Cold War national interests that are articulated more clearly with more meaningful interconnections between national interests and American foreign policy.[2] To be sure, the September 11 terrorist assaults underscore the mustiness of Cold War thinking about national security which is reified all too clearly in the so-called "Missile Defense Shield" program that was to be the gatekeeper of national security for the George W. Bush, Secretary of Defense Donald H. Rumsfeld, and Deputy Secretary of Defense Paul D. Wolfowitz crowd prior to the horrific events of September 11, 2001.

In my judgment, we have passed from the post-cold war world into an era of the "ghost war world" where interstate conflict continues to wane in favor of a "ghost war world" where perpetrators of terrorist assaults, like ghosts, coalesce to carry out a terrorist assault or set of terrorist assaults and then scatter, thereby in effect helping to blur the lines of accountability for terrorists and for nation-states that may support them. Seen from the vantage of terrorism and counterterrorism studies, while a significant terrorist assault against the United States was not an especially new or probing notion, the *modus operandi* and the level of planning and coordination demonstrated to execute a nearly simultaneous set of terrorist assaults against two or more targets was unexpected and seems to be unprecedented. While what Nef would call "insurgent" terrorist assaults with more than one target and with substantial geographical distance to separate venues are known to have happened, the degree of difficulty with respect to carrying out this set of terrorist assaults and, regrettably, the enormous loss of life, rate of injury, and level of property damage seems, at least to me, completely new.[3]

To be sure, all of the foregoing begs the question of why "higher order" terrorism, namely, chemical, biological, or nuclear terrorism was not used, assuming that such weapons could be acquired if not produced outright. As two of my colleagues at The College of Wooster repeatedly pointed out to me over lunch, the 5,500 persons presumed dead in the New York City terrorist assaults alone could easily be associated with the detonation of a low-yield nuclear device or the release of toxins into the environment. While the reasons why conventional terrorist assaults were used on September 11, 2001, remain shrouded in mystery, one interpretation of events suggests that the use of significant "higher order" terrorist assaults, like the prospect of the U.S. military making use of the "neutron bomb" in the European theater a generation ago, may cross a "nuclear threshold" thereby in effect helping to blur distinctions between conventional and non-conventional responses.

Equally important, those terrorist weapons of mass destruction may be held by terrorist chieftains in reserve, if they are available, as a type of "secondary strike capability force" (SSCF) for cities and other population centers, to control for targets and somehow partially offset the magnitude of counter-terrorist strikes when those strikes happen. To be sure, all of the aforementioned reflects the importance of analysts to attempt to wed strategic doctrine and terrorism in a new incarnation, this time with much less state centric emphasis to reflect the importance of non-state actors and, by extrapolation, state actors that use them in this new "ghost war world."

Unequivocally, perhaps the single most fundamental question distills down to how antecedent political and social conditions, with the potential to generate and sustain such terrorist assaults, seemingly did not deserve increased devotion from U.S. national security decision-makers in the larger world of action. This monograph demonstrates that it is possible to isolate and identify antecedent political and social conditions, and structural processes in particular political social systems that, in my judgment, are critical long haul and middle run factors with an enormous capacity to generate and sustain enormous pressures for political violence in general and terrorism in particular.

For example, this work highlights a broad array of terrorist groups in Turkey that seek to find a new niche in the post-Cold War world and which resonate with the enormous anger felt among some in Turkey that is directed at the Turkish ruling elite, "Turkish conglomerates" and the West with special focus on the United States. This work also highlights the problems in Egypt where hard-line counterterrorism policy, almost always a frequent visitor to the Middle East, has for one thing enforced the closure of "Islamic" banking and other religious social institutions thereby in effect helping to choke off relief from pressure that presupposes and derives from the growth in the "Islamization" of Egyptian society over the past few decades.

Compounding the matter even more, the significant reduction of Egyptian Islamic revivalist extremist terrorist assaults against the Mubarak regime in the late 1990's that is showcased in this work, coupled with long standing and widely recognized ties between al-Jihad's Dr. Ayman al-Zawahari and Shaykh Osama bin Laden ought to have become a significant part of the public discourse about American national security.[4] In a similar vein, the arrest of Ahmed Ressam in 1999 at the Canadian-American border ought to have signaled a condition fraught with peril for the United States insofar as there had been, as this work underscores, no terrorist assaults carried out by the Armed Islamic Group (GIA) of Algeria against American targets in the United States and only one chronicled incident against an American target in Algeria between 1994-1999. The fact that Ahmed Ressam had a set of interconnections to the GIA should have signaled American policy makers about a possible shift in strategy that may have revolved around the central idea of a broader dimension to a struggle that was largely confined to Algerian and French interests, thereby in effect helping to stimulate greater public discourse about a lurking national security problem.

Clearly, while the prediction of specific terrorist assaults is not possible, a closer, more carefully reasoned interpretation of antecedent events and conditions in specific nation-states, coupled with long range thinking about unresolved economic and political matters associated with "North-South relations" might work to alleviate pressures for structural political and economic change that have made violent action against the United States an emergent reality. In that context, this work on Middle East terrorism uses quantitative and qualitative analysis that, in my judgment, provides insight into the factors that help to generate and sustain Middle East terrorism at the "systems level," as well as the state, and sub-national actor levels, thereby in effect helping to give counterterrorism planners and policymakers more data to help shape the political and social discourse about counterterrorism plans for the future.

RICHARD J. CHASDI, PH.D.
The College of Wooster, Wooster, Ohio
October 3, 2001

Notes

1. Rohde 2001, B1, B2; Wines 2001a, A-1, B-2; Wines 2001b, section 4, 1, 2; Cooley 2000, 127, 144-149; Silke, 2001.
2. Kissinger 1999, 41-43; Brown 1994, 6-7.
3. Nef 1978, 19-20.
4. Jehl 2001, B-3.

Chapter One

Introduction

The analysis of political terrorism is one of the last frontiers of political violence that remains largely untouched by empirical investigation. This is a study of four systems of Middle East terrorism from 1994 through 1999 that is the second in a series of works that informs us about the dynamics of Middle East terrorism. My first book, *Serenade of Suffering: A Portrait of Middle East Terrorism, 1968-1993* lays the keel for this study of more contemporary Middle East terrorism set against the backdrop of the Israeli-Palestinian-Arab "peace process" and the continuously evolving post-Cold War environment.

The four Middle East terrorism systems under investigation in *Tapestry of Terror* include Algerian, Egyptian, Turkish, and "Israeli-Palestinian-Arab" terrorism. The analysis of those four Middle East terrorism systems is twofold. First, this analysis provides an empirical investigation of the targeting behavior of different types of Middle East terrorist groups in context specific settings. Those terrorism systems are chosen to study because Israeli-Palestinian-Arab and Turkish terrorism involve an array of different types of terrorist groups to analyze, while Egyptian terrorism and Algerian terrorism remain pronounced and dynamic Middle East terrorism systems in the Maghrib, namely the northern African area of the Middle East, with an enormous capacity to destabilize nation-state regimes with critical interconnections to parts of Europe and the United States. At a functional level, the inclusion of two Middle East terrorism systems from the Mashriq, namely the eastern part of the Middle East, and two from the Maghrib makes it possible to compare and contrast certain terrorist assault "attributes" and patterns of terrorist group and nongroup category behavior by region.[1]

Second, this work involves a qualitative analysis of what both Lasswell and Im, Cauley, and Sandler might call the terrorist group "maturity cycle."[2] To be more specific, there is increased devotion to the growth, maturity, and in many instances the "splintering" of terrorist groups and the formation of terrorist group "spin-offs" against the backdrop of the continuously evolving political and economic environment. In my first book, I introduced players and basic formative factors and dynamics essential to understanding the sources and origins of several Middle East terrorist groups. I do the same for terrorist groups not given treatment in my first work, and, for the remainder, expand on those basic discussions and interpretations.

From the start, what makes this analysis possible is the recognition and acceptance of the "rationality assumption" in decision making among terrorist group chieftains and tacticians insofar as without that, work that attempts to isolate and identify regular patterns of terrorist targeting behavior would be meaningless. The "rationality assumption" in decision making for terrorist group chieftains and tacticians has increasingly become generally recognizable in works about terrorism that eschew the notion of any particular "terrorism personality" or "terrorism mindset" that distinguishes the terrorist from rational decision makers. Authorities on terrorism who embrace the rationality of decision making assumption include, but are not limited to, Nef (1978), Crenshaw-Hutchinson (1972), Oots (1989), and Drake (1998).[3] For Nef, "unfortunate as it may seem from a moral viewpoint, terrorism turns out to be quite a 'rational' technique, if by rational, we assume an instrumental relationship between ends and means."[4]

Perhaps the single, most dominant theme of this study is the need to provide counterterrorism analysts with meaningful empirical data about what Middle East terrorism in those terrorist systems is all about. Hence, efforts are made to make a strong set of interconnections between national political initiatives and counterterrorism measures to terrorist assaults and the effects those events and dynamics might have on terrorism assaults. At first blush, I hope to be able to shed light on counterterrorism action time framing, with a special focus on picking from an array of counterterrorism instrument-types to use under certain select conditions.

The Threat of Terrorism

The single most fundamental question concerns why the empirical study of terrorism is so important in the first place. In the broadest sense, in the wake of the Cold War, empirical study of terrorism is increasingly important at several levels of analysis. First, with the demise of the Cold War, the use of terrorism will become, in my judgment, an increasingly important mode of political expression for nonstate actors as "a weapon of the weak," to use Crozier's term.[5] All too frequently, those terrorist organizations are supported by nation-state leaders who use terrorist groups to promote national interest in ways that blur lines of accountability and reduce the risk of punishment or capture for those ruling elites.[6]

At one level, terrorism is an instrument that often hinges on protracted communal conflict that happens within nation-states. What seems significant here is that Lederach reports the overall amount of war has not diminished or grown apace with the end of the Cold War.[7] For Lederach, "most current wars are intrastate affairs. The primary issues of contention concern governance and often involve the pursuit of autonomy or self-government for certain regions or groups."[8] In a similar vein, President William Jefferson Clinton framed the challenges and opportunities posed for the West at a New York UN summit in 2000. For Clinton, "these conflicts present us with a stark challenge . . . are they part of the scourge the UN was established to prevent? If so, we must respect sovereignty and territorial integrity, but still find a way to protect people as well as borders."[9]

Interestingly enough, the potential use of terrorism as an instrument of conflict can be expected within political contexts at either end of the socio-economic development spectrum. With respect to states starting along the road of socioeconomic development, disparities in modernization between articulated ethnic groups, and even the processes of socioeconomic development itself, have the enormous capacity to awaken or raise the political consciousness of segments of the populace, thereby in effect leading to political demands and aspirations that, if not met in some way by government, may result in violence and/or terrorism.[10] At the other extreme, there is the lurking prospect of terrorism in highly industrialized, primarily Western, countries over political issues where antigovernment protestors might use terrorist assaults to publicize political grievances. In my judgment, violent protest activities directed against the World Trade Organization (WTO) in Seattle, Washington, in 1999 and meetings in Quebec at the Summit of the Americas in April 2001 show a potential for terrorist assault activity in the future.

To be sure, the threat of Middle East terrorism to the United States and U.S. interests remains of particular concern to counterterrorism specialists. In the wake of the bombings in Nairobi, Kenya, and Dar es Salaam, Tanzania, in August 1998, Shaykh Osama bin Laden, the founder and leader of the al-Qaida organization, otherwise known as "the Base," remains "public enemy number one" on the Federal Bureau of Investigation's (FBI) "Most Wanted List." Somewhat ironically, bin Laden's military prowess presupposes and derives from U.S. support for Afghani resistance fighters against the forces of the former Soviet Union.[11]

It is commonplace to note a number of uncompleted terrorist assaults that may be linked to Shaykh Osama bin Laden. In December 1999, Ahmed Ressam, an Algerian with some interconnections to the Algerian-based Armed Islamic Group (GIA), was arrested on the Canadian-American border with bomb components in his car. During that same period, an Algerian with interconnections to the GIA and an arms-running operation, and his Canadian female companion were arrested at the Canadian-American border in Vermont.[12] Also, around 16 December 1999, eleven persons with suspected ties to bin Laden were arrested in Jordan for planning terrorist assaults.[13]

At the same time, the threat of Middle East terrorism is not by any means relegated only to the United States or Israel. It is commonplace to note accounts of Algerian terrorist groups like the GIA and other Islamic revivalist terrorist groups with infrastructure in countries like France, Switzerland, England, Spain, and Sweden. Clearly, terrorism perpetrated by some Kurdish groups or "proto-groups" and presumably by "lone operatives" has thrived in effective and sustained ways in Germany. One scripted account describes a report by the German intelligence organization BND that asserts the threat of "fundamentalist terrorism" in Germany and Europe will grow apace with the passage of time, first with relatively straightforward terrorist assaults against "soft" targets, perhaps followed with terrorist assaults by helicopters and non-manned flying platforms and with "higher order" nonconventional weapons. The German report, portions of which are found in *Welt am Sonntag*, goes on to report that American, Israeli, and European targets in Europe are faced with that looming catastrophe in that order.[14]

Undoubtedly, the darkest foreboding of all is the prospect of nonconventional "higher order" terrorism that includes chemical, biological, and nuclear weapons. At a functional level, the post-Cold War world system has an enormous capacity to influence the proliferation of biological, chemical, and nuclear components insofar as former Soviet technology and persons with skills in crafting or culling out weapons from available materials are "for sale" in the clandestine international marketplace.[15] Compounding the matter even further is the prospect of second- to third-party arms component or complete "arms transfers" to parties with interconnections to terrorist groups, or even to terrorist groups themselves.

One set of events seemingly fraught with danger is the decision by President Vladimir V. Putin and other Kremlin leaders to restart conventional arms sales to Iran within the context of Iranian efforts, supported by the Russians, to build a nuclear reactor presumably with a capacity to produce nuclear materials with military applications.[16] Still another problem revolves around a U.S. budget decline in support for Russian nuclear security.[17] In part, what seems significant here is the emphasis that Bush administration "hard-liners" like Vice President Richard B. Cheney and Secretary of Defense Donald H. Rumsfeld have placed on a "national missile defense" system that has fundamental problems that revolve around threat appraisal.

First, at a functional level, even if a "national missile defense system" is feasible from a technological perspective—and many, if not all, argue it is not—such a system seems completely inflexible and ineffective with respect to protection against other delivery systems, including persons armed with chemical, biological, or even nuclear devices. Second, seen from a political vantage, plans to forge a missile defense shield serve to destabilize further relations between the United States and Russia and between the United States and China, thereby in effect helping to reduce incentives for cooperation with the U.S. government in areas that include nuclear weapons proliferation and the curtailment of nuclear component availability.[18]

With respect to "higher order terrorism," namely chemical, biological, or nuclear terrorism, I make the argument in my prior work that the use of "higher order" terrorist assaults revolves around the central idea of terrorist group "purpose," the locale under consideration, and the continuously evolving international political landscape.[19] I suggest the level of threat is not evenly distributed, insofar as terrorist groups constrained by geographical site demographics or the desire for political accommodation with government over autonomy or independence outright would find the use of "higher order" terrorist assaults counterproductive. Conversely, the use of "higher order" terrorist assaults by "nihilistic or anarchistic" terrorist groups may be higher, even though the capacities of such groups to act using "higher order terrorism" may be lower.[20]

What seems significant here from the standpoint of this research on contemporary Middle East terrorism is strong evidence that at least one non-conventional "higher order" terrorist assault was committed in the United States between 1994 and 1999. In April 1997 an anonymous package was opened in the Washington, D.C., headquarters of the Jewish national organization B'nai B'rith and the chemical or biological material inside described as "red liquid" caused fifteen or more persons to require hospitalization.[21] While it is critical to recognize that "higher order" terrorist assaults are not necessarily more "spectacular" with respect to physical devastation rates than conventional terrorism, the use of a "higher order" weapon is significant and always "spectacular" in the sense that, like the neutron bomb, its use may cross a threshold, be it chemical, biological, or nuclear in nature, where perceptions of threat are altered and where there are ineluctable effects for the future direction of terrorist assault stratagems.[22] It remains to be seen whether or not that "higher order" anonymous terrorist assault against a Jewish-American facility in Washington, D.C. proves to be a harbinger of events to come.

International Law and Politics and a Definition of Terrorism

Perhaps the single most predominant theme about the relationship between international law and politics is captured by Professor Beres's notion that law follows politics, or to put it another way, that law is subordinate to geopolitical considerations.[23] The following discussion about international law and politics assumes the reader has an understanding of basic international law, and if that is not the case, the reader might review that brief portion of *Serenade of Suffering* that covers international law for background.[24]

In the world of praxis, the notion that law follows politics has profound and lasting effects on whether or not international law is upheld. First, as a result of that condition where geopolitical considerations predominate over international law, "self-help" measures taken by the leaders of nation-states may be law enforcing rather than law violating activity. For instance, the actions of Israel's Mossad agents in Argentina in 1960, that resulted in the trial of Adolf Eichmann in Israel for his involvement in planning the murder of six million Jews, can be thought of as law enforcing or lawmaking actions rather than law violating actions since the long-standing and time-honored principle of *aut dedere aut judicare* (extradite or prosecute) was not invoked by the Argentine government.[25]

Second, the actions of both subnational actors and national actors are often made opaque by proximate political needs within the context of structural political change. For example, as Beres tells us, the enormous capacity of nation-states to compromise international law in favor of political gain is underscored by the unwillingness of world political leaders to make Chairman Yasser Arafat accountable for his egregious Palestine Liberation Organization (PLO) crimes, like the massacre of Israeli athletes at the Munich Olympic Games in 1972 and the Ma'alot massacre of children in 1974.[26]

For Beres, efforts by nation-state leaders to work with Arafat, rather than to detain him, violate the Roman principle of *nullum crimen sine poena* or "no crime without a punishment" that ought to be upheld as a general principle of international law.[27] By the same token, political acquiescence to the contemporary political roles of former Israeli Prime Minister Yitzhak Shamir and Israeli Prime Minister Ariel Sharon has eclipsed Shamir's probable role in the 1948 assassination of UN negotiator Count Folke Bernadotte, and Sharon's pivotal role in the Qibya massacre in Jordan in 1953 and his role in the Sabra and Shatilla massacre in 1982, to promote geopolitical interests at the expense of international law.[28]

One fundamental question really boils down to why international law is important to consider in the first place when thinking about violent struggle that can be construed as terrorism. In part, the answer revolves around juris-prudential distinctions made between "justifiable insurgency" and terrorism. Those distinctions between "justifiable insurgency" and terrorism are important because members of a justifiable insurgency are afforded the protection of the laws of war codified by the Geneva Conventions of 1949 and Protocols I and II of 1977 that include prisoner of war (POW) status.[29] Seen from the vantage of politics, legitimacy for a violent struggle and its leaders is acquired through justifiable insurgency status that is critical in the pursuit of political goals. At the same time, political legitimacy can translate into political and economic benefits provided by nation-states that may include military assistance.

How are those jurisprudential distinctions made? As Beres suggests, those distinctions are made by an evaluation of an act of violence according to the juridical principles of *jus ad bello* (justice of war),[30] *jus in bello* (justice in war),[31] and the post-Nuremberg conception of the human rights regime.[32] With respect to *jus ad bello* (justice of war) we are told that the use of force is upheld under international law in four instances: in post-attack situations; for preemptive attacks; in humanitarian intervention efforts to protect nations or the nationals of another country from egregious violations of the human rights regime; to enforce collective security agreements.[33]

With respect to *jus in bello* (justice in war), we are told that three standards must be upheld to qualify for insurgency status: the norms of military discrimination, military necessity and proportionality. First, it is imperative that an insurgency abide by the norm of discrimination, namely that an insurgency distinguish between combatants and noncombatants as it operates, with the singular purpose of keeping non-combatants safe.[34] Second, military necessity has been described by Detter De Lupis as a rather hazy concept for shortening conflict, but in the broader sense, one that requires those who seek insurgent status to make a compelling case that the use of force is necessary after all peaceful avenues for political resolution have been exhausted without success.[35] Third, force used against an opponent must be proportional to the amount of force used against the group and as Beres tells us, the use of force must also be commensurate or proportional to the political goals pursued over the political landscape.[36]

If, for example, the Weatherman or some other "splinter group" of Students for Democratic Society (SDS) during the 1960's in the United States released chemical or biological toxins into the air at a Department of Defense facility to protest against the Vietnam War, that assault would be construed as terrorism insofar as the instrument used would exceed the force necessary to make political change and the amount of force used by the U.S. government against the group.[37] In sum, as Beres tells us, each and every act of violence is really judged twice—once from the vantage of *jus ad bello* (justice of war) and once from the vantage of *jus in bello* (justice in war).[38]

It is probably no exaggeration to say that Palestinian leaders could make a case that violent struggle against the Israeli government, such as the Intifadeh of 1987, met the criteria of *jus ad bello* (justice of war) before the "peace process" between Israelis and Palestinians began in earnest in 1991. Even though some, but certainly not all extrapolate, as Detter De Lupis reports, that those "laws of war" may apply to nonstate actors such as "nations" like the Kurds, for instance, she suggests that a more solid approach would be to invoke Chapter I Article 2 of the Charter of the United Nations and self-determination as a *jus cogens* norm. Where the Palestinian struggle failed to uphold international law, and thereby in effect relegated itself to the sphere of a terrorist movement, concerned the principle of *jus in bello* (justice in war) precisely because of the reason that the Palestine Liberation Organization (PLO) and other groups carried out terrorist attacks against civilian targets. The Kurdistan Workers' Party (PKK) is an example of another organization that might make the case for insurgency based on justice of war principles, while in effect relegating itself to the status of a terrorist group because it commits military actions against civilians and civilian targets.[39]

Bearing in mind the juridical principle of *jus ad bello*, Arafat's rejection of former Israeli Prime Minister Barak's set of concessions at Camp David have, in essence, undercut severely the notion that systemic violence perpetrated by Palestinians is justifiable under international law. That reality provides the Israelis with an opportunity to craft persuasive arguments in the court of public opinion about the "war of attrition" that Israel faces, and the tenor of actions taken or endorsed by the Palestinian National Authority (PNA).

It is commonplace to note in the literature on terrorism that, all too frequently, definitions of terrorism abound that are crafted with geopolitical considerations in mind. Illustrative of the problem is that Schmid "listed 109 different definitions of terrorism provided between 1936-1981 and there have been more since; the U.S. government alone has provided more than half a dozen, which are by no means identical."[40] In some instances, what qualifies or does not qualify as terrorism may differ within the context of the politics of conflict.[41] For example, the U.S. Department of State publication *1995 Patterns of Global Terrorism* does not list the Islamic Salvation Front (FIS) as a terrorist organization even though, as Martinez relates, acts of terrorism attributable to FIS are commonplace to note.[42]

Precisely because of that reason, a meticulous, comprehensive, widely recognized, and widely accepted definition of terrorism that is global in nature remains elusive.[43] Aside from UN resolutions such as United Nations General Assembly Resolution no. 538, that are not lawmaking, what is construed to be terrorism must be extrapolated from a cluster of nonconventional sources that are articulated in Article 38 of the Statute of the International Court of Justice, and from treaty law (i.e., conventions) that covers particular crimes, thereby in effect helping to confront terrorism in an indirect fashion.[44]

For example, several types of violent assaults, such as hostage taking, skyjacking, and sabotage, all commonly construed as terrorism, are prohibited under treaty law. Those treaties include, but are not limited to, the Convention on Offenses and Certain Other Acts Committed on Board Aircraft,[45] the Convention for the Suppression of Unlawful Seizure of Aircraft,[46] the Convention for the Suppression of Unlawful Acts Against the Safety of Civil Aviation,[47] and the International Convention Against the Taking of Hostages.[48]

Faced with the challenges and opportunities of the foregoing, a definition of terrorism in large part based on international law is used in this study as an operational definition to determine whether or not incidents commonly construed as terrorism, and by contrast, incidents construed as common criminal activity ought to be included in the data set. In my prior work, there is a more extensive discussion about the juridical concepts of *jus ad bello* (justice of war) and *jus in bello* (justice in war) that includes the principles of proportionality,[49] military necessity, and military discrimination.[50] The juridical touchstones of *jus ad bello* and *jus in bello* serve as cornerstones of that definition of terrorism, and the reader is advised to refer to that portion of *Serenade of Suffering* and my article "Terrorism: Stratagems for Remediation from an International Law Point of View" for additional discussion.[51] The conceptual definition of terrorism used here is the same as that used in my first book, and defines political terrorism as:

> the threat, practice, or promotion of force for political objectives by organizations or a person(s) whose actions are designed to influence the political attitudes or policy dispositions of a third party, provided that the threat, practice, or promotion of force is directed against (1) non-combatants; (2) military personnel in noncombatant or peacekeeping roles: (3) combatants, if the aforementioned violates juridical principles of proportionality, military necessity, and discrimination; or (4) regimes which have not committed egregious violations of the human rights regime that approach Nuremberg category crimes. Moreover, the act itself elicits a set of images that serve to denigrate the target population while strengthening the individual or group simultaneously.[52]

Qualitative Analysis

As in the case of my prior work, I use the Reiss and Roth "risk factor matrix" which those authors develop for understanding violent behavior in the domestic realm, and apply that scheme to Middle East terrorism. I use that "risk factor matrix" to evaluate the formative processes of terrorist groups, and terrorist "splinter" or "spin-off" groups and the maturation process of those groups against the backdrop of political and social events that help to give shape to the particular "Middle East terrorism system" under consideration (see figure 1.1).

Reiss and Roth skillfully break down causal factors along vertical and horizontal planes. The authors conceive a horizontal band of "risk factors" that include "predisposing," "situational," and "activating" factors.[53] In turn, Reiss and Roth cluster risk factor variables in groups of "social" and "individual" factors that are divided vertically into "macrosocial" and "microsocial" factors at the "social" level of analysis, and "individual" and "biological" factors at the "psychosocial" level of analysis. The presentation of factors in horizontal terms permits the analyst to isolate and identify political events according to longitudinal emphasis. A presentation of "risk factors" from the top of the schema downwards allows the analysis to posit watershed events in ever-narrower groups that consist of segments of society, smaller groups of persons, and individuals. The scheme makes it possible to place emphasis on "feedback loops" between levels of analysis and interconnections between levels or "cells" of analysis that proves to be extremely fruitful.[54]

An example that draws on an example in Reiss and Roth's work is illustrative of how a "feedback loop" works.[55] Imagine a situation where a young Palestinian mother living in an economic backwater condition in the Occupied Territories has precious little in the way of access to first-rate prenatal care and services. Reiss and Roth seem to suggest a "feedback loop" pathway to a "macrosocial" level of analysis insofar as if that mother were to have a difficult or problematic pregnancy and that child is damaged as a result of the delivery, that child as a young adult may have problems at the "psychosocial" or "individual" level of analysis or at both levels, thereby in effect helping to make that person very dangerous in a broader protracted conflict between ethnic groups.[56]

In a similar vein, Reiss and Roth point to interconnections between different matrix "cells" whereby factors at the "individual" level of analysis, such as "cognitive ability" problems, work in tandem with what the authors label "accumulated emotion," "alcohol" use, or use of other drugs to become a tinderbox for a broad array of "activating factors." Those "activating factors" can be as relatively straightforward as "opportunity recognition," such as a situation where two Israeli hikers are alone and isolated, or the highly publicized event where two Israeli military reservists took a wrong turn in Gaza and a crowd of Palestinians literally tore them to pieces before one of the terrorists spoke with the wife of Israeli army reservist Yossi Avrahami on his cell phone to tell her, "I just killed your husband."[57]

In a broader sense, the Reiss and Roth analysis is useful because it showcases how watershed political initiatives or events can have profound and lasting effects on terrorist group formation or the terrorist "splintering" or

Figure 1.1: Reiss and Roth's Risk Factors Matrix

Matrix for Organizing Risk Factors for Violent Behavior

Units of Observation and Explanation	Proximity to Violent Events and Their Consequences		
	Predisposing	Situational	Activating
Social macrosocial	Concentration of poverty Opportunity structures Decline of social capital Oppositional cultures Sex-role socialization	Physical structure Routine activities Access: weapons, emergency	Catalytic social event Medical services
Microsocial	Community organizations Illegal markets Gangs Family disorganization Preexisting structures	Proximity of responsible monitors Participants' social relationships Bystanders' activities Temporary communication impairments Weapons: carrying, displaying	Participants' communication exchange
Individual psychosocial	Temperament Learned social responses Perceptions of rewards/ Penalties for violence Violent deviant sexual preferences Cognitive ability Social, communication ability Self-identification in social hierarchy	Accumulated emotion Alcohol/drug consumption Sexual arousal Premeditation	Impulse Opportunity recognition
Biological	Neurobiologic[a] "traits" Genetically mediated traits Chronic use of psychoactive substances or exposure to neurotoxins	Transient neurobiologic "states" Acute effects of psychoactive substances	Sensory signal-processing errors Interictal events

[a]Includes neuroanatomical, neurophysiological, neurochemical, and neuroendocrine. "Traits" describes capacity as determined by status at birth, trauma, and aging processes such as puberty. "States" describes temporary conditions associated with emotions, external stressors, etc. Source: Albert J. Reiss, Jr., and Jeffrey A. Roth, *Understanding and Preventing Violence* National Academy Press (Washington, D.C., 1993.) Reprinted with the kind permission of the publisher.

"spin-off" process. This analysis will explore the tremendous effect potential of such events in the broader sense, and will describe and discuss particular events that include, but are not limited to, the Iranian revolution of 1979, the abrupt halt to the December 1991 national elections in Algeria, and Israeli Prime Minister Rabin's decision to ban outright the Kach and Kahane Chai parties. In addition, the analysis will highlight how the very personal experiences of future terrorists and their family members help to give structural shape to their way of thinking about struggle. In that context, the analysis will describe the experiences of the Islambouli brothers in Egypt, the Hattab brothers in Algeria, and Abduallah Öcalan in Turkey.

For readers with less interest in quantitative analysis, I hope that applications of the Reiss and Roth "risk factor matrix" to terrorism, political events linked to terrorism, and the fledgling development of terrorist groups provide excitement and insight about the sources and origins of terrorist groups and how those terrorist groups evolve. With that in mind, this analysis now turns to a review of quantitative approaches that I have taken to delve into the phenomenon of Middle East terrorism even further.

Continuity and Change: The Terrorist Group-Type Typology

In my prior work, a three-dimensional terrorist group-type typology has been crafted that presupposes and derives from three distinguishing character-istics that delineate types of terrorist groups Those distinguishing characteristics are political ideology, goals, and recruitment. That three-dimensional typology, which draws from Starr and Most's work on Third World conflicts, has three planes, and each plane encompasses one of the foregoing distinguishing charac-teristics (see figure 1.2).[58]

Along one axis is the distinguishing characteristic "goals" that comprises the first dimension, and along the second axis is the distinguishing characteristic of "recruitment" that comprises the second dimension. In turn, "political ideology" is found along the third axis, which comprises the third dimension of that typology. In terms of ideological distinctions, Middle East terrorist groups are broken down into nationalist-irredentist groups or "ethnocentric" groups, Islamic fundamentalist terrorist groups or "theocentric" groups that include Sunni (i.e., Egyptian) and Shi'ite organizations, nationalist-irredentist terrorist groups with Marxist-Leninist trappings, or "ideo-ethnocentric" groups, and Jewish fundamentalist terrorist groups, or "Jewish theocentric" groups. Precisely because of the reason there are four goal-types, three types of recruits, and three political ideology types, the structure of the typology is a 4x3x3 cube from which thirty-six combinations of terrorist group-types are possible. Those goal-types are themselves differentiated from tactical alternatives employed by terrorist groups.

Figure 1.2: A Three-Dimensional Typology Cube of Middle East Terrorist Group-Types

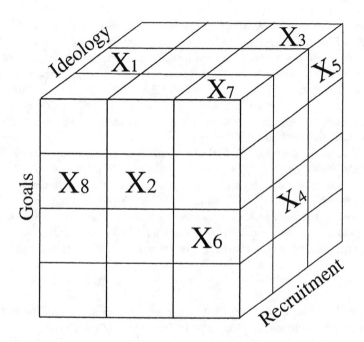

X₁ = Theocentric
X₂ = Theocentric charismatic
X₃ = Ethnocentric
X₄ = Ethnocentric charismatic
X₅ = Ideo-ethnocentric
X₆ = Ideo-ethnocentric charismatic
X₇ = Jewish theocentric
X₈ = Jewish theocentric charismatic

Source: Richard J. Chasdi.
"The Dynamics of Middle East Terrorism, 1968-1993:
A Functional Typology of Terrorist Group-Types"
(Ph.D. diss., Purdue University, 1995)

Eight terrorist group-types that are found in the larger world of action are derived from that typology, and each terrorist group-type is distinguished from one another based on political ideology, goals, and recruitment patterns. In terms of recruitment patterns, a distinction is made between terrorist groups led by charismatic leaders and terrorist groups led by noncharismatic leaders. In this study, this distinction between charismatic leaders and noncharismatic leaders is based on authoritative writings on charismatic leadership, authoritative works on Middle East terrorism, and on wide-ranging empirical observation of Middle East terrorist groups. In the broader sense, Middle East terrorist groups led by charismatic leaders include, but are not limited to, Dr. George Habash's Popular Front for the Liberation of Palestine (PFLP), Naif Hawatmah's Democratic Front for the Liberation of Palestine (DFLP), the Abu Nidal Organization of Sabri-Al-Banna, Rabbi Meir Kahane's Kach party, and the Kurdistan Workers Party (PKK) led by Abdullah Öcalan.[59]

In this book, the analysis format of Middle East terrorism is modified to isolate and identify particular types of Middle East "terrorism systems" that in this case include Algerian terrorism, Egyptian terrorism, Turkish terrorism, and "Israeli-Palestinian-Arab" terrorism. With that broader scope of empirical investigation, it becomes necessary to make certain modifications to the existing typology to account for broader variations found in the empirical data for some of the basic distinguishing characteristic descriptives, like "recruitment." In a similar vein, the term "nationalist" is broadened in this study to include the notions of "defense of the people" and/or "anti-establishment protest."[60]

To be more specific, in the case of the distinguishing characteristic "recruitment," two of the three following subcategories are modified. As the typology characteristics are articulated in *Serenade of Suffering,* "1 = clan; 2 = followers of a charismatic leader; 3 = Palestinian refugees." In the case of the first subcategory, "clan," a modification is made so that the subcategory reads "clan and/or disenfranchised," to take into account Algerian disenfranchised and other disenfranchised persons in other political systems who are not clan members. In the case of the third subcategory, "Palestinian refugees," it is adjusted slightly to read "Palestinians, Palestinian refugees, and/or disenfranchised Palestinians," to mirror the emergent reality of wealthy Palestinians who live in the Palestinian diaspora, and disenfranchised Palestinians in the Algerian, Turkish, and Egyptian political landscapes who are on the margins of society. With those modifications made, the typology has the capacity to capture dynamics of Middle East terrorism that emanates from various parts of the Middle East.[61]

Summary

In this chapter, an operational definition of terrorism and the basic constructs that underlie this study are reviewed. An operational definition of terrorism that presupposes and derives from international law is described and presented. Aside from the capacity of that operational definition of terrorism to move over and beyond politically generated definitions of terrorism that are all too frequently crafted with geopolitical considerations in mind, that operational definition is used to isolate and identify acts of violence, whether described as "terrorism" or "criminal activity" by others that ought to be included or excluded from the data bases crafted on Middle East terrorism used in this work.

The two basic constructs that serve as guideposts for this work include, first, a functional three-dimensional terrorist group typology that makes it possible to develop terrorist group-types based on three distinguishing characteristics.[62] In turn, those terrorist group-type categories make it possible to sort out types of terrorist groups and to run statistical tests to discern regular patterns of terrorist group targeting practices. The second construct that is used for qualitative analysis is an application of Reiss and Roth's "risk factor matrix" that makes it possible to explore terrorist group formation and growth, and to search for regular patterns that are associated with the growth and maturity of terrorist groups in different parts of the Middle East.

Having described the fundamental framework of this study in chapter 1, the study will now delve into modifications in format of analysis in more detail, the theory about "nonstructuralist" and "structuralist" Middle East terrorist groups that drives this study, data gathering and data methodology, and some newer theoretical work that describes terrorist group targeting behavior. It is to those areas that this analysis of Middle East terrorism now turns in chapter 2.

Notes

Material on terrorism and international law reprinted with the kind permission from *Shofar: An Interdisciplinary Journal of Jewish Studies,* volume 12, number 4 (pages 59-86) by permission of the University of Nebraska Press. Albert J. Reiss and Jeffrey A. Roth's "Risk Factor Matrix" reprinted with the kind permission of National Academy Press from their work, *Understanding and Preventing Violence.* Concepts about my Middle East terrorist group type typology and group type delineations first appeared in *The Journal of Conflict Studies,* Vol. XVII, No. 2, Fall 1997, 73-114, and permission is kindly extended for reuse in *Tapestry of Terror.*

1. Hourani 1991, xix. For Hourani, "the word 'Maghrib' is probably familiar enough to be used rather than 'North-west Africa' but 'Mashriq' is not so I have used 'Middle East' instead."

2. Lasswell 1935; Lasswell 1950; Lasswell 1978; Im, Cauley, and Sandler 1987; Ross and Miller 1997, 99.

3. Nef 1978, 19-20; Crenshaw-Hutchinson 1972; Oots 1989, 149-150; Drake 1998, 83, 15; Bremer 1988, 2; Chasdi 1999, 4, 16 n16, n17, 40, 61 n116, 67-68, 80 n20, 137, 197 n1, n2; Chasdi 1997, 73, 107 n1, n2; Chasdi 1995, 119-120.

4. Nef 1978, 19-20.

5. Crozier 1960, 158; Chasdi 1999 20, 43 n6.

6. Oots 1989, 146-147; Jenkins 1998, 241; Ranstorp 1997.

7. Lederach 1997, 7-8.

8. Lederach 1997, 7-8.

9. Sanger 2000, A-1.

10. Huntington 1968; Nordlinger 1968.

11. Kushner 1998, 12-13.

12. Burns and Pyes 1999, A-16.

13. Labaton 1999, A-30.

14. al-Khatib, *FBIS* 1999.

15. Jenkins 1998, 234-236, 238; Beres 1998; Williams 1995, as found in Kash 1998, 166.

16. Perlez 2001, A-15.

17. United States Congress, Freedom for Russia and Emerging Eurasian Democracies and Open Markets Support Act (P.L. 102-511.) *Office of Audits Memorandum Report 98-CG-014 Survey of US Information Agency, Freedom Support Act Funding To The New Independent States, June 1998;* "Freedom Support Act of 1992 Fact Sheet." At a functional level, "section III" informs us "the act promotes nuclear safety and demilitarization to prevent nuclear accidents and the spread of nuclear weapons. The bill would broaden the allowable use of $500 million appropriated for DOD last fall and provide authority to support defense conversion, non-proliferation efforts, nuclear weapons dismantlement, addressing the 'brain drain' problem, the relocation of former Soviet military forces, and nuclear plant-safety."

18. Seen from a jurisprudential vantage, the nullification of the ABM treaty (1972) in light of new technological developments might be viewed within the context of the principle of *"rebus sic stantibus"* or "a fundamental change of circumstances," insofar as Professor Lissitzyn tells us that "the doctrine of *rebus sic stantibus* has been regarded by some writers as justifying the repudiation of excessively burdensome treaty obligations. Indeed, it may be urged [sic] that the goal of stability and peace in the international community would be furthered rather than frustrated by the development of legal devises for putting an end to treaty obligations and other relationships which, first come to be resented as intolerably burdensome and which, second, the community is no longer strongly interested in protecting" (Lissitzyn, "Stability and Change: Unilateral Denunciation or Suspension of Treaties by Reason of Changed Circumstances," 61 Proceed. A.S.I.L. 186, 187, 189 [1967] as found in Weston, Falk, and D'Amato 1980, 141, 214).

Equally important, the foregoing argument to abolish the Treaty between the United States of America and the Union of Soviet Socialist Republics on the Limitation of Anti-Ballistic Missile Systems (23 U.S.T. 3435, T.I.A.S. no. 7503, reprinted in 11 I.L.M. 784 [1972] may be more than partially offset by an argument based on the principle *pacta sunt servanda* that conventions must remain in force between contracting parties insofar as a treaty, as Burns, Weston, and D'Amato suggest, crafts a norm of international law to be upheld (Weston, Falk, and D'Amato 1980, 26; Weston, Falk, and D'Amato 1990, 213).

19. Jenkins 1998, 230; Chasdi 1999, 7, 9.

20. Jenkins 1998, 230; Chasdi 1999, 7, 9.

21. *Jerusalem Post* 1997c, 2 (Israeli-Palestinian-Arab terrorism entry no. 441).

22. Drake tells us that Peter Gurney uses the term "spectaculars" as opposed to "potboiler" terrorist assaults (Drake, 1998, 10).

23. Beres 1988a; Beres 1988b; Beres 1987; Beres 1990; Chasdi 1994, 66-67.

24. Chasdi 1999, 21-24, 43-50.

25. Gal-Or 1985, 40, 134; Oppenheim 1948, 635-636, 643-645; Blakesley and Lagodny 1991, 46-47; Zagaris 1993, 192; Beres 1987, 104-105, 113-114; Beres 1988a; Beres 1988b; Beres 1990; Beres 1998; Nye 1993, 22-24, 135. Alternately, seen from a "state moralist" vantage, Bassiouni argues the "abduction" of Adolph Eichmann by Israeli Mossad agents is incompatible with one of the most fundamental principles under international law, namely, that of nation-state sovereignty. For Bassiouni, "the most serious threat to world public order lies in the practice of unlawful seizure of a person in a foreign state and his abduction. The *Eichmann and Tschombe* cases will remain landmarks of such abusive practice.(1) It is an affront of the asylum state and a challenge to the lawfulness of orderly world relations." ("3.Bassiouni, "International Extradition in American Practice and Public World Order," 36 Tenn.L.Rev. 1, 1-16 passim [1968] as found in Weston, Falk, and D'Amato 1980, 482-483, 479).

26. Beres 1988a; Beres 1988b; Beres 1990; Beres 1998; Blakesley 1992; Blakesley and Lagodny 1991.

27. Beres 1988a; Beres 1988b; Beres 1990; Beres 1998; Beres 1999c.

28. Kifner 1988, A-3; Gerner 1994, 44; Perdue 1989, 146-147.

29. UN 1950a; Weston, Falk, and D'Amato 1990, 147-154; UN 1950b; Weston, Falk, and D'Amato 1990, 155-159; UN 1950c; Weston, Falk, and D'Amato 1990, 160-169; UN 1950d; Weston, Falk, and D'Amato 1990, 170-180; UN 1978a; Weston, Falk, and D'Amato 1990, 230-246; UN 1978b; Weston, Falk, and D'Amato 1990, 247-252; Blakesley 1992, 75-76. For further discussion, see Chasdi 1995, 34 n8.

30. UN 1945a; Weston, Falk, and D'Amato 1990, 138-139; Beres 1990, 132; Intoccia 1985, 131-135; Wardlaw 1988, 235; Fenwick 1924, 438 n4; Chasdi 1994, 60; Weston, Falk, and D'Amato 1980, 35-36.

31. Beres 1988a, 293, Beres 1990, 133; Intoccia 1985, 136-137; Joyner 1988, 37; Wardlaw 1988, 235; UN 1978a; Weston, Falk, and D'Amato 1990, 230-246; Fried 1985, 107-108; Chasdi 1994, 60, 72-73; The juridical touchstone of *jus in bello* is codified in the 1977 Protocol of the Geneva Conventions in article 35 (UN 1978a, Weston, Falk, and D'Amato 1990, 230-246). Article 35. "Basic Rules." states: "1. In any armed conflict, the right of the Parties to the conflict to choose methods or means of warfare is not unlimited. 2. It is prohibited to employ weapons, projectiles, and material and methods of warfare of a nature to cause superfluous injury or unnecessary suffering. 3. It is prohibited to employ methods or means of warfare which are intended, or may be expected, to cause widespread, long term, and severe damage to the natural environment." Again, another example where geopolitical

considerations predominate over international law concerns the use of "flechette" shells by the Israeli military in Lebanon that may be in violation of subsection 2 of Protocol I. To be sure, Saddam Hussein's use of "eco-terrorism" during Persian Gulf War II is an infraction of subsection 3 of Protocol I.

For further discussion see Chasdi 1995, 31 n5. With respect to a document like the Hague Convention (1907), even though the state of Israel is obviously not a contracting party to Hague, Tunkin suggests that precisely because of the reason that Hague is upheld by an array of nations, that condition makes the convention an example of international customary law to be upheld by all nations (G. Tunkin, *Theory of International Law,* 127-131 [1974], as found in Weston, Falk, and D'Amato 1980, 55, 56, 64).

32. UN 1945c; Weston, Falk, and D'Amato 1990, 138-139. For a list of the numerous other conventions that serve to codify the human rights regime, see Chasdi 1995, 32-33; Chasdi 1994.

33. Brierly 1963, 405-406; Beres 1988a; Beres 1988b; Beres 1990; Chasdi 1994. For Brierly, the notion of preemptive attack presupposes and derives from the *Caroline* incident in 1837. In sum, Brierly relates that former U.S. Secretary of State Daniel Webster tells us about that condition where there is "a necessity of self defense, instant, overwhelming, leaving no choice of means and no moment of deliberation."

34. Beres 1988a, 293. The juridical touchstone of military discrimination is codified in the 1977 Protocol to the Geneva Conventions in article 51(4). (UN 1978a; Weston, Falk, and D'Amato 1990, 230-246). Article 51:(4) of Protocol I states: "Indiscriminate attacks are prohibited. Indiscriminate attacks are: (a) those which are not directed at a specific military objective; (b) those which employ a method or means of combat which cannot be directed at a specific military objective; or (c) those which employ a method or means of combat the effects which cannot be limited as required by this Protocol; and consequently, in each such case, are of a nature to strike military objectives and civilians or civilian objects without distinction."

35. Grotius (1604), Chapter VIII (Concerning the Forms to be Followed in Undertaking and Waging War). On Duties, I (xi.34), add 2 Samuel xx:19; Scott edition 1964, 97; Detter De Lupis 1987, 332-334; Chasdi 1994, 60; Beres 1990, 132-133.

36. Chasdi 1995, 31 n5; Chasdi 1994, 60; Detter De Lupis 1987, 74-75.

37. Beres 1990, 130, Intoccia 1985 121-146, Wardlaw 1988, 235; Jenkins 1998; Chasdi 1995, 34 n9.

38. Beres 1990, 130; Beres 1987, 35. In his work, Beres provides discussion and description of the Report of the Ad Hoc Committee on International Terrorism, 28 UN GAOR Supp. (no. 28) at 1, UN Doc. A/9028 (1973).

39. Detter De Lupis 1987, 127, 81-82; Gürbey 1996, 28.

40. Laqueur 1987, 380-381; Schlagheck 1988, 1; Kash 1998, 164-165; Chasdi 1999, 3, 16 n9.

41. Chasdi 1999, 3, 15 n 6.

42. That State Department account chronicles an entry for "Islamic Resistance Movement (see HAMAS)" followed by an entry for "Jamaat ul-Fuqra." USDOS 1996a; USDOS 1995; Martinez 2000, 45.

43. Laqueur 1987, 380-381; Chasdi 1994, 63, 68, 76-78; Gal-Or 1985, 231-275, 277, 78-79, 61-62; Wardlaw 1986, 283-284; Jenkins 1981, 171; Boyce 1977, 170; Kash 1998, 164-165. Conversely, particular crimes are classified as terrorism under the European Convention on the Suppression of Terrorism (ECST), such as, "(e) an offense involving the use of a bomb, grenade, rocket, automatic firearm or letter or parcel bomb if this use endangers persons."

44. UN 1945b, Weston, Falk, and D'Amato 1990, 33-38; Beres 1990, 130; Beres 1988a, 299; Boyce 1977, 170; Chasdi 1994, 68. To be sure, the works of Alberto Gentili, Hugo Grotius, (Hugo de Groot) Samuel von Pufendorf, and Emmerich de Vattel, are examples of work that fall in the sphere of Article 38 (d) of the Statute of the International Court of Justice that describes "the teachings of the most highly qualified publicists of the various nations as subsidiary means for the determination of the rules of law."

45. UN 1963; Weston, Falk, and D'Amato 1990, 357-362; Gal-Or 1985, 90-91; Chasdi 1994, 70.

46. UN 1970; Weston, Falk, and D'Amato 1990, 415-418; Gal-Or 1985, 90-91; Chasdi 1994, 70.

47. UN 1971; Weston, Falk, and D'Amato 1990, 419-422; Gal-Or 1985, 90-91; Wilkinson 1986, 255; Chasdi 1994, 70.

48. UN 1983; Weston, Falk, and D'Amato 1990, 439-442; Chasdi 1994, 70.

49. Beres 1988a, 293; UN 1978a; Weston, Falk, and D'Amato 1990, 230-246. The juridical touchstone of proportionality within the context of force used to pursue goals is codified in the 1977 Protocol to the Geneva Conventions in Article 57(b) which states that "an attack shall be cancelled or suspended if it becomes apparent that the objective is not a military one or is subject to special protection or that the attack may be expected to cause incidental loss of civilian life, injury to civilians, damage to civilian objects, or a combination thereof, which would be excessive in relation to the concrete and direct military advantage anticipated" (Weston, Falk, and D'Amato 1990, 239).

50. Grotius [1604] 1964, 97; Fried 1985, 107-108, 98 n4, n5; UN 1978a; Weston, Falk, and D'Amato 1990, 230-246; Beres 1988a, 293; Beres 1990, 133; Vattel [1758] 1964, 282; Gentili [1612] 1964, 252, 260; Fenwick 1924, 438 n4; Chasdi 1995, 11, 30-32; Chasdi 1994, 60, 72-73.

51. Chasdi 1999, 21-24, 42-50.

52. Beres 1987; Beres 1988a 293, 299 n14, Beres 1988b, 335; Beres 1990, 130, 132-133; Blakesley 1992, 35-37; Blakesley and Lagodny 1991; Detter De Lupis 1987, 75, 242, 242 n76; Gal-Or 1985; Intoccia 1985, 136-139; Joyner 1988, 37; Schmid 1983, 119-158; Wardlaw 1988, 235; Fried 1985, 98, 99-100, 107-108; Brierly 1963; Falvey 1986; Murphy 1978; Bassiouni 1978; Bassiouni 1986; Lasswell 1978, 258-259, 261-262; Crozier 1960, 159-160; Chasdi 1999, 24, 50 n25; Chasdi 1994, 65-66; Pearson and Rochester 1998, 448. For a discussion about the "esthetic component" of this definition, see Chasdi 1995, 38 n16, n17, n18; Chasdi 1994, 65-66.

53. Reiss and Roth 1993, 296.

54. Reiss and Roth 1993, 298, 304.

55. Reiss and Roth 1993.

56. Reiss and Roth 1993.

57. *Time,* 2000, 23.

58. Starr and Most 1985 32-52; Harkavy and Neuman 1985, 32-52; Chasdi 1997, 70; Chasdi 1999, 26, 17 n26; Chasdi 1995.

59. Willis 1996, 285, 287; Cobban 1984, 144-145; Chasdi 1999, 7, 17 n26, n27, 138-142, 201, n16, n17; Chasdi 1997, 73-74, 107 n3, n4, n5, n6, n7; Chasdi 1995, 97-100, 136, n3, n4, n5, n6.

60. Holsti 1970, 258, 264-265, 275-276, 286, 291. I draw on Holsti's phrase "defenders of the people" that is used to describe one of several role conceptualizations for nation-states. I am indebted to Professor Frederic S. Pearson for his suggestions and invaluable insight into the matter of typology modification.

61. Starr and Most 1985, 33-52, Chasdi 1999, 5-8, 14, 103, 139-142, 198-200 n15; Chasdi 1997, 73-74, 107, n5, 198; Chasdi 1995, 3-5, 100-105, 344-350. As I state in my first book, "the structural outline of this functional terrorist group typology derives from Starr and Most's quantitative analysis of third world conflicts, and was developed with the invaluable assistance of Professor Michael S. Stohl of Purdue University." I am also indebted to Patricia T. Morris for her help with theoretical development.

The modified coding scheme is as follows:

A = **Ideology:** 1 = Marxist-Leninist; 2 = religious; 3 = Palestinian nationalist

B = **Recruitment:** 1 = clan and/or disenfranchised persons; 2 = followers of a charismatic leader; 3 = Palestinians, Palestinian refugees, and/or disenfranchised Palestinians. (Although some overlap happens, groups are categorized according to discernable trends based on available data and/or information that can be extrapolated by newspaper accounts.)

C = **Goals:** 1= Islamic state in Palestine and/or other areas of the Middle East; 2 = secular Palestinian state; 3 = Marxist-Leninist state in Palestine and/or other areas of the Middle East; 4 = religious Jewish state in Israel.

The following is a list of the possible thirty-six combinations of terrorist group types:

$A^1 B^1 C^1$ 1, 1, 1 = a Marxist-Leninist terrorist group recruiting from a clan and/or disenfranchised persons, with the goal of an Islamic state in Palestine and/or other areas of the Middle East.

$A^1 B^1 C^2$ 1, 1, 2 = a Marxist-Leninist terrorist group recruiting from a clan and/or disenfranchised persons, with the goal of a secular Palestinian state.

$A^1 B^1 C^3$ 1, 1, 3 = a Marxist-Leninist group recruiting from a clan and/or disenfranchised persons, with the goal of a Marxist-Leninist state in Palestine and/or other areas of the Middle East (e.g., HADEP, TKP/MC Konferans, TIKKO, Dev Sol).

$A^1 B^1 C^4$ 1, 1, 4 = a Marxist-Leninist terrorist group recruiting from a clan and/or disenfranchised persons, with the goal of a religious Jewish state in Israel.

$A^1 B^2 C^1$ 1, 2, 1 = a Marxist-Leninist terrorist group recruiting from followers of a charismatic leader with the goal of an Islamic state in Palestine and/or other areas of the Middle East.

$A^1 B^2 C^2$ 1, 2, 2 = a Marxist-Leninist terrorist group recruiting from followers of a charismatic leader, with the goal of a secular Palestinian state.

$A^1 B^2 C^3$ 1, 2, 3 = a Marxist-Leninist terrorist group recruiting from followers of a charismatic leader, with the goal of a Marxist-Leninist state in Palestine and or other areas of the Middle East (e.g., the Kurdistan Workers Party [PKK] led by

Abduallah Ocalan; the Democratic Front for the Liberation of Palestine [DFLP] led by Naif Hawatmah; the Popular Front for the Liberation of Palestine [PFLP] led by Dr. George Habash).

$A^1 B^2 C^4$ 1, 2, 4 = a Marxist-Leninist terrorist group recruiting from followers of a charismatic leader, with the goal of a religious Jewish state in Israel.

$A^1 B^3 C^1$ 1, 3, 1 = a Marxist-Leninist terrorist group recruiting from Palestinians, Palestinian refugees, and/or disenfranchised Palestinians with the goal of an Islamic state in Palestine and/or other areas of the Middle East.

$A^1 B^3 C^2$ 1, 3, 2 = a Marxist-Leninist terrorist group recruiting from Palestinians, Palestinian refugees, and/or disenfranchised Palestinians with the goal of a secular Palestinian state.

$A^1 B^3 C^3$ 1, 3, 3 = a Marxist-Leninist terrorist group recruiting from Palestinians, Palestinian refugees, and/or disenfranchised Palestinians with the goal of a Marxist-Leninist state in Palestine or other areas of the Middle East .

$A^1 B^3 C^4$ 1, 3, 4 = a Marxist-Leninist terrorist group recruiting from Palestinians, Palestinian refugees, and/or disenfranchised Palestinians with the goal of a religious Jewish state in Israel.

$A^2 B^1 C^1$ 2, 1, 1 = a religious terrorist group recruiting from a clan and/or disenfranchised persons, with the goal of an Islamic state in Palestine and/or other areas of the Middle East (e.g., GIA, FIS-AIS, the Salafi Group for the Call and Combat [GPSC], Islamic Front of Great Eastern Raiders [IBDA-C], Anatolian Federal Islamic State [AFID], al-Gama'a el Islamiya [The Islamic Group], the Battalion of Death, Hamas, Amal).

$A^2 B^1 C^2$ 2, 1, 2 = a religious group recruiting from a clan and/or disenfranchised persons with the goal of a secular Palestinian state.

$A^2 B^1 C^3$ 2, 1, 3 = a religious terrorist group recruiting from a clan and/or disenfranchised persons with the goal of a Marxist-Leninist state in Palestine and/or other areas of the Middle East.

$A^2 B^1 C^4$ 2, 1, 4 = a religious terrorist group recruiting from a clan and/or disenfranchised persons with the goal of a religious Jewish state in Israel (e.g., Eyal, Sword of David, Hagai, Committee on Road Safety, Repression of the Traitors, Jewish Group of Vengance, Zo Artzenu, Jewish Avenging Organization [Ayin]).

$A^2 B^2 C^1$ 2, 2, 1 = a religious terrorist group recruiting from followers of a charismatic leader, with the goal of an Islamic state in Palestine or other areas of the Middle East (e.g., Turkish Hezbollah, Hezbollah, Ansarallah, Hezbollah-Palestine).

$A^2 B^2 C^2$ 2, 2, 2 = a religious group recruiting from followers of a charismatic leader, with the goal of a secular Palestinian state.

$A^2 B^2 C^3$ 2, 2, 3 = a religious group recruiting from followers of a charismatic leader, with the goal of a Marxist-Leninist state in Palestine and/or other areas of the Middle East.

$A^2 B^2 C^4$ 2, 2, 4 = a religious terrorist group recruiting from followers of a charismatic leader, with the goal of a religious Jewish state in Israel (e.g., JDL, Kach, Kahane Chai).

$A^2 B^3 C^1$ 2, 3, 1 = a religious terrorist group recruiting from Palestinians, Palestinian refugees, and/or disenfranchised Palestinians with the goal of an Islamic state in Palestine and/or other areas of the Middle East (e.g., Dr. Fathi Shkaki's Islamic Jihad).

$A^2 B^3 C^2$ 2, 3, 2 = a religious terrorist group recruiting from Palestinians, Palestinian refugees, and/or disenfranchised Palestinians with the goal of a secular Palestinian state.

$A^2 B^3 C^3$ 2, 3, 3 = a religious terrorist group recruiting from Palestinians, Palestinian refugees, and/or disenfranchised Palestinians with the goal of a Marxist-Leninist state in Palestine and/or other areas of the Middle East.

$A^2 B^3 C^4$ 2 ,3, 4 = a religious group recruiting from Palestinians, Palestinian refugees, and/or disenfranchised Palestinians with the goal of a religious Jewish state in Israel.

$A^3 B^1 C^1$ 3, 1, 1 = a Palestinian nationalist terrorist group recruiting from a clan and/or disenfranchised persons with the goal of an Islamic state in Palestine and or other areas of the Middle East.

$A^3 B^1 C^2$ 3, 1, 2 = a Palestinian nationalist terrorist group recruiting from a clan and/or disenfranchised persons with the goal of a secular state in Palestine.

$A^3 B^1 C^3$ 3, 1, 3 = a Palestinian nationalist terrorist group recruiting from a clan and/or disenfranchised persons, with the goal of a Marxist-Leninist state in Palestine and/or other areas of the Middle East.

$A^3 B^1 C^4$ 3, 1, 4 = a Palestinian nationalist terrorist group recruiting from a clan and/or disenfranchised persons with the goal of a religious Jewish state in Israel.

$A^3 B^2 C^1$ 3, 2, 1= a Palestinian nationalist terrorist group recruiting from followers of a charismatic leader with the goal of an Islamic state in Palestine or other areas of the Middle East.

$A^3 B^2 C^2$ 3, 2, 2 = a Palestinian nationalist terrorist group recruiting from followers of a charismatic leader, with the goal of a secular Palestinian state (e.g., Abu Nidal Organization [ANO] led by Sabri al-Banna; the Palestine Liberation Front [PLF] led by Abul al-Abbas; the Popular Front for the Liberation of Palestine General Command [PFLP-GC] led by Ahmed Jabril).

$A^3 B^2 C^3$ 3, 2, 3 = a Palestinian nationalist terrorist group recruiting from followers of a charismatic leader, with the goal of a Marxist-Leninist state in Palestine and/or other areas of the Middle East.

$A^3 B^2 C^4$3, 2, 4 = a Palestinian nationalist terrorist group recruiting from followers of a charismatic leader, with the goal of a religious Jewish state in Israel.

$A^3 B^3 C^1$ 3, 3, 1 = a Palestinian nationalist terrorist group recruiting from Palestinians, Palestinian refugees, and/or disenfranchised Palestinians with the goal of an Islamic state in Palestine and/or other areas of the Middle East.

$A^3 B^3 C^2$ 3, 3, 2 = a Palestinian nationalist terrorist group recruiting from Palestinians, Palestinian refugees, and/or other disenfranchised Palestinians with the goal of a secular Palestinian state (al-Fatah, the Arab Liberation Front [ALF], the Palestine Liberation Organization [PLO]).

$A^3 B^3 C^3$ 3, 3, 3 = a Palestinian nationalist terrorist group recruiting from Palestinians, Palestinian refugees, and/or other disenfranchised Palestinians with the goal of a Marxist-Leninist state in Palestine and/or other areas of the Middle East.

$A^3 B^3 C^4$ 3, 3, 4 = a Palestinian nationalist terrorist group recruiting from Palestinians, Palestinian refugees, and/or other disenfranchised Palestinians with the goal of a religious Jewish state in Israel.

62. Starr and Most 1985, 33-52.

Chapter Two

Methodology and Theoretical Developments

Introduction

The purpose of this chapter on methodology and theoretical development of Middle East terrorism analysis is twofold. First, this part of the work will provide a summary of research findings from prior work of mine to serve as a springboard for writing this monograph on the broader dynamics of Middle East terrorism. Those prior works include the book *Serenade of Suffering: A Portrait of Middle East Terrorism, 1968-1993,* and an article "Middle East Terrorism 1968-1993: An Empirical Analysis of Terrorist Group-Type Behavior."[1] At a substantive level, theoretical questions that have become clearer with the completion of the first monograph are extrapolated from those findings and explored in effective and sustained ways, framed for interpretation, description, and discussion.

Second, this chapter will describe the theoretical questions and analysis diagnostics that are used in this book to address adequately many of the questions that presuppose and derive from my prior research findings or were left unanswered by those earlier research results. Those extensions of the basic theory are presented along with carefully reasoned explanations as to why certain minor modifications of prior expectations are made.

The framework for discussion involves: summaries of basic qualitative and quantitative findings from my prior work; continuity and change in methodology; newer developments or work in the realm of terrorist group targeting behavior and data collection, and other extensions of the basic theory. From the start, it ought to be recognized that the data distribution format for *Tapestry of Terror* differs from the data format used in my prior work to provide additional insight into the dynamics of particular systems of Middle East terrorism.

In *Tapestry of Terror*, the data are broken down into specific "systems" of Middle East terrorism that include "Algerian terrorism," "Egyptian terrorism," "Turkish terrorism," and "Israeli-Palestinian-Arab terrorism." The advantage of the new format is that particular "terrorism systems" are isolated and identified, so that Middle East terrorist assaults, that are inextricably bound up with particular societies, that take place outside of a primary venue like Algeria, Egypt, Turkey, or outside of Israel, the Occupied Territories, or the jurisdiction of the fledgling Palestinian National Authority (PNA) are now no longer amalgamated or categorized into articulated geographical sites, such as "other," or "other Middle East state" locales without specific reference to primary venue and/or system of origin. In the process, the general contours of specific Middle East terrorist systems are revealed for the 1994 through 1999 period. What seems significant here is the findings presented in *Tapestry of Terror* that are broken down by specific types of Middle East terrorism systems seem to dovetail well with findings in my previous work.

At the same time, a breakdown of the data in this new format moves beyond the first monograph in three critical ways. First, this new format makes it possible to compare and contrast findings for specific terrorism systems across the regional areas of the Maghrib, or northern African areas, and the Mashriq regions of the Middle East.[2] Second, it is possible to contrast the dynamics of particular "terrorism systems" with the case study of Algerian terrorist assaults that are committed against the backdrop of "civil war." There is a predictive aspect to the analysis, insofar that making comparisons between the Algerian terrorism system and other Middle East terrorism systems may reveal unusual terrorist assault "attributes," if a political condition is permitted to deteriorate into a full-blown "civil war" replete with a decline in central power control.

Third, as mentioned previously, quantitative comparisons of findings presented in *Tapestry of Terror* with quantitative findings that presuppose and derive from the more amalgamated data set in my prior work dovetail well. In essence, that helps to reinforce the overall validity of the theory that drives my work insofar as the "Nonstructuralist-Structuralist" Middle East terrorist group-type continuum presented is able to help interpret findings for two time periods, namely the 1968 through 1993 period covered in my prior work, and the 1994 through 1999 period that is examined in this work.

Charismatic Leaders and Noncharismatic Leaders of Terrorist Groups: A Concept Revisited

As in prior work, this study makes distinctions between terrorist groups that are led by charismatic leaders and terrorist groups that are led by non-charismatic leaders. Seen from the vantage of history, there have been charismatic leaders interconnected to "phases" of the broader political-social movement of Arab nationalism for both pre-Arab nation-state and Arab nation-state polities.[3] One way of thinking about the importance of making distinctions between charismatic and noncharismatic leaders is to showcase the role of charismatic leaders in Middle Eastern events.

In the incarnations of Arab nationalism as Western-style nationalism, Arab socialism, and Islamic revivalism, there is a historical legacy of charismatic leaders that includes Sharif Hussien of Mecca and his sons Faisal and Abdullah who fought against the Ottoman Empire, President Gamal Abdul Nasser, and Colonel Muammar el-Quaddafi in the case of Arab socialism, and Ayatollah Ruhollah Khomeini in the case of Islamic fundamentalism. To be sure, they have captured and personified Arab nationalism's evolving temporal and ideological change and the continuity of each phase with what has come before.

That underlying theme of charismatic leadership can, in my judgment, be applied to terrorist groups as well. At the most basic level, charismatic leadership can capture the political-social discourse that "out-groups," that are defined largely by religion and ethnicity, have with other more mainstream (i.e., Sunni Islamic) groups.[4] Those strains and tensions between "out-groups" and groups that embrace the "prevailing social ideology" of Sunni Islam help, in my judgment, to shape the fierce struggle against a common enemy, in this case Israel and the West. As I suggest in my prior work, "one can draw on Starr and Most's work on war and look instead at cultural dissemination of conflict patterns to argue that if, within a region, one prevailing ideology such as Islam dominates, violent acts in the guise of terrorism committed by minority groups may resemble terrorism assaults committed by Islamic groups because of a *cultural* 'positive spatial diffusion' of social and religious ideology that would shape the modus operandi of non-majority (e.g., Christian) terrorist groups to resemble the modus operandi of majority Arab/Islamic terrorist groups."[5]

Distinctions between terrorist groups that embrace the "prevailing social ideology" of Islam and terrorist "out-groups" that embrace an alternate ideology like Marxist-Leninism seem to revolve in large part around recruitment patterns of religious minorities as followers of specific terrorist group leaders. For example, Long (1990) and Schiller (1988) both suggest that among Marxist-Leninist terrorist groups like the Popular Front for the Liberation of Palestine (PFLP) and the Democratic Front for the Liberation of Palestine (DFLP) those interconnections between Marxist-Leninism and Christian activism have helped to shape the fierce and protracted struggle against the State of Israel.[6] For Long, "their Marxist ideology can be explained at least in part in terms of a crisis of Christian identity in a largely Muslim Arab culture."[7] As is discussed in my first book, many of those terrorist group leaders are themselves members of religious or ethnic "out-groups," such as Dr. George Habbash of the PFLP, and Naif Hawatamah of the DFLP, who are Christian, as well as the late Dr. Wadi Hadad, once the leader of the Popular Front for the Liberation of Palestine-Special Operations Group (PFLP-SOG), and Sabri al-Banna (Abu Nidal) who is an Alawite.[8]

The foregoing underscores the underlying theme that distinctions among terrorist groups can be made by taking into account leadership quality criteria. Even though charismatic leadership, as one leading authority in international politics puts it, "is . . . not a dichotomous dependent variable" there are qualitative differences that include, but are not limited to, scope of influence, effects on recruitment, capacity to capture, awaken, or revitalize nationalist sentiments or other similar feelings, and feasibility of replacement that distinguishes someone like Dr. Fathi Shkaki of Islamic Jihad who was replaced within a week of his death in Malta by Ramadan Abdullah Shalah who is seemingly able to continue business as usual, from someone of the stature of Ayatollah Ruhollah Khomeini or, certainly in a narrower sense, Rabbi Meir Kahane.[9] Furthermore, there may be qualitative distinctions with respect to international dynamics and implications such as the allure, or lack thereof, for a "sponsor state" to provide foreign assistance such as money and/or weapons, thereby in effect helping to influence how foreign policy is crafted by nation-state actors.

As previously mentioned, the dynamics of "prevailing social ideology" and the behavior dynamics of terrorist groups that embrace alternate ideological systems such as Marxist-Leninism seem to be a good fit in the case of the Popular Front for the Liberation of Palestine (PFLP), the Popular Front for the Liberation of Palestine-Special Operations Group (PFLP-SOG) of Dr. Waddi Haddad, and the Democratic Front for the Liberation of Palestine (DFLP) of Naif Hawatamah. That way of thinking about terrorist group leadership in the Middle East is also a good fit with the case of the Kurdistan Workers' Party (PKK) in Turkey. Plainly, PKK leader Abdullah Öcalan has shaped the struggle of the Kurdistan Workers' Party against the Turkish government and the West along the lines of ethnic, regional, socioeconomic, and linguistic "fissures" between Kurds and Turks and injects those fault lines with high doses of traditional Marxist-Leninist thinking.

Serenade of Suffering: A Portrait of Middle East Terrorism, 1968-1993: A Summary of Findings

Causal Variables and Cross-Tabulation Analysis

The independent variables used in *Serenade of Suffering* and my other prior work were based on the generally recognizable importance that highly qualified terrorism specialists confer to them in the literature on terrorism. For the interested reader, a more in-depth discussion about those works sorted out by the particular explanatory variable under consideration is presented in *Serenade of Suffering: A Portrait of Middle East Terrorism, 1968-1993* in chapter 3, "Explanatory Variables for Terrorist Group Behavior and the Role of Prevailing Ideology."

This section provides a brief overview of the explanatory variables chosen to test in my prior work, and the works of terrorist specialists that isolate and identify those variables as influential with respect to terrorist group behavior. In some cases, the independent variables selected were not found embedded directly in the literature but were extrapolated from works that have a strong set of interconnections to terrorism by means of analysis of political violence broader in scope, such as communal conflict. In my first book, each of the following explanatory variables were found to have a statistically significant association with the dependent variable "target" when each was included with the dependent variable in a cross-tabulation test. It is to a brief description of the literature on terrorism and the explanatory variables those works showcase that discussion now turns.

The explanatory variable "political ideology" is written about as having a set of powerful interconnections to the type of target chosen by terrorist group tacticians or "lone operatives." Writers like Mickolus (1976), Bassiouni (1978), Ronchey (1978), Aston (1980), Crenshaw (1983), Della Porta (1985), Martin (1987), Rapoport (1987), Smart (1987), Harris (1989), Friedland (1992), and Flemming (1992) are among those who cite the influence of that variable on terrorist group behavior in direct terms. Seen from a slightly different angle, Della Porta views the role of the variable "political ideology" as an intervening variable that helps to influence the structural shape of the struggle.[10]

In addition to the rather obvious matter of determining whether or not statistically significant associations between "target" and "political ideology" exist in Middle East "terrorism systems" between 1994 and 1999, one fundamental question to delve into revolves around the effect of structural change in the system of international politics. In the wake of the Cold War, one underlying aim is to determine whether or not theocentric terrorist groups in their struggle against the West have, in effect, filled a similar niche in terms of target selection that was once a larger niche of Marxist-Leninist terrorist groups.

Seen from a different angle, as Nye might put it, is it possible to make conjecture about the effect of "structure," namely the end of the "Cold War" bipolar condition, on the "process" of interaction between terrorist groups and nation-states?[11]

The variable terrorist "group size" is another variable that is written about extensively in the literature on terrorism. Terrorism specialists such as Russell, Banker, and Miller (1979), Crenshaw (1983), Oots (1984; 1989), Smart (1987), and Drake (1998) describe the importance of that variable with respect to terrorist group behavior.[12] One way of thinking about that relationship that Flemming describes is to conceive of a positive relationship between terrorist assault sophistication and terrorist group size whereby more sophisticated terrorist assaults can be carried out with a larger group because of greater resources available.[13] One set of the findings in my prior work suggests the relationship between terrorist group size and target-type is not a linear relationship, but a curvilinear one, with a marked drop in terrorist assaults that involve civilian targets for "moderate" size terrorist groups. One implication of that finding is that multiple regression analysis may not be the type of model with the best fit for those data.

The variable terrorist "group-age" is another variable frequently cited with respect to what factors influence target selection by terrorist group chieftains.[14] For example, in my prior work, one basic conceptualization consistent with my research findings is that the more seasoned terrorist group tacticians become, the more they understand the utility of terrorist assaults against civilian targets. The quantitative relationship between the variables terrorist "group age" and "target" is explored in depth in Flemming's analysis of terrorism in Western Europe, and he suggests that a positive relationship exists between the age of the terrorist group under consideration and the capacity of that group to undertake successful and different types of terrorist assaults.[15]

In comparison, Long focuses on the enormous capacity for violence that grows apace as a terrorist group matures with the passage of time.[16] The problem with Long's approach, I think, is that he seems to equate "increasingly violent tactics" with success, namely the overall political effect, over and beyond the rage and hatred, that a terrorist act can generate and sustain. But what is success? Is a single terrorist assault successful in the middle run or long haul in the sense that it can shape structural political and economic change? Probably not.

Indeed, a terrorist assault with enormous violence can cross a "threshold of violence" thereby in effect helping to elicit counterterrorism acts or changes that have the capacity to more than offset any political or tactical gains made.[17] Seen from that vantage, the bombing of the Alfred P. Murrah Federal Building in Oklahoma City by Timothy J. McVeigh in 1995 is an example of a terrorist assault where the sheer physical devastation associated with 168 dead overshadowed and offset any effective political message-making. In a similar vein, as Harris, Jenkins, and Flemming all suggest, "constituent groups" themselves, in certain cases, may generate and sustain some form of what Ross and Gurr call "backlash" against terrorist group or "lone operative" perpetrators in the wake of very violent terrorist assaults perceived to be lurking calamities for the future.[18]

Location is another variable that is oftentimes cited in the terrorism literature as having a profound and lasting influence on target selection. Terrorism specialists that describe "location" as an explanatory variable for target selection include, but are not limited to, O'Neill (1978), Shultz (1978), Osmond (1979), Waugh (1982), Merari et al. (1986), Ross (1993), Ross and Miller (1997), and Flemming (1992).[19] One way of thinking about that matter concerns the variation in the quality or extensiveness of counterterrorism measures in place at various geographical locales. If counterterrorism measures in place are conceived of by terrorist group tacticians as more episodic and inconsistent than security measures elsewhere, that notion may influence the geographical site chosen for a terrorist assault.

To be more specific, many of those writers look at specific counter-terrorism institutions or policies in place at specific geographical sites, as well as the presence or absence of "constituent groups" as having a profound and lasting influence on the venue for terrorist assaults.[20] At the same time, a first pass at the data for the 1994 through 1999 period suggests that other more pedestrian factors such as opportunity availability, that itself can presuppose and derive from select conditions in place such as American government buildings not conforming to the "Inman standards," for example, may also be at work. Such was the case with respect to bin Laden's 1998 Kenya and Tanzania terrorist assaults.[21]

Several terrorism specialists describe the importance of "political events" such as the commemoration of holidays or anniversaries of watershed events as a variable that has an influence on terrorist group behavior. Those writers include, but are not limited to, Crenshaw-Hutchinson (1978), Ronchey (1978), Aston (1980), Fattah (1981), Karber and Mengel (1983), Ross (1993), Charters (1994), and Ross and Miller (1997).[22] Some writers, like both Fattah and Ronchey, emphasize that political events can shape the underlying tactics or stratagems of terrorist groups insofar as terrorist assaults are directed either at civilian targets or government targets.[23]

In his work on crafting a causal model for terrorism, Ross tells us that ". . . social, cultural, and historical precedents may be reinforced by naming terrorist cells after members who have died or people who rebelled under similar circumstances in the past, and committing actions on the anniversaries of past events which were significant to the group."[24] In a similar vein, but broader in scope, Ross and Miller tell us if terrorist groups, in pursuit of political goals over the political landscape, are hampered or shackled in their efforts, "then they may be motivated to *innovate* by acquiring or developing new technologies/hardware and explosive materials, utilizing different tactics and/or getting more or better training."[25]

Both Aston and Crenshaw-Hutchinson, by contrast, seem to put more of a premium on the set of interconnections between counterterrorism policies conceptualized in this study as political events, and the terrorist assaults that might presuppose and derive from them, thereby in effect suggesting that terrorist groups may be able to manipulate a situation and those counterterrorism policies to acquire political goals.[26] In turn, while Charters's argument is made in a broader sense, it has specificity insofar as it posits the relationship between terrorist assaults and political events within the parameters of foreign and domestic policy, thereby in effect helping to capture the dynamics associated with specific policy initiatives and vantages.[27]

Delving deeper, Karber and Mengel, and Ross all place a premium on the interconnections between political framework structures in place that serve as a backdrop to terrorist assaults. Karber and Mengel examine terrorist assaults within the context of greater and lesser degrees of "totalitarianism," "authoritarianism," and "democracy," and a real strength here is the presentation of a dynamic rather than static model.[28] In a similar vein, Ross argues that "oppositional terrorism. . . . is not as common, or enduring, in lesser developed nation-states and is quite uncommon in authoritarian and totalitarian left and right wing dominated countries."[29]

The first part of that assertion by Ross is, in my judgment, less persuasive than the latter part insofar as it fails to capture the horrors associated with terrorism in Sri Lanka (e.g., by the Tamil Tigers) or India (e.g., by the Sikhs) in the case of "lesser developed countries" (LDCs), or the terrorism in Egypt, Turkey, and Algeria in the case of more "authoritarian" nation-state regimes in lesser developed countries. Unequivocally, the foregoing observations revolve around the central idea of basic definition and operationalization of Ross's terms, "lesser developed nations" and "authoritarian . . . dominated countries." For example, a description of the threshold that delineates between "authoritarian" and "democratic" systems, or as Karber and Mengel would describe them, as systems "in transition," is needed.[30] Be that as it may, a real strength here for both of those works, as I mentioned previously, is the presentation of dynamic rather than static models of explanatory variables for terrorism.[31]

Insofar as there is for Karber and Mengel, as well as Ross, emphasis on an enormous capacity for change from one political system type to another, those works, as Ross suggests, seem to underscore Huntington's work on socioeconomic development, its importance, and the potential for "political institutionalization" by means of effective political parties.[32] In fact, in his work about an operational model for "oppositional terrorism," Ross isolates and identifies the variable "levels of modernization" as the single most important of his three "direct," or to use Crenshaw's phrase as he does, "permissive causes."[33]

In addition to works by both Fattah and Ronchey, the works of both Azar, Jureidini, and McLaurin, and Brecher and James serve as guideposts for crafting a theoretical proposition about the set of interconnections between terrorist assaults and political events. In Azar, Jureidini, and McLaurin's work about conflict in the Middle East, the authors suggest that the conflict system is regulated by dynamics that resemble a servo-mechanism that evokes negative actions in response to positive "cooperative" political events. Brecher and James's work also suggests emphasis on reactive initiatives when we are told that "the importance of the values at stake creates a disposition to initiate a crisis by violent acts, as well as to expect a violent trigger on the part of one's enemy."[34]

The problem with Azar, Jureidini, and McLaurin's way of thinking about the matter is it does not account for "breakout" or "breakthrough" events like the Northern Ireland power sharing arrangement hammered out in part by former U.S. Sen. George Mitchell that would recast power interconnections and relationships in Northern Ireland.[35] To be sure, terrorist assaults and terrorist group "splintering" has happened, but that is a phenomenon that happens apart from watershed events like the foregoing. It follows from Azar, Jureidini, and McLaurin's work that an event of such "cooperative" magnitude ought to evoke equally significant counterweight breakout events like a higher order "chemical" agent terrorist assault, for example, aimed at a specific target, insofar as biological or nuclear terrorist assaults are out of the question given the size of the geographical site under consideration. Plainly, a "higher order" terrorist assault of that nature has not, as far as I know, taken place.

The problem with Brecher and James's model of "protracted conflict," or "PC" conflict as they put it, is that it seems static. It does not seem as if that way of thinking is able to account for a protracted conflict system like the "Israeli-Palestinian-Arab" conflict that continuously evolves to the point where primary mainstream players like Yasser Arafat, Yitzak Rabin, and Shimon Peres seemingly understand that the relative costs of conflict have outweighed any political gains made, and hence seek to end perpetual conflict.[36] Seen from another angle, that model, in my judgment, does not take into account the concomitant development of newer "PC" systems like the one between the Israeli ruling elite and "hardline" groups like Hamas and Islamic Jihad that seemingly intersect or overlap with that larger "protracted conflict" system to destabilize it in the short run or even the "middle run," but perhaps not in the long haul. Models that evaluate perennial conflict need to take into account new developments like "PC" model offshoots that effect dynamic "protracted conflict systems" and need to explore whether or not the model takes into account temporal effects such as the impact or lack of impact that newer alternate "PC" systems might have in the long run as well as in the short term.

Some Qualitative Analysis Highlights from *Serenade of Suffering*

Seen from the vantage of qualitative analysis, perhaps the single most dominant theme of that work is that analysis of political context sheds light on the sources and origins, and growth of Middle East terrorist groups. At the heart of that analysis is the Reiss and Roth "Matrix for Organizing Risk Factors for Violent Behavior" that sorts out risk factors according to what can be interpreted as longitudinal factors and factors that range from societal factors in the broader sense to risk factors at the "individual" level of analysis (see figure 2.1).[37]

Long haul or "predisposing factors" in many cases seem to revolve around time-honored and longstanding religious and ethnic fissures in society that include, but are not limited to, schisms between Sunni and Shi'ite Muslims, Christians and Muslims, and Jews and Muslims.[38] The roles played by those "predisposing factors" suggest those factors generate and sustain relatively low level strains and tensions between groups articulated along societal "fault lines" and overall "pressurization" in the system susceptible to pressure from what Reiss and Roth call "situational" and "activating factors."[39]

In turn, "situational factors" can be conceived of as middle range factors that help, by means of their presence or implementation, to give shape to more proximate political and economic conditions, thereby in effect working to increase or decrease pressures associated with "predisposing factors." For example, the decision by the British during the mandate era to provide for a "quasi-government" system for both Jewish Palestinians and Arab Palestinians by means of "devolution of power" was one "situational factor" that introduced even more pressure into the political system and increased the enormous distance between Jewish-Palestinian and Arab-Palestinian ways of thinking about the continuously evolving environment in Palestine.[40] Middle range factors are also found to have profound and lasting influence on terrorist group "splintering" and the terrorist group "offshoot" processes.[41]

In turn, "activating factors" are immediate "catalytic" factors that may dovetail with the "predisposing factors" and "situational factors" previously mentioned, to ignite a condition fraught with peril, with violence as the direct outcome. In my prior work, qualitative analysis suggests that the debacle of the Six Day War of June 1967 had profound and lasting effects on terrorist group "splintering" and the "offshoot" process precisely because of the reason that President Gamal Abdul Nasser's standing as the leader of the Arab world was undercut and permanently besmirched by the totality of his defeat.[42] The qualitative analysis also illustrates that the death of a "charismatic" leader like Dr. Waddi Haddad of the PFLP-SOG or Rabbi Meir Kahane of the JDL and Kach may be an intrinsic "activating" event instrumental to the terrorist group "splintering" and terrorist group "offshoot" processes.[43]

Turning to the relationship between what Reiss and Roth call "social" and

Figure 2.1: Reiss and Roth's Risk Factors Matrix

Matrix for Organizing Risk Factors for Violent Behavior

Units of Observation and Explanation	Proximity to Violent Events and Their Consequences		
	Predisposing	Situational	Activating
Social macrosocial	Concentration of poverty Opportunity structures Decline of social capital Oppositional cultures Sex-role socialization	Physical structure Routine activities Access: weapons, emergency	Catalytic social event Medical services
Microsocial	Community organizations Illegal markets Gangs Family disorganization Preexisting structures	Proximity of responsible monitors Participants' social relationships Bystanders' activities Temporary communication impairments Weapons: carrying, displaying	Participants' communication exchange
Individual psychosocial	Temperament Learned social responses Perceptions of rewards/ Penalties for violence Violent deviant sexual preferences Cognitive ability Social, communication ability Self-identification in social hierarchy	Accumulated emotion Alcohol/drug consumption Sexual arousal Premeditation	Impulse Opportunity recognition
Biological	Neurobiologic[a] "traits" Genetically mediated traits Chronic use of psychoactive substances or exposure to neurotoxins	Transient neurobiologic "states" Acute effects of psychoactive substances	Sensory signal-processing errors Interictal events

[a]Includes neuroanatomical, neurophysiological, neurochemical, and neuroendocrine. "Traits" describes capacity as determined by status at birth, trauma, and aging processes such as puberty. "States" describes temporary conditions associated with emotions, external stressors, etc. Source: Albert J. Reiss, Jr., and Jeffrey A. Roth, *Understanding and Preventing Violence* National Academy Press (Washington, D.C., 1993.) Reprinted with the kind permission of the publisher.

"individual" levels of analysis, the qualitative analysis suggests a set of interconnections between factors found in "macrosocial" and "microsocial" cells at the "social" level of analysis, and "psychosocial" factor clusters at the "individual" level of analysis. In the narrower sense, it is possible to make interconnections between "societal" level realities or interpretations of those conditions and the processes, and wants and needs at the "psychosocial" level of analysis. For example, analysis suggests that many Kahanist types generate a skewed "holocaust" type reading of current events such as equating the former Soviet Union with Nazi Germany. For some, but certainly not all, activists who drift toward terrorist groups, the analysis suggests an interaction between "psychosocial factors" and physical abnormalities (e.g., hormone deficiencies, changes in brain function as a result of trauma) at what Reiss and Roth call the "biological" level of analysis.[44] One way of thinking about that interaction is that factors at the "social" level of analysis, at "microsocial" or "macrosocial" levels or both, coincide to exacerbate difficulties at the "individual" level of analysis with violent outcomes as the end product.[45]

The qualitative analysis also suggests there can be meaningful differences with respect to recruitment patterns between terrorist groups led by a charismatic leader like Haddad of the PFLP-SOG, Habash of the PFLP or Hawatamah of the DFLP, and terrorist groups led by non-charismatic leaders.[46] In the case of nationalist-irredentist groups with Marxist-Leninist trappings, it was found that a majority of activists were Christian, as is the case with Habash and Hawatamah.[47] With respect to ideology, the Marxist-Leninist political ideology of those types of terrorist groups are at odds with the "prevailing social ideology" of Sunni Islam that predominates over Shi'ites and other Islamic variants, as well as Christians and Druzes in the political fray.

Lastly, another significant finding revolves around the central idea that religious expression of dissent oftentimes masks an economic dimension of the political fray insofar as clarion calls for fundamental structural political and economic change are oftentimes found at the fringes of society from persons who have been plagued by economic discrimination and/or economic backwater conditions. For example, Auda and Gaffney both point to what Gurr would call "relative deprivation" as a factor that generates and sustains contemporary Sunni Islamic revivalist extremist rhetoric and behavior in Egypt.[48] In a similar vein, Livingstone and Halevy describe how PFLP recruitment efforts presuppose and derive from showcased discrepancies of wealth between oil-rich Gulf states and much of the Middle East to breathe life into traditional Marxist-Leninist interpretations of political events.[49] In this new monograph, the dynamics and processes associated with terrorist group growth and development will receive increased devotion to provide more insight into the process of terrorist group coalescence and maturity.[50]

Continuity and Change in Methodology

A Theory of "Nonstructuralist" and "Structuralist" Middle East Terrorist Group-Types and Quantitative Analysis: Some Applications in Serenade of Suffering

The purpose of this section is to chronicle some quantitative research findings from my prior work that will serve as guideposts for the basic framework of this second book about Middle East terrorism. The framework of analysis includes: a summary of underlying theory and methodology; quantitative findings; broad interpretations of bivariate testing results intermixed with brief discussion about variables chosen; other empirical findings and new developments.

In my first book, the dependent variable is "target," and independent and intervening variables under consideration include: "political ideology," "location," terrorist "group age," terrorist "group size," and "political events." Several theoretical propositions that revolve around the central role of those variables are crafted and tested by means of cross-tabulation analysis. Since the dependent variable "target" is really a dichotomous variable broken down into "government" and "civilian" terrorist targets for the purposes of bivariate testing, only bivariate analysis is used rather than standard multiple regression (OLS) to test the hypotheses under consideration.[51]

The theory about Middle East terrorist group-types that drives this work is threefold. First, a terrorist group-type continuum is crafted with "structuralist" terrorist groups found at one axis and "nonstructuralist" terrorist groups found at the other axis.[52] At a functional level, "structuralist" terrorist groups conceive of the opposition in terms of what Wallerstein would describe as "world systems," namely capitalism, imperialism, and/or colonialism.[53] Put another way, targets of terrorist assaults carried out by more "structuralist" terrorist groups are seen to represent aspects or symbols of Western society that are perceived to be antithetical to the interests of more traditional Arab nationalism or nationalism based on Islamic revivalist principles.[54] Accordingly, with respect to the targets of terrorist assaults, more emphasis ought to be placed on what both Drake and Hoffman would call "symbolic targets."[55] "Nonstructuralist" terrorist groups, by contrast, view the opposition more in terms of fierce struggle against individuals and groups of individuals who reside in land they do not legitimately own.[56] Hence, the underlying notion here is that terrorist assaults will focus increasingly on civilian targets.

At a second level, the theory postulates that the targeting behavior of Jewish fundamentalist terrorist groups, whether or not those terrorist groups are led by a charismatic leader, ought to present a radically different picture of terrorist group targeting behavior.[57] To be sure, those types of terrorist groups operate primarily in so-called "friendly areas" primarily in Israel, the Occupied

Territories, and sometimes in the United States.[58] Accordingly, in their role as informal political actors, Jewish fundamentalist terrorist groups ought to commit terrorist assaults with less intensity than their Arab and/or Islamic terrorist group counterparts to preclude the prospect of a "military backlash," thereby in effect helping to preserve their status as political actors.[59]

At a third level, it is proposed that the presence of a charismatic leader at the helm ought to amplify or intensify terrorist assaults for terrorist groups that embrace the "prevailing social ideology" of Sunni Islam. Conversely, the presence of a charismatic leader at the helm of a terrorist group that embraces an alternate system like Marxist-Leninism ought to intensify terrorist assaults precisely because of the reason that Christian or Shi'ite leaders of terrorist groups feel compelled to act in ways that ingratiate them to their Muslim or Sunni Muslim counterparts both at the state and subnational level, thereby in effect helping to solidify a set of interconnections between them.[60]

At a substantive level, the findings in *Serenade of Suffering* for non-charismatic group types reveal that ideo-ethnocentric terrorist groups have the highest rate of government target terrorist assaults, thereby in effect suggesting that those types of terrorist groups are the most "structuralist" of all group-types tested. Those findings for ideo-ethnocentric groups were the expected results.[61] Alternately, it was found that ethnocentric terrorist groups are more "non-structuralist" in nature, framing the context of the struggle as one more against individuals and groups of individuals.

At first, I conceived of ethnocentric groups as falling closer to the sphere of "structuralist" terrorist groups in comparison to theocentric terrorist groups that I thought would place the most emphasis against individuals and their religious belief systems.[62] As I report, I found that theocentric groups are more "structuralist" in nature than ethnocentric groups, and hence theocentric groups can be thought of as "hybrid types."[63] To be sure, those findings are justifiable insofar as Islamic fundamentalism not only focuses increased devotion to a person's religious affiliation and loyalties but also perceives the world as essentially divided up between an Islamic East and a Christian West.[64]

Analysis of terrorist assault "attributes" that presupposes and derives from terrorist attacks carried out by different types of Middle East terrorist groups and non-group actors is less supportive of the theory that drives that work.[65] What seems significant here is that the location where terrorist assaults happened seems to influence heavily the percentage rate of *numbers of deaths* that occurred. To be more specific, the comparatively low rate of death for ethnocentric terrorist group assaults may reflect or be inextricably bound up with the findings that 42.9 percent of ethnocentric terrorist group attacks happened in Israel.[66]

When the data are expanded to include terrorist groups led by charismatic leaders, and the findings are overlaid onto the continuum framework, it is found that the presence of a charismatic leader only slightly increases the propensity of theocentric terrorist groups to strike at civilian targets. In the case of ideo-ethnocentric groups, those data about target choice support strongly the notion that ideo-ethnocentric charismatic groups are more likely to attack civilian targets, thereby in effect acting in ways that more closely resemble terrorist assaults carried out by terrorist groups calling for a Pan-Arab or Pan-Islamic Middle East.[67]

In the case of ethnocentric groups, the presence of a charismatic leader at the helm seems to produce mixed results. For ethnocentric groups, a charismatic leader at the helm seems to decrease the percentage rate of ethnocentric terrorist assaults directed against civilian targets. In contrast, ethnocentric charismatic groups had a higher rate of terrorist assaults that caused deaths of between one and fifty persons. In a similar vein, ethnocentric charismatic groups had a higher rate of terrorist assaults that injured between one and fifty persons.[68] What seems significant here is that the explanatory variable "location" was found to be important in terms of explaining those findings. In the broader sense, however, data about the percentage rates for deaths, injuries, and property damage for different types of terrorist groups are less supportive of the theory.[69]

In the case of Jewish fundamentalist terrorist groups, the observed findings about terrorist assault intensity are strongly supportive of the central idea that Jewish theocentric charismatic terrorist groups and Jewish theocentric groups will commit terrorist assaults with less intensity than their Arab and/or Islamic terrorist group counterparts. It is found that Jewish theocentric charismatic groups carried out terrorist assaults with the highest rate of *non-lethal* attacks, while Jewish theocentric groups ranked second for non-lethal terrorist assaults. In turn, Jewish theocentric charismatic groups had the highest rate of *injury-free* terrorist assaults, followed by Jewish theocentric groups in second place.[70]

To be sure, trends in levels of property damage are consistent with the foregoing insofar as neither Jewish theocentric charismatic groups nor Jewish theocentric groups committed any terrorist assaults that caused high amounts of property damage, and only about 2 percent of terrorist assaults for each group-type caused moderate amounts of property damage.[71] The data suggest that the explanatory variable "location" is an influential variable insofar as most Jewish theocentric charismatic assaults took place in Israel, the Occupied Territories, and the United States, while all chronicled Jewish theocentric terrorist assaults happened in Israel and the Occupied Territories.[72]

For the purposes of review, two other significant groups of findings from my prior work ought to be described. First, terrorist assaults carried out by anonymous groups or "lone operatives" are found to comprise the single most common terrorist assault type from 1968 through 1993. Furthermore, nearly 90 percent of those unclaimed terrorist acts were directed at civilian targets. In my earlier work, an underlying theme that draws from Hoffman's portrayal of terrorist groups as "political pressure groups" within a political system, is that unclaimed acts serve to generate and sustain political pressure, from civilians primarily, to make structural political or economic change in response to the political demands and aspirations of terrorist group chieftains and their constituent groups.[73] Equally important, I draw from the works of Oots (1984), Shultz (1978), and Zariski (1989) to craft that argument about that role for unclaimed terrorist assaults in particular Middle East terrorism systems.[74]

Shultz really sets the stage for the following discussion when he describes "sub-revolutionary terrorism" as having ". . . to bring about certain changes within the body politic, not to abolish it in favor of a complete system change."[75] He goes on to tell us that sub-revolutionary terrorism ". . . means are employed primarily by groups or movements indigenous to the particular political system."[76]

In his analysis of extremist groups, Zariski goes on to illuminate the interactive processes that are at the heart of how and why terrorist groups can work as political players in a particular landscape. The author looks at the sources and origins of violence by skillfully breaking down groups that adopt an "extremist posture" as compared to others that remain reactive, not proactive, in nature. In describing what amounts to process, Zariski considers several factors across groups at one level, and the interconnections between the predominant ruling elite in government and groups at another level, that can generate and sustain violent outcomes or reduce them. For Zariski, some of those factors include the degree of group "exclusiveness" and "separatism" that is characteristic of the group under consideration, and whether or not a long-standing historical legacy of extralegal violence is a hallmark of the political system under scrutiny.[77]

Zariski, in ways reminiscent of Huntington's analysis of ethnic conflict, points to the underlying effects of variations in socioeconomic development that can, for the author, include immigration displacement and the perception or emergent reality that government favors one group over another.[78] Zariski tells us: "What stands out in our analysis, however, is . . . the key role played by the central government in fomenting or pacifying ethnoterritorial extremism. State discrimination, state violence, state repression, state concessions and reforms, timely or otherwise—these tend to be the decisive factors in the situation."[79] In other words, the author suggests that the interconnections between groups and between groups and government are dynamic, with an enormous capacity to influence the timing and nature of terrorist assaults. To be sure, Zariski suggests a "feedback loop," to use Reiss and Roth's phrase, where the timing and type of terrorist assaults undertaken may influence government actions as well.

What seems to be the problem here is that even with the emergent reality of episodic and inconsistent government attempts to respond to political demands and aspirations, terrorist assaults of either low intensity or high intensity can happen for reasons extraneous to government policy or even domestic factors altogether.[80] It follows that in a political system with widely recognized and utilized venues for political expression, unclaimed terrorist assaults that can be "low intensity" in nature can be used as the clandestine tools of terrorist groups acting, as Hoffman tells us, as underground "political pressure groups."[81] The relatively lower rates of deaths, injuries, and property damage for unclaimed terrorist assaults reported in my prior work are consistent with the foregoing point of view.[82] Plainly, one fundamental question really distills down to whether or not similar findings for unclaimed terrorist assaults, and by extrapolation a similar role in the political process, are found for unclaimed acts in different Middle East "terrorism systems" from 1994 through 1999.

Finally, the set of interconnections between terrorist assaults and different types of political events, as I have defined them, is analyzed. The results show that a vast majority of Middle East terrorist assaults from 1968 through 1993 are proactive or independent events rather than incidents carried out in reaction to political events. Those findings were unexpected results insofar as work by Azar, Jureidini, and McLaurin, and Brecher and James suggest, in my judgment, that terrorism ought to have powerful interconnections with "cooperative" political events, thereby in effect serving as a counterweight to those positive political events.[83]

It follows that the reason why those findings of mine seem at variance with appraisals of the broader phenomena of communal conflict which those authors offer is perhaps due to qualitative differences in the case of terrorism that are not captured by those ways of thinking about the broader concept of protracted conflict. Seen from a different angle, insofar as Osmond's findings suggest that Gurr's "relative deprivation theory" does not explain adequately the sources and origins of terrorism, support is available for that proposition and hence opens the door for some modifications of those conceptualizations.[84]

Data Collection and Other Extensions of the Basic Theory

Data Collection

One way this work moves over and beyond *Serenade of Suffering* concerns the fundamental matter of data collection. In *Tapestry of Terror* the data chronology is richer, having been put together from several sources that include the *Jerusalem Post, Foreign Broadcast Information Service (FBIS), and Joint Publications Research Service (JPRS)* scripted accounts found on the Internet service "World News Connection" (http://wnc.fedworld.gov/), Mickolus and Simmons' data base for the years 1994 and 1995, and *Keesings Record of World Events* found on the Internet service "Keesings Worldwide" (http://www. keesings.com). The underlying theme of that data collection modification revolves around the central idea that terrorism assaults that happen outside the geographical sites of Israel and the Occupied Territories may not be chronicled sufficiently, or even chronicled at all, thereby in effect falling short of the mark in terms of what type of data is needed for this study.[85]

In the case of scripted accounts from the *Jerusalem Post,* accounts on microfilm from 1994 through 1999 were reviewed by hand to find discrete events of Middle East terrorism and other forms of political violence that conform to the operational definition of terrorism presented in chapter 1, "Introduction."[86] In the case of *FBIS* and *JPRS* scripted accounts, "World News Connection" software provides for a "structured search" where the "term" "terrorism" was combined one at a time with the "terms" "Algeria," "Egypt," "Turkey," "Israel" and entered in the search grid sorted by "World News Connection" "publication dates" for the period 1994-1999.[87] Each account was then read, and if a description of an event was found that met the definitional criteria for a terrorist assault, it was added to the data chronology. In some cases, the names of terrorist groups themselves were used as a term combined with the term "terrorism" to generate chronicled accounts, to make certain that the data chronology would be more complete. In a similar vein, scripted accounts from the storehouse of data in *Keesings* were generated by using the word "terrorism" as a "keyword" and searching by country and by year.

Known acts of "independent" "state terrorism," as well as reactive acts that could be construed as state terrorism such as some of the Israeli-SLA ground assaults and shellings associated with Israel's "Operation Accountability" in southern Lebanon, are not included in the analysis.[88] Terrorist assaults that happen within the "security zone" in southern Lebanon are also excluded from the analysis unless the terrorist assault is directed at Israeli targets or other targets in Israel, or at targets in other geographical locales, by means of threats, for example.[89] To be sure, all chronicled threats or instances of violence promotion that emanated from Lebanon are included as discrete events in the data base.

To ensure data compatibility between entries from *Jerusalem Post* scripted accounts, from *FBIS* and *JPRS* found on "World News Connection," in Mickolus and Simmons' work, and in *Keesings,* I made efforts to try to find matching entries to *Jerusalem Post* articles if those were available. In terms of descriptions of numbers of deaths, numbers of injuries, levels of property damage, political event, nationality, ethnicity, and gender of victims, I would generally use statistics found in *Jerusalem Post* articles, followed by *FBIS, JPRS,* and *Keesings* accounts if all three types were available. In a few instances, accounts of discrete events are isolated and identified by reports in scholarly writings.[90] By the same token, Mickolus and Simmons' work from time to time provided a more complete description of terrorist assaults, and in those instances I relied more heavily, if not completely, on the Mickolus and Simmons' data chronology entries. At the same time, scripted accounts with precious little in the way of usable data were augmented by accounts from sources that include, but are not limited to, the *New York Times,* and the *Times* (London).

By contrast, within specific data sources, I was careful to try to follow up particular terrorist assaults by tracing an arc from new developments, such as the discovery of a underground terrorist cell and prison sentencing, to terrorist assault attribution when possible. Accordingly, certain unclaimed terrorist assaults became identifiable according to terrorist group and, by extrapolation, terrorist group-type or "lone operative" as the process of data collection progressed. Plainly, it ought to be clear that this data base, while comprehensive, does not represent or claim to represent every terrorist assault carried out in each terrorism system under consideration for the 1994 through 1999 period.[91]

Undoubtedly, as in my previous work, several acts of terrorism have been omitted from the data base because of the enormous number of terrorist assaults committed and human error that includes, but is not limited to, double counting, omitting terrorist assaults, wrongful inclusion of violent assaults mistakenly identified as "terrorism," and miscoding pieces of terrorism discrete event data.[92] In terms of thinking about source bias as a result of the use of English language data sources, it ought to noted that *FBIS* and *JPRS* data gathered by means of the "World News Connection" site include radio and scripted accounts translated into English from the original language when necessary. Seen from a different angle, as I mentioned in my prior work, some English language newspaper accounts of terrorist assaults, and presumably some accounts in Arabic, seem to suffer from source bias that may presuppose and derive from perennial struggles between pro-Western Sunni regimes and Islamic revivalist extremists.[93]

Coding Scheme: Summary and Update

The coding process transforms the data chronology so that each terrorist event has pieces of information like "location of event" or terrorist "group-type" that are coded by number in a specific data entry.[94] The data for each terrorism assault includes pieces of information for "event ID," "group-type," "group," "target," "property damage," "injuries," "deaths," "size," "age," "perpetrators," "political events," "location," "assault-type (MO)," "victim-type," "victim-nationality," "victim-ethnicity," and "discriminate/indiscriminate" terrorist assaults.

A coder reliability test is performed on nineteen terrorist assault entries.

Five of those events are from Turkish, "Israeli-Palestinian-Arab," and Egyptian terrorism data bases, while four events are extracted from the Algerian terrorism data base. The data categories used in this coder reliability test are the data categories subject to variation and therefore coder interpretation. Those seven data categories include "property damage," "location," "political events," "victim-type," "victim nationality," "victim ethnicity," and "discriminate/indiscriminate" terrorist assaults.[95]

The coder reliability coefficient is produced by using the formula

$$\frac{N(A)}{1+[(N-1)(A)]}$$

where A represents the ratio of agreement in pieces of information to the total number of pieces of information used in this test, which is 133 or 19 (the maximum score for each category) multiplied by the number of categories, which is seven.

$$A = \frac{112.7}{133} = 0.8473 \quad \frac{3(.8473)}{1+[(3-1)(.8473)]} = \frac{2.5419}{1+1.6946} = 0.9433$$

N represents the total number of judges used in this test that includes two Wayne State University graduate students in political science and myself.[96] The coder reliability coefficient obtained is .943 or 94.3 percent, which is a very favorable result.[97] That 94.3 percent statistic, that is well above the minimum acceptable rate of 80 percent, indicates that there were relatively few disagreements among the judges about how to interpret and code those data.[98]

The basic structure of the coding scheme is identical to the data coding scheme found in *Serenade of Suffering*.[99] The basic components for coding for target type include "government urban or government rural targets" (coded as "govt. targets"), "civilian targets," and "infrastructure targets" that are comprised of nongovernment urban and nongovernment rural infrastructure targets.[100] While in the very strictest sense, highways and bridges can be considered as government targets insofar as they are public works projects, there are qualitative distinctions between a court house, for example, and a road with respect to what Drake or Hoffman might call "symbolic value."[101] At the same time, the common wisdom of infrastructure as a distinct category of target is useful since infrastructure is oftentimes selected to attack to disrupt commerce and transportation, which may or may not reflect terrorist assaults against government.[102] Bearing those qualitative distinctions in mind, "government targets" and "infrastructure" targets are two distinct terrorist assault target categories in this study.

The category "government target" includes government buildings such as court houses, military administration and recruitment centers, noncombatant troops such as U.S. or UN peacekeepers, (e.g., UN "blue helmets" in the

Balkans), army recruiters, and senior military personnel in noncombatant roles. Other "government targets" include major religious figures like the pope, as head of the Vatican, for example, heads of state, parliament members, and police officials. In the case of Algerian terrorism, minor political actors as well as major ones are coded as government targets in part because the government officials at lower levels or echelons are inextricably bound up with national government within the context of what amounts to civil warfare. In the broader sense, local religious and political leaders who play minor political or religious roles in local settings, or who are non-state actors, such as a local Mufti or a local Jewish councilman, are coded as civilian targets.[103]

The category "civilian target" includes, but is not necessarily limited to, schools, civilian airports, civilian hospitals, commercial airliners, restaurants, commuter buses, and marketplaces.[104] In turn, "infrastructure targets" include oil tankers, oil pipelines, roads, bridges, highways, television and radio stations, and energy facilities. While the argument has been made to me that all of Israel's Israel Defense Forces (IDF) is comprised of a "civilian army" of sorts, distinctions between Israelis in uniform and/or on military duty from those Israelis in civilian roles clarify differences with respect to coding. In a similar vein, a state-run health clinic is coded as a civilian target ("3").[105] In turn, when a threat is made against "Israeli interests," for example, the target is coded as a civilian target.[106]

The three basic foregoing target-type categories can be put together to account for targets of terrorist assaults that share both civilian and government target "attributes" and those are labeled "multiple-type targets." In addition, combinations of those basic target component types can account for targets of terrorist assaults that have primary and secondary targets. For terrorist assaults that have "multiple claimants," a new scheme is devised that isolates and identifies those terrorist assaults by the types of terrorist groups claiming responsibility for the terrorist attack under consideration.

With respect to perpetrators, there are eight terrorist group-type categories in addition to categories for "unclaimed," "uncompleted," and identifiable "lone assailant" or "lone operative" terrorist assaults. In some cases, "proto-groups" of persons that coalesce to carry out terrorist assaults and then disburse within a more immediate time frame are placed under the rubric of noncharismatic terrorist group-types articulated, such as ethnocentric and Jewish theocentric group-types. What seems significant here with respect to making distinctions between anonymous terrorist assaults and "proto-group" terrorist assaults is a close reading in chronicled accounts of the sense or process of ad hoc coalescence that is illustrative of ethnocentric and Jewish theocentric terrorist "proto-group" dynamics. Terrorist assaults are linked to specific terrorist groups and, by extrapolation, to specific terrorist group-types either by claims of responsibility made, or attribution made by the governments of Algeria, Egypt, Turkey, Israel, the United States, or other nation-state governments or by the

Palestinian National Authority (PNA). In addition, *Jerusalem Post* sources, *FBIS* or *JPRS* sources, the work of Mickolus and Simmons, the work of other scholars, and *Keesings* accounts are sources used for linking together terrorist assaults with perpetrators.

In *Tapestry of Terror,* I used *Jerusalem Post* sources, *FBIS* and *JPRS* accounts, Mickolus and Simmons' work, and *Keesings* accounts to make interconnections between terrorist assaults and political events. In cases where no clear attribution is made, I rely on "contextual analysis" so that if a terrorist assault precedes a political event by a few days interconnections between those events may be made. As I relate in my prior work, the "contextual analysis" process can be relatively straightforward in some cases, while in other instances the terrorist assault needs to be viewed against the backdrop of political events such as national elections or the visit of diplomatic envoys.[107]

As in my prior work, in the case of "lone operatives" when attribution was not made by the foregoing sources, I used "contextual analysis" that included, but was not limited to, searching for "the presence or absence of a disclaimer of responsibility for" a specific terrorist assault "to classify events as to such criteria as the motivations of lone assailants and their interconnections, if any, to [specific] terrorist organizations."[108] For example, if a terrorist assault was an initiation rite, as in the case of the two youths seeking membership in the Fatah Hawks by trying to kill a mentally impaired man in Ramle in January 1994, the terrorist assault is classified as an ethnocentric attack committed by the Fatah Hawks.[109]

With respect to the size of terrorist groups, I have tried to acquire new information about terrorist group size for as many terrorist groups as possible. For example, while Hezbollah is in my prior work coded as a "moderate" size group ("3") of some 500 activists, Hezbollah is, by contrast, coded in *Tapestry of Terror* as a "very large" terrorist group of from 2,500 to 11,000 or more members to reflect the continuously evolving condition of Hezbollah.[110] Alternately, composition figures used in my prior work for Kach and Kahane Chai of less than 100 activists each are also used for coding purposes in this book.[111]

Seen from a different angle, new developments that presumably mirror richer data are incorporated into the analysis. For example, both Alexander and Sinai and the U.S. Department of State assert that Islamic Jihad is an analogue of Hezbollah and, as a result, Islamic Jihad was coded as a theocentric charismatic group in *Serenade of Suffering* and other prior work of mine.[112] Plainly, other information is now available from Eshel that describes Islamic Jihad as a rather loose-fitting marker for several smaller Islamic Jihad groups, with Dr. Fathi Shkaki's Islamic Jihad as perhaps the single most dominant of the Islamic Jihad organizations.[113] Accordingly, in *Tapestry of Terror* Islamic Jihad is now coded as a theocentric terrorist group rather than a theocentric charismatic terrorist group.

As in my prior work, I suggest that military and religious events that happen in the Middle East, or are inextricably bound up with Middle East affairs, generate and sustain influence with respect to "lone assailant" terrorist assaults and terrorist group behavior. It follows that political events, as I have defined them, are inclusive of military and religious events such as the anniversary of the Sabra and Shatilla massacre of Palestinians in Lebanon by Christian militia in 1982, the assassinations of Dr. Fathi Shaki of Islamic Jihad or Yiyhe Ayyash, the so-called "Engineer" of Hamas, "Operation Account-ability" carried out by the Israeli military against Hezbollah in Lebanon, Ramadan, Rosh Hashana, Yom Kippur, and Pesach (Passover).[114] With respect to coding, if there is no reference to a political or religious event the category "political event" is coded as "0" or "no relation to political events."[115]

Numbers of deaths and injuries that result from terrorist assaults are reported as interval type data that is recoded into ordinal categories of "0 = 0 deaths (injuries); 1 = 1 through 50 deaths (injuries), 2 = 51 through 100 deaths (injuries)" for the process of comparison and summary statistics interpretation. In terms of coding itself, most coding is a relatively straightforward matter of counting deaths and injuries, although in a few instances I had to extrapolate from reports of more than one terrorist assault in a single account reported along with a total figure for numbers of dead and/or injured. In those few cases, I would divide the total number of deaths and/or injuries by the number of terrorist assaults reported and enter attribute statistics in event entry categories.[116]

The variable "property damage" is made operational by using an ordinal measure that distinguishes between zero property damage ("1"), "slight" ("2"), "moderate" ("3"), "high" ("4"), and "severe" ("5") levels of property damage. "Slight" property damage is defined as less than or about U.S.$15,000, while "moderate" property damage is defined as from about U.S.$30,000 to U.S.$100,000. Moving across ordinal value label distinctions, "high" levels of property damage are defined as from about U.S.$100,000 to U.S.$1 million, while "severe" levels of property damage is defined as in excess of U.S.$1 million.[117] In the case of "Israeli-Palestinian-Arab terrorism, an Israeli shekel to U.S. dollar rate of NIS 3.21 to U.S.$1.00 is used to assist in coding.[118]

As previously mentioned, this work oftentimes relies on the use of "contextual analysis" to code data. The following is a brief description and discussion of some of the rules that are guideposts to the contextual analysis process. For example, if no reference is made to property damage, it is coded as "1" unless clear inferences are made. To be sure, if a person in an automobile is shot in a drive-by shooting and no property damage is referred to, the reader extrapolates, and the terrorist assault is coded "2" for level of property damage. To be sure, that is also the case, for example, if a bomb is placed under a truck and explodes.[119]

As other examples, the phrase "caused . . . damage" is coded a "2,"[120] while phrases like "burst of automatic . . . fire" to describe terrorist assaults with cars as targets are coded as a "2."[121] In turn, an airliner subjected to machine-gun fire, grenades, and stun grenades is coded a "3."[122] Emphasis is placed on conservative coding for property damage, so if a description of damage reads like "several buildings were damaged in the attack" without clearer reference, that terrorist act is coded a "2" or "slight" property damage.[123]

There is a series of context specific rules that are used to guide the coding for specific types of situations. In the broader sense, when the target of a terrorist attack is described in generic terms like "Croatia's interests," "Israeli interests," or "U.S. presence" the target is coded as a "civilian target" ("3").[124] If a state-run health clinic is attacked, the clinic is coded as a "civilian target" ("3") even though it is technically administered or owned by government.

If a terrorist dies in a terrorist assault, he or she is not counted among the dead. In terms of "discriminate" or "indiscriminate" terrorist assaults, distinctions are made based on whether or not the terrorist attack was intentional. Hence, for example, passengers of a commuter bus who are victims of a terrorist assault are coded as victims of a "discriminate" terrorist assault insofar as the bus is the intentional target, even though the passengers themselves are unknown to the terrorist(s) and therefore may be considered random targets.[125]

In terms of context specific situations that involve targets, the following rules are applicable: tourists who have been assaulted described only as "foreign nationals" are coded as "non-minorities" ("3") with respect to "victim ethnicity." Conversely, if the account offers no mention of the ethnicity of the victim(s), victim ethnicity is coded as "non-minority." If there is no mention of foreigners, the target is coded as "national" ("2") for "victim nationality." If a foreign embassy (e.g., the Greek embassy) is assaulted at a geographical site (e.g., in Ankara, Turkey) it is coded "foreign national" ("1") with respect to "victim nationality";[126] if a car of a foreign dignitary or official is assaulted (e.g., in Turkey) it is coded "foreign national" ("1") with respect to "victim nationality."[127]

In turn, if a threat is made by a nonindigenous group (e.g., the PKK in Germany) against a domestic government target (e.g., the German government), the target is coded "foreign national" ("1") for "victim nationality."[128] By contrast, if a threat is made by a nonindigenous group (e.g., Jama'at al-Jihad in Yemen) against a foreign government of the same nationality as the terrorist group (e.g., the Egyptian embassy in Yemen), the target is coded "national" ("2") for the "victim nationality" category.[129]

There is a range of other context specific coding classifications that involve targets of terrorist assaults. For example, prisoner trains are coded as "government targets" ("1");[130] "unarmed" police are coded as government targets ("1") if described as "unarmed" in the account;[131] munitions factories are coded as "government targets" ("1");[132] bombs placed on train tracks are coded as a terrorist assault against infrastructure ("2"); and former terrorists are coded as "civilian targets" ("3"). In terms of terrorist tactics, a verbal threat or a generic threat is coded as a threat;[133] if the threat is vandalism, the tactic is coded as vandalism;[134] if the threat is arson it is coded as arson.[135] In the case of a condition with both a threat and arson, the terrorist assault is coded as arson ("25") for assault-type.

In the case of coding for Israeli-Palestinian-Arab terrorism, the following guidelines about "victim nationality" and "victim ethnicity" apply: Palestinian-Arab victims in the Occupied Territories are coded as "national" ("2") for the "victim nationality" category. In other words, Palestinian-Arabs are coded as nationals in the Occupied Territories. In the Occupied Territories, Jewish victims are coded as "foreign nationals" ("1") for the "victim nationality" category. With respect to "victim ethnicity," Palestinian-Arab victims in the Occupied Territories are coded as "non-minority" ("3") persons,[136] while Jewish victims in the Occupied Territories are coded as "ethnic minority-foreign" ("2") for the category "victim ethnicity."[137]

If a threat is made against an Israeli leader (e.g., Prime Minister Rabin) by Jews who live in the Occupied Territories, "victim nationality" for that Israeli leader is coded as "foreign national" ("1") and "victim ethnicity" is coded "non-minority"("3").[138] With respect to geographical site, a terrorist assault that takes place in "Eastern Jerusalem" is coded as "Occupied Territories" ("48") and if the words "Jerusalem" or "West Jerusalem" are used, location is coded as "Israel" ("47").[139]

The framework of analysis moves over and beyond the statistical techniques used in *Serenade of Suffering* in several ways. As before, cross-tabulation analysis is performed where relative distributions measured in terms of frequencies and percentages by terrorist group-type are presented along with relevant significance test coefficients.[140] To be more specific, a "Pearson Chi Square" statistic is presented along with "p-values" and degrees of freedom, and in the case of 2x2 tables, a "Yates Continuity" correction measure is also generated with degree of freedom and "p-value" statistics.

As I mention in my prior work:

> For definition purposes, 'percent' indicates the percentage of the frequency of a value, like '0 injury,' for the total number of terrorist event entries. . . . In turn, a 'valid percent' is the percentage of terrorism cases for a value, like '0 injury,' with respect to the working data set for a particular test under consideration. . . . 'Cumulative percentage,' by contrast, is an aggregate percentage of the valid percent of a value, like '1-50 injuries,' coupled with the

valid percents of values that come before. In turn, 'cells with expected frequency less than 5' is a measure presented with some of the crosstabulation analysis findings that describes the percent and number of cells with expected values of less than five observations.[141] Finally, the minimum expected frequency figure presented with some crosstabulation tests under consideration, really serves as a threshold marker for the minimum value of the chi square necessary to appraise, in a meaningful way, whether or not statistical associations exist between 'terrorism variables.'[142]

To measure the strength of a statistically significant association, a "Phi" score and "Cramer's V" score along with significance scores for each are presented in the case of categorical or nominal data, and nominal and ordinal data. In addition, the diagnostic "Goodman and Kruskal Tau" is used to measure the strength of a statistically significant association between "target" and the independent and intervening variables under consideration. The non-Chi square based "Proportional Reduction in Error (PRE)" "Lambda" that determines the degree that one variable can be predicted from knowing the value of another is reported if and when appropriate.[143] In addition, the measure of "cells with an expected frequency of less than 5" is reported to help determine the usefulness of the Chi Square test in terms of validity.

To be sure, *Tapestry of Terror* pushes beyond *Serenade of Suffering* insofar as it seeks to flesh out a new dimension to the dynamics that constitute a set of interconnections between Middle East terrorist assaults and political events. In *Tapestry of Terror*, "independent" "T test" and ANOVA testing is performed to determine whether or not a statistically significant difference exists between the mean number of deaths caused by terrorist assaults that precede different types of political events (i.e., commemoration of landmark events, commemoration of religious holidays, ground assaults) by one month. At a functional level, ANOVA tests are performed when the means for number of deaths of three or more types of political events are under consideration, while "T tests" are also done when the means of two types of political events are under consideration and, in some cases, as "back-up" to ANOVA tests.

Another way that *Tapestry of Terror* pushes beyond my prior work is that measurement of terrorist assault "attributes" is expanded to include measurement of "victim nationality" and "victim ethnicity" as those attributes relate to the type of target in terrorist assaults in the data base.[144] As previously mentioned, type of terrorist assault is delineated between "discriminate" and "indiscriminate" terrorist assaults along the lines of whether or not the victims are intentionally targeted.

It follows that bivariate analysis that explores the relationship between target-type with respect to "victim nationality," or "victim ethnicity" can be performed in each case to reveal whether or not a statistically significant association exists between those variables and the target, using "discriminate/

indiscriminate" terrorist assault data as the control variable. In that way, cross-tabulation table "partials" can be generated to determine whether or not there are statistically significant differences between civilian and government targets based on "nationality" and whether or not there are statistically significant differences in the ethnic composition of civilian and government targets.

Newer Empirical Conceptualizations About Terrorist Group and Lone Assailant Behavior

In his work, Ross begins to craft an empirical model of the structural factors at the heart of "oppositional political terrorism."[145] For his dependent variable *Y*, Ross proposes to look at the amount of terrorist assaults carried out by terrorist groups and individuals. Notwithstanding that, for Ross, the dependent variable needs to be articulated more finely with respect to "scope," "amount," and "intensity."[146] At a functional level, Ross makes an important contribution insofar as he conceives of the dependent variable in not one but three ways: "state-sponsored" terrorism, "domestic" terrorism, and "international" terrorism. One of Ross's underlying themes is to run tests, presumably multiple regression analysis, using each of those types of terrorism and different terrorist groups in the process.[147]

In the case of the "independent variables" under consideration, Ross, who draws on Crenshaw's work, makes the distinction between "direct" or "permissive" structural causes, and "indirect" structural causes or "precipitant causes."[148] In the cases of the former, Ross focuses increased attention on three "permissive causes," namely "geographical location," a variable described as "least . . . important" of the "permissive causes" by the author, "type of political system," and the variable the author describes as most meaningful, "level of modernization."[149]

In the case of the latter, seven "precipitant causes" that work more indirectly are examined. Those "precipitant" causes are commonplace to note in various systems and include: "social, cultural, and historical facilitation," "availability of weapons and explosives," "grievances," "presence of other forms of unrest," "support," "organizational split and development," and "counterterrorist organization failure."[150] The framework for discussion involves, for both "permissive" and "precipitant" variables, the crafting of theoretical propositions to test, that build upon one another in sequential ways, thereby in effect increasing our understanding of the set of interconnections between causal variables.

Ross's central idea of skillfully breaking down terrorism into "domestic," "international," and "state-sponsored" types with respect to the dependent variable under consideration is insightful and important, and results from those analyses ought to be compared with analyses that do not make the foregoing distinctions with respect to the dependent variable. Nonetheless, as I have pointed out in my earlier work, terrorism classifications like the aforementioned are oftentimes not mutually exclusive categories, thereby in effect making empirical research difficult.[151] For example, the threshold that distinguishes between "transnational terrorism" and "international terrorism" can be very murky.[152] In a similar vein, the "domestic" terrorism of Dr. Fathi Shkaki's Islamic Jihad in the Occupied Territories is "state-sponsored" to some degree by the Syrians. Accordingly, sorting out the terrorism data in this way may serve to create trends or patterns in the data that presuppose and derive from the categorization process.

Another reaction I have to Ross's taxonomy revolves around his central idea of "grievances" as the most influential "precipitant cause" under consideration. For Ross, "grievances leading to terrorism can be divided into seven categories: economic, ethnic, racial, legal, political, religious, and social."[153] Ross goes on to suggest that extremist splinter groups that may engage in terrorism may themselves presuppose and derive from a condition where political demands and aspirations remain unrealized or ignored outright. Keeping that in mind, recall that the author tells us earlier that "the lion's share of terrorism takes place in democracies due to the strengths and limitations of this type of political system."[154]

What seems significant here is the case of the African American struggle where there has been no widespread and sustained "oppositional political terrorism" practiced even though Black America has endured a tortured historical legacy of slavery, political and economic discrimination, and systemic racism. To be sure, that experience easily fits into Ross's aforementioned "grievance" type categories, with the possible exception of the subgroup "religious grievances." Plainly, if a situation exists in a democracy where "grievance" types are at work either in a singular fashion, in tandem, or in combination, and terrorism has not happened in effective and sustained ways, that constitutes a "deviant case" thereby in effect suggesting that Ross's model as it is now depicted does not seem to capture all of the subtleties and nuances of terrorism that it needs to consider.

As I am fond of telling my students, one way of thinking about the absence of widespread and sustained "insurgent" terrorism in the United States, to use Nef's term, is to draw from Gordon's work on race, religion, and assimilation in America and his conception of "Eth-class."[155] For Gordon, "Eth-class" is "the subsociety created by the intersection of the vertical stratifications of ethnicity with the horizontal stratifications of social class."[156] Put another way, race and/or ethnicity intersect thereby in effect helping to fragment otherwise more monolithic ethnic and/or racial groups in the United States. As a result of a condition where an array of ethnic and racial groups in the United States are found among the working class, the middle class, and in the upper class nowadays, there are, seen from the vantage of Gordon, economic, political, and social dynamics that pull at racial or ethnic group cohesion.

Since terrorist group "constituency group" support, as Harris, Drake, and Flemming all tell us, is an intrinsic part of terrorist group success, the absence of such uniform and more monolithic ethnic and/or racial cohesion may help to take the wind out of the sails of what might really amount to "justifiable insurgency" in the face of White America's legacy of denial to Black Americans of political accommodation and change. In the narrower sense, the oftentimes brutal assaults used by police may in some instances, like the 1969 killing of Black Panther member Fred Hampton Sr. in Chicago, qualify as state terrorism.[157]

Plainly, one response to that foregoing condition might be that there are what Reiss and Roth might call wide-ranging "opportunity structures" that include venues for political expression in contemporary America following the Civil Rights Act of 1964 and Voting Rights Act of 1965 enacted during the administration of President Lyndon Johnson. But to be sure, that explanation does not suffice to explain the absence of sustained terrorism in earlier years, for example, between the years of 1945 and 1964.[158] In summation, a model that posits "grievances" as a crucial variable to consider needs to describe the workings of this "deviant case."

In his work on the processes of terrorist target choice, Drake offers us a framework that skillfully breaks down the dynamics of the "target selection process" into two phases. For Drake, the "first stage" revolves around the central idea that the "ideology" of the terrorist group under consideration, the "strategy" employed in pursuit of goals over the political landscape, and the "tactics" (i.e., types of terrorist operation) under consideration are of primary importance with respect to target choice.[159] For Drake, the variable "ideology" offers a "mental and moral framework within which the terrorists operate, and provides the terrorists with some sort of value system to which they can refer in deciding what actions they can take, or in seeking to justify them afterwards."[160] To be sure, "ideology" makes it possible to introduce in some, but certainly not all cases, flexibility of thought and a carefully reasoned rationale for terrorist assaults under consideration.[161] At a functional level, Drake delineates "ideology" into nine ideology classifications that include "religion," "separatism," "liberalism," "communist," "fascism," "single issue," "organized crime," "conservatism," and "anarchism."[162]

Moving from the broader construct of "ideology" that frames the parameters of fierce struggle, Drake tells us that taking different stratagems under consideration begins to narrow the range of target choice in effective and sustained ways. "The strategy of the group," the author tells us, "is based on an assessment of the reactions which the terrorists wish to evoke in certain psychological targets in order to promote their political objectives."[163] The strategy types that Drake uses—that he tells us presupposes and derives from the works of Crenshaw and Thornton—include "compliance," "threat elimination," "attrition," "disorientation," "provocation," "advertisement," and "endorsement."[164] Drake points out, correctly in my judgment, that simultaneously a terrorist assault has the enormous capacity to capture and fulfill the ends of multiple stratagem types.[165]

For Drake, the "strategy" that is crafted presupposes and derives from a discourse between political goals and the features of the political landscape, such as Drake's "external opinion" that presumably refers to constituency group support. To be sure, other factors such as the "personal characteristics" or "calibre" of terrorist group activists, coupled with other variables like "protective measures" and "current situation" that seem to fall under the sphere of what Drake calls the "security environment," narrows the funnel of choices for terrorist chieftains even further.[166] One notable underlying theme of Drake's analysis alludes to a cost-benefit analysis of sorts, where overall strategic importance at a moment in time may eclipse or partially offset the effect of ideology to elicit specific terrorist assault targets in a continuously evolving environment.[167]

The foregoing analysis by Drake provides a useful way of thinking about the dynamics of target choice. Drake's work highlights the rationality assumption for terrorist group chieftains by his emphasis on the process of cost-benefit analysis for what amounts to "stage two" or the actual selection of a particular target. Notwithstanding that, there are some difficulties with respect to operationalization of the "model" that, interestingly enough, Drake readily describes. First, some of Drake's ideology classifications are not mutually exclusive thereby in effect helping to pose problems for empirical research that demands more clear-cut categories for specific types of terrorism. The author also readily discusses the point that making a set of interconnections between a terrorist assault and a particular "strategy" is problematic with respect to reliance on official "communiqués."[168]

Equally important is that while ideology is a defining characteristic for different kinds of terrorist groups, "strategy" is not a defining characteristic, which brings into question any capacity of the model to showcase meaningful distinctions in terms of measurement with respect to different types of terrorism. If, for example, a strategy of "compliance" is used by terrorist groups with "separatist" and "religious" ideologies, that knowledge does not provide insight into the sources and origins of why, based on ideological differences between terrorist groups, that one selected "strategy" is used over another, especially if, for example, the variables "capabilities" or "security environment" are held constant.

To be sure, this work is a useful pedagogical tool illustrative of some of the subtleties and nuances of decisionmaking by terrorist group chieftains, but its use as a guidepost for empirical research as it now stands is somewhat limited because of category overlap problems, source bias by means of terrorist group "self reporting" about why terrorist assaults have happened, and the use of some variables that are not defining characteristics of terrorist groups.

Even though Im, Cauley, and Sandler's work is somewhat older than other works reviewed in this section, its emphasis on the use of economic theory to understand the dynamics inherent to cycles of terrorist assault activity provides notable insight about terrorist group targeting behavior seen from a slightly different vantage. From the start, the authors, for background, present earlier work that really describes the crafting of a set of "indifference curves" for terrorist chieftains that posit choices of stratagems in terms of a mixture between terrorist assaults and nonviolent actions, perhaps even actions that fall into the sphere of political activity within the parameters of the law, in pursuit of goals over the political landscape. We are told that Sandler, Tschirhart, and Cauley's model conceives of terrorists as "allocating a fixed amount of resources between terrorist activities and non-terrorist, legal activities so as to maximize utility."[169]

For Im, Cauley, and Sandler, the objective of their work is twofold. First, is to explore the "life cycles" of different types of terrorist assaults and the implications, with respect to predictive value of those life cycles that vary from a few to several months, for counterterrorism policy. Second, the authors delve deeply into the notion of "substitution effect" to determine whether or not that exists between and among terrorist assault types and the rate of substitution. In the case of the latter, Im, Cauley, and Sandler examine six pairs of time series data to determine whether or not there is the presence of "second best alternatives" with respect to terrorist assault substitutes and the type of those "second best alternatives."

The types of terrorist assaults under consideration include: "kidnappings (KN)," "barricade and hostage situations (BH)," "skyjackings (SJ)," "all international terrorist events (TL)," "other types of terrorist assaults (OT)."[170] For Im, Cauley, and Sandler, the findings suggest that different rates of substitution are found to happen according to the type of "mission" undertaken. The authors report: "If, therefore orthogonality is indeed consistent with substitution between events, then this substitution primarily occurs only between very short-run cycles in the two or three month range. . . . Only the pair SJ-KN showed no evidence of short-run substitution."[171]

One important conceptualization is that terrorist assault cycle "peaks" and "troughs" are associated with the emergent reality of "new issues" or the dynamic condition of counterterrorist measures and procedures in place that either dovetail nicely with the type of terrorist assault undertaken, thereby leading to "troughs" by means of counterterrorism that works in effective and sustained ways, or do not dovetail all that well to terrorist assaults.[172] Im, Cauly, and Sandler suggest that lulls in terrorist activity may correspond to counterterrorism measures that are a good fit against the type of terrorist assault happening, thereby in effect helping to make change in terrorist chieftain stratagems, that may contribute to "upturns" in the terrorist assault cycle.[173]

The foregoing is reminiscent of Lindblom's conception of policy "inputs" and "outputs" itself complete with a "feedback loop" that starts the policy-making process all over again.[174] Seen from a slightly different angle, the authors tell us about what amounts to distortions or dislocations in overall counterterrorism policy that presuppose and derive from focus by the ruling elite to hamper particular types of terrorism, such as skyjackings, at a specific time juncture for short-term political gain.[175] The authors go on to make the argument that counterterrorism actions must be conceived of in the long haul, taking into account the distortions inherent to short-term thinking on the part of politicians with "short-run time horizons."[176]

Im, Cauley, and Sandler present a powerful way of thinking about terrorist group targeting behavior that underscores the "rationality assumption" for terrorist group chieftain decisionmaking by means of reliance on a cost-benefit scheme in pursuit of what Sandler, Tschirhart, and Cauley call "maximum utility."[177] Notwithstanding that, there seem to be problems with the translation of those conceptions into the realm of counterterrorist policy proposals and applications. The underlying problem with thinking about long-haul counterterrorism policy that is somehow streamlined and coordinated among nations is, as the authors surely are aware, similar to problems that face any cartel insofar as there is always the temptation on the part of individual members to cheat, in this case for the political gain that presupposes and derives from national interest, rather than for profit.

For example, as Ranstorp suggests, French leaders, against the backdrop of American and British "no concessions" policy toward terrorists, and within the context of looming national elections that pitted the interests of François Mitterand and Jacques Chirac against one another, were able to take advantage of such seemingly stringent American and British positions to offer financial and political "positive sanctions," to use Baldwin's phrase, in exchange for hostage releases.[178] At the same time, rational decisionmaking among terrorist group chieftains can sometimes be clouded by what Drake calls the "clandestine" living of terrorist group activists on the run.[179] It seems, in my judgment, that for states, the power of geopolitical considerations that are generated and sustained by both domestic politics and international politics, and the geopolitical considerations for terrorist tacticians at the sub-national level, are somewhat underrated in this model as it now stands.

In turn, Hoffman provides a framework for thinking about terrorist assault target trends insofar as he presents ways of sorting out terrorist targets and some empirical findings associated with those classifications.[180] Hoffman's ways of sorting out terrorist target types and the empirical evidence he provides makes it possible to compare and contrast those results in effective and sustained ways to some of the methods and empirical results found in this study.

For the author, an underlying theme revolves around the central idea that while there has been a significant increase in terrorist assault fatalities in the 1980s through the 1990s, there has been, by contrast, precious little in the way of any structural change in tactics.[181] Hoffman tells us that while that trend may shift within the context of "religious" terrorist organizations that, for the author, are not bound by the same political and practical constraints as nationalist-irredentist groups, empirical trends reveal that conventional terrorism remains the single most predominant tactic of choice.[182]

Hoffman provides empirical findings that, as previously mentioned, will make it possible to make comparisons with findings to come in this work. First, the author suggests that terrorism manifests itself as cyclical activity when he reports, "the volume of worldwide terrorism fluctuates from year to year."[183] Second, Hoffman informs us that newer terrorist groups may engage in especially "spectacular" or "bloody" terrorist assaults to procure "publicity," namely "notoriety" or "international attention."[184] The author also reports that offspring terrorist groups become increasingly more resilient than their parent organization, "less idealistic," coupled with a greater capacity for "ruthless" actions and an enormous capacity to learn from the mistakes of their parent organizations. "An almost Darwinian principle of natural selection," says Hoffman, "also seems to affect all terrorist groups so that every new generation learns from its predecessors, becoming smarter, tougher, and more difficult to capture or eliminate."[185] As a result of terrorist assault tactics that remain largely conventional, and the fierce struggle of newer terrorist groups to make a name for themselves, Hoffman suggests that many of those terrorist groups engage in a very dynamic and ferocious "struggle for technological superiority" with counterterrorism authorities.[186]

One set of findings that seemingly contradicts findings in my prior work informs us that terrorist assaults against what Hoffman calls "symbolic" targets (i.e., diplomatic targets) are the single most predominant target type found, "followed by [assaults against] business, airline, military, and civilian targets."[187] At first blush, those findings seem to presuppose and derive from the way Hoffman categorizes events insofar as "business" and "airline" terrorist assaults are somehow distinguished from civilian terrorist target assaults. Hoffman's results and my own are more in agreement with respect to the paucity of terrorist assaults directed against infrastructure targets. The author asserts that, "attacks on energy, maritime, transportation, and communications targets [are] comparatively rare, if not statistically insignificant."[188]

Where I might take issue with the author concerns his placement of "airlines" and "business" as "symbolic targets," seemingly the same in qualitative texture to diplomatic or other government facilities. In contrast, I conceptualize "airline" and "business" terrorist assaults in a relatively straightforward manner, as having involved civilian targets. At the heart of the matter, many terrorist assaults are "symbolic" in some capacity, whether the terrorist assault is directed against an ethnic or racial or religious group, thereby in effect helping to preclude "symbolism" as a distinguishing characteristic of terrorist assaults.

Aside from that, "airline," "business," and "offices" are entities comprised of noncombatants, as in civilians, and in my judgment, reifying corporations and businesses detracts from the essential quality of terrorist assaults against civilian targets. In sum, a close reading of Hoffman's work is a fruitful way to close this section on newer empirical conceptualizations about terrorist targeting behavior insofar as that work provides a partial framework to view results to come in this research. It is to the empirical case studies of Algerian, Egyptian, Turkish, and Israeli-Palestinian-Arab terrorism that this study now turns.

Notes

1. Chasdi 1999; Chasdi 1997; Chasdi 1995.

2. Hourani 1991, xix.

3. Anderson, Seibert and Wagner 1998, 202-226.

4. Coser 1956, 110; Allport 1954, 145, 244-245; Norton 1988, 13-14; Long 1990, 22, 211; Schiller 1988, 96-97.

5. Chasdi 1999, 75, 201 n 19.

6. Long 1990; Schiller 1988.

7. Long 1990, 22, 211, Schiller 1988, 96-97.

8. Coser 1956, 110; Allport 1954, 145, 244-245; Cobban 1984, 140-141; Alexander and Sinai 1989, 41, 46-47, 159, 186, 189; Long 1990, 41-42; Dawisha 1986, 80; United States Department of Defense 1988, 9; Chasdi 1995, 112-113; Seale 1992, 58; Chasdi 1999, 75, 103-104, 81 n61.

9. Pinkas and Immanuel 1995, 1; Immanuel 1995a, 1; Immanuel 1995b, 2; Miller, *FBIS* 1997.

10. Chasdi 1999, 64-65; Flemming 1992.

11. Nye 1993, 98-131.

12. Russell, Banker and Miller 1979, 34; Smart 1987, 10, Oots 1984, 63, 65, 104, 86, 89, 90, 105, 91, 97; Oots 1989, 140; Drake 1998, 86, 79-80; Chasdi 1999, 68-69, 80-81.

13. Flemming 1992, 228.

14. Long 1990, 24; Karber and Mengel 1983, 29-30; Flemming 1992, 231; Chasdi 1999, 69-70, 81.

15. Flemming 1992, 231; Chasdi 1999, 69.

16. Long 1990, 24; Chasdi 1999, 69.

17. Chasdi 1999, 187; Chasdi 1997, 104; Jenkins 1998, 230.

18. Harris 1989, 95, 89-90, 92, 86; Ross and Gurr 1989, 409; Flemming 1992, 227; Chasdi 1995, 44, 80; Oots 1989, 141, 151 n17; Jenkins 1998, 231.

19. O'Neill 1978, 40, 25; Shultz 1978, 10; Osmond 1979, 57, 115, 90-93, 101-102, 117-118, 142-143, 145; Waugh 1982, 53; Merari et al. 1986, 6; Ross 1993, 320; Ross and Miller 1997, 89; Flemming 1992, 91; Gal-Or 1985, 91-92, 125; Chasdi 1995, 52-53, 54, 58 n6.

20. Ross 1993, Flemming 1992, 91-92; Gal-Or 1985, 91-92, 125; Chasdi 1999, 70, 81.

21. Shenon 1998, A-6. Those are guidelines crafted by a group under the aegis of Admiral Robert Inman of the United States Navy. Professor Michael Stohl of Purdue University has mentioned to me that "opportunity" is also factor to consider with respect to target selection. With respect to "opportunity" as a factor see Drake 1998, 8-9.

22. Fattah 1981, 29; Ronchey 1978, 152; Aston 1980, 81; Crenshaw-Hutchinson 1978, 32; Charters 1994, 218; Karber and Mengel 1983, 38, 35; Ross and Miller 1997, 95, 97,89-90.

23. Fattah 1981, 29; Ronchey 1978, 152; Chasdi 1999, 72, 81.

24. Ross 1993, 322.

25. Ross and Miller 1997, 83.

26. Aston 1980, 81; Crenshaw-Hutchinson 1978, 32; Chasdi 1999, 73-74, 81.

27. Charters 1994, 218; Chasdi 1999, 74, 81 n54.

28. Karber and Mengel 1983, 38, 35; Chasdi 1999, 74, 81 n55.

29. Ross 1993, 321.

30. Karber and Mengel 1983,

31. Karber and Mengel 1983, 38, 35; Chasdi 1999, 74, 81.

32. Ross 1993, 320, 322; Huntington 1968.

33. Ross 1993, 320, 322; Huntington 1968.

34. Brecher and James 1987, 9.

35. Chasdi 1999, 2.

36. Haberman 2001, 38-39. Seen from the vantage of the ruling elite, I suspect that cost-benefit analysis is more readily understood, by contrast to the masses, where nowhere is the problem more acute, precisely because no completed "socialization process of peace" has happened. While former "Special Middle East Coordinator" Dennis Ross puts more emphasis on the enormous capacity of Yasser Arafat to hamper and thwart peaceful resolution to the Israeli-Palestinian conflict than on the foregoing, I would put more emphasis on the foregoing rather than on Ross's interpretation that Arafat, "is not capable of negotiating an end to the conflict because what is required of him is something he is not able to do. It's simply not in him to go the extra yard."

37. Reiss and Roth 1993, 297-298.

38. Norton 1988, 13-14.

39. Reiss and Roth 1993, 291-326.

40. Chasdi 1999, 123, 208-209

41. Cobban 1984, 142; Yaari 1970; Chasdi 1999, 209, 219 n4.

42. Gresch 1983, 26-30; Nassar 1991, 19, 91; Chasdi 1999, 123-124, 209, 219 n5.

43. Chasdi 1999, 209. One way of thinking about the difference between the processes of terrorist group "splintering" and "offshoot" formation is that a terrorist group can coalesce as an "offshoot" with partial or complete outside membership evoked by admiration and other similar sentiments for an antecedent terrorist group, its leader(s) and/or its terrorist assault tactics. In turn, terrorist group "splintering" revolves around the central idea of current membership cohesion fraying at the edges that serves to generate and sustain "cliques" that simultaneously pursue different

political and/or tactical initiatives.

44. Reiss and Roth 1993, 291-326; Chasdi 1999, 209-210.

45. Reiss and Roth 1993, 291-326. To be sure, those dynamics are not unlike the dynamics associated with social fissures in society (e.g., by region, ethnicity, religion, socioeconomic development) that converge, a condition known as "coincidental cleavages" that is commonplace to note in the comparative politics literature. For example, see Huntington 1968; Horowitz 1985, Diamond 1990, 351-409; Theen and Wilson 1996.

46. Nassar 1991, 80-82; Gresch 1983, 18; Chasdi 1999, 111-112, 133 n181, n 183, 140, 210, 219 n 7; Chasdi 1997, 101-103.

47. Cobban 1984, 140-157; Alexander and Sinai 1989, 40-42, 46-47, 159, 186, 189; Long 1990, 22, 30, 41-42, 109, 115, 173-174, 195, 211 n13; Dawisha 1986, 80; US Directorate of Intelligence 1992; USDOD 1988, 24, 10; Taheri 1987, 76; Schiller 1988, 99; TVI Report Profile 1989b, 10; Chasdi 1995, 115-116; Chasdi 1999, 10, 109, 132 n65.

48. Auda 1994, 401; Gaffney 1997, 263-264; Chasdi 1999, 217, 220 n9.

49. Livingstone and Halevy 1990, 143; Chasdi 1999, 211, 220 n10.

50. Lasswell 1935; Lasswell 1978; Ross 1993, 322-323; Im, Cauley, and Sandler 1987.

51. Norusis 1991; George and Mallery 1995; Sirkin 1999; Wonnacott and Wonnacott 1990.

52. Chasdi 1999, 143, 201 n18, n19; Chasdi 1997, 74, 108; Chasdi 1995.

53. Wallerstein 1974; Cohen 1973.

54. Chasdi 1999, 143, 201; Chasdi 1997, 74, 107; Chasdi 1995, 103-105.

55. Drake 1998, 10-11, 25; Hoffman 1993, 14.

56. Chasdi 1995, 104.

57. Chasdi 1999, 143, 201; Chasdi 1997, 74, 108; Chasdi 1995, 104; Hoffman 1984, 19-15; Goodman 1971, 116, 118-119, 122; Lasswell 1978, 258; Pfaltzgraf 1986, 292; Lustick 1988, 67-71; Sprinzak 1988, 194-216; Merkel 1986, 25; Wilkinson 1986, 204-205.

58. Chasdi 1999, 164, 203 n47; Chasdi 1997, 74, 91, 108 n8; Chasdi 1995.

59. Hoffman 1984, 10-15; Ross and Gurr 1989, 408; Chasdi 1999.

60. Chasdi 1999, 14, 63, 75, 81-82 n65; Chasdi 1995, 102-104, 136 n4.

61. Chasdi 1999, 161, 185; Chasdi 1997, 88, 100; Chasdi 1995, 161.

62. Chasdi 1999, 182, 204 n72, 201; Taheri 1987, 121, 20, 21; Chasdi 1997, 100 n53, n54; Chasdi 1995, 314-315.

63. Drake 1998, 22-23; Chasdi 1995, 239, 277 n20; Taheri 1987, 121, 20, 21.

64. Chasdi 1999, 182, 204 n72; Chasdi 1997, 100, 11 n53, n54; Taheri 1987, 121, 20, 21; Chasdi 1995, 314-315.

65. Taheri 1987, 121, 20, 21; Chasdi 1999, 182; Chasdi 1997, 100; Chasdi 1995, 221-222.

66. Chasdi 1999, 191-192; Chasdi 1997, 102, 113-114; Chasdi 1995, 388.

67. Chasdi 1999, 185-186, 14, 67, 75-78, 109, 125, 143, 213.

68. Chasdi 1999, 165, 167, 186; Chasdi 1997, 103; Chasdi 1995, 325.

69. Chasdi 1999, 182, 186; Chasdi 1997, 100-101; Chasdi 1995, 315-316, 322-324.

70. Chasdi 1999, 164-165, 167, 186-187; Chasdi 1997, 103, 91; Chasdi 1995, 167, 169, 171, 177, 175.

71. Chasdi 1999, 168-170; Chasdi 1997, 93; Chasdi 1995, 185.

72. Chasdi 1999, 169, 191-192; Chasdi 1997, 113-114; Chasdi 1995, 388.

73. Hoffman 1984, 10-15; Flemming 1992, 227-228; Harris 1989, 95, 89-90, 92, 86; Chasdi 1995, 80, 44.

74. Hoffman 1984, 11; Oots 1984, 168; Shultz 1978, 10; Zariski 1989, 268-269; Chasdi 1995, 161, 167; Chasdi 1997, 92, 111, Chasdi 1999.

75. Shultz 1978, 10.

76. Shultz 1978, 10.

77. Zariski 1989, 268-269.

78. Huntington 1968.

79. Zariski 1989, 268-269.

80. Zariski really suggests, in my judgment, that terrorist group-to-group interconnections can affect the "attributes" of terrorist assaults directed at governments, and by extrapolation that international linkages, such as those between Iran and Hezbollah or Shaykh Osama bin Laden and the GIA in Algeria or al-Jama'a el Islamiya in Egypt, can determine the "attributes" of terrorist assaults as well.

81. Hoffman 1984, 10-15.

82. Chasdi 1999, 165, 167, 169.

83. Azar, Juredini, and McLaurin 1978; Brecher and James 1987

84. Osmond 1979, 115, 117-118, 57-58, 90-93, 10-102, 142-143, 145. In his work Osmond substitutes a schema to measure of terrorism levels according to country for the "Total Magnitude of Civil Strife (TMCS)" measure that Gurr has used.

85. Chasdi 1995, 145-146; Chasdi 1997, 75-76, 108 n11; Chasdi 1995, 123-126, 141 n29.

86. *Jerusalem Post* data for terrorist assaults from March 1995 through April 1995 were missing and unobtainable. Chasdi 1999, 21-26, 50-51 n23, n24, n25; Chasdi 1997, 74-75; Chasdi 1995, 11-16; Chasdi 1994, 66; Pearson and Rochester 1998, 448.

87. Since the maximum number of accounts produced at any one time by "World News Connection" searching is 510, the aim was to break down time periods under consideration to reflect the large number of scripted accounts that were generated.

88. Chasdi 1999, 143-144; Chasdi 1997, 75-76, 108.

89. Chasdi 1999, 144; Chasdi 1997, 75; Chasdi 1995, 126, 142 n31.

90. For example, see Mango 1995, 18.

91. Chasdi 1999, 144, 202 n23; Chasdi 1997, 75, 108 n11; Chasdi 1995, 123-126.

92. Chasdi 1999, 144, 202 n23; Chasdi 1997, 75, 108 n11; Chasdi 1995, 123-126.

93. Weimann and Winn 1994, 71; Chasdi 1999, 145, 202 n24, n25; Chasdi 1997, 76, 108, n12, n13.

94. Norusis 1991, 9, 269-270, 275-276, 229-230, 322, 325; Chasdi 1999, 147, 202 n29, n31, n32; Chasdi 1997, 77-78, 108-109 n17, n19, n20; White 1990, 350-354, 156; Wonnacott and Wonnacott 1990, 43, 262, 293-295, 549-560; Elifson, Runyon, and Haber 1982, 432-435, 161.

95. Drake 1998, 6. Drake suggests that discriminate terrorist assaults "contain a degree of discrimination with regard to the people or objects damaged, or the location of the attack."

96. Shimko 1991, 56-57; Anderson 1998, 292; Chasdi 1995, 130, 142 n35.

97. Chasdi 1999, 202, n34; Chasdi 1997, 109, n22; Chasdi 1995, 130, 142, 343.

98. I would like to thank Abdulahi Osman and Joseph Tenkorang of Wayne State University for their participation in the coder reliability test.

99. Chasdi 1999, 145-148; Chasdi 1997, 76-78.

100. Chasdi 1999, 145; Chasdi 1997, 76-78; Chasdi 1995, 126-127.

101. Drake 1998; Hoffman 1993.

102. Hoffman 1993.

103. Chasdi 1999, 145, 202; Chasdi 1995, 126-127, 342.

104. Chasdi 1999, 145, 202; Chasdi 1995, 126-127, 342.

105. *Jerusalem Post* 1999a, 7.

106. Makovsky 1994, 2 (Israeli-Palestinian-Arab terrorism entry no. 81).

107. Chasdi 1999, 146, 202; Chasdi 1997, 77, 108; Chasdi 1995; Kellet, Beanlands, and Deacon 1991, 40.

108. For discussion of "contextual analysis" see Kellet, Beanlands, and Deacon 1991, 40; Chasdi 1999, 145-146, 202 n27; Chasdi 1997, 76, 108 n15; Chasdi 1995, 126-130, 335-344.

109. Marcus 1994, 2.

110. Wege 1994, 155.

111. Nelan 1994, 39-41; Hutman 1994a, 1; *Jerusalem Post* 1992, 1; Keinon 1993, 3; Schacter and Rotem 1990, 1; Haberman 1994b; Chasdi 1999, 121, 135; Chasdi 1995, 117.

112. USDOD 1988, 15; Taheri 1987, 89; Alexander and Sinai, 1989; Chasdi 1999, 96, 128; Chasdi 1995, 109, 138-139.

113. Eshel 2000, 6.

114. Hutman 1996a, 2; Chasdi 1999, 146; Chasdi 1997, 77; Chasdi 1995, 130-131, 337-338.

115. *Chase's Annual.* 1993, 571; *Chase's Annual.* 1994, 572; *Chase's Annual.* 1995, 573; *Chase's Annual.* 1996, 718; *Chase's Annual.* 1997, 712. In the case of Algerian terrorism, where Ramadan is described as an especially important influence on terrorist assaults, events that took place during the Ramadan period are coded as "commemoration of religious holidays." To be sure, if there is a specific reference to Ramadan in accounts in other systems of terrorism, the event is coded "commemoration of religious holidays."

116. *Jerusalem Post* 1997g (Algerian terrorism entry no. 274).

117. Chasdi 1999, 155; Chasdi 1997, 86; Chasdi 1995, 156-157, 159, 336, 341.

118. *Jerusalem Post* 1996d, 1.

119. *Jerusalem Post.* 1997a, 5 (Algerian terrorism entry no. 183).

120. Mickolus and Simmons 1997 (entry nos. 17, 18).

121. Keinon 1994 (Israeli-Palestinian-Arab terrorism entry no. 158).

122. *Jerusalem Post.* 1994p, 1.

123. *Jerusalem Post.* 1995i, 4 (Algerian terrorism entry no. 104).

124. *FBIS* 1995d (Egyptian terrorism entry no. 71). By contrast, "official US presence" is coded as a government target. See Mickolus and Simmons 1997, 852 (Egyptian terrorism entry no. 63).

125. For "Victimization": 1=discriminate, 2=indiscriminate, 3=uncertain.

126. *FBIS* 1995j (Egyptian terrorism entry no. 82).

127. Mickolus and Simmons 1997, 611 (Turkish terrorism entry no. 7).

128. *JPRS* 1994h (Turkish terrorism entry no. 43).

129. *Jerusalem Post* 1995k, 2 (Egyptian terrorism entry no. 81).

130. *Jerusalem Post* 1994n, 4 (Egyptian terrorism entry no. 51).

131. *Jerusalem Post* 1995a, 1 (Egyptian terrorism entry no. 59).

132. *Jerusalem Post* 1997e, 12 (Turkish terrorism entry no. 124).

133. *Jerusalem Post* 1997b, 2 (Israeli-Palestinian-Arab terrorism entry no. 423).

134. Hutman 1994e, 12 (Israeli-Palestinian-Arab terrorism entry no. 14).

135. Siegel and Marcus 1994, 3 (Israeli-Palestinian-Arab terrorism entry no. 15).

136. Hutman and Pinkas 1994, 1, 2 (Israeli-Palestinian-Arab terrorism entry no. 5).

137. *Jerusalem Post* 1994, 2 (Israeli-Palestinian-Arab terrorism entry no. 8).

138. *Jerusalem Post* 1994, 2 (Israeli-Palestinian-Arab terrorism entry no. 9).

139. Chasdi 1995, 343.

140. Norusis 1991, 269-270, 275-276, 229-230, 322, 325; White 1990, 350-354, 156; Wonnacott and Wonnacott 1990, 43, 262, 293-295, 549-560; Elifson, Runyon, and Haber 1982, 432-435, 161; Chasdi 1999, 146, 202.

141. Norusis 1991, 270; Chasdi 1999, 147, 202 n31.

142. Norusis 1991, 85-87, 270, 132-133; Chasdi 1999, 147, 202 n32.

143. Norusis 1991, 315; Sirkin, 1999, 372; George and Mallery 1995; Wonnocatt and Wonnacott 1990.

144. For "Victim Nationality/State Affiliation": 1= Foreign national, 2=National, 3= Mixed. For "Victim Ethnicity": 1= Ethnic minority-national, 2=Ethnic minority-foreign, 3= Non-minority, 4= Ethnic minority-mixed (e.g., "Jewish institutions and Israeli institutions and Israeli institutions in France")* For "Victim Type": 1=Males, 2=Females, 3=Children, 4=Multiple: Predominantly male, 5=Multiple: Predominantly female, 6=Multiple: Predominantly children, 7=Multiple: Predominantly females and children, 8=Multiple: Predominantly males and children, 9= Multiple: Mixed. (*Mickolus and Simmons 1997, 748)

145. Ross 1993, 317; Ross and Miller 1997.

146. Ross 1993, 317; Ross and Miller 1997.

147. Ross 1993, 320; Ross and Miller 1997.

148. Ross 1993, 320, 327 n10; Ross and Miller 1997.

149. Ross 1993, 320, 322. Ross draws from Huntington's 1968 work, *Political Order in Changing Societies.*

150. Ross 1993, 320.

151. Chasdi 1995, 17-18.

152. Chasdi 1995, 17-18.

153. Ross 1993, 325.

154. Ross 1993, 321; Nef 1978.

155. Gordon 1964; Nef.

156. Gordon 1964, 51, 55, 160; Nef.

157. Harris 1989, 95, 89-90, 92, 86; Drake 1998, 174, 177; Chasdi 1999, 34; Gurr 1989b, 211-213.

158. To be sure, the fundamental question that boils down to whether or not that is due in part to the Cold War political framework that helped to mute ethnic conflict in other parts of the world deserves the increased devotion of empirical researchers. See Johnson, 1982.

159. Drake 1998, 175-182, 5-7.

160. Drake 1998, 175.

161. Drake 1998, 175.

162. Drake 1998, 16-17.

163. Drake 1998, 176, 39.

164. Drake 1998, 42-43.

165. Drake 1998, 176, 38, 43, 53.

166. Drake 1998, 80, 82-83, 175-179; Nye 1993.

167. Drake 1998, 139; Nye 1993.

168. Drake 1998, 9, 175, 181, 43, 53, 24-25.

169. Sandler, Tschirhart, and Cauley (1983) as found in Im, Cauley, and Sandler 1987, 242. At the same time, Duval and Stohl also suggest an economics theory based way of thinking about terrorist assault targeting behavior. Duval and Stohl 1983, 207-211; Stohl 1988, 161-163; Chasdi 1999, 203.

170. Im, Cauley, and Sandler 1987, 239.

171. Im, Cauley, and Sandler 1987, 251.

172. Im, Cauley, and Sandler 1987, 242.

173. Im, Cauley, and Sandler 1987, 241-242, 251.

174. Lindblom 1980.

175. Im, Cauley, and Sandler 1987, 243.

176. Im, Cauley, and Sandler 1987, 252.

177. Im, Cauley, and Sandler 1987, 239.

178. Ranstorp 1997, 204, 195-203, 205-206; Harris 1997; Winslow 1996; Baldwin 1971, 1985.

179. Drake 1998, 181-182, 35; Long 1990.

180. Hoffman 1993.

181. Hoffman 1993, 13.

182. Hoffman 1993; Shapiro 1996, 3. Seen from a different angle, Professor Ariel Merari suggests the role of religion may be exaggerated with respect to especially lethal suicide terrorist assaults insofar as the wish to die, not "religious fervor," is the single, most predominant impetus for suicide terrorist assaults.

183. Hoffman 1993, 24, 13.

184. Hoffman 1993, 15.

185. Hoffman 1993, 15.

186. Hoffman 1993, 15, 16, 19.

187. Hoffman 1993, 14.

188. Hoffman 1993, 14.

Chapter Three

The Case of Algerian Terrorism

Introduction

During the 1999 Christmas season, the looming catastrophe of full-blown transnational terrorism happening in the United States tarnished that otherwise ethereal moment of the twentieth century passing into eclipse. Nowhere was the problem more acute than in the state of Washington where an Algerian, living in Montreal, Canada, tried to cross over the Canadian-American border on a ferry from Victoria in a car that was a storehouse of the chemical fertilizer explosive RDX.[1] After a close reading of Ahmed Ressam's background, his powerful set of interconnections to Algeria's Armed Islamic Group (Groupe Islamique Arme or GIA) set off political shockwaves in the United States, France, and Canada.[2] Sometime later in Vermont, two persons, a Canadian woman accompanied by an Algerian man, also attempted to cross into the United States from Canada. They also had interconnections to the GIA and an affiliated arms running operation in Europe called the Algerian Islamic League.[3]

Those two events and the arrest of eleven Islamic activists in Jordan by Jordanian authorities around 16 December 1999 evoked a cacophony of voices about the underlying threat of terrorism to the United States.[4] Equally important is the fundamental question that really boils down to why leaders of Algeria's Armed Islamic Group (GIA), known for their terrorist assaults in Algeria, and

63

parts of Europe, would plan a terrorist assault against the United States.[5] In a way as perhaps never before since the bombing of the World Trade Center in New York City, the continuously evolving environment of worldwide terrorism confronted "soft" American targets separated only by the gatekeepers of travel and commerce at the Canadian-American border.

The purpose of this chapter is to provide an empirically based analysis of Algerian terrorism in the political landscape during the 1994-99 period. At a substantive level, it is important to move over and beyond episodic and inconsistent reports about particular atrocities happening in Algeria and to explore, rather than merely chronicle, what "insurgent terrorism" in Algeria is all about.[6] In the narrower sense, empirical analysis that captures some of those dynamics is critical for counterterrorism specialists, the policy-makers who rely on their judgment when crafting policy, and to persons inextricably bound up with Algeria's catastrophic condition.

In the broader sense, for students of political violence, this analysis attempts to fill gaps in empirically grounded knowledge about Algerian terrorism that now undoubtedly has profound and lasting implications for persons living outside of Algeria, itself shackled with unbridled violence and misery. For the lay observer of political violence, professional researchers, and counterterrorism policy-makers who shape their research agenda in both Europe and North America, the time to focus on empirical efforts to shed light on Algerian terrorism is now as a way to showcase what is happening in Algeria and beyond.[7] Before turning to the quantitative analysis, however, the framework of analysis here provides qualitative discussion and description about the following: Algerian terrorist group chieftains and colleagues; the coalescence and growth of the Islamic Salvation Front (FIS); the Armed Islamic Group (GIA); particular GIA "brigades"; certain GIA "splinter groups" or "proto-groups" that presuppose and derive from the Armed Islamic Group (GIA).

Islamic Salvation Front (FIS)
Al Jabha-al Islamiyya li-Inqadh

In the broader sense, the Islamic Salvation Front in its political party incarnation was crafted in 1989 by Shaykh Ali Belhadj (1956-), Dr. Abassi Madani (1931-), and Imam Hachemi Sahnouni against a backdrop of long-standing political and economic strains and tensions that came to fruition with the countrywide October 1988 riots.[8] In early 1994, the Islamic Salvation Front became affiliated with a paramilitary movement known as the Armed Islamic Movement (MIA) led by Abdelkader Chebouti.[9] The MIA officially changed its name around July 1994 to the Islamic Salvation Army (AIS), again under the aegis of Chebouti.[10] To be sure, the Islamic Salvation Army is a group now generally recognizable as the military branch of the Islamic Salvation Front.[11]

Available and reliable estimates about the number of FIS/AIS activists are practically nil. In the broadest sense, Willis refers to "foreign intelligence sources" that provide an estimate of between 800 and 1,000 "activists."[12] One scripted account quotes an anonymous Algerian general, "General X," who says that as of 1998 the number of Islamic Salvation Army (AIS) activists had been broken down to only "a few hundred men" before the Islamic Salvation Army announced a cessation of hostilities in October 1997.[13]

Accordingly, the number of Islamic Salvation Front-Islamic Salvation Army activists is estimated to constitute a moderate size terrorist group that in this study consists of between 101 and 700 activists. Lastly, for this research the FIS-AIS is coded as a terrorist group with non-charismatic leadership because for the 1994 to 1999 time period under consideration, while Madani and Belhadj were incarcerated or isolated, Abdelkader Hachani and his cohorts were presumably at the helm of the organization.[14]

Tracing an arc back to the late 1980s, both Ciment and Willis chronicle how following the 1988 riots, Imam Hachemi Sahnouni of the Al-Sunnah mosque, and Shajkh Belhadj, mulled over the prospect of putting together an Islamic political party that would pursue tangible political objectives over a political landscape fraught with peril and uncertainty.[15] In fact, Ciment and Roberts both suggest that the decision to craft an Islamic party was really a watershed event since among Islamists at this juncture, there had been predominant strains and tensions about the correct relationship between religious action and political action.[16]

On the one hand, as both Ciment and Roberts report, some leaders of Islamic revivalist movements in Algeria believed in carefully reasoned efforts to make "Islamic ethics" thrive in effective and sustained ways first, thereby in effect helping to facilitate societal transformation. That, Roberts tells us, reflects a tradition of Islam in Algeria where "the underlying purpose of radical Islamism [is] subordinating the political to the religious sphere."[17] On the other hand, we are told that other Islamists sought to craft an Islamic state outright, thereby in effect providing the political and legislative framework to promote effective and sustained "Islamic ethics" for the populace.[18]

To be sure, those bifurcating "strands of Islamic thought" about that ticklish question of political action was critical with respect to the structural shape of the fledgling Islamic Salvation Front.[19] Unequivocally, as Willis tells us, that emergent reality would insure that the scope of the Islamic Salvation Front with respect to its capacity to represent the "Islamic Movement" in Algeria was always makeshift and never complete.[20] At a substantive level, those differences have underlying implications for the range of political players and flexibility in the Algerian political system. In fact, Spencer makes a distinction based on the foregoing between groups strenuously competing with the government and one another, and "moderates" who work generally within the political framework.[21]

For example, Shaykh Ahmed Sahnoun (1909-) who as Roberts reports traces an arc to Shaykh Abdelhamid Ben Badis (1889-1940) and his Association of the Reform Ulema (1931) falls squarely into the sphere of that first "strand of Islamic thought" that places emphasis on continuing to weave Islamic ethics into the fabric of Algerian society.[22] Shaykh Sahnoun leads the nonpolitical and nonviolent association "al-Dawa al-Islamiya" or League of the Islamic Call that has as its single, most predominant theme a capacitated and revitalized Islamic ethical framework. Shaykh Sahnoun's enormous religious stature and charismatic authority that would have, according to Roberts, placed him above Dr. Madani in rank, did not offset the enormous ideological distance between him and political activists and, hence, his disaffection with the political processes associated with the Islamic Salvation Front.[23]

Likewise, Shaykh Abdallah Djaballah (1956-) who has led the Movement of the Islamic Renaissance (MNI) since 1989 is another pivotal figure who has disassociated himself from the Islamic Salvation Front.[24] Roberts tells us that with respect to weltanschauung, the Movement of the Islamic Resistance is "close in spirit and outlook to the Muslim Brotherhood."[25] Nowadays, Shaykh Djaballah is the leader of the Ennahda Movement, an organization that closely parallels the Movement of the Islamic Renaissance and was apparently crafted after the Algerian elections in June of 1997.[26]

In a similar vein, a third central leader on the Algerian landscape is Shaykh Manfoud Nanah (1942-) who has led the Movement for the Islamic Society ("al-Haraka li Mujtama Islaimi" or HAMAS) since around 1991.[27] The Movement for the Islamic Society has been described as a government-sanctioned and moderate party, again with a singular focus on what Roberts calls a "gradualist," or as Lindblom might put, an "incrementalist" approach to making structural change in Algerian society.[28] Accounts scripted in 1997 suggest the Movement for the Islamic Society or HAMAS changed its name to the Movement for Society of Peace (MSP) in part to distance itself from the Palestinian Hamas terrorist organization.[29]

At a functional level, Dr. Abbasi Madani, who earned a Ph.D. in education in England, would eventually become the predominant leader of the fledgling Islamic Salvation Front.[30] It is commonplace to note in the literature on Algeria that Abbasi Madani is a good concomitant to Ali Belhadj, a former high school teacher, who, unlike Madani, has sufficient religious background and training to serve as an imam.[31] In fact, Ciment suggests that interconnection between Madani and Belhadj reflects the "two faced" nature of FIS whose functional objectives are twofold. First, the Islamic Salvation Front (FIS) by means of Belhadj's vitriol, has to have the capacity to appeal to a constituency that is characterized by full-blown anger and other similar sentiments. Second, Madani's intellectual and especially probing nature gives the FIS the capacity to sound conciliatory with the tantalizing prospect of helping to make FIS into a vehicle to introduce flexibility into the political system.[32]

In any event, the Islamic Salvation Front became an emergent reality in February 1989.[33] In time, a "Majlis al-Shura" was put together to serve as a consultative council for the Islamic Salvation Front, thereby in effect helping to fulfill the important obligation of "ijma'" or "consensus" that both Hourani and Roberts suggest is an intrinsic aspect of Islamic Sharia.[34] As Roberts explains, the "Majlis al-Shura" of the Islamic Salvation Front was a national representative structure with five administrative subcomponents and that framework was an exemplar for similar FIS structures replicated according to more narrowly defined geographical locales.[35]

Notwithstanding that, sustained and concerted power was never really wrested away from Dr. Madani and Shaykh Belhadj by the "Majlis-al Shura" until the incarceration of the Madani and Belhadj in June 1991 by the Chadli Benjedid government, along with "hundreds if not thousands of Islamists," as Roberts puts it.[36] At a functional level, only after the incarceration of Madani and Belhadj did the influence of those two leaders on practical matters became episodic and inconsistent.

After their arrest on 30 June 1991, Abdelkader Hachani, a former petrochemical engineer whom Roberts describes as a non-charismatic figure, eventually became the predominant head of the FIS until his incarceration by the Algerian government in 1992.[37] In time, as one scripted account relates, Hachani was murdered while visiting his dentist, presumably by government counterterrorist operatives.[38] As Roberts reports it, a testament to the charisma and robust power of Madani and Belhadj and the "Algerianist" portion of FIS is that the "Majlis-al Shura" "affirmed its loyalty to Abbasi and Ben Hadj by reelecting them in their absence to the presidency and vice presidency of the party."[39]

At the same time, some of the Islamic Salvation Front's most notable chieftains are found either in Algeria or living in exile in Europe and other locales abroad.[40] Political rivalries, always a frequent visitor of fractured political leadership, have been a hallmark of the relations between the foregoing both outside and inside of Algeria.[41] For example, Willis tells us that Anwar Haddam who reportedly resided in Chicago, described himself as "the FIS Parliamentary Delegation to the U.S. and Europe" leader.[42] In a similar vein, as Willis relates, Rabah Kebir who reportedly resides in Germany calls himself "the official representative of the FIS abroad."[43]

Inside Algeria, by contrast, Mohammed Said conducted FIS business in tandem with his right-hand man Abderrazak Redjam.[44] Compounding the complexity of the situation even more, while in prison Madani and Belhadj appear to have endorsed, or at least strongly supported, different persons in terms of succession.[45] It seems that the continuously evolving Algerian environment has a strong effect on political loyalties and group membership, insofar as Willis reports that Haddam, Redjam, and Said jumped ship to the

Armed Islamic Group (GIA) in time precisely because of the reason that political rivalries and political tides ebbed and flowed in the direction of the GIA.[46]

Turning back to what Reiss and Roth might call the "activating event" of the 1988 riots, Roberts, Ciment, and Zoubir all make it clear the Islamists were not provocateurs, but seized on a groundswell of political instability and social unrest to promote an Islamic revivalist message of change.[47] Entelis, Ciment and Fuller all suggest that Islamists in Algeria deftly rode that wave of discontent using it to their advantage, in terms of grass roots organization and demonstrations.[48] In essence, "micro-social" factors, namely "community organization" channels, as Reiss and Roth might put it, were open and thrived in effective and sustained ways within the system of "free mosques," namely those mosques not shackled by government appointed imams, and thereby in effect serving as venues for political mobilization.[49]

Somewhat ironically, in the wake of the 1988 riots, the government of President Chadli Benjedid tried to fortify its position by acting as the gatekeeper of structural political change insofar as it promulgated the new Algerian 1989 constitution. Under the new guideposts of the 1989 constitution, article 40 expanded political participation, and as a result political legitimacy was guaranteed to "associations of a political character."[50] At the same time, the time-honored and long-standing set of powerful political interconnections between the ruling FLN and the Armee Nationale Populaire (ANP) was severed in the political arena.[51]

What seems significant here is that Islamists were allowed to participate in contesting elections even though we are told by both Roberts and Zoubir that participation of the Islamists was an infraction of article 40 of the constitution precisely because of the religious and divisive nature of the fledgling Islamist political movement.[52] With respect to political participation, article 40 states, "this right, nonetheless, cannot be invoked in order to attack fundamental freedoms, national unity, the integrity of the territory, the independence of the country or the sovereignty of the people."[53] Be that as it may, Ruedy, Spencer, Ciment, Roberts, and others all suggest that Chadli Benjedid's government planned to proceed with elections provided that the military-backed Algerian government had the capacity to manipulate, and if necessary control, the political power of the Islamists within the existing political framework.[54]

It is probably no exaggeration to say the political stability of President Chadli Benjedid's government was severely tarnished by the clarion call for political change that worked to generate and sustain an enormous FIS victory at both provisional assembly levels and communal assembly levels in the 1990 local elections.[55] In fact, as several writers tell us, such support was more a reflection of the disgust and other similar sentiments that so many Algerians felt towards the FLN rather than outright support for the Islamic Salvation Front.[56]

Be that as it may, nowhere was this confrontation between the FLN government and the Islamic Salvation Front more acute than during the national elections that followed in December 1991. It is commonplace to note that in December 1991 during the second round of national elections, the military superseded the Chadli government to stop the national electoral process outright.[57] In turn, President Chadli was removed from office by the Armee Nationale Populaire (ANP) and the five-man High Committee of State (Haut Comite d'Etat or HCE) was put into place under the aegis of Mohammed Boudiaf.[58] In turn, the High Committee of State breathed new life into a law that forbade any dosage of politics in the "free mosques," thereby in effect rending apart the FIS and it passed into eclipse as a legitimate political party in March 1992.[59]

What follows is a more in-depth analysis of the antecedents of the Islamic Salvation Front (FIS) in the context of Reiss and Roth's "risk factor matrix" for predicting violent outcomes.[60] Clearly, with respect to the Reiss and Roth analysis, the economic and political underpinnings of contemporary Algeria would constitute long-range "predisposing factors" that would fall primarily into "macrosocial" and "microsocial" spheres.[61] The analysis begins with fitting watershed events and processes happening in the 1980s into the Reiss and Ross framework, and then traces an arc to particular "predisposing" seminal events and processes that happen much earlier in time.

Several writers suggest that profound and lasting economic problems and hardships associated the Algerian condition started with the Ahmed Ben Bella (1962-65) and Hourai Boumediene (1965-78) "rentier state" system.[62] That system of "state capitalism" was based on oil production and oil revenue, without, as Vandewalle tells us, any meaningful economic distribution of those monies over and beyond Algeria's ruling elite. Compounding the matter even more but intrinsic to a "rentier state" system is the absence of a private sector that thrives in effective and sustained ways over and beyond what Vandewalle describes as the "parallel market" of Algeria's "trabendo" system.[63] Compounding the problem even more were President Chadli Benjedid's "economic liberalization" programs, all of which constituted perhaps the single, most predominant cornerstone of Algeria's looming calamity.[64]

For one thing, those long-standing "predisposing macrosocial" problems manifested themselves in what Reiss and Roth call "concentration of poverty effects," in this case in urban areas of Algeria, especially among the young unemployed "Hittistes" who have been resource pools for mass membership in the FIS.[65] Zoubir describes them as "those jobless people who lean against walls all day long; those with a diploma in Arabic (Arabophones) but who could not find work; Arabic teachers; students and graduates in the physical sciences."[66]

Here use of the Reiss and Roth construct shifts to interconnections and "feedback loops" between the "social" level of emphasis previously mentioned and the "individual" level of analysis. It is a pedagogical tool thereby in effect able to illustrate some of the dynamics that may occur among the most hardened

FIS-AIS activists or, for that matter, members of any organization that has committed terrorist assaults.[67] To be sure, this analysis does not apply to the overwhelming number of FIS constituents but more with respect to activists who commit violent outcomes that sometimes qualify as terrorist assaults.

For example, Reiss and Roth assert it is possible to make interconnections between the "macrosocial" conditions previously mentioned, and children raised in conditions of poverty or near poverty. The authors suggest that traumatic births and childhoods, that in large part presuppose and derive from those economic backwater conditions, could result in certain children with profound and lasting problems at Reiss and Roth's "individual" level of analysis.[68]

In turn, those children with particular "psychosocial" problems such as learned patterns of aggressive behavior towards women, and cognitive dysfunction, and perhaps working in tandem in some cases with "biological" problems like neurobiological disorders and/or genetic predispositions toward them, may complete the "feedback loop" between factors at the "individual" level of analysis and "social" levels by transforming aggressive impulses and obsessions into especially brutal terrorist assaults.[69] Seen from that vantage, the "sexual component" of violence in Algeria that Messaoudi, Roberts, Roy and Ciment all tell us about, that runs the gambit of violence ranging from the enforcement of "moral codes" about dress and behavior, to rape, mutilation, and murder can be viewed as a confluence of factors at several levels of analysis that closely parallels the foregoing description.[70]

Returning to broader "macrosocial" problems in society, the foregoing structural problems were exacerbated by a macroeconomic "structural" factor mix in the 1980s, such as the international debt crisis, the oil glut and the subsequent drop in oil revenues that helped to cause what Zoubir asserts was a "crumbling of the [ruling] bloc."[71] Zoubir suggests that political strains and tensions between President Chadli Banjedid and the National Liberation Front (Front de Liberation Nationale or FLN) exacerbated even further the underlying pressures associated with a broad and deep economic "macrosocial" condition afflicted with the twin ills of what Diamond might call "bloated" state capitalism and the dislocations in public services brought about by Chadli's reforms.[72]

In the broader sense, both Spencer and Roberts talk about the enormous distance between the capacity of the FLN to respond to the political and economic demands and aspirations of the Algerian populace.[73] We are told by Roberts that the rage and other similar feelings that, as previously mentioned, spanned across both "individual" and "social" levels of analysis, that focused special attention on Chadli in particular, were captured by 1988 street chants.[74] In fact, Zoubir and Vandewalle describe the totality of that lurking catastrophe as an unprecedented crisis of legitimacy for the National Liberation Front (FLN) government.[75]

Delving deeper, there are other "predisposing-macrosocial factors," as Reiss and Roth would describe them, that have had a profound and lasting effect on

Algeria's continuously evolving Islamic movement. Framing those "macrosocial factors" is the phenomenon of what writers like Fuller and Mortimer suggest is the fractured national identity of Algeria, rent apart by French and Arab influences with the passage of time.[76] Those historic "predisposing-macrosocial factors" that generate and sustain pressures in effective and sustained ways against that frame of fractured national identity include the "opportunity structure" of political expression that the First World War offered, as Entelis tells us, to the fledgling Arab nationalist movement, personified in the figures of Sharif Hussein of Mecca and his sons Faisal, Abdullah, and Ali.[77]

In the context of the pressure elicited by Arab nationalism in the Fertile Crescent at the turn of the nineteenth century, Roberts suggests that what Reiss and Roth might describe as "predisposing-macrosocial" factors were also inspired and buttressed in large part by exogenous "oppositional culture" influences in the writings of Egyptian reformist scholars, such as Muhammed Abduh, his mentor Jamal al-Din al-Afghani, and the Muslim Brotherhood movement of Hassan al-Banna founded in 1928.[78] To be sure, those writings had profound and lasting influence throughout the region, thereby in effect helping to shape the Algerian Salafiyya Movement, under the influence of Ben Badis and his devotees from the 1920s to the 1940s.[79] In more contemporary Algeria, to be sure, the Egyptian Islamic revivalist and martyr Sayyid Qutb had an enormous capacity to influence Algerian political thinkers and activists.[80]

Seen from a different angle, and this time endogenous to Algeria, is a historical legacy of what Reiss and Roth might call "community organizations," again at the "microsocial-predisposing" level, that in a broader sense really makes the prospect of volatility or change an ineluctable conclusion. At the heart of the matter is the Salafiyya Reform Movement and its twofold struggle in the early twentieth century. First, was the Salafaiya Reform Movement's ferocious fight against European influence that was inextricably bound up with a fierce struggle with Muslim "traditionalists," like the ulama, who were seen by the Salafiyya "reformers" as all too obsequious to the Europeans.[81]

Second, was the fierce competition with "Maraboutism," the Maghrib's incarnation of Sufi Islam, that was practiced by local holy men who combined Islam with indigenous religious traditions and other similar sentiments.[82] The Algerian "reformists" looked askance at the "marabouts," who in addition to corrupting Islam were perceived to be local instruments of French oppression.[83] In the context of that ferocious competition between European and indigenous forces, there is the rich historical legacy of Shaykh Abdulhamid Ben Badis and his Association of Reform Ulama that really makes for an Algerian morality tale about the protracted struggle against the corrupting influences of the West.

Compounding the analysis even more, there are, in my judgment, several important and more contemporary "situational" factors, to use Reiss and Roth's term, at the "macrosocial level" that influenced the continuously evolving

Algerian Islamist movement in the 1970s and 1980s.[84] First, it is commonplace to note in the literature on Algeria that the 1979 Iranian revolution has profound and lasting resonance in Algeria.[85] Spencer, Entelis, and Ciment all suggest that the success of the revolution had a powerful allure for Islamists who viewed the Algerian government as antithetical to the interests of Algerian Islamists.[86] As Spencer relates, "The Iranian revolution of 1979 stood out as an act of defiance within a Middle East seen to be increasingly controlled both economically and politically by the West."[87]

A second "situational" factor at the "macrosocial" level of analysis, in my judgment, was the 1979 invasion of Afghanistan by the Soviet Union, somewhat ironically within the context of the "detente" era between the United States and the Soviet Union.[88] As Roberts suggests, those aggressive set of assaults against Afghanistan evoked by the USSR, seemingly the quintessential "anti-imperialist" state, rent apart any notion that Algeria could continue to stoke the burners of loyalty to the socialist camp with the political goal of ideological and diplomatic distance from the West.[89] As Roberts suggests by extrapolation, the emergent reality of "socialist imperialism" in Afghanistan may have undercut the perception of FLN legitimacy and its perceived capacity to take Islamic interests into account.[90]

What seems significant here as well, and is best placed in the "macrosocial-situational" cell of the matrix, are the interconnections, sometimes fresh, sometimes less so, between FIS members and the "Afghani-Arabs" in Algeria.[91] As Willis reports, Kameredine Kherbane and Said Makhloufi, two former high-ranking members of FIS who were dismissed in 1991, had brought to the "Majlis al-Shura" council a wealth of military experience and set of interconnections to terrorist contacts in Afghanistan and Peshawar, Pakistan, a locale known as a training base for "Arab Mujahiden."[92]

A third "situational factor," this time at the "microsocial" level of analysis, is, in my judgment, the series of violent and contemporary internal Islamic uprisings that served as a bellwether of strength for extreme Islamic revivalism that Reiss and Roth might call a type of Algerian "oppositional culture."[93] The first of the foregoing was the 1982-87 insurrection of Mustapha Boyali's Algerian Islamic Armed Movement (MIA).[94] Spencer tells us that Boyali's goal was presumably to craft an Islamic state, and he was killed by Algerian counterterrorism forces in 1987.[95] According to Willis, it was the tattered remnants of Boyalis's "old" organization, freed from prison and fraying at the edges, that really made up a component of Abdelkader Chebouti's "new" Armed Islamic Movement (MIA or MAIA).[96]

Another example of a violent Algerian uprising, reported by both Willis and Fuller, is the obscure group al-Takfir Wa Hijra or "Anathematization and Refuge" that was led by Kamel Assamar and which started assaults against the Algerian government in 1992. The group al-Takfir Wa Hijra was skillfully broken down by the Algerian military and police soon after 1992. What seems significant here is that the group was liberally peppered with "Afghani Arabs" and that group presumably also had powerful interconnections with other "Afghani-Arabs" who fought in Afghanistan.[97]

In this analysis the sources and origins of the Islamic Salvation Front are overlaid against long-standing economic, cultural, and national identity or national integration problems associated with Algeria. In between lie the more contemporary economic and political problems associated with a shackled FLN government increasingly at loggerheads with the Algerian population. The analysis suggests that today's condition in Algeria, fraught with danger, is caused by a confluence of events at what Reiss and Roth would call "social" and "individual" levels of analysis.[98]

There is a temporal component here as elsewhere, where "activating" and "situational" factors become more entrenched and inclined towards becoming "predisposing" factors over time. That process sets the stage for "spin-off" terrorist group formation or terrorist group splintering that is a function of new "activating events" set against "predisposing factors." In essence one can conceive of that process as a sequence of splitting that closely parallels the formation of the parent organization. It is to those "splinter groups," most especially the Armed Islamic Group (GIA), that the direction of the analysis now turns.

Armed Islamic Group (GIA)
Jammat Islamiyya Mousalah

The Armed Islamic Group presupposes and derives from the Islamic Salvation Front (FIS), thereby in effect making it a FIS "spin-off" or "splinter" terrorist organization. It is commonplace to note that the "activating" factor responsible for the coalescence of the Armed Islamic Group (GIA) was the High Committee of State (Haut Comite d'Etat) decision to nullify the Algerian national elections in December 1991.[99]

The Armed Islamic Group has been described by the U.S. Department of State and Algerian sources as an overarching group that consists of a loose set of interconnections between smaller terrorist groups that Willis tells us mirror one another with respect to ideology.[100] Precious little in the way of solid information about the size of the Armed Islamic Group (GIA) is available. The U.S. Department of State reports that with respect to strength, GIA "strength [is] unknown, probably several hundred to several thousand."[101] Likewise, Ciment informs us in his analysis that "most observers suggest . . . numbering anywhere between several hundred and a few thousand in the country as a whole, with a few small cadres in France and other European countries."[102]

Alternatively, the anonymous Algerian general, "General X," provides a more specific range of from "1,300 to 2,000 men, supported by '5,000-6,000 individuals' who provide support and logistics."[103] Accordingly, the Armed Islamic Group (GIA) falls in the domain of a "large"-sized terrorist group that in this study has between 701 and 2,500 activists. In terms of terrorist group-type, the GIA is classified as a theocentric terrorist group precisely because its two charismatic leaders, Abdelhak Layada and Omar El-Eulmi, were either dead, as in the case of El-Eulmi or imprisoned as in the case of Layada during the 1994-99 time period under consideration.

In terms of recruitment patterns, Willis informs us that special focus is placed on central urban areas of Algeria.[104] With respect to what has been happening abroad, one scripted account tells us of GIA efforts in France in 1991-94 and perhaps afterwards, to recruit young persons "of north African origin" in and around "immigrant suburbs" near Paris to travel to Afghanistan and Pakistan to receive military training.[105] In the narrower sense, Willis also tells us that Adbuldhaak Layada, when he was at the helm of GIA leadership, put a premium on young recruits, precisely because of the reason they were more pliable in acceptance of Layada's authority.[106]

The GIA has had a cookie-cutter strategy of opposition to and noninvolvement with efforts undertaken by FIS at negotiation with the military-backed Algerian government of President Liamine Zeroual and his successor, President Abdelazziz Boutiflika. As if that condition was not enough, the GIA position has been to stoke the burners of conflict and violence against several segments of the Algerian populace as well as non-Algerian targets. Those perceived to be the enemies of GIA include the Algerian government, Algerian government interests, "intellectuals," Berber "Rai" singers whose sultry music and lyrics are seen as an affront to Muslim sensibilities, civilians who are perceived to be collaborators or sympathizers, foreign governments that support the Boutiflika regime, or even those seen as not sufficiently strident in opposition to the government.[107]

In addition to all that, the U.S. Department of State tells us the GIA began to commit terrorist assaults against foreign nationals in September 1993. As Willis suggests, that is in large part because of the symbolic importance of attacks against foreigners, the need for the GIA to garner "notoriety" as a fledgling terrorist group, and, in the broader sense, as a means to undermine the Algerian economy by curtailing foreign investment.[108]

Indeed, the Armed Islamic Group has continuously evolved into what Mickolus would describe as a "transnational" terrorist organization replete with sustained and concerted terrorist assaults done in effective and sustained ways in France against Algerian and French interests.[109] At the same time, there are scripted accounts that suggest that a flexible approach of compromise by the Algerian government at a substantive level might introduce flexibility into the system of negotiations. For example, there is a report that tells us that the GIA probably contributed to a FIS political platform during the Rome negotiations of 1995, thereby in effect making it possible to end GIA terrorist assaults upon the acceptance of that FIS platform by the Algerian government.[110] Delving deeper, another scripted account suggests that at least the Zourabi faction of the GIA had, in a close and carefully reasoned way, considered a 1999 truce to profit from the continuously evolving "Concord Law" that for one thing, provides a fledgling framework for partial or more complete amnesty for particular persons involved in Algerian terrorist assaults.[111]

Be that as it may, both Roberts and Willis tells us there were many former FIS personnel who defected to staff positions in the fledgling Armed Islamic Group (GIA).[112] In the narrower sense, Ciment tells us that from the start, those FIS defectors were "Afghani-Arabs," namely those Arabs who fought alongside the Afghani "Mujahadeen" in their fierce struggle against the Soviet Union and the pro-Soviet Najibullah regime in Kabul.[113] By the same token, defection to the GIA with a prior history of FIS affiliation apparently has severe costs. Evidently, a few important FIS defectors may have been myopic-like or politically naive to entrust their future to the GIA, since one scripted account tells us that Mohamed Said and Abderrezak Redjam, the two ranking FIS leaders previously mentioned, were killed by the GIA in Medea in 1994.[114]

In terms of historical analysis of the GIA, Willis provides a chronology and description of GIA leadership that traces an arc to a "first" GIA led by Mansour Melani, who is described as a follower of Mustapha Boyali's Islamic Group for the Defense of the Illicit. We are told this "first" GIA incarnation, that was comprised of three subcomponent groups, lasted until Melani's arrest by Algerian government forces in July 1992.[115] In turn, a "second" incarnation of GIA was put together by Abdulhak Layada and Omar el-Eulmi, both described by Willis as charismatic leaders.[116] It is Abdulhak Layada and Omar el-Eulmi and their activities that really define the historical parameters, sources, and origins of the contemporary GIA.

Omar el-Eulmi has been described by Willis as "the spiritual guide" of the fledgling Armed Islamic Group organization. He was killed by Algerian government forces soon after the incarnation of the "second" GIA. In turn, Abdulhak Layada fled Algeria and was eventually captured in Morocco and extradited to Algeria where he was imprisoned.[117] One scripted account quotes a very high-ranking Algerian official known as "General X," who tells us that Layada had been executed by the Algerian government in 1998.[118]

The qualitative analysis seems to suggest that an underlying theme of Algerian counterterrorism policy is to kill systematically high-ranking leaders in the hope that such efforts would cripple a terrorist group in the short run offsetting the radicalization process associated with "hard-line" counterterrorism actions. From the vantage of counterterrorism, what seems significant here is that the empirical evidence suggests those efforts are counterproductive and increase the pace if not the depth of radicalization. Willis provides us with a chronology of such counterterrorism actions when he reports that after the El-

Eulmi-Layada era the mantle of GIA leadership fell on Sid Ahmed Mourad, otherwise known as Djaffar Afghani, who was killed in 1994, followed in turn by Cherif Gousami who, as Mickolus and Simmons report, was killed by Algerian government forces on 26 September 1994.[119]

In more contemporary Algeria, both a 1996 newspaper account and Mickolus and Simmons' entry inform us about the continuously evolving GIA leadership as passing from Abou Khalil Mafoud, through Djamal Zitouni, Anwar Zouarbi, and Silmane Mahorzi, otherwise known as Abu Djamil.[120] At a substantive level, there are reports of GIA rivalries happening between the "Zouarbi Faction" and the "Djamil Faction," that may presuppose and derive in part from personal rivalries and perhaps because of disagreement over the enormous capacity of GIA main-line groups to kill, mutilate, sexually assault, and otherwise injure civilians ranging from men of all ages to women and children.

At a functional level, the organizational framework of the Armed Islamic Group (GIA) is perceived by some analysts to be rather freewheeling and relatively less institutionalized, sometimes pitting the interests of one set of GIA leaders against the interests of others.[121] Willis tells us that, over time, GIA leadership established a more formalized "Caliphate" in part to offset the political momentum generated and sustained by the official establishment of the Islamic Salvation Army (AIS) that, as previously mentioned, serves as the generally recognizable military branch of the Islamic Salvation Front (FIS).

As Willis suggests, that "Caliphate" is replete with individual "emirs" that comprise a "Majlis al-Shura" of sorts again presumably to invoke the Islamic tenet of "ijma'" or consensus.[122] We are told in scripted accounts of Algeria about GIA military wings and the "emirs" that are oftentimes delineated by particular geographical sites. For example, one scripted account informs us about seven Armed Islamic Group "wings" (GIA) that include the Mouloud Hibbi division, the 'Abd-al Rashid division, the al-Aqil division, the 'Ukashah division, the Farid al-Darki division, the Antar Zouabri division, and the Mustapha Kertali division.[123]

In the broader sense, what seems significant here is the Armed Islamic Group (GIA) has a set of interconnections that resonate, sometimes powerfully but sometimes with less force, throughout Europe. For example, over and beyond what has been previously mentioned about GIA infrastructure in relation to the 1999 Christmas-New Year incidents at the Canadian-American border, we are told in a scripted account by Martinez of one elaborate and sophisticated document theft and forgery network in Spain to benefit GIA activists throughout Europe that was skillfully broken down by the police General Intelligence Department.[124]

Likewise, descriptive accounts that Mickolus and Simmons provide inform us about GIA infrastructure that presumably presuppose and derive from constituent support in France and Belgium.[125] As if that were not enough of a problem, Zanini, in her analysis of terrorism and cyberspace, suggests that GIA groups are at the forefront of "Information Technology" or "IT" that allows GIA activists, by means of the Internet and other fledgling information technologies, to hamper the efforts of counterterrorist specialists.[126] For Ranstorp, that group of interconnected Islamic activists constitute a "cyber-umma."[127]

For one thing, those international structures facilitate terrorist assault operations both against government targets and civilian targets such as Algerian civilians with political backgrounds, and even Islamic Salvation Front (FIS) affiliated persons. For example, the elderly Shaykh Abdelbaki Sahraoui who was affiliated with FIS was gunned down in his northern Paris mosque in July 1995.[128] Simultaneously, there are accounts of a substantial Islamist presence in London and in Stockholm, thereby in effect making constituent group support for GIA and other Islamic revivalist extremist groups an emergent reality.[129] In that vein, Algerian Foreign Minister Ahmed Attaf of the Zeroual regime lambasted British and Swedish officials in 1998 for their rather freewheeling political asylum systems where persons known to have links with terrorist organizations were able to thrive in those countries in effective and sustained ways.[130]

Some Terrorist "Splinter Groups" of the Armed Islamic Group (GIA)

In turn, there seem to be some Armed Islamic Group (GIA) terrorist "splinter groups" or "spin-off" terrorist groups have come together in the wake of the continuously evolving terrorist assault activity of the GIA and the continuously evolving Algerian political landscape. To be sure, it is possible the first set of very opaque terrorist groups or "proto-groups" described in this section may simply be brigades of the Armed Islamic Group (GIA). Insofar as those fledgling groups or "proto-groups" claim terrorist assaults for themselves, commit terrorist assaults that show up in the data, and participate in the political fray, several of those "proto-groups" are described below.

In the broader sense, it is probably no exaggeration to say that a "situational factor," to use Reiss and Roth term, associated with the genesis of confirmed GIA "splinter" terrorist groups, is the indiscriminate and especially brutal use of force that has been a hallmark of GIA "military activity" in Algeria and elsewhere. That horrific violence has generated strains and tensions among Muslim revivalists, many of whom view the indiscriminate taking of life as antithetical to Islam. Precious little is known about particular "activating factors" for those fledgling groups or "proto-groups." It is likely that those proximate events such as personal rivalries work in tandem with the split in opinion about

GIA brutality to forge alliances between GIA people concerned with the morality and efficacy of GIA terrorist assaults.

Notwithstanding that, some data about possible GIA "splinter groups" or "spin-off" groups are available. One group that turns up in the data is the Phalanx of Supporters of the Sunnah or "Djamat Ansar al Sunnah."[131] At first blush, the Phalanx of Supporters of the Sunnah seems to have been a very small group or brigade led by the now-deceased Abu Ayoob who claimed to be involved in the assassination of an Algerian trade union leader, Abdelhak Benhamouda in 1997.[132] Another identifiable GIA brigade is the Partisans Phalanx or "Katib El-Ansar" whose leader, Farid Eddarki, is the GIA "emir" of Algiers.[133]

Another "splinter group" of the GIA is the Islamic Movement for Spreading the Faith and Holy War that was established on 22 July 1996 by Mustapha Kertali who was once a GIA "emir" in the Larbaa region of Algeria under the aegis of Djamel Zitouni before Zitouni's death in 1996.[134] One scripted account tells us that Kertali claims that some elements of the Islamic Front for Armed Holy War or FIDA and "GIA dissidents" have joined his ranks under the "Islamic Movement for Spreading the Faith and Holy War."[135] It is possible that a "situational factor," as Reiss and Roth might put it, associated with the formation the Islamic Movement for Spreading the Faith and Holy War is the GIA practice of terrorist assaults against civilian targets, for we are told "the announcement" of this new group, "comes amid evidence of splits in the GIA leadership."[136]

In a similar vein, we are told in another scripted account that Shaykh 'Ali Ben Hadjar's Islamic League of the Call and Holy War or "Ligue Islamique de la Da'wa et du Djihad" or LIDD is aligned at least in ideological terms with the Islamic Salvation Front (FIS). The Islamic League of the Call and Holy War was spawned on 5 February 1997 against the backdrop of strains and tensions associated with arguments among Islamist chieftains about the GIA behavior directed against noncombatants.[137]

Perhaps the single most predominant GIA "splinter group," known as the Salafi Group for the Call and Combat (GSPC), is associated with both its founder Hassan Hattab (1967-), otherwise known as Abou Hamza, and Shaykh Osama bin Laden.[138] Tizghart, whose article I draw from heavily, tells us that the Salafi Group for the Call and Combat was crafted in August 1998.[139] In the case of the Salafi Group for the Call and Combat, scripted accounts do suggest that the "situational" factor that generated and sustained its split from the GIA was a difference of opinion among leaders about the bloodletting that resulted from GIA terrorist assaults.[140] For Tizghart, another key risk factor with respect to Armed Islamic Group (GIA) splitting, that Reiss and Roth might describe as "situational," is the Islamic Salvation Front (FIS) "ceasefire" of October 1997.[141] The "activating" factor, as Tizghart suggests, was the death of the GIA's leader, Djamal Zitouni, in 1996, though the emergent reality of the

GSPC was not made official until 14 September 1998 with the proclamation of "Statement 'No. 1.'"[142]

Interestingly enough, the size of the Salafi Group for the Call and Combat (GSPC) has shifted dramatically over time and that is reflected in the coding scheme for terrorist group size. We are told by Tizghart that following the Islamic Salvation Front (FIS) ceasefire acceptance, and Hattab's lambasting of GIA practices against civilians, the size of the GSPC grew apace from some 700 activists to well into the range of 3,000 activists.[143] Clearly, that reflects the capacity of conflict dynamics to make structural change in terrorist group membership and policy direction.

What seems significant here is Tizghart's observation that Hassan Hattab has had an enormous capacity to generate and sustain support among some villages and even the assistance of some Berber supporters, thereby in effect substantiating Entelis's notion that Arab-Berber ethnic fissures and their implications ought not be exaggerated.[144] As Tizghart reports, the efforts of Hattab's constituent supporters have partially offset the effects of government forces and the so-called "Municipal Guard" units comprised of civilians that presumably work in ways similar to the 200,000-man "Patriot" counterterrorist civil guard units known since 1997 as "Groupes de Legitimate Defense."[145] As Tizghart really suggests, that pattern of political and group alignment he observes echoes similar underlying interconnections found in Algeria's war of independence of 1954-62.[146]

Tizghart provides some tantalizing background information about Hassan Hattab that resonates with the Reiss and Roth "risk factor matrix" at the "individual" level of analysis.[147] We are told by the author that Hassan Hattab's older brother, Mawlud Hattab, who was a devotee of Mustapha Boyali's Algerian Islamic Armed Movement (1982-87), joined the ranks of Abdelkader Chebouti's "new" MIA movement and crafted the "al-Fatah Battalion."[148] In turn, Tizghart asserts, another brother of Hassan Hattab known as 'Abd al Quadir also led another MIA brigade. A violent death—always a frequent visitor of terrorist activists and their terrorist assaults—claimed both brothers of Hassan Hattab. Tizghart suggests those profound and lasting, nay searing experiences, may have affected what Reiss and Roth might describe as Hassan Hattab's "self identification in social hierarchy" at the "predisposing-psychosocial level" of analysis.[149]

The foregoing seems plausible precisely because Tizghart suggests that Hassan Hattab romanticized Mustapha Boyali's Algerian Islamic Armed Movement and even tried to emulate some of its underlying themes and tactics. In the narrower sense, the proposition that Boyali's movement served as a blueprint for Hattab may have some predictive value. In the broader sense, that example, in my judgment, is illustrative of the usefulness of the Reiss and Roth "risk factor matrix" when applications are made to terrorist group chieftains and their terrorist groups. At a functional level, Hattab's leadership of the Salafi

Group for the Call and Combat passed into eclipse smoothly with the ascendancy of 'Abd al-Majid Disha.[150]

Perhaps the darkest foreboding of all, with respect to the West in general and the United States in particular, are Tizghart's assertions that there are strong interconnections between Shaykh Osama bin Laden and the Salafi Group for the Call and Combat (GSPC).[151] In the broader sense, Ranstorp suggests those interconnections can be seen within the context of bin Laden's set of powerful ties, replete with intricacies and nuances, between several militant Islamic revivalist groups with the capacity to coalesce at some level to confront Western influence in general and American influence in particular in the Middle East.[152]

In the narrower sense, and seen from a different angle, Tizghart asserts that bin Laden was a pivotal figure with respect to the formation and bankrolling of the Salafi Group for the Call and Combat (GSPC) precisely because GIA generates and sustains terrorist assaults against civilians with enormous carnage and deleterious political results. Equally important with respect to bin Laden's funding of GSPC are political rivalries with the GIA, that presuppose and derive from a continuously evolving political environment between FIS and the Algerian government, where Rabih Kabir of FIS had endorsed the Islamic Salvation Front cease-fire of October 1997.[153] With respect to the foregoing, Tizghart asserts that bin Laden's plan to confront Kabir and FIS revolved around the central idea of helping to provide a "middle of the road" alternative to the Islamic Salvation Front (FIS) in the Salafi Group for the Call and Combat and its European affiliates, which could still wage war against the Algerian regime.[154]

Undoubtedly, those and other interconnections help to weave a tapestry of terror that demands quantitative as well as qualitative analysis. Indeed, one aspect of that tapestry of terror is, as Tizghart asserts, the use of "Afghani-Arabs" to serve as interlocutors between bin Laden and the Salafiya Group for the Call and Combat to partially offset the effects of Western counterterrorism experts.[155] To be sure, both Zanini and Ranstorp suggest the Afghani-Arabs are a storehouse of activist support for several prolific Middle East terrorist organizations like the Armed Islamic Group (GIA) and the al-Jama'a al-Islamiya in Egypt.[156] It is that tapestry of terror that reflects what Avenarius calls "the privatization of terrorism," along with what Zanini suggests is a certain organizational decentralization, that is one hallmark of the differences that distinguish more contemporary or "new generation" Middle East terrorism from their "traditional" historical antecedents.[157]

In the case of interconnections between Islamic revivalist terrorist groups like the Salafi Group for the Call and Combat, and "Afghani-Arabs," bin Laden's financial and political support has an enormous capacity to develop a psychological imprinting of sorts that may evoke sentiments of obligation and other similar feelings from certain Islamic revivalist terrorist groups in Algeria toward him. In the broadest sense, the foregoing, coupled with bin Laden's morality tale of confrontation with the West in political, military, and economic terms, and equally important, generally recognizable opposition to American "cultural hegemony" in the world is, in my judgment, what poses a serious and fundamental set of challenges and opportunities for counterterrorism specialists nowadays.[158] In order to gauge that threat, an understanding of the dimensions of Algerian terrorism based on empirical analysis is required, and it is to that task that this work now turns.

Some General Observations about Algerian Terrorism

Relative Frequencies and Percentages of Algerian Terrorist Assaults by Year

For the five-year time period under consideration between 1994 and 1999, the data consist of 343 discrete events of Algerian terrorism that seem to be made up primarily of domestic and "transnational" terrorist assaults.[159] When the data are broken down by year of event, it is clear that Algerian terrorism has the peaks and troughs associated with cyclical activity. That finding about the cyclical nature of Algerian terrorism mirrors the findings of several broader studies on terrorism.[160]

With respect to the range of Algerian terrorist assaults, the smallest number happened in 1999 with 18 incidents or 5.2 percent (valid) percent of the working database that in this case is the complete database of 343 incidents. The largest number of Algerian terrorist assaults occurred in 1997 with 95 incidents or 27.7 percent of the total. Peak years include 1994, 1995, and 1997 while trough years include 1996 and 1999. During the peak years, 73 out of 343 events or 21.3 percent happened in 1994; 77 out of 343 acts or 22.4 percent were carried out in 1995; while a first place ranking of 95 out of 343 or 27.7 percent took place in 1997 (see figure 3.1).

Terrorist Assaults by Group-Type, Terrorist Group, and Location

A breakdown of Algerian terrorist assault data informs us that at 340 out of 342 acts, an overwhelming majority of Algerian terrorism, can be categorized into two types: terrorist assaults carried out by Islamic revivalist groups without charismatic leaders, known as "theocentric" terrorist groups, and by anonymous terrorist groups or declared "lone assailants." Certainly, the most glaring finding is that at 76.6 percent, over three-fourths or 262 out of 342 Algerian terrorist assaults, were carried out by anonymous groups or "lone assailants." Ranking

Frequencies

Statistics

Year of Event

N	Valid	343
	Missing	0

Year of Event

		Frequency	Percent	Valid percent	Cumulative percent
Valid	1994	73	21.3	21.3	21.3
	1995	77	22.4	22.4	43.7
	1996	37	10.8	10.8	54.5
	1997	95	27.7	27.7	82.2
	1998	43	12.5	12.5	94.8
	1999	18	5.2	5.2	100.0
	Total	343	100.0	100.0	

Year of Event

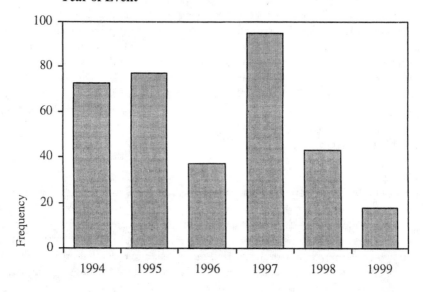

Figure 3.1: Relative Frequency of Algerian Terrorist Attacks by Year, 1994-1999

second are terrorist assaults carried out by theocentric terrorist groups that account for 21.9 percent or 75 out of 342 acts. In third place, three out of 342 acts by declared "lone assailants" make up some .9 percent. In fourth place are uncompleted acts that make up .6 percent or 2 out of 342 incidents. What seems significant here is that the only kind of terrorist group observable over the Algerian political landscape or where attribution is made by government or reliable nongovernment sources are theocentric terrorist organizations (see figure 3.2).

When the data are broken down more finely by identifiable Algerian terrorist groups, it is observed that among claimed or identifiable terrorist assaults, the Armed Islamic Group (GIA) committed the greatest number of terrorist acts with 62 out of 343 terrorist assaults or 18.1 percent of the total. The Islamic Salvation Army (AIS), that is, the military arm of the Islamic Salvation Front (FIS), placed a very distant second place, with only 6 out of 343 terrorist assaults or some 1.7 percent.[161] Clearly, there is enormous percentage distance between those first and second place rankings and it is possible, although it is certainly not definitive, that those findings may reflect the rather episodic and inconsistent negotiations between the FIS and the Algerian government that started in the summer of 1994, progressed through the Sant'Egidio talks in Italy, and continuously evolved through June 1999 and beyond.[162]

The Salafi Group for the Call and Combat (GSPC) ranked third with 5 out of 343 terrorist assaults or 1.5 percent, and that is notable precisely because of the rather public stance and very young age of the GSPC. A total of 5 out of 343 acts were carried out by more shadowy Algerian terrorist groups like Islamic Movement for Spreading the Faith and Holy War with one assault (.3 percent); the Phalanx of the Supporters of the Sunnah with two assaults (.6 percent); the Islamic Front for the Armed Jihad with one assault (.3 percent); the Union of Peaceful Citizens of Algeria with one assault (.3 percent).[163] To be sure, those Algerian terrorist groups accounted for one and a half percent (1.5 percent) of the total amount (see figure 3.3).

Analysis that breaks down those data by location reveals that an overwhelming majority of Algerian terrorist assaults are domestic in nature, happening within Algeria. Out of 343 cases, a full 315 terrorist assaults, or 91.8 percent of the total amount took place in Algeria. In Western Europe, a locale that is comprised of Great Britain, France, Germany, and Belgium in this study, 19 out of 343 terrorist assaults or 5.5 percent happened. In turn, 9 out of 343 events, or only 2.6 percent occurred in other or unknown geographical locales. Outside of the one thwarted terrorist assault in the United States previously mentioned, there are no recorded Algerian terrorist assaults against the United States or its citizens that happened in the United States between 1994 and 1999.[164] In sum, Algerian terrorism remains a largely self-contained phenomenon for the time period under consideration with the exception of some seepage into France (see figure 3.4).

Frequencies

Statistics

Category of Group

N	Valid	342
	Missing	1

Category of Group

		Frequency	Percent	Valid percent	Cumulative percent
Valid	Uncompleted acts	2	.6	.6	.6
	Unclaimed acts	262	76.4	76.6	77.2
	Theocentric claimed	75	21.9	21.9	99.1
	Lone assailant	3	.9	.9	100.0
	Total	342	99.7	100.0	
Missing	system	1	.3		
Total		343	100.0		

Category of Group

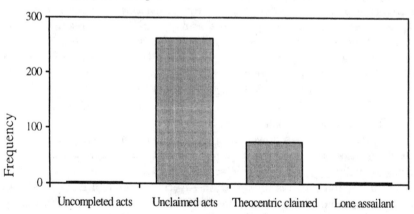

Figure 3.2: Relative Frequency of Algerian Terrorist Attacks by Group-Type, 1994-1999

Frequencies

Statistics

Name of Group

N	Valid	343
	Missing	0

Name of Group

		Frequency	Percent	Valid percent	Cumulative percent
Valid	FIS (AIS)	6	1.7	1.7	1.7
	GIA (Armed Islamic Group)	62	18.1	18.1	19.8
	Islamic Movement for Spreading the Faith and Holy War	1	.3	.3	20.1
	Phalanx of the Supporters of the Sunnah	2	.6	.6	20.7
	Uncompleted	1	.3	.3	21.0
	Unclaimed	261	76.1	76.1	97.1
	Salafi Group for the Call and Combat (GSPC)	5	1.5	1.5	98.5
	Islamic Front for the Armed Jihad	1	.3	.3	98.8
	Union of Peaceful Citizens of Algeria	1	.3	.3	99.1
	Lone assailant	3	.9	.9	100.0
	Total	343	100.0	100.0	

Name of Group

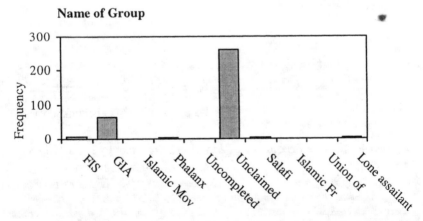

Figure 3.3: Relative Frequency of Algerian Terrorist Attacks by Terrorist Group, 1994-1999

Frequencies

Statistics

Locale

N	Valid	343
	Missing	0

Locale

		Frequency	Percent	Valid percent	Cumulative percent
Valid	Algeria	315	91.8	91.8	91.8
	Europe	19	5.5	5.5	97.4
	Other/Unknown	9	2.6	2.6	100.0
	Total	343	100.0	100.0	

Locale

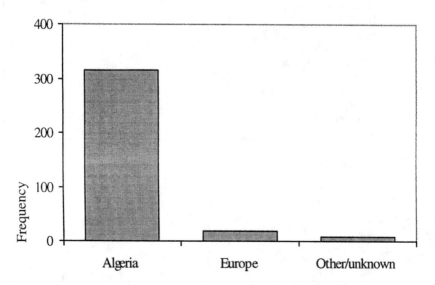

Figure 3.4: Relative Frequency of Algerian Terrorism by Location, 1994-1999

Terrorism Assault Attributes: Fatalities, Injuries, Property Damage, Target Preference

One of the single, most dominant themes that is commonplace to note in the literature on terrorism is that the enormous capacity of terrorism to create damage is more psychological in nature than physical in devastation.[165] The findings about death and injury rates support the research findings of many terrorism experts.[166] For Algerian terrorism, three-fourths of all terrorist assaults or 255 out of 338 acts killed between 1 and 50 persons. By contrast, 21.0 percent of Algerian terrorist assaults or 71 out of 338 events were non-lethal. Alternately, there are only 8 out of 338 events or 2.4 percent that resulted in the deaths of between 51 and 100 persons. There are 4 outlier cases that represent terrorist assaults with death rates of over 100 persons. In those terrorist assaults 113 persons, 176 persons, 200 persons in the Baraki section of Algiers, and in one instance 500 persons in an anonymous terrorist assault against the Relizane province "mountain" village of Had Chekala were killed in each case (see figure 3.5).[167]

Injury rate patterns, while not identical with the foregoing, mirror in a generally recognizable way the same relatively low patterns found in Algerian terrorist assault death rates. With respect to event injuries, 50.8 percent of the terrorist assaults committed, or 120 out of 236 acts, were injury-free events. Terrorist assaults that injured between 1 and 50 persons accounted for 44.1 percent of the total or 104 out of 236 acts, and was the second largest category. Terrorist assaults that resulted in injuries to 51 through 100 persons were rare, and comprise only 3.4 percent or eight of 236 cases. Lastly, there were four outlier cases that caused injuries to 104, 120, 125, and 286 persons, respectively, that comprise 1.6 percent of the total (see figure 3.6).

Turning to levels of property damage, analysis of 301 terrorist assaults reveals that most instances of Algerian terrorism cause relatively low amounts of property damage. Over one-half of all Algerian terrorist assaults, or 177 out of 301 events, caused no property damage. There were 79 out of 301 Algerian terrorist incidents or 26.2 percent that caused "slight" damage, while 22 out of 301 acts or 7.3 percent caused "moderate" damage. Moving towards the high end of the scale, it is observed that 20 out of 301 incidents or 6.6 percent caused "high" levels of property damage. It is observed that only three out of 301 incidents or 1.0 percent caused "severe" property damage, and that reflects the reality that terrorist assaults with "severe" property damage are very rare occurrences (see figure 3.7).

Analysis that breaks down the data by target type informs us that 84.2 percent or 287 out of 341 events involved civilian targets, as compared to 10.6 percent or 36 out of 341 events that involved government targets (see figure 3.8). Terrorist assaults against "infrastructure" was not especially common, with

Frequencies

Statistics

Event Deaths

N	Valid	338
	Missing	5

Event Deaths

		Frequency	Percent	Valid percent	Cumulative percent
Valid	0	71	20.7	21.0	21.0
	1	255	74.3	75.4	96.4
	2	8	2.3	2.4	98.8
	113	1	.3	.3	99.1
	176	1	.3	.3	99.4
	200	1	.3	.3	99.7
	500	1	.3	.3	100.0
	Total	338	98.5	100.0	
Missing	system	5	1.5		
Total		343	100.0		

Event Deaths

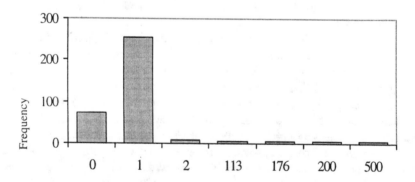

Figure 3.5: Relative Frequency of Numbers of Dead in Algerian Terrorist Incidents, 1994-1999   (0=0; 1=1 through 50; 2=51 through 100)

Frequencies

Statistics

Event Injuries

N	Valid	236
	Missing	107

Event Injuries

		Frequency	Percent	Valid percent	Cumulative percent
Valid	0	120	35.0	50.8	50.8
	1	104	30.3	44.1	94.9
	2	8	2.3	3.4	98.3
	104	1	.3	.4	98.7
	120	1	.3	.4	99.2
	125	1	.3	.4	99.6
	286	1	.3	.4	100.0
	Total	236	68.8	100.0	
Missing	system	107	31.2		
Total		343	100.0		

Event Injuries

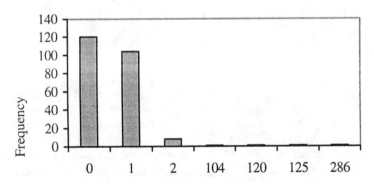

Figure 3.6: Relative Frequency of Numbers of Injured in Algerian Terrorist Incidents, 1994-1999   (0=0; 1=1 through 50; 2=51 through 100)

Frequencies

Statistics

Property Damage

N	Valid	301
	Missing	42

Property Damage

		Frequency	Percent	Valid percent	Cumulative percent
Valid	None	177	51.6	58.8	58.8
	Slight	79	23.0	26.2	85.0
	Moderate	22	6.4	7.3	92.4
	High	20	5.8	6.6	99.0
	Severe	3	.9	1.0	100.0
	Total	301	87.8	100.0	
Missing	system	42	12.2		
Total		343	100.0		

Property Damage

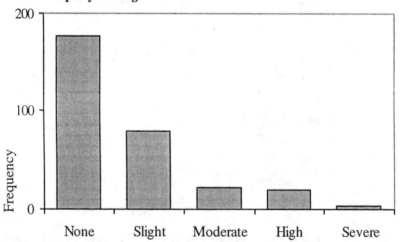

Figure 3.7: Levels of Property Damage Caused by Algerian Terrorist Attacks, 1994-1999

Frequencies

Statistics

Type of Target

N	Valid	341
	Missing	2

Type of Target

		Frequency	Percent	Valid percent	Cumulative percent
Valid	Govt. targets	36	10.5	10.6	10.6
	Infrastructure	12	3.5	3.5	14.1
	Civilian targets	287	83.7	84.2	98.2
	Govt.-civilian	2	.6	.6	98.8
	Civilian-govt.	3	.9	.9	99.7
	Infrastr.-civilian	1	.3	.3	100.0
	Total	341	99.4	100.0	
Missing	system	2	.6		
Total		343	100.0		

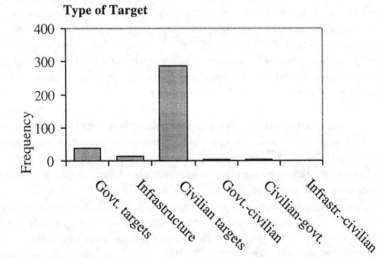

Figure 3.8: Relative Frequency of Algerian Terrorism Target-Types, 1994-1999

3.5 percent or 12 out of 341 acts. It is found that 58.3 percent or seven out of 12 infrastructure attacks were committed by anonymous terrorist groups or "lone assailants," while 1 out of 12 infrastructure terrorist attacks or 8.3 percent was carried out by an identifiable lone assailant. In turn, 33.3 percent or 4 out of 12 infrastructure terrorist attacks were carried out by theocentric groups (see table 3.1). While the amount remains low, 6 out of 341 terrorist assaults or 1.8 percent have "multiple targets," namely targets that contain both civilian and government attributes. For example, in one instance a car bomb detonated in the street enveloped civilian victims, but the bomb was exploded outside a police station.[168] It is observed that 1.2 percent or 3 out of 260 acts of unclaimed Algerian terrorist assaults involved "multiple targets," while Algerian assaults carried out by identifiable "lone assailants" never involved "multiple targets" between 1994 and 1999 (see table 3.1).

The foregoing analysis that gives shape to the general contours of Algerian terrorism leads to several conclusions, some that are consistent with prior findings about the general shape of terrorism, and some that showcase, in my judgment, notable variations for the Algerian terrorism data. First, Algerian terrorism, like terrorism in other parts of the world, exhibits cyclical activity replete with a regularity of ebbs and flows. What seems significant here is the only type of Algerian terrorist group in operation between 1994 and 1999 that makes claims for terrorist assaults or is attributed to having committed them are theocentric terrorist groups. What also stands out is the glaring finding about the predominance of anonymous terrorist group or "lone assailant" activity over the Algerian political landscape. A full 76.5 percent of the discrete events tested are anonymous terrorist assaults, while identifiable "lone assailant" terrorist assaults constitute .9 percent, with 3 out of 342 incidents.

Second, with respect to location, over 90 percent of all terrorist assaults related to the protracted battle between the military-backed Algerian government and Algerian Islamists happened within Algeria. There is some seepage into parts of Western Europe, but the analysis illuminates how Algerian terrorism remains in large part a self-contained phenomenon during 1994-99. Third is the finding that Algerian terrorism events, in the broader sense, cause relatively few casualties and relatively little property damage. At the same time, there are isolated cases of high-intensity conventional terrorism that happen and show up as outlier cases that echo the findings of other works on terrorism.[169]

Those findings are consistent with the results of several studies on terrorism that suggest that the psychological effect of terrorism, rather than full-blown physical devastation, is what generates and sustains the abject fear necessary to make terrorism an effective tool.[170] Lastly, the analysis informs us that practitioners of Algerian terrorism strongly favor civilian targets over government targets. To be specific, Algerian terrorist assaults favor civilian targets by about an 8:1 ratio over government targets, and that preference shown for civilian targets closely parallels findings of other works on terrorism and

Table 3.1: Relative Frequency of Algerian Terrorist Targets by Group-Type, 1994-1999

Type of Target * Category of Group Cross-Tabulation

			Category of group		
			Un-completed acts	Un-claimed acts	Theo-centric claimed
Type of target	Govt. targets	Count		22	13
		% within type of target		61.1%	36.1%
		% within category of group		8.5%	17.3%
		% of total		6.5%	3.8%
	Infra-structure	Count		7	4
		% within type of target		58.3%	33.3%
		% within category of group		2.7%	5.3%
		% of total		2.1%	1.2%
	Civilian targets	Count	2	228	55
		% within type of target	.7%	79.7%	19.2%
		% within category of group	100.0%	87.7%	73.3%
		% of total	.6%	67.1%	16.2%
	Govt.-civilian	Count		1	1
		% within type of target		50.0%	50.0%
		% within category of group		.4%	1.3%
		% of total		.3%	.3%
	Civilian -govt.	Count		1	2
		% within type of target		33.3%	66.7%
		% within category of group		.4%	2.7%
		% of total		.3%	.6%
	Infrastr-civilian	Count		1	
		% within type of target		100.0%	
		% within category of group		.4%	
		% of total		.3%	
Total		Count	2	260	75
		% within type of target	.6%	76.5%	22.1%
		% within category of group	100.0%	100.0%	100.0%
		% of total	.6%	76.5%	22.1%

Table 3.1 - continued

Type of Target * Category of Group Cross-Tabulation

			Category of lone assailant	Total
Type of target	Govt. targets	Count	1	36
		% within type of target	2.8%	100.0%
		% within category of group	33.3%	10.6%
		% of total	.3%	10.6%
	Infra-structure	Count	1	12
		% within type of target	8.3%	100.0%
		% within category of group	33.3%	3.5%
		% of total	.3%	3.5%
	Civilian targets	Count	1	286
		% within type of target	.3%	100.0%
		% within category of group	33.3%	84.1%
		% of total	.3%	84.1%
	Govt.-civilian	Count		2
		% within type of target		100.0%
		% within category of group		.6%
		% of total		.6%
	Civilian-govt.	Count		3
		% within type of target		100.0%
		% within category of group		.9%
		% of total		.9%
	Infrastr-civilian	Count		1
		% within type of target		100.0%
		% within category of group		.3%
		% of total		.3%
Total		Count	3	340
		% within type of target	.9%	100.0%
		% within category of group	100.0%	100.0%
		% of total	.9%	100.0%

squares with the aforementioned about the psychological import of terrorism (see figure 3.8).

Variable Analysis

Political Ideology and Target Type, Numbers of Deaths, Numbers of Injuries

From the start, it is important to acknowledge that analysis of Algerian terrorism is shackled by sketchy and incomplete data that makes any discussion and description of Algerian terrorist group-type behavior rather limited. As previously mentioned, the data suggest that for the 1994-99 period, theocentric terrorist groups are the only kind of terrorist group that operate in the Algerian political landscape and make claims for terrorist assaults or are attributed by government and nongovernment sources to having carried them out. At the same time, it is possible—nay likely—that some of the unclaimed terrorist acts recorded here are in fact carried out by Armed Islamic Group (GIA) terrorist organizations and even perhaps, as some writers have suggested, by Algerian government forces as a way to undercut the political and moral legitimacy of the Islamists.[171]

Plainly, limitations in those data that revolve around the central problem of terrorist group identification are a source of weakness for amalgamated data in general, and in the case of unclaimed Algerian terrorist acts in particular. In this case study, with amalgamated data that comprise such a large part of the Algerian terrorist assault data base, the differences normally associated with types of identifiable terrorist groups becomes blurred.[172] Bearing in mind that many unidentifiable GIA terrorist assaults may fall into the unclaimed category by default, it is possible that the following measures of statistical association for the variables "target" and "political ideology" do not reflect the population distribution with optimal precision. However, when data testing is performed on a few subsets of those data, invaluable insight into the parameters of Algerian terrorism is obtained.

Six theoretical propositions that presuppose and derive from the work of several authorities on terrorism and my own research findings are examined for validity. One standout finding from my prior work on Middle East terrorism is the very large number of unclaimed terrorist assaults carried out by anonymous terrorist organizations or "lone assailants." Accordingly, the following hypothesis about Algerian terrorist target choice and political ideology is proffered:

Hypothesis One: Unclaimed terrorist assaults will involve civilian targets more frequently than theocentric terrorist assaults.

The analysis of the relationship between "target type" and "political ideology" suggests that a statistically significant association exists between the political ideology of Islamic revivalist terrorist groups and the type of target selected. A Pearson Chi Square value of 5.353 with a "p-value" of .021, and a Yates Continuity Correction measure for a 2x2 table of 4.399 with a "p-value" of .036 at one degree of freedom (1 d.f.) makes it possible to reject the null hypothesis of no relation between the variables at the .05 confidence level.[173] Put another way, if we fail to reject the null hypothesis of no relation between the variables "political ideology" and "target," there is a 95 percent chance that that would be incorrect. In terms of the strength of the relationship, a Cramer's V score of .129 with a significance score of .021 and a "Phi" of -.129 with a significance score of .021 indicates a weak relationship between the variables (see table 3.2).

In the broader sense, 36 out of all 340 terrorist incidents or about 10.6 percent involved government targets, while 286 out of 340 incidents or 84.1 percent favored civilian targets. The data distribution shows that 8.5 percent of unclaimed acts or 22 out of 260 involved government targets, while 87.7 percent or 228 out of 260 involved civilian targets. In the case of theocentric terrorist assaults, 17.3 percent of theocentric assaults or 13 out of 75 involved government targets as compared with 73.3 percent or 55 out of 75 that involved civilian targets. Special focus on targets that do not fall into the realm of pure "civilian" or "government" targets devotes attention to outlier cases. It is observed that 3.5 percent or 12 out of 340 acts involved attacks against "infrastructure" targets such as power pylons, roads, or bridges. To be more specific, 7 out of 260 "unclaimed" terrorists assaults or 2.7 percent were aimed at infrastructure, while 5.3 percent or 4 out of 75 theocentric terrorist assaults, a rate nearly double the rate for anonymous terrorist activity, involved infrastructure targets.

By the same token, Algerian terrorist events that involved "multiple targets" were even more scarce, with only 1.8 percent or 6 out of 340 incidents. In the multiple target category, the "civilian-government" target type is the highest "multiple target" type recorded with three assaults or .9 percent of the total number of terrorist assaults. The foregoing results are supportive of Hypothesis One. I found that 87.7 percent of all unclaimed terrorist assaults (228/260) involved civilian targets, as compared with 73.3 percent (55/75) of theocentric terrorist assaults that were aimed at civilian targets (see table 3.2).

Table 3.2: Relative Frequency of Algerian Terrorist Targets by Group-Type, 1994-1999 (summary statistics)

Crosstabs

Case Processing Summary

	Cases					
	Valid		Missing		Total	
	N	Percent	*N*	Percent	*N*	Percent
Type of target * category of group	320	93.3%	23	6.7%	343	100.0%

Type of Target * Category of Group Cross-Tabulation

			Category of group		Total
			Unclaimed acts	Theo-centric claimed	
Type of target	Govt. targets	Count	23	13	36
		% within type of target	63.9%	36.1%	100.0%
		% within category of group	9.1%	19.1%	11.3%
		% of total	7.2%	4.1%	11.3%
	Civilian targets	Count	229	55	284
		% within type of target	80.6%	19.4%	100.0%
		% within category of group	90.9%	80.9%	88.8%
		% of total	71.6%	17.2%	88.8%
Total		Count	252	68	320
		% within type of target	78.8%	21.3%	100.0%
		% within category of group	100.0%	100.0%	100.0%
		% of total	78.8%	21.3%	100.0%

Chi Square Tests

	Value	df	Asymp. Sig. (2-sided)	Exact sig. (2-sided)	Exact sig. (1-sided)
Pearson Chi Square	5.353[b]	1	.021		
Continuity Correction[a]	4.399	1	.036		
Likelihood Ratio	4.782	1	.029		
Fisher's Exact Test				.029	.022
Linear-by-Linear Association	5.337	1	.021		
N of valid cases	320				

a. Computed only for a 2x2 table.
b. 0 cells (0%) have expected count less than 5. The minimum expected count is 7.65.

Table 3.2 - *continued*

Directional Measures

			value	Asymp. std. error[a]	Approx. t	Approx. sig.
Nominal by nominal	Lambda	Symmetric	.000	.000	b	b
		Type of target dependent	.000	.000	b	b
		Category of group dependent	.000	.000	b	b
	Goodman and Kruskal tau	Type of target dependent	.017	.017		.021[c]
		Category of group dependent	.017	.017		.021[c]

a. Not assuming the null hypothesis.
b. Cannot be computed because the asymptotic standard error equals zero.
c. Based on chi square approximation.

Symmetric Measures

		Value	Approx. sig.
Nominal by nominal	Phi	-.129	.021
	Cramer's V	.129	.021
N of valid cases		320	

a. Not assuming the null hypothesis.
b. Using the asymptotic standard error assuming the null hypothesis.

Political Ideology and Numbers of Dead

With respect to terrorist assault "attributes," the following theoretical proposition about the relationship between unclaimed Algerian terrorist assaults and numbers of deaths is examined for validity. The theoretical underpinning of this relationship, namely that unclaimed terrorist assaults will have lower rates of death, in part to offset the prospect of an enormous military backlash, presupposes and derives from the notion previously mentioned that unclaimed terrorist assaults play a role in a political system to pressure political leaders to make structural political change in reaction to the political demands and aspirations of segments the populace.

Hypothesis Two: Unclaimed terrorist assaults will result in a smaller percentage of deaths than terrorist assaults committed by theocentric groups.

In terms of the analysis of "category of group" and "numbers of dead," the cross-tabulation analysis suggests that a statistically significant association exists between numbers of dead that result from terrorist events that are claimed by theocentric groups and those that remain anonymous. The Pearson Chi Square is 19.899 at one degree of freedom (1 d.f.) with a "p-value" of less than .001 and a Yates Continuity Correction figure for a 2x2 table of 18.470 with a "p-value" of less than .001 at one degree of freedom (1 d.f.). To be sure, the null hypothesis of no relationship between the variables "category of group" and "numbers of deaths" is rejected at the .05 confidence level. With respect to the strength of the relationship, a Cramer's V score of .248 with a significance score of less than .001 and a "Phi" value of -.248 with a significance score of less than .001 suggests a relationship of slight strength between the two variables (see table 3.3).

A breakdown of the data reveals that 15.1 percent of unclaimed acts or 39 out of 258 were nonlethal terrorist assaults, while 84.1 percent of unclaimed acts or 217 out of 258 killed between one and fifty persons. By contrast, a full 38.7 percent of theocentric terrorist acts or 29 out of 75 were nonlethal, while 58.7 percent of theocentric claimed terrorist acts or 44 out of 75 killed between one and fifty persons. "Lone assailant" terrorist assaults were very rare, comprising only .9 percent or 3 acts out of 338 incidents, and in one instance 1 assault was nonlethal while the other two assaults killed between one and fifty persons. The sample mean for "event deaths" is 10.48, with a standard deviation of 33.44.

In terms of terrorist assaults with very high rates of death, the 4 outlier cases in the data comprise 1.2 percent, ranging from one case that resulted in 113 dead persons to another case that resulted in 500 dead persons. Two outlier cases were claimed or attributable to theocentric terrorist groups and two outlier cases were carried out by anonymous Algerian terrorist groups or "lone

Table 3.3: Relative Frequency of Numbers of Dead in Algerian Terrorist Incidents by Group-Type   (0=0; 1=1 through 50) (summary statistics)

Crosstabs

Case Processing Summary

	Cases					
	Valid		Missing		Total	
	N	Percent	*N*	Percent	*N*	Percent
Category of group * Event deaths	324	94.5%	19	5.5%	343	100.0%

Category of Group *Event Deaths Cross-Tabulation

			Event deaths		Total
			0	1	
Category of group	Unclaimed acts	Count	40	212	252
		% within category of group	15.9%	84.1%	100.0%
		% within event deaths	58.0%	83.1%	77.8%
		% of total	12.3%	65.4%	77.8%
	Theocentric claimed	Count	29	43	72
		% within category of group	40.3%	59.7%	100.0%
		% within event deaths	42.0%	16.9%	22.2%
		% of total	9.0%	13.3%	22.2%
Total		Count	69	255	324
		% within category of group	21.3%	78.7%	100.0%
		% within event deaths	100.0%	100.0%	100.0%
		% of total	21.3%	78.7%	100.0%

Chi Square Tests

	Value	df	Asymp. sig. (2-sided)	Exact sig. (2-sided)	Exact sig. (1-sided)
Pearson Chi Square	19.899[b]	1	.000		
Continuity Correction[a]	18.470	1	.000		
Likelihood Ratio	17.968	1	.000		
Fisher's Exact Test				.000	.000
Linear-by-Linear Association	19.838	1	.000		
N of valid cases	324				

a. Computed only for a 2x2 table.
b. 0 cells (0%) have expected count less than 5. The minimum expected count is 15.33.

Table 3.3 - continued

Directional Measures

			Value	Asymp. std. error[a]	Approx. T[b]	Approx. sig.
Nominal by nominal	Lambda	Symmetric	.000	.000	.[b]	.[b]
		Event deaths dependent	.000	.000	.[b]	.[b]
		Category of group dependent	.000	.000	.[b]	.[b]
	Goodman and Kruskal tau	Event deaths dependent	.061	.031		.000[c]
		Category of group dependent	.061	.030		.000[c]

a. Not assuming the null hypothesis.
b. Cannot be computed because the asymptotic standard error equals zero.
c. Based on chi square approximation.

Symmetric Measures

		Value	Approx. sig.
Nominal by nominal	Phi	-.248	.000
	Cramer's V	.248	.000
N of valid cases		324	

a. Not assuming the null hypothesis.
b. Using the asymptotic standard error assuming the null hypothesis.

assailants." Lastly, two uncompleted Algerian terrorist assaults chronicled here caused no loss of life as one might expect (see table 3.4). Undoubtedly, the empirical findings do not support Hypothesis Two, and hence it is rejected.

Political Ideology and Numbers of Injuries

It follows from the foregoing discussion about the role of unclaimed terrorist assaults to promote political change or accommodation that terrorist assaults designed to promote such change will have relatively low levels of injury rates, in part to prevent an enormous military backlash that would more than offset any political gains made. The following hypothesis that captures that idea is tested for validity:

Hypothesis Three: Unclaimed terrorist assaults will result in a smaller percentage of injuries than terrorist assaults committed by theocentric terrorist groups.

The bivariate analysis of "category of group" and "numbers of injuries" suggests that a statistically significant association exists between numbers of injuries that result from terrorist events, whether or not the act is a theocentric act or an unclaimed event. The analysis generates a Pearson Chi Square statistic of 5.106 and a "p-value" of .024 at one degree of freedom (1 d.f.), and a Yates Continuity Correction score for a 2x2 table of 4.359 with a "p-value" of .037 at one degree of freedom (1 d.f.). Hence, it is possible to reject the null hypothesis of no relation between the variables "category of group" and "number of injuries" at the .05 confidence level. A Cramer's V score of .152 with a significance score of .024, and a "Phi" value of -.152 with a significance score of .024, and a Goodman and Kruskal's *tau* score of .023 with a significance score of .024 when the event injuries is the dependent variable, all indicate a relationship of slight proportions between those two variables (see table 3.5).

The distribution of the data tell us that unclaimed terrorist assaults, at 87 out of 120 acts or 72.5 percent, have the highest number and the greatest percentage of terrorist attacks that were injury-free events. Ranking second with 24.2 percent or 29 out of 120 acts, theocentric terrorist assaults comprise the second highest number and percentage of injury-free Algerian terrorist assaults. In turn, identifiable "lone assailant" terrorist acts account for 1.7 percent or 2 out of 120 injury-free terrorist assaults (see table 3.6).

At the same time, anonymous terrorist acts comprise the largest portion of Algerian terrorist assaults that injure between one and fifty individuals, with 86.4 percent or 89 out of 103 acts. In turn, theocentric acts placed second with

Table 3.4: Relative Frequency of Numbers of Dead in Algerian Terrorist Incidents by Group-Type   (0=0; 1=1 through 100)

Crosstabs

Case Processing Summary

	Cases					
	Valid		Missing		Total	
	N	Percent	N	Percent	N	Percent
Category of group * event deaths	338	98.5%	5	1.5%	343	100.0%

Category of Group * Event Deaths Cross-Tabulation

			Event Deaths			
			0	1	113	176
Category of group	Uncompleted acts	Count	2			
		% within category of group	100.0%			
		% within event deaths	2.8%			
		% of total	.6%			
	Unclaimed acts	Count	39	217		
		% within category of group	15.1%	84.1%		
		% within event deaths	54.9%	82.5%		
		% of total	11.5%	64.2%		
	Theocentric claimed	Count	29	44	1	1
		% within category of group	38.7%	58.7%	1.3%	1.3%
		% within event deaths	40.8%	16.7%	100.0%	100.0%
		% of total	8.6%	13.0%	.3%	.3%
	Lone assailant	Count	1	2		
		% within category of group	33.3%	66.7%		
		% within event deaths	1.4%	.8%		
		% of total	.3%	.6%		
Total		Count	71	263	1	1
		% within category of group	21.0%	77.8%	.3%	.3%
		% within event deaths	100.0%	100.0%	100.0%	100.0%
		% of total	21.0%	77.8%	.3%	.3%

12.6 percent or 13 out of 103 incidents that injured between one and fifty persons. Identifiable "lone assailants" committed a total of 3 acts with 1 out of 235 of the total, or .4 percent, that injured between one and fifty persons. The sample mean for "event injuries" is 10.73 with a standard deviation of 26.61.

In my prior work on Middle East terrorism, one set of findings suggests that many unclaimed terrorist assaults are characterized by their low intensity.[174] One way of thinking about that matter is when generally recognizable issues of contention have been widely defined and articulated, unclaimed terrorist assaults acts as tools for, to use Hoffman's phrase, "political pressure groups" that seek to remind the ruling elite about the need for political change. Unequivocally, the high-intensity attributes in terms of numbers of deaths and injuries associated with unclaimed Algerian terrorist assaults fly in the face of that idea and leads to the fundamental question of what the role of unclaimed acts in the system of Algerian terrorism is all about.

Table 3.4 - continued

Category of Group * Event Deaths Cross-Tabulation

			Event deaths 200	Event deaths 500	Total
Category of group	Uncompleted acts	Count			2
		% within category of group			100.0%
		% within event deaths			.6%
		% of total			.6%
	Unclaimed acts	Count	1	1	258
		% within category of group	.4%	.4%	100.0%
		% within event deaths	100.0%	100.0%	76.3%
		% of total	.3%	.3%	76.3%
	Theocentric claimed	Count			75
		% within category of group			100.0%
		% within event deaths			22.2%
		% of total			22.2%
	Lone assailant	Count			3
		% within category of group			100.0%
		% within event deaths			.9%
		% of total			.9%
Total		Count	1	1	338
		% within category of group	.3%	.3%	100.0%
		% within event deaths	100.0%	100.0%	100.0%
		% of total	.3%	.3%	100.0%

Table 3.5: Relative Frequency of Numbers of Injured in Algerian Terrorist Incidents by Group-Type   (0=0; 1=1 through 50) (summary statistics)

Crosstabs

Case Processing Summary

	Cases					
	Valid		Missing		Total	
	N	Percent	N	Percent	N	Percent
Category of group * event injuries	221	64.4%	122	35.6%	343	100.0%

Category of Group * Event Injuries Cross-Tabulation

			Event injuries		Total
			0	1	
Category of group	Unclaimed acts	Count	89	90	179
		% within category of group	49.7%	50.3%	100.0%
		% within event injuries	75.4%	87.4%	81.0%
		% of total	40.3%	40.7%	81.0%
	Theocentric claimed	Count	29	13	42
		% within category of group	69.0%	31.0%	100.0%
		% within event injuries	24.6%	12.6%	19.0%
		% of total	13.1%	5.9%	19.0%
Total		Count	118	103	221
		% within category of group	53.4%	46.6%	100.0%
		% within event injuries	100.0%	100.0%	100.0%
		% of total	53.4%	46.6%	100.0%

Chi Square Tests

	Value	df	Asymp. sig. (2-sided)	Exact sig. (2-sided)	Exact sig. (1-sided)
Pearson Chi Square	5.106[b]	1	.024		
Continuity Correction[a]	4.359	1	.037		
Likelihood Ratio	5.239	1	.022		
Fisher's Exact Test				.026	.018
Linear-by-Linear Association	5.083	1	.024		
N of valid cases	221				

a. Computed only for a 2x2 table.
b. 0 cells (0%) have expected count less than 5. The minimum expected count is 19.57.

A total of 12 out of 235 outlier events makes up 5.1 percent of the total. Compounding the danger posed by anonymous events previously mentioned, it is found that anonymous practitioners of Algerian terrorism committed 8 out of 12 terrorist assaults that injured at least 51 persons. The remaining 4 of those 12 outlier cases were theocentric terrorist attacks. In the case of those anonymous terrorist assaults, the eight events previously mentioned injured 52, 56, 68, 70, 79, 85, 104, and 120 persons. In the case of the foregoing theocentric acts, those 4 outlier cases injured 60, 86, 125, and 286 persons. For anonymous acts, the size or "spread" of the data distribution is smaller since its

Table 3.5 - continued

Directional Measures

			Value	Asymp. std. error[a]	Approx. T[b]	Approx. sig.
Nominal by nominal	Lambda	Symmetric	.007	.092	.075	.940
		Event injuries dependent	.010	.129	.075	.940
		Category of group dependent	.000	.000	.[c]	.[c]
	Goodman and Kruskal tau	Event injuries dependent	.023	.019		.024[d]
		Category of group dependent	.023	.019		.024[d]

a.   Not assuming the null hypothesis.
b.   Using the asymptotic standard error assuming the null hypothesis.
c.   Cannot be computed because the asymptotic standard error equals zero.
d.   Based on chi square approximation.

Symmetric Measures

		Value	Approx. sig.
Nominal by nominal	Phi	-.152	.024
	Cramer's V	.152	.024
N of valid cases		221	

a.   Not assuming the null hypothesis.
b.   Using the asymptotic standard error assuming the null hypothesis.

range is 68 while the range for theocentric acts is 226.[175] It is found that 36.9 percent of theocentric terrorist assaults, or 17 out of 46 acts, caused some degree of injury, while a full 52.7 percent of unclaimed terrorist attacks, or 97 out of 184 acts, caused some degree of injury. Plainly, the data about terrorist assault injuries do not support Hypothesis Three and it is rejected. Those findings seem to suggest that the role played by anonymous Algerian terrorist assaults may not conform to the proposition that anonymous groups serve, to use Hoffman's phrase, as "political pressure groups."[176]

While many interpretations of the data are available, the findings are consistent with the notion that what really amounts to what Dunn calls full-blown "civil war" in Algeria since 1992 is an unusual situation where "opportunity structures" for legitimate political expression, as Reiss and Roth might describe them, seem to have been completely shattered.[177] If legitimate and broad-based modes of political expression are stifled in what Zoubir reports is an "authoritarian . . . political system," it seems plausible that what would in other circumstances serve to prod the political elite to make structural political change, could within the Algerian political and economic backwater landscape serve to express an overwhelming rage that presupposes and derives from that "civil war" coupled with what Dollard, et al. would describe as "frustration-aggression," and what Gurr, in turn, might describe as effects of "relative deprivation."[178] Further elaboration about the set of interconnections between high-intensity unclaimed Algerian terrorist assaults and structural factors that may shape those terrorist assault attributes are presented in the conclusions to this chapter.

Terrorist Group Age, Terrorist Group Size, and Target Selection

The aim of this section is to provide some description about the testing that explores whether or not a statistically significant relationship exists between the explanatory variables "terrorist group age" and "terrorist group size." The analysis reveals there is no statistically significant association between the dependent variable "target " and the independent variables terrorist "group age" or terrorist "group size." In the case of the bivariate analysis of "target" and "group age," a Pearson Chi Square statistic of 1.462 at one degree of freedom (1 d.f.) with a "p-value" of .227 is produced that makes it necessary to accept the null hypothesis. In the case of the analysis of "target" and "group size" a Pearson Chi Square value of .187 at one degree of freedom (1 d.f.) with a "p-value" of .666 is generated, and hence it is also not possible to reject the null hypothesis of no relation between the variables "target" and "group-size."

One issue that deserves increased devotion is whether or not these reported Chi square values are the result of a correlation between the variables "terrorist group age" and "terrorist group-size." A high correlations measure would suggest those independent variables may be capturing similar dynamics. One way of thinking about the matter is to run a bivariate correlations test to determine the relationship between the variables "group age" and "group size."[179]

Precisely because ordinal data is tested, Spearman's *rho* is used in the testing that is done with a one-tailed test because the theoretical relationship between the variables is understood, namely that for older terrorist groups, larger size is expected, and for younger terrorist groups, smaller size is

Table 3.6: Relative Frequency of Numbers of Injured in Algerian Terrorist Incidents by Group-Type, 1994-1999 (0=0; 1=1 through 50)

Case Processing Summary

	Cases					
	Valid		Missing		Total	
	N	Percent	N	Percent	N	Percent
Category of group * event injuries	235	68.5%	108	31.5%	343	100.0%

Category of Group * Event Injuries Cross-Tabulation

			Event injuries			
			0	1	52	56
Category of group	Uncompleted acts	Count	2			
		% within category of group	100.0%			
		% within event injuries	1.7%			
		% of total	.9%			
	Unclaimed acts	Count	87	89	1	1
		% within category of group	47.3%	48.4%	.5%	.5%
		% within event injuries	72.5%	86.4%	100.0%	100.0%
		% of total	37.0%	37.9%	.4%	.4%
	Theocentric claimed	Count	29	13		
		% within category of group	63.0%	28.3%		
		% within event injuries	24.2%	12.6%		
		% of total	12.3%	5.5%		
	Lone assailant	Count	2	1		
		% within category of group	66.7%	33.3%		
		% within event injuries	1.7%	1.0%		
		% of total	.9%	.4%		
Total		Count	120	103	1	1
		% within category of group	51.1%	43.8%	.4%	.4%
		% within event injuries	100.0%	100.0%	100.0%	100.0%
		% of total	51.1%	43.8%	.4%	.4%

expected.[180] It is observed there is a negative, rather than positive, relationship of -.239 with a significance score of .021 between the variables that suggests a weak relationship between the variables "group age" and "group size."[181] That small measure of correlation suggests the bivariate correlations results may stem from sketchy and incomplete data (see table 3.7).

To be more specific about the data for 1994-99, when terrorist groups are identifiable, there is no great degree of variation across group size, thereby in effect making data on terrorist group size an amalgam set of data. It is observed that the vast majority of identifiable Algerian terrorist assaults in the data are coded with respect to terrorist group size as either a "3," that is, a moderate size group from 101 to 700 activists, or a "4," that is, a large size group from 701 to 2,500 activists. With that as the emergent reality, differences among group size categories become more indistinct. In addition, it was sometimes necessary for me to make some estimations on terrorist group sizes and that may

Table 3.6 -continued

Category of Group * Event Injuries Cross-Tabulation

			Event Injuries			
			60	68	70	79
Category of group	Uncompleted acts	Count				
		% within category of group				
		% within event injuries				
		% of total				
	Unclaimed acts	Count		1	1	1
		% within category of group		.5%	.5%	.5%
		% within event injuries		100.0%	100.0%	100.0%
		% of total		.4%	.4%	.4%
	Theocentric claimed	Count	1			
		% within category of group	2.2%			
		% within event injuries	100.0%			
		% of total	.4%			
	Lone assailant	Count				
		% within category of group				
		% within event injuries				
		% of total				
Total		Count	1	1	1	1
		% within category of group	.4%	.4%	.4%	.4%
		% within event injuries	100.0%	100.0%	100.0%	100.0%
		% of total	.4%	.4%	.4%	.4%

also contribute to that condition.[182]

In a similar vein, a condition that resembles the foregoing problems with terrorist group size exists with respect to terrorist group age, where identifiable Algerian terrorist groups active between 1994 and 1999 all really have their genesis point between 1989, like FIS for example, and middle to late 1998, as in the case of the Salafi Group for the Call and Combat (GSPC). Accordingly, there is not a great deal of variation in terms of terrorist group age that would help to showcase differences in Algerian terrorist assault "attributes" isolated and identified by age. To be more specific, with respect to age, identifiable Algerian terrorist groups were coded either a "1" that represents terrorist groups that are one through three years old, or a "2" that represents terrorist groups that are four through nine years old at the time the terrorist assault is committed.

Table 3.6 - continued

Category of Group * Event Injuries Cross-Tabulation

			Event Injuries			
			85	86	104	120
Category of group	Uncompleted acts	Count				
		% within category of group				
		% within event injuries				
		% of total				
	Unclaimed acts	Count	1		1	1
		% within category of group	.5%		.5%	.5%
		% within event injuries	100.0%		100.0%	100.0%
		% of total	.4%		.4%	.4%
	Theocentric claimed	Count		1		
		% within category of group		2.2%		
		% within event injuries		100.0%		
		% of total		.4%		
	Lone assailant	Count				
		% within category of group				
		% within event injuries				
		% of total				
Total		Count	1	1	1	1
		% within category of group	.4%	.4%	.4%	.4%
		% within event injuries	100.0%	100.0%	100.0%	100.0%
		% of total	.4%	.4%	.4%	.4%

Location and Target Type

This section provides analysis of a theoretical proposition that examines the possibility that a relationship exists between target type and the geographical site where a terrorist assault is committed.

Hypothesis Four: Terrorist assaults carried out in Algeria will have a higher rate of attacks aimed at civilian targets than terrorist assaults carried out in Europe.

Analysis of the relationship between the variables "target" and "location" indicates that a statistically significant association exists between the two variables. A Pearson Chi Square value of 28.965 at two degrees of freedom (2 d.f.) along with a significance score or "p-value" of less than .001 reveals

Table 3.6 - continued

Category of Group * Event Injuries Cross-Tabulation

			Event injuries		Total
			125	286	
Category of group	Uncompleted acts	Count			2
		% within category of group			100.0%
		% within event injuries			.9%
		% of total			.9%
	Unclaimed acts	Count			184
		% within category of group			100.0%
		% within event injuries			78.3%
		% of total			78.3%
	Theocentric claimed	Count	1	1	46
		% within category of group	2.2%	2.2%	100.0%
		% within event injuries	100.0%	100.0%	19.6%
		% of total	.4%	.4%	19.6%
	Lone assailant	Count			3
		% within category of group			100.0%
		% within event injuries			1.3%
		% of total			1.3%
Total		Count	1	1	1
		% within category of group	.4%	.4%	100.0%
		% within event injuries	100.0%	100.0%	100.0%
		% of total	.4%	.4%	100.0%

Table 3.7: Bivariate Correlations Test for Explanatory Variables Terrorist Group Age and Group Size

Nonparametric Correlations

Correlations

			Size of group	Age of group
Spearman's *Rho* Size of group	Correlation Coefficient		1.000	-.239*
	Sig. (1-tailed)			
	N		73	73
	Age of group	Correlation Coefficient	-.239*	1.000
		Sig. (1-tailed)	.021	
		N	73	76

*   Correlation is significant at the .05 level (1-tailed).

a substantive relationship that makes it possible to reject the null hypothesis of no relation between the variables. It should be noted that 2 cells (33.3 percent) have an expected count of less than 5. While Norusis tells us that "in general, you should not use the chi-square test if more than 20 percent of the cells have expected values less than 5," the results are accepted because, if not, there is a strong possibility of making a "Type II" error.[183] In terms of measurement of the strength of the relationship, "Phi" and Cramer's V scores of .299 with significance scores of less than .001 suggests a slight relationship between the variables (see table 3.8).[184]

The data distribution reveals that 86.3 percent of Algerian terrorist assaults that were carried out in Algeria, or 270 out of 313 acts, involved civilian targets while only 8.9 percent or 28 out of 313 acts in Algeria were carried out against government targets. In contrast, 73.7 percent of Algerian terrorist assaults carried out in Europe, or 14 out of 19 incidents, were focused against civilian targets as compared to 10.5 percent or 2 out of 19 that involved government targets. While those findings are supportive of Hypothesis Four, the variation between civilian targets and government targets according to "locale" was smaller than I had expected. Lastly, 6 out of 36 acts or 16.7 percent of all Algerian terrorist assaults that involved government targets took place in other or unknown locales, while 3 out of 287 Algerian terrorist assaults or about 1.0 percent of the total that involved civilian targets happened in other or unknown

Table 3.8: Relative Frequency of Algerian Target Type by Location, 1994-1999 (summary statistics)

Crosstabs

Case Processing Summary

	Cases					
	Valid		Missing		Total	
	N	Percent	*N*	Percent	*N*	Percent
Type of target * locale	323	94.2%	20	5.8%	343	100.0%

Type of Target * Locale Cross-Tabulation

			Locale			Total
			Algeria	Europe	Other/ unknown	
Type of target	Govt. targets	Count	28	2	6	36
		% within type of target	77.8%	5.6%	16.7%	100.0%
		% with locale	9.4%	12.5%	66.7%	11.1%
		% of total	8.7%	.6%	1.9%	11.1%
	Civilian targets	Count	270	14	3	287
		% within type of target	94.1%	4.9%	1.0%	100.0%
		% with locale	90.6%	87.5%	33.3%	88.9%
		% of total	83.6%	4.3%	.9%	88.9%
Total		Count	298	16	9	323
		% within type of target	92.3%	5.0%	2.8%	100.0%
		% with locale	100.0%	100.0%	100.0%	100.0%
		% of total	92.3%	5.0%	2.8%	100.0%

Chi Square Tests

	Value	df	Asymp. sig. (2-sided)
Pearson Chi Square	28.965[a]	2	.000
Likelihood Ratio	16.577	2	.000
N of valid cases	323		

a. 2 cells (33.3%) have expected count less than 5. The minimum expected count is 1.00.

locations.

One notable finding is that the percentage of Algerian terrorist assaults against infrastructure targets in Europe, at 5.3 percent, or 1 act, is more than one and a half times greater than the 3.5 percent rate, or 11 out of 313 acts in Algeria, directed at infrastructure. In turn, "multiple target" terrorist assaults were rare in Algeria, and comprise only 4 out of 313 assaults or 1.3 percent. Of those "multiple target" assaults, the highest number recorded is 2 "civilian-government" terrorist assaults that make up .6 percent of the terrorist assaults that happened in Algeria. "Multiple target" terrorist assaults carried out in Europe, by contrast, comprise a much larger percentage of Algerian terrorist assaults there, and make up 10.5 percent or 2 out of 19 acts (see table 3.9).

Table 3.8 - *continued*

Directional Measures

			Value	Asymp. std. error[a]	Approx. T[b]	Approx. sig.
Nominal by nominal	Lambda	Symmetric	.049	.047	1.002	.317
		Type of target dependent	.083	.080	1.002	.317
		Locale dependent	.000	.000	c	c
	Goodman and Kruskal tau	Type of target dependent	.090	.049		.000[d]
		Locale dependent	.035	.026		.000[d]

a.   Not assuming the null hypothesis.
b.   Using the asymptotic standard error assuming the null hypothesis.
c.   Cannot be computed because the asymptotic standard error equals zero.
d.   Based on chi square approximation.

Symmetric Measures

		Value	Approx. sig.
Nominal by nominal	Phi	.299	.000
	Cramer's V	.299	.000
N of valid cases		323	

a.   Not assuming the null hypothesis.
b.   Using the asymptotic standard error assuming the null hypothesis.

Table 3.9: Relative Frequency of Algerian Target Type by Location, 1994-1999

Crosstabs

Case Processing Summary

	Cases					
	Valid		Missing		Total	
	N	Percent	N	Percent	N	Percent
Type of target * locale	341	99.4%	2	.6%	343	100.0%

Type of Target * Locale Cross-Tabulation

			Locale			Total
			Algeria	Europe	Other/unknown	
Type of target	Govt. targets	Count	28	2	6	36
		% within type of target	77.8%	5.6%	16.7%	100.0%
		% within locale	8.9%	10.5%	66.7%	10.6%
		% of Total	8.2%	.6%	1.8%	10.6%
	Infra-structure	Count	11	1		12
		% within type of target	91.7%	8.3%		100.0%
		% within locale	3.5%	5.3%		3.5%
		% of Total	3.2%	.3%		3.5%
	Civilian targets	Count	270	14	3	287
		% within type of target	94.1%	4.9%	1.0%	100.0%
		% within locale	86.3%	73.7%	33.3%	84.2%
		% of Total	79.2%	4.1%	.9%	84.2%
	Govt.-civilian	Count	1	1		2
		% within type of target	50.0%	50.0%		100.0%
		% within locale	.3%	5.3%		.6%
		% of Total	.3%	.3%		.6%
	Civilian-Govt.	Count	2	1		3
		% within type of target	66.7%	33.3%		100.0%
		% within locale	.6%	5.3%		.9%
		% of Total	.6%	.3%		.9%
	Infrastr-civilian	Count	1			1
		% within type of target	100.0%			100.0%
		% within locale	.3%			.3%
		% of Total	.3%			.3%
Total		Count	313	19	9	341
		% within type of target	91.8%	5.6%	2.6%	100.0%
		% within locale	100.0%	100.0%	100.0%	100.0%
		% of Total	91.8%	5.6%	2.6%	100.0%

Foreign Nationality and Target Type

It is commonplace to note in the literature about Algeria that the Armed Islamic Group (GIA) has targeted foreign nationals since September 1993.[185] For Willis, the underlying reasons for that special focus is to isolate and identify "'corrupting' non-Islamic influences" to strike at, and in the broader sense, to undercut that portion of the Algerian economy that relies heavily on foreign investment.[186] If follows that one portion of the analysis ought to tackle the question of to what degree foreign nationals have been made special targets during the 1994 through 1999 time period within the context of that protracted war between Islamist revivalists and the military-backed Algerian government. The following theoretical proposition captures the essence of that matter:

Hypothesis Five: In the case of "discriminate" terrorist assaults, Algerian civilian target terrorist assaults will involve a greater percentage of foreign nationals than Algerian government target terrorist assaults.

The bivariate analysis of "target" and "nationality of victim" generates cross-tabulation tables or "partials" of "discriminate," "indiscriminate," and "uncertain" Algerian terrorist assaults according to target type, each with its own set of summary statistics. Precisely because there is theoretical justification for an examination of "discriminate" terrorist assaults against target types, namely those assaults with intentional targets and non-random targets, the analysis devotes special attention to that "partials" table that showcases findings for "discriminate" Algerian terrorist assaults.

In terms of summary statistics, a Pearson Chi Square 4.331 with a "p-value" of .037 at one degree of freedom (1 d.f.) and a Yates Continuity Correction statistic of 3.336 with a "p-value" of .068 at one degree of freedom (1 d.f.) for the 2x2 table generated, makes it possible to reject the null hypothesis of no relation between the variables "target" and "nationality of victim" for discriminate Algerian terrorist assaults at the .05 level of confidence. In terms of the strength of the relationship, a Goodman and Kruskal *tau* of .026 with a "p-value" of .028 suggests a weak relationship between the variables "target" and "victim nationality" (see table 3.10).

The data distribution indicates that for civilian targets that are subject to discriminate Algerian terrorist assaults, 20.8 percent or 30 out of 144 events involve foreign nationals, while 79.2 percent or 114 out of 144 events directed at civilian targets involve Algerian nationals. In terms of government targets, a full 60.0 percent or 15 of 25 of government targets are Algerian in nature, while 40.0 percent or 10 of 25 of Algerian terrorist assaults directed against government targets involve foreign national targets. Clearly, the results are not supportive of Hypothesis Five and it is rejected. While a 20.8 percent or 30 out

Table 3.10: Relative Frequency of Algerian Terrorism Target Type by Victim Nationality – "Partials" ("discriminate"; "indiscriminate"; "uncertain")

Crosstabs

Case Processing Summary

	Cases					
	Valid		Missing		Total	
	N	Percent	N	Percent	N	Percent
Type of target * nationality of victim * victimization	192	56.0%	151	44.0%	343	100.0%

Type of Target * Nationality of Victim * Victimization Cross-Tabulation

Victim-ization	Type of target		Nationality of victim		Total
			Foreign national	National	
Dis-criminate	Govt. targets	Count	10	15	25
		% within type of target	40.0%	60.0%	100.0%
		% within nationality of victim	25.0%	11.6%	14.8%
		% of total	5.9%	8.9%	14.8%
	Civilian targets	Count	30	114	144
		% within type of target	20.8%	79.2%	100.0%
		% within nationality of victim	75.0%	88.4%	85.2%
		% of total	17.8%	67.5%	85.2%
	Total	Count	40	129	169
		% within type of target	23.7%	76.3%	100.0%
		% within nationality of victim	100.0%	100.0%	100.0%
		% of total	23.7%	76.3%	100.0%
Indis-criminate	Civilian targets	Count	1	7	8
		% within type of target	12.5%	87.5%	100.0%
		% within nationality of victim	100.0%	100.0%	100.0%
		% of total	12.5%	87.5%	100.0%
	Total	Count	1	7	8
		% within type of target	12.5%	87.5%	100.0%
		% within nationality of victim	100.0%	100.0%	100.0%
		% of total	12.5%	87.5%	100.0%
Un-certain	Govt. targets	Count	1	3	4
		% within type of target	25.0%	75.0%	100.0%
		% within nationality of victim	100.0%	21.4%	26.7%
		% of total	6.7%	20.0%	26.7%
	Civilian targets	Count		11	11
		% within type of target		100.0%	100.0%
		% within nationality of victim		78.6%	73.3%
		% of total		73.3%	73.3%
	Total	Count	1	14	15
		% within type of target	6.7%	93.3%	100.0%
		% within nationality of victim	100.0%	100.0%	100.0%
		% of total	6.7%	93.3%	100.0%

of 144 events rate for Algerian terrorist assaults against foreign national civilian targets is notable, those results indicate what Dunn and others suggest, namely, that most, but certainly not all, of the burden borne by civilian targets from Algerian terrorist assaults is shouldered by Algerian nationals themselves (see table 3.10).

Table 3.10 - *continued*

Chi Square Tests

Victimization	Value	df	Asymp. sig. (2-sided)	Exact sig. (2-sided)	Exact sig. (1-sided)
Discriminate					
Pearson Chi Square	4.331[b]	1	.037		
Continuity Correction[a]	3.336	1	.068		
Likelihood Ration	3.932	1	.047		
Fisher's Exact Test				.045	.038
Linear-by-Linear					
Association	4.306	1	.038		
N of valid cases	169				
Indiscriminate					
Pearson Chi Square	.[c]				
N of valid cases	8				
Uncertain					
Pearson Chi Square	2.946[d]	1	.086		
Continuity Correction[a]	.298	1	.585		
Likelihood Ration	2.849	1	.091		
Fisher's Exact Test				.267	.267
Linear-by-Linear					
Association	2.750	1	.097		
N of valid cases	15				

a. Computed only for a 2x2 table.
b. 0 cells (0%) have expected count less than 5. The minimum expected count is 5.92.
c. No statistics are computed because type of target is a constant.
d. 3 cells (75.0%) have expected count less than 5. The minimum expected count is 27.

Table 3.10 - *continued*

Directional Measures

Victimization			Value	Asymp. std. error[a]
Discriminate				
Nominal by nominal	Lambda	Symmetric	.000	.000
		Type of target dependent	.000	.000
		Nationality of victim dependent	.000	.000
	Goodman and Kruskal tau	Type of target dependent	.026	.028
		Nationality of victim dependent	.026	.028
Indiscriminate				
Nominal by nominal	Lambda	Symmetric	.[e]	
Uncertain				
Nominal by nominal	Lambda	Symmetric	.200	.139
		Type of target dependent	.250	.217
		Nationality of victim dependent	.000	.000
	Goodman and Kruskal tau	Type of target dependent	.196	.103
		Nationality of victim dependent	.196	.182

Table 3.10 - *continued*

Directional Measures

Victimization			Value	Asymp. std. error[a]
Discriminate				
Nominal by nominal	Lambda	Symmetric	.[c]	.[c]
		Type of target dependent	.[c]	.[c]
		Nationality of victim dependent	.[c]	.[c]
	Goodman and Kruskal tau	Type of target dependent		.038[d]
		Nationality of victim dependent		.038[d]
Indiscriminate				
Nominal by nominal	Lambda	Symmetric		
Uncertain				
Nominal by nominal	Lambda	Symmetric	1.035	.301
		Type of target dependent	1.035	.301
		Nationality of victim dependent	.[c]	.[c]
	Goodman and Kruskal tau	Type of target dependent		.097[d]
		Nationality of victim dependent		.097[d]

a. Not assuming the null hypothesis.
b. Using the asymptotic standard error assuming the null hypothesis.
c. Cannot be computed because the asymptotic standard error equals zero.
d. Based on chi square approximation.
e. No statistics are computed because type of target is a constant.

Symmetric Measures

Victimization			Value	Approx. sig.
Discriminate	Nominal by nominal	Phi	.160	.037
		Cramer's V	.160	.037
	N of valid cases		.169	
Indiscriminate	Nominal by nominal	Phi	.[c]	
		Cramer's V		
	N of valid cases		8	
Uncertain	Nominal by nominal	Phi	.443	.086
		Cramer's V	.443	.086
	N of valid cases		15	

a. Not assuming the null hypothesis.
b. Using the asymptotic standard error assuming the null hypothesis.
c. No statistics are computed because type of target is a constant.

Political Events and Target Type

In the broadest sense, an analysis of terrorism that is dynamic needs to explore the relationship between the intervening variable "political events" and the variable "target." Carefully reasoned thinking about the analysis leads to the fundamental question of whether or not political events generate and sustain terrorism events or whether terrorism activity, Algerian or otherwise, is largely independent of political event influence. In my prior work, one standout finding is that a majority of Middle East terrorism assaults are proactive events, rather than reactive ones inextricably tied together to political events.

In addition, I also found in my prior work that the basic thematic emphases of terrorist assaults with interconnections to political events are very similar. I found that what I call "symbolic" political enterprises or events seem to be paired in kind with what Drake might call "symbolic" terrorist activity.[187] In a similar vein, I found that violent government activity like air raids, with profound and lasting damage to persons or their treasured homes and property, evoked terrorist assaults against civilian targets that seemed to match the invasiveness and "intimacy" of the government perpetrated assaults.[188] Likewise, the results suggest religious holidays and holidays to commemorate landmark events that pull at the heartstrings of emotion, evoke terrorist assaults with special focus against civilian targets.[189] The following theoretical propositions capture the essence of the broader theoretical proposition that interconnections exist between the variables "target" and "political event." Those hypotheses also capture the dynamics of some earlier findings of mine that will be explored here for validity in the Algerian political context.

Hypothesis Six: Most terrorist activity will be unrelated to political events such as visits by major political figures, diplomatic initiatives, the commemoration of religious events, the commemoration of secular events, and counterterrorism activity.

Hypothesis Seven: Terrorist assaults in response to commemoration of religious holidays will have among the highest percentage rates of assaults against civilian targets.

Hypothesis Eight: Terrorist assaults in response to major political events will not have an especially sharp focus against civilian targets.

Hypothesis Nine: Terrorist assaults in response to landmark events will have among the highest percentage rate of terrorist assaults against civilian targets.

Hypothesis Ten: Terrorist assaults in response to government policy will involve a greater percentage rate of government targets than civilian targets.

The analysis suggests that a statistically significant association exists between the variables "target" and the intervening variable "political event." The bivariate analysis generates a Pearson Chi Square statistic of 11.838 at three degrees of freedom (3 d.f.) with a significance score or "p-value" of .008. At a functional level, those findings suggest that if repeated sampling was done the likelihood this distribution would appear if there is no relation between the variables is a little more than a thousandth of one percent. Accordingly, it is possible to reject the null hypothesis of no relation between the variables at the .05 confidence level. Again, it should be noted that 25 percent of the cells have an expected count of less than 5, but, as before, the findings, in my judgment, are worth reporting.[190] Since the variables "target" and "political events" are nominal measures, "Phi" and Cramer's V measures of association are reported with both scores of .203 with a significance score for "Phi" and Cramer's V of .008. Those .203 figures suggest a slight relationship between the variables "target" and "political events" (see table 3.11).

In terms of the breakdown of the data, it is evident that most Algerian terrorist assaults are unrelated to political events. Algerian terrorist assaults that are "independent" or unrelated to political events comprise 57.4 percent, over half of the total number of discrete events, or 193 out of 336 acts. Conversely, 143 out of 336 acts or 42.7 percent were "reactive" terrorist assaults, namely, those elicited in response to political events. Hence, the testing findings are supportive of Hypothesis Six. In the broader sense, a total of 164 out of 193 "independent" terrorist assaults, that comprise 84.9 percent of all Algerian "independent" terrorist assaults were aimed at civilian targets. In turn, it is observed that 118 out of 143 "reactive" terrorist assaults, or 82.5 percent of Algerian "reactive" terrorist assaults, a nearly identical percentage to the aforementioned, were aimed at civilian targets (table 3.12).

The data show that it is possible to accept the validity of Hypothesis Seven. The largest category of Algerian terrorist assaults related to political events is comprised of terrorist assaults committed to commemorate religious holidays, with 53 out of 143 incidents, that make up 37 percent of the total number of terrorist assaults with interconnections to political events. The smallest category of Algerian terrorist assaults related to political events is comprised of a single terrorist assault carried out to commemorate a secular holiday. Of the 53 terrorist assaults carried out to commemorate religious holidays, 47 out of 53 acts or about 89 percent involved civilian targets, putting it in second place among categories of terrorist assaults related to political events. It should be noted those 47 terrorist assaults carried out to commemorate religious holidays comprised by far the largest chunk of "reactive" terrorist events with a civilian target focus of over 88 percent (see table 3.12).

Table 3.11: Relative Frequency of Algerian Target Type by Political Event, 1994-1999 (summary statistics)

Crosstabs

Case Processing Summary

	Cases					
	Valid		Missing		Total	
	N	Percent	N	Percent	N	Percent
Political event * type of target	286	83.4%	57	16.6%	343	100.0%

Political Event * Type of Target Cross-Tabulation

			Type of target		Total
			Govt. targets	Civilian targets	
Political event	No relation to political events	Count	21	164	185
		% within political event	11.4%	88.6%	100.0%
		% within type of target	60.0%	65.3%	64.7%
		% of total	7.3%	57.3%	64.7%
	Commemoration of religious holidays	Count	4	47	51
		% within political event	7.8%	92.2%	100.0%
		% within type of target	11.4%	18.7%	17.8%
		% of total	1.4%	16.4%	17.8%
	Reaction to government policies	Count	6	9	15
		% within political event	40.0%	60.0%	100.0%
		% within type of target	17.1%	3.6%	5.2%
		% of total	2.1%	3.1%	5.2%
	Reaction to minor political events	Count	4	31	35
		% within political event	11.4%	88.6%	100.0%
		% within type of target	11.4%	12.4%	12.2%
		% of total	1.4%	10.8%	12.2%
Total		Count	35	251	286
		% within political event	12.2%	87.8%	100.0%
		% within type of target	100.0%	100.0%	100.0%
		% of total	12.2%	87.8%	100.0%

Chi Square Tests

	Value	df	Asymp. sig. (2-sided)
Pearson Chi Square	11.838[a]	3	.008
Likelihood Ratio	8.561	3	.036
Linear-by-Linear Association	.990	1	.320
N of valid cases	286		

a. 2 cells (25.0%) have expected count less than 5. The minimum expected count is 1.84.

There is a three-place tie for first place among "reactive" Algerian terrorist assaults with the most emphasis on civilian targets, but it should be noted that the total number of those attacks is low with only 16 assaults. Somewhat surprisingly, Algerian terrorist assaults carried out in relation to major political events like talks with the Islamic Salvation Army (FIS), French economic assistance to Algeria, or summits like the Organization for Security and Cooperation in Europe (OSCE) declaration in December 1996 always involved civilian targets (11 out of 11).[191] Accordingly, it is necessary to reject Hypothesis Eight. In turn, terrorist assaults that commemorated landmark events

Table 3.11 - *continued*

Directional Measures

			Value	Asymp. std. error[a]	Approx. T	Approx. sig.
Nominal by nominal	Lambda	Symmetric	.000	.000	b	b
		Political event dependent	.000	.000	b	b
		Type of target dependent	.000	.000	b	b
	Goodman and Kruskal tau	Political event dependent	.005	.005		.204[c]
		Type of target dependent	.041	.034		.008[c]

a.   Not assuming the null hypothesis.
b.   Cannot be computed because the asymptotic standard error equals zero.
c.   Based on chi square approximation.

Symmetric Measures

		Value	Approx. sig.
Nominal by nominal	Phi	.203	.008
	Cramer's V	.203	.008
N of valid cases		286	

a.   Not assuming the null hypothesis.
b.   Using the asymptotic standard error assuming the null hypothesis.

Table 3.12: Relative Frequency of Algerian Target Type by Political Event, 1994-1999

Crosstabs

Case Processing Summary

	Cases					
	Valid		Missing		Total	
	N	Percent	N	Percent	N	Percent
Type of target * political event	336	98.0%	7	2.0%	343	100.0%

Type of Target * Political Event Cross-Tabulation

Type of target		Political event			
		No relation to political events	Reaction to maj dip events	Commemoration of landmark events	Commemoration of religious holidays
Govt. targets	Count	21			4
	% within type of target	58.3%			11.1%
	% within political event	10.9%			7.5%
	% of total	6.3%			1.2%
Infra-structure	Count	7			
	% within type of target	58.3%			
	% within political event	3.6%			
	% of total	2.1%			
Civilian targets	Count	164	11	4	47
	% within type of target	58.2%	3.9%	1.4%	16.7%
	% within political event	85.0%	100.0%	100.0%	88.7%
	% of total	48.8%	3.3%	1.2%	14.0%
Govt.-civilian	Count				1
	% within type of target				50.0%
	% within political event				1.9%
	% of total				.3%
Civilian-govt.	Count	1			1
	% within type of target	33.3%			33.3%
	% within political event	.5%			1.9%
	% of total	.3%			.3%
Infrastr-civilian	Count				
	% within type of target				
	% within political event				
	% of total				
Total	Count	193	11	4	53
	% within type of target	57.4%	3.3%	1.2%	15.8%
	% within political event	100.0%	100.0%	100.0%	100.0%
	% of total	57.4%	3.3%	1.2%	15.8%

Table 3.12 - *continued*

Crosstabs

Case Processing Summary

	Cases					
	Valid		Missing		Total	
	N	Percent	*N*	Percent	*N*	Percent
Type of target * political event	336	98.0%	7	2.0%	343	100.0%

Type of Target * Political Event Cross-Tabulation

Type of target		Political event		
		Commemoration of secular holidays	Reaction to ground assaults	Reaction to government policies
Govt. targets	Count		1	6
	% within type of target		2.8%	16.7%
	% within political event		5.6%	35.3%
	% of total		.3%	1.8%
Infra-structure	Count		1	
	% within type of target		8.3%	
	% within political event		5.6%	
	% of total		.3%	
Civilian targets	Count	1	15	9
	% within type of target	.4%	5.3%	3.2%
	% within political event	100.0%	83.3%	52.9%
	% of total	.3%	4.5%	2.7%
Govt.-civilian	Count			1
	% within type of target			50.0%
	% within political event			5.9%
	% of total			.3%
Civilian-govt.	Count			1
	% within type of target			33.3%
	% within political event			5.9%
	% of total			.3%
Infrastr-civilian	Count		1	
	% within type of target		100.0%	
	% within political event		5.6%	
	% of total		.3%	
Total	Count	1	18	17
	% within type of target	.3%	5.4%	5.1%
	% within political event	100.0%	100.0%	100.0%
	% of total	.3%	5.4%	5.1%

Table 3.12 - *continued*

Type of Target * Political Event Cross-Tabulation

Type of target		Political event	Total
		Reaction to minor political events	
Govt. targets	Count	4	36
	% within type of target	11.1%	100.0%
	% within political event	10.3%	10.7%
	% of total	1.2%	10.7%
Infra-structure	Count	4	12
	% within type of target	33.3%	100.0%
	% within political event	10.3%	3.6%
	% of total	1.2%	3.6%
Civilian targets	Count	31	282
	% within type of target	11.0%	100.0%
	% within political event	79.5%	83.9%
	% of total	9.2%	83.9%
Govt.-civilian	Count		2
	% within type of target		100.0%
	% within political event		.6%
	% of total		.6%
Civilian-govt.	Count		3
	% within type of target		100.0%
	% within political event		.9%
	% of total		.9%
Infrastr-civilian	Count		1
	% within type of target		100.0%
	% within political event		.3%
	% of total		.3%
Total	Count	39	336
	% within type of target	11.6%	100.0%
	% within political event	100.0%	100.0%
	% of total	11.6%	100.0%

(4 of 4) always involved civilian targets, and hence it is possible to accept Hypothesis Nine as valid. Interestingly enough, it is observed that while there was only one terrorist assault that commemorated a secular holiday, that terrorist assault was directed at a civilian target.

Clearly, the results of the bivariate testing are not supportive of Hypothesis Ten. Algerian terrorist assaults undertaken in response to government policy at the national level, such as Algerian or French policy for the imprisonment of FIS leaders, Moroccan border policy vis-à-vis Algeria, and policy that revolves around Algeria's National Transition Council, comprised 17 out of 143 "reactive" terrorist assaults or 11.9 percent of all "reactive" terrorist assaults.[192] Still, the results are consistent with the basic essence of Hypothesis Ten. While over half of those types of terrorist assaults involved civilian targets (9 of 17 or 52.9 percent), a full 35.3 percent or over two-thirds were directed against government targets. That figure represented the highest number and greatest percentage of "reactive" terrorist assaults aimed at government targets.

Terrorist assaults that commemorate religious holidays comprise the highest percentage of "reactive" terrorist assaults overall, and have the second highest percentage of "reactive" terrorist assaults aimed at government targets. The third place position for "reactive" terrorist assaults against government targets is taken by terrorist assaults done in reaction to ground assaults, like the French anti-terrorist commando raid in Paris against a hijacked Air France airliner in 1994, and the killing of an Algerian bomb maker by French police in 1995.[193] For that category, it is observed that 1 out of 18 terrorist assaults was directed at government targets, or 5.6 percent of the total number that were committed in reaction to ground assaults.

Among "reactive" terrorist assaults, only five terrorist assaults focused on infrastructure targets. "Multiple target" terrorist assaults that were "reactive" to political events were equally rare, with 3.5 percent or 5 out of 143 acts. Both the "multiple target" type categories "government-civilian" and "civilian-government" each have 1 act that falls into the categories "commemoration of religious holidays" and "reaction to government policies." The single terrorist assault attributable to the multiple target type "infrastructure-civilian" happened in reaction to a government ground assault.

Undoubtedly, the deviant case here is that all 11 Algerian terrorist assaults undertaken in reaction to major political events focused on civilian targets 100 percent of the time. Although a definitive interpretation is not possible, this finding may reflect a set of very deep social fissures between Islamists who want to negotiate with the Algerian government and those who view any contact with the military-backed regime as anathema in moral terms, and a fundamental danger in functional terms since those efforts have the potential to create structural shifts that can only be deleterious to extremists among Islamists. Accordingly, to drive home the point about the importance of non-negotiation, civilian targets under those circumstances bear the brunt of punishment with respect to those "reactive" terrorist assaults.

In the broader sense, it is possible to make some comparisons about findings in this section with findings in my prior work on Middle East terrorism. In certain ways some of the results about the relationship between Algerian terrorism and "political events" echo results found in *Serenade of Suffering*. For example, the ratio of civilian and government targets for the category "commemoration of religious holidays" corresponds with the ratio found in the same category in my prior work. In *Serenade of Suffering*, the ratio of civilian targets to government targets for attacks in "commemoration of religious holidays" is a little less than 9.5:1 (86.4 percent to 9.1 percent) as compared to a ratio of about 11.5:1 (88.7 percent to 7.5 percent) found in this work.[194]

In a similar vein, the single recorded Algerian terrorist assault carried out to commemorate a landmark event in this study involved a civilian target (100.0 percent rate), while in *Serenade of Suffering* it was found that 92.7 percent of terrorist assaults to commemorate landmark events focused on civilian targets.[195] Further, in both studies, a little over one-third of "reactive" terrorist assaults committed in response to government policies focused on government targets. In this study that figure is 35.3 percent, as compared to a figure of 34.9 percent found in *Serenade of Suffering*.[196] In my prior work, that figure represents the second highest percentage of terrorist assaults with government targets recorded for any "reactive" terrorist assault category, while the 35.3 percent statistic found in this work represents the highest. In fact, with the exception of the category "reaction to ground assaults" that in my prior work had data that exhibits an especially sharp focus against civilian targets with 93.3 percent of terrorist assaults directed at civilian targets, the findings about "reactive" Algerian terrorist assaults are rather consistent with the results found in *Serenade of Suffering*.[197]

Compounding the matter of political events and their role even more, there are other indicators of the dynamic nature of the intervening variable "political event" that need to be examined. One underlying issue to explore that adds to the storehouse of knowledge about the interconnections between Algerian terrorism and political events is whether or not there are differences in the average number of persons killed in terrorist assaults leading up to the "commemoration of landmark events" and "political events" such as parliamentary or presidential elections.

Clearly, an examination of terrorist assault death rates during the month that precedes the event under consideration is different from a relatively straightforward breakdown of the data that reveals the number of events attributable to or claimed to be inextricably tied to political events. The following hypothesis captures the notion of dynamic effects of different types of political events on the number of deaths in terrorist assaults that precede those events by one month:

Hypothesis Eleven: The average number of persons killed in terrorist assaults that precede the commemoration of landmark events by one month will be greater than the average number of persons killed in terrorist assaults that precede internal political events by one month.

One way to tackle that matter is to perform an independent "T-Test" that will compare two sample means of terrorist assault deaths. One is the mean of the number of deaths in terrorist assaults linked to landmark events and the other is the mean of the number of deaths in terrorist assaults linked to internal political events (see table 3.13). The purpose of the independent T-Test is to determine whether or not there is a statistically significant difference between the mean number of deaths in these two samples that is not a function of sampling error.[198] In this test the assumption is made that the samples are independent samples, namely a condition where one sample does not presuppose and derive from the make-up of the other sample.[199]

In the case of "commemoration of landmark events," terrorist assaults are isolated and identified during the month preceding three different landmark events. Those "landmark events" include: the 30 June 1992 assassination of President Mohammed Boudiaf; the 2 November anniversary of the start of the Algerian war of independence that lasted from 1954 to 1962; the Algerian army takeover of 12 January 1992. With respect to the foregoing events, that one-month period is examined for the years 1994 through 1999 for the Boudiaf assassination and the anniversary of the beginning of Algeria's war of independence, and for the 12 December-12 January time period for 1994 to 1995, 1995-96, 1996-97, 1997-98, 1998-99, for the 12 January 1992 Algerian army takeover.[200]

In the case of "reaction to 'minor' political events," three different "minor" or internal political events are also earmarked for analysis. Those political events include: President Liamine Zeroual's "national dialogue" between opposition groups and the Algerian government that started on 8 August 1994; the 18 November 1995 presidential election victory that Zeroual "won" after his army appointment in 1994; and the parliamentary election of 5 June 1997.[201]

At a substantive level, to make sure that outlier cases of terrorist assaults with over 100 deaths do not skew the distribution of the curve for numbers of deaths, thereby in effect influencing "T-Test" assumptions and results, three outlier cases of Algerian terrorist assaults with 113, 176, and 500 deaths were trimmed from the analysis.[202] The "independent sample T-Test" performed suggests the population mean of deaths from terrorist assaults that precede the "commemoration of landmark" events by one month is different in a statistical sense from the population mean of deaths from terrorist assaults that precede the commemoration of internal political events by one month. The Levene's Test for Equality of Variance is interpreted, as Sirkin tells us, the same way as is an "F-Test" for homogeneity of variances, but is used because normality

Table 3.13: Independent "T-Test" for Difference of Means Test for Landmark Events and Internal Political Events in Algeria

T-Test

Group Statistics

	Event type	N	Mean	Std. deviation	Std. error mean
Number of dead	Landmark events	103	7.01	11.78	1.16
	Political events	19	3.42	4.21	.97

Independent Samples Test

		Levene's test for equality of variances	
		F	Sig.
Number of dead	Equal variances assumed	5.118	.025
	Equal variances not assumed		

Independent Samples Test

		T-test for equality of means			
		t	df	Sig. (2-tailed)	Mean fifference
Number of dead	Equal variances assumed	1.308	120	.193	3.59
	Equal variances not assumed	2.377	78.706	.020	3.59

Independent Samples Test

		T-test for equality of means		
			95% Confidence interval of the difference	
		Std. error difference	Lower	Upper
Number of dead	Equal variances assumed	2.74	-1.84	9.02
	Equal variances not assumed	1.51	.58	6.59

assumptions about sample distributions are less stringent.[203]

The Levene's test indicates with an obtained F of 5.118 and a significance score of .025 that it is possible to reject the null hypothesis of "equal variances assumed" in the population. Hence, the assumption of unequal variance is used as a guidepost for the "T-Test" and with a "T-Test" score of 2.377 at 78.706 degrees of freedom (78 d.f.) and a "p-value" of .020 it is possible to reject the null hypothesis of no difference in the population means of terrorist assaults that precede landmark events and political events by one month (table 3.13).[204]

In terms of the average number of deaths in terrorist assaults that precede the "commemoration of landmark events" by one month the mean is 7.01 (standard deviation 11.78) while the average number of deaths in terrorist assaults that precede "minor" or internal political events is 3.42 (standard deviation 4.21). Accordingly, Hypothesis Eleven that posited a difference in population means between events that lead up to landmark events and "minor" or internal political events by one month is accepted as valid.

Conclusions

General Patterns of Behavior

Analysis of relative frequencies of terrorist assaults by descriptive categories such as year, and numbers of dead, and cross-tabulation analysis, makes it possible to gain a greater understanding about the general contours of Algerian terrorism. Simultaneously, it is important to once again acknowledge that both the capacity to make in-depth interpretations of the data and even to run a really comprehensive analysis of Algerian terrorism is hampered by sketchy and incomplete data. At the same time, some broad trends in the data, that sometimes reverberate with earlier findings about terrorism behavior and sometimes resonate less so, have been discerned.

At the most fundamental level, it is observed that Algerian terrorism during the 1994-99 period is cyclical in nature, replete with a set of peaks and troughs. Another basic finding is that terrorist assaults over the political landscape were conducted, insofar as the sketchy and incomplete data reveal, by Islamic revivalist terrorist groups without charismatic leaders, by anonymous terrorist groups or "lone assailants," and "lone operatives" who were identifiable.

Perhaps the single most glaring finding is how predominant is anonymous "lone assailant" activity, with over three-quarters of all Algerian terrorist assaults that fall in that sphere. In terms of identifiable Algerian terrorist organizations, the greatest number of assaults were, to use Dunn's phrase, claimed or attributed to that "umbrella organization of Islamists," namely in this case the Armed Islamic Group (GIA).[205] The Islamic Salvation Army (AIS) that is recognized by many scripted accounts as the military branch of the Islamic Salvation Front (FIS) placed a very distant second, and a host of other, more shadowy terrorist groups or "proto-groups" trailed behind.

In addition to the cyclical pattern of Algerian terrorism that is illuminated by the analysis, another result, generally recognizable and consistent with other works, is that practitioners of Algerian terrorism prefer civilian targets over government targets by nearly a 8:1 ratio. That 8:1 ratio in favor of civilian targets nearly matches the 9.5:1 ratio of civilian to government target preference I found in my prior work in the case of terrorist assaults that happened in Israel and the Occupied Territories, and is greater than the 4.12:1 ratio found when other locales are included in the analysis.[206] In a similar vein, I found that "multiple target" type assaults are very rare and that Algerian terrorism really remains a relatively straightforward affair in terms of tactical complexity and coordination of attacks. To be specific "multiple target" type terrorist assaults comprised only 1.76 percent or 6 out of 340 acts for the 1994-99 time period (see table 3.2).

To be sure, Algerian terrorism still remains a largely self-contained phenomenon largely confined to Algeria, even though there has been some seepage into Europe, most notably France. Out of the total number of discrete events tested, a full 91.8 percent Algerian terrorism took place in Algeria, while 5.5 percent happened in France, Great Britain, Germany, and Belgium. In turn, 9 out of 343 events or a mere 2.6 percent of the total happened in other locales or unknown locations.

Still another set of findings about Algerian terrorism, that is consistent with the work of others, is revealed by a breakdown of the terrorist assault data by relative frequency. Here it is observed that the amount of physical devastation that is captured by an array of terrorist assault "attribute" measures is relatively small.[207] For one thing, we see from the relative frequency analysis that the bulk of Algerian terrorist assaults cause relatively low amounts of property damage. At the same time, a sample mean of 10.48 for numbers of dead and a sample mean of 10.73 for numbers of injuries seem to demonstrate the tendency for terrorist group tacticians to operate around the central idea that the use of abject fear rather than full-blown physical devastation is the most effective tool to pursue goals within the political environment.[208]

The Role of Political Ideology

Regrettably for scholars, the lay of the political land in Algeria is marked by only one identifiable type of terrorist group at work along with anonymous terrorist groups and "lone assailants," declared or otherwise. That condition does not make it possible to apply the empirical findings to the theoretical framework of "nonstructuralist" and "structuralist" terrorist group-types that is presented in chapter 1. What is possible to mull over is the role that political ideology may have with respect to the type of target chosen and some of the terrorist assault attributes associated with attacks by Islamic revivalist terrorist groups without charismatic leaders in the Algerian political and social context. Even though it is true there is some data weakness that presupposes and derives from data limitations, and while it is entirely possible this analysis has not been able to isolate and identify the effects of all causal factors identified here, the following results are offered.

Known political ideology is found to be influential in terrorist assaults when acts are made attributable to or claimed by Algerian theocentric terrorist organizations. Interestingly enough, what seems to be an almost S-shaped pattern in the data is observed. On the one hand, when assaults are attributed to or claimed by theocentric terrorist groups, the *death* percentage rate for terrorist assaults in the "mid-range," namely acts that kill one to fifty persons, is much less than the *death* rate percentage in that "mid-range" area for unclaimed Algerian terrorist assault activity. For example, it is observed that 82.5 percent of terrorist assaults that result in the deaths of between one and fifty persons are anonymous assaults. In comparison, only 16.7 percent of all theocentric terrorist assaults kill between one and fifty persons. At the same time, some 55 percent of unclaimed assaults are death-free, while only 40.8 percent of theocentric terrorist assaults are nonlethal events.

In terms of *injury* rates, it is observed that 86.4 percent of unclaimed acts result in injuries to between one and fifty persons, while a full 72.5 percent of unclaimed acts were injury-free. By comparison, 12.6 percent (13 of 103) of theocentric terrorist assaults *injured* between one and fifty persons, while 24.2 percent (29 of 120) of theocentric assaults are injury-free. While the trends of terrorist assaults that *injured* and *killed* one to fifty persons are consistent across theocentric group categories at 12.6 percent and 16.7 percent, respectively, and *injury* rates for unclaimed assaults at the "mid-range" (one through fifty persons) category parallels the percentage breakdown for *death* rates of unclaimed acts, around 86.4 percent and 82.5 percent, respectively, the one glaring difference is the high percentage of unclaimed acts that are injury-free events.

At the same time, the discrepancy between the percentage rate of anonymous assaults and theocentric terrorist assaults is greatly reduced for number of dead outlier cases, namely those terrorist assaults several standard deviations away from the mean number of deaths that is found to be about 10 persons. In that case, two theocentric terrorist assaults killed 113 and 176 persons, respectively, while two anonymous terrorist assaults killed 200 and 500 persons. In a similar vein, there are twelve outlier cases of terrorist events with *injury* rates of over fifty persons. Eight of those terrorist assaults were undertaken by anonymous terrorist groups or undeclared lone assailants, as compared with four terrorist assaults claimed by theocentric terrorist groups or attributed to them.

While the overall number of outlier cases is very low for interpretation, with a total of sixteen discrete events, it is possible to make some conjecture. The findings are consistent with the idea that terrorist groups do engage in terrorist activity that is sometimes claimed or attributable and in other cases is not claimed. It may be that in certain circumstances it is useful for terrorist groups to claim acts with high casualty rates (e.g., terrorist assaults with 113 and 176 dead) while falling back from an association with terrorist assaults with enormous amounts of carnage such as the actions in Algiers and the village of Had Chekala in Relazine province that killed 200 and 500 persons, respectively.[209] Finally, with respect to other terrorist assault attributes tested, it is found there is no statistically significant association between the variable "target" and the attribute variable "property damage."

Terrorist Group Age, Terrorist Group Size, and Target Selection

As reported previously, there is no statistically significant association found between the variables terrorist "target" and terrorist "group age," and the variables "target" and terrorist "group size." In the wake of those findings, a bivariate correlations test is administered to determine the relationship between the variables "group age" and "group size" that would suggest whether or not those variables really capture dynamics that are conceptually similar, thereby in effect contributing to that result. With a bivariate correlations score of -.239 and a significance score of .021, the findings suggest that the absence of a statistically significant association between the variable "target" and those two independent variables may presuppose and derive from incomplete and insufficient data about Algerian terrorist assaults.

Location

The data distribution makes it clear that Algerian terrorism is largely centered in Algeria, even though there is some seepage into parts of Western Europe. A total of 91.8 percent or 315 out of 343 assaults happened in Algeria, as compared to 5.5 percent or 19 out of 343 incidents that happened in Europe. In turn, it is observed that only 2.6 percent or 9 out of 343 acts happened in other or unknown locations. Several authorities on terrorism such as O'Neill, Osmond, Shultz, Waugh, Flemming, and Merari, et al. report that location is a powerful explanatory variable in terms of target selection.[210] Similarly, Algerian terrorism remains a largely self-contained phenomenon but it is uncertain as to why that is the case.

At the same time, those findings seem to presuppose and derive from the structural framework of the conflict that has continuously evolved into what Dunn and others have described as a "civil war."[211] While European and most notably French interests are sometimes targets in part because of the presence of Algerian nationals in exile, and precisely because of political and economic interconnections between European governments and the Algerian political-military regime, the dynamics of that protracted conflict and its implications remain centered in Algeria, at least for the present time.

Foreign Nationality and Target Type

The findings about the relationship between "target" and "nationality of victim" reveals a statistically significant association between the variables for "discriminate" Algerian terrorist assaults. The data distribution shows that 20.8 percent of all civilian target terrorist assaults involved foreign nationals as targets, while over three-quarters of all Algerian terrorist assaults directed against civilian targets involved Algerian nationals. What seems significant here is those findings suggest that while Algerian terrorism does place special emphasis on foreign nationals in the capacity of civilian targets as chronicled in several sources, the percentage of civilian target terrorist assaults against Algerian nationals is still over three times as large.

The Influence of Political Events

One subset of data that is more complete than data in other categories and thereby in effect provides more complete findings concerns the relationship between Algerian terrorism and political events. It is observed that Algerian terrorism is a largely proactive phenomenon in which some 57.4 percent or 193 out of 336 events bear no relationship to political events. In turn, it is observed that around 42.6 percent or 143 out of 336 events are dependent or "reactive" terrorist assaults with interconnections to political events.

What seems significant here is that the analysis suggests that terrorist assaults that are elicited in reaction to specific types of political events share similar thematic emphasis with them. For example, it is shown that what Drake and others would call "symbolic" terrorist assaults seem to have less emphasis on civilian targets, while terrorist assaults evoked in response to an array of profound and lasting, and even "intimate," political events and activities, share the same intensity as those political events that manifests itself in a greater proportion of terrorist assaults against civilian targets.

Another set of findings about political events revolves around the central idea that there is a statistically significant difference in the mean number of deaths in terrorist assaults that precede different types of political events by one month. An independent sample "T-Test" is administered to examine the mean number of deaths in terrorist assaults that preceded a set of "landmark events" and "minor" internal political events.

The underlying theme that the mean for "commemoration of landmark events" ought to be greater than the mean for terrorist assaults that precede "minor" internal political events presupposes and derives from the notion developed in my prior work that different types of political events, when they do evoke terrorist assaults, elicit terrorist assaults with different thematic emphases. The independent "T-Test" findings reveal there is a statistically significant difference between the two means under consideration, and that the mean for number of dead in terrorist assaults that precede "commemoration of landmark events" by one month is greater than the mean for number of dead in terrorist assaults that precede "minor" or internal political events by one month.

Terrorism By Anonymous Groups and Declared "Lone Operatives"

As previously mentioned, the largest cluster of Algerian terrorism is made up of anonymous terrorist activity for the 1994-99 period. The data show that at 76.5 percent, over three-fourths or 260 out of 340 of all Algerian terrorist assaults are carried out by anonymous terrorist groups or "lone assailants" (see table 3.2). It is also clear that at 79.7 percent, anonymous terrorist activity accounts for the largest portion of terrorist assaults directed at civilian targets when terrorist group and non-group categories are compared. While anonymous assaults have a heavy emphasis on civilian targets, the assault rate for unclaimed acts against infrastructure was mild, with only 7 out of 260 events that took place comprising only 2.7 percent of the total. Anonymous Algerian terrorist assaults directed against "multiple targets" were even more rare, with a total of 3 out of 260 events or 1.2 percent of the total.

In terms of physical destruction, it is observed that a high percentage of anonymous terrorist assaults (82.5 percent) *killed* between one and fifty persons, and that is the highest rate recorded for that category (see table 3.4). In a similar vein, 86.4 percent of unclaimed terrorist assaults *injured* between one and fifty persons. These findings tend to provide empirical support to an idea presented in my previous work that a "mixed bundle" of claimed or attributable terrorist assaults and anonymous assaults, in part to offset the prospect of enormous counterterrorism force, may be an advantageous way to practice terrorism if the themes, goals, and players in the political fray are sufficiently well known and articulated.[212]

Reflections

In the broadest sense, the enormous capacity for high-intensity Algerian terrorist assaults, some horrifically brutal in nature, begs the question of why that condition exists.[213] As Dunn relates, the emergent reality of "civil war" by 1993 is insufficient in itself to explain why generally recognizable slaughter of civilians by terrorist assaults has happened. Some scripted accounts about the war in Algeria estimate that some 75,000 persons or perhaps more have been killed since 1992.[214]

What, then, generates and sustains the kind of conflict in Algeria that evokes all too frequently such brutal, and in some cases, high-intensity terrorist assaults? While any sort of interpretation of events can only remain makeshift and incomplete at this stage, some fundamental reflections based on the writings of Algerian specialists is worth mulling over when thinking about that searing question. The continuously evolving environment in Nigeria, I think, provides a good counterexample to Algeria's tortuous historical legacy at several levels of analysis. In Nigeria, for example, during the federal government's war against the Republic of Biafra from 1968 to 1970, civilians were not the victims of systematic and sustained terrorist assaults by sub-national actors and equally important, as Theen and Wilson report, as that war passed into eclipse, the looming calamity of widespread government counterforce by General Yakubu Gowon against civilians never materialized.[215]

In contrast, civilian targets in Algeria have borne much of the yoke of horrors associated with that country's political instability and social unrest.[216] In terms of qualitative descriptions, two examples are as good as any to convey to the reader the qualitative brutality of murder in Algeria. For instance, at Haouche el-Hadj in the vicinity of Algiers, a group of Islamists in 1997 raided a farm killing fifteen persons with shovels, knives, and axes, and one woman had her severed breast inserted in her mouth and down her throat apparently either before or after she was killed.[217] In another event, a baby's head was severed from its body during a terrorist assault in the Chebli section of Blida province in September 1997 and put on the roof of the house while the body was placed in an oven in the kitchen.[218] All too frequently, there seems to be a process of torture and mutilation that moves over and beyond the act of killing itself. Many other horrific terrorist assaults, similar in nature and all too frequent in occurrence, afflict the Algerian populace.

One possible interpretation as to why that condition exists revolves around the central idea of a set of interconnections between brutal Algerian terrorist assaults carried out against opponents of intractable Muslim revivalist extremists, and a condition that several writers such as Fuller, Dunn, Ciment, and Ruedy suggest is Algeria's "fractured national identity," all played out against the backdrop of what Ruedy describes as an "economic backwater" condition.[219] In comparison to Nigeria, one striking difference in the Algerian environment, in my judgment, is what Fuller refers to as intrinsic "competing identities" between "Francophone" and "Arabophone" culture, and by extrapolation, the incomplete Algerian identity that may, as Fuller and Crenshaw-Hutchinson suggest, trace an arc to the profound and lasting experience of the "direct rule" approach of French colonialism that differed from the British approach of "indirect rule."[220] To be sure, Vandewalle really chronicles something similar when he suggests that fundamental processes and subcomponents necessary for robust national identity were ignored outright during Algeria's fledgling years. In his analysis, the author tells us that "many earlier observers gave little credence to the importance of cultural discourse, the power of ideas, and the wish for a more equitable and democratic society."[221]

To be more specific, Fuller draws on Soudan's work to explain the reasons for Algeria's "identity crisis" as threefold. In the broader sense, Fuller tells us of the ambiguous nature of Algerian identity where "Algeria in one sense suffers from a far less distinct and historically rooted identity than its more self confident neighbors Tunisia and Morocco. Indeed it was France that gave distinct 'national' boundaries to a modern state."[222] In fact, Dunn pursues the point further when he tells us, "Algerian identity was expressed not through the revival of some ancient culture or identification with a single national leader (as with Bourguiba in Tunisia), but through the glorification of the heroic and successful struggle against France."[223]

Fuller also asserts there is profound and lasting damage to the collective Algerian psyche associated with the temporal length and depth of French colonialism, pitting the character and interests of "Francophones" and "Arabophones" in fierce competition with one another.[224] To be sure, Crenshaw-Hutchinson tells us that "the traditional life of Algeria was literally destroyed and replaced with an alien system from which Algerians were excluded."[225] As mentioned previously, one aspect of discussion that deserves the increased devotion of Fuller and other scholars like him revolves around the central idea of long-haul effects associated with the different structural frameworks of British "indirect rule" where "tribal" group leaders were co-opted by colonial administrators and "direct French rule," that in the case of Algeria manifested itself in the French *pied noir* community, as the French were known in the vernacular, and the affluent *colon* community in particular.[226] Lastly, Fuller points to the enormous geographical space Algeria fills in the Maghreb that generates and sustains a "regional role" or hegemonic ranking fraught with uncertainty for policy makers.[227] He asserts that "Algeria as a new state and a 'new culture' was faced with the task of exploring its own national dimensions in the region after independence—a huge territorial presence with a new and uncertain regional role that had to be acquired."[228]

While I find Fuller's first two points to be tantalizing, the third seems much less persuasive precisely because of the reason that Nigeria also holds a regional hegemonic position in West Africa, there is no connection prima facie between regional hegemony and full-blown mass murder that I know of, nor are the interconnections between "fractured national identity" and hegemonic ranking explained adequately by Fuller. Be that as it may, the notion that brutal terrorist assaults, at least in part, presuppose and derive from a fragility of national identity that evokes a knee-jerk reaction of unbridled brutality against ideological opponents is worthy of study in the future.

All of the foregoing seems very different from Nigeria's historical legacy where divisions between "permanent majority" political groups like the Ibo, the Yoruba, and the Hausa Falani as well as between the foregoing and "permanent

minority" groups like the Ijaw, Tiv, and Edo, have not resulted in the same
degree of wholesale sweeping violence evident in Algeria, even though violence
that presupposes and derives from a host of "coincidental cleavages" has
certainly occurred in Nigeria between ethnic groups.[229] What seems
significant here is that this comparison between Algeria and Nigeria also
controls for the factors of regional hegemonic position previously mentioned by
Fuller, and the "economic malaise" brought on by public sector inefficiencies
and what Mortimer describes as the exogenous oil glut and international debt
factors in the 1980s that really spawned economic hardships in both
countries.[230]

Delving even deeper, that situation in Algeria of "competing identities," to
use Fuller's term, may contribute to what Spencer describes as a lawlessness
that may be inextricably bound up with very brutal terrorist assaults that have
happened in Algeria. For Spencer, "less explicable cases of individual violence
may in term be due to a generalized breakdown in law and order, in which
opportunistic reactions to the prolonged state of emergency have played as much
of a role as the pursuit of Islamist aims."[231]

Somewhat ironically, Spencer's passage, I think, is reminiscent of
Durkheim's "anomic condition," albeit with a twist. Durkheim's "anomic
condition," found in society characterized by economic specialization,
presupposes and derives from an unhealthy political social system where
individuals are increasingly removed from one another and unable to feel
"unity" or "solidarity."[232] If "government," that "independent organ . . . of
the social organism," as Durkheim puts it, cannot evoke an overarching unity
among persons, decay happens with persons feeling like "a lifeless cog."[233]

It seems possible that something similar to an "anomic state," described by
Durkheim as a function of Algeria's "fractured national identity" and blighted
economic condition, could help to generate and sustain especially brutal terrorist
assaults in Algeria.[234] That idea seems corroborated to some degree by
Zoubir's analysis, in which he quotes Bennoune who writes that corruptness
"has seized the entire social body and generates in it an ethical malaise which
leads to generalized cynicism."[235] In summation, Algeria as a case study
really showcases the importance of Huntington's notion that complete and
healthy identity formation is a necessary stage to go through and complete in a
successful way prior to socioeconomic development if the ruling elite is really
concerned about the overall and long-term political stability of the political-social
system.[236]

Notes

1. Labaton 1999, A30; Kifner 1999, A8; Kifner and Rashbaum 1999, A1, A17; Pyes, Kifner, Howe, Verhovek, and Burns 1999, A1, A22. Kifner and Rashbaum report "RDX (cylotrimethylene trinitrame) [is] widely used by military demolitions experts". Pyes *et al.* tell us, "one Montreal police investigator, Claude Paquette, this week said that the loose rules had turned Canada into 'a club Med for terrorists'."

2. Pyes et al. 1999, A1. Pyes et al. report that Ahmed Ressam had interconnections with Fateh Kemal, an Algerian "Afghani Arab" reported by French counterterrorism experts to be inextricably bound up with the assault by Algerian Islamists against French counterterrorism forces in Roubaix, France, in March 1996; Spencer 1996, 94, 95.

3. Johnston 1999, A24. Kifner and Rashbaum 1999, A1, A17; Burns and Pyes 1999, A-16; Stout and Olson 1999, A8: *FBIS* 1996g. Kifner and Rashbaum report that Said Atmani, another companion of Ms. Garafolo, also had interconnections with Ahmed Ressam. Interestingly enough, reports suggest Atmani himself seems to have powerful ties to Bosnia, where he fought with Bosnian Muslims during the war in Bosnia-Herzegovina during the 1990s. Stout and Olson tell us that the Algerian Action League is under the aegis of an Algerian who resides in Switzerland named Mourad Dhina.

4. *New York Times* 1999, A13; Labaton 1999, A30.

5. Labaton 1999, A30; Burns and Pyes 1999, A16.

6. Nef 1978, 13; Chasdi 1999, 54-55.

7. Pyes et al. 1999, A22.

8. Mortimer 1991, 577; Vandewalle 1997, 33; Dunn 1994, 28; Roberts 1994, 448; Martinez 2000, 8. For Martinez, the spelling is "Benhadj."

9. Willis 1996, 269, 272; Martinez 2000, 60.

10. Spencer 1996, 94-95; Willis 1996, 327-328; Roberts 1995, 254.

11. Spencer 1996, 94-95; Willis 1996, 327-328; Roberts 1995, 254.

12. Willis 1996, 297, 325. At the same time, 'Uthman Tizghart gives an AIS figure of some "2000 fighters" but that claim by contrast to Willis and "General X" seems rather high. Tizghart, *FBIS* 1999, 4.

13. *FBIS* 1998d.

14. Roberts 1991, 149; Roberts 1994, 448; According the U.S. Department of State, Madani and Belhadj were put under "house arrest" in September 1994. USDOS 1994.

15. Ciment 1997, 92-93; Willis 1996, 116.

16. Ciment 1997, 79-80; Roberts 1994, 449.

17. Roberts 1994, 449.

18. Ciment 1997, 79-80; Roberts 1994. In her analysis, Spencer (1996, 98) describes the former strand with Gilles Kepel's description of the "pietist" approach.

19. Willis 1996, 116-117, 110; Roberts 1994, 432.

20. Willis 1996, 116-117, 110; Roberts 1994, 451.

21. Spencer 1996.

22. Roberts 1994, 433, 450; Entelis 1986, 36; Gordon 1966, 30-33 Crenshaw-Hutchinson 1978, 3,4.

23. Roberts 1994, 450-452, 456.

24. Roberts 1994, 450-452, 456. Roberts reports that Djaballah claimed that the "Movement of the Islamic Resistance (MNI) was in fact an emergent reality in 1974" (Roberts 1991, 137).

25. Roberts 1991, 137.

26. Jamil, *FBIS* 1998.

27. Roberts 1994, 450; Roberts 1991, 136, 142; Spencer 1996, 94. The Movement for an Islamic Society (HAMAS) is not in any way interconnected or associated with Shaykh Ahmed Yassine's Hamas terrorist organization in Israel-Palestine.

28. Roberts 1994, 450; Roberts 1991, 136; Ciment 1997; Lindblom 1980.

29. Roberts 1991, 136; *FBIS* 1997m; *FBIS* 1998l; *FBIS* 1997h.

30. Roberts 1994, 449.

31. Mortimer 1991, 579; Entelis and Arone 1992, 28; Ruedy 1994, 242; Zoubir 1993, 88; Ciment 1997, 94. One scripted account asserts Belhadj falls more in the sphere of the Salafiyya or "reform" movement. *FBIS* 1997f.

32. Ciment 1997, 93-94; Roberts 1991, 136; Martinez 2000, 39-40. For Martinez, FIS was "legally authorized" in 1989, but established in 1982.

33. Roberts 1994, 448.

34. Hourani 1991, 68; Roberts 1994, 444; Willis 1996, 149. Anderson, Seibert, and Wagner define "Sharia" as "the Muslim social and legal code" (Anderson, Seibert, and Wagner 1998, 15, 44). Willis estimates the "Majlis al Shura" was comprised of some thirty to forty persons.

35. Roberts 1994, 448; Willis 1996, 149.

36. Roberts 1994, 471-472; Martinez 2000, 26.

37. Roberts 1994, 448; Martinez 2000, 26; *Jerusalem Post* 1999, 7; *Jerusalem Post* 1996a, 5.

38. Oufella 1999, 7.

39. Roberts 1994, 471, 466.

40. Spencer 1996, 94; Zoubir 1993, 102-104; USDOS 1994a.

41. Willis 1996, 270-276, 325; USDOS 1994a.

42. Willis 1996, 270-276, 325; USDOS 1994a.

43. Willis 1996, 270-276, 325; USDOS 1994a.

44. Willis 1996, 270-276, 325; USDOS 1994a.

45. Willis 1996, 273. Willis tells us Sahnouni was removed from the Majlis al-Shura in 1991.

46. Willis 1996, 273.

47. Roberts 1994, 430-431; Ciment 1997; Zoubir 1993; Spencer 1996, 93.

48. Entelis 1986, 87; Ciment 1997, 85; Fuller 1996, 33.

49. Roberts 1994, 444; Reiss and Roth 1993; Ciment 1987, 85. Ciment tells us those nongovernment appointed "imams" and "mullahs" are referred to as *"les barbes"* or "the bearded ones."

50. Roberts 1994, 431; Roberts 1991, 578; Mortimer 1991, 579.

51. Roberts 1994, 471. The National Popular Army (Armee Nationale Populaire) presupposes and derives from the National Liberation Army (Arme de Liberation Nationale) that was the military branch of the pre-independence National Liberation Front (FLN) until 1962. Entelis 1986, 58; Zoubir 1993, 97; Spencer 1996, 98;

Vandewalle 1997, 33.

52. Zoubir 1993, 95; Roberts 1994, 432.

53. Article 40 of Algeria's 1989 constitution as found in Roberts 1994, 431; Zoubir 1993, 90.

54. Spencer 1996; Roberts 1994, 464, 469-470; Ruedy 1992, 241; Ciment 1997, 41.

55. Roberts 1994, 428; Martinez 2000, 24.

56. Roberts 1994, 428; Martinez 2000, 23-47.

57. Fuller 1996, 29; Spencer 1996, 93.

58. Spencer 1996, 94-95, 102; Roberts 1994, 474; Zoubir 1993, 104; Martinez 2000, 42 n51.

59. Roberts 1994, 474; Spencer 1996, 94; Kapil 1998.

60. Reiss and Roth 1993, 297.

61. Reiss and Roth 1993; In the same vein, Ranstorp suggests that individual terrorist assaults can be analyzed in a similar way (Ranstorp 1996).

62. Vandewalle 1997, 34-35, 37-38; Zoubir 1993; Entelis and Arone 1992, 24; Entelis 1986, 49; Martinez 2000, 2-4.

63. Vandewalle 1997, 39; Martinez 2000, 25.

64. Zoubir 1993, 87-88.

65. Zoubir 1993, 94; Fuller 1996; Ciment 1997, 86; Hume and Quandt 1999, 149; Martinez 2000, 23, 46-47. *Jerusalem Post* writers tell us that the official government unemployment rate in Algeria was 28.1 percent as of 1998, or 2.1 million persons out of a total population of 29 million in Algeria *(Jerusalem Post* 1998c, 7).

66. Zoubir 1993, 94; Fuller 1996; Ciment 1997, 86; Hume and Quandt 1999, 149; Martinez 2000, 23, 46-47; *Jerusalem Post* 1998c, 7.

67. Willis 1996; Zoubir 1993; Roberts 1994; Reiss and Roth 1993.

68. Reiss and Roth 1993, 297-299.

69. Reiss and Roth 1993, 297-299; Roberts 1994, 452.

70. Messaoudi, 1995, 91-107; Roberts 1994, 436; Ciment 1997, 87-88; Entelis 1986, 85-87; Roy, as found in Ciment 1997, 70, 95, 87-88.

71. Mortimer 1991, 575; Zoubir 1993, 87-88; Ciment 1997, 85.

72. Zoubir 1983, 87-88; Mortimer 1991, 575; Spencer 1996; Roberts 1994, 430, 478.

73. Spencer 1996; Roberts 1994; Roberts 1991; Roberts 1995.

74. Roberts 1994, 459.

75. Zoubir 1993; Vandewalle 1997, 33; Mortimer 1991, 575.

76. Fuller 1996, 36, 8: Mortimer 1991, 575-577; Ciment 1987, 83; Entelis 1986, 59; Vandewalle 1997, 33; Spencer 1996; Roberts 1994, 435.

77. Entelis 1986, 35-36, 42.

78. Roberts 1994, 442, 440, 433; Spencer 1996, 97; Entelis 1986, 84; Ciment 1997, 77; Allen 1974, 149, 153.

79. Ciment 1997, 77-78; Entelis 1986, 84; Roberts 1994, 451, 433, 466. Reiss and Roth tell us that "there is tremendous variation in violence rates over short and long time periods and across macrosocial units — nations, cities, communities within cities, and addresses within communities" (Reiss and Roth 1993, 303). Roberts tells us the Salafiyya Movement types are also known as "Hanabalists." For Roberts,

Salafiyya reformers are more internationally oriented (i.e., "Pan-Arabic") while the "Algerianists" (Djeza'ara) are more oriented to Algerian Islam and crafting Algerian national identity.

80. Spencer 1996, 99; Ciment 1997, 77-78; Roberts 1994, 440-442.

81. Ciment 1997, 77-78; Roberts 1994, 433.

82. Ciment 1997, 74; Fuller 1996, 7; Gordon 1966, 30-33; Roberts 1994, 432.

83. Ciment 1987, 76-78; Entelis 1986, 42-43; Gordon 1966, 30-33; Roberts 1994, 433.

84. Reiss and Roth 1993; Chasdi 1999, 110.

85. Spencer 1996, 100; Ciment 1997, 90; Entelis 1986, 83; Ranstorp 1996, 58; Roberts 1994, 438.

86. Spencer 1996, 100; Ciment 1997, 90; Entelis 1986, 83.

87. Spencer 1996, 101; Ciment 1997, 90; Entelis 1986, 83.

88. Ranstorp 1996, 58; Roberts 1994, 439.

89. Roberts 1994, 439.

90. Roberts 1994, 439.

91. Willis 1996, 270; Zanini 1999.

92. Willis 1996, 270; Fuller 1996, 38; *FBIS* 1995e; Mickolus 1997, 661. Mickolus tells us that Kherbanne, after his expulsion from France in 1992, made his way to Croatia where he, as of 1997, spearheaded an arms smuggling operation tracing an arc from Algeria to Central Europe.

93. Spencer 1996, 96; Reiss and Roth 1993.

94. Willis 1996, 305, 327; Spencer 1996, 97. Somewhat paradoxically, Bayouli's movement is also referred to as the "Islamic Group for the Defense of the Illicit." Ruedy 1997, 242; Fuller 1996, 38; Martinez 2000, 49-50.

95. Spencer 1996, 97; Ciment 1997, 92; Roberts 1994, 428, 446; Mortimer 1991, 575; Entelis 1986, 36.

96. Willis 1996, 269, 272; Fuller 1996, 38; Martinez 2000, 70. Willis reports that Abdelkader Chebouti was in the process of starting to integrate Takfir wa Hirja persons with the MIA when a government counterterrorism assault stopped the process.

97. Willis 1996, 270; Fuller 1996, 38, 41; Martinez 2000, 70; Ranstorp 1998, 323-324. Ranstorp tells us there were some 7,000 to 9,000 Afghani-Arabs in Afghanistan.

98. Reiss and Roth 1993, 299.

99. Willis 1996, 285; Reiss and Roth 1993.

100. USDOS 1994a; Willis 1996, 279-280, 285; *FBIS* 1998d; Hume and Quandt 1994, 149.

101. USDOS 1998a.

102. Ciment 1997, 96.

103. *FBIS* 1998d, 2.

104. Willis 1996, 298.

105. *FBIS* 1995e; Mickolus and Simmons 1997, 819. To be sure, one Mickolus and Simmons discrete event or account suggests that GIA training is happening is the Sudan as well.

106. Willis 1996, 286 n52.

107. Roberts 1995, 254, 260; Willis 1996, 282; Kibble 1996, 357; Martinez 2000, 46 n67.

108. Willis 1996, 284; Martinez 2000, 11, 64-65, 13; Tizghart, *FBIS* 1999, 3. To be specific, Tizghart tells us of GIA *"fatwas,"* otherwise known as Islamic jurisprudential positions, that in that case authorized the killings of foreign nationals, "intellectuals," and, in the broader sense, supporters of the Algerian regime.

109. Mickolus 1980.

110. *JPRS* 1995a; Mickolus and Simmons 1997, 756; Roberts 1991, 259, 264.

111. *FBIS* 1999r.

112. Roberts 1995, 260 n21.

113. Ciment 1997, 95-96.

114. *FBIS* 1997d.

115. Willis 1996, 280-281.

116. Willis 1996, 280-281.

117. Willis 1996, 280-281.

118. *FBIS* 1998d.

119. Willis 1996, 328; Mickolus and Simmons 1997, 682.

120. *Jerusalem Post* 1996h, 4; Mickolus and Simmons 1997, 730.

121. Hume and Quandt 1999, 147; Zanini 1999, 250; Tizghart 1999.

122. Willis 1996, 328-329.

123. *FBIS* 1997f; Martinez 2000, 62.

124. Martinez, *FBIS* 1996.

125. Mickolus and Simmons 1997, 691-692, 776, 825.

126. In her analysis, Zanini tells us of a counterterrorism raid in Italy in which computers and floppy disks with instructions and component building directions were found. Zanini 1999, 251.

127. Ranstorp 1998, 323.

128. *Jerusalem Post* 1995g, 4; USDOS 1995; Willis 1996, 277; Mickolus and Simmons 1997, 844.

129. de Andres, *FBIS* 1998.

130. de Andres, *FBIS* 1998.

131. *FBIS* 1997c.

132. *FBIS* 1997c; Fuller 1996, 41. Fuller talks about a very opaque group in the Algerian political landscape called "The Sunnah and the Shari'a" that is backed by Iran.

133. *FBIS* 1997e; *FBIS* 1997f.

134. *FBIS* 1997k; Tizghart, *FBIS* 1999, 4-5; Mickolus and Simmons 1997, 856. Precious little in the way of available information is known about one GIA "splinter group" called the "GIA General Command" that Mickolus and Simmons refer to and tell us claimed responsibility for a bomb detonation in August 1995.

135. *FBIS* 1997k; Tizghart, *FBIS* 1999, 4-5. That scripted account tells us the "Armed Islamic Movement" otherwise known as the "MEI" is under the aegis of Said Makhloufi, a former ANP officer who first joined the Islamic Salvation Front (FIS) and in turn, broke away to craft MEI.

136. *FBIS* 1997k; Tizghart, *FBIS* 1999, 4-5; Reiss and Roth 1993.

137. *FBIS* 1997e.

138. Tizghart, *FBIS* 1999; *FBIS* 1998k.

139. Tizghart, *FBIS* 1999.

140. Tizghart, *FBIS* 1999.

141. Tizghart, *FBIS* 1999; Reiss and Roth 1993.

142. *FBIS* 1998k.

143. *FBIS* 1998k.

144. Entelis 1986, 55.

145. *FBIS* 1999h; Tizghart, *FBIS* 1999, 3.

146. Tizghart, *FBIS* 1999, 3; Martinez 2000, 10-11, 64-65, 13.

147. Tizghart, *FBIS* 1999; Reiss and Roth 1993.

148. Tizghart, *FBIS* 1999, 4-5.

149. Reiss and Roth 1993.

150. Tizghart, *FBIS* 1999; *Keesings* 1999.

151. Tizghart, *FBIS* 1999.

152. Ranstorp 1998.

153. Tizghart, *FBIS* 1999; Willis 1996, 238-239.

154. Tizghart, *FBIS* 1999.

155. Tizghart, *FBIS* 1999.

156. Zanini 1999, 250-252; Ranstorp 1998, 324-325.

157. Zanini 1999; Avenarius, *FBIS* 1998; Hume and Quandt 1999.

158. Zanini 1999; Ranstorp 1998; Avenarius, *FBIS* 1998.

159. Milibank 1976, 11-17. For Milibank, transnational terrorist assaults are "carried out by basically autonomous non-state actors, whether or not they enjoy some degree of support from sympathetic states" (Milibank 1976, as found in Elliot 1977, 7, 10). For Elliot's use and discussion of "transnational terrorism," "it becomes *trans* national by virtue of its mobility—it transcends national boundaries" (Eliott 1977, 11). Chasdi 1999, 59, 4, 17.

160. Enders, Parise, and Sandler 1992, 305-306; Flemming 1992, 133 n2; Jenkins 1988, 252, 246-266; Johnson 1978, 270; Mickolus, 1980, viii; National Foreign Assessment Center 1979, iv, 6; Johnson 1978, 270; Elliot 1977, 4; Milibank 1976, 11; FBI sources found in Smith 1994, 18-21; Chasdi 1997; Chasdi 1999.

161. Spencer (1996, 94-95) tells us that the Armed Islamic Movement (MIA) or Mouvement Islamique Arme evolved into the AIS in 1994.

162. Vandewalle 1997, 48; Spencer 1996, 95; Roberts 1995, 258-259, 264; *Jerusalem Post* 1999a, 5; *FBIS* 1997j.

163. Mickolus and Simmons 1997, 728-729. Mickolus and Simmons' scripted account suggests that the Union of Peaceful Citizens of Algeria was a one-shot type "proto-group" of three persons and accordingly the "group-type" column in that data entry was left blank. See *Times* (London), 1994; *Jerusalem Post* 1994m; *Keesings* 1994d.

164. USDOS 1996, section entitled "Algeria." One part of that United States Department of State account chronicles what was, in the department's judgment, probably a GIA terrorist assault against a U.S. warehouse in Algiers on 9 November 1995 in which the building was assaulted and an Algerian security guard was threatened.

165. Long 1990, 1; Flemming 1992, 164, 180, 194-195, 203-204; Gurr 1988, 45-46; Mickolus 1980, xxii-xxiii; Pflatzgraff 1986, 292; Hoffman 1984 10-15; Crozier 1960, 160; von der Mehden 1973; Horowitz 1985.

166. Long 1990, 1; Flemming 1992, 164, 180, 194-195, 203-204; Gurr 1988, 45-46; Mickolus 1980, xxii-xxiii; Pflatzgraff 1986, 292; Hoffman 1984 10-15; Crozier 1960, 160; von der Mehden 1973; Horowitz 1985.

167. Raitberger 1997, 5; *Jerusalem Post* 1998a, 1.

168. *Jerusalem Post* 1995a, 4.

169. Chasdi 1999.

170. Crozier 1960, 160; Flemming 1992.

171. *Jerusalem Post* 1997h, 6. For one thing, *Jerusalem Post* writers tell us a former Algerian government "secret agent" known as "Yussuf" reported to staff at the English newspaper the *Observer* that the Algerian government was inextricably bound up with so-called "Moslem fundamentalist[s]" terrorist assaults in France and in Algeria. Conversely, Algeria's ambassador to the United Nations, Abdallah Bali, dismisses the foregoing accusations outright. *FBIS* 1998b.

172. One scripted U.S. Department of State passage really alludes to that problem of measurement in its appraisal of a condition in which, "while the AIG was responsible for most of the attacks against foreigners in 1994 there are many extremist cells operating in Algeria that do not fall under a central authority that may also be responsible for such attacks" (USDOS 1995a).

173. Sirkin 1994, 383-427; Norusis 1991, 264-284, 311-330 Wonnacott and Wonnacott 1990, 778; George and Mallery 1995, 52-61; *SPSS*1999a, 234.

174. Chasdi 1999, 164, 203 n46; Chasdi 1997, 91, 110 n34; Chasdi 1995, 171, 228 n18, 377-387.

175. George and Mallery 1995, 49; Wonnacott and Wonnacott 1990, 39-40.

176. Hoffman 1984, 10-15.

177. Reiss and Roth 1993, 291-325; Dunn 1994.

178. Osmond explores "relative deprivation" to explain terrorism in his work that presupposes and derives from Gurr's work on "civil strife" and "relative deprivation." Osmond's findings suggest terrorism cannot be explained by Gurr's "relative deprivation" theory. Osmond 1979, 118, 116, 57, 144-145; Zoubir 1993, 84-86; Gurr and Harff; Gurr 1988; Gurr 1989a; Gurr 1989b; Dollard et al. 1939; Entelis and Arone 1992, 34.

179. George and Mallery 1995, 75-81.

180. George and Mallery 1995, 75-81; *SPSS* 1999a, 285-289.

181. George and Mallery 1995, 75-81.

182. *FBIS* 1998d; *FBIS* 1997f; Tizghart, *FBIS* 1999.

183. Norusis 1991, 270-71; Norusis 1988, 202.

184. Norusis 1991, 313-320.

185. USDOS 1995a; USDOS 1999d; Willis 1996, 284, 287; Dunn 1994, 146.

186. Willis 1996, 284, 287; Dunn 1994, 146.

187. Chasdi 1995, 211-219, 223; Chasdi, 1997, 98; Chasdi 1999, 175-180; Drake 1998, 10-11.

188. Chasdi 1995, 211-219, 223; Chasdi 1997, 97-98; Chasdi 1999, 175-180.

189. Chasdi 1995, 211-219, 223; Chasdi 1997, 97-98; Chasdi 1999, 175-180.

190. Norusis 1991, 270-271.

191. *Jerusalem Post* 1995h, 4; *Jerusalem Post* 1995n, 1; *Jerusalem Post* 1996g, 1.

192. *Jerusalem Post* 1994i, 4; *Jerusalem Post* 1994k, A-4; JPRS 1994d.

193. *Jerusalem Post* 1994p, 1; Mickolus and Simmons 1997, 848; *Jerusalem Post* 1995m, 3.

194. Chasdi 1999, 178.

195. Chasdi 1999, 178.

196. Chasdi 1999, 178. In *Serenade of Suffering,* it is found that 26 out of 66 terrorist attacks or 39.4 percent are associated with "reaction to government policy," while in this work 6 out 17 attacks or 35.2 percent are associated with "reaction to government policy."

197. Chasdi 1999, 178.

198. Sirkin 1999, 225, 298; Wonnacott and Wonnacott 1990, 302-303; Norusis 1991, 230. From the start, the plan was to perform a one-way ANOVA test to compare the three means of terrorist assault deaths linked to commemoration of landmark events, political events, and diplomatic initiatives such as the "EU Troika" visit to Algeria of European dignitaries from the Netherlands, Austria, and Luxembourg. Regrettably, the emergent reality was that those events were initiated only a very short time, in some cases only days, after the announcement of the event was made. To be sure, that emergent reality did not fit well with the contours of this analysis of variance.

With respect to other categories of death rates for Algerian terrorist assaults linked to political events, it would make no theoretical sense to compare the means of the foregoing with the mean of number of dead for ground assaults precisely because of the reason that such government activity is not announced in advance. Likewise, Algerian terrorist assaults linked to government polices were not included in the analysis. With respect to religious events, it is commonplace to note an underlying theme in the literature on Algerian terrorism that during the Ramadan holiday Algerian terrorist assaults would increase. Accordingly, it does not, in my judgment, seem theoretically useful to use an ANOVA test to account for Algerian terrorist assaults during the four-week period prior to Ramadan. *FBIS* 1998c; *Jerusalem Post* 1998b, 6; *FBIS* 1998a; *FBIS* 1997a; *FBIS* 1995a.

199. Sirkin 1999, 272; George and Mallery 1995, 83-84; *SPSS* 1999a, 251-252.

200. *Jerusalem Post* 1994d; Khiari 1994, 4; Willis 1996. For an example of an event to commemorate the Boudiaf assassination, see *Facts on File* 1994, 409.

201. Dunn 1994, 154; Roberts 1995, 257; Spencer 1996, 104, 95; *Jerusalem Post* 1995o, 4; *Jerusalem Post* 1995p, 3; Ganley 1997, 6.

202. When those terrorist assault outlier cases were included in the analysis, the standard deviation for numbers of dead in landmark events was 52.68 around a central measure of tendency, namely the mean of 14.25. By comparison, a standard deviation of 4.11 for number of dead for political events is associated with a mean of 3.35. To be sure, that extremely large standard deviation of 52.68 and the large difference in the means themselves suggest an influence of outlier cases on the distribution curve of numbers of dead.

203. Sirkin 1999, 290, 278, 282, 280 286; Norusis 1991, 289-291; *SPSS* 1999a, 227, 251, 268, 282.

204. As George and Mallery tell us, a two-tailed test is used irrespective of the directional nature of the difference in means (George and Mallery 1995, 84).

205. Dunn 1994, 149.

206. Chasdi 1999, 173, 175, 184, 212; Chasdi 1997, 101; Chasdi 1995, 390-391, 223.

207. Flemming 1992; Chasdi 1995; Chasdi 1997; Chasdi 1999; Drake 1998, 181.

208. Event deaths $N=339$, minimum 0, maximum 500, mean 10.45, standard deviation 33.39; event injuries $N=237$, minimum 0, maximum 286, mean 10.69, standard deviation 26.56.

209. Chasdi 1995; Chasdi 1997; Chasdi 1999; Raitberger 1997, 5; *Jerusalem Post* 1998a, 1.

210. O'Neill 1978, 34, 40, 25; Osmond 1979, 115-118, 57-58, 101-102, 90-93, 142-143; Shultz 1978, 10; Waugh 1982, 53-56; Flemming 1992, 95; Merari et al. 1986.

211. Dunn 1994.

212. Duvall and Stohl 1983, 207-211; Stohl 1988, 161-163; Chasdi, 1997, 105; Chasdi 1999, 188.

213. Dunn 1994, 150.

214. *Jerusalem Post* 1998d, 5. Another *Jerusalem Post* scripted account puts the figure at 60,000 persons (*Jerusalem Post* 1996i, 4). Other estimates include 40,000 persons as of 1998 provided by "General X" of the ANP *(FBIS* 1998d); a USDOS figure of some 75,000 since 1992 (USDOS 1999l, 2).

215. Theen and Wilson 1992, 553; Theen and Wilson 1986, 519-520; Theen and Wilson 1996, 533.

216. Dunn 1994, 146.

217. *FBIS* 1997b.

218. *Times* (London) 1997b, 11; *Jerusalem Post* 1997f, 6.

219. Fuller 1996, 5-7, 12, 17-19; Dunn 1994, 147-148; Ruedy 1992, 233, 241; Ciment 1997, 91; Mortimer 1991, 575-577.

220. Fuller 1996, 12, 17-19; Crenshaw-Hutchinson 1978, 1-8; Theen and Wilson 1986, 512-583, Theen and Wilson 1992, 546-613; Theen and Wilson 1996, 533.

221. Vandewalle, 1997, 34.

222. Fuller 1996, 17-18, 12.

223. Dunn 1994, 148.

224. Fuller 1996, 5-6, 12; Dunn 1994, 148; Ciment 1997, 91; Crenshaw-Hutchinson 1978, 2.

225. Crenshaw-Hutchinson 1978, 2, 1, 3-8. Faced with the lurking prospect of legislative change, Crenshaw-Hutchinson chronicles the affluent *colons'* opposition to 1947 legislation proposed under France's Fourth Republic that would have helped to promote greater electoral equity, thereby in effect helping to wrest away much of *colon* predominance over the Algerian political landscape.

226. Crenshaw-Hutchinson 1978, 2; Theen and Wilson 1986, 512-583; Theen and Wilson 1992, 546-613; Theen and Wilson 1996, 487-548; Diamond 1990, 351-409; Melson and Wolpe 1971, 1-42. Melson and Wolpe, in my judgment, suggest that "multiple communal identities" provide a source of strength as well as the prospect of

political instability and social unrest. The authors tell us, "the old identities in effect, coexist with the new, with the consequence that citizens come to hold multiple communal identities (for example, to their family, village, region, nationality, church and nation-state). By the same token, the internal differentiation . . . signals the proliferation of additional social reference points rather than the substitution of the new for the old" (Melson and Wolpe 1971, 28).

227. Fuller 1996, 5-6, 18; Dunn 1994, 148; Ciment 1997, 91.

228. Fuller 1996, 5-6; Dunn 1994, 148; Ciment 1997, 91.

229. Melson and Wolpe, 1971, 1-42; Diamond 1990, 341-409; Theen and Wilson 1986; Theen and Wilson 1992; Theen and Wilson 1996.

230. Mortimer 1991, 575; Diamond 1990, 371, 375, 391; Vandewalle 1997, 36, 39-4; Ruedy 1992, 239; Spencer 1996, 102.

231. Spencer 1996, 95.

232. Durkheim 1984 [1933], 295, 306, 171, 304; Ciment 1997, 89. Seen from a different angle, Barakat as found in Ciment's work, uses the term "anomie" to describe "alienation in religion" as persons are subsumed in Islamic fundamentalism.

233. Durkheim 1984 [1933], 295, 306, 171, 304; Ciment 1997, 89.

234. Durkheim 1984 [1933], 295, 301-309; Ciment 1997, 89.

235. Mahfoud Bennoune work as found in Zoubir 1993, 87, 107.

236. Huntington 1968; Entelis 1986, 45; Roberts 1994, 435.

Chapter Four

The Case of Egyptian Terrorism

Introduction

When nostalgia grows apace and I think about the tortured historical legacy of the Middle East, oftentimes I think of President Anwar el-Sadat. If I recall correctly, I was anchored in my college dormitory common room along with one or two friends closely watching Sadat's lumbering Boeing 707, resplendent in the colors of EgyptAir, land in Tel-Aviv, Israel. I seem to remember one pundit, mulling over what was transpiring, who evoked a comparison to man landing on the moon and, to be sure, that lurking analogy dovetailed nicely to capture what many described as the surrealistic texture of the trip. I devoted singular attention to the television screen as Sadat left his elegant jetliner to walk toward Prime Minister Menachem Begin of Israel and the diminutive older woman generally recognizable worldwide as "Golda." What seemed significant to me, and probably to all who remember, was that the old political order in the Middle East was passing into eclipse as those two once-fierce antagonists turned to welcome one another in front of an Israel Defense Forces (IDF) color guard.

It has been many years since that watershed political event, and while Begin, former Prime Minister Golda Meir, and Sadat are long dead, Egypt still remains a primary linchpin against political instability and social unrest in the Middle East region. Seen from the vantage of strategic thinking, Egypt, now

151

outside of the military fray, makes the likelihood of outright war between Israel and Arab confrontation states much smaller. Seen from the vantage of political diplomacy, it is all too frequently President Hosni Mubarak who helps to breathe new life into the episodic and inconsistent peace talks between Israelis and Palestinians.[1] Compounding the matter even more, Olson tells us that President Mubarak has a set of interconnections with Arab and Turkish leaders thereby in effect helping to promote overall stability in the region. For example, Olson reports that Mubarak's shuttle trip to Ankara in July 1996, ostensibly to lambast fledgling Turkish-Israeli military relations, was really carried out to prevent Turkish counterterrorist assaults against Kurdistan Workers' Party (PKK) training facilities in northern Syria.[2]

All of the foregoing is not lost on American foreign policy decisionmakers who are the gatekeepers to more than 1.2 billion U.S. dollars in military assistance and $800 million U.S. dollars of economic assistance to Egypt each year.[3] From the vantage of U.S. grand strategists and Israeli strategists who gauge the stability of the region in large part in terms of how vulnerable nations are to the threats of so-called "rogue states" like Iraq and Iran and the more insidious threat of Islamic revivalism, Mubarak's "secular" Egypt remains a cornerstone of American Middle East foreign policy.

An analysis of Egyptian terrorism and comparison of those quantitative findings to Algerian terrorism findings makes it possible to compare behavior trends in both systems of terrorism at several levels of analysis. First, a comparison of quantitative findings can be made within the context of region since Algeria and Egypt, the primary venues of both systems, are found in the Maghrib part of the Middle East. In addition, such comparison controls largely, if not completely, for "prevailing social ideology" since Sunni Islam predominates in both Algeria and Egypt.

Second, analysis of those two terrorism systems makes it possible to compare Algerian terrorism, which happens primarily within a rather isolated and self-contained political and social system, to Egyptian terrorism, which is more diverse in terms of social and political discourse. At one level, Egyptian terrorism revolves around religious differences such as the strains and tensions between Christian Copts and Sunni Muslims. At a more functional level, the discourse of Egyptian terrorism is involved more directly in contemporary Middle Eastern affairs as they relate to the long-standing, time-honored conflict between Israelis and Palestinians and the geopolitical considerations of the United States.

The framework of analysis for this chapter involves: a qualitative analysis of Egyptian terrorist groups and terrorist chieftains active in the political fray; some dynamics about the role of Islam in Egyptian society that continue to generate strains and tensions in the political system; quantitative analysis of Egyptian terrorism between 1994 and 1999; some reflections on ways of thinking about counterterrorism policy. It is to the analysis of Egyptian terrorist groups that the work now turns.

Qualitative Description and Analysis: Some Broader Aims

The purpose of this section is to delve into the sources and origins of three of the most predominant Egyptian terrorist groups active in the political fray between 1994 and 1999.[4] Those terrorist groups include al-Jama'a al-Islamiya or the "Islamic Group," al-Jihad Organization or "Holy War Organization," and the Vanguards of the Islamic Conquest Organization. The framework of analysis includes discussion about the following: antecedent political groups and social processes or movements; the emergent reality of specific antecedent terrorist groups that coalesced in the 1970s; political initiatives and dynamics like the struggle by President Gamal Abdul Nasser to spearhead Arab socialism, the fierce struggle between Nasser and the Muslim Brotherhood, and what Guenena and Esposito both call President Anwar-el-Sadat's "open door economic policy" programs.[5]

The Reiss and Roth "risk factors matrix" makes it possible to describe what Lasswell might call the "maturity cycle" of terrorist group evolution, and provides insight into the powerful set of interconnections between economic and political factors embedded in the Egyptian political system, that help to serve all too frequently as an impetus for Egyptian terrorist group formation, "splintering," and the process of terrorist "spin-off" formation.[6] What Reiss and Roth might call a set of "predisposing factors" at the "macrosocial" or societal level of analysis revolve around a sustained and unresolved conflict about the proper relationship between what Hatina tells us are the subcomponent strands of state, religion, and society in the Egyptian political-social framework.[7]

It is commonplace to note that al-Jama'a al-Islamiya, al-Jihad, and "splinter" group incarnations like the Vanguards of the Islamic Conquest Organization trace an arc to the Muslim Brotherhood or Jamayyat al-Ikhwan al-Muslimin.[8] As Hatina points out, that ticklish question about religion was never really resolved in Egypt from the start, unlike the case of modern Turkey where, during what Özbudun calls the 1925-45 "consolidation phase," Mustafa Kemal, otherwise known as Atatürk, injected a series of reforms into the political system directed against the Islamic establishment.[9] As Özbudun tells us, those reforms in Turkey included, but were not limited to, "the banning of religious orders; the adoption of the Swiss civil code to replace the *sharia;* acceptance of other Western codes in the fields of penal, commercial, and procedural law; the closing of religious schools; the outlawing of the fez."[10] Hatina tells us that perhaps the single, most dramatic reform happened a year before, with the abolishment of the Ottoman-Turkish Caliphate in 1924.[11]

By contrast, Hatina describes the arduous historical legacy of the struggle in Egypt at a functional level between Muslim "traditionalists" like the al-Azhar University *ulama* and those *ulama* of the state apparatus. There has also been struggle between Western-oriented students and student organizations of Jama'at al-Islamiya at college campuses in Egypt over the proper role of Islam in Egyptian society.[12] The struggle is even broader still, at a theoretical level between dissident Islamic revivalists, like members of the Muslim Brotherhood, and the secular state replete with "separation of powers" which is conceived of as a Western, Judeo-Christian construct.[13] To be sure, it is the struggle between the Jamayyat-al-Ikhwan Muslimin and the state that perhaps best epitomizes that unresolved sense of national identity that is a hallmark of the Egyptian polity.

What are the sources and origins of that condition in which the "national identity" phases of development, to use Huntington's terms, remain makeshift and never complete? Hatina and Sonbol both tell us that part of the problem presupposes and derives from what Hatina refers to as the position of "ambiguity" described for Islam in the original 1923 Egyptian constitution and echoed in the 1964, 1971, and 1980 amended versions of the constitution.[14] Hatina suggests that Islam, by means of the *sha'ria,* was seen as the centerpiece or central source of state authority but that exactly how that source would be transposed into political power and influence in the larger world of action was never spelled out with precision.[15] At a functional level, that schism was mirrored in the development of the Liberal Constitutionalist and Wafd parties, on the one hand, and the Muslim Brotherhood, on the other hand, which was crafted by Hassan al-Banna in 1928.[16]

The importance of epistemology within the Islamic tradition, as Hatina tells us, is seen from the vantage of the writings and positions of writers who inject the highest dosage of valid religious interpretation possible from the Qu'ran and the *hadiths* into their interpretations about the separation or indivisible unity of religion and state in Egypt.[17] Hatina points to the range of arguments that themselves trace an arc to the role and emphasis which the Prophet Mohammed is thought to have placed on setting up political infrastructure and whether or not that role was distinguishable from religious invectives and processes.

For example, the writings of "liberal nationalists" like Shaykh'Ali 'Abd al-Raziq (1888-1966), Shaykh Khalid Muhammed Khalid (1920-96) and, in the contemporary world, Faraj 'Ali Fuda (1945-92) provides close and carefully reasoned readings of Muslim sacred writings to illustrate and substantiate the point of view that religion ought to be separated at some level from the state.[18] Alternatively, conservative Islamist writers such as the Muslim Brotherhood's Muhammad al-Ghazali (1916-96) also crafted arguments of political theory that presuppose and derive from Islamic sacred texts.[19] It is important to note here that arguments within that "liberal nationalist" school varied somewhat with respect to interconnections between the polity, religion, and Egyptian society. But "liberal nationalist" ideas revolved around the generally recognizable notion of strengthening the political system not only against the lurking power of the West, but also to introduce flexibility into the political system to tackle the question of how to confront the challenges and opportunities associated with socioeconomic development or modernization.[20]

The Muslim Brotherhood:
Historical Antecedent and Blueprint for Action

The Muslim Brotherhood was crafted in 1928 by an Egyptian schoolteacher in Ismailia named Hassan al-Banna (1906-49) whose leitmotif was that Islam ought to serve as the guidepost to the revitalization of Egypt and the Muslim Middle East. A host of what Reiss and Roth might call "situational factors" at the "macrosocial" level of analysis were embedded in the Egyptian political landscape at that time, thereby in effect helping to generate and sustain the coalescence of the Muslim Brotherhood and other fledgling and similar Egyptian groups, like the antecedent group the Jamiyat al-Shubban al-Muslimin or Young Men's Muslim Association (YMMA).[21] At the heart of those causal factors are economic and political dynamics that Voll explains were associated with enormous substantive distance between the economic reality of most Egyptians and the ruling elite, under the aegis of the King Fu'ad monarchy and the British.[22]

Political instability and social unrest were hallmarks of the early Egyptian political landscape. Efforts to ameliorate the economic backwater condition of most Egyptians were eclipsed by political machinations where political rivalries and broader competition between political parties were predominant over the political landscape. For example, a set of "situational factors" prevailed as the Wafd Party, always in fierce competition with the Liberal Constitutionalist Party for political power, was, in the broader sense, shackled by limitations, as Voll tells us, imposed by the monarchy and perhaps at a more substantive level by British authorities.[23] The death of political leaders can also serve as a "situational factor" and Voll tells us that the death of Wafd Party leader Sa'd Zaghlul (1857-1927) diminished the potency and impact of the Wafd Party in Egyptian politics, and in Voll's words, "the party seemed reduced to a political interest group rather than a platform for national self-expression."[24]

It follows that one way of thinking about the matter is to view that set of interconnections between Egyptian "liberal nationalists" on the one hand, and the Egyptian monarchy and British officials on the other, as a condition afflicted with what Thucydides might describe as "stasis," where the political demands and aspirations of large segments of the population, in this case the disenfranchised, were not articulated in effective and sustained ways. For Thucydides that condition might lead to a condition of decline and decay.[25] In Reiss and Roth's lexicon, the foregoing economic and political conditions might constitute a political landscape characterized by the absence of meaningful political "opportunity structures" at the "predisposing-macrosocial" level of analysis for most of the populace.[26]

Compounding the problem even more was the emergent reality that Egypt, as Voll tells us, was also plagued in the 1930s by the worldwide Great Depression of the 1930's, that Reiss and Roth might call a transnational "situational" factor.[27] With political "opportunity structures" in Egypt makeshift and never really complete, overlaid against profound and lasting economic difficulties that were perceived to be a function of Western influence, Voll suggests the formation of a political-social group like the Muslim Brothers (Ikhwan al-Muslimin) or an Ikhwan antecedent group like YMMA was an ineluctable conclusion that reflected the fatigue and anger at shopworn slogans and symbols of Western style political organization.[28]

To be sure, it was within that political and economic context that the Muslim Brotherhood became an emergent reality in Ismailia near the Suez Canal. In fact, Husaini reports that al-Banna's service as a teacher in Ismailia was, to use Reiss and Roth's lexicon, the "activating factor" behind al-Banna's underlying theme to wed religious activism with political activism. "The political element," as Husaini writes, "never entered his reckoning during his student days, or while he was in Cairo, nor even in the beginning of his activity in Ismailia; or, more correctly, politics never was an outstanding element in his program during the preliminary stages. Here now, it is correct to say that there has been added to his social, Sufist tendency a political tendency born of a new environment."[29]

The story of the actual genesis of the group is itself intriguing precisely because of the reason that six followers of al-Banna, shackled with despair over economic and political conditions, and the torturous historical legacy of Egyptian life under foreign domination, came to al-Banna presumably with some conception of organization in mind.[30] In a similar vein, Mitchell reports that in four years Muslim Brotherhood leaders would set up organizations in abu-Suwayr, Suez, Port Said, and in western Nile delta locales.[31] In turn, al-Banna become the first gatekeeper or "spiritual guide" of the fledgling Muslim Brotherhood.[32] With respect to the early composition of the Muslim Brotherhood, we are told by Voll that the Muslim Brotherhood was an "urban based" organization composed of working-class persons, but Harris tells us the initial Muslim Brotherhood members were from poorer stock.[33]

One underlying theme for those leaders was to lambast Western decadence and corruption as a carefully reasoned instrument to constrain or suppress Egyptian political and economic demands and aspirations. Voll provides a passage from al-Banna's *Five Tracts of Hassan al-Banna* that is illustrative in a metaphorical sort of way of what the problem was all about. For al-Banna, the West introduced "their half-naked women into these regions, together with their liquors, their theaters, their dance halls, their amusements, their stories, their newspapers, their novels, their whims, their silly games, and their vices."[34] By the same token, Voll asserts that al-Banna did not condone violence as a vehicle to pursue the political goal of reform for the Egyptian political system.[35] In fact, Voll suggests that al-Banna's way of thinking about nonviolence and the reaction of some to that was what Reiss and Roth might call the "activating factor" behind the establishment of a militant Muslim Brotherhood spin-off group in the 1930s called Shabab Mohammed.[36]

Seen from the vantage of "conservative" Muslims, Islam had an enormous capacity to provide declarative and definitive answers to the political and economic problems in Egypt. In addition to the freewheeling political competition and economic conditions of the time, there were other "situational factors" or "situational" events that contributed to a condition ripe for Islamic revivalist group formation. In the narrower sense, one "situational" event was the rebellion of 1919 against the British that was quelled by British military forces.[37] There seems to be a dimension of that rebellion that pulled at the heartstrings of emotion for al-Banna, thereby in effect placing that rebellion as a "situational factor" in the sphere of the "individual-situational" level of analysis. In terms of interconnections to the "individual" level of analysis, the British military force response, as Mitchell and Husaini both relate, probably caused rage, anger, disorientation, and other similar sentiments. Mitchell tells us that "he was afterwards to remember with special bitterness the sight of British forces in occupation of his hometown at this time."[38]

In the broader sense, Mitchell, Husaini, and Abdelnasser all suggest that one seemingly "transnational" and "macrosocial-situational" event that had profound and lasting effects for Muslim "conservatives" was the abolishment of the Caliphate by Mustafa Kemel in 1924. Unequivocally, the abolishment of the Caliphate had profound and lasting implications for Muslim "conservatives" in Egypt and elsewhere and it is probably no exaggeration to say that those "conservatives" perceived that action by Atatürk as the quintessential manifestation of early twentieth century Western imperialism in the region.[39]

What seems significant here is that way of thinking about the abolishment of the Caliphate is an oversimplification of the Turkish political condition that really amounts to political game playing. Those with an allure to fundamentalist tenets of any kind may have a penchant to view political events in apocryphal ways, thereby in effect helping to preclude any realistic appraisal of Atatürk's needs to destroy the symbols and institutions of the Ottoman Empire in the wake of the First World War. That fundamentalist interpretation of political events seems to embody distortions, if not an outright misreading, of a watershed event, for many, but certainly not all, Muslim activists. In terms of the Reiss and Roth construct, those dynamics associated with that cognitive processing of information would fall into the realm of the "individual" level of analysis at the "predisposing-psychosocial" level, and perhaps for some persons, also at the "biological" level.[40]

In the case of al-Banna himself, Reiss and Roth's use of "predisposing" and "situational" factors at the "individual" level of analysis provides insight into the formative processes and dynamics that gave structural shape to al-Banna's way of thinking. In the broader sense, Mitchell tells us that al-Banna seems to have evoked a remarkable degree of self-importance and other similar sentiments as a young boy living in Mahmudiyya that somewhat ironically mirrors, in my judgment, the dynamics of Rabbi Meir Kahane's childhood.[41] Mitchell tells us: "[A] revealing instance of his religious ardour and convictions is the legendary tale, perhaps apocryphal but undoubtedly symbolic, of his single-handed and successful effort, at the age of ten, to have an 'obscene' statue of a semi-naked woman which was displayed on one of the river boats removed and destroyed by the police."[42]

That notion of self-importance did not seem to result in a cookie-cutter strategy of reactive protest that limited itself to struggle against inanimate symbols of Western decadence. The works of Mitchell, Husaini, and Harris all chronicle how the young al-Banna had a penchant for joining or crafting Islamic revivalist organizations.[43] As Harris reports, in al-Banna's capacity as secretary of "a benevolent society" called "the Benevolent Hasafiyat Society" or Jam'iyyat al-Hasafiyyah al-Khayriyyah, another incident involved his almost singular attention to three female Christian missionaries in Mahmudiyyah and his increased devotion to the removal of the mission precisely because of the reason it was seen as a venue for proselytizing by Christians.[44] Perhaps as a concomitant to life events like the foregoing, both Mitchell and Husaini recount how al-Banna as a boy enjoyed reading Islamic morality tales about time-honored pitched battles in Islamic history, "folk tales," and the extraordinary capacities of Islamic war heroes.[45]

Equally important to al-Banna with the passage of time was his profound and lasting interest in Sufism. Even though Sufism emphasizes a non-involvement from temporal matters, Sufism seems to have offered al-Banna a mystical epiphany about what Egypt's plight at the turn of the nineteenth century was all about and what was needed to make structural political and economic change.[46] It seems to follow that "temperament," "cognitive ability," or both of those "individual" level factors, and the power of "situational factors" were at work here, thereby in effect helping to influence al-Banna's very "un-Sufi-like" weltanschauung.[47] As Husaini relates, "he emphasized from the beginning of his mission, the foreigners' monopoly of the economy of the country, particularly in commerce and industry; he realized the affinity between politics and economics and saw the necessity of including them in his program."[48]

In the broader sense, Hassan al-Banna's increased devotion to Islamic religious education is illustrative of the influence of his father, himself a "traditionalist" scholar of note.[49] His father, Shaykh Ahmad 'Abd al-Rahman al-Banna, who was called "the watchmaker" for his mechanical talents, and generally recognizable as a scholar in the Hanbalist tradition for his work on Ahmad b. Hanbal, was a meticulous and conscientious father who provided the type of stable home atmosphere needed for al-Banna to lay a keel for his pursuits, and to thrive in effective and sustained ways.[50] What seems significant here is that the totality of al-Banna's childhood experience that falls in the realm of Reiss and Roth's "societal" and "individual" spheres would, for al-Banna, generate and sustain a conservative Islamic morality tale ethos. That ethos, peppered with mystical trappings and moral rectitude in effect helped to shape al-Banna's thinking, thereby in effect making it possible for him to peg-hole and compartmentalize complex life events into "moral" and "immoral" spheres.[51]

There seems to have been a confluence of what Reiss and Roth might call "societal" and "individual" factors that galvanized within Hassan al-Banna to help him inject the highest dosage of political activism possible into the strict Hanbalist essence of his approach. In the broadest sense, the emergent reality was a set of al-Banna-crafted "opportunity structures" for the expression of Egyptian political and economic demands and aspirations found both in the domestic sphere and the international sphere. In the case of international politics, the lurking catastrophe of Western "great power" domination remained, and Zionism with its European sources and origins and interconnections to the Jewish European elite like the Rothschild family, grew apace and culminated in the establishment of the state of Israel in 1948.

Against the backdrop of those watershed political events, the Muslim Brotherhood issued clarion calls to action to break the shackles of the subservient relationship between the Muslim East and the Christian West. Piscatori tells us there is a direct set of interconnections between the Muslim Brotherhood of the 1930s and what the author calls contemporary "neo-Ikhwanist groups" that call for an end to the Mubarak regime, U.S. support for Israel, the U.S. led embargo of Iraq, and, in the broader sense, Western and American presence in the Middle East.[52] Compounding the matter even more is the notion of American "cultural imperialism" within the context of the "technological revolution" or "information age" that includes satellite dishes, for instance, that is a Western artifact with an enormous capacity to disseminate underlying Western norms and values seen as antithetical, from the vantage of Islamic revivalists, to the true interests of the contemporary Muslim world.[53] It is to those contemporary political demands and aspirations of Islamic revivalist extremists, that have been captured by Islamic revivalist terrorist groups, that the analysis now turns.

Al-Jama'a al-Islamiya: the Islamic Group

Perhaps the single, most predominant Egyptian terrorist group in operation nowadays is al-Jama'a al-Islamiya, otherwise known as the Islamic Group (IG).[54] One way of thinking about al-Jama'a al-Islamiya is to place that terrorist group within the context of Ibrahim's classification scheme that sorts out various strands of the "Islamic resurgence" in Egypt into three categories, namely, "establishment Islam," "Sufi Islam," and "activist Islam."[55] To be sure, al-Jama'a al-Islamiya falls in the sphere of Ibrahim's "activist Islam" category. It is crucial to make distinctions as Ibrahim does, precisely because of the reason that the "Islamic resurgence" in Egypt is broad and multidimensional, with only a small sliver that consists of terrorist groups that commit terrorist assaults.

Among types of organizations that fall into Ibrahim's "activist Islam" category, the data show that al-Jama'a al-Islamiya has carried out the greatest number and highest percentage of Egyptian terrorist assaults between 1994 and 1999. At a functional level, the Islamic Group (IG) has been described as a "loosely organized" terrorist organization that seems to be skillfully broken down into subdivisions that resonate with a set of interconnections, sometimes powerful and sometimes more frail, oftentimes culled out according to geographical site.[56] In terms of leadership, one scripted account tells us that the more contemporary Islamic Group leadership includes Rifa'i Taha, who probably wrested away the helm of the Islamic Group after Shaykh Umar Abdul Rahman was imprisoned by the U.S. government for his role in the World Trade Center bombing of 1993.[57] A second leader, Muhammad Shawqi Islambouli, whose brother Lieutenant Khalid Islambouli spearheaded the al-Jihad team that assassinated President Anwar-el-Sadat in 1981, reportedly engages in terrorist activity from his crow's nest in Afghanistan.[58]

Other al-Jama'a al-Islamiya leaders who are reported to live in Egypt or outside of Egypt in exile include Mustafa Hamza, otherwise known as Abu Hazim, and Tal'at Fu'ad Qasim, also known as Abu Talal Qasimi.[59] Both of those persons are reported to have powerful interconnections to Shaykh Osama bin Laden and his al-Qaida organization, and both lived for a time in Afghanistan. Another scripted account written in October 1999 describes the "new military leadership" of the Islamic Group within Egypt as under the aegis of 'Ala' Abd-al Raziq and Rif'at Zaydan.[60] Prior to al-Raziq, Farid Kadwani was at the helm of IG's military leadership until his death in September 1999.[61] In turn, Kadwani had followed Tal'at Yasin Hammam who had led the military branch in Egypt since 1994.[62] Clearly, it is critical to differentiate between that new military ruling elite and the Islamic Group's old ruling elite who, as one scripted account reports, have been imprisoned in Liman Turah Prison since 1997.[63]

In a similar vein to what is observed in the case of Algerian terrorism, the aforementioned suggests that one underlying theme of Egyptian counterterrorism policy revolves around the assassination of al-Jama'a al-Islamiya terrorist chieftains, and that leads to the fundamental question of whether or not those assassinations are carried out alone or perhaps in tandem with other, perhaps less harsh counterterrorism measures. Regrettably, in-depth public information about Egyptian counterterrorism operations is practically nil, making it impossible to even make conjecture about that important matter.

Seen from the vantage of Sabri al 'Attar, an imprisoned IG member, the organizational framework of the Islamic Group consists of a "Shura Council" and a "military committee."[64] In the case of the "Shura Council," that al-Jama'a al-Islamiya member relates to Egyptian officials that the "Shura council" is comprised "of 'Isam Darbalah, 'Asim-'Abd-al-Majid, Najih Ibrahim, Usamah Hafiz, Abu-Talal al-Qasimi, and Abbud al-Zummar."[65] In the case of the "military committee" we are told that Mustafa Hamza, otherwise known as Abu Hazim, has been at the helm, along with Shihab-al Din and 'Asim Abu-Majid.[66] That scripted account, written by Sharaf-al-Din, also asserts that a treatise known as "The Islamic Action Charter" is perhaps the single most fundamental organizational tract of al-Jama'a al-Islamiya.[67]

The structural shape of the political framework of the Islamic Group reverberates with a set of powerful interconnections that are worldwide in scope. For example, in Sharaf-al-Din's scripted account, we are told by Islamic Group defendant Sabri al 'Attar that an al-Jama'a al-Islamiya storehouse presumably for media relations and logistics was located in Copenhagen, Denmark, and led by Talat Fu'ad Qasim until he vanished in Croatia in 1995.[68] In perhaps the darkest foreboding of all, al'Attar describes transit stations and military training facilities in Yemen, Peshawar, Pakistan, Albania, Afghanistan, and Sudan, as well as the participation of al-Jama'a al-Islamiya activists in Bosnian war, helping to stoke the burners of *jihad* against the West.[69] At the same time, Sharaf-al-Din sums up to tell us that while there are some twenty-eight Egyptian Islamic revivalist terrorist groups active in U.S. and European urban areas, effective and sustained counterterrorism efforts have generated enormous problems for the IG in terms of organization and communications infrastructure, thereby in effect helping to isolate IG activists and intensify personal rivalries among chieftains.[70]

The sources and origins of the al-Jama'a al-Islamiya or the Islamic Group are difficult to describe in a relatively straightforward way, insofar as there seem to be differences in description and discussion of al-Jama'a al-Islamiya and when that name was first used. Having said that, it is possible to trace an arc to the release of Muslim Brotherhood activists from Egyptian prisons by President Anwar-el-Sadat following the death of Nasser in 1970 to partially offset the political influence and underlying effects of Egyptian Arab Marxist student organizations and other groups who looked askance at Sadat precisely because of their full-blown support for Nasser's Arab-Marxist political agenda.[71] That practice of providing support to "enemies of your enemies" for short-term gain is a recurring theme in counterterrorist policy associated with deleterious long-haul results for the ruling elite. Seemingly, it is also a lesson that government counterterrorism policy makers find hard to master. The Israelis did almost exactly the same thing by supporting fledgling Islamic revivalist groups to offset the power of the Palestine Liberation Organization, while the Americans supported the Afghan mujhadeen or "freedom fighters," to use President Ronald Reagan's inaccurate term, against the Soviet Union in Afghanistan.[72]

The "new" Muslim Brotherhood—what Kepel calls the "neo-Muslim Brethren"—have had a different experience with the Egyptian government than did their older Muslim Brother counterparts. During the era of President Nasser, Ikhwan leaders were jailed, forced into exile, and in some cases killed, such as Sayyid Qutb who was murdered by the Egyptian government in 1966.[73] Nowadays by contrast, some groupings of the "neo-Muslim Brethren" devote almost singular attention to work within the Egyptian political framework, thereby in effect helping to elicit the tacit if not the outright support of the government.[74]

As Sonbol tells us, the contemporary Muslim Brotherhood speaks with a cacophony of voices, some that articulate a desire for greater political involvement and others that shun the formal political process outright.[75] For example, Azzam, Guenena, and Esposito all tell us about social services that include Muslim financial institutions *(sharikat tawzif al-amwal)* with "unusually high rates of return," schools, and high-quality and efficient hospital services that were provided by the Muslim Brotherhood to the Egyptian populace.[76] To be sure, those were not done for altruistic purposes, as one of the underlying Muslim Brotherhood goals was to generate and sustain full-blown support among college and university students for an Islamic revivalist agenda.[77]

With respect to the foregoing, the set of interconnections between the terrorist group al-Jama'a al-Islamiya and a set of university campus student organizations called "the Jama'at al-Islamiya" still remains somewhat unclear. For instance, Auda seems to suggest that the terrorist group al-Jama'a al-Islamiya presupposes and derives from university campus organizations also called al-Jama'a al-Islamiya.[78] Within the context of fierce competition with "young Islamic radicals," Auda tells us that the Muslim Brotherhood, by means of those groups, sought to introduce flexibility into the political-social system, thereby in effect helping to constrain and suppress the lurking challenge associated with more radical Islamic activity on campus.[79] In his analysis of the Muslim Brotherhood in the 1970s Auda tells us: "[T]he Brotherhood also moved to control university student unions and constitute al-Jama'a al-Islamiyya, or the Islamic Association, in the universities to represent its thinking. This strategy (which received some state assistance) entailed integrating the different Islamic societies in each university into one organization under the name al-

Jama'a al-Islamiyya."[80]

Seen from a slightly different angle, Azzam suggests the terrorist group al-Jama'a al-Islamiya presupposes and derives from a set of university campus organizations with a different name, called "the Jama'at al-Islamiya," and Azzam asks us to note the difference in spelling with the use of a "t" in Jama'at.[81] Both Azzam and Kepel suggest that those Islamic revivalist associations called "the Jama'at al-Islamiyya" which were crafted in the 1970s may have had interconnections to the Muslim Brotherhood and were generally recognizable as restricted to the parameters of the nonviolent political sphere.[82] But, as Kepel suggests, there were logistical problems insofar as the Jama'at al-Islamiya groups were anchored at campus settings and never had the capacity to operate over and beyond the university framework. In his analysis of al-Jihad leader Muhammed 'Abd al-Salam Faraj's criticism of the Jama'at, Kepel suggests that "the *jama'at islamiyya,* who were unable to move beyond the campuses and some of whose members dreamt of infiltrating the state apparatus in an effort to undermine it from within" were perceived by Faraj and al-Jihad to be impotent.[83]

As if that were not enough, Azzam points to another dimension, namely that the Jama'at al-Islamiya, as a social-political movement, was comprised of subcomponent groups that varied in approach with respect to the ticklish question of violence as a legitimate tool. For Azzam, "although the activities of the Jama'at throughout the country generally followed a similar pattern, activists nevertheless tended to follow the instructions of their particular amir (leader). Thus in one context, for example, Assyut, they would pursue more violent activities than in other areas."[84] By the same token, Voll chronicles how Sadat, faced with the lurking calamity of effective and sustained Islamic opposition, skillfully broke down the Jama'at al-Islamiya groups in 1980-81.[85]

Compounding the problem even more, Azzam also tells us that the term "Jama'a al-Islamiya" is used by activists in broad, generic terms to describe the group or movement, in contrast to the Egyptian government which has referred to the "Jama'a al-Islamiya" as "al-Jihad."[86] Be that as it may, what seems significant here is that there seems to be a degree of permeability, interpenetration, and nonexclusivity between and among Islamic groups or "proto-groups" in Egypt that makes it difficult to chronicle the precise parameters of Jama'a al-Islamiya, otherwise known as the Islamic Group.[87] For example, Abu-Sutyat reports how IG leader Muhammad Shawqi al-Islambouli recently jumped ship to join Dr. Ayman Zawahari's Jama'at al-Jihad (the Islamic Organization).[88]

To be sure, it may be more fruitful to focus special devotion to what Azzam and several other scholars tell us are the economic and political sources that generate and sustain the power of those movements in the first place.[89] In the broadest sense, both Auda and Gaffney as well as Piscatori suggest that the failures associated with modernization efforts under the aegis of Nasser and Sadat served to stoke the burners of discontent and anger against both of those regimes.[90] For Auda, "the Islamic movement in the 1970s was a sociopolitical expression of the contradiction and shortcomings of the modernization and transformation of state-society relations under Gamel Abdul Nasser (1952-70) and Anwar Sadat (1970-81)."[91] In a similar vein, in terms of the Camp David accords, Gaffney tells us that, "government spokesmen trumpeted assurances that peace would also bring prosperity, blaming the patent liabilities of a bloated and inefficient public sector and the poor performance of agricultural cooperatives on the exigencies of the long standing 'war' with Israel, which had been institutionalized decades before. But the promised prosperity would elude most Egyptians."[92]

Likewise, Guenena describes "the role of religion as an idiom of discontent."[93] In turn, Esposito elaborates to describe how the profound and lasting economic backwater conditions in Egypt nowadays that include but are not limited to acute unemployment and housing shortages, with government seemingly unable to respond adequately to those structural problems, helped to evoke feelings of loyalty and other similar sentiments for Islamic revivalism.[94] As Esposito reports: "[T]hese neorevivalists were more sweeping in their indictment of the West and their assertion of the total self-sufficiency of Islam. They maintained that Muslims should not look to Western capitalism or communism (white or red imperialism) but solely to Islam, the divinely revealed foundation of state and society."[95]

At a functional level, there are certain Egyptian government policy initiatives that have exacerbated the strains and tensions even further between the Mubarak government and Islamic revivalists. President Mubarak's regime, instead of using public policy as a lever to offset partially the effects of those foreboding economic backwater conditions, has tightened restrictions on Islamic institutions whose services dovetail nicely with the needs of a significant segment of the populace. In the economic realm, perhaps nowhere has the problem been more acute and dramatic than in the case of Islamic financial institutions, formerly unencumbered by Egyptian central banking supervision, that were able to attract enormous amounts of capital.[96] In the process, however, fear and other similar sentiments were elicited by government officials about Islamic economic clout. In response to that condition of unfettered "Islamic banking," Law 146 was enacted in 1988 to correct that condition, and one result was the perception that the secular government had undercut the social services which the Muslim Brotherhood had made an emergent reality.[97]

As if that were not enough of a problem, there is profound and lasting reluctance on the part of the Mubarak regime to generate and sustain further democratization whereby the Muslim Brotherhood, instead of having to make tacit alliances with "legal" opposition parties to confront the National Democratic Party (NDP), as it did in the national elections of 1984 and 1987, would be able to participate more freely in the electoral process.[98] An underlying maxim found in the work of both Huntington and Skocpol is that if government is unable or unwilling to respond to political demands and aspirations by means of reform, it may over time pass into eclipse in the wake of more profound structural political change.[99]

Even though revolution is not a likely scenario in the case of contemporary Egypt, profound and lasting political instability and social unrest may be evoked by public policy that exacerbates rather than assuages long-standing grievances generally recognizable as stemming from President Gamal Abdul Nasser's "Arab socialism" and President Anwar el-Sadat's "open door economic policy."[100] In summation, it would seem that in both economic and political spheres there are structural problems that will stoke the burners of political and economic discontent over the foreseeable future, thereby in effect helping to insure continued strains and tensions between Islamists and "secularists" in the Egyptian political fray.

As I wrote in my first book, many of the aforementioned scholars underscore what Reiss and Roth might call the absence of meaningful "opportunity structures," set against the backdrop of the economic backwater conditions described by Gaffney, Piscatori, Hatina, Azzam, Sonbol, and others.[101] If that were not enough of a problem, that set of economic backwater conditions for Egyptians contrasted sharply with the affluence acquired by many of their countrymen and others in the oil-rich Gulf states. Gaffney reports: "[C]omplicating the moral commentary from the mosques . . . was the fact that so much of the petroleum was located in lands that had not been developed into modern secular societies. Many Egyptians saw a connection between this vast wealth and the maintenance of an explicit Islamic identity."[102] Clearly, those Egyptian "opportunity structures" seem to have "failed" for segments of the Egyptian populace, thereby in effect helping to generate and sustain recruitment pools for Islamic revivalists, be they nonviolent or violent in nature.[103]

Jama'at Al-Jihad: the Jihad Association

Jama'at al-Jihad, or "the Holy War" association, is an al-Jama'a al-Islamiya "splinter" or "spin-off" terrorist group that began to coalesce between 1980 and 1981.[104] Some contemporary leaders of Jama'at al-Jihad include its leader, Dr. Ayman Rabi al-Zawahari, Muhammad Rabi al-Zawahari, and Tharwat Salah Shihata.[105] The common wisdom is that Zawahari, who is about fifty-one years of age, is a medical doctor by training who can trace an arc back to 1981 with his involvement in the Jama'at al-Jihad assassination of President Sadat.[106]

Zawahari, otherwise known as 'Abd al Mu'izz, Nur, and "the teacher," has been living in exile since he fled Egypt in the 1980s, and has been reported at several geographical sites that range from Afghanistan, Chechnya, Yemen, and Sudan, to Switzerland.[107] Perhaps the bleakest foreboding of all is that Zawahari has had profound and lasting interconnections to Shaykh bin Laden, reported to have started around 1983.[108] In turn, Muhammad Rabi al-Zawahari, who is a younger brother of Dr. Zawahari, spearheads the "military wing" of Jama'at al-Jihad, according to one scripted account. We are also told that Jama'at al-Jihad's "civil affairs committee" is under the aegis of Tharwat Salah Shihata.[109] After a long-standing period of strains and tensions between al-Jihad and the Islamic Group, there is a report that some contact, whether episodic and inconsistent or more sustained, has happened.[110] It is possible, in my judgment, that Shaykh Osama bin Ladin has the capacity to facilitate that relationship insofar as he has been reported to bankroll al-Jihad to some degree, and has had a long-standing relationship with Mustafa Hamza of the Islamic Group.[111]

It is probably no exaggeration to say that al-Jihad is best known as the Islamic revivalist terrorist group that assassinated President Sadat on 6 October 1981 during a parade to commemorate the 1973 October war.[112] What is less well publicized in the United States is the makeshift but never complete "revolution" that was somehow to spawn from that terrorist assault and the terrorist assault campaign that started with an attack against the police station in Asyut some hours later by al-Jihad.[113] At a functional level, Kepel relates that Lieutenant Khalid al-Islambouli, whose brother, Mohammed al-Islambouli, was incarcerated by Sadat's police, was the originator and gatekeeper for that bloodletting plan against Sadat. At a substantive level, the economic and political conditions that made a continuously evolving environment ripe for more Islamic revivalist terrorist assaults were already deeply embedded in the political landscape.[114]

Against the backdrop of what Reiss and Roth might call the "macrosocial-predisposing" factors of economic and political strife, the fledgling al-Jihad became an emergent reality under President Sadat's watch. In the broader sense, perhaps the single most dominant theme that has plagued "Muslim militants," to use Ibrahim's term, is how to make a broad and deep Islamic "revolution" an emergent reality as well.[115] Compounding the matter even more was the failure of two antecedent terrorist groups active in the political fray even before al-Jihad made its appearance. Insofar as a brief examination of those Egyptian terrorist groups helps to illuminate the antecedent political conditions for al-Jihad, the following descriptions about the Islamic Liberation Organization or ILO, and the Takfir wal Hijra or Repentance and Holy Flight (RHF), are provided.[116]

The first terrorist group under consideration is the Islamic Liberation Organization (ILO), otherwise known as Muhammad's Youth, Shabab Muhammad, the Technical Military Academy group (TMA), or "Military Academy groups" ("MA").[117] Esposito suggests that what Reiss and Roth might call the "activating factor" for the ILO's coalescence was the calamitous result of the 1967 Six Day War that rent apart President Gamal Abdul Nasser's "Arab socialism" as a vehicle to achieve the goals of Arab nationalism.[118] In the broader sense, Voll tells us that watershed event marked a structural shift in activism with "a return to religion" in the wake of Nasser's enormous incapacity to confront Israel and the West. "One interpretation," writes Voll, "of the defeat held that it was God's punishment on a people who had abandoned the straight path of Islam. In fact, the secularism of the era of Nasser was giving way to a heightened sense of religious awareness among Christians and Muslims."[119]

The Islamic Liberation Organization (ILO) was crafted around that time by its founder and leader, Dr. Salih Siriya, who was born in Palestine and had a set of interconnections to Islamic activists in Jordan. Esposito tells us the Islamic Liberation Organization is best known for its relatively straightforward terrorist assault against the Technical Military Academy in Cairo in April 1974 that was somehow to elicit full-blown revolution with the downfall of the Sadat regime.[120] To be sure, chances for some dialogue between the Sadat regime and the Islamic Liberation Organization were practically nil, and the ILO was decimated by Egyptian armed forces.

At an organizational level, Esposito states the Islamic Liberation Organization had an "executive council" that sought consensus about contentious issues under consideration.[121] The author suggests that nowhere was the problem more acute than within that "executive committee" framework, where less seasoned ILO activists could articulate, and by means of consensus, implement poorly reasoned-out assault plans. Esposito suggests the dynamics that were generated and sustained by that framework may have contributed to the catastrophic decision by ILO leaders to confront Egyptian forces head-on with the Technical Military Academy terrorist assault in 1974.[122]

Simultaneously, part of that problem, as Long and Guenena both suggest, may have been due to the dynamics associated with lower numbers of decision-makers and their interrelationships. At one level, as Guenena relates, the ILO recruitment pool was narrower than what al-Jihad's recruitment pool would be with acquaintances and friends made by means of religious activities.[123] As Long suggests, sub-national actors like terrorist groups are also prone to deleterious group dynamics among small numbers of decisionmakers that include Janis's "group-think," Jervis's "perception and misperception," and other dynamics that can skew the decisionmaking process of leaders.[124]

In terms of the sources and origins of the Islamic Liberation Organization, Esposito asserts that the Islamic Liberation Organization traces an arc to a broader ILO movement in Jordan, that itself seems to have been a spin-off movement of the Muslim Brotherhood.[125] The ILO put a premium on militant activity precisely because of the "microsocial-situational factor," as perceived by Siriya, that the "old leadership" of the Muslim Brotherhood had been skillfully broken down in psychological and physical terms by imprisonment under President Nasser.[126]

The Takfir wal 'Hijra, otherwise known as Repentance and Holy Flight (RHF), and Jama'at al-Muslimin, or Society of Muslims, revolved around the central idea of long-standing, effective, and sustained conflict against a corrupt society.[127] When Shukri Mustafa regained his freedom in 1971, Auda tells us that Takfir wal 'Hijra was crafted by Mustafa during the first part of the 1970s.[128] In fact, Sonbol tells us, "Shukri Mustafa, had been an active member of the Ikhwan and had spent time in prison after Qutb's plan failed against Nasser in 1965."[129] In terms of leadership dynamics, both Auda and Esposito chronicle that Mustafa's leadership style was profoundly "autocratic" in nature.[130]

At a substantive level, the cornerstones of Takfir wal 'Hijra were shaped differently from those of other Islamic revivalist extremist groups like al-Jihad. Ibrahim relates the underlying approach to *jihad* (holy struggle) was very different for Takfir wal 'Hijra precisely because Takfir wal 'Hijra advocated nonviolence and profound isolation from the start, to perfect the mores of its Islamic activists before a "final blow" at the Egyptian regime.[131] For Ibrahim, "the notion of removing oneself, literally or metaphorically, from the present corrupt society is akin to a Hijra—holy flight from *jahilliyya*, a condition of infidelity, decadence and oblivious ignorance similar to that prevailing in pre-Islamic Arabia."[132]

At a functional level, Auda suggests that Takfir wal 'Hijra's underlying theme of what Kepel calls "withdrawal" or "uzla" is, for one thing, even diametrically opposite to the world view of another nonviolent Egyptian Islamic revivalist group called al-Samawiyya, with Shaykh 'Abdallah al-Samawi at the helm.[133] For Ibrahim, the central idea that drove Takfir wal 'Hijra seems to have revolved around a blend of *da'wa* (i.e., the calling) coupled with a coup de grace of violence at the end point of the struggle. Ibrahim chronicles how Takfir wal Hijra, under the aegis of Shukri Mustafa, shrouded itself in isolation from Egyptian society in an unpopulated geographical site in the Nile region, while Auda's account gives more emphasis to "hijra" in other countries like Jordan, Libya, Saudi Arabia, and Yemen.[134]

It is probably no exaggeration to say that, at some juncture, the Egyptian government perceived Takfir wal 'Hijra to be a looming calamity and as a result moved against Takfir wal 'Hijra members. Many members were put in prison, some of them within the context of a preventive strike to elicit some pretext for government action.[135] Accordingly, Takfir wal 'Hijra activists engaged in "reactive terrorism" in 1977, first by kidnapping Hasayn al-Dhahabi, a teacher and former government official, thereby in effect helping to insure a government backlash that came following al-Dhahabi's murder. In essence, al-Dhahabi was murdered precisely because al Takfir wal 'Hijra stipulations to the government were ignored outright.[136] To be sure, the government response pulverized Takfir wal 'Hijra, thereby in effect leading to the execution of Shukri Mustafa at the hands of the Egyptian authorities.[137] In summation, it is unequivocally clear that a set of challenges and opportunities associated with how to wrest power away from Sadat were clearly articulated, along with a trail of blueprints of failed attempts against him from which future militant Islamic revivalist leaders might analyze and learn.

With the tortuous historical legacy of the Islamic Liberation Organization (ILO) and Takfir wal 'Hijra in the background, Jama'at al-Jihad (Holy War Association) was crafted as a vehicle to promote an effective, sustained, and ultimately successful challenge to the secular government of Egypt.[138] Guenena tells us that the central idea of al-Jihad organization revolved around the plans of Muhammad 'Abd al-Salam Faraj, Karem Muhammad Zudhi, Nabil Abdel Maguid al-Mughrabi, and Foud al-Dawalibi to put together a Majlis al-Shura Council that was crafted in October 1980.[139] At an ideological level, what seems significant here for Faraj, as Sonbol reports, was the underlying notion that Islamic revivalists follow one of the Prophet Muhammad's most fundamental tenets, namely ". . . order what is equitable and forbid the reprehensible. . . ."[140]

The literary vehicle that Muhammad 'Abd al-Salam Faraj crafted to capture the underlying notion of religious activism was his treatise about *jihad* called *Al-Faridah al-Ghai'bah* (The Forgotten Duty).[141] Kepel and Jansen both tell us that in that treatise Faraj chronicles underlying similarities between the Sadat regime and the Mongol invaders in the 1200s who were eventually thwarted by the Mamluks in Syria.[142] For Jansen, Faraj believed that Sadat evoked an illegitimate political and legal system similar to the Yasan system of Mongol law.[143] In the broader sense, the political goal that Jama'at al-Jihad activists pursue over the political landscape is the reestablishment of the Caliphate or "Khilafa" in Egypt.[144]

As Kepel reports, the framework of Jama'at al-Jihad is really an amalgam of two separate al-Jihad groups that were active in or around Cairo in southern Egypt and in "Middle Egypt."[145] The Cairo-based group was led by Muhammed Abd al-Salam Faraj, who served as a bellwether for about a half dozen smaller subgroups called "majmu'at" each with its own leader or *amir*. Both Guenena and Auda tell us that sometime before 1981 there was what appears to be another strand of al-Jihad under the aegis of Muhammed Salam Rahal and then by Kamal al-Sayed Habib, that actually blended into the Cairo based al-Jihad group under Mohammed Abd al-Salam Faraj.[146]

Kepel suggests that while both Faraj and Zuhdi shared a full-blown commitment to wage war against the pro-Western regime of Sadat, each had carefully reasoned differences in terms of how that goal ought to have been pursued.[147] The author goes on to chronicle that Karam Zuhdi was the leader of the middle Egypt or "Sa'id" group whose activities against the government presupposed and derived from his participation in al-Jama'at al-Islamiya.[148] Kepel describes personal rivalries and differences and suggests "contextual factors," namely the difference between urban and rural settings, as two reasons why those perspectives were so different. We are told by Kepel that Faraj devoted almost singular attention to Sadat and his assassination, thereby in effect promoting a "top down" approach to crafting an Egyptian Islamic polity while Zuhdi, by contrast, believed Egyptian Christians deserved the increased devotion of Islamic revivalist assaults.[149]

Seen from the vantage of the Reiss and Roth analysis, it is not possible to isolate and identify any one predominant "activating event" that was pivotal to compel Faraj's al-Jihad group in southern Egypt to cooperate, albeit in a loose way, with Zuhdi's al-Jihad group in "middle Egypt" with respect to terrorist assaults directed against the Egyptian government. Nonetheless, as Kepel suggests, there were underlying efforts to harmonize the actions of both al-Jihad branches by June 1980.[150] It is at that point that Shaykh Umar Abdul Rahman became a nexus point for both al-Jihad branches, thereby in effect helping to facilitate the overall consistency of Jama'at al-Jihad. Even though it is commonplace to note Shaykh Umar Abdul Rahman's role as Jama'at al-Jihad's "spiritual leader," Guenena tells us the major part that Shaykh Umar Abdul Rahman played in Jama'at al-Jihad remains open to interpretation.[151] Guenena relates that other al-Jihad chieftains like al-Dawalibi and al-Zomar claim that Abdul Rahman acted as al-Jihad's spiritual leader, while Faraj and Zuhdi, by contrast, refute that assertion.[152] One reason that is important concerns whether or not it was Abdul Rahman himself who issued the *fatwa* that called for the death for President Sadat because he was a "kafir" (unbeliever). For Kepel, the evidence about that important matter seems to remain inconclusive.[153]

In terms of recruitment patterns, Auda reports that Jama'at al-Jihad has held an allure for persons found shackled on the fringes of society. For Auda, "the Jihadist Islamic Jama'a is a grass-roots organization emphasizing the recruitment of individuals on the margins of society—the unemployed, the poor and the undereducated."[154] In a similar vein, Kepel suggests that persons who feel a powerful allure for Jama'at al-Jihad are less middle-class in nature than even the recruits of the Military Academy Group, otherwise known as the Islamic Liberation Organization (ILO).[155] Kepel, who draws on Cairo neighborhood demographics with respect to the places of residency of Jama'at al-Jihad trial defendants, reports that "these people are marginal in every sense of the word"[156]

The Vanguards of the Conquest (Tala'i al-Fateh)

The Vanguards of the Conquest, sometimes referred to as the Vanguards of the Islamic Conquest (Tala'i al-Fateh), is a Jama'at al-Jihad splinter group that was established around 1993 and was active until March 1997.[157] If the Vanguard of the Conquest organization presupposes and derives from one specific "activating event," that event remains, at least for me, shrouded in mystery. The two most predominant terrorist assaults that the Vanguards of the Conquest are best known for is the August 1993 assassination attempt against Egyptian Interior Minister Hassan al-Alifi and the November 1993 assassination attempt against the Egyptian prime minister, Dr. Atif Sidqi.[158]

The United States Department of State tells us that the Vanguards of the Conquest is under the aegis of Ahmad Hasyn Agiza, and Mickolus and Simmons assert that Mustafa Hamza, known for his prominent role in the Islamic Group, is "a senior officer" of the Vanguards of the Conquest.[159] Another chieftain of that group is reported to be Yasir Tawfiq al-Sirri who, having received "permanent residence" in Great Britain, became the head of "The Islamic Observation Center" in London. Seen from the vantage of Egyptian government counterterrorism experts, "The Islamic Observation Center" serves as a media outlet for the Vanguards of the Conquest.[160]

There seems to be some parallels between the contemporary Vanguards of the Conquest and an "activist" Islamic revivalist group called the Islamic Vanguards or Tali'a al-Islamyya, that was crafted by in 1979 by Fathi 'Abd al-Azizi in al-Sharqiyya Governate.[161] For example, one scripted account tells us that twenty-two persons who are accused of belonging to the Vanguards of the Conquest, in a case before an Egyptian military court known as the "Vanguards" case, were from the al-Sharqiyya Governate. At the same time, effective and sustained recruitment efforts for that group also happened in al-Sharqiyya Governate.[162]

In turn, scripted accounts inform us that the Vanguards of the Conquest and another Jama'at al-Jihad splinter "proto-group" coalesced or blended into what is known nowadays as the Jihad Group-Armed Vanguards of Conquest, otherwise known in Arabic as "jama'at al-jihad-tala'i' al Fateh al islami." To be sure, data about the Jihad Group-Armed Vanguards of Conquest remains rather sketchy but 'Abdallah Mansour appears to be acting in the capacity of "general secretary" of the group.[163]

Some General Observations about Egyptian Terrorism

Relative Frequencies and Percentages of Egyptian Terrorist Assaults by Year

The data set for Egyptian terrorist assaults that happened between 1994 and 1999 is comprised of 141 discrete events that are primarily domestic terrorist assaults. When the data are broken down in terms of relative frequency by year, it is observed that patterns of Egyptian terrorism, like patterns of Algerian terrorism, are cyclical, replete with peaks and troughs. In the case of Egyptian terrorism, peak years are 1994, 1995, and 1997, while the trough years are 1996, 1998, and 1999.

In the case of peak years, the highest number of Egyptian terrorist assaults happened in 1994 with 52 out of 141 assaults or 36.9 percent. The year 1995 has the second highest amount with 38 out of 141 events or 27.0 percent, while 1997 is the year with the third highest amount with 28 out of 141 assaults or 19.9 percent of the total. In the case of trough years, 1999 had the smallest number, with 1 out of 141 terrorist assaults or .7 percent of the total. That single terrorist assault, namely a threat against "the United States and the Jews," was made by Ahmad Ibrahim al-Naggar from his prison cage trial before a military court ostensibly on behalf of the al-Jihad Organization.[164] The year with the second lowest amount of Egyptian terrorism is 1998 with 3.5 percent or 5 out of 141 acts. The year 1996 ranked third lowest with 17 out of 141 terrorist incidents or 12.1 percent of the total (see figure 4.1).

Terrorist Assaults by Group-Type, Terrorist Group, and Location

In the broader sense, Egyptian terrorism is political terrorism related to the protracted struggle between President Hosni Mubarak's government and Islamic revivalist terrorist groups or "lone assailants," struggle between Islamic revivalist terrorist groups or "lone assailants" with ethnic minority groups like Egypt's Christian Copts, and political terrorism inextricably bound up with the larger conflict between Islamic revivalist activists, the West, and the state of Israel. In terms of format, as this analysis unfolds, certain findings about Egyptian terrorism are compared to counterpart findings for Israeli-Palestinian-Arab and Turkish terrorism for immediate comparisons. For full accounts of Turkish and Israeli-Palestinian-Arab terrorism, see chapters 5 and 6.

At first blush, there is an underlying theme similar in Algerian and Egyptian terrorism insofar as terrorist assaults for the 1994 through 1999 period in both terrorism systems are carried out by theocentric terrorist groups that are Islamic revivalist terrorist groups without charismatic leaders, by identifiable lone assailants, or by anonymous terrorist groups or lone assailants. Notwithstanding that, when the data are broken down by terrorist group-type, the emergent reality of Egyptian terrorism presents a rather different portrait than Algerian terrorism.

First, a full 54.2 percent of Egyptian terrorism or 77 out of 142 acts are claimed by or attributed to Egyptian theocentric groups. That compares with only 21.9 percent or 75 out of 342 acts for theocentric groups in the case of Algerian terrorism. In turn, only 19.3 percent or 119 out of 615 acts of Israeli-Palestinian-Arab terrorist assaults are theocentric acts. The results show that

Frequencies

Statistics

Year of Event

N	Valid	141
	Missing	1

Year of Event

		Frequency	Percent	Valid Percent	Cumulative Percent
Valid	1994	52	36.6	36.9	36.9
	1995	38	26.8	27.0	63.8
	1996	17	12.0	12.1	75.9
	1997	28	19.7	19.9	95.7
	1998	5	3.5	3.5	99.3
	1999	1	.7	.7	100.0
	Total	141	99.3	100.0	
Missing	system	1	.7		
Total		142	100.0		

Year of Event

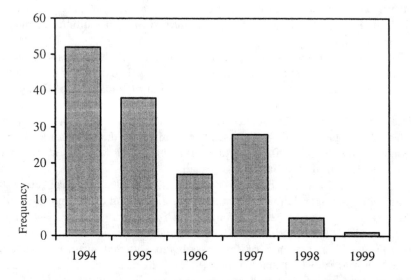

Figure 4.1: Relative Frequency of Egyptian Terrorist Attacks by Year, 1994-1999

36.6 percent of Egyptian terrorist acts or 52 out of 142 are anonymous incidents. Uncompleted terrorist assaults that account for 6.3 percent or 9 out of 142 acts is ten and one half times more frequent than the rate found for Algerian terrorism, where uncompleted acts make up only .6 percent or 2 out of 342 acts. The data show that 2.8 percent or 4 out of 142 Egyptian terrorist assaults were carried out by "declared" lone assailants by contrast to a rate of .9 percent or 3 out of 342 acts for "declared" lone assailants in the case of Algerian terrorism (see figure 4.2).

When the data are cut more finely by Egyptian terrorist groups, it is observed that al-Jama'a al-Islamiya, or the Islamic Group, carried out the highest rate of terrorist attacks at 41.5 percent or 59 out of 142 acts. What stands out here is that percentage and amount exceeds even the 52 out of 142 anonymous terrorist assaults that makes up the second place tally with 36.6 percent of the total. Terrorist assaults claimed by or attributed to Jama'at al-Jihad or Holy War Association, by contrast, have a mere 3 out of 142 acts terrorist assaults or 2.1 percent of the total (see figure 4.3).

As previously mentioned in chapter 2, terrorist groups that are generally recognizable as affiliates or "front organizations" of other more established terrorist groups are categorized as separate organizations in this analysis if those groups claim terrorist incidents or if government sources or other well-known or widely recognized sources provide attribution. Accordingly, a host of more shadowy Egyptian terrorist groups or "proto-groups" that in some cases may be "affiliate," "spin-off," or even "front organizations" for more time-honored and long-standing Egyptian terrorist groups or political movements like the Muslim Brotherhood comprise roughly 8.4 percent of the total. That percentage rate excludes the 3 out of 142 acts of Egyptian terrorism with multiple claimants found in the data.

Those Egyptian terrorist groups or "proto-groups" in the analysis include: the Vanguards of the (Islamic) Conquest or Tala'i' al-Fatah with 4 out of 142 terrorist assaults at 2.8 percent, the al-Jihad-Movement-Vanguards of Conquest with 2 out of 142 terrorist assaults or 1.4 percent, and al-Jama'a of International Justice, or the International Justice Association, with 4 out of 142 terrorist incidents or 2.8 percent. Terrorist assaults committed by the Islamic Battalions amounted to only .7 percent of the total or 1 out of 142 acts, as did terrorist assaults carried out by the Battalion of Death.

As mentioned earlier, there are 3 out of 142 recorded Egyptian terrorist assaults with "multiple claimants" that comprise 2.1 percent of the total amount. In the case of the 2 bombs detonated at the Nile Tower in al-Jizah in 1994, both al-Jama'a al-Islamiya and the Islamic Battalions issued statements of responsibility.[165] In the case of the assassination attempt against President Mubarak in Addis Ababa, Ethiopia, in 1995, both al-Jama'a al-Islamiya and the Vanguards of Conquest claimed responsibility for that terrorist assault.[166] In turn, al-Jama'a al-Islamiya or the Islamic Group in Arabic, Jama'at al-Jihad, and

Frequencies

Category of Group

N	Valid	142
	Missing	0

Category of Group

		Frequency	Percent	Valid percent	Cumulative percent
Valid	Uncompleted acts	9	6.3	6.3	6.3
	Unclaimed acts	52	36.6	36.6	43.0
	Theocentric	77	54.2	54.2	97.2
	Lone assailant	4	2.8	2.8	100.0
	Total	142	100.0	100.0	

Category of Group

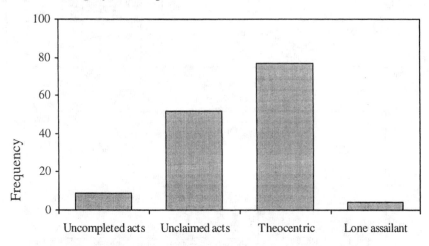

Figure 4.2: Relative Frequency of Egyptian Terrorist Attacks
by Group-Type, 1994-1999

Frequencies

Statistics

Name of Group

N	Valid	142
	Missing	0

Name of Group

	Frequency	Percent	Valid percent	Cumulative percent
Valid Uncompleted	9	6.3	6.3	6.3
Unclaimed	52	36.6	36.6	43.0
Lone assailant	4	2.8	2.8	45.8
al-Gama'a el Islamiya (Islamic Group)	59	41.5	41.5	87.3
al-Jihad (Egypt)	3	2.1	2.1	89.4
The Vanguards of Conquest (Egypt)	4	2.8	2.8	92.3
The Battalion of Death (Egypt)	1	.7	.7	93.0
al-Jam'ah of International Justice (Egypt)	4	2.8	2.8	95.8
Islamic Battalions (Egypt)	1	.7	.7	96.5
Multiple Egyptian Islamic Groups	3	2.1	2.1	98.6
al-Jihad/Movement/Vanguards of Conquest	2	1.4	1.4	100.0
Total	142	100.0	100.0	

Name of Group

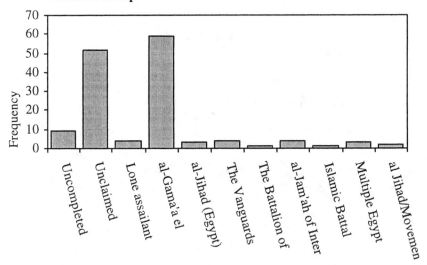

Figure 4.3: Relative Frequency of Egyptian Terrorist Attacks by Terrorist Group, 1994-1999

al-Jama'a of International Justice, otherwise known as the International Justice Association, issued statements of responsibility after the bombing of the Egyptian embassy in Islamabad, Pakistan in 1995.[167]

What seems significant here is that in two out of those three outlier cases, those "multiple claimant" terrorist assaults were "spectacular" in nature, either in terms of specific focus against a high-profile target like Mubarak, or with respect to comparatively large physical devastation rates and a degree of complexity that manifested itself in terrorist assault locales with geographical distance from Egypt as in the cases of those terrorist assaults in Ethiopia and Pakistan. The one rather "unspectacular" Egyptian terrorist assault committed against a civilian target was elicited by a "spectacular" terrorist event, namely the killing of over two dozen Palestinians during prayer in the Machpela Cave in Hebron by a Jewish revivalist, Dr. Baruch Goldstein.[168] Delving deeper into the source and origins of those terrorist assaults, one of those "spectacular" terrorist assaults was committed against a government target in reaction to government policy, while the terrorist assault against President Mubarak in Ethiopia is chronicled as an independent or non-reactive terrorist event.

An analysis of terrorist assault rates by location reveals that an overwhelming amount of Egyptian terrorism happened within Egypt at 78.9 percent, or over three-quarters, or 112 out of 142 acts. While a rate of 78.9 percent or 112 out of 142 acts is much less than the corresponding rate of 91.8 percent for Algerian terrorism, that rate is still rather high. Insofar as the central leitmotif of the conflict revolves around war with President Mubarak's regime, that finding for "domestic terror" rates is not all that unexpected. In Western Europe, only 6 out of 142 acts or 4.2 percent of Egyptian terrorism happened at that geographical site. The category, Western Europe, is comprised of France, Germany, Britain, Belgium, Austria, and Switzerland. It is found that 3.5 percent or 5 out of 142 acts were carried out in "other Middle Eastern states" that include Lebanon and Yemen.[169] In turn, 9 out of 142 acts or 6.3 percent occurred at other geographical sites.

The data reveal that 10 out of 142 acts or a full 7.0 percent of the total amount happened in the United States. Those 10 terrorist assaults include letter bombs sent to places like the federal penitentiary in Leavenworth, Kansas, the *Al-Hayat* newspaper offices at the United Nations in New York City, and the District of Columbia. The underlying theme of those terrorist assaults concerned violent protest directed against the United States for the imprisonment of Shaykh Umar Abdul Rahman, sometimes described as the "spiritual leader" of Jama'at al-Jihad because of his predominant role in the World Trade Center bombing in New York City in 1993.[170] It is also critical to report that the 1 terrorist assault outlier case recorded in which more than 51 persons were injured happened outside of Egypt in Islamabad, Pakistan.[171] In terms of Egyptian terrorism happening outside Egypt, 21.0 percent happened at geographical sites outside Egypt, the primary venue for conflict, as compared with a corresponding rate of 8.1 percent for Algerian terrorism. That 21.0 percent rate for Egyptian terrorism is virtually the same as the 20.3 percent rate found for Israeli-Palestinian-Arab terrorism found at locales other than Israel, the Occupied Territories, and the jurisdiction of the Palestinian National Authority (see figure 4.4).

Terrorist Assault Attributes: Fatalities, Injuries, Property Damage, Target Preference

When Egyptian terrorist assaults are broken down by ordinal measures of death and injury rates, the relatively low rates of physical devastation dovetail nicely with the notion that terrorism generates and sustains its power of effect primarily by means of the abject fear it promotes, thereby in effect helping to make structural political and social change possible. In the case of Egyptian terrorism, nearly two-thirds of all events at 63.7 percent or 86 out of 135 incidents, did not result in any deaths at all. A little more than one-third of all Egyptian terrorist assaults, at 36.3 percent or 49 out of 135 attacks, resulted in the deaths of between one and fifty persons. There are no outlier observations chronicled in the data on Egyptian terrorism (see figure 4.5).

In the broader sense, those findings for death rates are somewhat comparable to rates for Turkish terrorism. In the case of Turkish terrorism, the findings are similar with 72.6 percent of Turkish terrorist assaults that caused no deaths and 26.9 percent that caused the deaths of between one and fifty persons. The findings for Israeli-Palestinian-Arab terrorism differ somewhat in that a full 86.9 percent of Israeli-Palestinian-Arab terrorist acts were death-free events, while only 12.8 percent killed between one and fifty persons, a rate less than one-half of the Egyptian rate.

By contrast, some three-quarters of all Algerian terrorist assaults at 75.4 percent committed over the same period between 1994 and 1999 killed between one and fifty persons, a percentage figure some two times greater than that found for Egyptian terrorism. Furthermore, unlike the cases of Algerian terrorism, Turkish terrorism, and Israeli-Palestinian-Arab terrorism, there are no chronicled accounts of Egyptian terrorist assaults that killed between fifty-one and one hundred persons. There are also no Egyptian terrorist assaults found to have killed over one hundred persons (see figure 4.5).

In the case of injuries, the Egyptian terrorism results mirror the foregoing findings about Egyptian terrorist assault death rates but are not identical to them. The data show that three-quarters of all Egyptian terrorist assaults or 105 out of 140 incidents did not result in any injuries to persons. It is observed that only 24.3 percent or 34 out of 140 terrorist assaults were responsible for injuries to between one and fifty persons. There is one out of 140 Egyptian terrorist assaults or .7 percent that killed between fifty-one and one hundred persons (see figure 4.6).

Frequencies

Statistics

Locale

N	Valid	142
	Missing	0

Locale

		Frequency	Percent	Valid percent	Cumulative percent
Valid	Egypt	112	78.9	78.9	78.9
	Europe	6	4.2	4.2	83.1
	Other	9	6.3	6.3	89.4
	Other Middle East	5	3.5	3.5	93.0
	U.S.	10	7.0	7.0	100.0
	Total	142	100.0	100.0	

Locale

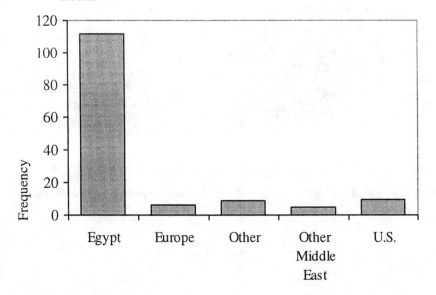

Figure 4.4: Relative Frequency of Egyptian Terrorism by Location, 1994-1999

Frequencies

Event Deaths

N	Valid	135
	Missing	7

· Event Deaths

		Frequency	Percent	Valid percent	Cumulative percent
Valid	0	86	60.6	63.7	63.7
	1	49	34.5	36.3	100.0
	Total	135	95.1	100.0	
Missing	system	7	4.9		
Total		142	100.0		

Event Deaths

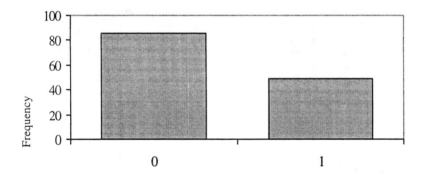

Figure 4.5: Relative Frequency of Numbers of Dead in Egyptian Terrorist Incidents, 1994-1999 (0=0; 1=1 through 50)

Frequencies

Statistics

Event Injuries

N	Valid	140
	Missing	2

Event Injuries

		Frequency	Percent	Valid percent	Cumulative percent
Valid	0	105	73.9	75.0	75.0
	1	34	23.9	24.3	99.3
	2	1	.7	.7	100.0
	Total	140	98.6	100.0	
Missing	system	2	1.4		
Total		142	100.0		

Event Injuries

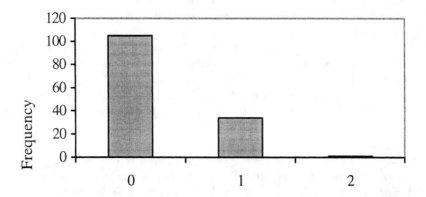

Figure 4.6: Relative Frequency of Numbers of Injured in Egyptian
Terrorist Incidents, 1994-1999 (0=0; 1=1 through 50; 2=51 through 100)

In comparison to Turkish terrorist assault rates, there is a slightly lower rate for Turkish terrorist assaults that are injury-free at 67.8 percent or 120 out of 177 acts. At the same time, there is a higher rate for Turkish terrorist assaults that injured between one and fifty persons at 31.6 percent as compared with the 24.3 percent rate for Egyptian terrorism. In the case of Israeli-Palestinian-Arab terrorism, the 69.8 percent rate for terrorist assaults that caused no injuries is very close to the 67.8 percent rate for Turkish terrorism. By contrast, it is found that 174 out of 606 Israeli-Palestinian-Arab terrorist attacks or 28.7 percent injured between one and fifty persons, and that result falls between the 31.6 percent rate for Turkish terrorism and the 24.3 percent rate for Egyptian terrorism.

The levels of injury rates for Egyptian terrorism are noticeably less than their Algerian counterpart rates. Only about half of all Algerian terrorist assaults at 50.8 percent were injury-free and 44.1 percent of Algerian terrorist assaults, as compared to the rate for Egyptian terrorist assaults of 24.3 percent, injured between one and fifty persons. As for other comparisons, it is found that Algerian terrorism has four outlier cases of terrorist assaults with injuries to over one hundred persons while Egyptian terrorism has none (see figure 4.6).

Turning to levels of property damage that stem from Egyptian terrorist assaults, the findings are illustrative of the idea that terrorism relies more on psychological import than the effects of physical damage. The findings reveal that almost three-quarters of all Egyptian terrorist assaults, at 74.1 percent or 103 out of 139 events, resulted in no property damage. There are 32 out of 139 Egyptian terrorist events or 23.0 percent that caused "slight" levels of property damage, while only one out of 139 terrorist events, that makes up .7 percent of the total, caused "moderate" damage. There are 3 recorded cases of Egyptian terrorism during this period, or 2.2 percent, that caused "high" levels of property damage, while none caused any "severe" damage (See figure 4.7).

Overall, the percentage of Algerian terrorist assaults that did not cause property damage, at 58.8 percent, is lower than the rate for Egypt, while rates for terrorist assaults that caused "slight" amounts of property damage are comparable. The real difference between Egyptian terrorism and Algerian terrorism with respect to property damage rates is seen moving into the realm of higher intensity terrorist assaults. For example, terrorist assaults in the Algerian case that caused "moderate" rates of property damage account for 7.3 percent, or 22 out of 301 events, as compared to a rate of .7 percent or one out of 139 events, for Egyptian terrorist assaults.

Some 6.6 percent of Algerian terrorist assaults caused "high" rates of property damage, a figure three times greater than the 2.2 percent or 3 out of 139 Egyptian terrorist assaults that caused "high" levels of property damage. With respect to "severe" property damage, it is found that 1.0 percent of all Algerian terrorist attacks caused "severe" property damage, while there are no chronicled cases of Egyptian terrorist assaults that caused "severe" property

Frequencies

Statistics

Property Damage

N	Valid	139
	Missing	3

Property Damage

		Frequency	Percent	Valid percent	Cumulative percent
Valid	None	103	72.5	74.1	74.1
	Slight	32	22.5	23.0	97.1
	Moderate	1	.7	.7	97.8
	High	3	2.1	2.2	100.0
	Total	139	97.9	100.0	
Missing	system	3	2.1		
Total		142	100.0		

Property Damage

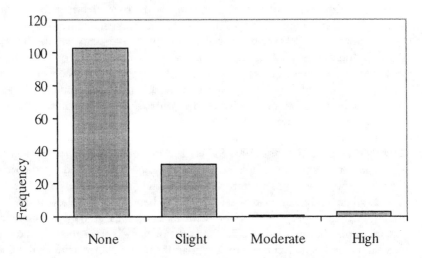

Figure 4.7: Levels of Property Damage Caused by Egyptian Terrorist Attacks, 1994-1999

damage. Those findings about levels of property damage are largely consistent with the foregoing comparisons about death and injury rates for Egyptian and Algerian terrorist assaults.

With respect to target preference, one notable finding is that perpetrators of Egyptian terrorist assaults between 1994 and 1999 seem to favor government targets nearly as much as civilian targets. The findings reveal that a full 45.0 percent of Egyptian terrorist assaults or 63 out of 140 events were aimed at government targets, while 55.0 percent or 77 out of 140 acts involved civilian targets. Those results are somewhat surprising since it appears more common to find patterns with a sharper preference for civilian targets. For example, a full 84.2 percent of Algerian terrorist assaults were aimed at civilian targets while only 10.6 percent of Algerian terrorist assaults were directed against government targets. Likewise, 77.7 percent of Israeli-Palestinian Arab terrorist assaults were directed at civilian targets, as compared with a rate of 66.1 percent in the case of Turkish terrorism. It is found there are no Egyptian terrorist assaults chronicled that involved "multiple type targets" or infrastructure targets for the five-year time period under consideration (see figure 4.8).

The analysis of the general contours of Egyptian terrorism is illustrative of some trends in terrorist assault behavior commonplace to note in the literature and, at the same time, serves to showcase patterns of Egyptian terrorism that differ with respect to patterns found in other systems of Middle East terrorism. First, as before, it is observed that Egyptian terrorism ebbs and flows in a cyclical fashion, much like the findings about Algerian terrorism and terrorism in many other geographical sites. The findings also reveal a scarcity of Egyptian terrorism events in 1998 and especially in 1999. While many interpretations of those findings are available, and a definitive explanation is beyond the scope of this study, one interpretation consistent with those findings concerns a truce called by certain imprisoned leaders of al-Jama'a al-Islamiya and other reports of a possible "deal" struck between the Mubarak government and some but certainly not all Islamic revivalists.[172]

In addition to the cyclical nature of Egyptian terrorism, another similarity to Algerian terrorism for 1994-99 is that the only chronicled incidents of Egyptian terrorism found involve terrorist assaults committed by theocentric terrorist groups, anonymous terrorist groups, and "lone operatives" or declared lone assailants. By contrast, what stands out here in stark relief to the set of findings about Algerian terrorism, with its enormous amount of anonymous terrorism that comprises some 76.6 percent of the Algerian total, is the higher percentage and actual number of Egyptian theocentric terrorist assaults that in fact exceed the percentage of anonymous Egyptian terrorist assaults by 17.6 percent.

It is observed that Egyptian terrorist assaults are largely confined to the home country, more so than in the case of Algerian terrorism, although there have been terrorist assaults in other locales such as Western Europe and the

Frequencies

Statistics

Type of Target

N	Valid	140
	Missing	2

Type of Target

		Frequency	Percent	Valid percent	Cumulative percent
Valid	Government	63	44.4	45.0	45.0
	Civilian	77	54.2	55.0	100.0
	Total	140	98.6	100.0	
Missing	system	2	1.4		
Total		142	100.0		

Type of Target

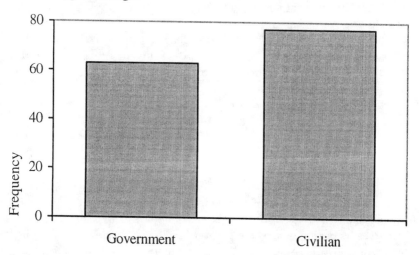

Figure 4.8: Relative Frequency of Egyptian Terrorism Target-Types, 1994-1999

United States.[173] The data show that 6 out of 142 events or 4.2 percent happened in Western Europe, 10 out of 142 events or 7.0 percent took place in the United States, 5 out of 142 events or 3.5 percent happened in other Middle Eastern states, while 9 out of 142 acts or 6.3 percent happened at "other" geographical sites that include Croatia, Ethiopia, and Pakistan. In the case of the United States, I found that terrorist assaults unrelated to the imprisonment of Shaykh Umar Abdul Rahman were nil.

In comparison to corresponding rates of death found for Turkish terrorism, Egyptian rates are roughly comparable. Conversely, the percentage rate of Israeli-Palestinian Arab terrorist assaults that killed between one and fifty persons is less than one-half the Egyptian rate. With respect to the 24.3 percent rate of Egyptian terrorist assaults that wounded between one and fifty persons, that finding for Egyptian terrorism fall between the 31.6 percent rate for Turkish terrorism and the 28.7 percent rate for Israeli-Palestinian-Arab terrorism. It is probably no exaggeration to say those percentage rates for Egyptian terrorism are noticeably less than comparable rates for Algerian terrorism, even though in the broader sense, levels of physical devastation from terrorism remain relatively low as compared to other forms of political conflict.[174]

What is unexpected in the case of Egyptian terrorism is the relative parity observed in terms of percentage rates for terrorist assaults against government targets and civilian targets. A full 45.0 percent or 63 out of 140 acts were directed at government targets, while 55.0 percent or 77 out of 140 incidents were aimed at civilian targets. Still, the generally recognizable preference for civilian targets, albeit less so in this case study on Egyptian terrorism, is consistent with the works of other terrorism specialists and my own work.[175]

Variable Analysis

Political Ideology and Target Type

Like the observations about Algerian terrorism that are presented in chapter 3, it is found in the case of the Egyptian terrorism that theocentric terrorist groups, anonymous terrorist groups and lone assailants, and declared "lone operatives" operate during the 1994 through 1999 period. With only one identifiable terrorist group-type that is operative, this set of findings does not have an enormous capacity to contribute to empirical description and qualitative discussion about the theory on "structuralist" and "nonstructuralist" Middle East terrorist group-types that drives this work.

As in the case of Algerian terrorism, data limitations about terrorist act attributes like group name, group size, and group age serve as a source of weakness for the amalgamated data. For example, in the case of anonymous

Algerian terrorist assaults, when bivariate analysis is performed, the likely combination of too many terrorist group-types placed into that one category contributes to a blurring of distinctions, thereby in effect helping to contribute to cross category variance. It is conceivable but, in my judgment, unlikely there is no relationship between the political ideology of Islamic revivalist terrorist groups without charismatic leaders, and the target chosen by terrorist group chieftains. The following hypothesis captures the idea that meaningful variation exists between the rate of civilian target terrorist assaults carried out by anonymous terrorist groups and "lone operatives" and the rate of civilian target assaults carried out by Egyptian theocentric terrorist groups:

Hypothesis One: Unclaimed Egyptian terrorist assaults will involve civilian targets more frequently than Egyptian theocentric terrorist assaults.

The bivariate analysis reveals that a statistically significant association exists between the variable "target" and the explanatory variable "political ideology," that in this case captures the Islamic revivalism of theocentric groups (see table 4.1). A Pearson Chi Square statistic of 6.434 and a "p-value" of .011, at one degree of freedom (1 d.f.), and a Yates Continuity Correction measure of association for a 2x2 cross-tabulation table of 5.558 with a "p-value" of .018 at one degree of freedom (1 d.f.) makes it possible to reject the null hypothesis of no relationship between the variables "target" and "political ideology" at the .05 level of confidence.[176] In other words, if repeated samplings were performed, the probability of this distribution of "political ideology" and "target" appearing by chance, namely without a statistically significant association between the variables is, using the Pearson Chi Square and "p-value" diagnostics, about one hundredth of one percent (.011). In terms of the strength of the relationship, a Cramer's V value of .221 with a significance score of .011 and a "Phi" value of .221 with a significance score of .011 indicate a slight relationship between the variables. A Goodman and Kruskal *tau* measure of .049 with a significance score of .012 when type of target is the dependent variable also indicates a weak relationship between the variables.

The data distribution reveals that 45.1 percent or 23 out of 51 of unclaimed Egyptian terrorist assaults involved civilian targets while 54.9 percent or 28 out of 51 unclaimed Egyptian terrorist assaults were directed against government targets. In terms of a breakdown of target type for theocentric terrorist assaults, it is observed that a full 67.5 percent or 52 out of 77 incidents were aimed at civilian targets while about only one-third at 32.5 percent or 25 out of 77 terrorist assaults were carried out against government targets. In the case of "lone assailant" terrorist assaults, it is found that there is an even split of 50.0 percent with 2 out of 4 terrorist assaults directed at civilian targets and 2 out of 4 terrorist assaults directed at government targets. For uncompleted terrorist assaults, all 8 thwarted terrorist attacks or a full 100.0 percent were aimed at

Table 4.1: Relative Frequency of Egyptian Terrorist Targets by Group-Type, 1994-1999   (summary statistics)

Crosstabs

Case Processing Summary

	Cases					
	Valid		Missing		Total	
	N	Percent	N	Percent	N	Percent
Type of target * category of group	132	93.0%	10	7.0%	142	100.0%

Type of Target * Category of Group Cross-Tabulation

Type of target		Category of group		Total
		Unclaimed acts	Theo-centric	
Government	Count	30	25	55
	% within type of target	54.5%	45.5%	100.0%
	% within category of group	54.5%	32.5%	41.7%
	% of total	22.7%	18.9%	41.7%
Civilian	Count	25	52	77
	% within type of target	32.5%	67.5%	100.0%
	% within category of group	45.5%	67.5%	58.3%
	% of total	18.9%	39.4%	58.3%
Total	Count	55	77	132
	% within type of target	41.7%	58.3%	100.0%
	% within category of group	100.0%	100.0%	100.0%
	% of total	41.7%	58.3%	100.0%

Chi Square Tests

	Value	df	Asymp. sig. (2-sided)	Exact sig. (2-sided)	Exact sig. (1-sided)
Pearson Chi Square	6.434[b]	1	.011		
Continuity Correction[a]	5.558	1	.018		
Likelihood Ratio	6.443	1	.011		
Fisher's Exact Test				.013	.009
Linear-by-Linear Association	6.385	1	.012		
N of valid cases	132				

a. Computed only for a 2x2 table.
b. 0 cells (0%) have expected count less than 5. The minimum expected count is 22.92.

government targets. Plainly, those test results make it necessary to reject the validity of Hypothesis One. As previously mentioned, there are no Egyptian terrorist assaults chronicled for the 1994 through 1999 time period that have "multiple-type targets" or infrastructure as targets (see table 4.2).

A comparison of Egyptian anonymous and theocentric assaults with Algerian anonymous and theocentric assaults is illustrative of the difference in burden that civilian targets bear in those two systems of Middle East terrorism. Egyptian terrorism carried out by anonymous perpetrators involve civilian targets 45.1 percent of the time or in 23 out of 51 acts, nearly half the percentage of the 87.7 percent or 228 out of 260 anonymous Algerian terrorist assaults directed at civilian targets. Conversely, the percentage rate of unclaimed Egyptian

Table 4.1 - *continued*

Directional Measures

			Value	Asymp. std. error[a]	Approx. T[b]	Approx. sig.
Nominal by nominal	Lambda	Symmetric	.091	.115	.769	.442
		Type of target dependent	.091	.129	.675	.499
		Category of group dependent	.091	.129	.675	.499
	Goodman and Kruskal tau	Type of target dependent	.049	.038		.012[c]
		Category of group dependent	.049	.038		.012[c]

a. Not assuming the null hypothesis.
b. Using the asymptotic standard error assuming the null hypothesis.
c. Based on chi square approximation

Symmetric Measures

		Value	Approx. sig.
Nominal by nominal	Phi	.221	.011
	Cramer's V	.221	.011
N of valid cases		132	

a. Not assuming the null hypothesis.
b. Using the asymptotic standard error assuming the null hypothesis.

Table 4.2: Relative Frequency of Egyptian Terrorist Targets by Group-Type, 1994-1999

Case Processing Summary

	Cases					
	Valid		Missing		Total	
	N	Percent	*N*	Percent	*N*	Percent
Category of group * type of target	140	98.6%	2	1.4%	142	100.0%

Category of Group * Type of Target Cross-Tabulation

Category of group		Type of target		Total
		Government	Civilian	
Uncompleted acts	Count	8		8
	% within category of group	100.0%		100.0%
	% within type of target	12.7%		5.7%
	% of total	5.7%		5.7%
Unclaimed acts	Count	28	23	51
	% within category of group	54.9%	45.1%	100.0%
	% within type of target	44.4%	29.9%	36.4%
	% of total	20.0%	16.4%	36.4%
Theocentric	Count	25	52	77
	% within category of group	32.5%	67.5%	100.0%
	% within type of target	39.7%	67.5%	55.0%
	% of total	17.9%	37.1%	55.0%
Lone assailant	Count	2	2	4
	% within category of group	50.0%	50.0%	100.0%
	% within type of target	3.2%	2.6%	2.9%
	% of total	1.4%	1.4%	2.9%
Total	Count	63	77	140
	% within category of group	45.0%	55.0%	100.0%
	% within type of target	100.0%	100.0%	100.0%
	% of total	45.0%	55.0%	100.0%

terrorist assaults against government targets at 54.9 percent or 28 out of 51 events is much higher than the 8.4 percent rate or 22 out of 260 acts of unclaimed Algerian terrorist assaults against government targets (see tables 4.2 and 3.2, and figure 3.8).

With respect to Egyptian theocentric groups, there is a marked preference for civilian targets at 67.5 percent as compared with a 32.5 percent rate for government targets that comprises a more than 2:1 ratio in favor of civilian targets. By contrast, in the case of Algerian terrorism, theocentric terrorist assaults are directed against civilian targets 73.3 percent of the time and against government targets 17.3 percent of the time. That preference for civilian targets by Algerian theocentric groups comprises a little more than a 4:1 ratio in favor of civilian targets.

In comparison, in the case of Turkish theocentric terrorist group attacks, the rate of civilian target terrorist assaults is much higher at 84.6 percent with theocentric attacks against government targets at only 15.4 percent. For Turkish theocentric terrorist groups, those findings represent a ratio of over 5:1 in favor of civilian targets. In the case of Israeli-Palestinian-Arab terrorism the 84.7 percent rate of civilian target attack for theocentric groups is virtually the same as the Turkish terrorism rate at 84.6 percent with Israeli-Palestinian Arab theocentric government attacks at 11.6 percent. By the same token, the civilian target rate for Egyptian theocentric terrorist assaults is still less than the civilian target rate for Algerian, Turkish, and Israeli-Palestinian-Arab theocentric terrorist groups.

Foreign Nationality and Target Type

It is commonplace to note that terrorist assaults by Islamic revivalist terrorist groups in upper Egypt regions of the country like El-Minya, Assyut, Sohag, Quana, and Luxor devote special focus to foreign nationals to showcase and undercut the roles those foreign nationals play in strengthening the Egyptian economy by means of tourism.[177] It follows that one facet of Egyptian terrorism that needs investigation is to determine the degree that foreign nationals are targeted within the context of "discriminate" Egyptian terrorist assaults. The following theoretical proposition captures that foregoing notion:

Hypothesis Two: In the case of "discriminate" terrorist assaults, Egyptian terrorist assaults will have a greater percentage of civilian targets that involve foreign nationals than Egyptian nationals.

The bivariate analysis of "victim nationality" and "target type" distinguishes among categories of "discriminate," "indiscriminate," and "uncertain" types of terrorist assaults, thereby in effect making it possible to produce a set of cross-tabulation table "partials" each with its own set of summary statistics. When data produced by that bivariate analysis for "discriminate" terrorist assaults are analyzed, the summary statistics inform us that a statistically significant association exists between terrorist assault victim "nationality" and "target-type" in the case of "discriminate" terrorist assaults.

For that bivariate analysis "partials" table, a Pearson Chi Square statistic of 21.886 with a "p-value" of less than .001 at one degree of freedom (1 d.f.) and a Yates Continuity Correction measure of association for that 2x2 "partials" table of 20.049 with a "p-value" of less than .001 at one degree of freedom (1 d.f.) makes it possible to reject the null hypothesis of no relationship between the variables at the .05 level of confidence (see table 4.3). In terms of the strength of the relationship, a Cramer's V value of .463 with a significance score of less than .001, and a "Phi" of -.463 with a significance score of less than .001, suggests a moderate relationship between the variables. Moreover, the non-Chi Square based Proportional Reduction in Error (PRE) measure of association "Lambda," with type of target as the dependent variable is found to be .429 with a significance score of .005, and that suggests a moderate type of relationship between the variables "target" and "nationality of victim."

The data distribution reveals that among Egyptian terrorist assaults that are "discriminate" in nature, a full 64.2 percent or 34 out of 53 terrorist assaults against civilian targets are directed at foreign nationals, while 35.8 percent or 19 out of 53 civilian target terrorist assaults were directed against Egyptian

Table 4.3: Relative Frequency of Egyptian Terrorism Target-Types by Victim Nationality – "Partials" ("discriminate"; "indiscriminate"; "uncertain" terrorist assaults)

Case Processing Summary

	Cases					
	Valid		Missing		Total	
	N	Percent	N	Percent	N	Percent
Type of target * nationality of victim * victimization	104	73.2%	38	26.8%	142	100.0%

Table 4.3 - *continued*

Type of Target * Nationality of Victim
* Victimization Cross-Tabulation

Victimization	Type of target		Nationality of victim - Foreign national	Nationality of victim - National	Total
Discrim-inate	Government	Count	9	40	49
		% within type of target	18.4%	81.6%	100.0%
		% within nationality of victim	20.9%	67.8%	48.0%
		% of total	8.8%	39.2%	48.0%
	Civilian	Count	34	19	53
		% within type of target	64.2%	35.8%	100.0%
		% within nationality of victim	79.1%	32.2%	52.0%
		% of total	33.3%	18.6%	52.0%
	Total	Count	43	59	102
		% within type of target	42.2%	57.8%	100.0%
		% within nationality of victim	100.0%	100.0%	100.0%
		% of total	42.2%	57.8%	100.0%
Indiscrim-inate	Government	Count	1		1
		% within type of target	100.0%		100.0%
		% within nationality of victim	100.0%		100.0%
		% of total	100.0%		100.0%
	Total	Count	1		1
		% within type of target	100.0%		100.0%
		% within nationality of victim	100.0%		100.0%
		% of total	100.0%		100.0%
Uncertain	Civilian	Count		1	1
		% within type of target		100.0%	100.0%
		% within nationality of victim		100.0%	100.0%
		% of total		100.0%	100.0%
	Total	Count		1	1
		% within type of target		100.0%	100.0%
		% within nationality of victim		100.0%	100.0%
		% of total		100.0%	100.0%

Table 4.3 - *continued*

Chi Square Tests

Victimization		Value	df	Asymp. sig. (2-sided)	Exact sig. (2-sided)	Exact sig. (1-sided)
Discriminate	Pearson Chi Square	21.886[b]	1	.000		
	Continuity Correction[a]	20.049	1	.000		
	Likelihood Ratio	22.974	1	.000		
	Fisher's Exact Test				.000	.000
	Linear-by-Linear Association	21.672	1	.000		
	N of valid cases	102				
Indiscriminate	Pearson Chi Square	.[c]				
	N of valid cases	1				
Uncertain	Pearson Chi Square	.[c]				
	N of valid cases	1				

a. Computed only for a 2x2 table
b. 0 cells (0%) have expected count less than 5. The minimum expected count is 20.66.
c. No statistics are computed because type of target and nationality of victim are constants.

Directional Measures

Victimization				Value	Asymp. std. error[a]
Discriminate	Nominal by nominal	Lambda	Symmetric	.391	.113
			Type of target dependent	.429	.118
			Nationality of victim dependent	.349	.137
		Goodman and Kruskal tau	Type of target dependent	.215	.079
			Nationality of victim dependent	.215	.080
Indiscriminate	Nominal by nominal	Lambda	Symmetric	.[d]	
Uncertain	Nominal by nominal	Lambda	Symmetric	.[d]	

Table 4.3 - *continued*

Directional Measures

Victimization				Approx. T^b	Approx. sig.
Discriminate	Nominal by nominal	Lambda	Symmetric	3.072	.002
			Type of target dependent	2.840	.005
			Nationality of victim dependent	2.105	.035
		Goodman and Kruskal tau	Type of target dependent		$.000^c$
			Nationality of victim dependent		$.000^c$
Indiscriminate	Nominal by nominal	Lambda	Symmetric		
Uncertain	Nominal by nominal	Lambda	Symmetric		

a. Not assuming the null hypothesis.
b. Using the asymptotic standard error assuming the null hypothesis.
c. Based on chi square approximation
d. No statistics are computed because type of target and nationality of victim are constants.

Symmetric Measures

Victimization			Value	Approx. sig.
Discriminate	Nominal by nominal	Phi	-.463	.000
		Cramer's V	.463	.000
	N of valid cases		102	
Indiscriminate	Nominal by nominal	Phi	$.^c$	
	N of valid cases		1	
Uncertain	Nominal by nominal	Phi	$.^c$	
	N of valid cases		1	

a. Not assuming the null hypothesis.
b. Using the asymptotic standard error assuming the null hypothesis.
c. No statistics are computed because type of target and nationality of victim are constants.

nationals. In turn, when "discriminate" Egyptian terrorist assaults were carried out against government targets, a full 81.6 percent or 40 out of 49 acts were directed against Egyptian "national" targets as compared to only 18.4 percent or 9 out of 49 acts against "foreign national" government targets. It would seem that in the case of Egyptian terrorist assaults directed against civilian targets, terrorist planners place a special focus against foreign nationals. Plainly, with foreign nationals involved in 64.2 percent or 34 out of 53 "discriminate" civilian target terrorist assaults, it is now permissible to accept the validity of Hypothesis Two (see table 4.4).

Seen from the vantage of articulated Egyptian Islamic revivalist themes, the finding that 81.6 percent of government targets are Egyptian "national" targets is not an unexpected finding precisely because of the reason that almost singular attention is devoted to President Mubarak and his regime as the primary target in that conflict. In terms of nationality patterns for Egyptian civilian targets, the generally recognizable direction in favor of foreign nationals was not unexpected but the percentage degree that civilian foreign nationals were targeted was indeed unexpected. What seems significant here and makes those findings especially intriguing is that the percentage rate of civilian targets that are foreign nationals for Egyptian terrorism, at 64.2 percent or 34 out of 53 events, exceeds the rate for Algerian terrorism that was found to be 20.8 percent or 30 out of 144 acts, by a margin of three to one. That gap in percentage rates is quite a glaring finding since one aspect of Algerian terrorist assaults against foreigners reportedly revolves around the central idea of hampering foreign investment in that country to undercut the economic stability of Algeria and, by extrapolation, to promote political instability and social unrest under the watch of the Algerian regime.[178]

Terrorist Group Age, Terrorist Group Size, and Target Selection

The purpose of this section is to explore the underlying theme that within the context of Egyptian terrorism, there are meaningful relationships between the variables terrorist "group age" and "target," and terrorist "group size" and "target." As previously mentioned in chapter 2, several terrorist specialists have described and discussed the relationship between the dependent variable "target" and the causal variables terrorist "group age" and terrorist "group size."[179] The following hypothesis captures the notion that a positive relationship exists between "target" and terrorist "group age":

Hypothesis Three: Older Egyptian terrorist groups will have a higher percentage of civilian target attacks than younger Egyptian terrorist groups.

Table 4.4: Relative Frequency of Egyptian Terrorism Target-Type by Terrorist Group Age, 1994-1999 (summary statistics)

Case Processing Summary

	Cases					
	Valid		Missing		Total	
	N	Percent	N	Percent	N	Percent
Age of group * type of target	70	49.3%	72	50.7%	142	100.0%

Age of Group * Type of Target Cross-Tabulation

			Type of target		Total
			Government	Civilian	
Age of group	1 thru 3 years	Count	8	2	10
		% within age of group	80.0%	20.0%	100.0%
		% within type of target	36.4%	4.2%	14.3%
		% of Total	11.4%	2.9%	14.3%
	16 thru 20 years	Count	14	46	60
		% within age of group	23.3%	76.7%	100.0%
		% within type of target	63.6%	95.8%	85.7%
		% of Total	20.0%	65.7%	85.7%
Total		Count	22	48	70
		% within age of group	31.4%	68.6%	100.0%
		% within type of target	100.0%	100.0%	100.0%
		% of Total	31.4%	68.6%	100.0%

Chi Square Tests

	Value	df	Asymp. sig. (2-sided)	Exact sig. (2-sided)	Exact sig. (1-sided)
Pearson Chi Square	12.771[b]	1	.000		
Continuity Correction[a]	10.277	1	.001		
Likelihood Ratio	11.947	1	.001		
Fisher's Exact Test				.001	.001
Linear-by-Linear Association	12.589	1	.000		
N of valid cases	70				

a. Computed only for a 2x2 table
c. 1 cells (25.0%) have expected count less than 5. The minimum expected count is 3.14.

The cross-tabulation table analysis indicates that a statistically significant association exists between the variable terrorist "group age" and "target." The bivariate analysis generates a Pearson Chi Square statistic of 12.771 with a "p-value" of less than .001 at one degree of freedom (1 d.f.). In addition, a Yates Continuity Correction value of 10.277 with a "p-value" of .001 at one degree of freedom (1 d.f.) is produced. Accordingly, it is possible to reject the null hypothesis of no relation between the variables terrorist "group age" and "target" at the .05 level of confidence (see table 4.4).

Put in other words, the Pearson Chi Square statistic and "p-value" suggest

Table 4.4 - *continued*

Directional Measures

			Value	Asymp. std. error[a]	Aprox. T[b]	Approx. sig.
Nominal by nominal	Lambda	Symmetric	.188	.079	1.948	.051
		Type of target dependent	.273	.123	1.948	.051
		Age of group dependent	.000	.000	[c]	[c]
	Goodman and Kruskal tau	Type of target dependent	.182	.091		.000[d]
		Age of group dependent	.182	.098		.000[d]

a. Not assuming the null hypothesis.
b. Using the asymptotic standard error assuming the null hypothesis.
c. Cannot be computed because the asymptotic standard error equals zero.
d. Based on chi square approximation.

Symmetric Measures

		Value	Approx. sig.
Nominal by nominal	Phi	.427	.000
	Cramer's V	.427	.000
N of valid cases		70	

a. Not assuming the null hypothesis.
b. Using the asymptotic standard error assuming the null hypothesis.

that if the null hypothesis of no relationship is not rejected there is a 95 percent chance that it would be incorrect, thereby in effect constituting a "Type II" or "Beta" error. It should be noted that 25.0 percent of the total number of cells, or one cell, has an expected value of less than five but those findings, in my judgment, need to be reported or it is very likely that a "Type II" or "Beta" error will be made in terms of failing to reject the null hypothesis of no relation between the variables when the null hypothesis ought to be rejected.[180] In terms of the strength of that relationship, a Cramer's V score of .427 with a significance score of less than .001 and a "Phi" statistic of .427 with a significance score of less than .001 suggests a moderate relationship between the variables. Alternatively, a Goodman and Kruskal *tau* value of .182 with a significance score of less than .001 suggests a weak relationship between the variables under consideration.

In terms of the data distribution, fledgling terrorist groups of between one and three years old carried out 80.0 percent or 8 out of 10 terrorist assaults against government targets, while 20.0 percent or 2 out of 10 events were aimed at civilian targets (see table 4.5). Terrorist groups of between ten and fifteen years old have only 1 chronicled terrorist assault and that 1 act involved a government target that makes up a mere 1.4 percent of the total. Terrorist groups between sixteen and twenty years old also have a more uneven distribution with respect to terrorist targets with 14 out of 60 acts or 23.3 percent directed at government targets, and a full 76.7 percent or 46 out of 60 acts aimed at civilian targets.

To be sure, as terrorist groups mature, the rate of terrorist assaults against government targets declines and the rate of civilian target terrorist assaults grows apace. In fact, that 4:1 ratio in favor of government targets among "young" terrorist groups that are one through five years old is almost a mirror image with respect to civilian target type and percentage difference between target types for "older" terrorist groups of between sixteen and twenty years old. It is observed that "older" terrorist groups attack civilian targets 76.7 percent of the time, while terrorist assaults against government targets happen only 23.3 percent of the time. That ratio favors civilian targets by about a 3.3:1 ratio. (see table 4.5). As previously mentioned, there are no Egyptian terrorist assaults chronicled that involve infrastructure or any "multiple-type" targets for the 1994-99 period. Seen from a different angle, the results reveal that the largest portion of Egyptian terrorism, at 82.2 percent or 60 out of 73 acts, were committed by older terrorist groups between sixteen and twenty years old. In turn, terrorist assaults committed by "young" terrorist groups between one and three years old comprise the second highest percentage at 13.7 percent or 10 out of 73 acts, while "old" terrorist groups that are between twenty-one and twenty-five years old carried out only 2.7 percent or 2 out of 73 acts.

It is entirely possible, nay probable, that this analysis about the relationship between terrorist "group age" and "target" has not captured all the causal

Table 4.5: Relative Frequency of Egyptian Terrorism Target-Type by Terrorist Group Age, 1994-1999

Case Processing Summary

	Cases					
	Valid		Missing		Total	
	N	Percent	*N*	Percent	*N*	Percent
Age of group * type of target	73	51.4%	69	48.6%	142	100.0%

Age of Group * Type of Target Cross-Tabulation

			Type of target		Total
			Government	Civilian	
Age of group	1 thru 3 years	Count	8	2	10
		% within age of group	80.0%	20.0%	100.0%
		% within type of target	34.8%	4.0%	13.7%
		% of total	11.0%	2.7%	13.7%
	10 thru 15 years	Count	1		1
		% within age of group	100.0%		100.0%
		% within type of target	4.3%		1.4%
		% of total	1.4%		1.4%
	16 thru 20 years	Count	14	46	60
		% within age of group	23.3%	76.7%	100.0%
		% within type of target	60.9%	92.0%	82.2%
		% of total	19.2%	63.0%	82.2%
	21 thru 25 years	Count		2	2
		% within age of group		100.0%	100.0%
		% within type of target		4.0%	2.7%
		% of total		2.7%	2.7%
Total		Count	23	50	73
		% within age of group	31.5%	68.5%	100.0%
		% within type of target	100.0%	100.0%	100.0%
		% of total	31.5%	68.5%	100.0%

factors at work that might compel terrorist groups increasingly to focus sharper attention on civilian target terrorist assaults. To be sure, other variables might include the degree of monetary support, or nation-state backing as measured in monetary or arms transfers to terrorist organizations.[181] Another idea consistent with those data revolves around the central notion, put forward in my prior work, that as terrorist chieftains become more seasoned with experience and the passage of time, there is a generally recognizable trend in favor of civilian targets precisely because of the abject fear that terrorist assaults elicit from civilians. That profound and lasting fear is perhaps more intense among civilians than government personnel or military forces and, equally important, is able to provide political pressure against the ruling elite in effective and sustained ways that is necessary to make structural political change. It follows that, with the passage of time, terrorist group chieftains may have an epiphany of sorts, understanding in more profound and lasting ways the utility of terrorist assaults against civilian targets.[182]

In the case of bivariate testing to determine whether or not an association between terrorist "group size" and "target" exists, the results are found to be not significant and suggest that no statistically significant association exists between those two variables. Taken together, those results about terrorist "group size" and "target" that are found to be not significant, and the findings about a statistically significant association between the variables terrorist "group age" and "target" suggest the results of the bivariate testing for terrorist "group size" and "target" presuppose and derive from a condition of not having more available and complete data about Egyptian terrorism, and, in the narrower sense, the size of Egyptian terrorist groups that target civilian, government, and other types of targets.[183]

Conclusions

General Patterns of Behavior

A breakdown of the data by relative frequencies of Egyptian terrorist assaults provides a picture of the general shape of Egyptian terrorism. When the data on Egyptian terrorist assaults are clustered according to year of event, it is found that Egyptian terrorism, like Algerian terrorism, is characterized by cycles of activity replete with peaks and troughs. With respect to the types of terrorist groups that are active between 1994 and 1999, the data suggest that Egyptian terrorism is conducted by theocentric groups or Islamic revivalist terrorist groups without charismatic leaders, anonymous terrorist groups and "lone operatives," and declared "lone assailants."

One standout finding that differs from the Algerian case is the much larger proportion of Egyptian terrorist assaults linked to theocentric groups that have waged protracted warfare against what theocentric terrorist leaders consider is the "pharaoh-like" regime of President Mohammed Hosni Mubarak.[184] To be sure, theocentric terrorist assaults over the Egyptian political landscape comprise a much larger proportion of the total amount than do unclaimed terrorist assaults.

In a broader sense, analysis of relative frequency by target type reveals that Egyptian terrorist assaults involve civilian targets only 10 percent more than terrorist assaults that strike at government targets (see figure 4.8). That finding is in glaring contrast to the same analysis done for Algerian terrorist assaults that reveals a preference for civilian targets by what amounts to about an 8:1 ratio (see figure 3.8). Those findings, with respect to Egypt, are consistent with perhaps the single most dominant theme prevalent among terrorist groups that perpetrate Egyptian terrorist assaults, namely, that war is waged primarily against the regime of President Mubarak as well as against the underlying interests of the West in general and the United States and Israel in particular. In terms of other types of terrorist assault targets, I found there are no chronicled Egyptian terrorist assaults against infrastructure or "multiple-type" targets for the 1994-99 period.

With respect to geographical site, over three-quarters of the total amount of Egyptian terrorism that happened between 1994 and 1999 took place in Egypt. The United States is the venue with the second highest rate of Egyptian terrorism between 1994 and 1999 at 7.0 percent. Those terrorist assaults are comprised of a spate of letter bombs terrorist assaults against the offices of the Saudi Arabian newspaper *Al-Hayat* and the U.S. federal penitentiary in Leavenworth, Kansas, all with a set of interconnections to the incarceration of Shaykh Umar Abdul Rahman of the Jama'at al-Jihad for his role in the World Trade Center bombing in 1993.

In turn, geographical sites that fall under the category "other" like Pakistan and Croatia have, at 6.3 percent, the third highest amount, while Western Europe, with 4.2 percent, is the venue with the fourth largest amount of Egyptian terrorism. At the other extreme, "other Middle East states" was the aggregate venue with the least amount of Egyptian terrorism. That 4.2 percent finding for Western Europe is less than the 5.5 percent of Algerian terrorist assaults that happened in Western Europe, which is comprised in large part by Algerian terrorist assaults that took place in France.[185] Unequivocally, Egyptian terrorist assaults remain confined largely to Egypt, but there is much more focus against geographical sites outside of the country with a total of 21.0 percent that occurred outside Egypt as compared to 8.1 percent of Algerian terrorist assaults that happened outside Algeria.

In terms of terrorist assault "attributes" such as number of dead and injured that result from terrorist assaults, analysis of relative frequencies provides a way to compare and contrast levels of deaths and injury in Egyptian terrorist assaults with levels of death and injury in Algerian terrorist assaults. With respect to deaths, it is observed that a full 63.7 percent of Egyptian terrorist assaults are death-free events while a little more than one-third (36.3 percent) result in the deaths of between one and fifty persons. Those findings reveal levels of death and injury for Egyptian terrorism that are less than corresponding rates for Algerian terrorist assaults. In the case of Algerian terrorism, only 21.0 percent of Algerian terrorist assaults were death-free events and a full three-quarters of all Algerian terrorist assaults (75.4 percent) killed between one and fifty persons.

It is found that similar differences are observable with respect to injury rates when Egyptian and Algerian terrorism are compared. In the case of Egyptian terrorism, three-quarters of all events are injury-free, while 24.3 percent injured between one and fifty persons. In contrast, only half of Algerian terrorist assaults (50.8 percent) are found to be injury-free events as compared to a full 44.1 percent, nearly twice the Egyptian rate, that injured between one and fifty persons (see table 3.6). However, in the case of property damage, the findings for Egyptian and Algerian terrorist assaults are more comparable. For example, nearly three-quarters of Egyptian terrorist assaults (74.1 percent) resulted in no property damage, while 23.0 percent caused "slight" levels of property damage. In the Algerian case, by contrast, 58.8 percent of terrorist assaults caused no property damage, a figure somewhat comparable to the Egyptian figure of 74.1 percent, and rates of "slight" damage were virtually the same with the Egyptian rate at 23.0 percent and the Algerian rate at 26.2 percent.

In the case of Egyptian terrorism, the sample mean of 1.36 deaths (standard deviation of 3.00) and the sample mean of 2.05 injuries (standard deviation of 7.95) also highlight the underlying theme that the effectiveness of terrorism revolves around its enormous capacity to generate and sustain abject fear rather than severe physical devastation.[186] Notwithstanding that, a comparison to corresponding statistics for Algerian terrorism reveals the mean number of deaths for Algerian terrorism is a little more than *seven and a half* times greater than for Egyptian terrorism. In a similar vein, the mean number of injuries for Algerian terrorism assaults is a little more than *five* times as high as the mean number of injuries for Egyptian terrorist assaults. Clearly those measures reveal a large degree of variation with respect to devastation and risk for persons when Algerian terrorism is compared with Egyptian terrorism.

The Role of Political Ideology

Regrettably, like the analysis of Algerian terrorism that is presented in chapter 3, this analysis of Egyptian terrorism has precious little to offer for an evaluation of the underlying theory about "structuralist" and "nonstructuralist"

Middle East terrorist group-types that drives this study. That is the case precisely because of the reason that, as in the case of Algerian terrorism, only theocentric terrorist groups, anonymous terrorist groups or "lone operatives," and declared lone assailants are found to be active during the 1994 through 1999 period. Nonetheless, what is possible is to tie together findings about Egyptian terrorism and the relationship between terrorist assaults carried out by Islamic revivalist terrorist groups without charismatic leaders, anonymous terrorist groups or persons, and "declared" lone assailants. When those comparisons are made, it is possible to make a broader analysis, to distinguish terrorist assault attribute patterns for theocentric groups and other perpetrators within the Egyptian system of terrorism and within the Algerian system of terrorism and beyond, as I attempt in chapter 7.

In the case of political ideology, it is found that a statistically significant association exists between the dependent variable "target" and the causal variable "political ideology." That means that clear and meaningful patterns exist between targets that Egyptian theocentric terrorist groups choose, and the type of target that is chosen by anonymous Egyptian terrorist groups or non-group actors. The data show that in the case of Egyptian theocentric terrorist assaults, there is, at 67.5 percent or 52 out of 77 acts, a notable preference for civilian targets. In the case of Egyptian unclaimed terrorist assaults, by contrast, there is a more even distribution between civilian targets at 45.1 percent or 23 out of 51 acts and government targets at 54.9 percent or 28 out of 51 acts. Those data suggest that even though civilian targets are targets of preference for Egyptian theocentric terrorist assaults, Egyptian civilian targets are involved less frequently in Egyptian theocentric attacks than in Algerian theocentric group attacks.

Foreign Nationality and Target Type

One important set of findings concerns the relationship between "discriminate" Egyptian terrorist assaults against civilian targets and the basic composition of those Egyptian civilian targets by "nationality." The bivariate testing that generates "partials" showcase the special focus that Egyptian terrorist assaults seem to place on foreign nationals as targets. The data show that at 64.2 percent, nearly two-thirds of Egyptian terrorist assaults against civilian targets, or 34 out of 53 acts, are directed at foreign nationals, thereby in effect helping to lend support to the common wisdom that a significant aspect of the protracted conflict against the Mubarak regime revolves around the central idea of targeting foreign tourists and those others perceived to be fortifying the regime by infusions of monies. Compounding the matter even more, those findings reveal the emergent reality that at 64.2 percent, Egyptian terrorist assault preference for foreign nationals in the context of civilian target terrorist assaults exceeds the corresponding rate for Algerian terrorist assaults at 20.8 percent by a margin of three to one.

Egyptian Terrorist Assault "Attribute" Indicators

In terms of Egyptian terrorism, there is an array of attribute indicators like numbers of dead, numbers of injury, levels of property damage, and location of event designed to capture Egyptian terrorist assault "attributes" or characteristics. It is found that no statistically significant association exists between each of those terrorist assault attribute indicators and the variable "target." In addition, there is no statistically significant association found between the intervening variable "political events" and the variable "target." A one-way Analysis of Variance (ANOVA) was performed to determine whether or not there is a statistically significant difference in the mean number of deaths that result from Egyptian terrorist assaults that precede "political events" by one month. Political event categories tested include "commemoration of religious events," "minor" or internal political events, and "commemoration of landmark events." The results of that ANOVA test indicate no statistically significant difference among the three means examined for those categories of political events under consideration.[187]

Terrorist Group Age and Target Selection

Another notable set of findings suggests that a statistically significant association exists between the variable terrorist "group age" and "target." In terms of strength, that relationship is found to be a moderate to rather strong one, and suggests rather vividly that, with the passage of time, terrorist group planners increasingly favor Egyptian terrorist assaults against civilian targets. One possible interpretation of the data revolves around the central idea that terrorist chieftains, as they become more experienced, increasingly understand that abject fear produced by terrorist assaults against civilian targets may generate and sustain the type of "political pressure," as Hoffman suggests, that makes it an almost ineluctable conclusion that the ruling elite will respond to at least some aspect of the political demands and aspirations articulated.[188]

In fact, similar types of dramatic findings about the relationship between the variables terrorist "group age" and "target" are showcased in my prior work that explores Middle East terrorism between 1968 and 1993, although Middle East terrorism in those works is not broken down within the context of specific nation-states or particular systems of Middle East terrorism.[189] Finally, bivariate testing informs us there is no statistically significant association found between the variables terrorist "group-size" and "target." While it is conceivable that no relationship between those two variables exists, it seems more likely those findings presuppose and derive from data limitation such as sketchy, incomplete, or unavailable data that serves as a source of weakness.

Reflections

The protracted struggle between Islamic revivalist groups and President Mubarak's regime, that has resulted in what Nef calls "insurgent terrorism" by Islamic revivalist extremists, takes place within the context of emergency laws that were invoked by Mubarak following the assassination of President Anwar-el-Sadat by Jama'at al-Jihad activists on 6 October 1981.[190] Nonetheless, as both Esposito and Azzam and other writers tell us, the heavy-handed and shop-worn approach of harsh counterterrorism measures allows precious little in the way of meaningful political expression.[191] Equally important, those measures belie and do not address the underlying institutionalization of Islam that has happened across many sections of Egyptian society during the 1980s, thereby in effect helping to pose a set of fundamental challenges and opportunities for the Egyptian regime.[192]

Political instability and social unrest in Egypt seem to be an ineluctable outcome of that condition as it stands, and the reason for that is twofold. First, at what Nye might call the "domestic" level of analysis, the Egyptian government seems unable or unwilling to respond to political demands and aspirations that cluster around the role of a revitalized Islam in Egyptian society.[193] One predominant theme in the literature is how to help the Egyptian government introduce more flexibility into the Egyptian political system. As Baker really suggests, one way of thinking about that matter is to make certain from the start that American policy makers recognize it is consistent with their geopolitical interests to make distinctions between Islamic "centrists" or *Wasittiyyah* and Islamic revivalist extremists who carry out terrorist assaults, thereby in effect helping to provide an opportunity for U.S. government and nongovernment actors make interconnections with Islamist "centrists."[194]

For Baker, the *Wasittiyyah* of Egypt approach structural political and social change in incremental, and nonviolent ways and the author suggests that the Mubarak regime, perhaps with American leaders to spur on the process, ought to begin to make what Reiss and Roth might call meaningful "opportunity structures" for "centrist" Islamic revivalists in the political sphere, perhaps coupled with some real efforts to reduce corruption and improve economic conditions.[195] To be more specific, Baker tells us of one *Wasittiyyah* group known as the "New Islamists" that has what the author calls a rational interpretation approach to the Qu'ran and *hadiths* and who seemingly look askance at the zero-sum approach of certain other Islamic revivalist organizations active in the fray.[196] The New Islamists have been active since the 1980s in the grassroots political fray helping to ameliorate economic backwater conditions by means of social service provisions, but the burden remains heavy for that organization and its leaders under the Mubarak regime.[197]

Second, political instability and social unrest in Egypt seem to have sources and origins at what Waltz might call the "third image," and Nye might call a "systems level" of analysis.[198] In the wake of the Cold War, structural change in the international political system has happened whereby "pure bipolarity," to use Nye's phrase, has given way to a return to a new "multi-polar" condition.[199] In turn, that has amplified concerns about the United States and its political role that, seen from the vantages of both Lasswell and Gilpin as well as Modelski, may constitute a "cultural hegemony" in the late twentieth century and early twenty-first century world system.[200] Again, as Baker suggests, the central idea of efforts to make a set of interconnections by means of government or nongovernment actors to more moderate elements of Islamic movements to help mute that perception is a powerful tool both for American and Egyptian policy makers to consider.[201]

While the foregoing challenges and opportunities are daunting, it appears the Egyptian government has chosen a harder line military approach more narrow in scope and, perhaps for the short run only, there are indications the counter-terrorist force campaign against Islamic revivalist terrorist groups in Egypt has met with some tactical successes, even though the political legitimacy of the Mubarak regime has been besmirched by effective and sustained human rights violations.[202]

Seen from a slightly different angle, Guenena skillfully breaks down what options the Egyptian government might have in the short run and long haul to somehow "change the direction" of the "Islamic Trend."[203] Guenena, who draws from Ibrahim's work, tells us that in the short term the Egyptian government ought to embrace democracy, if only "as a safety valve while in the meantime starting a national plan."[204] That "national plan," as Guenena puts it, would work as a long-term income redistribution mechanism that, as Guenena tells us, ". . . is more structurally oriented towards pacifying and hence reducing the volatility which it [the government] deems to be destabilizing."[205]

In addition, what seems significant here and ought to be amenable to the Mubarak regime as rather benign public policy is a set of nonmilitary social responses aimed at Egyptian "centrists" with respect to education, Islamic economic and political institutions, and public discussion or critiques about aspects of U.S. foreign policy like the efficacy and morality of UN sanctions against Iraq.[206] American policy makers and leaders might not like some of those initiatives with respect to the short-term political horizon, but within the context of long-haul U.S. strategic national interests, those initiatives have an allure precisely because of the reason it appears to begin the process of response to the concerns that Islamists, and perhaps others, for that matter, have about the nature and role of the American presence in Egypt and the Middle East.[207]

Seen from a quantitative vantage, one glaring set of findings is the notable drop-off in Egyptian terrorism for the years 1998 and 1999. While it is beyond the scope of this work to provide authoritative interpretations of those quantitative findings, what seems significant here is that some scripted accounts suggest the leaders of al-Jama'a al-Islamiya may have undertaken some type of "structural shift" with respect to tactics that perhaps includes more than an episodic and inconsistent alignment with Shaykh Osama bin Laden's al-Qaida organization. As Ranstorp suggests, such a step would conform to expected behavior as a logical next step in the sequence of a broader struggle against the West.[208] That is the case, as the author points out, because Sayyid Qutb's notion of a "vanguard" directed against the world of ignorance (*jahiliyya*) has influenced bin Laden in profound and lasting ways.[209]

It seems clear the Mubarak regime intends to inject the highest dosage of stability possible into the political system by means of counterterrorism force and aspects of state terrorism that include military trials for civilians and what in practice can amount to indefinite periods of prison confinement for persons with alleged involvement in political activities or movements deemed illegal.[210] While Mubarak chooses to generate and sustain such tactics that may serve him in the short and middle run, heavy reliance on those instruments to partially offset the effects of Islamic revivalist extremists seems antithetical to the political goal of long-term political stability in Egypt.[211] Perhaps the darkest foreboding of all concerns the set of interconnections between bin Laden, his al-Qaida organization, and certain Islamic revivalist extremist chieftains. Somewhat ironically, the almost singular official focus by the Egyptian government on terrorism as an international phenomenon replete with domestic manifestations may, with the passage of time, take on greater structural shape and become an emergent reality for Egyptians to confront.

Notes

1. For one of several examples, see Perlez 2000.
2. Olson 1997, 17.
3. Kuttler 1998, 3; Azzam 1996, 118.
4. Kepel 1985, 191. In Kepel's work, the translation of al-Jihad is "Sacred Combat."
5. Esposito 1992, 95, 133, 134; Guenena 1986, 78; Ibrahim 1988, 643, 649; Sonbol 1988, 26; Hammoud 1998, 305.

6. Harold Lasswell coins the term "maturity cycle" to describe the growth of the power of political entities and, in my judgment, it can apply to sub-national actors as well. See Lasswell 1935, 37, 107, 110, 252, 253; Lasswell 1978, 261-263; Long 1990, 24; Crozier 1960, 127; Ibrahim 1988, 649; Flemming 1992, 231; Chasdi 1999, 173, 204.

7. Hatina 2000, 36, 50.

8. Guenena 1997; Guenena 1986; Hatina 2000; Kepel 1985, 202, 204; Voll 1991; Auda 1994, 383; Auda 1994, 406 n10; Esposito 1992, 130; Ibrahim 1988, 654; Anderson, Seibert, and Wagner 1998, 75-76; Abu-Amr 1997, 227, 235; Smith 1996, 95-98.

9. Hatina 2000, 35-36, 41, 50; Özbudun 1990, 184; Husaini 1956, 5; Heyworth-Dunne 1950, 8-9.

10. Hatina 2000, 35-36, 41, 50; Özbudun 1990, 184; Husaini 1956, 5; Heyworth-Dunne 1950, 8-9.

11. Hatina 2000, 36, 39-40; Ibrahim 1988, 636; Huntington 1968; Abdelnasser 1994, 32-33; Kepel 1985, 196.

12. Hatina 2000, 37; Ibrahim 1988, 637; Ibrahim 1988, 632, 637-638. Ibrahim calls this set of interconnections between state and al-Azhar religious authorities "establishment Islam." For Ibrahim, "establishment Islam" is one of three Islamic "tendencies" in Egypt.

13. Esposito 1992, 135; Hammoud 1998, 323, 329.

14. Hatina 2000, 50, 37, Sonbol 1988, 29; Voll 1991, 377.

15. Hatina 2000, 36-37; Azzam 1996, 112, 110. Presumably, the foregoing "ambiguity" about the set of interconnections between the state and Islam was, seen from the vantage of the constitutional framers, the most practical way to proceed with the emergent reality of an Egyptian constitution and constitutional monarchy.

16. Hatina 2000, 41, 50; Voll 1991, 357, 361; Anderson, Seibert, and Wagner 1998; Auda 1994, 406 n10; Husaini 1956, 1; Mitchell 1969, 8; Abdelnasser 1994, 32-33; Harris 1964b, 150; Ibrahim 1988, 640; Heywood-Dunne 1950, 15. Heywood-Dunne tells us the Muslim Brothergood was crafted in 1929.

17. Hatina 2000, 39, 43, 45, 49; Hammoud 1998, 328.

18. Hatina 2000, 35, 38, 44, 55; Hammoud 1998, 321-322. Faraj 'Ali Fuda was killed by Jama'at al-Jihad activists in June 1992, and Hammoud tells us that he was portrayed as a person influenced by the leaders of the Copts.

19. Hatina 2000, 37-38, 44, 46, 55-57; Voll 1991, 358, 397; Husaini 1956, 5-6; Huntington 1968.

20. Hatina 2000, 41-42.

21. Husaini 1956, 1, 2; Heyworth-Dunne 1950, 11-14; Mitchell 1969, 8; Harris 1964b, 147; Reiss and Roth 1993. Husaini suggests that the notion of YMMA presupposed and derived from the Christian organization, Young Men's Christian Association (YMCA) that was crafted in Cairo in 1927. At the same time, Heyworth-Dunne, drawing on section 2 of the YMMA "oath," tells us "there is a great deal of difference between the character of this group and that of the YMCA." That "statement" of oath issues a clarion call "to be active as a warrior (mujahid) fighting for the revival of the glory of Islam by restoring its religious law and its supremity" (Heyworth-Dunne 1950, 11, 13).

22. Voll 1991, 359-360; Abdelnasser 1994, 32.

23. Voll 1991, 359; Husaini 1956, 6; Azzam 1999, 110; Mitchell 1969, 4.

24. Voll 1991, 359; Hatina 2000, 36.

25. For example, see Cochrane's *Thucydides* 1929, 79, 132, 135, 136-137.

26. Reiss and Roth 1993, 291-305.

27. Voll, 1991, 360.

28. Voll, 1991, 360.

29. Husaini 1956, 11; Mitchell 1969, 7; Harris 1964, 148, 150-151.

30. Harris 1964, 149-151; Mitchell 1969, 8; Abdelnasser 1994, 32. Harris relates the names of those six followers as "Hafiz 'Abd al-Hamid, Ahmad al-Misri, Fu'ad Ibrahim, 'Abd al-Rahman Hasab Allah, Ismail 'Izz, and Zaki al Mughrabi" (Harris 1964, 149).

31. Mitchell 1969, 9.

32. Ibrahim 1988, 645-648, 649 n29; Esposito 1992, 131; Abdelnasser 1994, 37; Sonbol 1998, 30. The second "spiritual guide" was Maamoun H. al-Hudhaiby; the third was Omar el-Telmassani who died in 1986, followed by Supreme Guide Hamid Abul-Naser.

33. Voll 1991, 366; Mitchell 1969, 10; Heywood-Dunne 1950, 15; Abdelnasser 1994, 34; Harris 1964, 155, 158.

34. Voll 1991, 360-361, 397 n37. See Charles Wendell's translation of al-Banna's *Five Tracts of Hasan al-Banna (1906-1949)*, 28-29, as cited in Voll.

35. Voll 1991, 362.

36. Voll 1991, 362.

37. Harris 1964, 144; Voll 1991, 357; Husaini 1956, 5; Mitchell 1969, 3; Hatina 2000, 16; Hammoud 1998, 314.

38. Mitchell 1969, 3; Husaini 1956, 3. It is possible to mull over, as I am sure others have done before me, whether or not that experience helped make it possible for al-Banna to somehow isolate and identify with Adolf Hitler's need for "living space" faced with the same lurking colonial powers under consideration, namely England and France.

39. Mitchell 1969, 4; Husaini 1956, 5; Abdelnasser 1994, 33-34; Voll 1991, 636.

40. Reiss and Roth 1993. What seems significant here is that for some persons, but certainly not all, "psychosocial" factors like "learned social responses" and "cognitive ability" about the West and Western hegemony in Egypt could exacerbate biological problems in certain persons, and in turn, those biological problems could affect underlying cognition about the West.

41. For an analysis of Rabbi Meir Kahane's youth using the Reiss and Roth "risk factor matrix," refer to my earlier book, *Serenade of Suffering*.

42. Mitchell 1969, 4.

43. Mitchell 1969, 2; Husaini 1956, 4; Harris 1964, 144-145.

44. Harris 1964, 145; Husaini 1956, 9, 29; Mitchell 1969, 2.

45. Husaini 1956, 26-27; Mitchell 1969, 4; Harris 1964, 144.

46. Mitchell 1969, 2; Ibrahim 1988, 638-639; Husaini 1956, 3-4; Harris 1964, 144.

47. Husaini 1956, 29-30.

48. Husaini 1956, 27.

49. Husaini 1956, 26, 31; Mitchell 1969; Heyworth-Dunne 1950, 16; Harris 1964, 143.

50. Heyworth-Dunne 1950, 16; Mitchell 1969, 1, 3; Harris 1964, 143; Husaini 1956, 26.

51. Husaini 1956, 4, 9-10, 26-30; Mitchell 1969, 2-3; Harris 1994, 152; Hammoud 1998, 324-325.

52. Piscatori 1994, 362; Guenena 1997, 137; Esposito 1992, 95.

53. Guenena 1997, 137.

54. Abu-Sutayt, *FBIS* 1999.

55. Ibrahim 1988, 632, 635.

56. USDOS 1999d, 4.

57. *FBIS* 1999w.

58. Sharaf-al-Din, *FBIS* 1999; Kepel 1984. To be sure, the incarceration of Muhammad al-Islambouli by the Sadat regime led to Lieutenant Khalid al-Islambouli's terrorist assault against Sadat, and it is likely that first event, certainly in tandem with the volcanic-like shockwave of Islambouli's execution by the Mubarak regime, was what Reiss and Roth might call an "activating factor" for Muhammad Shawqi Islambouli.

59. Sharaf-al-Din, *FBIS* 1999; Kepel 1984.

60. Abu-Stit, *FBIS* 1999.

61. Abu-Stit, *FBIS* 1999.

62. Abu-Stit, *FBIS* 1999; *FBIS* 1997l.

63. Abu-Sutayt, *FBIS* 1999, 2. Abu Sutyat tells us those incarcerated leaders include Hamdi 'Abd al Rahman, Najih Ibrahim, Karam Zuhdi, Fu'ad al-Dawalihi, 'Ali al- Sharif, 'Abbud al- Zummur, Tariq al-Zummur, and Salih Jahin.

64. Sharaf-al-Din, *FBIS* 1999.

65. Sharaf-al-Din, *FBIS* 1999.

66. Sharaf-al-Din, *FBIS* 1999, 7, 5.

67. Sharaf-al-Din, *FBIS* 1999, 5, 3-4.

68. Sharaf-al-Din, *FBIS* 1999, 2-3.

69. Sharaf-al-Din, *FBIS* 1999, 4-5, 8-9.

70. Sharaf-al-Din, *FBIS* 1999, 9.

71. Ibrahim 1988, 644, 641; Voll 1991, 377; Sonbol 1988, 28; Esposito 1992, 94-95, 131; Hammoud 1998, 317.

72. Fuller 1996, 30 n3.

73. Ibrahim 1988, 654; Hammoud 1998, 325-326; Voll 1992.

74. Kepel 1985, 201; Voll 1991, 372, 380; Azzam 1996, 110; Esposito 1992, 98, 131, 133.

75. Sonbol 1988, 30.

76. Azzam 1996, 112, 117; Guenena 1997, 130, 134; Ibrahim 1988, 641-643; Esposito 1992, 98, 133; Voll 1997, 346, 386.

77. Auda 1994, 380.

78. Auda 1994, 380.

79. Auda 1994, 380; Ibrahim 1988, 644.

80. Auda 1994, 380; Guenena 1997, 133.

81. Azzam 1994, 121 n1, n2.

82. Azzam 1996, 111-112 ; Kepel 1985, 201, 205.
83. Kepel 1985, 201; Esposito 1992, 124.
84. Azzam 1996, 121 n2.
85. Voll 1991, 381.
86. Azzam 1996, 121 n1, n2.
87. Azzam 1996, 121 n1, n2.
88. Abu-Sutyat, *FBIS* 1999, 2.
89. Azzam 1996, 113.
90. Auda 1994, 375; Piscatori 1994, 361, 362; Gaffney 1997, 263-264; Chasdi 1999, 92, 127.
91. Auda 1994, 375; Piscatori 1994, 361, 362; Gaffney 1997, 263-264; Chasdi 1999, 92, 127.
92. Gaffney 1997, 263-264; Chasdi 1999, 92, 127.
93. Guenena 1997, 130.
94. Esposito 1992, 99.
95. Esposito 1992, 125; Harris 1964, 155.
96. Azzam 1996; Guenena 1997, 130, 134; Ibrahim 1988, 642.
97. Guenena 1997, 130, 134; Ibrahim 1988, 642.
98. Azzam 1996, 110-111; Esposito 1992, 100; Ibrahim 1988, 646; Sonbol 1988, 28; Guenena 1997, 133; Hammoud 1998, 329.
99. Skocpol 1979; Huntington 1968.
100. Esposito 1992, 95, 133, 139; Guenena 1986, 78; Ibrahim 1988, 643. 649; Sonbol 1988, 26; Hammoud 1998, 332.
101. Gaffney 1997, 263-264; Piscatori 1994, 361, 363, 366; Hatina 2000, 42, 44; Azzam 1996, 118; Sonbol 1988; Kepel 1985, 206.
102. Gaffney 1994, 265; Chasdi 1999, 92, 127.
103. Reiss and Roth 1993, 291-305; Gaffney 1997; Kepel 1985, 206; Esposito 1992, 99; Sonbol 1988, 26; Chasdi 1999, 92, 127.
104. Auda 1994, 379; Guenena 1986, 52-53; Kepel 1985, 206.
105. *FBIS* 1999g.
106. *FBIS* 1998i.
107. *FBIS* 1999g; *FBIS* 1998h; *FBIS* 1999q; *FBIS* 1999u, 2.
108. *FBIS* 1998i.
109. *FBIS* 1999g, 2.
110. Saharaf-al-Din, *FBIS* 1999, 2.
111. *FBIS* 1999g; *FBIS* 1999d.
112. Kepel 1985, 191-192; Schmid and Jongman 1988, 531.
113. Kepel 1985, 192, 211, 214; Auda 1994, 383; Ibrahim 1988, 650; Sonbol 1988, 34, 31. Sonbol suggests there had to be a set of interconnections between al-Jihad and the Muslim Brotherhood to make that complex plan come to fruition.
114. Kepel 1985, 205, 210; Guenena 1986, 56.
115. Ibrahim 1988, 635; Kepel 1985, 202.
116. Esposito 1992, 134; Auda 1994, 382; Guenena 1988, 650.
117. Esposito 1992, 133, 137, 94; Guenena 1986, 63; Ibrahim 1988, 650, 650 n30.
118. Esposito 1992, 133, 137; Ibrahim 1988, 637, 640.
119. Voll 1991, 376; Esposito 1992; Hammoud 1998, 314, 317.

120. Esposito 1992, 133-134; Voll 1991, 383; Ibrahim 1988, 650.

121. Esposito 1992, 136-137.

122. Esposito 1992, 136-137.

123. Guenena 1986, 63. Guenena cites an Ibrahim work (Ibrahim 1980, 437-438).

124. Long 1990, Janis 1972; Jervis 1976.

125. Esposito 1992, 137, 133, 136-137.

126. Esposito 1992, 137, 133, 136-137.

127. Guenena 1997, 133, 141 n7; Auda 1994, 381-382; Voll 1991, 382; Schmid and Jongman 1988, 531-532.

128. Auda 1994, 381.

129. Auda 1994, 381-382; Sonbol 1988, 31; Esposito 1992, 129.

130. Esposito 1992, 136-137; Auda 1994, 381.

131. Ibrahim 1988, 653; Auda 1994, 397.

132. Ibrahim 1988, 653; Auda 1994, 397.

133. Auda 1994, 399-400; Kepel 1985, 203.

134. Ibrahim 1988, 653, 652 n40; Auda 1994 381-382; Voll 1991; Kepel 1985, 193. Kepel reports that Mustafa Shukri was executed by Egyptian authorities in 1978.

135. Ibrahim 1988, 650, 653-654; Kepel 1985, 193, 201; Esposito 1992; Auda 1994.

136. Esposito 1992, 134; Guenena 1997, 141 n7; Auda 1994, 380-382. To be sure, Auda's chronicle of events differs from Esposito's account with respect to Auda's emphasis on Takfir wal 'Hijra's structural and organizational problems as the cause of its demise.

137. Ibrahim 1988, 653-654.

138. Voll 1997, 381.

139. Guenena 1986, 52-54, 56.

140. Sonbol 1988, 32. Sonbol tells us that Faraj's brand of activism closely parallels Wahabist and Shi'ite doctrine in certain ways.

141. Kepel 1985, 193; Esposito 1992, 95-96, 134; Voll 1991, 383; Ibrahim 1988, 654, 651; Sonbol 1988, 32; Jansen 1986, 1, 6-8; Hammoud 1998, 328 . In Kepel's analysis, the translation of Faraj's work is *The Hidden Imperative,* while Esposito's translation is *The Neglected Obligation.* In turn, Ibrahim's translation of the "booklet" is *The Absent Commandment,* or *al-Faridha al-Ghaeba.* Esposito (1992, 96) describes Faraj as the "ideologue" of al-Jihad.

142. Kepel 1985, 194-197; Jansen 1986, 6-8; Hourani 1991, 85, 88.

143. Jansen 1986, 8,7; Kepel 1985, 196-97. Jansen and Kepel both report that al-Jihad chieftain Muhammad 'Abd al-Salam Faraj draws heavily in his work from the works of Ibn Taymiyah (1263-1328 AD) and Abu Hanifah (?-767 AD).

144. Guenena 1986, 59, 53, 70; Guenena 1997, 137; Jansen 1986, 6-9; Esposito 1992, 135; Abdelnasser 1994, 34, 28; Kepel 1985, 199; Jansen 1986, 6-8. The passage in Guenena (1986, 59) draws from the work of "Ayubi: 1982-1983, 277."

145. Kepel 1985, 205-206, 194; Guenena 1986, 52.

146. Guenena 1986, 52, 70; Guenena 1997; Auda 1994, 382; Kepel 1985, 214, 193. Faraj was executed on 15 April 1992 for his role in President Sadat's assassination on 6 October 1981.

147. Guenena 1986, 52, 70; Guenena 1997; Auda 1994, 382; Kepel 1985, 214, 193.

148. Kepel 1985, 206, 207, 204.

149. Kepel 1985, 206-208, 202, 209-210; Esposito 1992, 129; Hammoud 1998, 314, 317. Hammoud tells us the "Coptic conspiracy" theory that Copts serve to hamper the crafting of an Islamic state in Egypt generates and sustains discrimination and terrorist assaults against the Coptic community. Hammoud also asserts that the political activism of Pope Shenouda III helped to exacerbate strains and tensions between Islamic revivalists and Egyptian Copts.

150. Kepel 1985, 207; Azzam 1996, 119.

151. Guenena 1997, 131; Guenena 1986, 59.

152. Guenena 1986, 59-61.

153. Kepel 1985, 207, 210, 214; Guenena 1986, 60-61; Auda 1994, 382-383; O'Ballance 1997, 26; Voll 1997, 387; Esposito 1992, 137. Esposito refers to Shaylh Umar Abdul Rahman as the "religious adviser" to Jama'at al-Jihad.

154. Auda 1994, 401; Guenena 1986, 66-68.

155. Kepel 1985, 217.

156. Kepel 1985, 217-218; Guenena 1986, 67.

157. al-Shafi'i 1998; *Jerusalem Post* 1996b; *FBIS* 1997o.

158. *FBIS* 1999g; USDOS 1999d.

159. USDOS 2000e; Mickolus and Simmons 1997, 830.

160. *FBIS* 1999g.

161. Auda 1994, 382; Ibrahim 1988, 632, 635.

162. *FBIS* 1999p.

163. al-Shafi'i 1998.

164. *FBIS* 1999b; Azzam 1996, 115. Azzam points to "a lull in the violence" with respect to al-Jama'a al Islamiya and al-Jihad terrorist assault activity.

165. Mickolus and Simmons 1997, 572.

166. *Jerusalem Post* 1995g, 4; Mickolus and Simmons 1997, 828; *Jerusalem Post* 1995e, 1; *Jerusalem Post* 1995f, 4; *Jerusalem Post* 1995j, 6; *FBIS* 1996d; *FBIS* 1995c; Baligh 1995, 4.

167. *Jerusalem Post* 1995q, 1; *FBIS* 1995i; *FBIS* 1995f; *FBIS* 1995g; *FBIS* 1995h; *Keesings* 1995c; Mickolus and Simmons 1997, 890-893.

168. Mickolus and Simmons 1997, 572; Chasdi 1999, 61.

169. Mickolus and Simmons 1997, 572; *FBIS* 1995j; *FBIS* 1996b; Mickolus and Simmons 1997, 890. Since Mickolus and Simmons code threats against Egyptian embassies in the U.S., Germany, China, and France as one terrorist assault event, the same was done in my coding. Since "al-Dammon's AL-YAWM" is the source of those threats, location is coded as "other Middle Eastern states."

170. Auda 1994, 382, 397; Esposito 1992; USDOS 1999l, 2; USDOS 1996b, 3; Halawi 1998, 1.

171. *Jerusalem Post* 1995q, 1.

172. *FBIS* 1998s; *FBIS* 1998p.

173. Eltahawy 1995, 1. Egyptian terrorist assaults that happened in Croatia are coded as "other" with respect to location.

174. Horowitz, 1985; von der Mehden 1973; Chasdi 1999, 155, 202.

175. Mickolus 1980, xviii; Flemming 1992, 133 n2: Enders, Parise, and Sandler 1992, 305-306; Johnson 1978, 270; Jenkins 1988, 252; Chasdi 1995; Chasdi 1997; 78-79; Chasdi 1999, 148-149, 202.

176. Sirkin 1999, 400-402.

177. Azzam 1996, 113-115; Guenena 1997, 131; Ibrahim 1988, 651.

178. Willis 1996, 284, 287.

179. Chasdi 1999, 172-173; Chasdi 1997; Chasdi 1995.

180. Noursis 1991, 270. To be sure, a rate of 25.0 percent for cells with an expected frequency of less than five is not far beyond the general rule that Noursis informs us about with respect to valid Chi Square tests not having more than 20 percent of cells with an expected frequency of less than five.

181. Professor Frederic S. Pearson of Wayne State University and I have discussed this point as it relates to work that revolves around the central idea of "border effects" for U.S. and Canadian terrorism patterns.

182. Hoffman 1984, 10-15; Chasdi 1999; Chasdi 1997; Chasdi 1995.

183. The bivariate analysis test results for terrorist group "age" and "target type" include a Pearson Chi Square value of 12.771 at one degree of freedom (1 d.f.) and a "p-value" of less than .001.

184. Kepel 1985, 192; Esposito 1992, 93, 96. This is the description that Lieutenant Khalid Islambouli, the leader of the al-Jihad terrorists who assassinated President Anwar-el-Sadat on 6 October 1981 used to describe the late president.

185. See chapter 3. The fifteen Algerian terrorist assaults chronicled in France account for some 79 percent of the total amount of nineteen terrorist assaults recorded for Europe.

186. "Event deaths $N = 135$, 'minimum 0'; 'maximum 19'; mean 1.36, standard deviation 3.00"; "event injuries $N = 140$; 'minimum 0'; 'maximum 80'; 'mean 2.05, standard deviation 7.95."

187. For the ANOVA test, the mean for "landmark event" is 1.15 with a standard deviation of 2.18; the mean for "political event" is 2.28 with a standard deviation of 5.61; the mean for "religious holiday" is 1.00 with a standard deviation of 2.66, and the Scheffe test produces a significance score or "p-value" of .491, thereby in effect making it impossible to reject the null hypothesis of no statistically significant difference between the means. In addition, two independent sample "T-Tests" were performed; the means for "landmark event" and "political event" are 1.15 and 2.28, respectively, and the means for "political event" and "religious holiday" are 2.28 and 1.00, respectively, with "p-values" of .294 and .273 generated in each test, thereby in effect making it impossible to reject the null hypothesis of no statistically significant difference between the means in each test.

188. Hoffman 1984, 10-15.

189. Chasdi 1999; Chasdi 1997; Chasdi 1995.

190. Azzam 1996, 111; Kepel 1985, 191-192; Hammoud 1998, 329; Nef 1978, 13.

191. Sonbol 1988, 33-34; Guenena 1997, 136, 139; Hammoud 1998, 330-331; Baker 1997, 128.

192. Esposito 1992, 97,94, 100, 132, 139; Azzam 1996, 118-121; Guenena 1997, 130-131; Ibrahim 1988, 632, 648; Voll 1991, 346; Kepel 1985, 193.

193. Azzam 1996, 116.

194. Baker 1997, 127. To be sure, Baker is a subscriber to what K. J. Holsti calls the "theory of global society" but his ideas about the "Wasittiyyah" in Egypt are also fruitful within the context of realist and neorealist frameworks.

195. Baker 1997, 122, 126-127; Reiss and Roth 1993.

196. Baker 1997, 128.

197. Baker 1997, 126-127. Baker tells us the treatise of the New Islamists was made public in 1992.

198. Waltz 1959, 159-186; Nye 1993.

199. Nye 1997, 120.

200. Esposito 1992, 95; Hammoud 1998, 323; Baker 1997, 117, 118, 120; Waltz 1959, as found in Nye 1993, 122; Lasswell 1935; Lasswell 1978; Gilpin, 1981; Modelski 1978.

201. Baker 1997, 128-131.

202. Azzam 1996, 116-117; Esposito 1992,99: Guenena 1997, 136; Guenena 1986, 79; Hammoud 1998, 330; Baker 1997, 122, 128; Sonbol 1988, 33.

203. Guenena 1986, 76, 78

204. Guenena 1986, 79; Guenena 1997, 139, 136; Hammoud 1998, 332.

205. Guenena 1986, 79, Guenena 1997, 139, 136.

206. Baker 1997, 122-128; Sonbol 1988, 34-36.

207. Esposito 1992, 95; Sonbol 1988, 35-36; Hammoud 1998, 323. Some public policy measures to confront the lurking catastrophe of U.S. "cultural hegemony" have been crafted in geographical sites such as France, Canada, and Israel (Voll 1991, 361). In Voll's work, it seems, in my judgment, that Hassan al-Banna hints at "cultural imperialism." Allport 1954; Coser 1956.

208. Ranstorp 1998; Voll 1997, 369-371.

209. Ranstorp 1998; Voll 1997, 369-371; Esposito 1992, 126-128, 135; Hatina 2000, 51; Jansen 1986, 7.

210. Azzam 1996, 111; Hammoud 1998, 330. Hammoud tells us about the 1992 antiterrorism law that imposes the death penalty for members of terrorist groups and allows persons to be detained for up to three days before police are required to notify the prosecutor's office.

211. Sonbol 1988, 33-34; Baker 1997.

Chapter Five

The Case of Turkish Terrorism

Introduction

Seen from the vantage of American strategic planners, Turkey remains a gemstone for U.S. foreign policy in the Middle East. Illustrative of the enormous importance of Turkey are the major roles that American and NATO military forces play over the Turkish landscape. At the same time, there is a historical legacy of what Nef would call "insurgent" terrorism in and around Turkey and a series of cooperation and conflict points at the nation-state and sub-national level that have the potential to destabilize further relations between nations and subnational actors in that part of the Middle East.

For example, in the wake of the terrorist assault against the USS *Cole* in Aden, Yemen, on 12 October 2000, the armed forces of the United States were placed on highest, "Delta" alert against the lurking catastrophe of terrorism at other geographical sites with interconnections to U.S. interests.[1] The Incirlik air force base compound in Turkey, with an effective and sustained allure for Islamic revivalist terrorists, was almost certainly among those facilities placed on highest "Delta" alert.[2]

In the case of Incirlik, that air force base is one of the single most dominant tactical and strategic military sites for the United States and NATO. For one thing, in a non-NATO capacity, the Incirlik air base has been used to administer the "no-fly zones" established in Iraq at the end of the Persian Gulf War

217

primarily to protect Iraqi Kurds in northern Iraq, and Shi'ite Muslims in the southern part of Iraq from the military forces of President Saddam Hussein.[3] In a broader sense, Turkey serves as the venue for "Operation Poised Hammer," otherwise known as "Operation Provide Comfort" (OPC), that is a "multinational [military] force" that, as Aykan tells us, serves "as a deterrent" force against the Iraqi military in northern Iraq.[4] What seems significant here is the cost-benefit debate about "Operation Provide Comfort" that presents a microcosm of the greater debate about the subtleties and nuances and overall value of Western presence in Turkey and the Middle East.

For example, as Aykan reports, the Turkish government views "Operation Provide Comfort" as a vehicle to promote underlying "security" and facilitate the implementation of humanitarian assistance to Kurdish refugees upheld by UN Security Council Resolution 688 and not, by contrast, to support or promote in any way an independent Kurdish state or a "federalist confederation" between a Kurdish state and Turkey.[5] By the same token, Aykan points to an underlying theme that reverberates among some but certainly not all Turkish leaders that "Operation Provide Comfort" really serves as a cornerstone or "beachhead" to increase the capacity of the United States ruling elite to pursue American "national interests" in Iraq and elsewhere in the Middle East.[6]

Turkish politics and the stability of the Turkish political system have a strategic importance that moves over and beyond the role of a proximate counterweight to Iraqi, Syrian, and Iranian politics and actions. First, as Mango tells us, Turkey remains the single "Muslim" democracy in the region.[7] As Hale reports, the Turkish military, which views itself as the "guardianship of the state," supports the political system to make certain that Islam is constrained to the sphere of temporal affairs.[8] In essence, the military supports a nonsectarian Islamic hue to the Turkish political framework that is captured by the sometimes predominant role of the Welfare Party or Refa Partisi under the aegis of Necmettin Erbakan in more contemporary Turkish politics.[9] Otherwise, the Turkish military places enormous ideological distance between Islam and the state. Indeed, Turkey has an allure for the West precisely because of its secular "Kemalist" approach to religious and political compartmentalization with respect to the political system.

Second, precisely because of its geographical locale, a strong pro-Western Turkey serves as a buffer partially to offset the effects of political instability that presupposes and derives from sub-national actors active in the Caucasus and, in the broader sense, from the prospect of time-honored and long-standing Russian challenges that stem from the geographical proximity and political ambitions of the Russian Federation in the so-called "near abroad" areas.[10] At the same time, Turkey has a set of interconnections to the political elite in pro-Western Arab nation-states that serves partially to offset the political effects of extreme Arab nationalism and Islamic revivalism, thereby in effect helping to promote the interests of the United States and Israel. Nowadays, there is also a fledgling relationship between Turkey and Israel that includes joint military activities and commercial interests.[11]

Third, the geographical locale of Turkey, positioned as it is between Eastern Europe in the west, and Iraq, Syria, Iran, Armenia, and Georgia in the east and northeast, makes Turkey a crossroads and potential gatekeeper for the effects of political events and dynamics that happen elsewhere that have the potential to evoke political instability and social unrest in European nations. For example, Turkish political positions taken with respect to Kurdish refugees from Iraq not only affect Turkey but have the potential to cause economic dislocations in Eastern and Western Europe.

As if all that were not enough, Olson points out that Turkish leaders have control over much of the precious resource of water insofar as those elite have the enormous capacity to control water flows that stem from the Tigris and Euphrates rivers that are found in the southeastern part of Turkey, and the Ceyhan and Seyhan rivers that are found in what the author describes as the south-central part of Turkey.[12] To be sure, the particular state leaders who have control over water resources are critical, but episodic and inconsistent control over that resource can also have a significant destabilizing effect. What seems to bode ill for long-term stability between Turkey and Syria, for example, is that the Syrians, in turn, have control over the Orantes or al-Asi River in the northern part of Syria before it flows into the Turkish province of Hatay, itself a part of Syria before 1939.[13]

One of the underlying themes of politics, namely that political issue areas are interconnected and interpenetrating in effect, is showcased in that all too frequently access to what is perceived to be sufficient amounts of water by countries like Syria and Iraq have been hinged on political issues. For instance, in the case of Syria, support from President Hafaz el-Assad for the Kurdistan Workers' Party or PKK, served to increase the lurking prospect of confrontation between Turkey and its Arab neighbors and even Iran.[14] Interestingly enough, there is potential to use the water resource as a form of what Baldwin would call a "positive sanction" to compel the leaders of states to conform their political behavior to what Holsti might call "classical paradigm" political expectations, in addition to international law, thereby in effect helping to promote political stability.[15]

Finally, the loss of Iran as a strategic partner as a result of the Iranian revolution of 1979 amplifies the strategic role of Turkey even more, and helps to give structural shape to American national interest objectives that are pursued in the post-Cold War world.[16] The overall strategic importance and effect of Turkey is also captured in the contemporary U.S. political domestic sphere. A U.S. House of Representatives resolution introduced by Representative James E. Rogan (R-Calif.) to recognize the Armenian genocide of 1.5 million persons that happened under the watch of the Ottoman Young Turks between 1915 and 1923 was thwarted on 20 October 2000. According to one scripted account by

Schmitt, House Speaker J. Dennis Hastert stopped a vote on the floor of the House from taking place precisely because of the reason President William Jefferson Clinton strongly understood the enormous capacity of the resolution to "harm national security and hurt relations with Turkey, a NATO ally."[17]

All of the foregoing highlights the importance of Turkey for U.S. and Western policy makers and the potential for terrorism to destabilize a complex and delicate set of conditions with cooperation and conflict points at both national and sub-national actor levels. The purpose of the next section is to provide qualitative discussion and description of some of the terrorist groups, their major players, and the dynamics that those groups and some Turkish government counterterrorist policies generate over the Turkish political landscape.

The framework of analysis involves: exploration into the sources and origins of the PKK within the context of the Reiss and Roth "risk factor matrix"; analysis of some other well-known "leftist" terrorist organizations that have waged political struggles against the Turkish government during the 1994-99 period; brief description and discussion of more opaque terrorist groups in the system of Turkish terrorism. In the process, the analysis seeks to isolate and identify from a qualitative point of view what some of the outstanding challenges and opportunities are with respect to Turkish terrorism for the 1994-99 period.

Kurdistan Workers' Party
(Partia Kakaren-i-Kurdistan or PKK)

It is commonplace to note that the Kurdistan Workers' Party (PKK) was crafted by Abdullah Öcalan, Cemil Bayik, and Kemal Pir in 1978 overlaid against the time-honored and long-standing Kurdish resistance against the Republic of Turkey.[18] That Kurdish resistance traces an arc to the establishment of the republic in 1923 and before to the time of the Ottoman Empire.[19] At a substantive level, the time-honored political goal of the Kurdistan Workers' Party of an independent Kurdish state has, as Gürbey and Mango both suggest, probably passed into eclipse with an increasing recognition of the internal divisions that have rent apart the Kurds and the geopolitical considerations of nation-state leaders in the Middle East that preclude such a step.[20]

Consequently, as Gürbey and Mango both tell us, the contemporary goals of the PKK probably revolve around a federalist structure with a Kurdish state inextricably bound up with Turkey.[21] At a functional level, PKK military action inclusive of the use of terrorism as a tactic became an emergent reality in 1984.[22] For coding purposes, the PKK is classified as an ideo-ethnocentric charismatic terrorist group because of its underlying Marxist-Leninist/nationalist irredentist standpoint and the charismatic nature of its founder and leader,

Chairman Abdullah Öcalan, who was eventually imprisoned in Turkey following his capture in Kenya in 1999.[23]

Available data related to estimates about PKK size suggest that, by contrast to many other terrorist groups under consideration, the Kurdistan Workers' Party is a very large terrorist organization that resonates with a set of interconnections between groups or branches, be they more formal at home or perhaps less so outside of Turkey.[24] For example, Criss tells us that PKK activists numbered 10,000 as of 1992.[25] In a similar vein, Gunter reports that PKK activists in Germany alone are comprised of around 4,800 persons.[26] Gunter also reports that it is commonplace to note the People's Liberation Army of Kurdistan (ARGK), a PKK appendage, has some 10,000 activists as of 1997.[27] As a result, the PKK is coded as a very large terrorist organization, that in this study is a category for terrorist groups of between 2,500 and 11,000 or more activists.

The political framework of the Kurdistan Workers' Party mirrors the traditional "top down" bureaucratic structures of Marxist-Leninist nation-states. Gunter tells us the basic framework of the PKK consists of a "Central Committee" (CC) and a "Leadership Council" that the author compares to a Politburo.[28] In the past, that "Central Committee" has been under the aegis of Chairman Öcalan, known previously as General Secretary Öcalan. In turn, several administrative "bureaus" with authority over different spheres of operation are subordinate to the PKK Central Committee.[29]

With respect to administrative logistics, one scripted account written in July 1994 reports that Abdullah Öcalan had skillfully broken down areas of combat into three "field commands" to include the "north, central and south field commands" by contrast to the old system of regional areas or "regional states."[30] In terms of interconnections to exogenous links, a set of international political interconnections between the Kurdistan Workers' Party and contemporary state actors and, in the past, non-state actor terrorist organizations, are discernable.

Accounts of PKK interconnections to state actors abound. Gunter and Olson both report that the PKK has been able to generate and sustain interconnections with the late Syrian President Hafaz al-Assad.[31] In turn, both Criss and Dunn talk about PKK interconnections to the fledgling state of Armenia with special focus that is placed on the Nagorno-Korbagh region, while Gunter also reports about military interconnections between PKK and Iran.[32] Gunter and others also report a set of time-honored PKK-Greek interconnections. Gunter tells us those interconnections include very significant amounts of financial aid, military training, and gunrunning done in part by means of the "Greek Cypriot administration."[33] In terms of PKK interconnections to subnational actors (i.e., other terrorist groups) Gunter describe a robust relationship between the PKK and Naif Hawatamah's Popular Democratic Front for the Liberation of Palestine (PDFLP) in earlier days during the 1970s.[34]

What seems significant here is to frame the continuously evolving condition
of the Kurdistan Workers' Party with political dynamics and movements that
have come before. It is commonplace to note that the Turkish political "left"
really presupposes and derives from a continuously evolving post-Second World
War environment increasingly plagued with political and economic ills that
served to generate and sustain generally recognizable dissatisfaction with the
Turkish political system.[35] In the political sphere, a hallmark of the Kemalist
political framework was the Turkish authoritarianism that failed to introduce any
flexibility into the political system and that, for many, defined what the Turkish
political system was all about. In essence, those deleterious patterns of political
and economic conditions share some similarities with respect to what is found
in the case of the political systems in Algeria and Egypt.

That authoritarian bent to the political system traces a curve to the inception
of the republic. For example, Özbudun chronicles the political legacy of contemporary Turkey where Mustapha Kemal's People's Party, otherwise known as the
Republican People's Party (RPP) in times to come, became the single most
predominant political party after 1925 with the suppression of the Progressive
Republican Party.[36] To be sure, it was the only official Turkish political party
to operate in the Turkish political landscape until the Democratic Party (DP),
itself crafted by RPP renegades in 1946, wrested power away from the RPP in
1950.[37] In time, the Democratic Party passed into eclipse in favor of its
successor, the Justice Party (JP).[38]

Equally important, as both Barkey and Criss suggest, were the economic
conditions where a few urban-based business "conglomerates" were the single
most predominant force in the Turkish economic sphere, thereby in effect
helping to exacerbate urban and rural fissures in Turkish society.[39] Criss tells
us, "leftist students viewed the JP government of Süleyman Demierl as
supporting the 'monopolist bourgeoisie,' which collaborated with 'US
imperialism' and subordinated the Turkish economy to it. Hence, it was
impossible to develop heavy industry and become self sufficient."[40] Likewise,
in his analysis of the Islamic Welfare Party or Refah Partisi, Barkey asserts that,
"the party has made the most out of the prevalent fear of big business in the
countryside and among small entrepreneurs, harping not only on the role of
Istanbul based conglomerates in the Turkish economy but, with the [European]
customs union agreement, on the threat posed by European corporations."[41]

In the broader sense, Karpat describes how socioeconomic development in
Turkey during the 1950s and 1960s worked to generate and sustain economic
dislocations and "social change" and caused people from rural locales to move
into urban areas.[42] We are told by Karpat of the *gcekondu* or "shantytowns"
where very poor persons had to live and face the enormous challenges posed by
urban life that was rent apart by political instability and social unrest by the
1970s.[43] Against that backdrop of structural economic change, Gunter suggests
that perhaps the single, most dominant theme for the genesis of the Kurdistan

Workers' Party was the long-standing inability or unwillingness of other so-called Turkish "leftist" political organizations to nurture, generate, and sustain responsibility for Kurdish nationalist sentiments and other similar feelings.[44]

For Gunter, the PKK presupposes and derives from what Reiss and Roth might call "macrosocial-situational factors" of specific and immediate "leftist" Turkish resistance to Turkish political and economic realities that Kurds, among others, were forced to confront. Extending the analysis further, that resistance on the part of the leftist circles really mirrored, as Esman might suggest, the emphasis placed on traditional Marxist-Leninist interpretations of economic conditions at the expense of the ethnic component that is at the heart of Kurdish political demands and aspirations.[45]

Seen from a slightly different angle, Mango focuses on the inadequacies of government response to what Huntington might describe as "political decay" where effective political institutionalization, perhaps always makeshift and never complete with the single predominance of Atatürk's and President İsmet İnönü's RPP party until 1950, began to fray at the edges even more.[46] In his work, Mango describes the ensuing condition: "when the promise of free parliamentary rule dissolved in financial mismanagement, parliamentary skullduggery and Islamic rumblings; then in the late 1960s when the 'social state' promised by the new Constitution failed to materialize."[47]

Within the context of an array of political demands and aspirations made on government, Criss divides the emergent reality of Turkish terrorism framed according to specific time periods. For Criss, terrorism that presupposes and derives from the political instability and social unrest of the 1960s comprises a "first wave" that passed into eclipse around 1972. In turn, a "second wave" of Turkish terrorism commenced around 1974.[48] For Criss, student activism to promote a socialist Turkey continuously evolved insofar as that "by 1969," the author tells us, "mass movements had ceased, and terrorist acts had begun."[49] Criss reports that student debate societies known as the Federation of Debate Clubs, or what Scherer calls the Intellectual Club Federation continuously evolved into the Dev Genç or Devrimci Gencier Organization, otherwise known as the Revolutionary Youth Organization, by 1969.[50]

For a more complete understanding of the sources and origins of the PKK and other "leftist" Turkish terrorist groups, the analysis turns to description and discussion of certain PKK antecedent organizations. Scherer states that Dev-Genç was an organization comprised of perhaps some 600 activists with interconnections to the Palestine Liberation Organization (PLO) that trained Dev Genç activists.[51] That organization was skillfully dismantled, as Scherer reports, by Turkish authorities in 1970.[52]

Interestingly enough, the Turkish government's skillful breakdown of Dev Genç in 1970 could be seen as an "activating factor," to use Reiss and Roth's term, for the crafting of Dev Genç's successor group known as the Turkish People's Liberation Army or TPLA, that was a terrorist group with strong support from Marxist-Leninist nation-states. To be more specific, Scherer reports the TPLA was characterized by strong interconnections to Marxist-Leninist "second world" countries like East Germany, North Korea, and Bulgaria.[53] Insofar as Turkish government counterterrorism policy may have helped to induce the formation of TPLA, replete with international inter-connections to national actors from the start, the fundamental matter really distills down to a reappraisal of the common wisdom of a wholesale crackdown against the TPLA or terrorist groups like that under similar conditions.

Gunter reports that many antigovernment activists were freed from prison after the 1974 amnesty offered by Prime Minister Bülent Ecevit that followed the military takeover in 1971 that wrested power away from the Demeriel government.[54] Those "second wave" activists, to use Criss's term, were able to put together many of the terrorist groups under consideration in this study as gatekeepers of a continued struggle, waged in effective and sustained ways, against the Turkish government that itself remained the symbol of the political and economic ills that plagued the republic.[55] In that context, Gunter tells us about the Kurdistan Workers' Party antecedent group that was crafted by university students in 1974 known as Ankara Higher Education Association or AYOD. The Ankara Higher Education Association (AYOD) was itself one of several political offshoots of the Dev-Genç (Devrimci Gencier) or Revolutionary Youth Organization that, as previously mentioned, was crafted in 1969.[56]

At a substantive level, Gunter traces an arc from several Turkish "leftist" terrorist groups to that overarching parent organization Dev-Genç. Besides the AYOD, those terrorist groups include, but are not limited to, the Turkish Communist Party Marxist-Leninist (TKP/ML), its military branch TIKKO, and the Dev-Yol or Revolutionary Group crafted in 1975 or 1976 that Schmid and Jongman describe as a TPLA splinter group.[57] In turn, Dev-Yol spawned its own political offshoot or splinter group in 1978 known as Dev-Sol.[58] Criss reports those aforementioned groups were either "Marxist-Leninist" in nature, presumably insofar as "wage earners" or the proletariat are envisioned to coalesce over time to wrest political and economic power away from "wage holders" or the bourgeoisie and petit bourgeoisie like small merchants, or "Maoist" insofar as the peasantry takes the place of the proletariat in rural settings to spearhead the revolution.[59]

The underlying theme of the Ankara Higher Education Association was to confront the Turkish government over the twin themes of the "Kurdistan question" against the backdrop of the Marxist themes of "social justice" and "economic inequality."[60] To be sure, Gunter suggests that seen from the vantage of Kurds, Marxist ideas were necessary but not sufficient insofar as the political and economic demands and aspirations of the Kurds were ignored outright by some Turkish political "leftist groups" and certainly not placed at the forefront of the political agendas by any of the aforementioned.[61] Seen from the vantage of Gurr and Harff, much of the foregoing, and the economic and political hardships that are generally recognizable in the case of Kurds living in Turkey nowadays, might constitute, as Criss suggests, a powerful example of "relative deprivation" replete with examples of persons and groups of persons that react to those sustained conditions with violence.[62]

Imagine a situation that emphasizes Reiss and Roth's "microsocial-situational factors" in which the concrete effects of Kurdish political isolation, even among dissident Marxist-Leninist "leftist groups," are at work in effective and sustained ways. In addition, the mind-set of other Turkish political "leftist group" leaders can be viewed as an example of the Reiss and Roth "bystander activities" descriptive and that relative indifference would exacerbate even more the urgency of the fledgling Kurdish struggle in Turkey during the 1970s.[63] Compounding the matter even more, all of the foregoing is set against the backdrop of the tortuous historical legacy of the Kurdish resistance that has come before.

For Mango, Kurds are delineated from other ethnic groups in Turkey in large part by the languages of "Kurmanji," otherwise known as "Badinani" and "Dimili" or "Zaza."[64] Unequivocally, to be Kurdish also means to understand the full-blown effects of the historical legacy of momentous political events on more contemporary Kurdish political action movements and the Turkish government responses to them. Examples of such events include, but are not limited to, the Shaykh Said Rebellion of 1925, and the Shaykh Ubeydullah Rebellion in the 1870s that Yegen suggests might be viewed as the "first nationalist uprising" of Kurdish nationalists.[65]

As Mango relates, those movements were never inclusive of all Kurds, but the influence of those movements is profound and lasting all the same.[66] For example, the Shaykh Said Rebellion from 8 February 1925 through 15 April 1925, under the aegis of Shaykh Said and others, pitted the interests of Kurdish nationalists, themselves comprised of specific Kurdish peoples like the Cibran, the Sasunah, and the Tatkun, against the armies of the Kemalists in Ankara and their allies in battle places like Diyarbakir, Voton, and Elazığ.[67] Watershed historical events like those might be considered for the more contemporary Kurdish struggle as a set of "predisposing factors" at the "macrosocial" level of analysis.[68] The ethnic strains and tensions between groups and subgroups of Kurdish peoples might be captured by the Reiss and Roth descriptive "oppositional cultures" found at the "predisposing" level of analysis.[69]

Equally important, as Olson chronicles, is absence of what Reiss and Roth might call political and economic "opportunity structures" for Kurds in the wake of the rebellion, insofar as the Turkish government showcased an enormous capacity for revenge and retribution with the execution of Shaykh Said after his Diyarbakir independence tribunal conviction of 1925 and the wholesale depopulation and destruction of Kurdish villages following the end of the Shaykh Said rebellion.[70] All of the foregoing and other watershed historical events might have influenced Abdullah Öcalan and other like him, in more contemporary times in Turkey, to devote almost singular attention to the generally recognizable needs associated with the Kurdish struggle.

Turning to analysis of the origins of the AYOD by means of Reiss and Roth's work, it is difficult to isolate and identify one single "activating event" for the coalescence of the AYOD and its successor group, the Kurdistan Workers' Party, but particular events in Abdullah Öcalan's life, at the "individual" level of analysis, stand out with respect to his need to develop stratagems of remediation for Kurdish political demands and aspirations. If one single event may qualify as an "activating factor" for Öcalan's political activism in the broader sense, Gunter suggests perhaps that event was his incarceration in 1970 while still a young man precisely because of his protests against the "social injustice" and "economic inequality" that was a hallmark of the Kurdish experience in Turkey.[71] Gunter suggests it was that experience that compelled him to understand that the Kurdish dilemma deserved his increased devotion and almost singular attention.[72]

Notwithstanding that, there seems to be what Reiss and Roth might call "predisposing factors" at the "individual-psychosocial" level of analysis that may be equally important to illustrate the matter of Öcalan's emotional and political development. In the broader sense, Gunter tells us of the life experiences and strong personality of Abdullah Öcalan's great-grandfather Husune Oce, who articulated the fundamental matter as one that really distilled down to forceful confrontation with the Turks, that had profound and lasting effect on Öcalan who seems to have gravitated towards strong male figures.[73] Seen from the vantage of the Reiss and Roth analysis at the "individual" level of analysis, such effective and sustained indoctrination might fall within the sphere "psychosocial factors," perhaps along the lines of "learned social responses" and "perception of rewards/penalties for violence."[74]

Interestingly enough, the effects of that strong personality may have been amplified even more by what Gunter tells us was the generally recognizable weakness of Öcalan's father. Gunter reports Öcalan said that "his father was 'such a weak person that his reaction to injustices was to go up to the roof of the house and scream and swear.'"[75] Although it is only conjecture, a "feedback loop" between "social" and "individual" levels of analysis might have existed, where seemingly clear-cut approaches articulated by the great-grandfather, for one, perhaps captured by Reiss and Roth's notion of "perceptions of rewards/penalties for violence" may have been magnified by some "family disorganization" that presupposed and derived from the father's notable weakness of character and family reactions to that condition.

In turn, from the vantage of "microsocial" factors, that "family disorganization" may have amplified or distorted a variety of "psychosocial" factors that might include: "learned social responses," "perceptions of rewards/penalties for violence," and at a most basic level, "cognitive ability."[76] In that vein, it ought to be noted that Öcalan had a reputation for especially brutal assaults against fellow Kurds perceived to be rivals or tacit collaborators that, from Gunter's vantage, may have served as an "activating factor" for an intra-group struggle between Öcalan and one of his chieftains, Duran Kalkan, thereby in effect helping to facilitate the process that resulted in the demise of one PKK appendage called the Kurdistan Freedom Brigades (HRK) described below.[77]

An underlying theme interwoven into the lives of many who have become violent political activists is the university setting that has an enormous capacity to galvanize persons, thereby in effect helping to provide legitimacy to inner conflicts that presuppose and derive from the interactions and interconnections between family, the "outside environment," and the individual. In that respect Abdullah Öcalan's continuously evolving pathway was similar to others insofar as he formed, as previously mentioned, the AYOD and met Kemal Pir and Cemil Bayik, two other originators of the Kurdistan Workers' Party in that context.[78] Indeed, it is Jung who tells us life experiences in a university setting, for example, affect the development of persons through middle age, by contrast to Freud who would have us believe development stops after the very early years of childhood.[79]

For Öcalan, Kurdish nationalism was the single most predominant factor to generate and sustain action and there was a continuously evolving environment from the student-comprised Ankara Higher Education Association (AYOD) to a new political action group framework. It was Kurdish nationalism that stoked the burners of change and galvanized like-minded persons with the end result that a more "formal party," to use Gunter's term, namely, the Kurdistan Workers' Party, was crafted and established on 27 November 1978.[80] Plainly, it was at some juncture here that Öcalan was marked with the nickname "Apo" that Gunter reports can translate into the word "uncle."[81] That is notable precisely because of the reason that Öcalan's group was known from the start as "Apocular" or "followers of Apo," also known later as the National Liberation Army or Ulusal Kurtulus Ordusu (UKU).[82] After Öcalan crafted "Apocular" in Ankara, Gunter, who draws on the work of van Bruinessen, tells us that Öcalan relocated into what Gunter calls "Kurdish areas," presumably with special focus on consolidation and recruitment, especially from recruitment pools of persons on the economic fringes of society.[83]

As a blueprint for action, one prevailing notion commonplace to note among "leftist" Turkish political groups that came before the PKK was what Gunter describes as "armed propaganda," a concept that revolved around the central idea of armed assaults against Turkish forces to underscore their ineptitude and singular incapacity to protect Turkish interests. In essence, "armed propaganda" was practiced to evoke uncertainty and other similar feelings about the legitimacy of Turkish government political and military institutions.[84] That "prevailing ideology" of "armed propaganda" among Turkish "leftist" political action groups served to elicit the PKK's first terrorist assault, a botched assassination attempt in 1978 against a Justice Party member of parliament and local official named Mehmet Celal Bucak.[85]

Analysis of a later phase of the "growth cycle" of PKK indicates there is evidence that the absence of Abdullah Öcalan, while on the run from the Turkish government, had profound and lasting effects on the PKK terrorist group splintering process.[86] One scripted account tells us of an October 1998 memo that may have served as an "activating factor," against the backdrop of "situational factors" associated with Öcalan's absence, to spawn at least one new PKK "splinter organization" comprised of women that itself presupposes and derives from the Free Women's Union (YAJK), a women's brigade formed by Öcalan in 1978.[87] One way of thinking about Abdullah Öcalan's physical absence because of his efforts to escape capture is to reflect about whether or not strenuous efforts to apprehend him were conceived of within the context of efforts to promote terrorist group splitting. Regrettably, analysis of that facet of Turkish counterterrorism policy remains shrouded in mystery.

Appendages of the Kurdistan Workers' Party (PKK):

- Kurdistan National Liberation Front or Eniye Rizyariye Nevata Kurdistan (ERNK)

- People's Liberation Army of Kurdistan or Artes- i Rizyariye Gel Kurdistan (ARGK)

- Metropolitan Revenge Brigade

At a functional level, Olson tells us that the Kurdistan Workers' Party is skillfully broken down into several organizational sections that include the Kurdistan National Liberation Front, also known as ERNK, and the People's Liberation Army of Kurdistan, otherwise known as ARGK.[88] Both Gunter and Olson as well as Criss report that Cemil Bayik is the leader of the ARGK.[89] In this study, the ARKG is coded as "PKK" since the PKK is the military gatekeeper of the armed struggle against the Turkish government. With respect to size, Gunter estimates that the ARGK is comprised of around 10,000 activists.[90]

In the case of the ERNK, Gunter tells us that "although it usually masks itself in the West as solely a peaceful popular front, the ERNK has also been involved in armed actions from its inception."[91] In contrast to the ARGK, the ERNK is coded as a separate organization precisely because of its official status as a political organ and the reason that its relationship to PKK, as described below, is circumscribed. With respect to size, Gunter relates that some "50,000 formal members" may comprise the ERNK, which places more of an emphasis on an urban venue for its activities.[92]

To be sure, there appears to be some difference between chronicles of the historical legacy of the Kurdistan Workers' Party as it pertains to the ERNK and ARGK, and those differences are illuminated by scripted accounts written by both Gunter and Criss.[93] For Gunter, the Kurdistan National Liberation Front (ERNK) was crafted in 1985 to serve as the political branch of the PKK, while the People's Liberation Army of Kurdistan (ARGK) was crafted and operational as a "professional guerrilla army" by the late 1980s.[94] Somewhat paradoxically, the boundaries of both of those groups are permeable, if not strictly interpenetrating. Gunter tells us that "a member of the ERNK is not necessarily a formal member of PKK, while by definition a member of the ARGK is."[95]

Interestingly enough, Gunter asserts that an antecedent terrorist group to both ERNK and ARGK was actually crafted in 1984 under the name Kurdish Freedom Brigades, otherwise known as Hazen Rizgariyu Kurdistan (HRK). The Hazen Rizgariyu Kurdistan (HRK), under the direction of Duran Kalkan, had an enormous capacity for terrorist assaults against Kurdish villages, presumably to shape and conform constituency group support for the PKK.[96] As Gunter relates, that group was broken down in 1986 by PKK officials with the development of ARGK after HRK leader Duran Kalkan looked askance at Öcalan's continued support of that freewheeling violence against the Kurdish community.[97]

For Criss, the continuously evolving development of PKK complete with military as well as political appendages is somewhat different than what is described in the foregoing accounts. Criss reports that the ERNK was crafted in 1984 as a military unit but was undercut by the absence of constituency group backing that was evoked by what Criss calls ERNK's "hit and run missions."[98] In turn, Criss reports that the People's Liberation Army of Kurdistan or ARGK, under the aegis of Cemil Bayik, was put together in or around 1984 to fill the vacuum that presupposed and derived from the ERNK's ineffectiveness, presumably from both a military, and equally important, a political point of view.[99]

Since the works of both Gunter and Criss give approximately the same time period for the genesis of ERNK, it is coded in this study as a terrorist group between ten and fifteen years old. What seems significant here about ERNK development, from a theoretical vantage, is that empirical evidence of eroding support for that organization is a good fit with Harris's underlying theme articulated in her work on Northern Ireland that constituency group mores and values can generate and sustain the structural shape of terrorist group assaults and tactics.[100]

Precisely because of the reason Turkish terrorist assaults are claimed by PKK "front" organizations or "offshoot" groups clearly delineated from PKK by claims of responsibility, or attribution from government or media sources, the quantitative analysis isolates and identifies terrorist assaults for each "front organization" of PKK or PKK "offshoot" whenever possible. Hence, the

Metropolitan Revenge Brigade described in one *Jerusalem Post* scripted account as a previously "unknown branch of the Kurdistan Workers Party (PKK)" and listed by Mickolus and Simmons as an "'underground revenge group' of the Popular Army for the Liberation of Kurdistan" is coded separately.[101] In a similar vein, very shadowy terrorist groups or "proto-groups" such as the Independent Work Group are coded as ideo-ethnocentric terrorist groups based on brief description about them found in scripted accounts and the absence of any evidence of leaders who fall in the sphere of charismatic leaders.[102]

Revolutionary Left or Dev-Sol (Devrimci Sol); Revolutionary Peoples' Forces; Turkish Communist Party/Marxist-Leninist Conference Organization or TKP/MC Konferans; Turkish Worker's Peasants Liberation Army or Türkkiye Isçi Köylü Kurtulus Ordusu (TIKKO)

To recapitulate, Criss tells us the Dev-Genç or Revolutionary Youth Organization that evolved from the Turkish student movement of the 1960s spawned several Turkish "leftist" political groups that carried out terrorist assaults against the Turkish government and Turkish interests.[103] As previously mentioned, Dev-Sol or the Revolutionary Left was crafted in 1978 and is, as Gunter reports, a political offshoot of the Dev-Yol or Revolutionary Group that was established in 1976 that itself traces a curve to the Dev-Genç movement.[104]

It is commonplace to note that Dev-Sol, nowadays sometimes called the Revolutionary People's Liberation Front-Revolutionary Left, or DHKP-C, was put together in 1978 by Dursun Karatas.[105] According to Mickolus and Simmons' work and other scripted accounts, Bedri Yagan, Karatas' right hand man and deputy commander of Dev-Sol perished in 1993 during a Turkish police counter-terrorism assault in Istanbul.[106] With respect to its organizational framework, Dev-Sol seems to have been broken down according to geographical locales with the Ankara area under the aegis of Semih Genc, himself incarcerated in February 1992 by the Turkish government.[107] That scripted account suggests that Dev-Sol activist numbers have dwindled in the face of effective and sustained Turkish counterterrorism activity.[108] Interestingly enough, Gunter asserts there has been some set of interconnections or cooperation between Dev-Sol and PKK.[109]

For Schmid and Jongman, one underlying theme of Dev-Sol's stratagems in the late 1970s was to carry out terrorist assaults against the right-wing extremist political party National Action Party (NAP), that was founded in 1948 and led by Colonel Alparsian Türkes, and presumably his "paramilitary" unit known as the Grey Wolves.[110] Those terrorist assaults carried out by Dev-Sol may be considered by extrapolation to be terrorist assaults directed against the state as well, because of the generally recognizable accusations of NAP interconnections with the Turkish government, insofar as it is claimed by some that NAP engages in extralegal activities against government opponents.[111]

In the broader sense, while Dev-Sol has a long-standing and time-honored legacy of carrying out terrorist assaults against the Turkish government, there are some reports in scripted accounts that Dev-Sol broadened the struggle during the 1990-91 Persian Gulf War to include terrorist assaults against American, British, and French targets in Turkey.[112] As this book goes to press, what is known about Dursun Karatas is that he and some of his Dev-Sol associates were arrested by French authorities in 1997. Faced with the looming catastrophe of extradition to Turkey, Karatas disappeared from the political landscape after French authorities granted him what amounted to a "conditional" release pending legal proceedings against him.[113] In the case of the Revolutionary People's Forces, a group that was probably fashioned in 1994, that group is considered to be a "splinter group" or front organization of Dev-Sol insofar as a terrorist assault was claimed by the former and subsequently by the latter sometime soon afterwards.[114]

The Turkish Communist Party Marxist-Leninist (TKP/ML) also presupposes and derives from the Dev-Genç political organization of the 1960s. Schmid and Jongman tell us the Turkish Communist Party Marxist-Leninist (TKP/ML) was crafted in 1973 and was led, as both Gunter and Schmid and Jongman relate, by Ibrahim Kaypakkuya.[115] Schmid and Jongman report that Kaypakkuya was killed while he was detained in prison following the September military coup in Turkey in 1980.[116] Presumably, Kaypakkuya also crafted the military branch of TKP/ML called Türkiye Isçi Köylü Kurtulus Ordusu (TIKKO), otherwise known in English as the Turkish Workers Peasants Liberation Army.[117] Schmid and Jongman report that TKP/ML is Maoist in nature, thereby in effect putting a premium on the peasantry as the central player in a "peasant revolution" to set up a Marxist-style state. Presumably, the Turkish Communist Party/Marxist-Leninist Conference Organization, also known as the TKP-MC Konferans, is a spin-off terrorist group of TKP/ML and, in a broader sense, from the Turkish radical "leftist" movement in general.[118]

The Islamic Groups: Great Eastern Islamic Raiders (IBDA-C); Turkish Hezbollah; Anatolian Federal Islamic State (AFID)

There is precious little in the way of clear-cut and available data associated with many of the Turkish Islamic revivalist terrorist groups under consideration in this study. In the broader sense, Turkish Islamic revivalist terrorist groups seem to be broken down into an older set that traces an arc to the early 1970s, and a newer set that traces a curve to the late 1980s. In the case of the former, one terrorist group under consideration is the Great Eastern Islamic Raiders or IBDA-C that was probably crafted in the "mid 1970's" and is described in one scripted account as an Islamic fundamentalist group that is small in size.[119]

A scripted account by Pacal states the IBDA-C is under the aegis of Salih Mirzabeyoglu and has been so since its inception.[120] For Pacal, the IBDA-C presupposes and derives from what is known as the ideology of "the Greater East [of Turkey]," itself crafted in large part by Necip Fazil Kisakurek, described by Pacal as "the intellectual father of the Islamists."[121] Pacal describes long-standing stints in prison that the author suggests helped to shape the contours of Mirzabeyoglu's way of thinking about effective and sustained political struggle and those life experiences might be considered by Reiss and Roth in their totality as an "activating event."[122]

Pacal points out that the organizational structure of the Great Eastern Islamic Raiders (IBDA-C) is rather freewheeling and loose, with "cells" of small numbers of activists that have a profound and lasting capacity to influence, plan, and execute terrorist assaults. To be sure, IBDA-C's underlying organizational framework of rather autonomous group "cells" is in stark contrast to the authoritarian top-down bureaucratic nature of many of Turkey's so-called "leftist" terrorist groups.[123] Interestingly enough, certain scripted accounts point to interconnections between the IDBA-C and, what might be at that stage in 1996, a "proto-group" called the Caucasian Chechen Solidarity Committee that commandeered the Russian ferry boat *Avrasya*.[124]

As previously mentioned, there are different and sometimes conflicting accounts about the sources and origins of Islamic revivalist extremist terrorist groups in Turkey. For example, Criss tells us Turkish Hezbollah appears to be "an armed protector of the pro-Islamic Welfare Party."[125] Seen from a very different vantage, Gunter is one writer who suggests the IBDA-C may in fact be a Turkish government artifact designed to be one of what Gunter calls the "Hizbullah-Contra" organization put together to combat Islamic groups in part by helping to make them appear very extremist, especially in terms of tactics.[126] In a similar vein, the author suggests the Anatolia People's Front may be a component of that "Hizbullah-Contra" organization.[127]

The Anatolian Federal Islamic State organization (AFID) presupposes and derives from the Islamic Society and Communities Union (ICCB) that was crafted by Cemalettin Kaplan in 1984 or 1985.[128] According to one scripted account, the establishment of an Islamic state in what is now the Republic of Turkey is the political goal the AFID pursues over the Turkish political landscape.[129] Another scripted account reports that the "ICCB-AFID" center of operations is in Germany.[130] In the wake of Cemalettin Kaplan's death in 1992, the AFID has been under the aegis of his son, "Caliph" Metin Kaplan.[131] In the absence of more definitive information about recruitment and leadership, the AFID, like the IBDA-C, is coded as a Turkish theocentric terrorist group.

Be that as it may, Gunter does point out that the Turkish government has confirmed the existence of a Turkish Hezbollah organization.[132] With respect to its organizational framework, Gunter suggests the term "Turkish Hizbullah" seems to be a rather generic umbrella label to delineate Hezbollah type organizations, some of which have generally recognizable "pro-PKK" sentiments presumably within the context of a common struggle against the state, while others are "anti-PKK" in nature, that lambast the Marxist-Leninism and equality of the sexes approach inherent to the PKK.[133] One scripted account reports that Kemal Donmez, leader of the Turkish government's Struggle Against Terrorism Department, suggests that Turkish Hezbollah was crafted within the context of what is called the "Islamic Movement" in Batman province around 1987.[134] Gunter also suggests that some set of interconnections exists between what amounts to Turkish Hezbollah and the Iranian intelligence service Savama, but, as Gunter also suggests, if those interconnections do exist, they remain shrouded in mystery.[135]

Other Subnational Actors in the Kurdish/Turkish Political Fray: A Brief Overview

- The Kurdish Democratic Party (KDP)

- The Patriotic Union of Kurdistan (PUK)

- HADEP

- November 17

One aspect of the intricacies and nuances associated with the workings of political systems in general is the set of interconnections between subnational actors and national actors. Perhaps nowhere else in the Middle East than in the context of Turkish and Iraqi politics is that condition more acute. In the case of the Kurdish resistance in Iraq, the Kurdistan Democratic Party (KDP) and the Patriotic Union of Kurdistan (PUK) are predominant in the political landscape.[136] Both Dunn and Gunter, as well as both Criss and Olson, suggest that the enormous capacity for the foregoing groups to shift alliances is in part a function of nation-states like Iraq and Iran that seek to promote national interests, oftentimes at the expense of groups of Kurdish peoples all too frequently riddled with fierce internal competition and struggle.[137]

What seems significant here is that those dynamics between nations, nations and subnational actors, and in some cases between subnational groups, help to comprise a dynamic political condition ripe with political instability that is always a frequent visitor in that context, with the potential to disrupt relations between nation-states as well as between subnational actors.[138] The analysis now turns to a brief discussion about those two most important subnational actors in the Kurdish political fray. The Kurdish Democratic Party (KDP) and the Patriotic Union of Kurdistan (PUK) are pivotal players, and both Dunn and Gunter suggest that "coincidental cleavages" of region and ethnicity, as delineated in part by language and "tribal" affiliation, contribute to the distinctions between the KDP and the PUK.[139]

The Kurdish Democratic Party (KDP) was, as Gunter reports, crafted in 1946 by the Iraqi Kurdish leader Mullah Mustafah Barzani (1903-1979) and is now under the aegis of his son Mursaud Barzani.[140] Gunter reports the KDP has been characterized "as rightist, conservative, feudal, tribal, and nationalist."[141] In turn, Dunn tells us that Barzani was once a general of the ephemeral Kurdish Republic of Mahbad in northern Iran that lasted from 1945 to 1946 with effective and sustained backing from the Soviet Union before Stalin was pressured to remove Soviet forces from Iran.[142] Seen from the vantage of the Reiss and Roth analysis, the fall of the Mahbad Republic might be seen as one of several "situational factors" that were involved in the establishment of the KDP.[143]

What Reiss and Roth might call a host of "situational factors" also made conditions ripe for KDP group splitting. At one level, those subnational actors were exploited in effective and sustained ways by leaders of nation-states like Iraq and Iran to promote geopolitical interests. For example, against the backdrop of those strains and tensions, Barzani crafted a sometimes fragile set of political interconnections to a succession of Iraqi regimes, thereby in effect seeking greater autonomy and rights for Kurds in Iraq, that culminated in a rebellion against Iraq that received support from the Shah of Iran and tacit support from the United States.[144]

As Dunn informs us, insofar as then-Vice President Saddam Hussein worked in tandem with his Iranian counterparts in 1974 to resolve that dilemma, the ineluctable conclusion was a quid pro quo arrangement in 1975 to withdraw Iranian support from Barzani in exchange for Iranian rights with respect to the Shat-al-Arab waterway system, thereby in effect helping to destroy Barzani's rebellion.[145] That "activating factor," to use Reiss and Roth's term, namely the failure of Barzani's war against Iraq, helped to reify divisions in the KDP that are discussed at length in the works of both Dunn and Gunter.[146]

In addition, Dunn reports that a set of strains and tensions between Barzani and other members of the KDP ruling elite, themselves possibly, as Dunn suggests, exacerbated by urban/rural distinctions between members, helped to create conditions that would over time help generate and sustain the formation of the Patriotic Union of Kurdistan (PUK), a KDP "splinter group."[147] In 1975, Jalal Talabani led a breakaway faction of KDP that coalesced into the Patriotic Union of Kurdistan (PUK), while the KDP remained under the aegis of Hashim Aqrawi.[148]

According to one scripted account, the current leader of the PUK, Celal Talabani, seeks to craft a "federation" between a fledgling "Kurdistan" in northern Iraq and Turkey.[149] As Aykan and Criss both report, Barzani's KDP has been what Aykan calls "the main ally" of Turkey in its war against the PKK, while Dunn reports by contrast, that Talabani's group, in part because of what Gunter suggests is its "socialist" orientation, has cooperated or taken sides with Iraq.[150] Moreover, Aykan reports that within the context of geostrategic struggles between Turkey, Syria, and Iran, the PUK has also received support from Iran and Syria.[151] Notwithstanding that, insofar as those alignments are not etched in stone it is difficult to describe time-honored, long-standing, clear-cut examples of alliances.[152]

The Kurdish People's Democracy Party, otherwise known as HADEP, committed one recorded terrorist assault of vandalism against business establishments between 1994 and 1999 that revolved around the central idea of political support for the Kurdistan Workers' Party (PKK).[153] HADEP was fashioned in May 1994, and is described by Gürbey as a "pro-Kurdish" political party that traces an arc to its immediate antecedent party, known as the Democratic Party (DP).[154] In turn, the DP was itself a short-lived political party that was crafted in 1992 and broken down by Turkish authorities, namely the Constitutional Court, in 1994, in large part precisely because of allegations that a set of interconnections existed between the DP and the PKK.[155]

The Democratic Party, the parent organization of HADEP, traces a curve to the People's Labor Party or HEP that was fashioned in 1990 and broken down in 1993 by the Constitutional Court.[156] To be sure, all three of those Kurdish-oriented political parties have been shackled by effective and sustained government harassment that in some instances could be construed as state terrorism, and those actions have included, but are not limited to, numerous arrests of high-ranking members.[157] In the 1995 national elections HADEP did not receive sufficient numbers of votes to pass the 10 percent lower limit needed to claim representation in Turkey's parliament.[158]

There is one nonindigenous terrorist group that is found to operate within the system of Turkish terrorism during the 1994-99 period. The November 17 Revolutionary Organization, otherwise known as Epanastatiki Organosi 17 Novemvr or Epamastikos Laikos Ayonas, is a Greek "Marxist-Leninist" terrorist group that first appeared in 1975 over the political landscape.[159] The November 17 group has devoted almost singular attention to a protracted struggle against the West both in Greece and elsewhere. At the heart of the matter, as some scripted accounts suggest, is a political struggle against perceived Western imperialism in the Mediterranean and Middle East areas and Western, especially U.S., influence at those geographical sites. Accordingly, terrorist assaults against government targets such as policemen and government officials that symbolize traditional pro-Western regimes, oftentimes carried out with a .45 caliber handgun, have been the special, almost singular focus of November 17 terrorist tacticians.[160]

The one terrorist assault chronicled for the November 17 group between 1994 and 1999 happened in Athens, Greece, in July 1994 when a Turkish government official was assassinated. Mickolus and Simmons's compilation and one scripted account report that November 17 has targeted Turkish interests precisely because of the reason that the Ecevit government spearheaded the Turkish invasion of Cyprus in 1974 and set up the Turkish Republic of Northern Cyprus (TRNC).[161] While available data about November 17 Organization chieftains and political frameworks are sketchy, a United States Department of State publication scripted in 1989 estimates the size of November 17 to be very small, with activists that range from some twenty to twenty-five persons.[162] Accordingly, November 17 is coded as an ideo-ethnocentric terrorist group that is "very small" in size.

Some General Observations about Turkish Terrorism

Relative Frequencies and Percentages of Turkish Terrorist Assaults by Year

The data for Turkish terrorist assaults consist of 192 discrete events, the majority of which are domestic terrorist assaults. As in the case studies of Algerian and Egyptian terrorism that come before, the time period under consideration are the years 1994 through 1999. When relative frequency statistics for Turkish terrorist assaults are generated according to year of event, it is evident that Turkish terrorism exhibits the same kind of cyclical ebbs and flows that characterize corresponding breakdowns of data for Algerian and Egyptian terrorism. In the case of Turkish terrorism, peak years are 1994, 1995, and 1999, as compared to its trough years of 1996, 1997, and 1998. Interestingly enough, Algerian, Egyptian, and Turkish terrorism all share the peak years 1994 and 1995 while variation occurs across Middle East terrorism systems for trough years.[163]

In the case of peak years for Turkish terrorism, the years 1994 and 1995 experienced the greatest amount and frequency of Turkish terrorism with 49 out of 181 events or 27.1 percent in 1994, and 48 out of 181 act or 26.5 percent in 1995. The third highest amount of Turkish terrorism happened in 1999, with 45 out of 181 incidents or 24.9 percent of the total. In the case of trough years, 1997 exhibited the least amount of Turkish terrorism with only 8 out of 181 acts or a paltry 4.4 percent of the total. The year with the second lowest amount of Turkish terrorism is 1996, with 21 out of 181 acts or 11.6 percent of the total (see figure 5.1)

Frequencies

Statistics

Year of Event

N	Valid	181
	Missing	11

Year of Event

		Frequency	Percent	Valid percent	Cumulative percent
Valid	1994	49	25.5	27.1	27.1
	1995	48	25.0	26.5	53.6
	1996	21	10.9	11.6	65.2
	1997	8	4.2	4.4	69.6
	1998	10	5.2	5.5	75.1
	1999	45	23.4	24.9	100.0
	Total	181	94.3	100.0	
Missing	system	11	5.7		
Total		192	100.0		

Year of Event

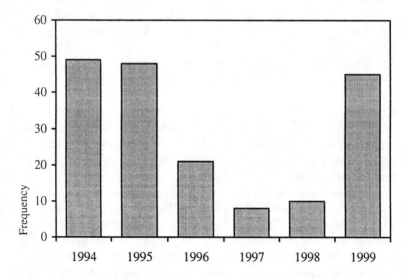

Figure 5.1: Relative Frequency of Turkish Terrorist Attacks by Year, 1994-1999

Terrorist Assaults by Group-Type, Terrorist Group, and Location

What seems significant here is that political terrorism in Turkey, namely terrorist assaults related to the Turkish political and historical legacy that oftentimes revolve around ethnic or religious fissures and conflict in society, is liberally peppered with an array of terrorist groups that comprise several Middle East terrorist group-types.[164] Perhaps the single most dominant reason that is important is precisely because of the reason those data are able to provide empirical evidence to test the underlying theory that drives this study and to help make some comparisons to the findings in my prior work.[165]

A breakdown of Turkish terrorist assaults by terrorist group-type reveals that the largest amount of Turkish terrorism that happened between 1994 and 1999, a full 50.0 percent in fact, was undertaken by ideo-ethnocentric charismatic groups, with 96 out of 192 acts. Unclaimed Turkish terrorist assaults ranked second in terms of frequency and percentage, with 38 out of 192 terrorist assaults or 19.8 percent of the total. In third place are ideo-ethnocentric terrorist groups that carried out 16 out of 192 incidents that make up 8.3 percent of the total. In turn, Turkish theocentric groups ranked fourth with 13 out of 192 terrorist assaults or 6.8 percent, while ethnocentric "proto-groups," that usually consist of relatively large numbers of violent protestors with looser ties to one another, ranked a very close fifth with 12 out of 192 terrorist assault or 6.3 percent of the total. Lastly, there are two acts of identifiable "lone assailant" terrorism recorded for the foregoing time period, one a terrorist assault carried out against the newspaper offices of the nonreligious periodical *Hurryet* on 14 May 1997, and the other a terrorist assault where a Kurdish activist commandeered a Turkish Airlines aircraft on 30 October 1998 (see figure 5.2)[166]

When the data on Turkish terrorism are broken down by terrorist group, it is observed that the Kurdistan Workers' Party (PKK) was the most prolific Turkish terrorist group for the 1994 through 1999 period, carrying out a recorded 89 out of 182 terrorist assaults that comprised nearly a full one-half of all Turkish terrorist acts with 48.9 percent of the total. That first-place ranking in terms of relative percentage outstrips the second place ranking of unclaimed terrorist acts, with 20.3 percent or 37 out of 182 acts, by well over a two-to-one margin (see figure 5.3).

Uncompleted acts, by contrast, comprised a little under 8.0 percent of the total, at 7.8 percent or 15 out of 192 acts, but that rate for uncompleted acts was quite high when compared to the uncompleted act rate for Egyptian terrorism at 6.3 percent and the miniscule rate of .6 percent for uncompleted Algerian terrorist assaults. (See figure 5.2.) At a substantive level, insofar as several distinct but interpenetrating explanatory factors like levels of government control, relatively low in the case of Algeria, levels of counterterrorism

Frequencies

Statistics

Category of Group

N	Valid	192
	Missing	0

Category of Group

		Frequency	Percent	Valid percent	Cumulative percent
Valid	Ideo-ethnocentric charismatic	96	50.0	50.0	50.0
	Uncompleted acts	15	7.8	7.8	57.8
	Unclaimed acts	38	19.8	19.8	77.6
	Theocentric	13	6.8	6.8	84.4
	Ethnocentric	12	6.3	6.3	90.6
	Ideo-ethnocentric	16	8.3	8.3	99.0
	Lone assailant	2	1.0	1.0	100.0
	Total	192	100.0	100.0	

Category of Group

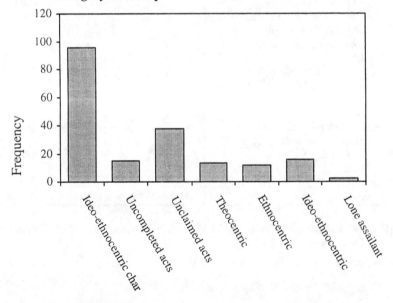

Figure 5.2: Relative Frequency of Turkish Terrorist Attacks by Group-Type, 1994-1999

Frequencies

Statistics

Name of Group

N	Valid	182
	Missing	10

Name of Group

		Frequency	Percent	Valid percent	Cumulative percent
Valid	Uncompleted	16	8.3	8.8	8.8
	Unclaimed	37	19.3	20.3	29.1
	Lone assailant	2	1.0	1.1	30.2
	PKK (Kurdistan Workers Party)	89	46.4	48.9	79.1
	ERNK (Nat. Front for the Liberation of Kurdistan)	5	2.6	2.7	81.9
	Dev-Sol (Revolutionary Left)	5	2.6	2.7	84.6
	Islamic Front of Great Eastern Raiders (IBDA-C)	5	2.6	2.7	87.4
	Hezbollah/Turkey	6	3.1	3.3	90.7
	Anatolian Federal Islamic State (AFID)	1	.5	.5	91.2
	TKP/MC Konferans	4	2.1	2.2	93.4
	Metropolitan Revenge Brigade	2	1.0	1.1	94.5
	Revolutionary People's Forces	2	1.0	1.1	95.6
	HADEP	2	1.0	1.1	96.7
	TIKKO	1	.5	.5	97.3
	Kourken Yans'kian (Armenian)	1	.5	.5	97.8
	Organization for Solidarity with Chechen Resistance Fighters	1	.5	.5	98.4
	November 17	1	.5	.5	98.9
	Kurdish Patriotic Union	1	.5	.5	99.5
	Independent Work Group (Turkey)	1	.5	.5	100.0
	Total	182	94.8	100.0	
Missing	system	10	5.2		
Total		192	100.0		

Figure 5.3: Relative Frequency of Turkish Terrorist Attacks by Terrorist Group, 1994-1999

Name of Group

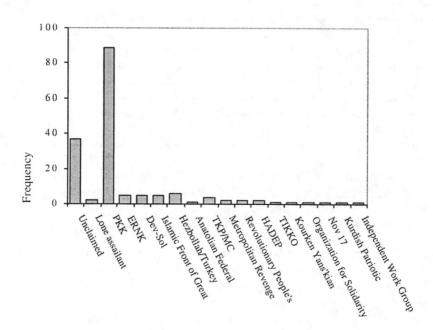

proficiency, seemingly higher for Egypt, Turkey, and Western Europe, and in the narrower sense, geographical site (i.e., urban/rural venues, actual terrain texture) may help to account for the foregoing variations in findings about uncompleted terrorist assaults, those results, by extrapolation, inform us about the underlying theme that location seems to be an important explanatory variable for counterterrorism outcomes as well a terrorist assault actions.[167]

In turn, the remainder of Turkish terrorist assaults were committed by an array of terrorist groups and are outlier or extreme outlier cases, several standard deviations from the mean number of Turkish terrorist assaults committed by the PKK and anonymous groups or non-group actors. That total comprises 20.4 percent of Turkish terrorism recorded, virtually the same amount as all unclaimed acts.[168] If increased attention is focused on those outlier cases, it is apparent that the highest number of incidents, 6 out of 182 events or 3.3 percent, were carried out by Hezbollah/Turkey, followed by the National Front for Liberation of Kurdistan (ERNK) that is an appendage of PKK with 5 out of 182 assaults or 2.7 percent, Dev-Sol otherwise known as the Revolutionary Left with 5 out of 182 assaults or 2.7 percent, the Islamic Front of Great Eastern Raiders (IBDA-C) with 5 out of 182 assaults or 2.7 percent, and the leftist group TKP/MC Konferans with 4 out of 182 assaults or 2.2. percent.

Other extreme outlier cases include terrorist assaults perpetrated by the Metropolitan Revolutionary Brigade with 2 out of 182 assaults or 1.1 percent; the Revolutionary People's Forces with 2 out of 182 acts or 1.1 percent; HADEP, which is actually a Kurdish-based political party, with 2 out of 182 acts or 1.1 percent; TIKKO with 1 out of 182 acts or .5 percent; Kourken Yans'kian with 1 out of 182 acts or .5 percent; the Organization for Solidarity with Chechen Resistance Fighters with 1 out of 182 acts or .5 percent; the Greek terrorist group November 17 with 1 out of 182 acts or .5 percent; the Kurdish Patriotic Union (PUK) with 1 out of 182 acts or .5 percent; the Anatolian Federal Islamic State (AFID) with 1 out of 182 acts or .5 percent; and the Independent Work Group, that is perhaps a "front-group" or "proto-group," with 1 out of 182 acts or .5 percent (see figure 5.3). It ought to be noted the only terrorist assault related to the Armenian struggle against Turkey that is recorded for the 1994 through 1999 period was carried out by Kourken Yans'kian.[169]

Analysis that breaks down data on Turkish terrorist assaults by location shows the single most predominant venue for Turkish terrorism is Turkey itself, where 139 out of 192 acts or 72.4 percent of the total happened. In Western Europe, a location category comprised of Britain, France, Germany, Belgium, Switzerland, Austria, the Netherlands, and Greece, 40 out of 192 terrorist assaults took place that make up 20.8 percent of the total. The third highest amount of Turkish terrorism by location with 7 out of 192 acts or 3.6 percent of the total happened in other Middle East states. Middle East states that make up that category include Iraq, Lebanon, and Syria. Terrorist assaults that happened in other locales ranked fourth, with 6 out of 192 terrorist incidents or 3.1 percent of the total. What seems significant here is Turkish terrorism, that remains in very large part domestic in nature, takes place in areas outside of Turkey 27.5 percent of the time. In comparison, 5.5 percent of Algerian terrorism happens in Europe, and 2.6 percent of Algerian terrorism happens in other or unknown locales. In a similar vein, Egyptian terrorism seeps into areas outside of Egypt 21.0 percent of the time.

For Turkish terrorism, the rate of terrorist assaults outside of Turkey comprises 27.5 percent of the total and that figure is certainly consistent with the notion that internecine fighting between Turks and Kurds is a significant problem in Europe in general and Germany in particular. At the same time it is incumbent upon me to mention that in the case of the 25 unclaimed terrorist assaults chronicled in Germany between 1994 and 1999, it is possible some of those acts might have been neo-Nazi terrorist assaults or assaults carried out by other German ultra-nationalists against non-German persons and property. There are no chronicled acts of Turkish terrorism in the United States for the time period under consideration, although it is commonplace to note that acts of Armenian terrorism have been carried out in the United States in cities like Boston and Los Angeles.[170]

In summation, while Turkish terrorism remains largely confined to Turkey itself, the aggregate rate of terrorist assaults outside Turkey is noticeably higher at 27.5 percent, or 53 out of 192 acts, than the aggregate rate for Algerian terrorism at 8.1 percent, the Egyptian rate of 21.0 percent, and the rate for Israeli-Palestinian-Arab terrorism that happens outside of Israel, the Occupied Territories, and the jurisdiction of the PNA, at 20.3 percent. At the same time, a comparison of findings reveals that, at 7.2 percent or 45 out 623 acts, Israeli-Palestinian-Arab terrorism has the highest percentage of terrorist assaults that happened in "other" locations outside of articulated location categories (see figure 5.4).

Terrorism Assault Attributes: Fatalities, Injuries, Property Damage, Target Preference

A breakdown of the data into ordinal categories of death-free terrorist assaults, terrorist assaults responsible for one through fifty deaths, and terrorist assaults that killed fifty-one through one hundred persons, reveals a pattern of death rates for Turkish terrorism that is consistent with the death rates found in the cases of Egyptian and Algerian terrorism analyzed in this work, and, in the broader sense, with the findings of my prior work.[171] In the case of Turkish terrorism from 1994 to 1999, a full 72.6 percent of all terrorist assaults or 135 out of 186 events resulted in no deaths. In turn, 50 out of 186 assaults that comprise 26.9 percent of the total resulted in the deaths of between one and fifty persons.

There is only one terrorist assault recorded for the 1994 to 1999 period that caused the deaths of over fifty persons, and that event was a car bomb explosion in February 1999 in the Kurdish-run Iraqi town of Zakho.[172] What seems significant here is that in comparison to the percentage rate of Algerian terrorist assaults that claimed the lives of over fifty persons, at 3.6 percent, or 12 out of 338 acts, the rate for Turkish terrorist assaults of that magnitude is exceedingly small, at 1 out of 186 acts or .5 percent of the total. In comparison, there are no acts of Egyptian terrorism recorded for this time period that killed over fifty persons (see figure 5.5).

Frequencies

Statistics

Locale

N	Valid	192
	Missing	0

Locale

		Frequency	Percent	Valid percent	Cumulative percent
Valid	Europe	40	20.8	20.8	20.8
	Other	6	3.1	3.1	24.0
	Other Middle East	7	3.6	3.6	27.6
	Turkey	139	72.4	72.4	100.0
	Total	192	100.0	100.0	

Locale

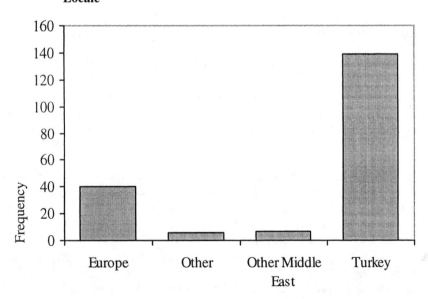

Figure 5.4: Relative Frequency of Turkish Terrorism by Location, 1994-1999

Frequencies

Statistics

Event Deaths

N	Valid	186
	Missing	6

Event Deaths

		Frequency	Percent	Valid percent	Cumulative percent
Valid	0	135	70.3	72.6	72.6
	1	50	26.0	26.9	99.5
	54	1	.5	.5	100.0
	Total	186	96.9	100.0	
Missing	system	6	3.1		
Total		192	100.0		

Event Deaths

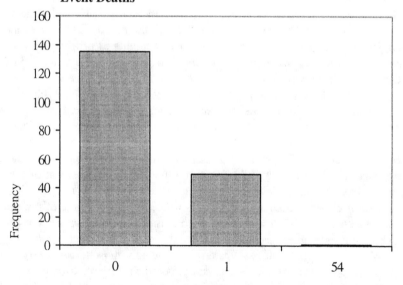

Figure 5.5: Relative Frequency of Numbers of Dead in Turkish Terrorist Incidents, 1994-1999   (0=0; 1=1 through 50)

In the case of injury rates for Turkish terrorism, the data show similar if not identical patterns when compared to trends in Turkish terrorist assault death rates. A full 67.8 percent or 120 out of 177 Turkish acts were injury-free events. In turn, 31.6 percent of all Turkish terrorist assaults or 56 out of 177 acts caused injuries to between one and fifty persons. The one extreme outlier case that wounded eighty persons is the same car bomb terrorist assault in Zakho, Iraq, previously mentioned, that claimed the lives of fifty-four persons.[173] In the broader sense, those findings conform to earlier findings that a majority of terrorist events are characterized by relatively few deaths and injuries or none at all (see figure 5.6).

Turning to analysis of property damage caused by Turkish terrorism, relative frequency measures of property damage make it clear that most Turkish terrorism chronicled in this work is characterized by relatively little in the way of property damage or none at all. A full 56.7 percent or 72 out of 127 acts did not result in any property damage. A full 38.6 percent or 49 out of 127 Turkish terrorist assaults caused "slight" property damage, while 3 out of 127 terrorist assaults or 2.4 percent caused "moderate" property damage. Turkish terrorist assaults that resulted in "high" or "severe" levels of property damage are outlier cases that make up 3 out of 127 acts or 2.4 percent of the total. To be more specific, terrorist assaults that caused "high" levels of property damage accounts for only 1.6 percent or 2 out of 127 events, while Turkish terrorist assaults that caused "severe" damage were even more scarce with 1 out of 127 acts or a mere .8 percent of the total (see figure 5.7). In the broader sense, the findings that Turkish terrorism causes relatively small amounts of property damage are consistent with previous findings presented in this study and with findings in other works on terrorism.[174]

Analysis of Turkish terrorist assaults that isolate and identify assaults by target type indicate that some two-thirds at 66.1 percent, or 125 out of 189 terrorist assaults, involve civilian targets. In comparison, a little more than one-fourth at 27.5 percent, or 52 out of 189 acts were carried out against government targets. Terrorist assaults against infrastructure constituted the third largest target type category, with 9 out of 189 events or 4.8 percent of the total amount (see figure 5.8). That 4.8 percent infrastructure rate for Turkish terrorism is closer to the Algerian terrorism rate of 3.5 percent and is in sharper contrast to the Israeli-Palestinian-Arab infrastructure rate of 1.5 percent and the Egyptian infrastructure target rate that is nil.

With respect to "multiple-type targets," namely those terrorist targets that seem to blend together both civilian and government target attributes, there are 3 out of 189 recorded Turkish terrorist assaults against "government-civilian" terrorist targets that comprise only 1.6 percent of the total. That finding about terrorist assaults with "multiple-type targets" is consistent with the very low percentage rate of terrorist assaults with "multiple-type targets" found in the case of Algerian terrorism at 1.8 percent, and the absence of any multiple-type

Frequencies

Statistics

Event Injuries

N	Valid	177
	Missing	15

Event Injuries

		Frequency	Percent	Valid percent	Cumulative percent
Valid	0	120	62.5	67.8	67.8
	1	56	29.2	31.6	99.4
	80	1	.5	.6	100.0
	Total	177	92.2	100.0	
Missing	system	15	7.8		
Total		192	100.0		

Event Injuries

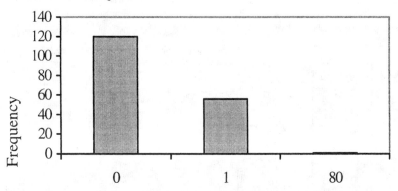

Figure 5.6: Relative Frequency of Numbers of Injured in Turkish Terrorist Incidents, 1994-1999   (0=0; 1=1 through 50)

Frequencies

Statistics

Property Damage

N	Valid	127
	Missing	65

Property Damage

		Frequency	Percent	Valid percent	Cumulative percent
Valid	None	72	37.5	56.7	56.7
	Slight	49	25.5	38.6	95.3
	Moderate	3	1.6	2.4	97.6
	High	2	1.0	1.6	99.2
	Severe	1	.5	.8	100.0
	Total	127	66.1	100.0	
Missing	system	65	33.9		
Total		192	100.0		

Property Damage

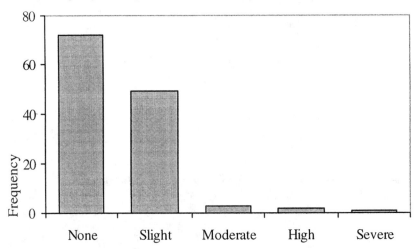

Figure 5.7: Levels of Property Damage Caused by Turkish Terrorist Attacks, 1994-1999

Frequencies

Statistics

Type of Target

N	Valid	189
	Missing	3

Type of Target

		Frequency	Percent	Valid percent	Cumulative percent
Valid	Government	52	27.1	27.5	27.5
	Infrastructure	9	4.7	4.8	32.3
	Civilian	125	65.1	66.1	98.4
	Govt.-Civilian	3	1.6	1.6	100.0
	Total	189	98.4	100.0	
Missing	system	3	1.6		
Total		192	100.0		

Type of Target

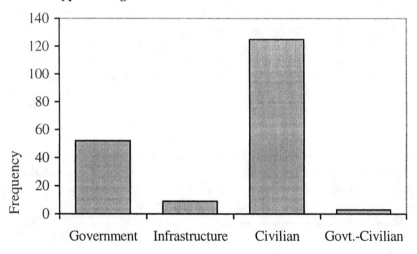

Figure 5.8: Relative Frequency of Turkish Terrorism Target-Types, 1994-1999

target terrorist assaults in the case of Egyptian terrorism.

The aforementioned analysis makes it possible to craft some broad-brush conclusions about the general contours of Turkish terrorism. From the start, it is apparent that trends found in Turkish terrorism conform to the cyclical patterns of ebbs and flows that are a hallmark of Algerian terrorism and Egyptian terrorism. Alternatively, perhaps the single most fundamental difference between Turkish terrorism and the foregoing is that an array of different types of terrorist groups speckle the Turkish political landscape thereby in effect making it possible to test an array of theoretical propositions for empirical validity. Another standout finding concerns the high amount of Turkish ideo-ethnocentric charismatic terrorist activity that undoubtedly mirrors the effective and sustained struggle against the Turkish government waged by the Kurdistan Workers' Party.

Analysis of Turkish terrorism by location also reveals that while Turkish terrorism remains largely contained inside Turkey, there is significant seepage into parts of Western Europe that is broader in scope than the seepage found in the cases of Algerian and Egyptian terrorism. The findings reveal that 20.8 percent or 40 out of 192 acts of Turkish terrorism happened in Western Europe, 3.6 percent or 7 out of 192 acts happened in other Middle East states, and 3.1 percent or 6 out of 192 events happened in other locations. In sum, over one-quarter of all Turkish terrorist events happened outside of Turkey.

The findings inform us that Turkish "insurgent" terrorist assaults, as with Algerian and Egyptian terrorist assaults, caused relatively little in the way of numbers of deaths, injuries, and amounts of property damage when compared to other forms of ethnic conflict such as conventional war.[175] To be more specific, in the case of Turkish terrorism there is only one act of terrorism that killed and wounded more than fifty persons, and that assault happened in the Iraqi town of Zakho.[176] In the broader sense, that finding mirrors the results of other works on terrorism with respect to the relatively infrequent amount of terrorism that causes comparatively high rates of deaths and injuries.[177]

In the case of target selection, the findings on Turkish terrorism reveal that civilian targets are the target of choice for terrorist planners who undertake Turkish terrorist assaults. Illustrative of the problem faced by potential civilian targets is that Turkish terrorist groups and non-group actors are found to favor civilian targets over government targets by about a 2.4:1 ratio for the 1994 to 1999 period. Seen from the vantage of comparative analysis, that 2.4:1 ratio in favor of civilian targets is higher than the relative parity at 1:.81 in favor of civilian targets for Egyptian terrorism, but pales in comparison to the nearly 8:1 ratio in favor of civilian targets that is a hallmark of Algerian terrorism. Another standout finding is that Turkish terrorism has a larger component of infra-structure terrorist assaults than in the case of Algerian terrorism, Egyptian terrorism, or Israeli-Palestinian-Arab terrorism. In the broader sense, those findings for Turkish terrorism about the preference for civilian targets are not only consistent with other findings in this work and results from my prior work, but also square with the findings of other works on terrorism.[178]

Variable Analysis

Political Ideology and Target Type, Numbers of Injuries

In this section of the analysis, several theoretical propositions about the relationship between the political ideology of Turkish terrorist groups and the dependent variable "target" will be tested for validity. Those theoretical propositions presuppose and derive from the works of several widely recognized authorities on terrorism and my own research findings found in my prior work.[179] The sources and origins that those theoretical propositions presuppose and derive from are referenced in chapter 2. The following hypotheses about Turkish terrorist group target choice and political ideology are presented for examination:

Hypothesis One: Ideo-ethnocentric terrorist groups will attack government targets (i.e., courthouses, military administration facilities, military recruitment centers, and non-combatant troops such as UN peacekeepers) more often than ethnocentric and theocentric groups.

Hypothesis Two: Ethnocentric terrorist groups will attack civilian targets more often than theocentric terrorist groups.

The analysis of the relationship between "target" and "political ideology" suggests a statistically significant association exists between those two variables. A Pearson Chi Square value of 14.791 with a "p-value" of .005 at four degrees of freedom (4 d.f.) makes it possible to reject the null hypothesis of no relationship between the variables "target" and "political ideology" at the .05 level of confidence. In other words, if the null hypothesis of no relation between the variables is not rejected, there is a 95 percent chance of making a "Type II" error, namely the failure to reject the null hypothesis of no relation when it ought to be rejected. It needs to be mentioned that three cells have expected frequencies less than five that corresponds to 30.0 percent having an expected count less than five. Nonetheless, the Chi Square statistic and "p-value" suggest that it would be imprudent to fail to reject the null hypothesis insofar as the possibility of a "Type II" error would be strong.

With respect to the strength of the relationship between the variables "target" and "political ideology," a Cramer's V score of .299 and a "Phi" score of .299, both with a significance score of .005, suggests a weak relationship between the variables. In addition, a Goodman and Kruskal *tau* score of .090 with a significance score of .005 when "target" is the dependent variable also indicates a weak relationship between those variables. (See table 5.1).

Bivariate analysis of the data reveals a data distribution where ethnocentric terrorist groups have the highest percentage of terrorist assaults against government targets, with 58.3 percent or seven out of twelve acts (see table 5.2). Ideo-ethnocentric terrorist organizations had the second highest rate with 43.8 percent of terrorist assaults or seven out of sixteen acts aimed at government targets. In turn, 21.1 percent or eight out of thirty-eight unclaimed or unattributable acts were directed against government targets. Turkish theocentric terrorist groups, by contrast, had the lowest rate of terrorist assaults directed against government targets with two out of thirteen acts or a mere 15.4 percent, and that figure is consistent with the central conception about theocentric groups that I first developed in my prior work.[180] The underlying theme of that theoretical proposition is that theocentric terrorist groups will place less of a premium on government targets than will ideo-ethnocentric terrorist groups that are more "structuralist" in nature precisely because those groups view the struggle against the enemy in a "hybrid" manner that focuses on both an individual's declared loyalties and belief system and a "worldview" that perceives the world as rent apart by fundamental religious fissures between an Islamic East and a Christian West.[181]

Accordingly, Hypothesis One about Turkish terrorism is rejected. But further analysis about the nature of ethnocentric terrorist groups reveals the findings are much closer to the mark set by Hypothesis One. A second place finish for ideo-ethnocentric terrorist groups is, in my judgment, a result consistent with the general idea behind that foregoing hypothesis precisely because of the reason that most ethnocentric groups with terrorist assaults recorded in the data base are really "proto-groups" of Kurdish individuals that coalesced with the specific and immediate aim of protest against European governments and Israel for the alleged participation of those governments in the capture in Kenya of Abdullah Öcalan, the charismatic leader of the Kurdistan Workers' Party.[182] If the analysis factors that dimension into an appraisal of the high rate of ethnocentric government targets, it seems clear that a specific type of terrorist action (i.e., mobs, protests against government embassies) may have skewed the results in favor of the ethnocentric government target rate.

The cross-tabulation table analysis also reveals that, in the case of Turkish terrorism, theocentric terrorist groups focused attention on civilian targets 86.4 percent of the time or in eleven out of thirteen events. In contrast, 25.0 percent of ethnocentric terrorist assaults or three out of twelve events were aimed at civilian targets. Plainly, those findings about the rate of civilian target terrorist assaults for theocentric and ethnocentric groups are not the expected findings and, as a result, Hypothesis Two is rejected.

At the same time, with respect to data interpretation, one factor at work

Table 5.1: Relative Frequency of Turkish Terrorist Targets by Group-Type, 1994-1999   (summary statistics)

Crosstabs

Case Processing Summary

	Cases					
	Valid		Missing		Total	
	N	Percent	*N*	Percent	*N*	Percent
Type of target * category of group	165	85.9%	27	14.1%	192	100.0%

Type of Target * Category of Group Cross-Tabulation

Type of target		Category of group			
		Ideo-ethnocentric charismatic	Unclaimed acts	Theo centric	Ethno centric
Govern-ment	Count	19	8	2	7
	% within type of target	44.2%	18.6%	4.7%	16.3%
	% within category of group	21.3%	21.6%	15.4%	70.0%
	% of total	11.5%	4.8%	1.2%	4.2%
Civilian	Count	70	29	11	3
	% within type of target	57.4%	23.8%	9.0%	2.5%
	% within category of group	78.7%	78.4%	84.6%	30.0%
	% of total	42.4%	17.6%	6.7%	1.8%
Total	Count	89	37	13	10
	% within type of target	53.9%	22.4%	7.9%	6.1%
	% within category of group	100.0%	100.0%	100.0%	100.0%
	% of total	53.9%	22.4%	7.9%	6.1%

Table 5.1 - *continued*

Type of Target * Category of Group Cross-Tabulation

Type of target		Category Ideo-ethnocentric	Total
Govern-ment	Count	7	43
	% within type of target	16.3%	100.0%
	% within category of group	43.8%	26.1%
	% of total	4.2	26.1%
Civilian	Count	9	122
	% within type of target	7.4%	100.0%
	% within category of group	56.3%	73.9%
	% of total	5.5%	73.9%
Total	Count	16	165
	% within type of target	9.7%	100.0%
	% within category of group	100.0%	100.0%
	% of total	9.7%	100.0%

Chi Square Tests

	Value	df	Asymp. sig. (2-sided)
Pearson Chi Square	14.791[a]	4	.005
Likelihood Ratio	13.075	4	.011
Linear-by-Linear Association	5.407	1	.020
N of valid cases	165		

a. 3 cells (30.0%) have expected count less than 5. The minimum expected count is 2.61.

Directional Measures

			Value	Asymp. std. error[a]	Approx. T[b]	Approx. sig.
Nominal by nominal	Lambda	Symmetric	.034	.026	1.271	.204
		Type of target dependent	.093	.070	1.271	.204
		Category of group dependent	.000	.000	.[c]	.[c]
	Goodman and Kruskal tau	Type of target dependent	.090	.048		.005[d]
		Category of group dependent	.015	.011		.046[d]

a. Not assuming the null hypothesis.
b. Using the asymptotic standard error assuming the null hypothesis.
c. Cannot be computed because the asymptotic standard error equals zero.
d. Based on chi square approximation.

here to account for those findings may be the very nature of the Turkish ethnocentric "proto-groups" in the 1994 through 1999 period. As previously mentioned, it is possible those results may be skewed to the degree that they are precisely because of the unusual nature of the Turkish ethnocentric "proto-groups" under consideration. In essence, those ethnocentric "proto-groups" may have constituted a one-shot condition of very emotionally laden and widespread ethnocentric "proto-group" riots against government targets that were elicited precisely because of the capture of PKK leader Abdullah Öcalan. There is only one ethnocentric terrorist assault recorded with interconnections to the Armenian struggle for the 1994-99 period, thereby in effect providing some indication of the influence of the time period under consideration for research findings.[183]

As previously mentioned in chapter 3 on Algerian terrorism, I draw on the writings of several authorities on terrorism to suggest that anonymous terrorist assaults ought to involve civilian targets more often than government targets.[184] At a functional level, that notion revolves around the central idea that anonymous terrorism serves to generate and sustain political pressure for structural political or economic change, thereby in effect helping to elicit responses from government to the political demands and aspirations of terrorist group chieftains. The following hypothesis about anonymous terrorism captures the essence of that notion:

Hypothesis Three: Anonymous terrorist assaults will involve civilian targets more frequently than theocentric terrorist assaults.

The cross-tabulation table analysis informs us that theocentric terrorist groups have the highest rate of civilian target attacks with 11 out of 13 incidents

Table 5.1 - *continued*

Symmetric Measures

		Value	Approx. sig.
Nominal by nominal	Phi	.299	.005
	Cramer's V	.299	.005
N of valid cases		165	

a. Not assuming the null hypothesis.
b. Using the asymptotic standard error assuming the null hypothesis.

Table 5.2: Relative Frequency of Turkish Terrorist Targets by Group-Type, 1994-1999

Category of Group * Type of Target Cross-Tabulation

Category of group		Type of target		
		Government	Infrastructure	Civilian
Ideo-ethnocentric charismatic	Count	19	4	70
	% within category of group	19.8%	4.2%	72.9%
	% within type of target	36.5%	44.4%	56.0%
	% of total	10.1%	2.1%	37.0%
Uncompleted acts	Count	9		3
	% within category of group	75.0%		25.0%
	% within type of target	17.3%		2.4%
	% of total	4.8%		1.6%
Unclaimed acts	Count	8	3	27
	% within category of group	21.1%	7.9%	71.1%
	% within type of target	15.4%	33.3%	21.6%
	% of total	4.2%	1.6%	14.3%
Theocentric	Count	2		11
	% within category of group	15.4%		84.6%
	% within type of target	3.8%		8.8%
	% of total	1.1%		5.8%
Ethnocentric	Count	7	2	3
	% within category of group	58.3%	16.7%	25.0%
	% within type of target	13.5%	22.2%	2.4%
	% of total	3.7%	1.1%	1.6%
Ideo-ethnocentric	Count	7		9
	% within category of group	43.8%		56.3%
	% within type of target	13.5%		7.2%
	% of total	3.7%		4.8%
Lone assailant	Count			2
	% within category of group			100.0%
	% within type of target			1.6%
	% of total			1.1%
Total	Count	52	9	125
	% within category of group	27.5%	4.8%	66.1%
	% within type of target	100.0%	100.0%	100.0%
	% of total	27.5%	4.8%	66.1%

Table 5.2 - *continued*

Category of Group * Type of Target Cross-Tabulation

Category of group		Type of target	
		Govt.-Civilian	Total
Ideo-ethnocentric charismatic	Count	3	96
	% within category of group	3.1%	100.0%
	% within type of target	100.0%	50.8%
	% of total	1.6%	50.8%
Uncompleted acts	Count		12
	% within category of group		100.0%
	% within type of target		6.3%
	% of total		6.3%
Unclaimed acts	Count		38
	% within category of group		100.0%
	% within type of target		20.1%
	% of total		20.1%
Theocentric	Count		13
	% within category of group		100.0%
	% within type of target		6.9%
	% of total		6.9%
Ethnocentric	Count		12
	% within category of group		100.0%
	% within type of target		6.3%
	% of total		6.3%
Ideo-ethnocentric	Count		16
	% within category of group		100.0%
	% within type of target		8.5%
	% of total		8.5%
Lone assailant	Count		2
	% within category of group		100.0%
	% within type of target		1.1%
	% of total		1.1%
Total	Count	3	189
	% within category of group	1.6%	100.0%
	% within type of target	100.0%	100.0%
	% of total	1.6%	100.0%

or 84.6 percent of all theocentric terrorist assaults. In second place, Turkish ideo-ethnocentric charismatic terrorist assaults were directed against civilian targets 72.9 percent of the time with 70 out of 96 events. Ranking third, right on the heels of the aforementioned, anonymous Turkish terrorism assaults targeted civilian targets in 71.1 percent of terrorist assaults or in 27 out of 38 events. Ranking fourth, 56.3 percent of ideo-ethnocentric terrorist assaults, or nine out of 16 events, were directed against civilian targets, as compared with ethnocentric terrorist assaults that ranked fifth, with only 25.0 percent or 3 out of 12 ethnocentric terrorist assaults that focused singular attention on civilian targets (see table 5.2).

Ideo-ethnocentric charismatic groups are found to be the only type of terrorist group to include "multiple-type targets" in their repertoire, with 3 out of 96 events or 3.1 percent of the total. The 2 out of 189 terrorist assaults committed by declared "lone assailants" that comprise 1.1 percent of the total were both directed at civilian targets (see table 5.2). Plainly, the foregoing results are not the expected findings and Hypothesis Three is rejected.

One important dimension of analysis of Turkish terrorism and, in the narrower sense, the process of target selection concerns the fundamental question of whether or not there is a special emphasis placed against foreign nationals for "discriminate" Turkish terrorist assaults. By "discriminate" terrorist assaults I mean terrorist assaults that are not random with respect to target selection, such as the strangulation of a particular person rather than a roadside bomb explosion detonated by a time devise attached to the explosive charge. In the case of Algerian terrorism, and especially in the case of Egyptian terrorism, it is found that special emphasis has been placed with respect to the targeting of foreign nationals as a component in the broader struggle waged by

Table 5.2 - *continued*

Case Processing Summary

	Cases					
	Valid		Missing		Total	
	N	Percent	*N*	Percent	*N*	Percent
Category of group * type of target	189	98.4%	3	1.6%	192	100.0%

Islamic fundamentalists against the West and governments perceived to be Western outposts or, at the very least, heavily dependent on Western economic and military assistance.

In the cases of Algerian and Egyptian terrorism, the generally recognizable trends revealed by the bivariate testing in favor of some emphasis against foreign nationals were not unexpected results. However, in the case of Turkish terrorism, the bivariate analysis makes it clear there is no statistically significant association between the dependent variable "target" and the independent variable "nationality of victim."[185] Put another way, it is found there is no statistically significant relationship with respect to the national or foreign composition of civilian and government targets for Turkish terrorism.

Political Ideology and Numbers of Injuries

Bivariate analysis of the relationship between "numbers of injuries" and "category of group" suggests a statistically significant association between number of injuries that result from Turkish terrorist assaults and whether or not terrorist assaults are carried out by ideo-ethnocentric charismatic terrorist groups, anonymous actors, or ideo-ethnocentric terrorist groups. A Pearson Chi Square statistic of 9.539 and a "p-value" of .008 at two degrees of freedom (2 d.f.) make it possible to reject the null hypothesis at the .05 level of confidence. In this test, it is found that no cells (0%) have an expected frequency of less than five.

In terms of measurement of the strength of that relationship, a Goodman and Kruskal's *tau* score of .067 with a significance score of .009 when "event injuries" is the dependent variable suggests a weak relationship between the dependent variable "event injuries" and the independent variable "category of group." In addition, a Cramer's V measure of .258 with a significance score of .008 and a "Phi" measure of .258 with a significance score of .008 also indicates a weak relationship between those variables (see table 5.3).

Earlier, in chapter 3 that provides treatment of Algerian terrorism, I put together the proposition about the role of anonymous terrorist assaults helping to introduce change and some flexibility into the political system by drawing on the works of Hoffman (1984), Shultz (1978), Lasswell (1978), and Pfaltzgraf (1986).[186] To test another dimension of that proposition with respect to Turkish terrorism, the following hypothesis is offered for examination:

Hypothesis Four: Anonymous terrorist assaults will result in a smaller percentage of injuries than terrorist assaults committed by theocentric terrorist groups.

Table 5.3: Relative Frequency of Numbers of Injured in Turkish Terrorist Incidents by Group-Type (0=0; 1=1 through 50) (summary statistics)

Case Processing Summary

	Cases					
	Valid		Missing		Total	
	N	Percent	N	Percent	N	Percent
Event injuries * category of group	143	74.5%	49	25.5%	192	100.0%

Event Injuries * Category of Group Cross-Tabulation

Event injuries		Category of group			Total
		Ideo-ethnocentric charmismatic	Unclaimed acts	Ideo-ethnocentric	
0	Count	59	16	13	88
	% within event injuries	67.0%	18.2%	14.8%	100.0%
	% within category of group	66.3%	42.1%	81.3%	61.5%
	% of total	41.3%	11.2%	9.1%	61.5%
1	Count	30	22	3	55
	% within event injuries	54.5%	40.0%	5.5%	100.0%
	% within category of group	33.7%	57.9%	18.8%	38.5%
	% of total	21.0%	15.4%	2.1%	38.5%
Total	Count	89	38	16	143
	% within event injuries	62.2%	26.6%	11.2%	100.0%
	% within category of group	100.0%	100.0%	100.0%	100.0%
	% of total	62.2%	26.6%	11.2%	100.0%

Chi Square Tests

	Value	df	Asymp. sig. (2-sided)
Pearson Chi Square	9.539[a]	2	.008
Likelihood Ratio	9.629	2	.008
Linear-by-Linear Association	.000	1	.995
N of valid cases	143		

a.   0 cells (0%) have expected count less than 5. The minimum expected count is 6.15.

The distribution of the data about terrorist assault injuries reveals that theocentric and ethnocentric terrorist groups have the highest percentage of injury-free terrorist assaults with 10 out of 10 events or 100.0 percent in the case of theocentric group type assaults, and 8 out of 8 events or 100.0 percent in the case of ethnocentric terrorist assaults. It is observed that ideo-ethnocentric terrorist assaults ranked second for injury-free terrorist assaults with 13 out of 16 events or 81.3 percent, as compared with 59 out of 89 ideo-ethnocentric charismatic terrorist assaults or 66.3 percent of all ideo-ethnocentric charismatic terrorist acts. (See table 5.4).

Table 5.3 - *continued*

Directional Measures

			Value	Asymp. std. error[a]	Approx. T[b]	Approx. sig.
Nominal by nominal	Lambda	Symmetric	.055	.055	.977	.329
		Event injuries dependent	.109	.106	.977	.329
		Category of group dependent	.000	.000	.[c]	.[c]
	Goodman and Kruskal tau	Event injuries dependent	.067	.041		.009[d]
		Category of group dependent	.032	.023		.010[d]

a.   Not assuming the null hypothesis.
b.   Using the asymptotic standard error assuming the null hypothesis.
c.   Cannot be computed because the asymptotic standard error equals zero.
d.   Based on chi square approximation.

Symmetric Measures

		Value	Approx. sig.
Nominal by nominal	Phi	.258	.008
	Cramer's V	.258	.008
N of valid cases		143	

a.   Not assuming the null hypothesis.
b.   Using the asymptotic standard error assuming the null hypothesis.

Table 5.4: Relative Frequency of Numbers of Injured in Turkish Terrorist Incidents by Group-Type, 1994-1999 (0=0; 1=1 through 50)

Crosstabs

Case Processing Summary

	Cases					
	Valid		Missing		Total	
	N	Percent	N	Percent	N	Percent
Category of group * event injuries	177	92.2%	15	7.8%	192	100.0%

Category of Group * Event Injuries Cross-Tabulation

Category of group		Event injuries			Total
		0	1	80	
Ideo-ethnocentric charismatic	Count	59	30		89
	% within category of group	66.3%	33.7%		100.0%
	% within event injuries	49.2%	53.6%		50.3%
	% of total	33.3%	16.9%		50.3%
Uncompleted acts	Count	14	1		15
	% within category of group	93.3%	6.7%		100.0%
	% within event injuries	11.7%	1.8%		8.5%
	% of total	7.9%	.6%		8.5%
Unclaimed acts	Count	16	20	1	37
	% within category of group	43.2%	54.1%	2.7%	100.0%
	% within event injuries	13.3%	35.7%	100.0%	20.9%
	% of total	9.0%	11.3%	.6%	20.9%
Theocentric	Count	10			10
	% within category of group	100.0%			100.0%
	% within event injuries	8.3%			5.6%
	% of total	5.6%			5.6%
Ethnocentric	Count	8			8
	% within category of group	100.0%			100.0%
	% within event injuries	6.7%			4.5%
	% of total	4.5%			4.5%
Ideo-ethnocentric	Count	13	3		16
	% within category of group	81.3%	18.8%		100.0%
	% within event injuries	10.8%	5.4%		9.0%
	% of total	7.3%	1.7%		9.0%
Lone assailant	Count		2		2
	% within category of group		100.0%		100.0%
	% within event injuries		3.6%		1.1%
	% of total		1.1%		1.1%
Total	Count	120	56	1	177
	% within category of group	67.8%	31.6%	.6%	100.0%
	% within event injuries	100.0%	100.0%	100.0%	100.0%
	% of total	67.8%	31.6%	.6%	100.0%

When terrorist assaults that caused injuries are considered, it is found that anonymous Turkish terrorist assaults have the second largest share of terrorist assaults that wounded between one and fifty persons with 54.1 percent or 20 out of 37 terrorist events. That falls behind the 100.0 percent rate or 2 out of 2 acts for declared "lone assailant" terrorist assaults that injured between one and fifty persons. Ranking third are the 33.7 percent of terrorist assaults or 30 out of 89 acts committed by ideo-ethnocentric charismatic terrorist groups that wounded between one and fifty persons. Actually, the only terrorist assault that resulted in injuries to over fifty persons was an anonymous terrorist assault. Plainly, those results make it is necessary to reject the validity of Hypothesis Four.

What is notable here is those results about anonymous Turkish terrorist assaults that caused injuries to between one and fifty persons are very similar to what is found for anonymous terrorist assaults in the Algerian context. In the case of Algerian terrorism, anonymous terrorist acts have, at 48.4 percent or 89 out of 184 acts, the highest rate of terrorist assaults that injured between one and fifty persons. Furthermore, in the case of Algerian terrorism 8 out of 184 anonymous acts were outlier observations, namely terrorist assaults that injured over fifty persons. Insofar as there is only 1 Turkish terrorist assault that is an outlier case, it is not possible to discuss or describe any empirical support for an anonymous terrorist assault injury "threshold" in place for most anonymous terrorist assaults that would be consistent with the central idea that anonymous terrorist assaults serve as political signal sending to government for terrorist groups or non-group actors. However, those findings about injury rates are consistent with findings about Algerian terrorism and, in the broader sense, the foregoing interpretation of results.

Terrorist Group Age, Terrorist Group Size, and Target Selection

The purpose of this section of the analysis is to examine whether or not a statistically significant association exists between the variable "target" and the explanatory variables terrorist "group age" and terrorist "group size." Bivariate analysis testing in both cases produced test results that are not significant, that indicate there is no statistically significant association between either "target" and terrorist "group age," or "target" and terrorist "group size." In the case of bivariate testing for "target" and "group age," a Pearson Chi Square value of 2.622 with a "p-value" of .270 at two degrees of freedom (2 d.f.) is produced. In the case of bivariate testing for "target" and "group size," a Pearson Chi Square value of .011 with a "p-value" of .917 at (1 d.f.) is produced.

The fundamental question boils down to whether those findings for "target" and "group age," and "target" and "group size" found to be not significant presuppose and derive from a strong correlation between the explanatory variables "age" and "size" or some other set of factors. In order to determine whether or not "group age" and "group size" are capturing similar dynamics, a bivariate correlations test is performed. Spearman's *rho* is used precisely because both "group age" and "group size" categories of data are ordinal in nature. The bivariate correlations test performed is a one-tailed test because the theoretical direction of the relationship between the variables is understood, namely, that when a terrorist group is younger it ought to be smaller in size whereas when a terrorist groups matures it ought to be larger in size (see table 5.5).

The findings of the bivariate correlations test between the explanatory variables terrorist group "age" and terrorist "group size" indicate there is no statistically significant correlation between those two variables at the .05 level

Table 5.5: Bivariate Correlations Test for Explanatory Variables Terrorist Group Size and Group Age

Correlations

Correlations

		Size of group	Age of group
Size of group	Pearson Correlation	1.000	.033
	Sig. (1-tailed)		.369
	N	105	105
Age of group	Pearson Correlation	.033	1.000
	Sig. (1-tailed)	.369	
	N	105	126

Nonparametric Correlations

Correlations

			Size of group	Age of group
Spearman's *rho*	Size of group	Correlation coefficient	1.000	.037
		Sig. (1-tailed)		.353
		N	105	105
	Age of group	Correlation coefficient	.037	1.000
		Sig. (1-tailed)	.353	.
		N	105	126

of confidence. The findings are not significant insofar as a correlation figure of .037 with a significance score of .353 is generated. As a result, it would be imprudent to accept the notion that "size" and "age" as explanatory variables essentially capture overlapping or the same dynamics with respect to influence on the type of terrorist target chosen. The absence of any statistically significant correlation between the variables "age" and "size" suggests those findings about the relationship between terrorist group "age" and "target," and terrorist group "size" and "target" that are found to be not significant presuppose and derive from the nature of the data.

One characteristic of those data is that there is not a great deal of variation found between the age of terrorist groups since most identifiable terrorist groups are older groups that in some cases chronicle their beginnings to the middle or late 1970s. In a similar vein, there is a large amount of identifiable terrorist assaults that is carried out by very large terrorist groups (i.e., the Kurdistan Workers Party) that involve civilian and government targets, while there are comparatively few such assaults for very small terrorist groups. The sketchy data about terrorist group size in general, and the amalgamated nature of data for more mid-sized terrorist groups, may contribute to a condition where summary statistics that are not significant are generated.

Conclusions

General Observations

Analysis of the data when relative frequencies are generated for year of event, group-type, numbers of dead, numbers of injured, target-type, and location makes it possible to discern the general outlines of Turkish terrorism at the end of the twentieth century. At the most basic level, it is clear that Turkish terrorism, as with Algerian and Egyptian terrorism, is characterized by a series of peaks and troughs thereby in effect comprising a cyclical pattern of terrorism with ebbs and flows.[187] From the start, what seems significant here is that the variety of terrorist groups active in the system of Turkish terrorism is sufficiently rich to evaluate the theory that drives this work within the context of empirical trends in the data on Turkish terrorism.

With respect to data distribution, one standout finding is the high amount of ideo-ethnocentric charismatic terrorist assaults, at 96 out of 192 events or a full 50.0 percent that are largely comprised of PKK terrorist incidents. Alternatively, there is a very low number of "lone operative" assaults, with 2 out of 192 events that comprise only 1.0 percent of the total. Seen from the vantage of case study comparisons, that 1.0 percent figure for "lone operative" assaults is virtually the same as the corresponding rate of "lone assailant" assaults in the case of Algerian terrorism at .9 percent, but nearly three times less than the rate for Egyptian terrorism at 2.8 percent of the total. At the same time, it is observed the rate of uncompleted assaults for Turkish terrorism is, at 7.8 percent, or 15 out of 192 acts, much higher than the rate of uncompleted terrorist assaults of 6.3 percent for Egyptian terrorism and far greater than the paltry .6 percent of uncompleted terrorist assaults chronicled in the case of Algerian terrorism.

With respect to terrorist target preference, planners of Turkish terrorism favor terrorist assaults against civilian targets over government targets by a ratio of about 2.4:1. In the case of Turkish terrorism that 2.4:1 ratio is substantially greater than the 1:.81 ratio found in the case of Egyptian terrorism. That 2.4:1 ratio in favor of civilian targets is much less than the nearly 4:1 ratio in favor of civilian target terrorist assaults found for Israeli-Palestinian-Arab terrorism, but it pales in comparison to the nearly 8:1 ratio in favor of civilian targets found in the case of Algerian terrorism. Plainly, civilian targets shoulder more than twice the burden as do government targets in terms of percentage rates, but are not burdened nearly to the same degree as Algerian civilian targets have been.

In terms of geographical site, the data show that 72.4 percent or 139 out of 192 acts of Turkish terrorism happened inside Turkey. Be that as it may, there is a more significant amount of Turkish terrorism seepage across national borders than found in the case studies of Algerian, Egyptian, and Israeli-Palestinian-Arab terrorism.[188] In the case of Western Europe, 40 out of 192 terrorist assaults happened, that comprise nearly one-quarter of the total amount. That figure is noticeably greater than the 4.2 percent or 6 out of 142 acts of Egyptian terrorism that happened at that locale, and the 5.5 percent of Algerian terrorism that happened in Western Europe. Turkish terrorist assaults that took place in "Other Middle Eastern states" account for 3.6 percent or 7 out of 192 acts. That rate is virtually the same as the rate for Egyptian terrorism, at 3.5 percent or 5 out of 142 acts, and is greater than the rate for Algerian terrorism where no terrorist assaults at "other Middle Eastern" state locations are found. A slightly different pattern holds true in the case of "other" locales, where 3.1 percent or 6 out of 192 acts of Turkish terrorism occurred as compared with the corresponding figures of 2.6 percent for Algerian terrorism, and a full 6.3 percent, or 9 out of 142 acts, in the case of Egyptian terrorism. If those data are aggregated, a full 27.5 percent or 53 out of 192 acts of Turkish terrorism happened outside of Turkey, by contrast to the 21.0 percent of Egyptian terrorism that happened outside of Egypt, the 20.3 percent of Israeli-Palestinian-Arab terrorism that happened outside of Israel, the Occupied Territories, and the jurisdiction of the PNA, and the 8.1 percent that happened outside of Algeria.

Still another set of diagnostics show that the physical devastation caused by Turkish terrorism remains relatively small, thereby in effect helping to reinforce the generally recognizable notion that the abject fear that terrorism evokes, especially sharp when civilian targets are involved, is what makes terrorism an instrument that can be used in effective and sustained ways. The findings reveal that only 50 out of 186 acts, or 26.9 percent of all Turkish terrorism terrorist assaults caused the deaths of between one and fifty persons, while 135 out of 186 acts or 72.6 percent, almost three-quarters of all events, did not result in any deaths. There is only one outlier event that happened, in the Iraqi town of Zakho where 54 persons were killed in a terrorist car bomb assault.[189]

Similar patterns hold true in the case of numbers of injured associated with Turkish terrorism. For example, only 31.6 percent of all Turkish terrorist assaults resulted in injuries to between one and fifty persons in comparison to the 67.8 percent of terrorist assaults, over two-thirds of the total, that caused no injuries. Again, the one outlier case is the same outlier where a bomb in an anonymous terrorist assault exploded in Zakho, Iraq, and injured 80 persons. The sample mean for "event deaths" is 1.36 with a standard deviation of 4.81. The sample mean for "event injuries" is 2.81 with a standard deviation of 7.70.[190]

The Role of Political Ideology

At a theoretical level, what seems significant here about the Turkish findings is the capacity of those results to test the theoretical conceptualizations that drive this study against empirical evidence for the time period 1994 through 1999. In the process, it will be possible to make some close and carefully reasoned comparisons between Algerian, Egyptian, and Turkish terrorism. Equally important, those findings will make it possible to make some comparisons later on in this work to some findings about Middle East terrorism between 1968 and 1993 that are chronicled in my previous work on Middle East terrorism.

In the case of the explanatory variable "political ideology," it is observed there is a statistically significant association between that causal variable and the variable "target." In the narrower sense, as previously mentioned, the data show that perpetrators of Turkish terrorism favor civilian targets 66.1 percent of the time or in 125 out of 189 events, while government targets are favored 27.5 percent of the time or in 52 out of 189 assaults. That 2.4:1 ratio in favor of civilian targets is, in the broader sense, consistent with the findings of other studies about terrorism and is a good fit between the findings for Egyptian terrorism that only slightly favors terrorist assaults against civilian targets by an 1:.81 ratio, and the 8:1 ratio in favor of civilian targets for Algerian terrorism with 287 out of 341 acts or 84.2 percent that involved civilian targets, and 36 out of 340 acts or 10.6 percent that involved government targets.

How do those data support the underlying theoretical framework about "structuralist" and "nonstructuralist" terrorist group-types? At a theoretical level, it is possible to overlay the data about non-charismatic Turkish terrorist group-types onto a continuum of "structuralist" and "nonstructuralist" Middle East terrorist group-types that I developed in my prior work.[191] The data reveal that in the case of Turkish terrorism, ideo-ethnocentric groups have a 56.3 percent rate of terrorist assaults against civilian targets and a full 43.8 percent rate of terrorist assaults against government targets. Those government target-civilian target ratios are the expected findings for ideo-ethnocentric groups, with Turkish ideo-ethnocentric terrorist groups falling into the sphere of "structuralist" terrorist groups-types at the left axis of the "structuralist-nonstructuralist" Middle East Group-Type Continuum (see figure 5.8).

In turn, theocentric terrorist groups have a terrorist assault rate directed at government targets of 15.4 percent and a rate of 84.6 percent for terrorist assaults directed at civilian targets. Those findings place theocentric groups to the right of ideo-ethnocentric terrorist groups, moving left to right from the "structuralist" axis towards the "nonstructuralist" axis. To be sure, that position is consistent with the idea of theocentric terrorist groups as a "hybrid" group-type that combines elements of both a "worldview" struggle against opponents and a view that perceives the fierce struggle against opponents as one against persons and groups of individuals.

While the foregoing results are expected findings and fit well into the continuum framework, the findings about ethnocentric target attacks comprise a set of deviant findings that requires interpretation. It is observed that Turkish ethnocentric terrorist assaults were directed at civilian targets only 25.0 percent of the time or in 3 out of 12 acts, and were directed against government targets 58.3 percent of the time or in 7 out of 12 acts. As previously mentioned, when those ethnocentric terrorist assaults are scrutinized it is apparent that the majority of those terrorist assaults were carried out by "proto-groups" of the Kurdish resistance that came together with the specific and immediate aim of political protest against government targets in response to the capture of PKK leader Abdullah Öcalan.

It seems likely those "proto-group" terrorist assaults skewed the results for ethnocentric groups in particular and the relationships between terrorist group types in the case of Turkish terrorism in general precisely because of the singular focus those ethnocentric terrorist "proto-group" attacks had on government targets. Be that as it may, it is also evident there was precious little in the way of more standard ethnocentric terrorist assaults, thereby in effect helping to showcase the importance of the time period under consideration with respect to the results obtained. Plainly, if the unusual nature of ethnocentric terrorist assaults for the 1994 through 1999 period are taken into account, there is good fit between the expected findings of terrorist group-types along the terrorist group-type continuum and the observed results (see figure 5.9).

Another cornerstone of the theory that drives this work is the central idea first described in my prior work that "leaders of terrorist groups with religious and social ideologies somewhat antithetical to Islam might encourage their terrorist groups to act in ways more like other terrorist groups that are more in sync with the prevailing social-political ideology"[192] For example, the Kurdistan Workers' Party (PKK), a group whose terrorist assaults make up a majority of terrorist acts found in the ideo-ethnocentric charismatic category, has been at odds with "the prevailing social ideology" of Kemalist "secularism" on the one hand, and, as a Marxist-Leninist organization, with Islam on the other hand. In the broader sense, it would be expected that with Abdullah Öcalan in place, ideo-ethnocentric charismatic group assaults would have a much greater degree of civilian target attacks. The findings about ideo-ethnocentric charismatic terrorist assaults in the Turkish context strongly support that central notion developed in my prior work (see figure 5.10).

As previously mentioned, ideo-ethnocentric terrorist groups are found to fall squarely in the realm of "structuralist" terrorist groups, with a government target terrorist assault rate of 43.8 percent and a civilian target rate of 56.3 percent. In turn, ideo-ethnocentric charismatic groups place to the right of the aforementioned along that continuum with a government target assault rate of 19.8 percent and a civilian target rate of 72.9 percent, thereby in effect providing strong support for the central idea that charismatic leaders of terrorist groups outside the "prevailing social ideology" compel tacticians and the terrorist activists who work for them to act in ways more like terrorist groups that embrace the prevailing social ideology of Islam.[193]

The deviant case of Turkish ethnocentric terrorist groups described and

"Structuralist"		"Nonstructuralist"	
	Ideo-ethnocentric	Theocentric	Ethnocentric*
Civilian targets	56.3% (9/16)	84.6% (11/13)	25.0% (3/12)*
Government targets	43.8% (7/16)	15.4% (2/13)	58.3% (7/12)*

Figure 5.9: Continuum of "Structuralist" and "Nonstructuralist" Turkish Terrorist Group-Types for Non-Charismatic Group Types and Target (Jewish Fundamentalist Terrorist Group-Types Excluded)

discussed above falls at the "structuralist" axis of the model, diametrically opposite to its expected place along the continuum (see figure 5.9). Clearly, there were no ethnocentric charismatic or theocentric charismatic terrorist assaults chronicled in the data base on Turkish terrorism to evaluate. In sum, when the data for terrorist group-types are sorted out with respect to percentage rates of civilian target and government target assault rates, it is apparent that the observed findings dovetail extremely well with the expected continuum rankings provided that the ethnocentric group-type is once again understood to be a deviant case.

Turning to the findings about unclaimed terrorist assaults for Turkish terrorism, the data reveal there is a 71.1 percent rate for unclaimed civilian target terrorist assaults. The comparatively low amount of civilian target attacks for unclaimed groups or non-group actors is not the expected finding. Nonetheless, the rate of civilian target attacks at 71.1 percent is high enough to make it imprudent, in my judgment, to reject outright the underlying theme about the role of anonymous terrorist assaults.[194] To be sure, a civilian target attack rate of 71.1 percent, nearly three-quarters of all anonymous terrorist activity, is still a substantial component of the total amount of unclaimed or unattributable terrorist assaults.

The fundamental issue under consideration is why that 71.1 percent civilian target terrorist assault rate for anonymous terrorist groups or non-group actors ranks less than the rate for civilian target terrorist assaults for all terrorist group-types except ideo-ethnocentric groups. To be sure, while there is certainly no definitive answer or interpretation for those data, one idea revolves around a

"Structuralist"			"Nonstructuralist"	
	Ethnocentric*	Ideo-ethnocentric	Ideo-ethnocentric charismatic	Theocentric
Civilian targets	25.0% (3/12)*	56.3% (9/16)	72.9% (70/96)	84.6% (11/13)
Government targets	58.3% (7/12)*	43.8% (7/16)	19.8% (10/96)	15.4% (2/13)

Figure 5.10: Continuum of "Structuralist" and "Nonstructuralist" Turkish Terrorist Group-Types and Target (Jewish Fundamentalist Terrorist Group-Types Excluded)

theme developed in my previous work that if political issues and goals of contention are sufficiently clear-cut and widely recognized, terrorist organizations may commit some anonymous terrorist assaults against civilian targets to generate and sustain structural political or economic change. It follows that interpretation, which is clearly not the only interpretation available, suggests that specific political objectives in the Turkish political system may not be as clearly articulated or well defined as political issues of contention in other political systems.

In the broader sense, the many terrorist groups that operate within the system of Turkish terrorism have their own difficulties in terms of articulation of particular goals and political grievances because they have to work in what has been described as an authoritarian "secularist society" supported by the Turkish armed forces that is the very antithesis of what many political conceptions or objectives of those terrorist groups are all about. At a functional level, a host of terrorist groups operative in the Turkish political fray have political goals with enormous ideological and functional distance between them, that blurs the picture of "who did what, when, and how," thereby in effect helping to militate against the practice of anonymous terrorist assaults. For example, there is enormous ideological space between the political goals of Turkish Hezbollah, and those of the Kurdistan Workers' Party (PKK) and other "leftist" groups like Dev-Sol and TIKKO.[195] Compounding the matter even more, Gunter reports there have been allegations, that he suggests are dubious in nature, of some "cooperation" between Armenian groups and the PKK that in actuality may blur distinctions even more.[196]

Other so-called "leftist groups," aside from the PKK, may have an increasingly difficult time making a set of interconnections between their subnational actor interests (i.e., political goals) and terrorist group tactics. Somewhat ironically, that mirrors the problem that both Brown and Kissinger describe with respect to nation-states having to make and articulate interconnections between "national interest" and foreign policy in the post Cold War world.[197] Plainly, such a condition may require terrorist assaults with claims of responsibility even though the risk of effective counterterrorism activity against them is probably greater. In turn, the comparatively smaller role that perpetrators of Islamic revivalist terrorist assaults have played in the Turkish political landscape may necessitate claims of responsibility if only to avoid confusion with terrorist assaults committed by terrorist groups of the Kurdish resistance, where political issues and goals are more clearly articulated and understood.

Terrorist Assault "Attribute" Indicators

There are a number of "attribute" indicators that are used in bivariate analysis tests designed to capture the attributes of Turkish terrorist assaults. In the case of Turkish terrorism, it is found that there is no statistically significant association between the attribute variables "numbers of deaths," "location," "property damage," the intervening variable "political events," and the variable "target-type." A bivariate analysis for the variables "target-type" by "victim nationality" with "assault type" (i.e., "discriminate," "indiscriminate," and "uncertain" terrorist assaults) as a control variable is performed to examine whether or not there is a statistically significant association between the variables "target-type" and "victim nationality" for "discriminate" terrorist assaults. The findings generated in one of the "partials" tables produced shows the association between the variables is found to be not significant.

At the same time, bivariate analysis tests are performed to determine whether or not statistically significant associations exist between the variable "target" and terrorist "group age," and "target" and the variable terrorist "group size." In both cases, the test results indicate that no statistically significant association exists. The next step is to determine whether or not those two explanatory variables, terrorist group "age" and terrorist group "size," capture overlapping or similar dynamics. Hence, the fundamental matter is to explore whether or not there is a statistically significant correlation between those two explanatory variables. A one-tailed bivariate correlations test is run because the theoretical direction of the relationship between the variables "size" and "age" is understood. In turn, Spearman's *rho* is used because data for both "size" and "age" are ordinal in nature. The absence of any statistically significant correlation between those two variables seems to suggest that the cross-tabulation table correlation results that are found to be not significant may be due to sketchy or incomplete data.

Reflections

In the broader sense, the likelihood of full-blown political change in the fundamental secularist orientation of the Turkish state remains, in my judgment, practically nil. At the same time, seen from the vantage of a counterterrorism point of view, the Turkish ruling elite are faced with looming political and economic problems that have an enormous capacity to cause very serious problems for both Turkish and regional stability, especially with respect to subnational actor potential to exploit those problems.

To be sure, part of the potential for political instability and social unrest in the Turkish political landscape presupposes and derives from factors that stem from the structural changes in the international political system that occurred as the Cold War passed into eclipse.[198] The end of the Cold War and the subsequent time lag between the period 1987-91 and the present has made it possible for residual effects of that structural change to work their way through political systems with proximate effects at the subnational actor level for terrorist groups and nongroup actors.[199] In the case of Turkish terrorism, those effects seem to include a continuously evolving "niche" for Islamic revivalist terrorist groups and some change in ideology emphasis for Turkish ideo-ethnocentric groups.

What seems significant with respect to target selection is that terrorist attacks by Turkish ideo-ethnocentric groups against targets that represent Western cultural mores and Western democratic capitalism are augmented, but certainly not replaced outright, by Islamic fundamentalist terrorist groups whose chieftains are at least as passionate about the ills associated with democratic capitalism and its perceived decadence.[200] One way of thinking about the matter is that the "niche" of Marxist-Leninist groups, overtaken by the pace of events since 1987, has been filled to some degree by Islamic revivalist extremist organizations who also conceive of the West as antithetical to core values. At least in part, that notion presupposes and derives from results found in my prior work. In those works certain results suggest that ideo-ethnocentric groups like the Arab Communist Organization (ACO) and the Lebanese Armed Revolutionary Faction (LARF) in Lebanon seem to place more of a premium against government targets.[201] In that context, one important observation gleaned from the qualitative analysis is that the Kurdistan Workers' Party (PKK), while staying close in ideological distance to its Marxist-Leninist underpinnings, has in recent years made some makeshift if never complete modifications to address the ticklish matter of Islamic revivalist thought that permeates through much of the Middle East and elsewhere in places like Pakistan, the Philippines, and Tajikistan, thereby in effect through its behavior helping to acknowledge the power of Islamic revivalism as an instrument to confront the West in general and the United States in particular.[202]

Accounts of that PKK process are relatively straightforward and commonplace to note. For Criss, "nevertheless, PKK had to flirt with religion for a number of reasons. First by 1990 it had become obvious that the Marxist-Leninist (hence atheist) PKK was unable to draw the mass support from a society in which religious sentiment was very strong. Third, Öcalan suddenly realized the importance of religion as another support mechanism. As of 1989 PKK propaganda leaflets and brochures began and ended with prayers."[203] In turn, in his analysis of PKK party platforms, Gunter describes the "continuing . . . de-emphasis on the strident Marxism that marked its earlier days. . . . symbolically, the hammer and sickle were dropped from the party's flag."[204]

In his analysis of the Kurds in Turkey and the absence of an Islamic response to their plight, Houston asserts there are several factors behind why there has been no Islamic response to the ticklish question of Turkish ethnic discrimination against the Kurds.[205] Houston cites and describes the work of Bulaç that points to the tortuous historical legacy of persecution by the Turkish state apparatus against Turkish Islamists during the "single party period," and to the structural component of the Cold War where nationalist and Islamists forged what can be described as an arrangement of convenience.[206] Clearly, what seems significant here is that a structural component of the international political system has passed into eclipse, thereby in effect helping to increase the prospect that Islamists and anti-Kemalist groups could forge their own alliance of convenience.

Compounding the matter even more, less well-known ideo-ethnocentric terrorist groups in the Turkish political system, replete with their rather anachronistic political platforms, seem to be increasingly unable to fashion persuasive political agendas in the post-Cold War world, thereby in effect helping to create more potential for the manipulation of those Marxist-Leninist terrorist organizations, perhaps by exogenous forces. After all, the single most dominant difference between the PKK and those other groups is that the PKK, like Kurdish nationalist movements that have come before, works within the context of what Muller might call full-blown "ethnic-nationalistic" rebellion that itself is able to generate and sustain support by means of the capacity to evoke Kurdish nationalist sentiments and other similar feelings. At the same time, Kurdish nationalists, opposed to the Marxist-Leninism of the PKK and the PKK emphasis on equality of the sexes that stems from that standpoint, seem to be open to even more direct influence from contemporary Islamic revivalist sources.[207]

Taking the argument one step further, it is commonplace to note that Shaykh Osama bin Laden and his organization al-Qa'ida, otherwise known as the Base organization, have a powerful set of interconnections to Middle East terrorist organizations in many political landscapes that include al-Jama'a al-Islamiya (the Islamic Group) in Egypt and the Jammat Islamiyya Mousalah or Armed Islamic Group (GIA) in Algeria. One aspect of al-Qa'ida potency is its enormous capacity to marshal the human capital of several terrorist organizations with its own resources for particular terrorist assault missions. Consider the reflections of Nigogosian when he tells us, "the PKK will . . . attempt to broaden its struggle, perhaps through the mediation of Alevi Kurds and/or by making alliances with the large and increasingly unhappy, both Kurdish and Turkish, Alevi population."[208] A bleak foreboding to be sure, concerns the role bin Laden or someone like him might have as an interlocutor between PKK and the Alevis who are Shi'ite, working in effective and sustained ways.[209]

In fact, it need not be Shaykh Osama bin Laden or a person like him who could seek to exploit some of the problems associated with Turkish terrorist group political objectives in the contemporary world. Nation-state actors in the Middle East with political goals to pursue might be able to exploit the antipathy that some Kurdish resistance movements like the KDP have to the "secularism" of the Turkish state and the "Marxist-Leninism" of the PKK, to fashion a stratagem of assaults for political gain in the name of a unified front against the Turkish government and the West.[210]

To be sure, organized activity to unify particular Turkish terrorist groups, as well as terrorist groups within a specific group-type such as all ideo-ethnocentric groups, could be crafted or manipulated by the ruling elites in countries like Iraq, Iran, or Syria with political destabilization as a goal or attempts to change aspects of the existing distribution of power in the Mashriq region, with profound and lasting implications for both nation-states and sub-national actors in the Middle East and nation-states in the West.[211] Perhaps the bleakest foreboding of all might be some coordinated effort that is effective and sustained between bin Laden or persons like him with the apparatus of a Middle East nation-state, where the ruling elite in that nation seek to pursue national interest objectives in tandem with bin Laden or someone like him.[212]

All of the aforementioned really distills down to the fundamental question of what stratagems for remediation are available to the ruling elite of Turkey for more controllable events that happen at home. If, as Criss suggests, much of the political instability, social unrest, and terrorism observed in Turkey presuppose and derive from economic backwater conditions, then the strategy needs to be twofold. First, there needs to be some wholesale infusion of monies into the system and the implementation of a series of what Baldwin would call "positive sanctions" perhaps to create fissures in constituency group support thereby in effect helping to promote meaningful dialogue. If constituent groups are buttressed with the tangible assets associated with nonlethal technologies under the rubric of "positive sanctions," distance ought to be created between hard-core ideologues and "hanger on" types that might help generate further contacts between groups of constituent supporters and government officials.[213]

At a substantive level, as Mango and others suggest, egregious and sometimes seemingly arbitrary restrictions on Kurdish political demands and aspirations need to be lifted to help legitimize the political and moral capacity of the Turkish government.[214] Moreover, political parties associated with the Kurdish nationalist movement need to be unfettered to operate in effective and sustained ways.[215] As Huntington tells us, "political decay" begins when "political institutionalization," namely the absence of effective political parties able to respond to political demands and aspirations of segments of society, is not found.[216] Insofar as party frameworks are concerned, "cross-cutting" political parties to further national integration goals, as opposed to parties that amplify "coincidental" cleavages based on ethnic regional, religious, and other similar sentiments or feelings are preferable.[217]

As Reiss and Roth might put it, the need to have effective "macro-social" level "opportunity structures" in place for Kurdish communities in both political and economic spheres is critical to act as a safety valve for the ineluctable conclusion of conflict associated with political demands and aspirations unsatisfied or ignored outright. Plainly, if those political demands and aspirations are not met at some level, low-level conflict and terrorism, almost always a frequent visitor to democratic political systems without flexibility, will continue. In a broader sense, low-level conflict or what in today's parlance is called "asymmetrical warfare" does not, in my judgment, pose the direct threat of revolution or even fundamental political change in Turkey. But that does not mean that Turkish terrorism, perhaps reconfigured, does not have the potential to cause enormous problems for government stability and effectiveness.

The lurking prospect of a burgeoning front of certain Marxist-Leninist terrorist groups, Kurdish nationalist terrorist groups, and Islamic revivalist terrorist groups that operate over the Turkish political landscape, perhaps spearheaded by Osama bin Laden or someone like him, poses a set of challenges and opportunities for counterterrorism specialists. Picture a situation like the foregoing coupled with a nation-state like Syria, Iran, or Iraq lurking in the background with national interests of its own to fulfill and the conditions become even more complex. In its totality, the foregoing set of conditions must really compel Turkish policy makers and policy makers from the United States to pause and reflect on the interpenetrating dynamics between structural change in our contemporary world and the dynamic effects that presuppose and derive from that change that may influence terrorist group behavior in particular settings.

Notes

1. Myers 2000a, A-1, A-12; Gordon 2000, A-9; Myers 2000b, A-10; Becker 2000, A-12.
2. Mango 1994, 44; Becker 2000, A-12.
3. Aykan 1996, 343, 349-350; Gunter 1997, 117; Criss 1995, 31; *Keesings* 1995a.
4. Aykan 1996, 343, 349-350; Gunter 1997, 100, 97; Criss 1995, 31; Dunn 1995, 72, 82; Barkey 1996, 7; Olson 1997, 15-16.
5. Aykan 1996, 346, 348-340, 351, 360; Nigogosian 1996, 39.
6. Aykan 1996, 348-349, 360, 346, 348, 354, 350; Gunter 1997, 97; Barkey 1996, 7.
7. Mango 1994, 53; Muller 1996, 194; Criss 1991, 124.
8. Hale as found in Mango 1995, 6, 1; Barkey 1996, 1, 3, 5; Gürbey 1996, 10, 4; Nigogosian 1996, 47; Karpat 1981, 11; Muller 1996, 177; Houston 1997; Criss 1991, 128, 133, 144.
9. Criss 1991, 128, 144; Hale as found in Mango 1995, 6, 1; Barkey 1996, 1, 3, 5; Gürbey 1996, 10, 4; Nigogosian 1996, 47; Karpat 1981, 11; Muller 1996, 177; Houston 1997; Criss 1991, 128, 133, 144.

10. Dunn 1995, 72, 74; Barkey 1996, 2, 7; Nigogosian 1996, 41; Gunter 1997, 95, 112-113, 96, 114. Those challenges and opportunities are perhaps best captured by the dynamics of the Crimean War (1853-56) where Britain and France had to form an alliance against Czarist Russia, precisely because of Russian encroachment against areas of the Ottoman Empire, "the sick man of Europe," itself in the process of passing into eclipse (Nye 1993).

11. Olson 1997, 9-10, 19; Gunter 1997, 94.

12. Criss 1995, 32-33, 29; Olson 1997, 4, 2, 11, 15, 19.

13. Olson 1997, 2, 4, 11, 15, 19; Mango 1994, 33. Olson tells us that with the lurking catastrophe of the Second World War, Hatay/Alexandretta was given to Turkey in the hope that Turkey would remain neutral. To be sure, Olson's example of the transfer of sovereignty in the case of Hatay/Alexandretta seems as good as example as any of the dynamics associated with "artificial boundaries" set up by the great powers and the enormous capacity for conflict that presupposes and derives from those "artificial boundaries" (Yegen 1996, 220, 223).

14. Mango 1994, 29; Gunter 1997, 94, 27; Criss 1995, 26; Olson 1997, 2-3.

15. Baldwin 1971, 1985, Holsti 1985; Nigogosian 1996, 39; Gürbey 1996, 30-32. To be sure, one could conceive of water as part of quid pro quo arrangements designed to promote balance of power and thereby in effect helping to hamper efforts at regional hegemony.

16. Brown 1994, 6-7; Kissinger 1999, 41-43.

17. Schmitt 2000, A-15; Karpat 1981, 25. As Karpat tells us, Turkey has been a NATO member since 1952.

18. Gunter 1997, 24, 29; Dunn 1995, 79; Criss 1995, 18; Olson 1997, 2; Mango 1994, 42, 40. Mango tells us the PKK was fashioned in 1974.

19. Gunter 1997, 24, 29; Dunn 1995, 79; Criss 1995, 18; Olson 1997, 2; Mango 1994, 42, 40.

20. Gürbey 1996, 23-24; Mango 1994, 47; Gunter 1997, 45-46, 96, 124-125; Dunn 1995, 85; Aykan 1996, 360; Olson 1997, 4; Khashan 1997, 4; Criss 1995, 22, 28, 31; Dunn 1995, 85.

21. Gürbey 1996, 23-24; Mango 1994, 47; Gunter 1997, 45-46, 96, 124-125; Dunn 1995, 85; Aykan 1996, 360; Olson 1997, 4; Khashan 1997, 4; Criss 1995, 22, 28, 31; Dunn 1995, 85.

22. Gunter 1997, 49; Barkey 1996, 8; Mango 1994, 42; Gürbey 1996, 23.

23. Gürbey 1996, 25; Bell 1999, 2; Gunter 1997, 32-33. Gunter tells us that Öcalan's title shifted from "general secretary" to "chairman" after the fifth PKK Congress in 1995.

24. In the broadest sense, Criss (1995, 25, 27) tells us there is the significant matter of how representative the PKK is of the Kurdish population in general. In contrast, Gürbey (1996, 24) asserts there is enormous support for the PKK.

25. Criss 1995, 20.

26. Gunter 1997, 101, 120; Gürbey 1996, 24. In turn, Gürbey reports some 6,900 PKK activists in Germany.

27. Gunter 1997, 37-38, 101, 120; Gürbey 1996, 24.

28. Gunter 1997, 26, 31-33.

29. Gunter 1997, 26, 31-33.

30. *JPRS* 1994a; Gunter 1997, 40, 46. By contrast, Gunter tells us that PKK restructure initiative "failed to be carried out."

31. Gunter 1997, 27; Criss 1995, 26; Olson 1997, 2-3. Olson tells us that Syrian support for the PKK involved broader Syrian geopolitical considerations and may have been in retaliation to fledgling Turkish-Israeli interconnections and conflict with Turkey about water in Hatay province.

32. Gunter 1997, 26, 123; Olson 1997, 2-8; Criss 1991, 129, 131; Criss 1995, 31-32; Dunn 1995, 84.

33. Gunter 1997, 110-112; Karpat 1981, 21.

34. Gunter 1997, 26, 123; Olson 1997, 2-8; Criss 1991, 129, 131; Criss 1995, 31-32; Dunn 1995, 84.

35. Karpat 1981, 18, 19, 17; Gunter 1997, 23; Barkey 1996, 2.

36. Özbudun 1990, 182-183; Criss 1995, 124.

37. Özbudun 1990, 189-190; Karpat 1981, 28; Houston 1997.

38. Criss 1991, 125-126; Karpat 1981, 12.

39. Barkey 1996, 5; Criss 1991, 127; Mango 1994, 45; Gunter 1997, 24.

40. Criss 1991, 127; Mango 1995, 2; Mango 1994, 45; Huntington 1968. Zurcher, as Mango reports, really draws on "dependency theory" as espoused by Andre Gunder Frank and others in effective and sustained ways to explain Turkey's enormous problems that hamper socio-economic development or modernization.

41. Barkey 1996, 5; Mango 1994, 45.

42. Karpat 1981, 18, 19, 17.

43. Karpat 1981, 18, 19, 17; Criss 1991, 135. Criss tells us that the "rightists" also conceived of the *gcekondu* or "shantytowns" as a recruitment pool for their own paramilitary organizations.

44. Criss 1995, 18; Criss 1991, 129-133; Gunter 1997, 24-25, 32-33.

45. Gunter 1997, Reiss and Roth 1993, Mango 1995, 2; Mango 1994, 40, 45; Criss 1995, 18; Esman 1994.

46. Huntington 1968, 43, 84, 12-14, 78-79, 34-36.

47. Mango 1995, 2; Mango 1994, 37.

48. Criss 1991, 123-124, 131.

49. Criss, 1991, 129.

50. Criss 1991, 131, 128-129; Criss 1995, 18; Scherer 1982, 139; Gunter 1997, 24.

51. Scherer 1982, 139; Karpat 1981, 21; Gunter 1997, 23.

52. Scherer 1982, 139; Gunter 1997.

53. Scherer 1982, 139; Mango 1994, 42; Criss 1991, 129-130; Criss 1995, 18.

54. Gunter 1997, 23-24; Criss 1991, 131; Criss 1995; Özbudun 1990; Mango 1994, 41-42; Karpat 1981, 14, 19.

55. Criss 1995; Gunter 1997, 23-24.

56. Gunter 1997, 24-25; Scherer 1982, 139.

57. Gunter 1997, 24; Schmid and Jongman 1988, 677; Karpat 1981, 21, 20; Criss 1991, 131.

58. Gunter 1997, 24; Schmid and Jongman 1988, 677; Karpat 1981, 21, 20; Criss 1991, 131.

59. Criss 1991, 129; Hobsbawm 1987.

60. Holsti 1985, Gunter 1997, 24-25; Nye 1993.

61. Gunter 1997, 25, 29; Mango 1994, 42; Criss 1995, 18.

62. Criss 1991, 135, 124; Criss 1995, 20, 35; Gurr and Harff 1994, 82-95; Mango 1994, 37; Karpat 1981, 17; Gunter 1997, 23.

63. Reiss and Roth 1993; Gunter 1997, 24-25, 32-33, 29; Esman 1994; Mango 1994, 42, 40, 45; Mango 1995, 2.

64. Mango 1994, 34-35; Criss 1995, 24-25. Conversely, Criss tells us of a "Kurdish linguist" who asserts particular Kurdish groups are indistinct precisely because of the reason that the Kurdish languages Karmanji and Zaza "are mutually unintelligible."

65. Olson 1999, 109-110; Yegen 1996, 219; Muller 1997, 175-76. For Yegen, the Shaykh Said Rebellion of 1925 may presuppose and derive from the Kurdish understanding that the elimination of the Caliphate in 1924 and, consequently, what Yegen calls the Turkish "tyranny of the centre" would have deleterious consequences for Kurds (Yegen 1996, 221, 223-224).

66. Mango 1994, 40; Gürbey 1996, 25; Muller 1996, 175-76.

67. Olson 1999, 109-110; Yegen 1996, 219; Gürbey 1996, 13.

68. Reiss and Roth 1993.

69. Reiss and Roth 1993.

70. Olson 1999, 125; Yegen 1996, 219; Mango 1994, 40; Karpat 1981, 17.

71. Gunter 1997, 28-29; Karpat 1981, 17; Holsti 1985.

72. Gunter 1997, 28.

73. Gunter 1997, 27-29.

74. Reiss and Roth 1993,

75. Gunter 1997, 28.

76. Reiss and Roth 1993.

77. Gunter 1997, 33-35, 37, 47-48.

78. Gunter 1997, 34.

79. Reiss and Roth 1993; Jung 1933, 58. Jung tells us, "In handling younger people I generally find the familiar viewpoints of Freud and Adler applicable enough, for they offer a treatment which brings the patient to a certain level of adaptation and normality, apparently without leaving any disturbing after-effects. With older people, according to my experience, this is not often the case. It seems to me that the elements of the psyche undergo in the course of life a very marked change—so much so, that we may distinguish between a psychology of the morning and a psychology of its afternoon" (Jung 1933, 58).

80. Gunter 1997, 25-26; Karpat 1981, 19; Mango 1994, 42, 39. Mango tells us the PKK was fashioned in 1974.

81. Gunter 1997, 27; Karpat 1981, 19; Mango 1994, 42, 39.

82. Gunter 1997, 25.

83. Gunter 1997, 25; Karpat 1981, 19.

84. Gunter 1997, 24, 47; Karpat 1981, 19.

85. Gunter 1997, 24, 47; Karpat 1981, 19; Criss 1995, 20-21.

86. FBIS 1999b.

87. FBIS 1999b; Gunter 1997, 32.

88. Olson 1997, 9, 5; Gürbey 1996, 23; Gunter 1997, 35-37.

89. Olson 1995, 5; Olson 1997, 9 Gunter 1997, 128, 121; Criss 1995.

90. Gunter 1997, 37; Criss 1995, 20; Nigogosian 1996, 40. Nigogosian asserts the size of ARGK may expand to 50,000-60,000 by 1995.

91. Gunter 1997, 36-38, 33; Criss 1995, 20; Nigogosian 1996, 40. Nigogosian asserts the size of ARGK may expand to 50,000-60,000 by 1995.

92. Gunter 1997, 37, 33. In this discussion, Gunter draws on the work of Ismet G. Imset.

93. Gunter 1997; Criss 1995.

94. Gunter 1997, 36-37, 32, 43; Criss 1995, 19; Gürbey 1996, 23; Nigogosian 1996, 43. For Criss, the establishment of ERNK is sometime after 1984.

95. Gunter 1997, 37.

96. Gunter 1997, 34, 47.

97. Gunter 1997, 34-35, 48.

98. Criss 1995, 19; Gürbey 1996, 23. Gürbey tells us the date is 1985.

99. Criss 1995, 19.

100. Harris 1989, 95, 89-90, 92, 86.

101. *Jerusalem Post* 1994a, 3; Mickolus and Simmons 1997, 559.

102. *FBIS* 1999r.

103. Criss 1995, 18.

104. Criss 1995, Criss 1991, Gunter 1997, 24-25, 53-54; Karpat 1981, 20.

105. Gunter 1997, 24-25, 53; *Keesings* 1994c.

106. *JPRS* 1994e; Mickolus and Simmons 1997, 676; *JPRS* 1994f.

107. *JPRS* 1994e.

108. *JPRS* 1994e.

109. Gunter 1994, 53, 94.

110. Criss 1991, 127, 135-136; Schmid and Jongman 1988, 676-677; Gürbey 1996; Gunter 1997, 72; Karpat 1981, 5, 12. Criss (1991, 144-145, 139) tells us that Colonel Türkes is now inextricably bound up with the Islamic movement in Turkey.

111. Criss 1991, 137-138, 142; Karpat 1981, 5, 12; Gunter 1997, 72.

112. Criss 1991, 137-138, 142; Karpat 1981, 5, 12; Gunter 1997, 72.

113. *JPRS* 1995b.

114. *JPRS* 1994g; *Keesings* 1994c; *Keesings* 1996; Cevik, *FBIS* 1995.

115. Gunter 1997, 24; Schmid and Jongman 1988, 697.

116. Schmid and Jongman 1988, 697; Mango 1994, 42.

117. Gunter 1997, 24.

118. *FBIS* 1998q.

119. *Keesings* 1995b, 2; Pacal, *FBIS* 1998.

120. Pacal 1998, 2, 4.

121. Pacal 1998, 2, 4.

122. Pacal 1998, 2, 4; Reiss and Roth 1993.

123. Pacal 1998, 2, 4.

124. Pacal 1998, 2. In Pacal's scripted account, he tells us of "Circassians." *FBIS* 1996a; Barkey 1996, 2-3.

125. Criss 1995, 21; Criss 1991, 144.

126. Gunter 1997, 68-71; Gürbey 1996, 18; Muller 1996, 182; Houston 1997, 16.

127. Gunter 1997, 68-71; Gürbey 1996, 18; Muller 1996, 182; Houston 1997, 16.

128. *FBIS* 1998o.

129. *FBIS* 1998o.

130. *FBIS* 1998r.

131. *FBIS* 1999a.

132. Gunter 1997, 70.

133. Gunter 1997, 70-71; Gürbey 1996, 18.

134. *FBIS* 1999a; Gunter 1997, 71.

135. Gunter 1997, 70-71.

136. Dunn 1995, 80-84; Mango 1994, 43. Insofar as this study focuses on terrorist assaults carried out between 1994 and 1999 in specific locales, more in-depth discussion about other political players such as the Kurdish Democratic Party of Iran (KDPI) is omitted.

137. Dunn 1995, 74-75, 78, 85-86; Gunter 1997, 100, 96-97, 125 Criss 1995, 30-33; Olson 1997, 18; Mango 1994, 43, 55; Ali 1997, 521.

138. Criss 1995, 30-31, Yegen 1996, 224; Gunter 1997, 115-116.

139. Dunn 1995, 74-75; Gunter 1997, 161 n2, 115; Diamond 1990; Mango 1994, 34; Criss 1995, 30-31.

140. Gunter 1997, 161 n2, 115.

141. Gunter 1997, 161 n2, 115.

142. Nye 1993, Criss 1991, 125; Dunn 1995, 78, 80; Mango 1994, 34; Mango 1995, 7; Olson 1997, 1; Gürbey 1996, 21.

143. Dunn 1995, 78, 80; Reiss and Roth 1993, 293.

144. Dunn 1995, 80-81, 72. The one chronicled terrorist assault that may or may not be attributable to the PUK was carried out in Turkey by the "Kurdish Patriotic Union." Be that as it may, that "group" is described as "a PKK affiliate," thereby in effect placing it in the "ideo-ethnocentric" category for coding purposes.

145. Dunn 1995, 80-81.

146. Dunn 1995, 80-83; Gunter 1997.

147. Dunn 1995, 80; Gunter 1997, 161 n2, n3; Criss 1995.

148. Dunn 1995, 80-81; Gunter 1997, 161 n2, 115, 26; Mango 1994, 43.

149. Mango 1994, 55; Gürbey 1996, 23-24; *FBIS* 1998j.

150. Aykan 1995, 360; Dunn 1985, 80, 82; Gunter 1997, 161 n2, 115, 120-121; *FBIS* 1999e.

151. Aykan 1996, 361; Gunter 1997, 96.

152. Criss 1991, 360; Criss 1995, 30; Aykan 1996, 345-346, 360, 361-362; Gunter 1997, 116, 120-121, 124-125 ; Dunn 1995, 81-83. For example, Gunter tells us of a PKK-KDP relationship (1983-87); Dunn tells us of a short-lived Iraqi Kurdistan Front (1987-88); Dunn and Aykan tell us of a full-blown Kurdish revolt against Saddam Hussein in 1991; Gunter tells us of a "KDP-PUK 'civil war' in 1994"; Gunter, Aykan, and Dunn tell us of a joint ceasefire declared between the PUK and Barzani's KDP in December 1995 that followed the "Dublin agreement" or "Drogheda agreement" of August 1995. In turn, the Drogheda agreement has passed into eclipse (Olson 1997, 17).

153. *FBIS* 1999j; Mango 1994, 46; Gürbey 1996, 28, 14-15.

154. Barkey 1996, 8, 2, 5; Mango 1994, 46-47; Gürbey 1996, 28; *FBIS* 1995b.

155. Criss 1995, 26-27; Gunter 1997, 35, 44, 73; Mango 1994, 46-47; Gürbey 1996, 27; Nigogosian 1996, 40-41; Muller 1996, 188; Barkey 1996, 8.

156. Criss 1995, 25-26; Gürbey 1996, 26, 14; Muller 1996, 187; Gunter 1997, 73.

157. Gunter 1997, 73; Barkey 1996, 8-10.

158. Barkey 1996, 2, 8; Gürbey 1996, 28; Nigogosian 1996, 46; Criss 1991, 143.

159. USDOD 1988, 69-72; Schmid and Jongman 1988.

160. USDOD 1988, 69-72; Schmid and Jongman 1988.

161. *Jerusalem Post* 1994e, 5; *Jerusalem Post* 1998h, 7; Mango 1995, 14-15.

162. *Jerusalem Post* 1994e, 5; *Jerusalem Post* 1998h, 7; Mango 1995, 14-15.

163. Starr and Most 1983; Starr and Most 1976; Gunter 1986, 233; Gürbey 1996, 21; Mango 1994, 34. At first blush, one way of thinking about that includes the possibility that some "contagion effect," as Starr and Most write about, perhaps, as Gürbey suggests, associated with the fledgling "peace process" between Israelis and Palestinians is at work here. Gürbey (1996, 21), Khashan (1997, 11), and Mango (1994, 34) are three writers who discuss the effects of "contagion effect" with respect to Turkish terrorism. To be sure, that matter which poses a tantalizing research project, is over and beyond the realm of this study.

164. Chasdi 1999; Chasdi 1997; Chasdi 1995.

165. Chasdi 1999; Chasdi 1997; Chasdi 1995.

166. *Jerusalem Post* 1997e, 5; *Keesings* 1998.

167. Terrorism specialists who cite location as an explanatory variable for terrorist group behavior include, but are not limited to: O'Neill 1978, Shultz 1978, Osmond 1979, Waugh 1982, Merari et al. 1986, Ross 1993, and Flemming 1992.

168. ERNK (2.7 percent) + Dev Sol (2.7 percent) + Islamic Front of Great Eastern Raiders (2.7 percent) + Hezbollah Turkey (3.3 percent) + Anatolian Federal Islamic State (.5 percent) + TKP/MC Konferans (2.2 percent) + Metropolitan Revenge Brigades (1.1 percent) + Revolutionary People's Forces (1.1 percent) + HADEP (1.1 percent) + TIKKO (.5 percent) + Kourken Yans'kian (.5 percent) + Organization for Solidarity with Chechen Resistance Fighters (.5 percent) + November 17 (.5 percent) + Kurdish Patriotic Union (.5 percent) + Independent Work Group (.5 percent) = 20.4 percent.

169. To be sure, that finding may reflect incomplete data rather than a true representation of the dynamics of Armenian terrorism for the 1994-99 period.

170. Gunter 1986, 229, 235, 240.

171. Chasdi 1999; Chasdi 1997; Chasdi 1995.

172. *Jerusalem Post* 1995c, 8.

173. *Jerusalem Post* 1995c, 8.

174. Hoffman 1984, 10-15; Gurr 1988, 45-46; Mickolus 1980, xxii-xiii; Jenkins 1998, 230; Crozier 1960, 160; Pfaltzgraff 1986, 292; Flemming 1992, 164, 180, 194-195, 203-204; Chasdi 1999, 150, 181, 202 n35; Chasdi 1995, 153, 156, 171, 228 n18, 221; Chasdi 1997, 90, 110 n30.

175. von der Mehden 1973; Horowitz 1985; Silber and Little 1997; Chasdi 1997, 155, 202 n38; Nef 1978, 13; Jenkins 1998, 230.

176. *Jerusalem Post* 1995c, 8.

177. Hoffman 1984, 10-15; Gurr 1988, 45-46; Mickolus 1980, xxii-xxiii; Crozier 1960, 160; Pfaltzgraff 1986, 292; Flemming 1992, 164, 180, 194-195, 203-204; Chasdi 1999, 150, 181, 202 n35; Chasdi 1995, 153, 156, 171, 228 n18, 221; Chasdi 1997, 90, 110 n30; Drake 1988, 181.

178. For example, see the works of Hoffman 1984, 11; Oots 1984, 168; Shultz 1978; Zariski 1989, 268-269.

179. Chasdi 1999, 160, 143, 181.

180. Chasdi 1999, 181-183; Chasdi 1997, 100; Chasdi 1995, 221, 322-323.

181. Taheri 1987, 20, 21, 121; Chasdi 1999, 181-182, 204 n72, 213; Chasdi 1997, 100, 111 n54; Chasdi 1995, 100-104, 136 n4, n5, 239, 277 n20; Drake 1988, 22-23.

182. A breakdown of Turkish terrorism ethnocentric terrorist assaults shows that eight out of twelve ethnocentric terrorist assaults or some 67.0 percent are "proto-group" terrorist assaults, while the four ethnocentric group assaults were carried out by HADEP (2), the Organization for Solidarity with Chechen resistance fighters, and Kourken Yans'kian.

183. Gunter 1986, 222, 227, 228; Gunter 1997, 109. To be sure, for the underlying theme of ideology, Gunter reports there is variation with respect to Armenian terrorist groups. Gunter tells us ASALA, otherwise known as the Armenian Secret Army for the Liberation of Armenia, is "Marxist" in nature that stopped its terrorist assaults around 1983. JCAG by contrast, otherwise known as the Justice Commandos for the Armenian Genocide, and known after 1983 as the Armenian Revolutionary Army, is described by Gunter as a "right wing, nationalist terrorist organization."

184. Hoffman 1984, 10-15; Flemming 1992; Shultz 1978, 10; Lasswell 1978, 258; Lasswell 1935; Pfaltzgraff 1986, 282; Goodman 1971; Chasdi 1995, 171, 228 n18; Chasdi 1997, 90, 110 n30.

185. The findings are not significant: Chi Square .743 and a "p-value" of .389 at one degree of freedom (1 d.f.).

186. Hoffman 1984, 11; Shultz 1978, 10, Lasswell 1978, 258; Pfaltzgraff 1986, 292; Chasdi 1999, 164, 187, 203 n48, 213; Goodman 1971.

187. Gunter 1986, 233. As an example of another study that demonstrates a cyclical configuration with respect to terrorist assaults by year, see Gunter's analysis of Armenian terrorism between 1973 and 1984.

188. In the case of Algerian terrorism, the total amount of terrorism outside Algeria is 5.5 percent for "Europe," plus 2.6 percent for "Other/Unknown" locales, for a total of 8.1 percent. In the case of Egyptian terrorism, the total amount of terrorism outside of Egypt is 4.2 percent for "Europe," plus 6.3 percent for "Other/Unknown" locales, plus 3.5 percent for "Other Middle East states" plus 7.0 percent for the "United States," for a total of 21.0 percent. In the case of Israeli-Palestinian-Arab terrorism, the total amount of terrorism outside Israel, the Occupied Territories, and the jurisdiction of the PNA is 2.8 percent for Europe, plus 7.1 percent for "Other," plus 7.8 percent for "Other Middle East states" plus 2.3 percent for the "United States," for a total of 20.0 percent.

189. See notes 171 and 175.

190. "Event deaths N=186, 'Minimum: 0'; 'Maximum: 54'; 'Mean: 1.36';
Standard Deviation: 4.81; "Event Injuries N=177, 'Minimum: 0'; 'Maximum: 80';
'Mean: 2.81'; 'Standard Deviation: 7.70."
   191. Chasdi 1999, 182.
   192. Chasdi 1999, 76.
   193. Starr and Most 1976, 110-111; Starr and Most 1983; Seale 1992; Parsons
1964, 328, 358-363, 363-386; Long 1990, 18-19, 22, 211; Schiller 1988, 96-97;
Dollard et al. 1939; Gal-Or 1985, 14; Lasswell 1935, 107, 37; Coser 1956, 110,
Allport 1954, 154, 244-245; Nye 1993; Anderson, Seibert, and Wagner 1998, 202-
226; Wallerstein 1974; Chasdi 1995, 136 n4; Chasdi 1999, 75-78, 14, 63, 109, 125,
143, 213. As I mention in my prior work: "[A]n underlying fact of Middle East life
is that religion permeates political and social institutions and has a profound and
lasting effect on political outcomes. The reasoning here is that Christian leaders of
terrorist groups may feel pressure to act in ways that ingratiate them to their Moslem
counterparts, thereby in effect solidifying the set of political interconnections between
them." To be sure, Öcalan is not Christian, but Turkish-Kurdish ethnic fissures, by
extrapolation, can be seen as at the heart of similar dynamics. Seen from a slightly
different angle in *Serenade of Suffering*, I argue that "one can draw on Starr and
Most's work on war and look instead at cultural dissemination of conflict patterns to
argue that if, within a region, one prevailing ideology such as Islam dominates,
violent acts in the guise of terrorism committed by minority groups may resemble
terrorism assaults committed by Islamic groups because of a *cultural* 'positive spatial
diffusion' of social and religious ideology that would shape the modus operandi of
non majority . . . terrorist groups to resemble the modus operandi of majority
Arab/Islamic terrorist groups" (Chasdi 1999, 75).
   194. Harris 1989, 95, 89-90, 92, 86; Chasdi 1999, 65-66, 79 n10, n11.
   195. Criss 1995, 28; Gunter 1997, 124-125; Dunn 1995, 85. Interestingly
enough, not even aspects of the political objectives of the PKK are characterized by
especially sharp focus. For example, Criss describes "the many ambiguous demands
of Öcalan," while Gunter talks about Öcalan's "rather vague goal of somehow
establishing a 'revolutionary democratic federation' in northern Iraq that would lay
the groundwork for a federation in Turkey." In turn, Dunn seems to place more of an
emphasis on the underlying theme of an independent Kurdish state when he reports,
"although the PKK seems to still demand independence from Turkey it has offered to
talk with Ankara." It seems plausible that less than pristine political objectives not
only between Turkish terrorist groups but even within the single most predominant
one during the 1994-99 period under consideration may shackle the full-blown effect
of anonymous terrorist assaults found in other geographical sites.
   196. Gunter 1997, 108-109.
   197. Brown 1994, 6-7; Kissinger 1999, 41-43.
   198. Nye 1993; Waltz 1959; Gürbey 1996, 21; Nigogosian 1996, 39; Karpat
1981; Bulaç as found in Houston 1997, 11.
   199. Brown 1996, 6-7.
   200. Baker 1997; Esposito 1992.
   201. Chasdi 1999, 213.
   202. Mickolus and Simmons 1997, 622, 623, 636, 751-752, 755; Gürbey 1996;
Houston 1997, 16; Olson 1997, 6.

203. Criss 1995, 23; Dahl 1957; Gunter 1997, 51, 36.
204. Gunter 1997, 51, 36; Nigogosian 1996, 43; Gürbey 1996.
205. Houston 1997, 10, 11, 4.
206. Ali Bulaç as cited and described in Houston 1997, 10-11.
207. Gürbey 1996, 22, 25; Nigogosian 1996, 39, 44; Muller 1996, 175; Mango 1994, 34-36, 47.
208. Nigogosian 1996, 44.
209. Karpat 1981, 16, 19.
210. Gunter 1997, 71; Nigogosian 1996, 49; Khashan 1997, 11. Khashan points to "contagion effect" with respect to the seepage of Islamic revivalism, and at one level that is a good fit with Starr and Most's notion of "contagion effect."
211. Aykan 1996, 361; Gunter 1997, 100, 47-48, 53; Criss 1991, 145; Olson 1997, 18. *JPRS* 1994b. To be sure, there are scripted accounts seemingly at odds with one another with respect to Iran's longstanding position on PKK support. On the one hand, there is a 1994 scripted account that suggests Iran is supportive of Turkey in its struggle against PKK, while on the other hand, both Aykan and Gunter tell us that the PUK, which engaged in full-blown combat against the KDP in 1994, has received support from Iran after July 1996.
212. Williams 1988, 203-275; Kolko 1988; Nye 1993. The central idea of that notion might revolve around a twist on William Appelman Williams's revisionist notion of an "open door policy" with respect to the United States, where a Middle East rogue nation-state might use the activities of a sub-national actor to "walk through" with respect to influence, if not control outright of, new geographical sites.
213. Criss 1995, 25, 28-29; Criss 1991; Nigogosian 1996, 39; Baldwin 1971; Baldwin 1985; Gürbey 1996, 31-32; Chailand (1994) as found in Mango 1995, 8; Sprinzak 1991.
214. Mango 1994, 49-50, 46; Nigogosian 1996, 42.
215. Aykan 1996, 347; Gunter 1997, 66-67; Mango 1994, 49-50, 46.
216. Huntington 1968, 43, 84, 12-14, 78-79, 34-36.
217. Diamond, Linz, and Lipset 1990; Huntington 1968; Theen and Wilson 1986, 522-532; Theen and Wilson 1996, 497-505; Karpat 1981, 41-42; Criss 1995, 34-36; Gürbey 1996, 30; Muller 1996, 193-195; Mango 1994, 49-50. Alternatively, Mango tells us Kurdish-based political parties would help generate and sustain an effective Turkish political system.

Chapter 6

The Case of Israeli-Palestinian-Arab Terrorism

Introduction

The empirical analysis of Israeli-Palestinian-Arab terrorism in this work is performed against the backdrop of the fledgling Israeli-Palestinian "peace process" that is now confronted with the challenges and opportunities posed by the election of Prime Minister Ariel Sharon in 2001, and the seemingly more "hands off" approach to U.S. participation elicited by President George W. Bush. The tortuous historical legacy of the "peace process" is comprised of several watershed events that include the Declaration of Principles (DOP) - Oslo Agreement of 13 September 1993; the Oslo I Agreement or Cairo Agreement of 4 May 1994; the Oslo II Agreement or Taba Agreement of 26 September 1995; the Hebron Agreement of 1997; the Wye River Memorandum of 23 October 1998.[1]

The purpose of this section is to serve as a primer, to familiarize the reader with some highlights of certain "peace process" agreements, and the dynamics that undergird them, thereby in effect helping to place quantitative findings in a dynamic political context. The framework for discussion involves: discussion and description of antecedent political events and political dynamics to the "peace process"; some basic components and aims of the foregoing agreements;

analysis of particular Israeli-Palestinian-Arab terrorist organizations and their growth within the context of the "peace process" and other new political frameworks like the Taif Accord of 1989.

Political Dynamics and Antecedent Political Events

It is probably no exaggeration to say that the long-standing and time-honored conflict between Jews and Palestinians that really traces an arc to the 1880s has reached the point of full-blown exhaustion for both parties.[2] That exhaustion has really been encapsulated by events that presuppose and derive from the Israeli military occupation of the West Bank and Gaza since the defeat of Egypt, Syria, Jordan, and other Arab confrontation states in the 1967 Six Day War. In 1971 Israel's first prime minister, David Ben-Gurion, was on the right track to articulate long-haul concern about the emergent reality of Israeli control over the Occupied Territories, but, perhaps as a function of his Labor Zionist background, his focus on effects that Palestinian birthrates would have on the labor force, besmirched with a jingoist hue, were wide of the mark precisely because they failed to capture the dynamics and significance of unmet Palestinian demands and aspirations.[3]

Compounding that problem even more is what Rubin and others describe as the effects of the end of the Cold War and the breakup of the Soviet Union and the alliances between the Soviet Union, Soviet client states, and subnational actors that were a hallmark of regional and international politics in the Middle East.[4] As if that was not enough of a problem, the second Persian Gulf War in 1990-91 drove home the ineluctable conclusion that the "old politics" in the Middle East was passing into eclipse.

In a broader sense, that protracted conflict between Israelis and Palestinians evoked sentiments of resignation and other similar feelings on both sides, grounded in a seedbed of stark emergent realities. At a substantive level, the State of Israel has, as some have remarked, continuously evolved into what Lasswell calls a "garrison-police state" helping to rend apart the promise of a tranquil, thriving Jewish homeland and a secure, safe haven for Jews worldwide.[5] At a functional level, Israel's economy has been hampered in large part because of the enormous amount of revenue invested in weapons that have no rate of return associated with them, and which become obsolete, thereby in effect requiring the infusion of even more money.

From the Palestinian vantage, the land of "Paradise"[6] was rent apart by *al-Nakbah* or "the catastrophe" of the 1947-48 Israeli war of independence, and that watershed event was compounded by one disaster after the next, such as the manipulations of the Palestinian cause and the Palestinian elite by leaders of Arab nation-states, and several military conflicts such as the Six Day War of

1967, King Hussein's "Black September" expulsion of Palestinians from Jordan in 1970, the October War of 1973, the war in Lebanon in 1982, the Persian Gulf War in 1990-91, and the war between Israel and Hezbollah and other terrorist groups in southern Lebanon.

To be sure, the abject miseries associated with the horrors of the occupation and the economic backwater condition found in the Occupied Territories have had profound and lasting psychological effects and costs that are even inter-generational in effect among both the "inside" Palestinian community and the "outside" Palestinian diaspora. In turn, many Israelis have been scarred by the experiences of having to serve as members of a military of an occupying power in a role that is not compatible with the generally recognizable vision of what the Israel Defense Forces (IDF) are all about.

It is against that tortuous historical legacy that Israeli and Palestinian pragmatists in the late 1970s and 1980s began to conceptualize and cull out cornerstones for breaking that cycle of zero-sum political and military gains and losses in pursuit of the goal of "mutual gain" for both Israelis and Palestinians.[7] Those cornerstones include the acceptance among many Palestinians of the "two-state solution" within the context of United Nations Security Council Resolutions 242 and 338, and the recognition by former Israeli Prime Minister Menachem Begin at Camp David in 1978 of a Palestinian autonomy plan.[8]

With the passage of time, the United States, always a frequent visitor when helping to promote more even-handed or symmetrical negotiations and interconnections between Israelis and Palestinians, entered into a "dialogue" with the PLO in 1988 in exchange for a commitment from the PLO to stop the use of terrorism in the political fray. Both Israeli and Palestinian ruling elite, shackled with the deleterious effects of communal conflict, were seemingly prepared, both in psychological and political terms, to tackle the ticklish question of compromise in pursuit of "the peace of the brave."[9]

The Makeshift and Never Complete Political Structure of the "Peace Process": Background and Review

The Declaration of Principles and Oslo Agreement of 1993

The Declaration of Principles (DOP), that presupposes and derives from the Madrid talks in 1991, was elicited by Israeli and Palestinian negotiators in the summer of 1993. The Oslo Agreement was signed on the White House lawn by Prime Minister Yitzhak Rabin, PLO Chairman Yasser Arafat, and Foreign Minister Shimon Peres on 13 September 1993.[10] In turn, the Oslo I Agreement of 1994 was implemented to serve as a guidepost or gatekeeper for the effective and sustained implementation of the original Oslo Agreement. As Anderson,

Seibert, and Wagner, as well as Rubin, tell us, Oslo I is an "interim agreement" that worked to lay a keel for Palestinian autonomy in Gaza and the West Bank, as stipulated in Article I, for an interim period of no longer than five years.[11]

The Oslo Agreement provides a basic framework where mechanisms and procedures for a set of fledgling Israeli-Palestinian interconnections are articulated.[12] In the Oslo Agreement, the rudiments of what is called in Article I, "a Palestinian Interim Self-Government Authority, the elected Council (the "Council"), for the Palestinian people in the West Bank and the Gaza Strip" are delineated in more specificity in Article 7 and Article 9 that follow.[13] Some predominant features that those provisions describe involve the crafting of "a strong police force, while Israel will continue to carry the responsibility for defending against external threats" as stipulated in Article VIII, and the "transfer of authority" to the Palestinian National Authority in the realm "education and culture, health, social welfare, direct taxation, and tourism" as stipulated in Article VI (2) of the Oslo Agreement.[14]

The Oslo Agreement also provides for political and economic forums to augment the fledgling "peace process" that include "a Joint Israeli-Palestinian Liaison Committee" described in Article X to address "disputes," "coordination," and matters of "common interest," and, as stipulated in Article XI, "an Israeli-Palestinian Economic Cooperation Committee."[15] In a similar vein, participation of the governments of Egypt and Jordan are ensured in Article XII that provides for mechanisms whereby the governments of Egypt and Jordan can serve as gatekeepers for "liaison and cooperation arrangments between the Government of Israel and the Palestinian representatives." In addition, the governments of Egypt and Jordan may facilitate review of the status of "persons displaced" in 1967 by means of crafting or "constitution of a Continuing Committee".[16]

The Oslo I Agreement of 1994

One way of thinking about the Oslo I Agreement[17] of 4 May 1994 is how it expands further the scope of many of the political, military, and economic forums and processes that remain somewhat makeshift and incomplete in the Oslo Agreement.[18] For example, under Article III, some of the processes associated with the transfer of civil control from the Israeli Civil Administration and military government to the Palestine National Authority (PNA) are delved into more deeply in the Protocol Concerning Civil Affairs as found in Annex II.[19] In addition, the "Joint Israeli-Palestinian Liaison Committee" described in Article X of the Oslo Agreement is dealt with in more detail in Article XV (2) (3) (4) of the Oslo I Agreement.[20]

Regrettably, one of the underlying problems with Oslo I, like the Oslo

Agreement that comes before, is that certain mechanism procedures are couched in language that is sometimes so open-ended or vague as to make some of the mechanisms for conflict resolution essentially inoperative.[21] For example, Article XVII (2) stipulates that "disputes which cannot be settled by negotiations may be settled by a mechanism of conciliation to be agreed between the Parties."[22] But that clause seems to beg the question insofar as if Israelis and Palestinians cannot agree on issues at a substantive level, it seems likely that at a functional level non-agreement might also prevail with respect to the method of "conciliation" chosen, or if arbitration ensues, the group of arbitrators selected.

What seems significant here is that Oslo I makes it clear that the Palestine Liberation Organization (PLO) and not the Palestinian National Authority (PNA) has the authority to "conduct negotiations and sign agreements with states or international organizations for the benefit of the Palestinian Authority" as stipulated in Article VI (2) (a) and (2) (b) of the Oslo I Agreement.[23] Under Article VI (2) (c), what does, interalia, fall in the realm of the PNA is the implementation of PLO agreements that includes, but is not limited to, the creation of "representative offices" for international organizations and foreign states other than the types of "representative office" listed in Article VI (2) (a) of the Oslo I agreement, such as "embassies, consulates or other types of foreign missions and posts.[24]

With respect to the promulgation of Palestinian National Authority legislation, Article VII of Oslo I describes mechanisms put into place to give the Israeli government an opportunity to review and consider whether or not particular legislation is "otherwise inconsistent" with the Oslo I Agreement or "exceeds the jurisdiction of the Palestinian authority."[25] Article XII (1) informs us that Israel and the PNA are not to act as provocateurs with respect to one another and shall carry out legal actions to prevent provocative actions evoked by third parties.[26] Another section of the Oslo I Agreement deals with the treatment and status of collaborators where, as found in Article XX (4), "until an agreed solution is found, the Palestinian side undertakes not to prosecute these Palestinians or to harm them in any way."[27]

In the broadest sense, and by design, the most contentious issues at the heart of the Israeli-Palestinian conflict—that include, but are not limited to, the final status of Jerusalem, borders, the final status of Israeli settlers, and the so called "right of return" for Palestinians in the diaspora—are never delved into in the Oslo I Agreement.[28] To be sure, that stratagem revolved around the central idea that by "front-loading" interim agreements on crucial matters, the "peace process" would have the capacity to generate and sustain a momentum that would provide reason enough for compromise on those critical issues with the passage of time.[29]

The Oslo II Agreement of 1995

The Oslo II interim Agreement[30] supercedes the Oslo I interim agreement as stipulated in Article XXXI (2) of the Oslo II Agreement.[31] This new interim agreement replicates and in some cases builds on forums that were previously delineated in the Declaration of Principles and augmented under the Oslo I Agreement. Examples of such forums that are replicated in Oslo II include "The Joint Israeli-Palestinian Liaison Committee" found under Article XXVI (1), and as stated in Article XXI (2), the capacity to craft a dispute "mechanism of conciliation to be agreed between the Parties." In turn, provisos for "arbitration" are found in Article XXI (3), while Article IX (5) (a), and (5) (b) of the Oslo II Agreement delineate the realms of PLO and PNA jurisdiction and responsibility.[32]

Notwithstanding that, there are modifications in Oslo II to existing structures and processes set out in the Declaration of Principles. For instance, under Article XVIII, modifications are made that provide greater specificity to the political power of Yasser Arafat with respect to making legislative initiatives, and "secondary legislation."[33] Article XVIII (3) states:

> [W]hile the primary legislative power shall lie in the hands of the Council as a whole, the Ra'ees of the Executive Authority of the Council shall have the following legislative powers: a. the power to initiate legislation or to present proposed legislation to the Council; b. the power to promulgate legislation adopted by the Council; and c. the power to issue secondary legislation, including regulations, relating to any matters specified and within the scope laid down in any primary legislation adopted by the Council.[34]

In addition, in Article XXII (2), on "Relations between Israel and the Council," education curricula offered in schools need to revolve around the central idea of helping to promote, "peace between the Israeli and Palestinian peoples."[35] In a similar vein, under Article XXVI (5), Oslo II calls for the establishment of a "monitoring and steering committee" under the aegis of "The Joint Israel-Palestine Liaison Committee" to oversee the fulfillment of the agreement.[36]

Seen from a historical vantage, one of the most significant aspects of Oslo II is the agreement, under "Final Clauses," Article XXXI (9), to change clauses of the 1964 and 1968 Palestinian National Charter that, as Butenschon relates, denied the State of Israel "legitimacy as a state."[37] For example, Article 9 of the Palestinian National Charter of 1968 states:

> Armed struggle is the only way to liberate Palestine. Thus it is the overall strategy, not merely a tactical phase. The Palestinian Arab people assert their absolute determination and firm resolution to continue their armed struggle and to work for an armed popular revolution for the liberation of their country and

their return to it. They also assert their right to normal life in Palestine and to exercise their right to self determination and sovereignty over it.[38]

Still another example of how the scope of Oslo II exceeds the scope of the Declaration of Principles is found under Article XXVIII (2), entitled "Missing Persons," where clauses that relate to finding Israeli soldiers and the bodies of Israeli soldiers are articulated.[39]

One underlying theme of Oslo II revolves around articulated efforts to constrain and suppress terrorism that are seemingly twofold in nature. At a substantive level, under Article XIII (2)(a), Oslo II delegates primary responsibility to "confronting the threat of terrorism" to the State of Israel. That article presupposes and derives from Article VIII of the Declaration of Principles.[40] At a functional level, under Article XV, both Israelis and Palestinians in more proximate terms, are required "to prevent acts of terrorism, crime and hostilities directed against each other, against individuals falling under the other's authority and against their property, and shall take legal measures against offenders."[41]

Under Oslo II, the issue of administrative framework composition in different geographical sites in the Occupied Territories is addressed. Under the agreement, the Occupied Territories are skillfully broken down into three administration types that involve "Area A," "Area B," and "Area C." In the case of "Area A" all geographical sites, that include all Palestinian towns and the Arab section of Hebron, fall under the aegis of the Palestine National Authority with the proviso that the Israeli military participate in Israeli-Palestinian "joint patrols."[42]

In turn, "Area B" locales are under a mixed system of administration where the Palestine National Authority has jurisdiction over civil matters and can retain a police force, but those administrative units and police remain under the aegis of Israeli military forces. In turn, geographical sites that do not fall in the spheres of "Area A" or "Area B" make up "Area C" which is under Israeli control. Those geographical sites include Israeli military bases, Israeli settlements, some areas without habitation, and locales deemed to be of strategic importance to the Israeli government.[43]

The Hebron Agreement of 1997

The Hebron Agreement was initialed on 15 January 1997 within the context of Oslo II after agreement between the government of Israel, led by Prime Minister Benjamin Netanyahu, and the Palestine Liberation Organization, led by PLO Chairman Yasser Arafat. The framework of that agreement revolves around the partition of Hebron into areas "H-1" and "H-2" and includes sections of that agreement that deal with security matters like "Joint Mobile Units"

(JMU) and "Rapid Response Teams" (RRT).[44] Area H-1 is comprised of "areas of Palestinian self rule" in Hebron. In turn, under section 10(b), H-2 areas are under Palestinian National Authority civil control except for "civil powers and responsibilities" that are maintained by the Israeli military government to promote and ensure the security of Israelis and Israeli property.

Under the Hebron Agreement areas that fall in the realm of H-2 include, but are not limited to, Beit Hadassah, the Arab Market, the Casba, Tel Rumeida, the Tomb of the Patriarchs, and the Machpela Cave, which is the site of the 1994 massacre of over two dozen Palestinians shot by Dr. Baruch Goldstein of Kiryat Arba. A sizable portion of the agreement deals with logistical and infrastructure matters such as joint patrols on roads and construction codes.[45] The Hebron Agreement skillfully breaks down administration of the city where 80 percent of city administration passes from Israeli to Palestinian National Authority control and where the Israeli government maintains military obligations for an area much smaller in size where some twenty thousand Palestinians and four hundred Jewish settlers live.[46] Seen from a chronological vantage, after the Hebron Agreement was agreed to, Prime Minister Netanyahu's plan to build a Jewish settlement at Har Homa in East Jerusalem was the impetus for full-blown suspension of the implementation of the Oslo II Agreement.[47]

The Wye River Memorandum of 1998

The underlying theme of the Wye River Memorandum concerns its use as an instrument to aid in the implementation of the Oslo II Agreement, rather than as a vehicle to supersede the provisions of the Oslo II Agreement.[48] Perhaps the single, most predominant part of the Wye River Memorandum is the agreement where the Israeli government is to transfer 13 percent of "Area C" land under Israeli control to "Area B" (12 percent) and "Area A" (1 percent) with the stipulation that three percent of the land transferred to "Area B" be put aside for "Green Areas and/or Nature Reserves."[49] In those areas it is the responsibility of the State of Israel for "protecting Israelis and confronting the threat of terrorism."[50]

In turn, stipulations about security issues that are more specific than what is found in Oslo II are found in "Section II" entitled "Security" under the Wye River Memorandum. For example, under "Security Actions (1)," a U.S.-Palestinian committee to discuss terrorism is set up to meet every two weeks, presumably to exchange information and plan counterterrorism stratagems.[51] In addition, under section B entitled "Security Cooperation," a trilateral committee comprised of American, Palestinian and Israeli representatives will meet to exchange information and plan strategy no less than every two weeks.[52] Under section C of Wye River, entitled "Other Issues," legal mechanisms and procedures for the "arrest and transfer of suspects and defendants" are described in section 3, "Legal Assistance in Criminal Matters," within the context of the Oslo II Agreement.[53] At a functional level, the reason why those provisions are critical is that many suspected terrorists, after carrying out terrorist assaults, have fled into areas under Palestinian National Authority control, thereby in effect helping to create problems for the Israelis with respect to arrest and prosecution.

Seen from the vantage of politics, what seems significant here is that the Wye River Memorandum was antithetical to the interests of Prime Minister Benjamin Netanyahu and other members of the right wing part of the Israeli body politic.[54] Faced with the strains and tensions generated and sustained by Israel's hard-liners, the Wye River Memorandum was not put into effect by the agreed date by Netanyahu ostensibly because of the reason it had not been ratified by the Israeli Knesset.[55] The execution of the Wye River Memorandum has remained makeshift and never complete, with the Israeli government having completed only one phase of redeployment, before Prime Minister Netanyahu stopped implementation of the Wye River Memorandum in 1998.[56]

Wye River Memorandum II: The Sharm-el Shaykh Agreement

A new incarnation of the Wye River Memorandum document, otherwise known as "Wye River II" or the Sharm el-Shaykh Agreement, was agreed to by PLO Chairman Yasser Arafat and Israeli Prime Minister Ehud Barak and put into effect on 5 September 1999, but the "peace process," fraught with peril, began to fray at the edges soon afterwards. Nowhere was the problem more acute than the disagreement over what lands to transfer to the PNA and the ticklish question of Israeli settlement construction.[57] At a functional level, one out of three redeployment stages had been completed before "Wye River II" was suspended.[58] With precious little in the way of accomplishment, President William Jefferson Clinton met with Prime Minister Ehud Barak and Chairman Arafat at Camp David in 2000 to re-ignite the "peace process," but the entire framework collapsed over their disagreement about the gemstone of Jerusalem.[59]

With the Camp David talks having reached a critical juncture, Likud Knesset member Ariel Sharon evoked rage and other similar feelings among Palestinians with his visit to the Temple Mount, also known as al-Haram al-Sharif, on 28 September 2000. What has been called the new "Intifadah" presupposes and derives from that visit and the continuously deteriorating political and military condition that followed in the wake of the failed Camp David negotiations. Accordingly, the "peace process" was tabled by Prime Minister Ehud Barak on 22 October 2000.[60] With the perception that Israeli security demands and aspirations were left unmet by Prime Minister Barak and

Israeli government officials, a generally recognizable call for an Israeli election for prime minister resulted in an overwhelming election victory for Ariel Sharon, and continued violence. The analysis now turns to discussion and description of significant actors in the system of Israeli-Palestinian-Arab terrorism within the context of emergent political realities.

Al-Qaida or "The Base"

The al-Qaida or "The Base" organization was established by Shaykh Osama bin Laden probably in 1988 and, according to the United States Department of State, consists of between "several hundred and several thousand members."[61] Engelberg is more specific in his estimation and puts the number of al-Qaida activists at "5,000 militants."[62] Predominant terrorist organizations that have "factions" involved with al-Qaida include Egypt's al-Jihad organization, Egypt's al-Jama'a al-Islamiya or the Islamic Group (IG), the Armed Islamic Group (GIA) of Algeria, and the Pakistani Islamic revivalist group known as Harakat ul-Ansur or Harakat ul-Mujahidin (HUM).[63]

The set of interconnections between al-Qaida and other terrorist groups that have been interwoven by bin Laden and his associates are extensive and reverberate powerfully, not only between various group wings but between various geographical sites that include, but are not limited to, Afghanistan, Pakistan, Saudi Arabia, Yemen, Jordan, Algeria, Egypt, Sudan, Kenya, Tanzania, parts of Europe, Canada, and the United States.[64] What seems significant here is the enormous capacity of al-Qaida to put together activists from a variety of backgrounds to carry out terrorist assaults and then disband that particular terrorist team in favor of others as new opportunities and political goals present themselves.[65]

The sources and origins of al-Qaida can be sorted out into clusters of factors that fall into Reiss and Roth's "predisposing," "situational," and "activating" factor categories.[66] In terms of "predisposing" factors at the "macrosocial" level of analysis, the time-honored and long-standing involvement of Western nations in the Middle East, strenuously competing with one another over natural resources and areas of strategic advantage, may be the single most basic "predisposing" factor to spur on contemporary Islamic revivalist extremists like Shaykh Osama bin Laden.

The role of Western intrigue in the twentieth century alone traces an arc to the McMahon-Hussein correspondence of 1915-16, the Sykes-Picot Agreement of May 1916, and the betrayal of Sharif Hussein of Mecca and his son Faisel by the French and eventually the British over an independent Arab state following the First World War.[67] That tortuous historical legacy and other events to come, like the U.S. overthrow of Iranian Prime Minister Dr.

Mohammad Mossadegh in 1953 and continued U.S. support for the State of Israel and pro-Western Sunni regimes like the al-Sa'ud dynasty in Saudi Arabia, helped to spur on not only Osama bin Laden but great Islamic revivalist leaders before him such as Sayyid Qutb of the Muslim Brotherhood in Egypt.[68] Indeed, as Ranstorp reports, it was Sayyid Qutb's notion of "dedicated vanguard," designed to confront the West that remained in a perennial condition of ignorance or *jahiliyya*, that had a profound and lasting effect on bin Laden.[69]

Seen from the vantage of late twentieth century events, it is possible to understand the way of thinking, if not condoning the methods, behind Islamic revivalist terrorist groups. The USSR passing into eclipse in 1991, the plunge of Russia almost willy-nilly into making efforts at rapid privatization replete with calamitous consequences, the slower but more steady pace of privatization in China, and the expansion of NATO into parts of Eastern Europe elicit generally recognizable credence to the argument that it is Islam and only Islam that stands up against the onslaught of American "cultural imperialism," in much the same way as Salah al-Din (1169-93) stood up to the Crusaders.[70] To be sure, Western instruments of dissemination have become even more dangerous and destructive in the eyes of many with the Internet of today, a quantum leap from the printing press, which according to Lewis played an important part in the downfall of the Ottoman Empire.[71]

Several political events fall into the sphere of what Reiss and Roth might call "situational" factors in the context of analysis of the coalescence of the al-Qaida group. First, was the Soviet Union ruling elite's invasion of Afghanistan in 1979 and subsequent rise of the American-backed "mujahdeen" who were trained to fight against both the Soviets and the pro-Soviet regime in Kabul. Those "mujahdeen" were augmented by several thousand so-called "Afghan-Arabs."[72] As Engleberg reports, it was that conflict that would create well-trained and battle-seasoned soldiers and, equally important, the infrastructure in Peshawar, Pakistan, itself a safe haven and launching pad for American and other Western-sponsored assaults against Soviet forces.[73] To be sure, that infrastructure would later serve as mechanisms to generate and sustain training facilities for many Islamic revivalist extremists.

In that context, Engelberg reports that an antecedent group to bin Laden's al-Qaida organization, called the Makhtab al Khadimat or "the Office of Services," was set up by a Jordanian Palestinian soldier-scholar known as Abdullah Azzam in 1984. One underlying theme of the "Office of Services" was to increase the allure for young persons to fight against Soviet forces in Afghanistan, presumably with American support, tacit or otherwise. For the author, bin Laden worked in tandem with Azzam, and with his wealth of some $300 million, bin Laden was able donate substantial amounts of money to the project.[74]

Another "situational" factor that led to the coalescence of al-Qaida revolves around the strains and tensions between many pro-Western Sunni governments in the Middle East and Islamic revivalists in countries like Algeria, Egypt, Morocco, Saudi Arabia, Pakistan, and Jordan.[75] Compounding that matter even more at the "individual-psychosocial" level of analysis was the "accumulated emotion" of some, but certainly not all "Afghani-Arabs" who wanted to expand the scope of "the Office of Services" to engage those regimes. Engleberg relates to us that Dr. Ayman al-Zawahari and perhaps Shaykh Umar Abdul Rahman of the al-Jihad group in Egypt had profound and lasting influence on bin Laden's fledgling notion of a greater scope and depth for the struggle against the enemies of Islam. One scripted account by Shafi'i reports that Zawahari's al-Jihad crafted a joint front with bin Laden called the World Front for the Liberation of the Holy Places.[76]

Perhaps it was this disagreement between Azzam, with his singular focus against the Soviets in Afghanistan, and those Egyptians over the path to take that served as an "activating" factor for bin Laden to craft a Makhtab al-Khadimat "splinter group" known as al-Qaida in or around 1988. After Azzam's car bomb assassination in 1989, the more extremist element of "the Office of Services" pushed what was left of Makhtab al-Khadimat into the fold of Shaykh bin Laden's al-Qaida organization. In turn, as al-Qaida grew apace, an "umbrella" like organization of many bin Laden-supported terrorist groups known as the International Islamic Front for Jihad against Jews and Crusaders was formed probably in 1998.[77] Simultaneously, al-Qaida may also use the name the Islamic Army for the Liberation of the Holy Places.[78] In this study, acts attributable to the International Islamic Front for Jihad against Jews and Crusaders, or the Islamic Army for the Liberation of the Holy Places, or claims of responsibility made by those groups are coded as al-Qaida terrorist assaults.

Hezbollah, within the Context of the Taif Accord of 1989

The purpose of this section is provide some insight into what amounts to Hezbollah's continuously evolving condition into what Lasswell might call the "maturity" phase of its development.[79] To be sure, some understanding of Hezbollah's development requires a discussion against the backdrop of Lebanon's continuously evolving political landscape, itself marked by the end of the Lebanese civil war of 1975-90 and the implementation of the Taif Accord in 1989.[80] The framework for discussion involves: discussion and description of more contemporary Lebanese politics as background and introduction; dynamics between Hezbollah, Iranian religious leaders, and Syrian leaders in Damascus; some basic Hezbollah players; the fitting of watershed political events into Reiss and Roth's schema for understanding "risk factors for violent behavior"; international linkages.[81]

The exact date of Hezbollah's beginnings seem shrouded in some uncertainty, with some scripted accounts that suggest Hezbollah was crafted under Iranian tutelage in 1983, even though Ranstorp's work, for example, tells us that the date July 1982 is closer to the mark.[82] At a substantive level, while Hezbollah is reported to have had some 500 armed activists during the 1980s, newer estimates that reflect the emergent reality of Hezbollah's increasingly predominant political and military position in southern Lebanon suggest that the figure has increased into the thousands.[83] For example, in his work about the Israeli and South Lebanon Army (SLA) conflict with Hezbollah, Harris reports that starting from 1991, and presumably through May 2000 when the Israelis withdrew willy-nilly from southern Lebanon, "Hizballah deployed about 700 fighters along the front, with several thousand in reserve in Beirut and the Biqa'. They faced about 2,800 SLA militiamen, principally Christians and Shi'is, and 1,000 Israeli troops, although the Israelis quickly brought large reinforcements from time to time."[84]

Accordingly, Hezbollah is coded as a "very large" terrorist group of between 2,500 and 11,000 or more members activists in *Tapestry of Terror*, by contrast to earlier work of mine that coded Hezbollah as a "moderate" size terrorist group.[85] The Believers Resistance Movement or al-Mukawama al-Moumna is a terrorist group described by Ranstorp as "close to the [Hezbollah] movement," while the Islamic Resistance can be viewed as a Hezbollah sub-component.[86]

As Ranstorp informs us, in the wake of Ayatollah Ruhollah Khomeini's death in 1989, Ayatollah Sayyid Muhammed Husayn Fadlallah wears the robes of "spiritual leader" of Hezbollah, even though it is commonplace to note that Ayatollah Fadlallah often puts distance between the set of interconnections between Hezbollah and himself, presumably for political and security reasons.[87] For Ranstorp, a "national Majlis al-Shura" council with an emphasis on top-down decision making characterized Hezbollah until, following Ayatollah Khomeini's death, an "Executive Shura" and "Politbureau" were culled out that helped to decentralize decision making somewhat by means of particular "portfolio" divisions.[88] With respect to specialized assaults, Ranstorp tells us about the Special Security Apparatus (SSA) of Hezbollah that carried out terrorist assaults against foreign nationals during the 1980s in Lebanon.[89]

At the most basic level, the fundamental matter of Hezbollah's increasing role in Lebanese politics really distills down to why Lebanon's system of confessional politics came to an end, at least in the formal sense, in 1989-90. In a broader sense, the aim here is to frame some pivotal Lebanese events and dynamics into a context to understand more completely the "window of opportunity" that helped to contribute to the shape and depth of Hezbollah's political involvement in Lebanese politics under the Taif political system.

As Wege explains, the National Pact of 1943 was a political framework that, in a broader sense, stemmed from Lebanon's constitution of 1926, and the

1932 census to generate and sustain Maronite Christian predominance over Sunnis and Shi'ites.[90] To be sure, it is possible to view the National Pact of 1943 and its enormous incapacity to stabilize Lebanon's system of "confessional politics" as a "predisposing factor" at the "macro-social" level of analysis that contributed to the emergent reality of Hezbollah in Lebanon and Hezbollah's significant political role under the Taif system.[91] In the narrower sense, Hezbollah's political role seems to have hinged on what Reiss and Roth might call "situational events" associated with the outcome of the Lebanese civil war. Such "situational events" include, but are not limited to, the defeat of General Michel Aoun in 1990 that was made possible in part by the support received by President Elias Hirawi, Syrian President Hafaz el-Assad's chosen leader of Lebanon, from Lebanese Forces (LF) Christian militia leader Dr. Samir Ja'Ja, done at General Aoun's expense.[92]

Both Ranstorp and Winslow, as well as Harris, seem to suggest that the dynamics of Lebanon's "confessional politics" is nowadays subsumed under a Syrian political superstructure generated and sustained by the late President Hafaz el-Assad, and his successor and son, President Bashar el-Assad.[93] That political system revolves around the central idea of what Winslow refers to as the "dual executive" system with former President Hirawi, who is a Maronite Christian, at the helm, sharing power with a series of Sunni prime ministers. Those Lebanese prime ministers have included Salim al-Hoss, Rashid Kharmi, as well as the current Prime Minister Rafiq al-Hirari, himself a person who has accrued billions of dollars of wealth and who has an almost singular focus on the reconstruction and economic revitalization of Lebanon.[94]

Equally important is the Syrian stratagem of working to install other leaders who are malleable and who help to promote Syrian geopolitical considerations. For example, Amal leader Nabhi Berri is a Shi'ite leader who primarily represents the Shi'ite community in southern Lebanon as Speaker of Parliament, and also serves in his capacity as leader of that Syrian "proxy group" as a counterweight to Iranian geopolitical interests.[95] In turn, Druze leader Wadi Jumblatt of the Progressive Social Party (PSP) was placed in the position of "Minister for War Displaced" in part to placate the Druzes of the mountainous Shuf region, thereby in effect making it possible for him to pursue the goal of better Druze-Christian relations in the political fray.[96] Prior to the emergent reality of President Emile Lahoud's election in 1998, President Hirawi, Prime Minister Hirari, and Speaker of the House Berri comprised what Harris calls a "troika" system of Lebanese authority under the aegis of Syrian President Bashar Assad.[97]

One of the underlying themes of Ranstorp's work is that a set of interconnections exists between Iranian clergy in civil and military positions in Iran and Hezbollah clergy that reverberates with profound and lasting effects on Hezbollah and its policy directions.[98] To be sure, a prevailing faction of religious clerics in Iran generates and sustains volcanic-like effects that influence

Hezbollah "institutions" and the path of Hezbollah activity pursued in the political fray.[99] At the same time, as Ranstorp, Harris, and Taheri all suggest, Iranian control over Hezbollah is makeshift and never complete, and particular Hezbollah "cells" may act with greater or lesser degrees of independence.[100] What also seems significant here is that understanding the interconnections between Hezbollah religious chieftains and Iranian religious leaders may, as Ranstorp suggests, serve as an indicator of "clergy factionalism" in Iran thereby in effect helping to reveal dynamics within the ruling elite of the Islamic Republic of Iran.[101]

Compounding the matter even more, those dynamics are set against the backdrop of what Ranstorp calls the Iranian-Syrian-Hezbollah "triangular relationship" in which Hezbollah promotes both Iranian and Syrian geopolitical interests on the ground in Lebanon, while both Syria and Iran promote Hezbollah's political and military stature in contemporary Lebanon under the Taif Accord.[102] To be sure, that arrangement, as Ranstorp tells us, is critical to both the Iranian and Syrian ruling elite insofar as the Syrian ruling elite remains heavily dependent on Iranian oil and relies in part on Hezbollah to help anchor its political agenda in the political fray that is Lebanese politics.[103] In turn, Winslow tells us that Iranian strength in Lebanon serves the Syrian ruling elite well as a counterweight to Saddam Hussein's Iraq.[104]

In turn, the Iranian ruling elite needs the cooperation of the Syrian ruling elite to promote its bridgehead among Lebanese Shi'ites, and to make certain that both Hezbollah and the Iranian Pasdaran (Revolutionary Guard) unit in the Biqa, there to augment Hezbollah, are allowed to thrive in effective and sustained ways.[105] The Syrian-Iranian alliance, as Ranstorp tells us, makes it possible for Iranian and Syrian leaders to use Hezbollah to inject a high dosage of political instability and social unrest to disrupt the fledgling Israeli-Palestinian "peace process" as it unfolds with the passage of time.[106] In the broader sense, and as a concomitant to the above, Iran's political elite, as Winslow suggests, needs to have carefully reasoned interconnections with President Assad to serve a counterweight to Iraq, its fierce rival in Middle East regional political affairs.[107] At a functional level, Harris tells us that the Iranians need those interconnections to maintain routes of financial and military assistance to Hezbollah in the Biqa Valley and beyond to the suburbs in the southern part of Beirut.[108]

There have been three Hezbollah "General Secretaries" who trace an arc to the fledgling years of Hezbollah during the early 1980s. Those three persons are Shaykh Subhi Tufeili (1987-91), Shaykh Abbas al-Musawi (1991-92), and the current leader of Hezbollah, Shaykh Hassan Nasserallah. A scripted account penned in 1996 reports that Hezbollah's "deputy leader" in Lebanon is Shaykh Naim Qassem.[109] A fourth person critical to the continuously evolving nature of Hezbollah was the religious cleric Shaykh Ragheb Harb, who was killed in fierce fighting that presupposed and derived from efforts to craft Hezbollah.[110]

An underlying theme in accounts by Ranstorp and others about Hezbollah revolves around the central idea that Hezbollah is not monolithic, but characterized by political rivalries that often presuppose and derive from competing alliances.[111] Within the context of Ranstorp's substantive discussion about a tapestry interwoven between Iran and Hezbollah, the author reports that Shaykh Subhi Tufeili, himself a "radical" who put a premium on the political goal of an Islamic Lebanon, was able to generate and sustain a close relationship with Ayatollah Montazari, himself a member of the more extremist camp of Iranian clergy that also includes Hojjat al-Islam Muhammad Musavi Kho'inihan, Musavi Khoeiniha, Medhi Hashemi, Hojjat al-Islam Ali Akbar Mohtashemi, and Ayatollah Ali Meshkeni.[112]

One way of thinking about Shaykh Subhi Tufili's ascendancy to Hezbollah's general secretary position is to view that event as one that at least in part presupposes and derives from what Reiss and Roth might call the "activating factor" of Israel's war in Lebanon in 1982.[113] During Israel's invasion of Lebanon, then-Defense Minister Ariel Sharon, seemingly pitting the interests of Prime Minister Menachem Begin against his own interests, spearheaded an Israel Defense Forces military assault that pressed deeply into Lebanon stopping just outside of Beirut. In fact, that "macro-social activating factor" and its probable effect on the composition of Hezbollah's chieftains may be one example that showcases the deleterious effects of heavy-handed, "hard-line" military or counterterrorism responses to terrorism, that in this case manifests itself in all-too-frequent Palestinian terrorist assaults against northern Israeli towns.

It may be that the political fray of Lebanese politics may have helped to elicit efforts to place a person like Shaykh Tufeili, with his vision of an Islamic Lebanese state, in the position of general secretary from the start. What Reiss and Roth might term the "situational-macro-social" factors at work here seem to revolve around the central idea of protracted conflict between Israelis and Palestinians and the availability of weapons in southern Lebanon and in Lebanon as a whole. To make further conjecture, "micro-social factors" at the "situational" level of analysis that may help to generate and sustain political instability and social unrest, might include strains and tensions between Sunnis and Shi'ites, and strains and tensions between Shi'ites and Palestinians in Lebanon, who precisely because of the reason they continue their ferocious struggle against Israel from Lebanese soil, make segments of the Lebanese populace targets of Israeli counterterrorist assaults as well.

Those dynamics between groups in Lebanon, seen from the vantage of Reiss and Roth's framework of analysis, might be viewed within the context of "participants social relationships" that are, in this case, frayed at the edges.[114] If the analysis is extended further, "predisposing factors" at the "macro-social" level of analysis would involve structural characteristics at both the domestic and international systems level.[115] First, the economic backwater condition of many in the Shia community in southern Lebanon that can be seen as an example of Reiss and Roth's "concentration of poverty," and second, in a broader sense, the clash between "oppositional cultures" found within the context of Islamic revivalist struggles against Israel and the West.[116]

In turn, Shaykh Tufeili's control over Hezbollah passed into eclipse with the ascendancy of Shaykh Abbas al-Musawi in 1991. As Ranstorp reports, Shaykh Musawi was a supporter of Ayatollah Khamani and former Iranian President Ayatollah Hashemi Rafsanjani, and, for Ranstorp, Musawi's capture of the general secretary position of Hezbollah echoed the prevailing strength of Iran's more "pragmatic" if not more moderate branch of religious clergy.[117] What seems significant here about Winslow's account is that he really suggests that the Persian Gulf War of 1990-91, replete with coalition partners from the Middle East, was, to use Reiss and Roth's terminology, an "activating macro-social factor" that could be construed to be what Reiss and Roth describe as a "catalytic social event."[118]

Compounding the matter even more was that the Persian Gulf War happened against the backdrop of a more profound and lasting "predisposing-macro-social" event, namely the end of the Cold War in 1989 and the passing into eclipse of the Soviet Union on 25 December 1991 while under the aegis of General Secretary Mikhail Gorbachev.[119] It could be argued, as both Ranstorp and Harris suggest, that both the "macro-social-activating factor" of the Persian Gulf War and the "macro-social-predisposing factor" of the Cold War's end helped to reconfigure Middle East politics, thereby in effect making it necessary for Hezbollah chieftains to elicit cooperative interactions over the hostage situation that reached its apex with the release of all the American, French, British, and German hostages held by Hezbollah or its affiliates.[120]

All of the foregoing really boils down to the fundamental matter of why the Israelis assassinated Shaykh Abbas al-Musawi in a helicopter gunship assault in 1992, knowing that any political gains made by killing him might be more than offset by the emergent reality of an even more extremist Hezbollah chieftain like Shaykh Nasserallah taking the helm. To be sure, as Ranstorp points out, the answer may be twofold. At one level, Shaykh Musawi stoked the burners of conflict with the Israelis and, as Ranstorp suggests, he may have been killed precisely because of the reason that negotiations between the Israelis and Hezbollah over captured Israel Defense Forces personnel and Israeli pilot Rod Arad had foundered. At another level, Ranstorp suggests that the Americans were enraged over the hanging of Lieutenant Colonel William Higgens who served the United Nations as a peacekeeper in Lebanon.[121]

At the same time, we are told by Ranstorp that Shaykh Musawi was less extremist than others like Shaykh Tufeili insofar as he had a capacity to introduce pragmatism into a political landscape fraught with peril.[122] Seen from that vantage, "hard-line" Israeli counterterrorism assaults, presumably to match the aggressiveness of Musawi's increased focus on conflict against the State of Israel in southern Lebanon, may have been costly in the long haul, falling short of the mark of suppression or constraint of Hezbollah. To be sure, some public political recognition by the Israeli government about Lebanese political demands and aspirations, coupled with prisoner exchanges, perhaps in tandem with some "third party" negotiations about long-haul consensus issues, may have provided some leverage that might have helped to bring about at least a lengthening of the time horizon where pragmatism might have been able to predominate over radicalism.[123]

Perhaps the single most dominant indicator of Hezbollah's evolving life-cycle into its "maturity phase" was its formal foray into Lebanese politics during the August through September 1992 Lebanese national elections.[124] The underlying reasons for the decision by Hezbollah chieftains to contest that election remain oblique and open to interpretation. On the one hand, Ranstorp places emphasis on Shaykh Hassan Nasserallah's problems with control over the Islamic Resistance and his view that saw more mainstream political participation as a vehicle to pursue his goal of an Islamic state in Lebanon.[125] For Ranstorp, Nasserallah continues to generate and sustain military activities that sometimes include terrorist assaults against the Israelis by means of the Islamic Resistance.[126]

On the other hand, Wege seems to place more emphasis on the dynamics of Iran's political elite, within the context of personal differences between Tufeili and Nasserallah, skillfully breaking down Hezbollah into a political faction and a military appendage known as the Islamic Resistance.[127] Be that as it may, in its incarnation as a thriving political party with the support of the Syrians, Hezbollah was able to garner twelve out of one hundred twenty-eight seats in the Lebanese National Assembly.[128] Harris tells us that a combined Hezbollah-Amal ticket list was able to generate and sustain strong support among the 1.3 million Shiites in southern Lebanon.[129]

During the 1996 national elections, Hezbollah was able to garner four seats in national elections, again working with Amal on a combined ticket put together willy nilly by the Syrians at the last possible juncture.[130] That combined Hezbollah-Amal party list had the capacity to capture all twenty-three seats apportioned to south Lebanon.[131] While the historical legacy of Hezbollah's role in Lebanese politics began under the aegis of Musawi, it was, as Ranstorp reports, Shaykh Hassan Nasserallah who decided that Hezbollah ought to delve into the national political arena in 1992, even though Shaykh Tufeili looked askance at that idea precisely because of the reason that, from Tufeili's vantage, Hezbollah's political participation in national elections detracted from the goal of an Islamic state in Lebanon.[132] In large part, the future role of Hezbollah will presuppose and derive from intersecting and at time antithetical Syrian, Iranian, and Iraqi geopolitical interests, themselves determined in large part by the future direction of the Israeli-Palestinian "peace process."

The Palestinian National Authority and Palestine Liberation Organization: Interconnections and the Response of the "Rejectionist" Camp

In this section that informs us about new developments for the Palestinian National Authority and the Palestine Liberation Organization, the purpose is to explore the continuously evolving environment against the backdrop of the Israeli-Palestinian "peace process." The framework of discussion involves: the continuously evolving condition of the Palestinian National Authority (PNA or PA); the dynamics between "inside" and "outside" Palestine communities that generate and sustain strains, tensions, and growth; interconnections between the Palestine Liberation Organization, the Palestinian National Authority, and al-Fatah; dynamics of PLO-PNA growth and maturity within the context of the Reiss and Roth analysis; the response of the hard-line "rejectionists" to the unfolding "peace process" and the fledgling proto-government in Gaza and Jericho.

The Palestinian National Authority, oftentimes called the Palestinian Authority, became an emergent reality in May 1994.[133] As Parker reports, the single, most predominant role for the Palestinian National Authority is to implement Israeli-PLO agreements in geographical sites under PA jurisdiction, while it is the PLO that forges agreements between Israel and the fledgling Palestinian state.[134] For Parker, "the PLO, which no longer able to effectively represent its traditional constituency, is still the official partner in negotiations, and not the PA, which is responsible for administering the accords in the self-rule areas."[135]

As both Hilal and Hassassian report, the Palestinian National Authority is a fledgling proto-government or what Parker describes as a "provisional regime," where the "executive authority" remains the single most dominant part of government with respect to the Palestinian Legislative Council (PLC) elected on 20 January 1996, and the judicial part of government.[136] While the "executive branch" of the Palestinian National Authority has been active in the political fray since the PA bloomed in 1994, presidential elections were also held on 20 January 1996 and Arafat won the electoral vote, beating his one competitor, Samihah Khalil, by 88 percent to the 9.3 percent garnered by Khalil.[137]

For Hilal, precisely because of the reason that the "executive branch" under the aegis of President Arafat emerged from the start, Arafat was and is still able to pull at the strings of control to ensure the predominance of "outside" al-Fatah, insofar as al-Fatah persons hold positions in the security system and the military courts, thereby in effect helping to promote Arafat's own political interests as well as Israeli and American interests that hinge on the constraint and suppression of Hamas and Islamic Jihad.[138] For Jad, what seems significant here is that there is no clear-cut procedure for succession when the Arafat era passes into eclipse. Jad relates that the Basic System of Law of the Palestinian National Authority stipulates in Articles 6 and 9 that the Speaker of the Palestinian Legislative Council (PLC) is at the helm of power until a new election is held within a two-month time period.[139] Jad, in my judgment, is correct when he tells us that the final decision will be influenced heavily by the Israeli ruling elite.[140]

Perhaps the single, most dominant set of dynamics that undergird the continuously evolving condition of the Palestinian National Authority revolve around the central notion of strains and tensions between the "inside" Palestinian community that lives in the "refugee camps," "villages," and "towns" in the Occupied Territories and the "outside" Palestinian community of the Palestinian diaspora that lives in places like Lebanon, the Gulf states, Tunisia, Europe, and the United States.[141] Compounding the matter even more, strains and tensions between the "inside" and "outside" Palestinian communities involve fissures at several levels over and beyond simple demographic distinctions.

For instance, we are told by Parker that Lindholm Schultz's conceptualization involves defining characteristics that revolve around emphasis that the "inside" Palestinian community places on civil structures like trade unions, women's movements, and family, while "outside" Palestinians with their "Tunis mentality" place emphasis on bureaucratic and military organizations.[142] Further still, it is commonplace to note a "Kulturekampf" between "inside" and "outside" Palestinian communities strenuously competing with one another over fledgling political power. For example, it is commonplace to hear about differences between Palestinian "outsiders" who, as Parker states, have been oriented towards "conspicuous consumption" by contrast to "insiders" who, with the exception of the elite, have been fettered by the economic backwater conditions of the Occupied Territories.[143] Compounding the matter even more, the author suggests that life experiences for Palestinians under Israeli occupation have an enormous capacity to differ, in part because of the reason that Palestinian locales have become increasingly isolated from one another. For Parker, "a complex patchwork of varying jurisdictions and varying degrees of political autonomy mean that Palestinians are experiencing self rule differently, even within the 'autonomous areas.'"[144]

As Frisch, Parker, Hilal, and Butenschon all point out, higher-level leadership positions in the Palestinian National Authority have been garnered by al-Fatah "outsiders" from the Palestinian diaspora who have in effect wrested power away from Palestinian "insiders."[145] For Frisch and certainly for others, what seems significant here is that al-Fatah is, at a functional level, "depoliticized" as high-ranking al-Fatah personnel coming from places like Tunis are drawn into PNA institutions and the political fray of politics in Gaza City.[146] Indeed, as Frisch points out, both Palestinian "insiders" and Palestinian "outsiders" did not want al-Fatah to contest the January 1996 elections as a political party.[147] The author goes on to explain that Arafat has increasingly relied on kinship ties among predominant Palestinian families to generate and sustain support in pursuit of what Frisch describes as a "neopatriarchy" with Arafat at the helm.[148]

At a functional level, al-Fatah officials who function as PLO mouthpieces evoke the hard-line nationalist sentiments and similar feelings that the PLO would find imprudent to express. For example, in an interview, al-Fatah Central Committee member Muhammad Ghunaym, otherwise known as Abu-Mahir, tells us, "the Zionist entity. . . . has ignored international legitimacy and its resolutions, threatened security and peace, backtracked on the signed agreements, and continued to confiscate Palestinian land, build colonies, confiscate freedoms, close borders, and prevent people from moving between the West Bank and the Gaza Strip and from reaching their workplaces merely to compel the Palestinian people to accept the fait accompli policy the Zionist enemy is trying to implement on Palestinian territory."[149] It is also commonplace to note that al-Fatah personnel at are the heart of Tanzim paramilitary activities in the Occupied Territories. At a substantive level, younger al-Fatah members from the "inside" who were born and raised in the Occupied Territories find themselves increasingly at the fringes of higher-echelon political power and are relegated into the sphere of middle-level institutional actors. As Frisch reports, it is within the context of the foregoing that persons like al-Fatah official Marwan al-Barghuthi lambast Yasser Arafat for his "top-down" autocratic style of political control.[150]

One way of thinking about the continuously evolving condition of the PLO and its increasingly pragmatic approach to conflict with Israel is to frame some watershed political events into the Reiss and Roth taxonomy of "risk factors" for violence.[151] In terms of "macrosocial-predisposing" events that compelled the PLO to embrace a more pragmatic approach, perhaps the single most predominant factor is the Six Day War of 1967 that besmirched the reputation of President Gamal Abdul Nasser's military as a robust threat to the Israel Defense Forces (IDF).[152] In the wake of the Six Day War of 1967, a profound and lasting crisis, about whether a Pan-Arab or Palestinian perspective ought to predominate in the fierce struggle against Israel played out, involving Nasser's offer of resignation and the December 1967 resignation of the PLO's first chairman of its executive Committee, Ahmad Shuqairy, who favored a Pan-Arab emphasis for the struggle, and who is perhaps best known for his clarion call "to drive the Jews into the sea."[153]

Compounding the problem even more is what can be thought of as another "predisposing factor," namely Israel's victory over Arab confrontation states in the October War of 1973, where Arafat, as Seale and Gresch both tell us, now understood that the Israelis would not be destroyed by military force and, equally important, that President Nixon and Secretary of State Kissinger were both inextricably bound up with the idea of laying a keel for more symmetrical

negotiations between Israelis and Arabs, and Arab-Palestinians.[154] To extend
the analysis even more, that epiphany for Yasser Arafat might be viewed within
the context of a "predisposing factor" at the "individual-psychosocial" level of
analysis where at the level of "cognitive ability," shop-worn romantic notions
of a full-blown liberation of all of Palestine were eclipsed, and where this shift
in cognitive capacity might be framed within the context of "perceptions of
rewards/penalties for violence."[155]

Hence, both Butenschon and Hassassian report it is possible to trace an arc
from what Hassassian says is the end of the PLO's "maximalist position," that
issued the clarion call for the complete physical destruction of the State of
Israel, to the lurking catastrophe of the Six Day War of 1967.[156] In turn, both
Butenschon and Hassassian trace a curve from the PLO idea of a "democratic
and secular state" passing into eclipse to the Israeli victory over Arab
confrontation states in the October War of 1973.[157] Seen from the vantage of
both Butenschon and Hassassian, what was to come was the emergent reality of
a "two state approach" that called for an independent Palestinian state that
abutted the State of Israel consistent with United Nations Security Council
resolutions 242 and 338, that in reality breathed new life into the United Nations
General Assembly Resolution 181 of 1947 that calls for the partition of Palestine
into Jewish and Arab states.[158]

Turning to an analysis of "macrosocial-situational factors," what seems
significant here is what both Parker and Cubert describe as the influence of the
Intifadeh of 1987-91 on the enormous capacity of Yasser Arafat and the PLO
to introduce flexibility into their reactions to the continuously evolving mass
struggle in the Occupied Territories against the Israeli occupation.[159] For
Parker, Arafat, from his crow's nest in Tunis, had the enormous capacity to
shift almost singular attention away from an emphasis on activity that emanated
from the "outside" Palestinian community or Palestinian diaspora, to working
to establish a beachhead in the political and military fray of politics and action
in the Occupied Territories.[160] Cubert provides us with a Palestinian account,
accepted by some but certainly not all, that suggests local PLO officials in the
Occupied Territories, working in tandem with the PLO in Tunis, may have been
inextricably bound up planning the Intifadeh.[161]

Another "situational" factor at the "macrosocial" level of analysis
instrumental with respect to the changing stratagems of the PLO might be the
Persian Gulf War of 1990-91.[162] Nowhere were the problems posed by the
end of the Cold War more acute for Middle East politics than in the case of the
Persian Gulf War, where Arab nation-states such as Egypt and Syria were part
of a coalition of forces spearheaded by the United States and marshaled against
the military forces of another Arab state.

As both Hilal and Cubert tell us, the old politics of the Middle East had
passed in eclipse in the wake of the Cold War and the breakdown of the Soviet
Union, along with the economic assistance that had been provided by the Soviet

ruling elite to its "proxy states" and sub-national clients.[163] For Hilal, the enormous pressures generated and sustained with that structural shift in the international political system, coupled with the full-blown defeat of President Saddam Hussein of Iraq and Arafat's blunder of siding with Saddam Hussein in the Persian Gulf War, led to the Madrid Conference talks of 1991 between Israelis and non-PLO Palestinians, and remains a powerful impetus for PLO leaders to practice pragmatic negotiations with the Israeli ruling elite.[164]

PNA Opposition: The "Rejectionist Front"

The single most predominant theme of the "Rejectionist Front," that was originally crafted in 1974, revolves around its opposition to the fledgling "peace process" between Israelis and Palestinians, and thereby in effect, as Cubert puts it, its opposition to "the PLO's authority."[165] The organizations that comprise the "Rejectionist Front" include George Habash's Popular Front for the Liberation of Palestine, Ahmed Jabril's Popular Front for the Liberation of Palestine-General Command, the Democratic Front for the Liberation of Palestine of Naif Hawatamah, the Arab Liberation Front, Al-Sa'iqa, Fatah-the Uprising, Fatah-the Revolutionary Council, the Tal'at Yaqub Faction of the PLF, the Islamic Resistance Movement, the National Salvation Front, Hamas and Islamic Jihad.[166] Another cornerstone of this way of thinking portrays the framework of the Oslo agreements as helping to place the United States and Israel in a predominant position over the struggle of Palestinians, Palestinian leaders in their pursuit of political goals over the landscape, and, in a broader sense, the struggle of Arabs and other Muslims against the West.[167]

What seems significant here, and from the vantage of PLO leaders especially fortuitous, is that the hard-line Palestinian opposition has not been able to respond in effective and sustained ways to the challenges and opportunities posed by the Oslo accords and the Wye River Memorandum, even though the fledgling Palestinian National Authority remains fettered with political and economic problems of its own.[168] As Hilal reports, part of the problem presupposes and derives from the enormous inability of the "rejectionist" organizations, many of which are far removed from the Occupied Territories in "outside" Palestinian communities such as those in Syria and Lebanon, to come together to craft a thriving parallel structure that might pose an alternate challenger to the power of the Palestinian National Authority (PNA).[169]

Cubert makes the important point that among "rejectionist" terrorist groups there are grades of rejection ranging from complete rejection of Israel outright by the Popular Front for the Liberation of Palestine (PFLP) and Hamas, to what the author terms the "reluctant rejection" of the Democratic Front for the Liberation of Palestine (DFLP).[170] In a similar vein, Cubert explains that there are differences with respect to why Hamas and PFLP chieftains reject Israeli-PNA talks, insofar as Hamas views the struggle as an unbreachable one with Jews and Muslims strenuously competing with one another, while the PFLP views the "two state solution" only as a springboard for further political and military gains made against Israel to stoke the burners for a final lethal assault against Israel.[171]

Notwithstanding that, both Parker and Cubert report two attempts by "rejectionist" groups to form such a mirror alternative to the PNA-PLO framework with the coalescence of the Alliance of Palestinian Forces that was put together in 1994, and the Palestinian Independence Front that was crafted in 1996.[172] As Hilal, Parker, and Cubert all suggest, one of the underlying themes that revolves around those organizations and, by extrapolation similar organizational efforts, are the visceral personal rivalries and ideological strains and tensions between Hamas and the PFLP, for example, that really presuppose and derive from the eclectic range of ideological standpoints of the participant groups.[173]

As if that was not enough of a problem, Hilal reports that the radical PLO opposition groups embraced a myopic-like approach to the Palestinian Legislative Council elections by abstaining from that January 1996 election, thereby in effect frittering away any chance to influence unfolding political events in effective and sustained ways. We are told that particular individuals who did contest and win seats in the election ran as "independents" and did not contest that election as representatives of specific Islamic groups like Hamas or Islamic Jihad.[174]

Following the 1996 election, the emergent reality is a PNA government with a Palestine Legislative Council (PLC) with eighty-eight seats that includes six seats allotted to those with what Hilal describes as having "an Islamic background (five from a radical background)."[175] Be that as it may, Arafat in his quest to exert full-blown executive control over the legislative body of the PNA has, according to Haidar Abdul Shufi, himself a "Fatah independent" or non-al-Fatah slate candidate and subsequent Palestinian Legislative Council member, relegated the Palestine Legislative Council to the fringes of political power.[176] In the broader sense, both Parker and Cubert tell us that Arafat has had acute problems in his efforts to bring the Palestinian hard-line opposition into the sphere of the Palestinian National Authority political framework.[177]

Jewish Fundamentalist Terrorism: The Case of the Kahanist Movement

One way of thinking about the continuously evolving condition of Kach, Kahane Chai, and its spin-off groups is to view developments within the context of the Reiss and Roth risk factor matrix.[178] With respect to Kach and its continuously evolving condition, ranging from political maturity as an official Knesset political party to its more clandestine role in the Israeli political fray today as an illegal organization, the analysis chronicles political structural decline at one level but, from a qualitative view, seemingly more vitriolic terrorist assaults as it moves forward within the context of the time period of the Oslo agreements.[179]

In a broader sense, cumulative pressures on Jewish fundamentalist extremists have been generated and sustained by what Reiss and Roth might call several "predisposing factors" at the "macrosocial" level of analysis. With respect to Kach ("Thus" or "the Way"), one pivotal "macrosocial-predisposing" factor was the "anti-racist" amendment passed by Israel's Central Election Committee in 1985, thereby in effect making it possible for Israel's supreme court to ban Kach from official political participation in the Israeli national elections of 1988.[180] Seen from the Reiss and Roth vantage, political "opportunity structures" at the national level of politics were wrested away from Kach, perhaps contributing to what Thucydides might describe as some sort of "stasis" or "blockage" where the interests of a segment of Israeli society were thwarted with the potential for more seepage of Kach undertakings into the sphere of extralegal activity.[181]

Even though Kahanist movement membership and Gush Emunim membership are sometimes interpenetrating, but sometimes distinct from one another, the generally recognizable political condition of the Gush Emunim is, I think, inextricably bound up with the extremist Jewish fundamentalists of Kach and Kahane Chai.[182] Bearing that in mind, another "predisposing factor" that may have spurred on change so that Kahane-types found themselves or perceived themselves to be increasingly undercut and/or isolated in the political fray revolves around what Sprinzak calls the "deradicalization of [the] Gush Emunim" or "Bloc of the Faithful" movement in the early 1990s.[183]

For Sprinzak, the underlying reasons why the ideological core of the Gush Emunim began to fray at the edges are threefold. First, the Gush Emunim settler lifestyle, as the author reports, became more affluent, pitting the interests of effective and sustained political participation that requires time, sacrifice, and the threat of imprisonment, among other things, against the interests and comforts associated with an Israeli incarnation of the "American dream."[184]

Second, Sprinzak asserts that "technocrats" with less extremist political positions began to staff administrative positions starting in the 1970s in political institutions like Amana and the Yesha Council thereby in effect spreading a view of the world more concerned about more immediate political and material gain than with ideological commitment.[185] Third, we are told by Sprinzak that there has been a "decline in charismatic leadership" among rabbis in the wake of the death of Rabbi Zvi Yehuda Kook (1891-1982) insofar as the Merkaz ha-rav Yeshiva which he headed set an example for other yeshivas for a more singular focus on Torah study rather than full-blown expression of nationalist sentiments and other similar feelings.[186]

From the vantage of the Reiss and Roth taxonomy, what seems significant here is there may be interconnections between those foregoing "macrosocial-predisposing factors" and a set of "microsocial-predisposing factors" on the one hand, as well as to "individual" level "psychosocial factors" on the other. For example, what Sprinzak calls the "'bourgeoisification' of [the] Gush Emunim," here labeled a "macrosocial predisposing factor," may have caused strains and tensions or even rent apart what Reiss and Roth call "microsocial-preexisting structures," whether formal or informal, between members of the Gush Emunim and members of the Kahanist camp.[187]

In turn, the continuously changing condition of Gush Emunim may have triggered in Kahane-type persons interpretations of abandonment at the individual level of analysis where "cognitive ability" processes may have interpreted those dynamics with a holocaust reading of abandonment of the Jewish people, that culminated with the Second World War. Extending the analysis even further, it is possible that against the backdrop of the foregoing, persons like Dr. Baruch Goldstein may have more severe problems at the "psychosocial" level of analysis, perhaps coupled with some risk factor at the "biological" level of analysis, that contributes to the commission of terrorist assaults generally recognizable as moving over and beyond other acts of terrorism practiced against Palestinian-Arabs such as beatings, vandalism, intimidation, and stone-throwing.[188]

There are several of what Reiss and Roth might call "situational" factors that may have compounded pressures even more for Kahane types to engage in terrorist assaults to demonstrate "staying power," itself associated with the "predisposing factors" previously mentioned. Those "situational factors" include the assassination of Rabbi Meir Kahane in New York by el-Sayyid al-Nosair on 5 November 1990, the election victory of the Labor Party in 1992 over the Likud Party under the aegis of Prime Minister Yitzhak Shamir, and the outright ban of Kach and Kahane Chai in 1994 in the wake of the Hebron massacre.

Unequivocally, the assassination of Rabbi Meir Kahane, the founder and charismatic leader of Kach who traces an arc to the Jewish Defense League that he also founded in 1968, disrupted "participants' social relationships" within Kach at the "microsocial-situational" level of analysis. As Schlein of the Hebrew newspaper *Maariv* tells us, in the wake of Kahane's murder it was for Kach chieftain Tiran Pollack "still unclear how the future leadership of the movement will appear, if one man or the leadership group is to be elected."[189] In a broader sense, Kahane's murder would help to alter the Israeli political landscape insofar as Kach splinter or spin-off groups or proto-groups were spawned.

To be sure, the assassination of Rabbi Meir Kahane by el-Sayyid al-Nosair, an Islamic fundamentalist extremist inextricably tied to Shaykh Umar Abdul Rahman in the New York City area, may have further helped to exacerbate the influence of "macrosocial-predisposing factors," namely "oppositional cultures" dynamics in Israel between Jews and Arabs and perhaps even other non-Jews. In turn, the foregoing may have helped to generate and sustain the influence of "psychosocial factors" at the individual level of analysis. It seems plausible that Kahane's murder helped to generate and sustain enormous anxiety and/or pressure with respect to "self identification in the social hierarchy" insofar as the murder seemed to reinforce distinctions between Kahane types and the rest of Israeli society.[190] In sum, those sets of interconnections described above are as good examples as any of how interconnections in the Reiss and Roth schema connect factors between "units of observation" such as "predisposing" and "situational" factors, as well as among them.

Another two "situational factors" under consideration here in the context of the Reiss and Roth schema are the 1992 Israeli national election and the outright ban against Kach and Kahane Chai on 13 March 1994 following the Hebron massacre by Dr. Baruch Goldstein of Kiryat Arba. In the case of the 1992 election, the confidence that Jewish fundamentalists had in the Likud government to thrive in an effective and sustained way in spite of the lurking calamity of the Intifadeh and its aftermath was, as Sprinzak suggests, rent apart. Equally important, the lucrative political "macrosocial-opportunity structures" connected to the center of Israeli political power that the Likud government provided to Israeli hard-liners passed into eclipse with the Labor party victory.[191]

Equally important, that shift from a Likud-dominated government to a Labor-dominated government may have also, for some Jewish fundamentalists, enhanced feelings of "self identification in the social hierarchy" at the "predisposing-psychosocial" level of analysis insofar as many of their fellow citizens betrayed them by a vote for the Labor Party.[192] Be that as it may, the cabinet of Prime Minister Rabin compounded those dynamics even more when it imposed a full-blown ban on Kach and Kahane Chai on 13 March 1994 in the wake of the Hebron massacre.[193] At a substantive level, that ban was put into effect under the 1948 Ordinance for the Prevention of Terror, paragraph eight, itself promulgated after the 1948 assassination of UN mediator Count Folk Bernadotte who was shot by members of the Stern Gang.[194] To be sure, the emergent reality of that ban on Kach and Kahane Chai was to help stoke the burners of discontent and conflict among some, but certainly not all, Israelis.

For Sprinzak, the Declaration of Principles (DOP)-Oslo Agreement of 1993 was the triggering event for what he calls the Gush Emunim "revitalization," and it was, in my judgment, the same "activating factor" for terrorist assaults seemingly designed to demonstrate the Kahanist movement's "staying power" as well as its continued political opposition to the "peace process."[195] It was that watershed political event and the Oslo II five-year interim agreement that followed, that could be viewed as a type of "macrosocial-catalytic social event," as well as a catastrophic political event by Israeli hard-liners committed to the idea of a Greater Israel to encompass the lands of Judea and Samaria. Seen from a slightly different angle, there are interconnections between those watershed political events and "psychosocial-activating factors" such as "impulse" and "opportunity recognition" that compel a relatively small number of persons to transform their rage and frustration into the emergent reality of terrorist assaults.[196]

Within the context of the Declaration of Principles-Oslo Agreement of 1993, Prime Minister Rabin should have known that his decision to make those organizations illegal in the name of robust counterterrorism policy, nay to make illegal even any showing of their symbols like the "clenched fist" of Kach in public, was a glaring mistake insofar as it took away any legal venues for political expression, thereby in effect helping to introduce even more inflexibility and pressure into the political system.[197] As to why that ban may have happened at that particular juncture, Gordon's scripted account reports that both Minister of Knesset Yael Dayan of the Labor Party and Minister of Knesset Avraham Ravitz of United Torah Judaism Party blame pressure from the Clinton administration for Rabin's generally recognizable action against Kach and Kahane Chai within the context of the unfolding "peace process."[198]

As if that was not enough of a problem, another ripple effect of Rabin's outright ban against Kach and Kahane Chai was its contribution to the process of causing terrorist group spin-offs or terrorist group-splitting to happen, processes that are neither new nor especially unfamiliar to Israeli counterterrorist experts. Another underlying process at work that is discerned by empirical observation revolves around the central idea of role augmentation for existing terrorist groups. In the case of the "spin-off" process for Kach and Kahane Chai, Keinon and Hutman report that Kach chieftain Baruch Marzel and Shmuel Sackett, the executive director of Kahane Chai, were relatively straightforward in their inference that extralegal activities commonly construed as terrorism would continue within the context of another spin-off organizational framework.[199] In that context, a Kach "spin-off" organization called the Ideological Front was founded in 1996 and its one of its chieftains, Rabbi Michael Ben Horin, in essence told a group of followers at Prime Minister Rabin's gravesite that if Prime Minister Benjamin Netanyahu chose to take the same path as Rabin, "he will bury himself, his blood will not be on our hands."[200]

What seems significant here is that the broader political context also reverberates with powerful interconnections and effects for terrorist group splitting and role augmentation for terrorist groups already having split from parent organizations. The process of terrorist group splitting is discernable in the case of the Kach splinter Noar Meir and the Kach splinter group Eyal.[201] One scripted account reports that leaders of Noah Meir describe Noah Meir as a Kahanist youth group with direct interconnections to Kahane Chai that promotes summer camp activities. It promotes the use of violence, defined in a narrower sense in this study as terrorism, by means of pamphlets that laud the Rabin assassination.[202] In the case of the latter, the Jewish fundamentalist terrorist group Eyal otherwise known as the Israeli Fighting Organization, was spawned as a Kach splinter group that, as Sprinzak reports, purports to be even more extremist than its parent organization Kach.[203]

Eyal was established by Tel Aviv University student Avishai Raviv in 1992, and Sprinzak tells us that its origins trace an arc to Prime Minister Rabin's outright ban on Kach and Kahane Chai in 1994, seen in the narrower sense here as the "activating event" for the genesis of Eyal.[204] Perhaps the bleakest foreboding of all is there seems to be some evidence of interconnections between Avishai Raviv, other Jewish extremists, and Yigal Amir, the young student who shot Rabin in the back with a pistol at a Tel Aviv rally for peace on 4 November 1995.[205] It is not possible to overstate the point that analysis suggests that Rabin's ban on Kach and Kahane Chai was a powerful impetus for Jewish fundamentalist terrorist group radicalization, and in retrospect, a glaring mistake to make.

In the case of role augmentation, the Committee on Road Safety is an example of an existing Kach spin-off organization that has undergone role augmentation as a function of the continuously evolving environment. The Committee on Road Safety, led by Shmuel Ben Yishai, was originally crafted in 1986 to assist persons in need of protection as they traveled to and from locales in the Occupied Territories.[206] It is probably no exaggeration to say the "situational factors" described above probably contributed to this organization expanding its activities into the realm of proactive actions, some of which can be construed as terrorism.[207] For example, chieftains of the Committee on Road Safety stated the group had burned down five Arab-owned stores around February 1994.[208] One way of thinking about interconnections between the Israeli government counterterrorism measures previously described, and role augmentation, is that existing organizations like the Committee on Road Safety may experience "mission creep" in much the same way as government forces do in responding to changing political conditions.

In a similar vein, what seems significant here is the emergence of parallel structure organizations to terrorist groups that, as Sprinzak informs us, revolve around the central idea of "civil disobedience."[209] In the Israeli political landscape, the underlying problem with some of those organizations is that some of their actions really qualify as terrorist assaults with the threat of force implicit in their actions. Equally troublesome, leaders of those groups are all too frequently former terrorists themselves. For example, the group Chai Ve-Kayam ("Alive and Existing"), an organization of some three dozen or less members, is led by Yehuda Etzion, once a prominent member of the so-called "Jewish underground" or Terror Against Terror (TNT).[210] One scripted account describes the forceful efforts of Chai Ve-Kayam members to enter illegally onto the Temple Mount or Haram al-Sharif to pray and presumably confront anyone who would hamper their efforts.[211]

The Zo Artzenu ("This is Our Land") organization is another example of a movement that has as its underlying theme the notion of "civil disobedience" but has in reality carried out at least one terrorist assault chronicled in this analysis.[212] Zo Artzenu was crafted in 1993 by Moshe Feiglin and former Kahane Chai Executive Director Shmuel Sackett and has focused almost singular attention on government protest and the illegal construction of settlements in the Occupied Territories. As Sprinzak suggests, the aim of "Operation Duplicate" and "Operation Duplicate II" initiatives was to generate and sustain momentum for settlement construction irrespective of the Israeli government stance on that matter.[213]

According to Sprinzak, Zo Artzenu chieftains claim to draw on the non-violent principles of the Reverend Dr. Martin Luther King Jr., but, as the author suggests, there seems to be what Reiss and Roth might call "cognitive process" distortions associated with that way of thinking. For Sprinzak, at the heart of the problem is the seeming inability of Zo Artzenu leaders to make distinctions between a persecuted racial minority, in the case of African-Americans during the 1950s and 1960s, and the proactive efforts that straddle and sometimes enter into the realm of terrorist assaults, in my judgment, practiced by persons basically devoted to a Jewish state at the expense of Palestinian human rights.[214]

For Sprinzak, perhaps the single, most predominant contribution of the Zo Artzenu movement to the Israeli political fray is its capacity to tarnish the reputation of the Israeli government insofar as it is helping to pit the interests of Jewish revivalists against more mainstream Israelis.[215] As with Chai Ve-Kayam that is previously mentioned, the underlying problem with Zo Artzenu is that Zo Artzenu activists engage in activities that in some circumstances really qualify as terrorism precisely because of the reason that, at the very least, those activists sometimes promote violence and disruption as vehicles for political expression.

For example, a Zo Artzenu demonstration in August 1995 designed to disrupt traffic on Israeli highways and in Jerusalem resulted in the beating of Israeli Police Chief Commander Arye Amit and police charges against Zo Artzenu leaders of "inciting rebellion."[216] During that summer, Zo Artzenu chieftains issued a set of directives in pamphlet form that promoted violence against Israeli police, and public disruption incidents that led to the arrest of Moshe Feiglin, Shmuel Sackett, and Rabbi Danny Elon on charges of sedition and the conviction of Feiglin and Sackett in December 1995.[217]

Some General Observations about Israeli-Palestinian-Arab Terrorism

Relative Frequencies and Percentages of Israeli-Palestinian-Arab Terrorist Assaults by Year

The database for Israeli-Palestinian-Arab terrorism constitutes the largest subset of empirical data in this study, with a total of 623 discrete terrorist assaults. The terrorist assault entries for the 1994 through 1999 time period are comprised largely of domestic terrorism and international or "transnational" terrorism.[218]

At first blush, what seems significant here is that terrorist assaults inextricably bound up with the Israeli-Palestinian conflict are carried out against the backdrop of a continuously evolving "peace process" environment which, as this book goes to press, has perhaps hit its nadir. Illustrative of "peace process" events and the influence of dynamics that presuppose and derive from those events are the terrorist assaults carried out within the context of the 1994 Israeli-Jordanian peace agreement, further development of the violent sector of the Jewish right wing in the Israeli political landscape, phases of Israeli military "redeployment" in the Occupied Territories in areas such as Gaza, Jericho, Nablus, Bethlehem, and Hebron, the election of Israeli Prime Minister Benjamin Netanyahu in 1996, and the 1998 Wye River Memorandum.[219]

When the data for the 1994 through 1999 years are broken down according to year of event, it is clear the trends that appear are not typical of the empirical trends seen earlier in this work with respect to Algerian, Egyptian, or Turkish terrorism and, to be sure, with empirical trends seen in terrorism with a set of interconnections to the Israeli-Palestinian-Arab conflict before the Declaration of Principles in Oslo in 1993.[220] In the foregoing case studies, terrorism has been marked by a series of peaks and troughs that constitute cyclical terrorist event activity. Indeed, those findings, as previously mentioned, are consistent with the findings of other empirical studies about terrorism.[221]

Analysis of relative frequencies of terrorist assaults by year seems to paint a different portrait of Middle East terrorism associated with the struggle between Israel and the Palestinians. With respect to the range of terrorist assaults, the largest number and percentage happened in 1994 with 175 terrorist events or 28.1 percent of the 622 discrete events included in this test. The smallest number and percentage of terrorist assaults took place in 1999 with 40 events or 6.4 percent of the total. In between, there were 143 terrorist events or 23.0 percent that occurred in 1995, and 104 incidents or 16.7 percent that were carried out in 1996. In turn, there were 91 terrorist assaults or 14.6 percent that happened in 1997, as compared with 69 terrorist events or 11.1 percent that happened in 1998 (see figure 6.1). To be sure, there has been a steady decline in the amount and percentage of terrorism associated with the Israeli-Palestinian-Arab conflict since the start of 1994.

Terrorist Assaults by Group-Type, Terrorist Group, and Location

At a functional level, "Israeli-Palestinian-Arab" terrorism, as I have defined it, is inclusive of terrorist assaults with a set of interconnections to the Israeli-Palestinian struggle or otherwise tied together to that by means of fierce struggle between Israel and Arab confrontation states or between Israel and Iran. At the same time, also placed under the rubric of Israeli-Palestinian-Arab terrorism is a smaller portion of terrorist assaults that presuppose and derive from intra-national conflicts, with perhaps more indirect interconnections to the foregoing struggle, such as conflict between Israelis and Druzes, Jewish Israelis or tourists and "Israeli-Arabs," and between "secular Jews" and "religious and/or right-wing" Jews in Israel.[222] From the start, it is apparent that a wealth of different types of terrorist groups operate over the Israel-Palestine political landscape thereby in effect providing empirical data that will, as in the case study of Turkish terrorism that comes before, make it possible to delve into several theoretical propositions about terrorist group behavior. It follows that those findings will help breathe life into the theory that drives this study for the 1994 through 1999 time period under consideration.

As previously suggested, when the data are broken down by terrorist group-type and other non-group categories, the emergent reality more closely parallels the Turkish terrorism case study findings than the results for Algerian and Egyptian terrorism. For the 1994 through 1999 time period under consideration, the most prolific type of terrorist groups were theocentric groups with 119 out of 615 terrorist assaults or 19.3 percent of the total (see figure 6.2). Theocentric charismatic groups were the second most dynamic type of terrorist group with 97 events that comprise 15.8 percent of the total. Nonetheless, the largest amount of terrorist assaults was carried out by anonymous groups or "lone assailants" with 140 out of 615 incidents or 22.8 percent of the total.

In turn, the 80 identifiable "lone assailant" terrorist assaults that comprise 13.0 percent of the total, and the 79 uncompleted acts or 12.8 percent of the whole, virtually tied for third place. Seen from a slightly different vantage, the foregoing terrorist group-type and non-group categories comprise 83.7 percent of all terrorist assaults recorded, while the remainder, some 16.3 percent, is comprised of events committed by an eclectic array of different types of terrorist groups.[223] Those types of groups include: Jewish theocentric and Jewish theocentric charismatic terrorist assaults with 40 terrorist events (6.5 percent) and 25 terrorist events (4.1 percent), respectively, 20 ethnocentric terrorist assaults (3.3 percent), 14 ideo-ethnocentric charismatic terrorist attacks (2.3 percent), and one ethnocentric-charismatic terrorist incident (.2 percent).

Frequencies

Statistics

Year of Event

N	Valid	622
	Missing	1

Year of Event

		Frequency	Percent	Valid percent	Cumulative percent
Valid	1994	175	28.1	28.1	28.1
	1995	143	23.0	23.0	51.1
	1996	104	16.7	16.7	67.8
	1997	91	14.6	14.6	82.5
	1998	69	11.1	11.1	93.6
	1999	40	6.4	6.4	100.0
	Total	622	99.8	100.0	
Missing	system	1	.2		
Total		623	100.0		

Year of Event

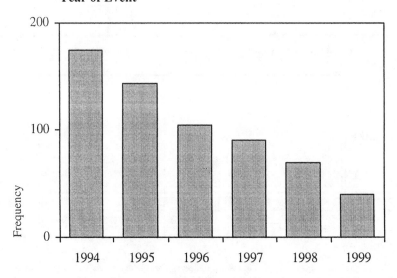

Figure 6.1: Relative Frequency of Israeli-Palestinian-Arab Terrorist Attacks by Year, 1994-1999

Frequencies

Statistics

Category of Group

N	Valid	615
	Missing	8

Category of Group

		Frequency	Percent	Valid percent	Cumulative percent
Valid	Theocentric charismatic	97	15.6	15.8	15.8
	Jewish theocentric charismatic	25	4.0	4.1	19.8
	Ideo-ethnocentric charismatic	14	2.2	2.3	22.1
	Jewish theocentric	40	6.4	6.5	28.6
	Uncompleted acts	79	12.7	12.8	41.5
	Unclaimed acts	140	22.5	22.8	64.2
	Theocentric	119	19.1	19.3	83.6
	Ethnocentric	20	3.2	3.3	86.8
	Ethnocentric charismatic	1	.2	.2	87.0
	Lone Assailant	80	12.8	13.0	100.0
	Total	615	98.7	100.0	
Missing	system	8	1.3		
Total		623	100.0		

Category of Group

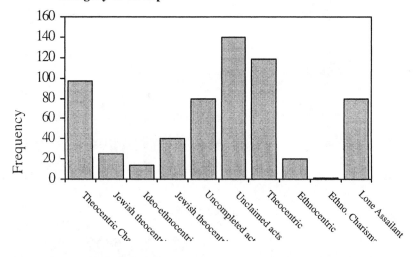

Figure 6.2: Relative Frequency of Israeli-Palestinian-Arab Terrorist Attacks by Group-Type, 1994-1999

Multiple claimant terrorist assaults were very rare, and comprise 8 out of 575 events or only 1.4 percent of the total (see figure 6.3). Terrorist assaults claimed by a theocentric and theocentric charismatic group account for 4 out of 575 acts or .7 percent, while 2 terrorist assaults are claimed by two Jewish theocentric terrorist groups, that is .3 percent of the total. In turn, one terrorist assault was claimed by two different theocentric groups (.2 percent) as compared to only 1 terrorist assault (.2 percent) that was claimed by both an ideoethnocentric charismatic and a theocentric terrorist group.

Several trends in those data are noteworthy and some of those findings dovetail nicely with results found in *Serenade of Suffering*.[224] For example, analysis found in my earlier work informs us that 27.7 percent of Middle East terrorist assaults committed from 1968 through 1993 were unclaimed acts as compared to a comparable rate of 22.8 percent for Israeli-Palestinian-Arab terrorism for the 1994 through 1999 time period.[225] Seen from the vantage of comparison between the Maghrib and Mashriq areas of the Middle East, that 22.8 percent figure for anonymous Israeli-Palestinian-Arab terrorist assaults is over three times less than anonymous terrorist assaults inextricably bound up with protracted conflict in Algeria. It is also notably less than the 36.6 percent of anonymous terrorism found in the case of Egyptian terrorism, and somewhat more than the 19.8 percent of Turkish terrorist assaults that remain anonymous.

Another compelling finding concerns the much lower percentage of ethnocentric terrorist assaults carried out between 1994 and 1999, at 3.3 percent, in stark contrast to the 18.1 percent rate found for ethnocentric groups that practiced Middle East terrorism between 1968 and 1993.[226] At a substantive level, that finding informs us that a five-fold-plus drop in ethnocentric terrorist assaults corresponds to a comparison between a "pre-peace process" time period and data for terrorism from 1994 through 1999 chronicled since the Oslo Accord of 1993. Still another, perhaps more unexpected finding, against the backdrop of glaring opposition to the "peace process" and its tortuous historical legacy, is the relatively consistent findings for uncompleted terrorist assaults at 12.8 percent for the 1994 through 1999 period, and the 10.6 percent rate found for Middle East terrorism for the 1968 through 1993 time period.[227]

Again, seen from the vantage of comparison between Maghrib and Mashriq areas and within particular "terrorism systems," that 12.8 percent mark for uncompleted events is greater than the 7.8 percent figure found in the case of Turkish terrorism, twice as high as the 6.3 percent rate found in the case of Egyptian terrorism, and about twenty times greater than the miniscule .6 percent rate of uncompleted terrorist assaults found for Algerian terrorism. To be sure, those findings suggest strongly that the variable location, be it because of counterterrorism measures in place or for other factors that might include, but are not necessarily limited to, qualities of constituency support or more basic demographic features, has an effect on terrorist group and non-group assault success rates.

Frequencies

Statistics

Name of Group

N	Valid	575
	Missing	48

Name of Group

		Fre-quency	Per-cent	Valid percent	Cumu-lative percent
Valid	Uncompleted	79	12.7	13.7	13.7
	Unclaimed	140	22.5	24.3	38.1
	Lone Assailant	80	12.8	13.9	52.0
	Hezbollah	89	14.3	15.5	67.5
	Hamas	85	13.6	14.8	82.3
	Islamic Jihad	28	4.5	4.9	87.1
	Ansarallah (Partisans of God) (Hezbollah ass.)	1	.2	.2	87.3
	Believers Resistance (Hezbollah assoc.)	1	.2	.2	87.5
	Fatah	5	.8	.9	88.3
	Black 13 of September Faction	2	.3	.3	88.7
	ANO (FRC)	1	.2	.2	88.9
	PFLP	7	1.1	1.2	90.1
	PFLP-GC	1	.2	.2	90.3
	DFLP	5	.8	.9	91.1
	Kach	17	2.7	3.0	94.1
	Kahane Chai	3	.5	.5	94.6
	Committee for Road Safety	3	.5	.5	95.1
	Repression of the Traitors	1	.2	.2	95.3
	Eyal	2	.3	.3	95.7
	Sword of David	3	.5	.5	96.2
	Jewish Group of Vengeance	1	.2	.2	96.3
	Hagai	1	.2	.2	96.5
	Multi: Theo; Theo-Char	4	.6	.7	97.2
	Multi: Jewish Theo	2	.3	.3	97.6
	Multi: Theo; Theo	1	.2	.2	97.7
	Osama bin Laden (al-Qaida)	4	.6	.7	98.4
	United Command of the Global Uprising	1	.2	.2	98.6
	Zo Artzenu	1	.2	.2	98.8
	Ayin (Jewish Agency Organization)	1	.2	.2	99.0
	Multi: Ideoethno-Char; Theocentric	1	.2	.2	99.1
	Students of Musa Abu Marzouq	1	.2	.2	99.3
	Islamic Revolutionary Army	1	.2	.2	99.5
	Pales Resistance Jafa	2	.3	.3	99.8
	Org. of Oppressed on Earth	1	.2	.2	100.0
	Total	575	92.3	100.0	
Missing	system	48	7.7		
Total		623	100.0		

Figure 6.3: Relative Frequency of Israeli-Palestinian-Arab Terrorist Attacks by Terrorist Group, 1994-1999

When the analysis of terrorist assaults is broken down by identifiable terrorist groups, it is observed that among identifiable terrorist groups the greatest number and highest percentage of terrorist assaults were carried out by Hezbollah with 89 out of 575 events and 15.5 percent of the total, followed by Hamas that committed 85 out of 575 terrorist assaults or 14.8 percent of the total amount (see figure 6.3). In turn, the 28 terrorist assaults committed by Islamic Jihad, that comprise a paltry 4.9 percent of the total, place Islamic Jihad in a distant third place. In terms of terrorist group activity, some 12.9 percent of the terrorist assaults that remain are comprised of terrorist assaults committed by an array of terrorist groups and "multiple terrorist group events," namely those terrorist assaults claimed by more than one terrorist group.

To be sure, many of those terrorist groups chronicled are widely recognized and oftentimes venerable organizations such as al-Fatah with .9 percent, the PFLP with 1.2 percent, the PFLP-GC with .2 percent, the DFLP with .9

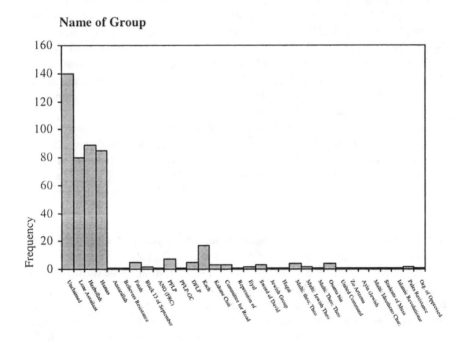

Figure 6.3 — *continued*

percent, Kach with 3.0 percent, and Kahane Chai with .5 percent of the total. In addition, Ansarallah acts represent .2 percent of the total, while terrorist assaults carried out by the Believers Resistance also represent .2 percent of the total. In turn, the Organization for the Oppressed on Earth, another Hezbollah-associated group, carried out .2 percent of all terrorist acts chronicled. Interestingly enough, Shaykh bin Laden's al-Qaida organization with 4 terrorist assaults accounts for only .7 percent of the total amount.[228] To be sure, there is, at 3.5 percent, a small amount of Israeli-Palestinian-Arab terrorism that could be the product of front organizations or "splinter groups" of more generally recognizable terrorist groups that operate in the political fray.[229]

Analysis of relative frequencies that sorts data by location informs us that Israel has the highest number and percentage of Israeli-Palestinian-Arab terrorist assaults, with 210 events or a full one-third (33.7 percent) of the 623 incidents involved in this test (see figure 6.4). Terrorist assaults that happened in the Occupied Territories rank second with 192 events or 30.8 percent of the total, by contrast to the 15.1 percent or 94 out of 623 terrorist assaults that happened in the jurisdictional area of the Palestinian National Authority (PNA). In fourth place with 8.0 percent of the total or 50 out of 623 acts are terrorist events that occurred in "other Middle East" locales such as Lebanon, Syria, Jordan, and Egypt. In fifth place with 7.2 percent of the total or 62 out of 623 acts are terrorist events that occurred in "other" locales such as Buenos Aires, Argentina; Colon, Panama; Nairobi, Kenya; Dar es Salaam, Tanzania; Chiang Mai-Bangkok, Thailand; Cyprus; Santiago, Chile; Asuncion, Paraguay; Tashkent, Uzbekistan; and New Delhi, India.

In sixth place, Western Europe experienced 17 terrorist assaults that comprise 2.7 percent of the total.[230] The United States ranked seventh with 2.4 percent or 15 out of 623 acts. With respect to a comparison of findings about Middle East terrorism from 1968 through 1993, there is rough parity in terms of the terrorist assault percentage rate in Israel, insofar as 35.4 percent rather than 33.7 percent of the total events occurred in Israel.[231] Turning to the Occupied Territories, there is also rough equivalency in findings, with 30.8 percent of all terrorist events happening there for the period 1994 through 1999, by contrast to the 29.9 percent figure for the 1968-93 period.[232]

Alternately, European states were shackled with Middle East terrorism from 1968 through 1993 some 12.6 percent of the time, and that is some four and a half times the 2.7 percent rate found in this work.[233] In contrast, the percentage of Israeli-Palestinian-Arab terrorism that took place in the United States for the 1994-99 time period under consideration is one-half, at 2.4 percent, of the corresponding rate of 4.8 percent found for Middle East terrorist assaults committed in the U.S. between 1968 and 1993.[234] Seen from a different angle, while the overall frequencies of Israeli-Palestinian-Arab terrorism by year have diminished between 1994 and 1999, the percentage of Israeli-Palestinian Arab terrorism happening in Israel and the Occupied

Frequencies

Statistics

Locale

N	Valid	623
	Missing	0

Locale

		Frequency	Percent	Valid percent	Cumulative percent
Valid	Europe	17	2.7	2.7	2.7
	Israel	210	33.7	33.7	36.4
	Occupied	192	30.8	30.8	67.3
	Other	45	7.2	7.2	74.5
	Other Middle East	50	8.0	8.0	82.5
	PA	94	15.1	15.1	97.6
	U.S.	15	2.4	2.4	100.0
	Total	623	100.0	100.0	

Locale

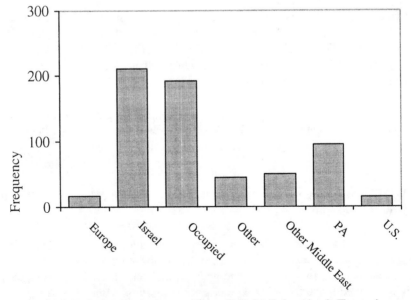

Figure 6.4: Relative Frequency of Israeli-Palestinian-Arab Terrorism by Location, 1994-1999

Territories has, percentage-wise, stayed roughly the same even during the years of the unfolding Israeli-Palestinian "peace process."

In sum, the data suggest a noteworthy decrease in the percentage of terrorist assaults directly related to the Israeli-Palestinian-Arab struggle in both Western Europe and the United States from 1994 through 1999. One way of thinking about the matter is that the Israeli-Palestinian "peace process" years correspond to a significant decline in terrorism percentage rates in Western European states and the United States, thereby in effect helping to provide some impetus by the Europeans and Americans to spur on negotiations between the Israeli and Palestinian ruling elites. However, the terrorist assault percentage rates have remained virtually the same in the case of Israel and the Occupied Territories during the "peace process" years. Put another way, those findings suggest precious little in the way of tangible benefits for Israelis living in Israel and the Occupied Territories as an inducement to make structural political change.

In terms of a comparison with the findings for the case studies of Algerian, Egyptian, and Turkish terrorism, what seems significant here are the differences in relative percentages of terrorist assaults outside the primary venue of conflict. With respect to Algerian terrorism, 5.5 percent or 19 terrorist assaults related to the fierce, underlying struggle between Algerian Islamists and the military-backed Algerian government happened in Western Europe, as compared to 2.8 percent or 17 terrorist assaults in the case of Israeli-Palestinian-Arab terrorist attacks.

While there are no chronicled acts of completed Algerian terrorism that happened in the United States, 2.3 percent of Israeli-Palestinian-Arab terrorism happened there. By contrast, the 4.2 percent of Egyptian terrorist assaults that happened in Western Europe is about one and one-half the 2.8 percent rate of Israeli-Palestinian-Arab terrorism found in Western Europe. The 7.0 percent of Egyptian terrorism that happened in the United States is a rate some three times the amount of Israeli-Palestinian-Arab terrorism found in the United States. Lastly, in the case of Turkish terrorism, the rate of Turkish terrorism in Western Europe, at 20.8 percent, far outstrips the foregoing rates for Western Europe, but the rate of Turkish terrorism in the United States for the 1994-99 period is nil, as in the case of completed Algerian terrorism.

Terrorism Assault Attributes: Fatalities, Injuries, Property Damage, Target Preference

In the case of Israeli-Palestinian Arab terrorism, when the data are broken down into ordinal categories of terrorist assaults with zero deaths, deaths of between one and fifty persons, and between fifty one and one hundred persons, it is observed that the lion's share of terrorist assaults, namely 531 acts or a full

86.9 percent of the total of 611 events, were terrorist assaults that did not cause any fatalities (see figure 6.5). In turn Israeli-Palestinian-Arab terrorist assaults that caused the deaths of between one and fifty persons are 12.8 percent or 78 out of 611 acts. Alternately, there is only 1 Israeli-Palestinian Arab terrorist assault chronicled that killed between fifty-one and one hundred persons. Finally, the bombing of the U.S. embassy in Nairobi, Kenya, in August 1998 by bin Laden's al-Qaida organization, with 247 deaths, is the 1 outlier case many standard deviations away from the mean number of deaths chronicled in those data.[235]

To be sure, those findings are largely consistent with results about terrorism assault fatalities in the case of Turkish terrorism, but suggest lower lethality levels for Israeli-Palestinian Arab than for Egyptian terrorism or Algerian terrorism. Some 36.3 percent of Egyptian terrorist assaults or 49 out of 135 acts are found to have resulted in the deaths of between one and fifty persons, while a full 75.4 percent of Algerian terrorist assaults or 255 out of 338 acts killed between one and fifty persons. When comparisons are made between the aforementioned findings for Israeli-Palestinian-Arab terrorism and comparable findings for Middle East terrorism during the 1968-93 period, it is observed there has been a percentage rate increase in terrorist assaults that are death-free from 68.6 percent to 86.9 percent, while the rate of terrorist assaults responsible for the deaths of between one and fifty persons also has dropped from 31.0 percent to 12.8 percent.[236]

In the case of patterns of injuries for Israeli-Palestinian-Arab terrorist assaults from 1994 through 1999, a similar if not identical set of trends is revealed (see figure 6.6). A full 69.8 percent of terrorist assaults or 423 out of 606 incidents did not injure a single person, while 174 out of 606 terrorist events or 28.7 percent injured between one and fifty persons. There were 7 outlier terrorist events that injured more than one hundred persons, that comprise 1.4 percent of the total with a range of injuries of between 106 and 4,257 persons. In comparison to the analysis of Algerian, Egyptian, and Turkish terrorism that comes before, it is observed those trends are largely consistent with comparable result patterns for Algerian, Egyptian, and Turkish terrorism. At the same time, those findings about injuries are also consistent with data about injury rates for Middle East terrorism conducted between 1968 and 1993.[237]

With respect to property damage, the relative frequency analysis sorts data into ordinal categories of no property damage, "slight," "moderate," "high," and "severe" levels of property damage. The data inform us that 397 out of 580 acts or 68.4 percent of terrorist assaults caused no property damage, as compared with 149 out of 580 acts or 25.7 percent that resulted in a "slight" amount of property damage, defined as less than or about U.S.$15,000 (see Figure 6.7). Seen from a slightly different vantage, the data show that a full 94.1 percent of all Israeli-Palestinian-Arab terrorist assaults chronicled caused

Frequencies

Statistics

Event Deaths

N	Valid	611
	Missing	12

Event Deaths

		Frequency	Percent	Valid percent	Cumulative percent
Valid	0	531	85.2	86.9	86.9
	1	78	12.5	12.8	99.7
	2	1	.2	.2	99.8
	247	1	.2	.2	100.0
	Total	611	98.1	100.0	
Missing	system	12	1.9		
Total		623	100.0		

Event Deaths

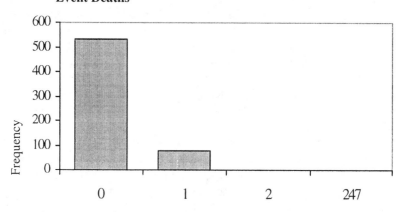

Figure 6.5: Relative Frequency of Numbers of Dead in Israeli-Palestinian-Arab Terrorist Incidents, 1994-1999   (0=0; 1=1 through 50; 2=51 through 100)

Frequencies

Statistics

Event Injuries

N	Valid	606
	Missing	17

Event Injuries

		Frequency	Percent	Valid percent	Cumulative percent
Valid	0	423	67.9	69.8	69.8
	1	174	27.9	28.7	98.5
	2	2	.3	.3	98.8
	106	1	.2	.2	99.0
	109	1	.2	.2	99.2
	168	1	.2	.2	99.3
	192	1	.2	.2	99.5
	200	1	.2	.2	99.7
	231	1	.2	.2	99.8
	4257	1	.2	.2	100.0
	Total	606	97.3	100.0	
Missing	system	17	2.7		
Total		623	100.0		

Event Injuries

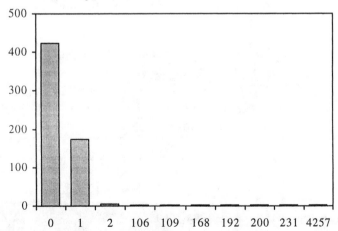

Figure 6.6: Relative Frequency of Numbers of Injured in Israeli-Palestinian-Arab Terrorism Incidents, 1994-1999 (0=0; 1=1 through 50; 2=51 through 100)

Frequencies

Statistics

Property Damage

N	Valid	580
	Missing	43

Property Damage

		Frequency	Percent	Valid percent	Cumulative percent
Valid	None	397	63.7	68.4	68.4
	Slight	149	23.9	25.7	94.1
	Moderate	17	2.7	2.9	97.1
	High	13	2.1	2.2	99.3
	Severe	4	.6	.7	100.0
	Total	580	93.1	100.0	
Missing	system	43	6.9		
Total		623	100.0		

Property Damage

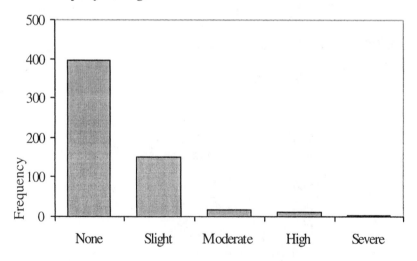

Figure 6.7: Levels of Property Damage Caused by Israeli-Palestinian-Arab Terrorist Attacks, 1994-1999

either slight levels of property damage or no property damage at all. Moderate levels of property damage, defined as from about U.S.$30,000 to U.S.$100,000 were caused 2.9 percent of the time, while high levels of property damage, defined as from about U.S.$100,000 to U.S.$1 million happened in only 13 cases or 2.2 percent of the time. There are only 4 terrorist assaults out of 580 acts recorded or .7 percent that resulted in "severe" levels of property damage that is defined as in excess of U.S.$1 million.[238]

In the narrower sense, those findings about property damage closely parallel the property damage levels found for Algerian, Egyptian, and Turkish terrorism. In the broader sense, the foregoing findings, like many of the findings that are presented for Algerian, Egyptian, and Turkish terrorism that came before, suggest the power of terrorism to make structural political change presupposes and derives from its psychological impact and import rather than from enormous amounts of physical devastation.[239] Seen from the vantage of a longitudinal perspective, the aforementioned findings about levels of property damage are largely consistent with results about property level damage found in my earlier work about Middle East terrorism from 1968 through 1993.[240]

In the analysis of target type preference, categorical data is broken down into several target-types, but a full 97.8 percent of terrorist assault targets are found to involve civilian or government targets. A full 77.7 percent, slightly over three-quarters of all terrorist assaults, or 468 out of 602 terrorist acts, involved civilian targets (see figure 6.8). Terrorist assaults directed against government targets, by contrast, amounted to 121 out of 602 acts or 20.1 percent. The remainder of those terrorist assaults are found to have been directed at infrastructure targets in 9 out of 602 acts that amounts to 1.5 percent of the total, and "multiple targets," namely "civilian-government" targets, in 4 out of 602 instances or .7 percent of the total. Those findings, that reveal about a 3.8 :1 ratio in favor of civilian targets over government targets, are not as dramatic as the ratio of civilian targets to government targets found in Algerian terrorist assaults at 8:1, but that ratio in favor of civilian targets is greater than in the case of Turkish terrorism, where the ratio is found to be 2.4:1, and certainly greater than in the case of Egyptian terrorism, where the ratio of civilian-government targets is found to be a mere 1:.81. Seen from a different vantage, a longitudinal comparison of the 3.8:1 ratio for civilian targets over government targets found here as compared with the 4.1:1 ratio for the Middle East data for the 1968 through 1993 period suggests that ratio has remained virtually the same over time, dipping slightly from about 4.1:1 between 1968 and 1993, to about 3.8:1 for the 1994 through 1999 period.[241]

Frequencies

Statistics

Type of Target

N	Valid	602
	Missing	21

Type of Target

		Frequency	Percent	Valid percent	Cumulative percent
Valid	Government	121	19.4	20.1	20.1
	Infrastructure	9	1.4	1.5	21.6
	Civilian	468	75.1	77.7	99.3
	Civilian-Govt	4	.6	.7	100.0
	Total	602	96.6	100.0	
Missing	system	21	3.4		
Total		623	100.0		

Type of Target

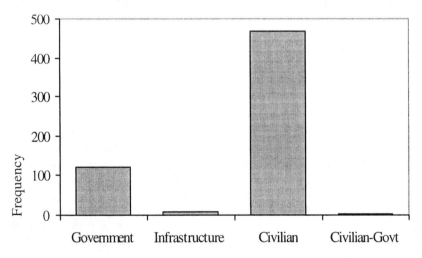

Figure 6.8: Relative Frequency of Israeli-Palestinian-Arab Terrorism Target-Types, 1994-1999

Variable Analysis

Political Ideology and Target-Type, Numbers of Deaths

The findings about the targeting behavior of "structuralist" and "non-structuralist" Middle East terrorist groups in my prior work reveals that ethnocentric terrorist groups are more "nonstructuralist" in nature than ideo-ethnocentric groups and that theocentric groups can be conceived of as a "hybrid type" with "structuralist" and "nonstructuralist" strands of thinking.[242] At the same time, findings in my prior work reveal that in the case of nationalist-irredentist terrorist groups, the presence of a charismatic leader seems to alter the behavior of ethnocentric groups to emphasize terrorist assaults against government targets.[243]

It is observed that ideo-ethnocentric terrorist group assaults are not chronicled for the 1994 through 1999 time period under consideration, presumably because those types of terrorist groups were not operative over the political landscape. Taking the aforementioned results from my prior work into account, the following hypotheses are modified here to reflect the emergent reality of the absence of ideo-ethnocentric terrorist assaults. The following modified hypotheses that capture the proposed dynamics between target-type and political ideology are presented for analysis:

Hypothesis One: Ethnocentric charismatic terrorist groups will attack government targets (i.e., court houses, military administration facilities, military recruitment centers, and noncombatant troops such as UN peacekeepers) more often than ethnocentric, theocentric, and Jewish theocentric terrorist groups.

Hypothesis Two: Ethnocentric terrorist groups will attack civilian targets more often than theocentric terrorist groups.

The bivariate analysis of "target-type" and "category of group" includes terrorist acts perpetrated by terrorist groups with differences in political ideology, anonymous terrorist assaults, and uncompleted terrorist assaults.[244] The bivariate analysis suggests there is a statistically significant association between different categories of terrorist groups and the type of target that is selected (see table 6.1). A Pearson Chi Square statistic of 33.552 with a "p-value" of less than .001 at seven degrees of freedom (7 d.f.) makes it possible to reject the null hypothesis of no relation between the variables "target-type" and "category of group" at the .05 level of confidence. The results reveal that two cells or 12.5 percent had an expected frequency of less than five. In terms of the strength of the association, a Goodman and Kruskal's *tau* value of .058 with a "p-value" of less than .001 when "type of target" is the dependent

Table 6.1: Relative Frequency of Israeli-Palestinian-Arab Terrorist Targets by Group-Type, 1994-1999   (summary statistics)

Crosstabs
Case Processing Summary

	Cases					
	Valid		Missing		Total	
	N	Percent	N	Percent	N	Percent
Type of target * category of group	580	93.1%	43	6.9%	623	100.0%

Type of Target *Category of Group Cross-Tabulation

Type of target		Category of group			
		Theocentric charismatic	Jewish theocentric charismatic	Ideo-ethnocentric charismatic	Jewish theocentric
Govern-ment	Count	6	8	1	9
	% within type of target	5.0%	6.7%	.8%	7.5%
	% within category of group	6.4%	32.0%	7.1%	25.0%
	% of total	1.0%	1.4%	.2%	1.6%
Civilian	Count	88	17	13	27
	% within type of target	19.1%	3.7%	2.8%	5.9%
	% within category of group	93.6%	68.0%	92.9%	75.0%
	% of total	15.2%	2.9%	2.2%	4.7%
Total	Count	94	25	14	36
	% within type of target	16.2%	4.3%	2.4%	6.2%
	% within category of group	100.0%	100.0%	100.0%	100.0%
	% of total	16.2%	4.3%	2.4%	6.2%

Type of Target * Category of Group Cross-Tabulation

Type of target		Category of group				
		Un-completed acts	Un-claimed acts	Theo-centric	Ethno-centric	Total
Govern-ment	Count	17	63	14	2	120
	% within type of target	14.2%	52.5%	11.7%	1.7%	100.0%
	% within category of group	26.6%	29.6%	12.3%	10.0%	20.7%
	% of total	2.9%	10.9%	2.4%	.3%	20.7%
Civilian	Count	47	150	100	18	460
	% within type of target	10.2%	32.6%	21.7%	3.9%	100.0%
	% within category of group	73.4%	70.4%	87.7%	90.0%	79.3%
	% of total	8.1%	25.9%	17.2%	3.1%	79.3%
Total	Count	64	213	114	20	580
	% within type of target	11.0%	36.7%	19.7%	3.4%	100.0%
	% within category of group	100.0%	100.0%	100.0%	100.0%	100.0%
	% of total	11.0%	36.7%	19.7%	3.4%	100.0%

Table 6.1 — *continued*

Chi Square Tests

	Value	df	Asymp. sig. (2-sided)
Pearson Chi Square	33.552[a]	7	.000
Likelihood Ratio	37.015	7	.000
Linear-by-Linear Association	3.811	1	.051
N of valid cases	580		

a. 2 cells (12.5%) have expected count less than 5. The minimum expected count is 2.90.

Directional Measures

			Value	Asymp. std. error[a]	Approx. T[b]	Approx. sig.
Nominal by nominal	Lambda	Symmetric	.000	.000	.[b]	.[b]
		Type of target dependent	.000	.000	.[b]	.[b]
		Category of group dependent	.000	.000	.[b]	.[b]
	Goodman and Kruskal tau	Type of target dependent	.058	.017		.000[c]
		Category of group dependent	.015	.005		.000[c]

a. Not assuming the null hypothesis.
b. Cannot be computed because the asymptotic standard error equals zero.
c. Based on chi square approximation.

Symmetric Measures

		Value	Approx. sig.
Nominal by nominal	Phi	.241	.000
	Cramer's V	.241	.000
N of valid cases		580	

a. Not assuming the null hypothesis.
b. Using the asymptotic standard error assuming the null hypothesis.

variable suggests a weak relationship between the variables. In addition, a Cramer's V score of .241 and a "Phi score" of .241 with significance scores of less than .001 also suggests a weak relationship between the variables "target-type" and "category of group."

The cross-tabulation tables reveal a data distribution that shows ideo-ethnocentric charismatic groups have the highest rate of terrorist attacks directed at civilian targets with 92.9 percent or 13 out of 14 acts. Theocentric charismatic terrorist groups have the second highest percentage rate of civilian target terrorist assaults with 92.6 percent or 88 out of 95 terrorist incidents (see table 6.2). Ranking third among types of terrorist groups are ethnocentric terrorist groups that have a 90.0 percent rate of civilian target attack or 18 out of 20 terrorist assaults.

Alternately, in the case of terrorist group-types, ethnocentric charismatic groups had the lowest percentage of civilian target attacks with 0 percent, followed by Jewish theocentric charismatic terrorist groups with the second lowest rate of civilian target terrorist assaults at 68.0 percent or 17 out of 25 acts. Jewish theocentric groups have the third lowest rate of terrorist assaults directed at civilian targets with 69.2 percent or 27 out of 39 terrorist incidents. Lastly, 73.8 percent of declared lone assailant terrorist assaults or 59 out of 80 acts are directed at civilian targets, by contrast to 26.3 percent or 21 out 80 acts of declared lone assailant attacks directed against government targets.

What seems significant here in terms of a comparison with 1968 through 1993 findings is that Jewish theocentric terrorist groups, once with a relatively high percentage rate of terrorist assaults against civilian targets at 76.4 percent, is now found to have the third lowest percentage rate of civilian target terrorist assaults among terrorist group-types at 69.2 percent for the 1994 through 1999 time period.[245] Equally important is another standout finding that while the lion's share of unclaimed terrorist assaults were aimed at civilian targets for the 1968 through 1993 period with 89.7 percent or 279 out of 311 acts, thereby in effect making it the highest ranking category for that time period, unclaimed acts directed at civilian targets for the 1994 through 1999 period account for only 65.9 percent or 91 out of 138 events, making it the lowest ranked of all categories for civilian target terrorist attacks.[246] Those results are dramatic insofar as they reveal a complete, rank reversal with respect to the relationship between unclaimed acts and civilian targets for the 1968 through 1993 period and the 1994 through 1999 time period that is covered in this work.

In contrast, ethnocentric charismatic terrorist groups are found to have the highest rate of government target assaults at 100.0 percent, but that rate reflects only one successful terrorist assault that was committed. In second place are Jewish theocentric charismatic groups with 32.0 percent or 8 out of 25 terrorist assaults. Jewish theocentric groups have the third highest rate of attacks against government targets with 23.1 percent or 9 out of 39 terrorist assaults. The percentage rate of unclaimed terrorist assaults directed at government targets is

Table 6.2: Relative Frequency of Israeli-Palestinian-Arab Terrorist Targets by Group-Type, 1994-1999

Case Processing Summary

	Cases					
	Valid		Missing		Total	
	N	Percent	*N*	Percent	*N*	Percent
Type of target * category of group	594	95.3%	29	4.7%	623	100.0%

Type of Target * Category of Group Cross-Tabulation

Type of target		Category of group			
		Theocentric charismatic	Jewish theocentric charismatic	Ideo-ethnocentric charismatic	Jewish theocentric
Govern ment	Count	6	8	1	9
	% within type of target	5.0%	6.6%	.8%	7.4%
	% within category of group	6.3%	32.0%	7.1%	23.1%
	% of total	1.0%	1.3%	.2%	1.5%
Infra structure	Count				3
	% within type of target				33.3%
	% within category of group				7.7%
	% of total				.5%
Civilian	Count	88	17	13	27
	% within type of target	19.1%	3.7%	2.8%	5.9%
	% within category of group	92.6%	68.0%	92.9%	69.2%
	% of total	14.8%	2.9%	2.2%	4.5%
Civilian -Govt.	Count	1			
	% within type of target	25.0%			
	% within category of group	1.1%			
	% of total	.2%			
Total	Count	95	25	14	39
	% within type of target	16.0%	4.2%	2.4%	6.6%
	% within category of group	100.0%	100.0%	100.0%	100.0%
	% of total	16.0%	4.2%	2.4%	6.6%

somewhat higher at 30.4 percent or 42 out of 138 terrorist acts. Lastly, it is observed there are no ideo-ethnocentric terrorist assaults recorded for the 1994 through 1999 period under consideration.

It follows from the foregoing results that Hypothesis One and Hypothesis Two are accepted as valid. In the case of Hypothesis One, ethnocentric charismatic groups are found to assault civilian targets a full 100.0 percent of the time, as compared to 90.0 percent or 18 out of 20 events for ethnocentric groups, and 84.7 percent or 100 out of 118 terrorist assaults for theocentric groups. In turn, it is observed that Jewish theocentric groups direct terrorist assaults against civilian targets in 69.2 percent or 27 out 39 of Jewish theocentric terrorist assaults. In the case of Hypothesis Two, the data inform us that 90.0 percent or 18 out of 20 ethnocentric terrorist assaults are directed

Table 6.2 — *continued*

Type of Target * Category of Group Cross-Tabulation

Type of target		Category of group			
		Un-completed acts	Un-claimed acts	Theo centric	Ethno centric
Govern-ment	Count	17	42	14	2
	% within type of target	14.0%	34.7%	11.6%	1.7%
	% within category of group	26.6%	30.4%	11.9%	10.0%
	% of total	2.9%	7.1%	2.4%	.3%
Infra-structure	Count		4	2	
	% within type of target		44.4%	22.2%	
	% within category of group		2.9%	1.7%	
	% of total		.7%	.3%	
Civilian	Count	47	91	100	18
	% within type of target	10.2%	19.8%	21.7%	3.9%
	% within category of group	73.4%	65.9%	84.7%	90.0%
	% of total	7.9%	15.3%	16.8%	3.0%
Civilian-Govt.	Count		1	2	
	% within type of target		25.0%	50.0%	
	% within category of group		.7%	1.7%	
	% of total		.2%	.3%	
Total	Count	64	138	118	20
	% within type of target	10.8%	23.2%	19.9%	3.4%
	% within category of group	100.0%	100.0%	100.0%	100.0%
	% of total	10.8%	23.2%	19.9%	3.4%

against civilian targets, while 84.7 percent or 100 out 118 of all theocentric terrorist assaults involve civilian targets.

Plainly, a first pass devoted to Israeli-Palestinian-Arab outlier cases makes it apparent that a comparatively low percentage of terrorist assaults, some 2.2 percent or 13 out of 595 events, involved infrastructure or "multiple-type" targets.[247] To be more specific, infrastructure targets account for 1.5 percent of the total or 9 out of 595 acts, while only one kind of "multiple-type" target attack is found, namely 4 "civilian-government" target terrorist assaults, 2 carried out by theocentric group(s), 1 anonymous act, and 1 theocentric charismatic group act. In the broadest sense, with respect to a comparison to the outlier patterns discerned for the 1968 through 1993 time period, that ratio of infrastructure and "multiple-type" targets has remained relatively constant. For

Table 6.2 — *continued*

Type of Target * Category of Group Cross-Tabulation

Type of target		Ethnocentric charismatic	Lone assailant	Total
Govern-ment	Count	1	21	121
	% within type of target	.8%	17.4%	100.0%
	% within category of group	100.0%	26.3%	20.4%
	% of total	.2%	3.5%	20.4%
Infra-structure	Count			9
	% within type of target			100.0%
	% within category of group			1.5%
	% of total			1.5%
Civilian	Count		59	460
	% within type of target		12.8%	100.0%
	% within category of group		73.8%	77.4%
	% of total		9.9%	77.4%
Civilian-Govt.	Count			4
	% within type of target			100.0%
	% within category of group			.7%
	% of total			.7%
Total	Count	1	80	594
	% within type of target	.2%	13.5%	100.0%
	% within category of group	100.0%	100.0%	100.0%
	% of total	.2%	13.5%	100.0%

example, for the 1968 through 1993 period, infrastructure terrorist assaults took place 1.7 percent of the time as compared to 1.5 percent of the time for the 1994 through 1999 period, while "civilian-government" attacks increased in a miniscule fashion from .3 percent to .7 percent.[248] At the same time, other variations of "multiple-type" target terrorist attacks found in that earlier 1968-93 time period that comprise .7 percent do not exist for the 1994 through 1999 time period. What seems significant here is those data suggest a percentage rate increase in infrastructure terrorist assaults for theocentric groups from 0 percent or no chronicled terrorist assaults for the 1968 through 1993 period to two out 118 acts for the 1994 through 1999 period, that accounts for 1.7 percent of all theocentric group terrorist incidents.

The findings for outlier target-type terrorist assaults for Israeli-Palestinian-Arab terrorist attacks are consistent in generally recognizable ways with comparable findings for Algerian, Egyptian, and Turkish terrorism, replete with some notable exceptions. For example, in the case of Algerian terrorism, there are many more "multiple target-type" combinations observed and the terrorist attack rate against infrastructure targets is over twice as much at 3.5 percent or 12 out of 340 acts, by contrast to the 1.5 percent rate found in this analysis.[249] In contrast, in the case of Turkish terrorism, the only "multiple target-type" assaults found are three "government-civilian" terrorist assaults that comprise 1.6 percent or 3 out of 189 acts. For Turkish terrorism, terrorist assaults against infrastructure targets ranks highest with 4.8 percent or 9 out of 189 events. In turn, there are no "multiple target-type" terrorist assaults chronicled in the Egyptian terrorism data, nor are there any terrorist assaults against infrastructure targets.

One of the underlying themes of this study is that unclaimed terrorist assaults primarily against civilian targets serve to generate and sustain concerted political pressure on the ruling elite that is necessary to make structural political change an emergent reality. Hypothesis Three captures the essence of that central idea, and allows the reader to make comparisons to targeting behavior among unclaimed and theocentric types of groups found in the context of Algerian and Egyptian terrorism, as well as in the case of Turkish terrorism.

Hypothesis Three: Unclaimed terrorist assaults will involve civilian targets more frequently than theocentric terrorist assaults.

To recapitulate, in the analysis of Algerian terrorism performed in chapter 3 of this work, it is found that unclaimed terrorist assaults that are directed at civilian targets 87.7 percent of the time, or in 228 out of 260 acts, are more frequent than the 73.3 percent rate or 55 out of 75 civilian target terrorist acts for theocentric attacks. Those findings are consistent with an underlying theme of this work, namely that unclaimed acts against civilian targets serve to generate and sustain political pressure on the ruling elite to make structural political change.

In the case of Egyptian terrorism, by contrast, it is found that only 29.9 percent of unclaimed acts or 23 out of 77 acts involved civilian targets, as compared to theocentric incidents with a full 67.5 percent or 52 out of 77 acts directed at civilian targets. To be sure, those comparative findings about Egyptian terrorist assaults do not constitute the expected outcome within the context of the proposed role that unclaimed terrorist assaults play in the political fray. In the case of Turkish terrorism, the results again conform with the expected findings with 71.1 percent or 27 out of 38 unclaimed acts that involve civilian targets. Theocentric groups in the context of Turkish terrorism committed attacks against civilian targets 84.6 percent of the time or in 11 out of 13 terrorist assaults.

In the case of Israeli-Palestinian-Arab terrorism, it is found that 65.9 percent of unclaimed terrorist incidents or 91 out of 138 acts were carried out against civilian targets, as compared to 84.7 percent or 100 out of 118 theocentric acts that were directed against civilian targets. Interestingly enough, that 65.9 percent rate of unclaimed terrorist assaults against civilian targets ranks last in comparison to the corresponding rates for other terrorist group-type and non-group-type categories. As previously mentioned, what seems significant here from a longitudinal point of view is the diametrically opposite ranking order for civilian target attacks by unclaimed terrorist assaults in the context of Israeli-Arab-Palestinian terrorism for the 1994 through 1999 time period under consideration. Plainly, those findings are also at variance with the expected findings, and hence it is necessary to reject the validity of Hypothesis Three.

Political Ideology and Numbers of Dead

The following hypothesis presupposes and derives from data findings presented in my earlier work within the context of description and discussion about "nonstructuralist" and "structuralist" Middle East terrorist groups. At a theoretical level, the findings suggest that ethnocentric group-types are found near the "nonstructuralist" axis of the continuum developed in *Serenade of Suffering* and other works of mine.[250] Those findings suggest the percentage rate of ethnocentric terrorist assaults with deaths of between one and fifty persons ought to be high. With earlier findings of mine found in my prior work that serve as a backdrop, Hypothesis Four is presented for empirical investigation:

Hypothesis Four: Ethnocentric terrorist groups will have a higher percentage of terrorist acts that cause deaths than terrorist acts committed by theocentric terrorist groups.

A bivariate correlations test for the variables "category of group" and "numbers of dead" suggests that a statistically significant association exists between those two variables.[251] A Pearson Chi Square statistic of 49.728 with a "p-value" of less than .001 at five degrees of freedom (5 d.f.) is generated, thereby in effect making it possible to reject the null hypothesis of no relation between the variables at the .05 level of confidence (see table 6.3). It is found that three cells or 25.0 percent of the cells have an expected frequency of less than five and as before it is, in my judgment, prudent to accept the validity of those findings for fear of making a "Type II" error. In terms of the strength of that association a Goodman and Kruskal *tau* diagnostic value of .162 with a significance value of less than .001 when "event deaths" is the dependent variable suggests a weak relationship between those variables. In addition, a "Phi" score of .402 with a significance score of less than .001 and a Cramer's V score of .402 with a significance score of less than .001 are other diagnostics that suggest a weak relationship between the variables.

In terms of the data distribution, ideo-ethnocentric charismatic groups are found to have the highest rate of terrorist incidents that killed between one and fifty persons with nearly two-thirds at 64.3 percent or 9 out of 14 acts (see table 6.4). Theocentric terrorist groups placed a distant second with 29.7 percent or 35 out of 118 acts that caused the deaths of between one and fifty persons. In turn, ethnocentric terrorist groups had the third highest rate of terrorist assaults that killed between one and fifty persons with 15.0 percent or 3 out of 20 acts. At the other extreme, ethnocentric charismatic groups had the lowest percentage of terrorist assaults that killed between one and fifty persons with zero, while theocentric charismatic groups had the second lowest percentage with 3.3 percent or 3 out of 92 acts. Theocentric charismatic terrorist groups also had the second highest rate of nonlethal terrorist assaults with 95.7 percent or 88 out of 92 acts. In turn, Jewish theocentric charismatic groups had the highest rate of nonlethal terrorist assaults with 96.0 percent or 24 out of 15 acts.[252]

Plainly, the empirical evidence makes it necessary to reject the validity of Hypothesis Four. As previously mentioned, ethnocentric terrorist groups are found to have a relatively low rate of terrorist assaults that killed between one and fifty persons. Theocentric terrorist groups, by contrast, have a rate that is nearly double that ethnocentric group rate. To be sure, it ought to be mentioned again there are no ideo-ethnocentric terrorist assaults chronicled in the data for the 1994 through 1999 time period. Seen from a longitudinal angle, it is observed the 15.0 percent ethnocentric group-type rate is a little more than one-half the 35.2 percent rate for ethnocentric terrorist assaults that killed between one and fifty individuals during 1968-93 found in my earlier works.[253] With respect to theocentric group-type ratio differences, terrorist assaults that resulted in the deaths of between one and fifty persons for the 1994 through 1999 period at 29.7 percent is almost one-half the corresponding rate of 57.3 percent for the 1968-93 time period.[254]

Table 6.3: Relative Frequency of Numbers of Dead in Israeli-Palestinian-Arab Terrorist Incidents by Group-Type, 1994-1999 (0=0; 1=1 through 50) (summary statistics)

Crosstabs

Case Processing Summary

	Cases					
	Valid		Missing		Total	
	N	Percent	N	Percent	N	Percent
Category of group * event deaths	307	49.3%	316	50.7%	623	100.0%

Category of Group * Event Deaths Cross-Tabulation

Category of group		Event deaths		Total
		0	1	
Theocentric charismatic	Count	88	3	91
	% within category of group	96.7%	3.3%	100.0%
	% within event deaths	34.9%	5.5%	29.6%
	% of total	28.7%	1.0%	29.6%
Jewish theocentric charismatic	Count	24	1	25
	% within category of group	96.0%	4.0%	100.0%
	% within event deaths	9.5%	1.8%	8.1%
	% of total	7.8%	.3%	8.1%
Ideo-ethnocentric charismatic	Count	5	9	14
	% within category of group	35.7%	64.3%	100.0%
	% within event deaths	2.0%	16.4%	4.6%
	% of total	1.6%	2.9%	4.6%
Jewish theocentric	Count	35	4	39
	% within category of group	89.7%	10.3%	100.0%
	% within event deaths	13.9%	7.3%	12.7%
	% of total	11.4%	1.3%	12.7%
Theocentric	Count	83	35	118
	% within category of group	70.3%	29.7%	100.0%
	% within event deaths	32.9%	63.6%	38.4%
	% of total	27.0%	11.4%	38.4%
Ethnocentric	Count	17	3	20
	% within category of group	85.0%	15.0%	100.0%
	% within event deaths	6.7%	5.5%	6.5%
	% of total	5.5%	1.0%	6.5%
Total	Count	252	55	307
	% within category of group	82.1%	17.9%	100.0%
	% within event deaths	100.0%	100.0%	100.0%
	% of total	82.1%	17.9%	100.0%

Table 6.3 — *continued*

Chi Square Tests

	Value	df	Asymp. sig. (2-sided)
Pearson Chi Square	49.728[a]	5	.000
Likelihood Ratio	49.445	5	.000
Linear-by-Linear Association	18.811	1	.000
N of valid cases	307		

a. 3 cells (25.0%) have expected count less than 5. The minimum expected count is 2.51.

Directional Measures

			Value	Asymp. std. error[a]	Approx. T[b]	Approx. sig.
Nominal by nominal	Lambda	Symmetric	.037	.055	.662	.508
		Category of group dependent	.026	.068	.382	.702
		Event deaths dependent	.073	.066	1.071	.284
	Goodman and Kruskal tau	Category of group dependent	.042	.011		.000[c]
		Event deaths dependent	.162	.041		.000[c]

a. Not assuming the null hypothesis.
b. Using the asymptotic standard error assuming the null hypothesis.
c. Based on chi square approximation.

Symmetric Measures

		Value	Approx. sig.
Nominal by nominal	Phi	.402	.000
	Cramer's V	.402	.000
N of valid cases		307	

a. Not assuming the null hypothesis.
b. Using the asymptotic standard error assuming the null hypothesis.

Table 6.4: Relative Frequency of Numbers of Dead in Israeli-Palestinian-Arab Terrorist Incidents by Group-Type, 1994-1999   (0=0; 1=1 through 50)

Crosstabs

Case Processing Summary

	Cases					
	Valid		Missing		Total	
	N	Percent	N	Percent	N	Percent
Event deaths * category of group	603	96.8%	20	3.2%	623	100.0%

Event Deaths * Category of Group Cross-Tabulation

Event deaths		Category of group			
		Theocentric charismatic	Jewish theocentric charismatic	Ideo-ethnocentric charismatic	Jewish theocentric
0	Count	88	24	5	35
	% within event deaths	16.7%	4.5%	.9%	6.6%
	% within category of group	95.7%	96.0%	35.7%	89.7%
	% of total	14.6%	4.0%	.8%	5.8%
1	Count	3	1	9	4
	% within event deaths	4.1%	1.4%	12.2%	5.4%
	% within category of group	3.3%	4.0%	64.3%	10.3%
	% of total	.5%	.2%	1.5%	.7%
247	Count	1			
	% within event deaths	100.0%			
	% within category of group	1.1%			
	% of total	.2%			
Total	Count	92	25	14	39
	% within event deaths	15.3%	4.1%	2.3%	6.5%
	% within category of group	100.0%	100.0%	100.0%	100.0%
	% of total	15.3%	4.1%	2.3%	6.5%

Table 6.4 — *continued*

Event Deaths * Category of Group Cross-Tabulation

Event deaths		Category of group			
		Un-completed acts	Un-claimed acts	Theo-centric	Ethno-centric
0	Count	76	130	83	17
	% within event deaths	14.4%	24.6%	15.7%	3.2%
	% within category of group	98.7%	94.9%	70.3%	85.0%
	% of total	12.6%	21.6%	13.8%	2.8%
1	Count	1	7	35	3
	% within event deaths	1.4%	9.5%	47.3%	4.1%
	% within category of group	1.3%	5.1%	29.7%	15.0%
	% of total	.2%	1.2%	5.8%	.5%
247	Count				
	% within event deaths				
	% within category of group				
	% of total				
Total	Count	77	137	118	20
	% within event deaths	12.8%	22.7%	19.6%	3.3%
	% within category of group	100.0%	100.0%	100.0%	100.0%
	% of total	12.8%	22.7%	19.6%	3.3%

Event Deaths * Category of Group Cross-Tabulation

Event deaths		Category of group		Total
		Ethnocentric charismatic	Lone assailant	
0	Count	1	69	528
	% within event deaths	.2%	13.1%	100.0%
	% within category of group	100.0%	86.3%	87.6%
	% of total	.2%	11.4%	87.6%
1	Count		11	74
	% within event deaths		14.9%	100.0%
	% within category of group		13.8%	12.3%
	% of total		1.8%	12.3%
247	Count			1
	% within event deaths			100.0%
	% within category of group			.2%
	% of total			.2%
Total	Count	1	80	603
	% within event deaths	.2%	13.3%	100.0%
	% within category of group	100.0%	100.0%	100.0%
	% of total	.2%	13.3%	100.0%

Political Ideology and Property Damage

The following theoretical proposition about the relationship between terrorist group-type and property damage presupposes and derives from Flemming's work and my own research findings from my prior work.[255] In my prior work, I found that theocentric group attacks caused some degree of property damage in 46.6 percent of attacks, as compared to ethnocentric terrorist attacks that caused some type of property damage 45.9 percent of terrorist assaults.[256] However, ethnocentric groups had higher rates of terrorist assaults that caused "moderate" and "high" rates of property damage, while the rate of theocentric terrorist assaults that caused "severe" property damage was found to be almost three times greater than the rate for ethnocentric groups.[257]

In my prior work, even though Middle East terrorist assaults that caused "moderate" damage (6.4 percent) and "high" rates of damage (3.8 percent) account for 10.2 percent of the total, and terrorist assaults that result in "severe" damage only represent a sliver at 1.5 percent, it seems those findings are consistent with the central idea that major property damage is more pronounced in terrorist assaults committed by more "structuralist" terrorist groups that, as I describe in length in *Serenade of Suffering*, seem to place more of a premium on assaults against government targets rather than civilian targets.[258] With the foregoing discussion and description in mind, the following hypothesis, to capture the relationship between terrorist group-type and levels of property damage caused by terrorist assaults, is offered:

Hypothesis Five: Ethnocentric terrorist groups will commit terrorist acts that result in lesser amounts of property damage than terrorist acts committed by theocentric terrorist groups.

A bivariate correlations test generates summary statistics that inform us there is a statistically significant association between the variables "category of group" and "property damage."[259] A Pearson Chi Square statistic of 27.394 with a "p-value" of less than .001 at six degrees of freedom (6 d.f.) makes it possible to reject the null hypothesis of no relation between the variables at the .05 level of confidence. With respect to the strength of the association, a Goodman and Kruskal *tau* score of .059 with a significance score of less than .001 when property damage is the dependent variable suggests a weak relationship between the variables. In addition, a Cramer's V score of .243 with a "p-value" of less than .001 and a "Phi" score of .243 with a "p-value" of less than .001 also indicate a weak relationship between the variables "property damage" and "category of group" (see table 6.5).

In the broader sense, the data distribution reveals that over two-thirds or 68.8 percent or 395 out of 574 terrorist assaults did not cause generally

Table 6.5: Level of Property Damage Caused in Israeli-Palestinian-Arab Terrorist Incidents by Group-Type, 1994-1999 (summary statistics)

Crosstabs

Case Processing Summary

	Cases					
	Valid		Missing		Total	
	N	Percent	N	Percent	N	Percent
Property damage * category of group	463	74.3%	160	25.7%	623	100.0%

Property Damage * Category of Group Cross-Tabulation

Property damage		Category of group			
		Theocentric charismatic	Jewish theocentric charismatic	Ideo-ethnocentric charismatic	Jewish theocentric
None	Count	43	10	10	15
	% within property damage	13.4%	3.1%	3.1%	4.7%
	% within category of group	60.6%	43.5%	71.4%	46.9%
	% of total	9.3%	2.2%	2.2%	3.2%
Slight	Count	28	13	4	17
	% within property damage	19.6%	9.1%	2.8%	11.9%
	% within category of group	39.4%	56.5%	28.6%	53.1%
	% of total	6.0%	2.8%	.9%	3.7%
Total	Count	71	23	14	32
	% within property damage	15.3%	5.0%	3.0%	6.9%
	% within category of group	100.0%	100.0%	100.0%	100.0%
	% of total	15.3%	5.0%	3.0%	6.9%

Property Damage * Category of Group Cross-Tabulation

Property damage		Category of group			
		Unclaimed acts	Theocentric	Ethnocentric	Total
None	Count	155	77	10	320
	% within property damage	48.4%	24.1%	3.1%	100.0%
	% within category of group	74.9%	79.4%	52.6%	69.1%
	% of total	33.5%	16.6%	2.2%	69.1%
Slight	Count	52	20	9	143
	% within property damage	36.4%	14.0%	6.3%	100.0%
	% within category of group	25.1%	20.6%	47.4%	30.9%
	% of total	11.2%	4.3%	1.9%	30.9%
Total	Count	207	97	19	463
	% within property damage	44.7%	21.0%	4.1%	100.0%
	% within category of group	100.0%	100.0%	100.0%	100.0%
	% of total	44.7%	21.0%	4.1%	100.0%

Table 6.5 — *continued*

Chi Square Tests

	Value	df	Asymp. sig. (2-sided)
Pearson Chi Square	27.394[a]	6	.000
Likelihood Ratio	26.362	6	.000
Linear-by-Linear Association	10.716	1	.001
N of valid cases	463		

a. 1 cell (7.1%) has expected count less than 5. The minimum expected count is 4.32.

Directional Measures

			Value	Asymp. std. error[a]	Approx. T[b]	Approx. sig.
Nominal by nominal	Lambda	Symmetric	.013	.018	.675	.500
		Property damage dependent	.035	.051	.675	.500
		Category of group dependent	.000	.000	.[c]	.[c]
	Goodman and Kruskal tau	Property damage dependent	.059	.023		.000[d]
		Category of group dependent	.011	.005		.000[d]

a. Not assuming the null hypothesis.
b. Using the asymptotic standard error assuming the null hypothesis.
c. Cannot be computed because the asymptotic standard error equals zero.
d. Based on chi square approximation.

Symmetric Measures

		Value	Approx. sig.
Nominal by nominal	Phi	.243	.000
	Cramer's V	.243	.000
N of valid cases		463	

a. Not assuming the null hypothesis.
b. Using the asymptotic standard error assuming the null hypothesis.

recognizable property damage, as compared to about one-quarter of terrorist assaults or 146 out of 574 acts that caused "slight" amounts of property damage (see table 6.6). When the data are broken down by terrorist group-type, however, it is found that exactly one-half of ethnocentric terrorist assaults did cause property damage and one half did not.

Ethnocentric charismatic groups, by contrast, have the highest rate of attacks that did not cause property damage at 100.0 percent, but that rate reflects only one successful chronicled terrorist assault. In turn, for terrorist group-types, theocentric groups have the second highest rate of terrorist assaults that did not damage property at 73.3 percent or 77 out of 105 acts. Ideo-ethnocentric charismatic groups ranked third for damage-free terrorist acts with 71.4 percent or 10 out of 14 acts. In turn, Jewish theocentric charismatic groups have the highest rate of "slight" property damage at 52.0 percent or 13 out of 25 acts, while Jewish theocentric groups follow closely behind in second place with 50.0 percent or 17 out of 34 acts.

Notwithstanding that, the foregoing results are not completely wide of the mark. In terms of "moderate" amounts of property damage, theocentric charismatic groups rank first with a rate of 11.4 percent or 10 out of 88 acts, while ethnocentric groups did not carry out terrorist assaults with "moderate" property damage. In turn, while Jewish theocentric charismatic groups rank first in the percentage of terrorist assaults that caused "high" rates of property damage, ethnocentric groups ranked second highest. In the case of "severe" property damage, theocentric charismatic groups rank first with 3.4 percent of all theocentric charismatic attacks responsible for "severe" damage or in 3 out of 88 events. To be sure, precisely because there are no recorded ideo-ethnocentric terrorist assaults, those first-place rankings for theocentric and theocentric charismatic groups for "moderate" property damage and a first place ranking for "severe" theocentric assaults are expected findings within the context of the "structuralist" and "nonstructuralist" terrorist group-type continuum.

Nonetheless, the data results are not consistent with Hypothesis Five and it is rejected. At low rates of damage, the findings are unexpected insofar as theocentric groups had a rate of 19.0 percent or 20 out of 105 for terrorist assaults that caused "slight" amounts of property damage, while the rate for ethnocentric terrorist assaults that caused "slight" damage is nearly two and a half times that rate at 45.0 percent or 9 out of 20 acts. At the "moderate" ordinal level, the picture is different and more expected, insofar as 4.8 percent of theocentric attacks or 5 out of 105 events caused "moderate" amounts of property damage as compared to an ethnocentric group rate of nil. Still, the rate of ethnocentric terrorist assaults that caused a "high" level of property damage, at 5.0 percent or 1 out of 20 acts, is nearly twice the rate of theocentric groups at 2.9 percent or 3 out of 105 acts. Hence, a full 50.0 percent of ethnocentric terrorist assaults caused some type of property damage, while the rate is only 26.7 percent for theocentric groups. Finally, neither ethnocentric nor theocentric

Table 6.6: Level of Property Damage Caused in Israeli-Palestinian-Arab Terrorist Incidents by Group-Type, 1994-1999

Crosstabs

Case Processing Summary

	Cases					
	Valid		Missing		Total	
	N	Percent	N	Percent	N	Percent
Property damage * category of group	574	92.1%	49	7.9%	623	100.0%

Property Damage * Category of Group Cross-Tabulation

Property damage		Category of group			
		Theocentric charismatic	Jewish theocentric charismatic	Ideo-ethnocentric charismatic	Jewish theocentric
None	Count	43	10	10	15
	% within property damage	10.9%	2.5%	2.5%	3.8%
	% within category of group	48.9%	40.0%	71.4%	44.1%
	% of total	7.5%	1.7%	1.7%	2.6%
Slight	Count	28	13	4	17
	% within property damage	19.2%	8.9%	2.7%	11.6%
	% within category of group	31.8%	52.0%	28.6%	50.0%
	% of total	4.9%	2.3%	.7%	3.0%
Moderate	Count	10			1
	% within property damage	58.8%			5.9%
	% within category of group	11.4%			2.9%
	% of total	1.7%			.2%
High	Count	4	2		
	% within property damage	33.3%	16.7%		
	% within category of group	4.5%	8.0%		
	% of total	.7%	.3%		
Severe	Count	3			1
	% within property damage	75.0%			25.0%
	% within category of group	3.4%			2.9%
	% of total	.5%			.2%
Total	Count	88	25	14	34
	% within property damage	15.3%	4.4%	2.4%	5.9%
	% within category of group	100.0%	100.0%	100.0%	100.0%
	% of total	15.3%	4.4%	2.4%	5.9%

terrorist groups engaged in terrorist assaults that caused "severe" property damage.

In an earlier analysis of "category of group" and "target-type" for Israeli-Palestinian-Arab terrorism, it is found that a full 90.0 percent of ethnocentric terrorist assaults were directed at civilian targets, as compared to a civilian target rate of 84.7 percent for theocentric groups. At a theoretical level, those are expected findings insofar as in my prior work ethnocentric terrorist groups were found to be more "nonstructuralist" in nature, framing the context of their struggle more against individuals and groups of individuals, more so than "hybrid" type theocentric groups, and certainly more so than "nonstructuralist" groups that wage war against a "world system" like capitalism or imperialism where terrorist assaults are more inclined to have special focus on government

Table 6.6 — *continued*

Property Damage * Category of Group Cross-Tabulation

Property damage		Category of group			
		Un-completed acts	Un-claimed acts	Theo-centric	Ethno-centric
None	Count	74	84	77	10
	% within property damage	18.7%	21.3%	19.5%	2.5%
	% within category of group	96.1%	64.6%	73.3%	50.0%
	% of total	12.9%	14.6%	13.4%	1.7%
Slight	Count	3	43	20	9
	% within property damage	2.1%	29.5%	13.7%	6.2%
	% within category of group	3.9%	33.1%	19.0%	45.0%
	% of total	.5%	7.5%	3.5%	1.6%
Moderate	Count		1	5	
	% within property damage		5.9%	29.4%	
	% within category of group		.8%	4.8%	
	% of total		.2%	.9%	
High	Count		2	3	1
	% within property damage		16.7%	25.0%	8.3%
	% within category of group		1.5%	2.9%	5.0%
	% of total		.3%	.5%	.2%
Severe	Count				
	% within property damage				
	% within category of group				
	% of total				
Total	Count	77	130	105	20
	% within property damage	13.4%	22.6%	18.3%	3.5%
	% within category of group	100.0%	100.0%	100.0%	100.0%
	% of total	13.4%	22.6%	18.3%	3.5%

targets.[260]

It follows that one way to add depth to the foregoing analysis is to look at the quality of the terrorist act itself, to examine whether or not terrorist attacks against government targets result in less emphasis on property damage consistent with their "symbolic" nature and role, as compared with terrorist assaults against civilian targets. The following hypothesis captures those dynamics and is tested:

Hypothesis Six: Terrorist attacks against government targets will be associated with lower amounts of property damage than terrorist assaults against civilian targets.

Table 6.6 — *continued*

Property Damage * Category of Group Cross-Tabulation

Property damage		Category of group: Ethnocentric charismatic	Category of group: Lone assailant	Total
None	Count	1	71	395
	% within property damage	.3%	18.0%	100.0%
	% within category of group	100.0%	88.8%	68.8%
	% of total	.2%	12.4%	68.8%
Slight	Count		9	146
	% within property damage		6.2%	100.0%
	% within category of group		11.3%	25.4%
	% of total		1.6%	25.4%
Moderate	Count			17
	% within property damage			100.0%
	% within category of group			3.0%
	% of total			3.0%
High	Count			12
	% within property damage			100.0%
	% within category of group			2.1%
	% of total			2.1%
Severe	Count			4
	% within property damage			100.0%
	% within category of group			.7%
	% of total			.7%
Total	Count	1	80	574
	% within property damage	.2%	13.9%	100.0%
	% within category of group	100.0%	100.0%	100.0%
	% of total	.2%	13.9%	100.0%

A bivariate analysis informs us there is a statistically significant association between the variables "target-type" and "property damage."[261] A Pearson Chi Square statistic of 25.492 with a "p-value" of less than .001 at two degrees of freedom (2 d.f.) is produced, thereby in effect making it possible to reject the null hypothesis of no relation between the variables at the .05 level of confidence (see table 6.7). It is observed that one cell or 16.7 percent has an expected frequency of less than five. With respect to the strength of the association, a Goodman and Kruskal *tau* measure of .043 with a "p-value" of less than .001 when "property damage" is the dependent variable indicates a weak relationship between those two variables. In turn, a Cramer's V score of .218 with a "p-value" of less than .001 and a "Phi" score of .218 with a "p-value" of less than .001 also suggests a weak relationship between the variables "property damage" and "target-type."

The data distribution informs us that across almost every ordinal measure of property damage, terrorist assaults against civilian targets are associated with greater amounts of property damage than terrorist assaults against government targets (see table 6.8). The findings support strongly Hypothesis Six and accordingly it is accepted as valid. It is observed that 30.9 percent or 134 out of 434 terrorist assaults directed at civilian targets created "slight" amounts of property damage, as compared to a rate of 10.1 percent, or 12 out of 119 acts, directed against government targets that caused "slight" levels of damage.

In the case of "moderate" property damage, 3.7 percent of civilian target terrorist attacks or 16 out of 434 incidents caused "moderate" damage, while there is no "moderate" damage recorded for terrorist assaults against government targets. In a similar vein, 2.8 percent of the 434 civilian target terrorist assaults in this test, or 12 out of 434 acts, caused "high" levels of property damage, as compared with only .8 percent of terrorist assaults directed at government targets or 1 out of 119 acts that caused a "high" level of damage. Lastly, the percentage rate of terrorist assaults aimed at civilian targets and government targets that caused "severe" property damage is virtually the same, at .5 percent or 2 out of 434 in the case of the former and .8 percent or 1 out of 119 in the case of the latter. Be that as it may, the findings for terrorist assaults that cause "severe" levels of property damage are rather marginal insofar as terrorist attacks that cause that type of massive physical devastation only make up .7 percent of the total, or 4 out of 565 incidents.

Terrorist Group Age, Terrorist Group Size, and Target Selection

Based on the works of Long,[262] Karber and Mengel,[263] and Flemming,[264] as well as my own findings,[265] the following theoretical proposition that captures the relationship between terrorist group age and target-type is

Table 6.7: Relative Frequency of Property Damage by Israeli-Palestinian-Arab Target-Type, 1994-1999 (summary statistics)

Case Processing Summary

	Cases					
	Valid		Missing		Total	
	N	Percent	N	Percent	N	Percent
Type of target * property damage	534	85.7%	89	14.3%	623	100.0%

Type of Target * Property Damage Cross-Tabulation

Type of target		Property damage			Total
		None	Slight	High	
Govern-ment	Count	105	12	1	118
	% within type of target	89.0%	10.2%	.8%	100.0%
	% within property damage	28.0%	8.2%	7.7%	22.1%
	% of total	19.7%	2.2%	.2%	22.1%
Civilian	Count	270	134	12	416
	% within type of target	64.9%	32.2%	2.9%	100.0%
	% within property damage	72.0%	91.8%	92.3%	77.9%
	% of total	50.6%	25.1%	2.2%	77.9%
Total	Count	375	146	13	534
	% within type of target	70.2%	27.3%	2.4%	100.0%
	% within property damage	100.0%	100.0%	100.0%	100.0%
	% of total	70.2%	27.3%	2.4%	100.0%

Chi Square Tests

	Value	df	Asymp. sig. (2-sided)
Pearson Chi Square	25.492[a]	2	.000
Likelihood Ratio	29.331	2	.000
Linear-by-Linear Association	19.524	1	.000
N of valid cases	534		

a. 1 cell (16.7%) has expected count less than 5. The minimum expected count is 2.87.

offered for empirical analysis:

Hypothesis Seven: Older terrorist groups in the Israeli-Palestinian-Arab terrorism context will have a higher percentage of civilian target attacks than younger terrorist groups.

In terms of bivariate testing, the summary statistics generated suggest a statistically significant association between the variables "target-type" and terrorist "group age" (see table 6.9). A Pearson Chi Square statistic of 15.265

Table 6.7 — *continued*

Directional Measures

			Value	Asymp. std. error[a]	Approx. T	Approx. sig.
Nominal by nominal	Lambda	Symmetric	.000	.000	.[b]	.[b]
		Type of target dependent	.000	.000	.[b]	.[b]
		Property damage dependent	.000	.000	.[b]	.[b]
	Goodman and Kruskal tau	Type of target dependent	.048	.014		.000[c]
		Property damage dependent	.043	.013		.000[c]

a. Not assuming the null hypothesis.
b. Cannot be computed because the asymptotic standard error equals zero.
c. Based on chi square approximation.

Symmetric Measures

		Value	Approx. sig.
Nominal by nominal	Phi	.218	.000
	Cramer's V	.218	.000
N of valid cases		534	

a. Not assuming the null hypothesis.
b. Using the asymptotic standard error assuming the null hypothesis.

Table 6.8: Relative Frequency of Property Damage by Israeli-Palestinian-Arab Target-Type, 1994-1999

Crosstabs

Case Processing Summary

	Cases					
	Valid		Missing		Total	
	N	Percent	N	Percent	N	Percent
Type of target * property damage	565	90.7%	58	9.3%	623	100.0%

Type of Target * Property Damage Cross-Tabulation

Type of target		Property damage					Total
		None	Slight	Moderate	High	Severe	
Govern-ment	Count	105	12		1	1	119
	% within type of target	88.2%	10.1%		.8%	.8%	100.0%
	% within property damage	27.3%	8.2%		7.7%	25.0%	21.1%
	% of total	18.6%	2.1%		.2%	.2%	21.1%
Infra-structure	Count	7				1	8
	% within type of target	87.5%				12.5%	100.0%
	% within property damage	1.8%				25.0%	1.4%
	% of total	1.2%				.2%	1.4%
Civilian	Count	270	134	16	12	2	434
	% within type of target	62.2%	30.9%	3.7%	2.8%	.5%	100.0%
	% within property damage	70.3%	91.2%	94.1%	92.3%	50.0%	76.8%
	% of total	47.8%	23.7%	2.8%	2.1%	.4%	76.8%
Civilian-Govt.	Count	2	1	1			4
	% within type of target	50.0%	25.0%	25.0%			100.0%
	% within property damage	.5%	.7%	5.9%			.7%
	% of total	.4%	.2%	.2%			.7%
Total	Count	384	147	17	13	4	565
	% within type of target	68.0%	26.0%	3.0%	2.3%	.7%	100.0%
	% within property damage	100.0%	100.0%	100.0%	100.0%	100.0%	100.0%
	% of total	68.0%	26.0%	3.0%	2.3%	.7%	100.0%

Table 6.9: Relative Frequency of Israeli-Palestinian-Arab Target-Type by Terrorist Group Age, 1994-1999 (summary statistics)

Crosstabs

Case Processing Summary

	Cases					
	Valid		Missing		Total	
	N	Percent	N	Percent	N	Percent
Type of target * age of group	246	39.5%	377	60.5%	623	100.0%

Type of Target * Age of Group Cross-Tabulation

Type of target		Age of group			
		1 - 3 years of age	4 - 9 years of age	10 - 15 years of age	16 - 20 years of age
Government	Count	3	6	12	1
	% within type of target	10.3%	20.7%	41.4%	3.4%
	% within age of group	42.9%	10.7%	9.8%	4.0%
	% of total	1.2%	2.4%	4.9%	.4%
Civilian	Count	4	50	110	24
	% within type of target	1.8%	23.0%	50.7%	11.1%
	% within age of group	57.1%	89.3%	90.2%	96.0%
	% of total	1.6%	20.3%	44.7%	9.8%
Total	Count	7	56	122	25
	% within type of target	2.8%	22.8%	49.6%	10.2%
	% within age of group	100.0%	100.0%	100.0%	100.0%
	% of total	2.8%	22.8%	49.6%	10.2%

Type of Target * Age of Group Cross-Tabulation

Type of target		Age of Group		Total
		21 thru 25 years of age	26+ years of age	
Government	Count	5	2	29
	% within type of target	17.2%	6.9%	100.0%
	% within age of group	33.3%	9.5%	11.8%
	% of total	2.0%	.8%	11.8%
Civilian	Count	10	19	217
	% within type of target	4.6%	8.8%	100.0%
	% within age of group	66.7%	90.5%	88.2%
	% of total	4.1%	7.7%	88.2%
Total	Count	15	21	246
	% within type of target	6.1%	8.5%	100.0%
	% within age of group	100.0%	100.0%	100.0%
	% of total	6.1%	8.5%	100.0%

Table 6.9 — *continued*

Chi Square Tests

	Value	df	Asymp. sig. (2-sided)
Pearson Chi Square	15.265[a]	5	.009
Likelihood Ratio	11.609	5	.041
Linear-by-Linear Association	.012	1	.913
N of valid cases	246		

a. 4 cells (33.3%) have expected count less than 5. The minimum expected count is .83.

Directional Measures

			Value	Asymp. std. error[a]	Approx. T	Approx. sig.
Nominal by nominal	Lambda	Symmetric	.000	.000	.[b]	.[b]
		Type of target dependent	.000	.000	.[b]	.[b]
		Age of group dependent	.000	.000	.[b]	.[b]
	Goodman and Kruskal tau	Type of target dependent	.062	.043		.010[c]
		Age of group dependent	.006	.005		.205[c]

a. Not assuming the null hypothesis.
b. Cannot be computed because the asymptotic standard error equals zero.
c. Based on chi square approximation.

Symmetric Measures

		Value	Approx. sig.
Nominal by nominal	Phi	.249	.009
	Cramer's V	.249	.009
N of valid cases		246	

a. Not assuming the null hypothesis.
b. Using the asymptotic standard error assuming the null hypothesis.

with a "p-value" of .009 at five degrees of freedom (5 d.f.) makes it possible to reject the null hypothesis of no relation between the variables at the .05 level of confidence (see table 6.9). It is observed that four cells or 33.3 percent of the cells have an expected frequency of less than five but it is, in my judgment, necessary to report the results for fear of making a "Type II" error of failing to reject the null hypothesis when it ought to rejected. In terms of the strength of the association, a Goodman and Kruskal *tau* statistic of .062 with a "p-value" of .010 suggests a weak relationship between the variables. Likewise, a "Phi" score of .249 with a significance value of .009 and a Cramer's V score of .249 with a significance score of .009 also suggests that a weak relationship exists between the variables "target-type" and terrorist "group age."

In the broadest sense, Israeli-Palestinian-Arab terrorist groups of from ten through fifteen years of age are found to have carried out the highest number and percentage terrorist attacks with 123 out of 249 acts or, at 49.4 percent, about one-half of the terrorist assaults used in this test. Very young terrorist groups of between one and three years old have the lowest number and rate of terrorist assaults with 7 terrorist attacks or 2.8 percent of the total (see table 6.10).

In a narrower sense, older terrorist groups between sixteen and twenty years of age have the highest rate of civilian target terrorist assaults, with 92.3 percent or 24 out of 26 acts. Terrorist groups over twenty-six years of age have the second highest rate of civilian target attacks, with 90.5 percent or 19 out of 21 attacks. In third place are terrorist groups of between ten and fifteen years old with 89.4 percent or 110 out of 123 events. At the same time, it is found that terrorist groups of between four and nine years old have the fourth highest rate of civilian target terrorist attacks with 87.7 percent or 50 out of 57 events, while an older set of terrorist groups of between twenty-one and twenty-five years of age have a lower rate of civilian target terrorist assaults at 66.7 percent or 10 out of 15 acts. It follows that ranking order is the reverse of the ranking for government target terrorist assault rates.

Those findings are largely consistent with Hypothesis Seven, even though the expected findings predict terrorist groups of between twenty-one and twenty-five years of age to have a higher rate of civilian target terrorist assaults than terrorist groups of between four and nine years old. Notwithstanding that, those findings for the 1994 through 1999 time period are supported by results found in my prior work that in similar ways demonstrate a similar and generally recognizable relationship between increasing terrorist group age and an increasing likelihood of civilian target terrorist assaults.

At a theoretical level, what seems significant here is those findings are a good fit with the underlying notion that presupposes and derives from the works of Lasswell, Long, and others that as terrorist group leaders become more seasoned with experience those leaders understand more fully the utility of terrorist assaults that strike at civilian targets.[266] That "maturity cycle," to

Table 6.10: Relative Frequency of Israeli-Palestinian-Arab Target-Type by Terrorist Group Age, 1994-1999

Crosstabs

Case Processing Summary

	Cases					
	Valid		Missing		Total	
	N	Percent	N	Percent	N	Percent
Type of target * age of group	249	40.0%	374	60.0%	623	100.0%

Type of Target * Age of Group Cross-Tabulation

Type of target		1 - 3 years of age	4 - 9 years of age	10 - 15 years of age	16 - 20 years of age
		Age of group			
Govern-ment	Count	3	6	12	1
	% within type of target	10.3%	20.7%	41.4%	3.4%
	% within age of group	42.9%	10.5%	9.8%	3.8%
	% of total	1.2%	2.4%	4.8%	.4%
Infra-structure	Count				1
	% within type of target				100.0%
	% within age of group				3.8%
	% of total				.4%
Civilian	Count	4	50	110	24
	% within type of target	1.8%	23.0%	50.7%	11.1%
	% within age of group	57.1%	87.7%	89.4%	92.3%
	% of total	1.6%	20.1%	44.2%	9.6%
Civilian-Govt.	Count		1	1	
	% within type of target		50.0%	50.0%	
	% within age of group		1.8%	.8%	
	% of total		.4%	.4%	
Total	Count	7	57	123	26
	% within type of target	2.8%	22.9%	49.4%	10.4%
	% within age of group	100.0%	100.0%	100.0%	100.0%
	% of total	2.8%	22.9%	49.4%	10.4%

employ Lasswell's phrase that he uses to describe the continuously evolving condition of nations, is an idea that, with respect to terrorism organizations, deserves the increased devotion of scholars who explore terrorism group dynamics both in the Middle East and at other geographical sites.[267]

Delving into the analysis even more, it is found that the single infrastructure terrorist assault chronicled in the data was carried out by a terrorist group of between sixteen and twenty years of age and that event comprises a mere .4 percent of the total or 1 out of 249 acts (see table 6.10). With respect to "multiple-type target" terrorist assaults, there are only two recorded "civilian-government" terrorist assaults, 1 committed by a terrorist group of between four and nine years of age, and 1 terrorist assault carried out by a terrorist group of between ten and fifteen years old.

Table 6.10 — *continued*

Type of Target * Age of Group Cross-Tabulation

Type of target		Age of group: 21 - 25 years of age	Age of group: 26+ years of age	Total
Government	Count	5	2	29
	% within type of target	17.2%	6.9%	100.0%
	% within age of group	33.3%	9.5%	11.6%
	% of total	2.0%	.8%	11.6%
Infra-structure	Count			1
	% within type of target			100.0%
	% within age of group			.4%
	% of total			.4%
Civilian	Count	10	19	217
	% within type of target	4.6%	8.8%	100.0%
	% within age of group	66.7%	90.5%	87.1%
	% of total	4.0%	7.6%	87.1%
Civilian-Govt.	Count			2
	% within type of target			100.0%
	% within age of group			.8%
	% of total			.8%
Total	Count	15	21	249
	% within type of target	6.0%	8.4%	100.0%
	% within age of group	100.0%	100.0%	100.0%
	% of total	6.0%	8.4%	100.0%

Group Size and Target Selection

Based on the works of Crenshaw,[268] Russell, Banker, and Miller,[269] Smart,[270] Oots,[271] and my own findings in my prior work, the following hypothesis is offered to capture the relationship between terrorist "group size" and "target" selection:

Hypothesis Eight: Very small and small terrorist groups will have a higher percentage of civilian target attacks than large and very large terrorist groups.

A bivariate analysis of the variables terrorist "group size" and "target-type" suggests that a statistically significant association exists between those two variables.[272] A Pearson Chi Square value of 7.220 with a "p-value" of .027 at two degrees of freedom (2 d.f.) makes it possible to reject the null hypothesis of no relation between those variables at the .05 level of confidence (see table 6.11). It is found that 33.3 percent or two cells have an expected frequency of less than five, and the results are reported precisely because of the reason that it is likely a "Type II" error of failing to reject the null hypothesis when it ought to be rejected would be made otherwise. In terms of the strength of the association, a Goodman and Kruskal's *tau* measure of .033 with a "p-value" of .027 when "type of target" is the dependent variable suggests a weak relationship between the variables. In addition, a Cramer's V score of .182 with a "p-value" of .027 and a "Phi" score of .182 with a "p-value" of .027 also indicates a slight relationship between the variables terrorist "group-size" and "target-type."

In the broader sense, the data distributions inform us that "small" terrorist groups of between fifty-one and one hundred activists carried out the largest chunk of terrorist assaults, with 47.5 percent or nearly one-half of all events, or 104 out of 219 acts (see table 6.12). "Moderate" size groups that consist of 101 through 700 activists, by contrast, carried out the smallest sliver of terrorist events at .9 percent or 2 out of 219 acts. In addition, the only two "multiple-type target" attacks recorded when terrorist assaults committed are broken down by terrorist group size were carried out by "small" terrorist groups, and in both cases those "multiple-type target" attacks are "civilian-government" terrorist assaults.

In the narrower sense, "large" terrorist groups of between 701 and 2,500 activists have the highest rate of civilian target attacks at 100.0 percent or 11 out of 11 acts. "Very large" terrorist groups that range from between 2,501 activists through 11,000 or more activists rank second with 92.9 percent of terrorist assaults directed at civilian targets or 91 out of 98 events. In third place are "small" terrorist groups that are found to have carried out terrorist assaults against civilian targets in 83.7 percent of all assaults or in 87 out of 104

Table 6.11: Relative Frequency of Israeli-Palestinian-Arab Target-Type by Terrorist Group Size, 1994-1999 (summary statistics)

Crosstabs

Case Processing Summary

	Cases					
	Valid		Missing		Total	
	N	Percent	N	Percent	N	Percent
Type of target * size of group	217	34.8%	406	65.2%	623	100.0%

Type of Target * Size of Group Cross-Tabulation

Type of target		Size of group			Total
		Small	Moderate	Large	
Govern-ment	Count	16	1	7	24
	% within type of target	66.7%	4.2%	29.2%	100.0%
	% within size of group	15.1%	50.0%	6.4%	11.1%
	% of total	7.4%	.5%	3.2%	11.1%
Civilian	Count	90	1	102	193
	% within type of target	46.6%	.5%	52.8%	100.0%
	% within size of group	84.9%	50.0%	93.6%	88.9%
	% of total	41.5%	.5%	47.0%	88.9%
Total	Count	106	2	109	217
	% within type of target	48.8%	.9%	50.2%	100.0%
	% within size of group	100.0%	100.0%	100.0%	100.0%
	% of total	48.8%	.9%	50.2%	100.0%

Chi Square Tests

	Value	df	Asymp. sig. (2-sided)
Pearson Chi Square	7.220[a]	2	.027
Likelihood Ratio	6.221	2	.045
Linear-by-Linear Association	4.099	1	.043
N of valid cases	217		

a. 2 cells (33.3%) have expected count less than 5. The minimum expected count is .22.

incidents. In fourth place, "very small" terrorist groups commit terrorist assaults that involve civilian targets 75.0 percent of the time or in three out of four events. In fifth and last place, "moderate" terrorist groups have the lowest civilian target terrorist assault rate with 50.0 percent or 1 out of 2 incidents. Plainly, the foregoing results suggest that during the 1994 through 1999 time period, at least, larger terrorist groups rather than smaller terrorist groups have a higher percentage of civilian target terrorist assaults and, accordingly, Hypothesis Eight is rejected as invalid.

Table 6.11 — *continued*

Directional Measures

			Value	Asymp. std. error[a]	Approx. T[b]	Approx. sig.
Nominal by nominal	Lambda	Symmetric	.068	.036	1.814	.070
		Type of target dependent	.000	.059	.000	1.000
		Size of group dependent	.083	.043	1.892	.058
	Goodman and Kruskal tau	Type of target dependent	.033	.030		.027[c]
		Size of group dependent	.019	.017		.017[c]

a. Not assuming the null hypothesis.
b. Using the asymptotic standard error assuming the null hypothesis.
c. Based on chi square approximation.

Symmetric Measures

		Value	Approx. sig.
Nominal by nominal	Phi	.182	.027
	Cramer's V	.182	.027
N of valid cases		217	

a. Not assuming the null hypothesis.
b. Using the asymptotic standard error assuming the null hypothesis.

Table 6.12: Relative Frequency of Israeli-Palestinian-Arab Target-Type by Terrorist Group Size, 1994-1999

Crosstabs

Case Processing Summary

	Cases					
	Valid		Missing		Total	
	N	Percent	*N*	Percent	*N*	Percent
Type of target * size of group	219	35.2%	404	64.8%	623	100.0%

Type of Target * Size of Group Cross-Tabulation

Type of target		size of group					
		Very small	Small	Moderate	Large	Very large	Total
Govern-ment	Count	1	15	1		7	24
	% within type of target	4.2%	62.5%	4.2%		29.2%	100.0%
	% within size of group	25.0%	14.4%	50.0%		7.1%	11.0%
	% of total	.5%	6.8%	.5%		3.2%	11.0%
Civilian	Count	3	87	1	11	91	193
	% within type of target	1.6%	45.1%	.5%	5.7%	47.2%	100.0%
	% within size of group	75.0%	83.7%	50.0%	100.0%	92.9%	88.1%
	% of total	1.4%	39.7%	.5%	5.0%	41.6%	88.1%
Civilian-Govt.	Count		2				2
	% within type of target		100.0%				100.0%
	% within size of group		1.9%				.9%
	% of total		.9%				.9%
Total	Count	4	104	2	11	98	219
	% within type of target	1.8%	47.5%	.9%	5.0%	44.7%	100.0%
	% within size of group	100.0%	100.0%	100.0%	100.0%	100.0%	100.0%
	% of total	1.8%	47.5%	.9%	5.0%	44.7%	100.0%

Location and Target Selection

Based on the works of Merari et al., Waugh, Shultz, O'Neill, Osmond, and Flemming,[273] I develop, in my previous work, a theoretical proposition about location as an explanatory variable to capture the dynamics of terrorist targeting behavior within the context of Middle East terrorism.[274] I explored the relationship between geographical site and terrorist target-type and found that that the highest rate of civilian target terrorist assaults happened in the Occupied Territories, followed closely by the rate of civilian target terrorist assaults committed in Israel.[275] In turn, European states placed a distant third in the civilian target terrorist assault rankings. The following hypothesis is used within the context of Israeli-Palestinian-Arab terrorism for the 1994 through 1999 time period:

Hypothesis Nine: Terrorist attacks in the Occupied Territories will have the highest percentage of attacks aimed at civilian targets, while terrorist attacks in Israel will have the second highest percentage of attacks aimed at civilian targets.

Cross-tabulation table analysis suggests that a statistically significant association exists between the variables "location" and "target-type."[276] A Pearson Chi Square statistic of 7.825 with a "p-value" of .050 at three degrees of freedom (3 d.f.) makes it possible to reject the null hypothesis of no relation between the variables "location" and "target-type" at the .05 level of confidence (see table 6.13). It is found that 12.5 percent of the cells or one cell has an expected frequency of less than five. With respect to the strength of the association, a Goodman and Kruskal's *tau* of .013 with a "p-value" of .050 when type of target is the dependent variable indicates a weak relationship between those two variables. To be sure, a "Phi" measure of .115 with a "p-value" of .050 and a Cramer's V score of .115 with a "p-value" of .050 are other diagnostic measures that suggest a weak relationship between the variables "location" and "target-type."

In the broader sense, in terms of the data distribution, it is apparent that Israel experienced the largest portion of terrorist assaults with over one-third (34.2 percent) or 206 out of 602 incidents. At the other extreme, the United States experienced the lowest rate of Israeli-Palestinian-Arab terrorism with 2.3 percent or 14 out of 602 incidents (see table 6.14). In the narrower sense, the highest rate of civilian target terrorist attacks is claimed by "other Middle East states" with 87.2 percent or 41 out of 47 acts. The Occupied Territories has the second highest rate of civilian target terrorist assaults at 81.3 percent or 152 out of 187 attacks. The rate of such attacks for Israel follows closely behind at 77.6 percent or 160 out of 205 acts. In the case of the jurisdiction of the Palestinian

Table 6.13: Relative Frequency of Israeli-Palestinian-Arab Target-Type by Location, 1994-1999 (summary statistics)

Crosstabs

Case Processing Summary

	Cases					
	Valid		Missing		Total	
	N	Percent	*N*	Percent	*N*	Percent
Type of target * locale	589	94.5%	34	5.5%	623	100.0%

Type of Target * Locale Cross-Tabulation

Type of target		Locale				Total
		Europe	OT	Oth mid	Other	
Govern-ment	Count	6	29	80	6	121
	% within type of target	5.0%	24.0%	66.1%	5.0%	100.0%
	% within locale	35.3%	16.0%	23.3%	12.8%	20.5%
	% of total	1.0%	4.9%	13.6%	1.0%	20.5%
Civilian	Count	11	152	264	41	468
	% within type of target	2.4%	32.5%	56.4%	8.8%	100.0%
	% within locale	64.7%	84.0%	76.7%	87.2%	79.5%
	% of total	1.9%	25.8%	44.8%	7.0%	79.5%
Total	Count	17	181	344	47	589
	% within type of target	2.9%	30.7%	58.4%	8.0%	100.0%
	% within locale	100.0%	100.0%	100.0%	100.0%	100.0%
	% of total	2.9%	30.7%	58.4%	8.0%	100.0%

Chi Square Tests

	Value	df	Asymp. sig. (2-sided)
Pearson Chi Square	7.825[a]	3	.050
Likelihood Ratio	7.835	3	.050
N of valid cases	589		

a. 1 cell (12.5%) has expected count less than 5. The minimum expected count is 3.49.

National Authority, nearly three-quarters of all terrorist assaults, at 73.9 percent or 65 out of 88 acts, were aimed at civilian targets.

Both the United States and Western Europe were virtually tied for the lowest rate of civilian target terrorist assaults with 64.3 percent or 9 out of 14 acts, and 64.7 percent or 11 out of 17 incidents, respectively. In the case of "other" geographical sites, the rate of civilian target terrorist attack is 69.8 percent or 30 out of 43 acts. Those "other" geographical sites include Chiang Mai-Bangkok, Thailand, Buenos Aires, Argentina, Colon, Panama, Cyprus, Santiago, Chile, Asuncion, and San Antonio, Paraguay, along Argentina's border with Paraguay, Nairobi, Kenya, Dar es Salam, Tanzania, Cape Town, South Africa, Tashkent, Uzbekistan, and New Delhi, India.[277]

Table 6.13 — continued

Directional Measures

			Value	Asymp. std. error[a]	Approx. T	Approx. sig.
Nominal by nominal	Lambda	Symmetric	.000	.000	.[b]	.[b]
		Type of target dependent	.000	.000	.[b]	.[b]
		Locale dependent	.000	.000	.[b]	.[b]
	Goodman and Kruskal tau	Type of target dependent	.013	.009		.050[c]
		Locale dependent	.006	.005		.021[c]

a. Not assuming the null hypothesis.
b. Cannot be computed because the asymptotic standard error equals zero.
c. Based on chi square approximation.

Symmetric Measures

		Value	Approx. sig.
Nominal by nominal	Phi	.115	.050
	Cramer's V	.115	.050
N of valid cases		589	

a. Not assuming the null hypothesis.
b. Using the asymptotic standard error assuming the null hypothesis.

Table 6.14: Relative Frequency of Israeli-Palestinian-Arab Target-Type by Location, 1994-1999

Crosstabs

Case Processing Summary

	Cases					
	Valid		Missing		Total	
	N	Percent	N	Percent	N	Percent
Type of target * locale	602	96.6%	21	3.4%	623	100.0%

Type of Target * Locale Cross-Tabulation

Type of target		Locale							
		Europe	Israel	OT	Oth mid	Other	PA	US	Total
Govern-ment	Count	6	45	29	6	12	19	4	121
	% within type of target	5.0%	37.2%	24.0%	5.0%	9.9%	15.7%	3.3%	100.0%
	% within Locale	35.3%	21.8%	15.5%	12.8%	27.9%	21.6%	28.6%	20.1%
	% of total	1.0%	7.5%	4.8%	1.0%	2.0%	3.2%	.7%	20.1%
Infra-structure	Count		1	4		1	2	1	9
	% within type of target		11.1%	44.4%		11.1%	22.2%	11.1%	100.0%
	% within Locale		.5%	2.1%		2.3%	2.3%	7.1%	1.5%
	% of total		.2%	.7%		.2%	.3%	.2%	1.5%
Civilian	Count	11	160	152	41	30	65	9	468
	% within type of target	2.4%	34.2%	32.5%	8.8%	6.4%	13.9%	1.9%	100.0%
	% within Locale	64.7%	77.7%	81.3%	87.2%	69.8%	73.9%	64.3%	77.7%
	% of total	1.8%	26.6%	25.2%	6.8%	5.0%	10.8%	1.5%	77.7%
Civilian-Govt.	Count			2			2		4
	% within type of target			50.0%			50.0%		100.0%
	% within Locale			1.1%			2.3%		.7%
	% of total			.3%			.3%		.7%
Total	Count	17	206	187	47	43	88	14	602
	% within type of target	2.8%	34.2%	31.1%	7.8%	7.1%	14.6%	2.3%	100.0%
	% within Locale	100.0%	100.0%	100.0%	100.0%	100.0%	100.0%	100.0%	100.0%
	% of total	2.8%	34.2%	31.1%	7.8%	7.1%	14.6%	2.3%	100.0%

The foregoing data do not support Hypothesis Nine and accordingly it is rejected as invalid. At the same time, it ought to be noted as a caveat that the high rate of civilian target terrorist attacks committed at "other Middle East states" geographical sites may mirror the amount of threats or clarion calls to promote violence issued by various groups such as Hezbollah that is based in Lebanon, and Islamic Jihad that is based in Damascus, Syria.[278] Accordingly, the second and third place tallies for civilian target terrorist assaults for the Occupied Territories and Israel respectively are not, in my judgment, really at variance with the broader underlying theme of Hypothesis Nine.

Political Events and Target Selection

The following hypothesis about whether or not terrorist assaults are largely proactive or independent from political events is based in large part on results found in my prior research. In those works of mine, work of both Azar, Jureidini and McLaurin, and Brecher and James are springboards or guideposts used to develop a theoretical proposition that delves into an underlying set of interconnections between political events and terrorist assaults. In Azar, Jureidini and McLaurin's study about political-social violence in the Middle East, the authors suggest a servo mechanism of sorts at work where political events that are "cooperative" in nature evoke non-cooperative events like terrorist assaults for example, to offset and political gain made.[279]

Seen from a different angle, Brecher and James, in their discussion about international crises within "Protracted Conflict (PC)" conditions and non-"PC" conditions, tell us, "the importance of the values at stake creates a disposition to initiate a crisis by violent acts, as well as to expect a violent trigger on the part of one's enemy."[280] Insofar as those works suggest, in my judgment, possible interconnections between terrorism and political events in communal conflict contexts, I tested in my prior work the theoretical proposition that most terrorist assaults will have interconnections to political events. I found my findings about Middle East terrorist assaults and political events to be inconsistent with that hypothesis. Hence, the following modified hypothesis about the proactive or reactive nature of terrorist assaults is offered:

Hypothesis Ten: Most terrorist assaults will be proactive terrorist assaults not linked to political events in the region, such as wars, visits by major political figures, diplomatic initiatives, the commemoration of religious and secular holidays, and counterterrorism activity.

The bivariate analysis indicates a statistically significant association exists between the variables "target-type" and "political event" (see table 6.15). A

Table 6.15: Relative Frequency of Israeli-Palestinian-Arab Target-Type by Political Event, 1994-1999 (summary statistics)

Crosstabs

Case Processing Summary

	Cases					
	Valid		Missing		Total	
	N	Percent	N	Percent	N	Percent
Type of target * political event	555	89.1%	68	10.9%	623	100.0%

Type of Target * Political Event Cross-Tabulation

		Political event			
Type of target		No relation to political events	Reac. diplomatic event	Reac. shellings	Reac. govt. assass.
Govern-ment	Count	59	7	1	1
	% within type of target	48.8%	5.8%	.8%	.8%
	% within political event	18.7%	23.3%	5.9%	6.7%
	% of total	10.6%	1.3%	.2%	.2%
Civilian	Count	256	23	16	14
	% within type of target	59.0%	5.3%	3.7%	3.2%
	% within political event	81.3%	76.7%	94.1%	93.3%
	% of total	46.1%	4.1%	2.9%	2.5%
Total	Count	315	30	17	15
	% within type of target	56.8%	5.4%	3.1%	2.7%
	% within political event	100.0%	100.0%	100.0%	100.0%
	% of total	56.8%	5.4%	3.1%	2.7%

Type of Target * Political Event Cross-Tabulation

		Political event			
Type of target		Comm. landmark events	Comm. secu. holi	Reac. terrorism	Reac. grnd. assau.
Govern-ment	Count	3	1	12	6
	% within type of target	2.5%	.8%	9.9%	5.0%
	% within political event	20.0%	33.3%	27.3%	12.8%
	% of total	.5%	.2%	2.2%	1.1%
Civilian	Count	12	2	32	41
	% within type of target	2.8%	.5%	7.4%	9.4%
	% within political event	80.0%	66.7%	72.7%	87.2%
	% of total	2.2%	.4%	5.8%	7.4%
Total	Count	15	3	44	47
	% within type of target	2.7%	.5%	7.9%	8.5%
	% within political event	100.0%	100.0%	100.0%	100.0%
	% of total	2.7%	.5%	7.9%	8.5%

Table 6.15 — *continued*

Type of Target * Political Event Cross-Tabulation

Type of target		Political event		Total
		Reac. govt. policies	Reac. min. pol. events	
Govern ment	Count	21	10	121
	% within type of target	17.4%	8.3%	100.0%
	% within political event	38.9%	66.7%	21.8%
	% of total	3.8%	1.8%	21.8%
Civilian	Count	33	5	434
	% within type of target	7.6%	1.2%	100.0%
	% within political event	61.1%	33.3%	78.2%
	% of total	5.9%	.9%	78.2%
Total	Count	54	15	555
	% within type of target	9.7%	2.7%	100.0%
	% within political event	100.0%	100.0%	100.0%
	% of total	9.7%	2.7%	100.0%

Chi Square Tests

	Value	df	Asymp. sig. (2-sided)
Pearson Chi Square	36.571[a]	9	.000
Likelihood Ratio	33.118	9	.000
Linear-by-Linear Association	11.002	1	.001
N of valid cases	555		

a. 6 cells (30.0%) have expected count less than 5. The minimum expected count is .65.

Directional Measures

			Value	Asymp. std. error[a]	Approx. T[b]	Approx. sig.
Nominal by nominal	Lambda	Symmetric	.014	.011	1.293	.196
		Type of target dependent	.041	.031	1.293	.196
		Political event dependent	.000	.000	.[c]	.[c]
	Goodman and Kruskal tau	Type of target dependent	.066	.023		.000[d]
		Political event dependent	.008	.004		.000[d]

a. Not assuming the null hypothesis.
b. Using the asymptotic standard error assuming the null hypothesis.
c. Cannot be computed because the asymptotic standard error equals zero.
d. Based on chi square approximation.

Pearson Chi Square of 36.571 with a "p-value" of less than .001 at nine degrees of freedom (9 d.f.) makes it possible, nay necessary, to reject the null hypothesis of no relation between the variables at the .05 level of confidence. It is found that 30.0 percent or six cells have an expected frequency of less than five. As before, those results ought to be reported for fear of making a "Type II" error that involves failing to reject the null hypothesis when it ought to be rejected. In terms of the strength of the association, a Goodman and Kruskal's *tau* of .066 with a "p-value" of less than .001 when type of target is the dependent variable suggests a weak relationship between those two variables. Likewise, a Cramer's V measure of .257 with a "p-value" of less than .001 and a "Phi" measure of .257 with a "p-value" of less than .001 also indicate a weak relationship exists between the variables. Put another way, a statistical association between political event type and target-type is evident.[281]

The data distribution informs us that a full 54.5 percent of all terrorist assaults or 322 out 591 acts are proactive events, not related to political events (see table 6.16). That figure of 54.5 percent is quite a bit less than the corresponding figure of 71.1 percent for Middle East terrorism from 1968 through 1993.[282] The remaining categories for "political events" are filled with outlier observations that total 45.5 percent. In the case of "reactive" terrorism, terrorist assaults in response to government policy elicited the largest portion of the total at 9.5 percent or 56 out of 591 incidents. Terrorist attacks in response to ground assaults evoked the second highest portion of "reactive" terrorism with 8.1 percent or 48 out of 591 acts. Ranking third are terrorist assaults committed in reaction to terrorism itself that comprise 7.6 percent or 45 out of 591 acts.

Table 6.15 — *continued*

Symmetric Measures

		Value	Approx. sig.
Nominal by nominal	Phi	.257	.000
	Cramer's V	.257	.000
N of valid cases		555	

a. Not assuming the null hypothesis.
b. Using the asymptotic standard error assuming the null hypothesis.

Table 6.16: Relative Frequency of Israeli-Palestinian-Arab Target-Type by Political Event, 1994-1999

Crosstabs

Case Processing Summary

	Cases					
	Valid		Missing		Total	
	N	Percent	N	Percent	N	Percent
Type of target * political event	591	94.9%	32	5.1%	623	100.0%

type of target * political event Cross-Tabulation

Type of target		Political event			
		No relation to political events	Reac. diplomatic event	Reac. shellings	Reac. air strikes
Govern-ment	Count	59	7	1	
	% within type of target	48.8%	5.8%	.8%	
	% within political event	18.3%	23.3%	5.9%	
	% of total	10.0%	1.2%	.2%	
Infra-structure	Count	6			
	% within type of target	75.0%			
	% within political event	1.9%			
	% of total	1.0%			
Civilian	Count	256	23	16	12
	% within type of target	55.9%	5.0%	3.5%	2.6%
	% within political event	79.5%	76.7%	94.1%	100.0%
	% of total	43.3%	3.9%	2.7%	2.0%
Civilian-Govt.	Count	1			
	% within type of target	25.0%			
	% within political event	.3%			
	% of total	.2%			
Total	Count	322	30	17	12
	% within type of target	54.5%	5.1%	2.9%	2.0%
	% within political event	100.0%	100.0%	100.0%	100.0%
	% of total	54.5%	5.1%	2.9%	2.0%

The data show there is a three-way tie for types of political events that spawn terrorist assaults with the highest rate of civilian target attack. Terrorist assaults in reaction to air strikes, kidnappings, and the commemoration of religious holidays all have a rate of 100.0 percent. As I discuss in my previous work, personal and even "intimate" types of political events such as war, air strikes, and the commemoration of landmark events seem to evoke especially personal and "intimate" terrorist assaults in kind. In this analysis, terrorist assaults committed in reaction to shellings ranked second with a rate of 94.1 percent or 16 out of 17 acts. Ranking third are terrorist assaults carried out in response to government assassinations with 93.3 percent or 14 out of 15 acts. In fourth place are terrorist assaults carried out in response to ground assaults with a rate of 85.4 percent of 41 out of 48 incidents. In fifth place are the 80.0

Table 6.16 — continued

Type of Target * Political Event Cross-Tabulation

Type of target		Political event			
		Reac. govt. assass.	Reac. kidnappings	Comm. landmark events	Comm. relig. holidays
Govern-ment	Count	1		3	
	% within type of target	.8%		2.5%	
	% within political event	6.7%		20.0%	
	% of total	.2%		.5%	
Infra-structure	Count				
	% within type of target				
	% within political event				
	% of total				
Civilian	Count	14	1	12	11
	% within type of target	3.1%	.2%	2.6%	2.4%
	% within political event	93.3%	100.0%	80.0%	100.0%
	% of total	2.4%	.2%	2.0%	1.9%
Civilian-Govt.	Count				
	% within type of target				
	% within political event				
	% of total				
Total	Count	15	1	15	11
	% within type of target	2.5%	.2%	2.5%	1.9%
	% within political event	100.0%	100.0%	100.0%	100.0%
	% of total	2.5%	.2%	2.5%	1.9%

percent of terrorist assaults carried out against civilian targets in response to the commemoration of landmark events like the anniversary of the death of Fathi Shkaki, the Islamic Jihad leader presumably killed by the Israelis in Malta.

Conversely, terrorist assaults done in response to "minor" political events, such as elections, are not at all characterized by an especially sharp focus against the populace insofar as only 33.3 percent or 5 out of 15 acts involved civilian targets, while a full 66.7 percent involved government targets. In turn, terrorist assaults committed in reaction to the commemoration of secular holidays has the second lowest rate of civilian target attacks at 50.0 percent or 2 out of 4 incidents. Terrorist assaults committed in response to government policy elicited the third lowest rate against civilian targets at 58.9 percent or 33 out of 56 incidents, and the second highest rate at 37.5 percent or 21 out of 56 acts against government targets.[283] As I describe in my prior work, those

Table 6.16 — *continued*

Type of Target * Political Event Cross-Tabulation

Type of target		Comm. secu. holi.	Reac. terrorism	Reac. grnd. assau	Reac. govt. policies	Reac. min. pol. events	Total
Govern-ment	Count	1	12	6	21	10	121
	% within type of target	.8%	9.9%	5.0%	17.4%	8.3%	100.0%
	% within political event	25.0%	26.7%	12.5%	37.5%	66.7%	20.5%
	% of total	.2%	2.0%	1.0%	3.6%	1.7%	20.5%
Infra-structure	Count		1		1		8
	% within type of target		12.5%		12.5%		100.0%
	% within political event		2.2%		1.8%		1.4%
	% of total		.2%		.2%		1.4%
Civilian	Count	2	32	41	33	5	458
	% within type of target	.4%	7.0%	9.0%	7.2%	1.1%	100.0%
	% within political event	50.0%	71.1%	85.4%	58.9%	33.3%	77.5%
	% of total	.3%	5.4%	6.9%	5.6%	.8%	77.5%
Civilian-Govt.	Count	1		1	1		4
	% within type of target	25.0%		25.0%	25.0%		100.0%
	% within political event	25.0%		2.1%	1.8%		.7%
	% of total	.2%		.2%	.2%		.7%
Total	Count	4	45	48	56	15	591
	% within type of target	.7%	7.6%	8.1%	9.5%	2.5%	100.0%
	% within political event	100.0%	100.0%	100.0%	100.0%	100.0%	100.0%
	% of total	.7%	7.6%	8.1%	9.5%	2.5%	100.0%

terrorist target dynamics may reflect the largely "symbolic" nature of terrorist assaults evoked by secular holidays and government policy, with almost singular focus on protest against the meaning of those holidays and against government policy and process.[284]

Seen from a longitudinal vantage, one standout finding is the apparent percentage increase in terrorist assaults that presuppose and derive from some, but certainly not all, political events. In some cases, there is a concomitant increase in the terrorist assault focus on the general population echoed in the terrorist assault rate against civilian targets. For example, the percentage rate of terrorist assaults carried out in reaction to government assassinations has increased some threefold, from .7 percent for Middle East terrorist assaults or 8 out of 1,208 incidents for the 1968 through 1993 period to 2.5 percent or 15 out of 591 events.[285] As previously mentioned, government assassinations, an intimate political event, evoke terrorism with a sharper focus against the general population, with a civilian target rate of 93.3 percent for the 1994 through 1999 period, up from 75.0 percent. In turn, terrorist assaults in reaction to shellings have increased as a proportion of the whole from .3 percent between 1968 and 1993 to 2.9 percent for the 1994 through 1999 time period. In terms of emphasis on civilian target attack, there has been a dramatic overall increase as well, from 75.0 percent found for the 1968 through 1993 time period in my earlier work, to a rate of 94.1 percent for the contemporary period.

Conversely, the rate of terrorist assaults carried out in response to landmark events has declined from a rate of 3.4 percent for the 1968 through 1993 time period to a rate of 2.5 percent or 15 out of 591 incidents for the 1994 through 1999 period. There has also been a decrease in focus against civilian targets, from a rate of 92.7 percent found for the 1968 through 1993 period to a rate of 80.0 percent or 12 out of 15 events for the 1994 through 1999 period. Likewise, the rate of terrorist assaults carried out in commemoration of secular holidays has decreased from 1.4 percent of the total between 1968 and 1993, to a rate of .7 percent or 4 out of 591 acts. Again, there has also been a decrease in focus against the civilian targets from a rate of 82.4 percent to a rate of 50.0 percent or 2 out of 4 events. As if that were not enough, the percentage of terrorist assaults carried out in commemoration of religious holidays has stayed virtually the same but a sharper focus against civilian targets is observed, with a rate of 86.4 percent for the 1968 through 1993 period increasing dramatically to a full 100.0 percent or 11 out of 11 events for the 1994 through 1999 period.

One way of thinking about the set of interconnections between Israeli-Palestinian-Arab terrorism and political events as I have defined them is to explore whether or not there are statistically significant differences in the mean number of persons killed in terrorist assaults that precede different types of political events. As previously mentioned, an examination of the difference in means for death rates for terrorist assaults linked to different types of political events may reveal a new dimension about the relationship between terrorist events and political events in a broader sense, thereby in effect helping to provide more predictive power to the analysis. The following hypothesis explores the dynamics of political events on death rates caused by terrorist assaults for a one-month period prior to the political event under consideration:

Hypothesis Eleven: The average number of persons killed in terrorist assaults that precede anniversaries of major political-diplomatic events such as peace accords or agreements by one month will be greater than the average number of persons killed in terrorist assaults that precede minor or internal political events such as national elections by one month.

An independent sample "T-Test" is performed to compare the sample mean for deaths from terrorist assaults associated with major political-diplomatic events to the sample mean for deaths from terrorist assaults associated with minor or internal political events.[286] In the case of major diplomatic-political terrorist assaults used in that analysis, terrorist assaults are isolated and identified as having taken place one month prior to the anniversary of the Israeli-Jordanian peace accord of 26 October 1994 for the years 1995 through 1999. The other event categories with data is the one-month period that precedes the anniversary of the Oslo Agreement of 13 September 1993 for the years 1994 through 1999, and the month period that precedes the anniversary of the Oslo II Agreement of 28 September 1995.[287] It is found there are no data events that correspond to a one-month period prior to the Wye River Memorandum of 25 October 1998 for the 1999 year.

In the case of minor or internal political events, discrete events for the one-month period before two political elections are isolated and identified in the data set to use in that "T-Test." Those events include the Palestinian Council election of 20 January 1996 and the Israeli national election of 29 May 1996. In keeping with the format used, terrorist events used in that test were culled out of the larger data base for the 20 December 1995 through 20 January 1996 period in the case of the Palestinian Council election, and for the 29 April 1996 through 29 May 1996 period in the case of the Israeli national election.[288]

The "T-Test" performed indicates there is a statistically significant difference in the mean number of deaths for terrorist assaults that precede major political-diplomatic events by one month and the mean number of deaths for terrorist assaults that precede minor or internal political events by a one-month period. The mean number of deaths that are caused by terrorist assaults in the one-month period prior to major political-diplomatic events is .30 as compared with a mean of .0909 or 9.09E-02 for minor or internal political events (see table 6.17).

The Levene's test for equality of variances generates an "F" value of 5.770 with a significance score of .018, thereby in effect making it possible to reject the null hypothesis of equal variances assumed in the population for the

Table 6.17: Independent "T-Test" for Difference of Means Test for "Political Event" and "Major Political Event" Israeli-Palestinian-Arab Terrorism

Group Statistics

	Event type	N	Mean	Std deviation	Std error mean
Number of deaths	Political event	22	9.09E-02	.29	6.27E-02
	Major political event	92	.30	.84	8.71E-02

Independent Samples Test

		Levene's test for equality of variances	
		F	Sig
Number of deaths	Equal variances assumed	5.770	.018
	Equal variances not assumed		

Independent Samples Test

		T-Test for equality of means			
		t	df	Sig (2-tailed)	Mean difference
Number of deaths	Equal variances assumed	-1.178	112	.241	-.21
	Equal variances not assumed	-1.989	96.881	.050	-.21

Independent Samples Test

		T-Test for equality of means		
		Std error difference	95% confidence interval of the difference	
			Lower	Upper
Number of deaths	Equal variances assumed	.18	-.57	.15
	Equal variances not assumed	.11	-.43	-4.34E-04

"T-Test." Hence, the "unequal variance assumption" is used in the "T-Test," and with a "T" score of -1.989 with a significance score of .050 at 96.881 degrees of freedom, it is possible to reject the null hypothesis that no statistically significant difference in means for numbers of deaths due to terrorist assaults exists in samples for the foregoing two political events. Accordingly, Hypothesis Eleven that posited a difference in population means between numbers of deaths caused by terrorist assaults one month prior to anniversaries of major political-diplomatic events and one month prior to minor or internal political events is accepted as valid.

Conclusions

General Trends

The cross-tabulation analysis reveals several important trends about the basic parameters of Israeli-Palestinian-Arab terrorism between 1994 and 1999. At the most fundamental level of analysis, the data reveal there has been a steady decline in the amount of terrorism taking place by year from 1994 through 1999. Apart from the decline in relative amounts of Israeli-Palestinian-Arab terrorism by year, those findings are also a departure from other findings insofar as there is no cyclical activity discerned with any peaks or troughs to report.

The analysis reveals that the single most prolific type of terrorist group between 1994 and 1999 was theocentric groups. Theocentric terrorist groups carried out 19.3 percent or 119 out of 615 recorded terrorist acts, while theocentric charismatic terrorist groups carried out the second largest percentage of terrorist assaults at 15.8 percent with 97 acts. Conversely, the smallest number of terrorist assaults for a group type was the 1 terrorist incident committed by an ethnocentric charismatic group, and the second lowest amount was carried out by ideo-ethnocentric charismatic groups with 14 out of 615 terrorist acts.

As in the case of my earlier research findings, the largest number of Israeli-Palestinian-Arab terrorist assaults was carried out by anonymous terrorist groups or "lone operatives." Those findings, in my judgment, are not surprising because issues of contention are clearly delineated and articulated in the political fray. In short, it is Islamic revivalist terrorist groups and Jewish revivalist terrorist groups, both with and without charismatic leaders, that are opposed to a negotiated settlement between the Palestine Liberation Organization and the government of Israel. When the analysis is broken down further by terrorist group, a similar breakdown of the data is revealed with Hezbollah as the most dynamic group with eighty-nine terrorist assaults, followed by eighty-five terrorist assaults claimed or attributable to Hamas. By contrast, the number and percentage of terrorist assaults carried out by Shaykh bin Laden's al-Qaida organization were very low with four out of 575 events or .7 percent of the total. In a similar vein, terrorist assaults with multiple claimants were also very low with eight out of 575 acts or a mere 1.4 percent.

As my earlier work suggests, terrorist groups and "lone operatives" in pursuit of political goals over the political environment favor terrorist assaults against civilian targets. The results suggest that those who commit Israeli-Palestinian-Arab terrorism favor civilian targets over government targets by a ratio of about 3.8:1, which is about two and one-half times less than the approximately 10:1 ratio in favor of civilian targets for the 1968-93 time period when only Israel and the Occupied Territories are included in the analysis.[289] The finding that "multiple target-type" terrorist assaults are extremely rare at .7 percent closely parallels results in my earlier work, suggesting that terrorist assaults remain relatively straightforward affairs, with almost singular focus against one type of target.[290] In a similar vein, terrorist assaults against infrastructure targets between 1994 and 1999 are found to be very low with only 9 out of 602 events or 1.5 percent of the total.

It is difficult to measure the cost of terrorism, in part because "imputed costs," as Reiss and Roth might put it, are hard to gauge and can even be intergenerational in effect.[291] However, if one evaluates the physical costs in terms of measurement of numbers of deaths, numbers of injured, and degree of property damage caused by terrorist assaults, the cost is comparatively low. The sample mean for numbers of dead for Israeli-Palestinian-Arab terrorism is 1.09 and the sample mean for numbers of injured is 10.28.[292] With respect to property damage, there were low levels of damage recorded that closely parallel death and injury rates. For example, over two-thirds of all incidents caused no property damage whatsoever, while only 5.1 percent caused "moderate" and "high" amounts of property damage. "Severe" property damage was extremely rare, accounting for less than 1.0 percent of the total.

The Role of Political Ideology

The variable "political ideology" is found to be influential with respect to what type of terrorist target was selected. For one thing, the analysis reveals that ethnocentric terrorist groups attacked civilian targets more often than did theocentric terrorist groups. Those findings are consistent with the results of my earlier work that suggests that ethnocentric terrorist groups are more "non-structuralist" than theocentric groups. Theocentric terrorist groups are considered "hybrid" types with both "nonstructuralist" and "structuralist" strands of thinking about the struggle against the enemy.[293] Clearly, when these results are overlaid against the basic framework of the continuum, there is a very good fit between them (see figure 6.9).

The analysis of terrorism "attribute" variables is only somewhat supportive of the underlying theory that guides this work. By extrapolation from the theory about target choice, more "nonstructuralist" terrorist groups such as ethnocentric groups ought to have higher rates for death since their emphasis is on attacks against civilian targets. That pattern ought to hold true for ideo-ethnocentric charismatic groups precisely because of the notion that terrorist groups with Marxist-Leninist trappings led by charismatic leaders will demonstrate behavior more in conformance with terrorist groups that embrace the "prevailing social ideology" of Islam.

Keeping that in mind, the results show that ideo-ethnocentric charismatic terrorist groups have the highest rate of terrorist acts that killed between one and fifty persons, followed by the rate for theocentric groups. It is found in my prior work that the presence of a charismatic leader at the helm of ethnocentric groups increases the frequency of ethnocentric government target attacks.[294] While there may be a set of interconnections between the "prevailing social ideology" of Islam embraced by ethnocentric groups coupled with the effects of charismatic leadership at work here, those dynamics remain shrouded in uncertainty. Be that as it may, ethnocentric charismatic groups, as expected, with their emphasis on government targets, had the lowest percentage of terrorist assaults that killed between one and fifty persons with nil. With respect to the relationship between terrorist group-type and degree of property damage caused by terrorist assaults, the results are not supportive of the theory that distinguishes between "structuralist" and "nonstructuralist" terrorist group-types.

"Structuralist"		"Nonstructuralist"
Ideo-ethnocentric	Theocentric	Ethnocentric
Civilian targets	84.7% (100/118)	90.0% (18/20)
Government targets	11.9% (14/118)	10.0% (2/20)

Figure 6.9: Continuum of "Structuralist" and "Nonstructuralist" Israeli-Palestinian-Arab Terrorist Group-Types for Non-Charismatic Group-Types and Target (Jewish Fundamentalist Terrorist Group-Types Excluded)

Location

Another basic finding concerns the geographical locales where Israeli-Palestinian-Arab terrorism has happened. The bulk of that terrorism happened in Israel, the Occupied Territories, and areas administered by the PNA, respectively, followed by geographical sites labeled "other Middle East states." Those "other Middle East states" include Syria, Lebanon, Egypt, and Jordan. In fifth place, is the percentage ranking for terrorist assaults that took place in "other locales." Those "other locales" include, but are not limited to, Argentina, Panama, Kenya, Tanzania, Cyprus, and Thailand. In turn, the data reveal that the relative frequency rate for Israeli-Palestinian-Arab terrorism is virtually the same in Western European nations and the United States.

What seems significant here is there has been a sizable increase in the relative percentage rate of terrorist assaults from 1.5 percent that happen in "other locales" between the 1968 through 1993 time period that my prior work covers and the 7.1 percent for the 1994 through 1999 time period analysis found in this monograph. Taken together, those findings are consistent with the notion there has been more emphasis placed on "other locales," perhaps either as a function of a strategy shift on the part of some terrorist groups, the differences in counterterrorism measure quality by locale, or both.

Charismatic Leadership: Impact on Islamic Fundamentalist, Marxist-Leninist, and Nationalist-Irredentist Terrorist Groups

The analysis also indicates that ethnocentric charismatic terrorist groups attacked government targets more often than did ethnocentric, theocentric, and Jewish theocentric terrorist groups. The findings also show that ideo-ethnocentric charismatic terrorist groups have, at 92.9 percent, the highest rate of civilian target terrorist assaults.

When the basic framework of the "structuralist-nonstructuralist" continuum is overlaid against those findings, there is good fit between the expected and observed results (see figure 6.9). It is observed that ethnocentric charismatic groups fall at the far end of the "structuralist" axis, while ethnocentric groups are placed much closer to the "nonstructuralist" axis. In turn, ideo-ethnocentric charismatic terrorist groups fall at the far end of the "nonstructuralist" axis. Finally, the placement of theocentric and theocentric charismatic terrorist groups towards the middle of the "structuralist-nonstructuralist" continuum is consistent with the notion that theocentric terrorist groups are "hybrid" terrorist group types that have both "structuralist" and "nonstructuralist" strands of thinking associated with them.

Those findings strongly support the results found in my prior work about ethnocentric groups with charismatic leaders, and how the presence of a charismatic leader for ethnocentric groups is associated with targeting behavior with greater emphasis on government targets. Clearly, my explanation offered in earlier works that this trend reflects the targeting practices of the Abu Nidal Organization is consistent with these data, since the ANO carried out that one recorded terrorist assault (see figure 6.10).[295]

With respect to the relationship between the political ideology of a terrorist group and property damage, the analysis is mixed and fails to reveal any consistent patterns. By extrapolation from the theory about terrorist group-type targeting practices, terrorist groups that fall in the sphere of "structuralist" terrorist groups ought to have higher rates of property damage while terrorist groups that fall in the sphere of "nonstructuralist" terrorist groups ought to have lower rates of property damage.[296] When terrorist assaults are analyzed apart from the type of groups that perpetrates them, the results indicate terrorist attacks directed at government targets are associated with less property damage than terrorist assaults aimed at civilian targets.

For ethnocentric terrorist groups, the results are mixed. On the one hand, ethnocentric terrorist groups have a higher rate of terrorist acts that caused "slight" damage than theocentric groups, and that is an expected finding. On the other hand, theocentric groups have a higher rate of terrorist attacks that caused "moderate" levels of property damage. One expected finding is that ideo-ethnocentric charismatic groups, found at the extreme end of the "non-structuralist" axis, have the second highest rate of terrorist assaults that do not cause any property damage. By contrast, one unexpected result is that theocentric terrorist groups are found to have the highest rate of damage-free terrorist assaults.

"Structuralist"					"Nonstructuralist"
	Ideo-ethnocentric	Ethnocentric charismatic	Theo-centric	Ethno-centric	Theocentric charismatic	Ideo-ethnocentric charismatic
Civilian targets		0.0%	84.7% (100/118)	90.0% (18/20)	92.6% (88/95)	92.9% (13/14)
Government targets		100.0% (1/1)	11.9% (14/118)	10.0% (2/20)	6.3% (6/95)	7.1% (1/14)

Figure 6.10: Continuum of "Structuralist" and "Nonstructuralist" Israeli-Palestinian-Arab Terrorist Group-Types and Target (Jewish Fundamentalist Terrorist Group-Types Excluded)

The Relationship of Terrorist Group Age and Size to Target Selection

With respect to the relationship between terrorist group age and target selection, the findings reveal a weak to modest relationship between those two variables. The relationship is basically linear in this case, with incremental increases in the percentage rate of civilian target terrorist assaults for ordinal categories that reflect increasing terrorist group age. There is a marked drop in the percentage rate of civilian target attacks when comparison is made between terrorist groups 16 through 20 years old, and terrorist groups 21 through 25 years old, but the rate returns to about the same high level for terrorist groups 26 years old or older.

In the broader sense, those findings are generally consistent with the underlying notion that as terrorist group tacticians become more seasoned, they understand increasingly the importance of civilian terrorist assaults as a vehicle to compel the ruling elite to respond to political demands and aspirations for change. By the same token, there are other interpretations of the data available, such as the possibility that government-target terrorist assaults involve greater risk of capture or death for terrorists than do civilian target attacks.

The findings suggest a weak to modest relationship between terrorist group size and target choice. Plainly, there is a curvilinear relationship between terrorist group size and terrorist group target that appears in the results. Interestingly enough, those findings mirror the same type of curvilinear relationship between those variables found in my previous work.[297] In this analysis, it is evident there is a modest increase in focus on civilian targets when "very small" and "small" terrorist groups are compared. That is followed by a decrease for "moderate" groups, and an upswing for "large" terrorist groups that tapers off a bit for "very large" terrorist groups.

In a similar vein, the reasons why there is an increase in focus on government targets by "moderate" groups remain shrouded in uncertainty. One possible explanation, but certainly not the only one, revolves around the central idea that at some stage in the "maturity cycle" as terrorist groups increase in size, there is some need to focus on government targets, perhaps either within the context of a struggle for survival, or a need for recognition, or both. In sum, the reasons for the shape of that relationship deserve the increased devotion of scholars.

The Behavioral Patterns of Jewish Fundamentalist Terrorist Groups

One cornerstone of the theory that drives this work is that Jewish fundamentalist terrorist groups will commit terrorist assaults with less intensity than their Islamic counterparts because they operate predominately in Israel and the Occupied Territories.[298] One basic question to confront is whether or not there has been a measurable increase in terrorist assault intensity from 1994 through 1999, a period that really corresponds to the birth and unfolding of the "peace process" between Israelis and Palestinians.

For the 1994 through 1999 time period, Jewish theocentric charismatic groups had the second lowest rate of civilian target terrorist attacks for any terrorist group-type, putting aside uncompleted acts and "lone assailant" acts. That rate is followed by Jewish theocentric terrorist groups with the third lowest rate of civilian target terrorist attacks. Of course, that also means that among identifiable terrorist group-types, Jewish theocentric charismatic groups have the second highest rate of government target terrorist assaults at 32.0 percent followed by Jewish theocentric terrorist groups with 23.1 percent.

Those very high rates of terrorist assaults with focus against government targets are consistent with the government actions and the dynamics of the continuously evolving political environment where phases of Israeli military redeployment and the transfer of civil authority to the Palestine National Authority (PNA) have happened. What seems significant here with respect to comparison between rates for the 1968-93 period is that Jewish theocentric terrorist groups, once with a relatively high rate of civilian target terrorist assaults, now have the third lowest rate overall at 69.2 percent, while Jewish theocentric charismatic groups have the second lowest rate at 68.0 percent.

Another set of standout findings revolve around the matter of whether or not there are quantitative differences in terrorist assault intensity levels for Jewish fundamentalist terrorist group assaults carried out between 1994 and 1999 and Jewish fundamentalist terrorist group assaults carried out between 1968 and 1993. In the case of terrorist assaults that caused *deaths*, the findings in this research reveal the percentage rates for Jewish theocentric and Jewish theocentric charismatic groups remained virtually the same for the 1968-93 period and the 1994-99 period.[299] In turn, that would suggest that the essential baseline of "Jewish terror" as measured in percentage rates of *deaths* has not really changed much, even with the seemingly heightened intensity of the vitriol associated with some terrorist assaults such as threats of death and the promotion of violence, that is commonplace to note among observers of the Israeli-Palestinian-Arab political arena from 1994 through 1999.[300]

In terms of *property damage,* Jewish theocentric charismatic terrorist assaults led the way with 52.0 percent of its attacks that resulted in "slight" property damage, while Jewish theocentric groups followed closely behind with 50.0 percent of attacks that caused "slight" property damage. Seen from a different angle, less than one-half of Jewish fundamentalist terrorist assaults, or 40.0 percent of Jewish theocentric charismatic attacks and only 44.1 percent of Jewish theocentric terrorist assaults, were damage-free events. Seen from a longitudinal vantage, there has been a marked increase in the percentage of terrorist attacks that result in "slight" property damage for Jewish theocentric groups, but a slight drop in Jewish theocentric charismatic terrorist assaults that cause "slight" property damage.[301] Those findings are also supportive of the notion that while the baseline of death rates for Jewish fundamentalist terrorist groups has remained virtually the same between time periods, there has been an upswing in Jewish theocentric assaults resulting in "slight" property damage.

The Influence of Political Events

The results show that Israeli-Palestinian-Arab terrorism remains in large part a proactive process rather than a reactive enterprise. However, findings in *Tapestry of Terror* suggest the rate of reactive terrorist assaults, namely those terrorist assaults linked to political events, as I have defined them, has increased substantially between the 1968-93 period covered in *Serenade of Suffering* and the 1994-99 period given treatment in *Tapestry of Terror*.

One of the underlying themes of the theory presented in *Serenade of Suffering* revolves around the central idea that government political initiatives, inclusive of particular military actions, pull at the heartstrings of emotion in personal and even "intimate" ways thereby in effect helping to evoke highly intensive terrorist assaults in kind. The findings in *Tapestry of Terror* support that notion and, as before, those findings have implications for counterterrorism policy.

For instance, the timing of political initiatives can be framed to avoid highly charged anniversaries of religious and landmark events for example, and the counterterrorism methods or tactics used may be dovetailed with avoidance of high casualty rates in mind. For example, one tack to take might be to use counterterrorism tactics that do not elicit terrorist assaults with especially sharp focus against civilian targets if counterterrorist actions must be carried out around the time of highly emotional watershed events like the commemoration of religious holidays happen.

By extrapolation, another tactic would revolve around the use of personal or intimate methods of counterterrorism actions like air strikes or kidnapping only during time frames that are far removed from such highly emotional events. Extending the analysis further, it is possible to think about the manipulation of the foregoing with the aim of fostering or hampering terrorist group splitting or group cohesion when it is desirable from the vantage of counterterrorism specialists and policy makers. The rudiments of a dynamic counterterrorism policy matrix will be augmented in chapter 7.

One way that *Tapestry of Terror* moves beyond *Serenade of Suffering* concerns the use of independent "T-Tests" to determine whether or not there are statistically significant differences in the average number of deaths in terrorist assaults linked to different types of political events. To be sure, that testing which evaluates terrorist assaults one month prior to different political event types is different from the relatively straightforward tabulations of terrorist events with interconnections to political events by claims of responsibility, attribution by government sources, or the use of contextual analysis. In the case of Israeli-Palestinian-Arab terrorism, it is found that a statistically significant difference in the average number of deaths in terrorist events exists for terrorist assaults that precede major political-diplomatic events by one month, and for terrorist assaults that precede minor or internal political events by one month.

Terrorism by Anonymous Groups and "Lone Operatives"

Terrorist assaults perpetrated by anonymous terrorist groups or "lone operatives" are found to be the most pervasive type of terrorist act taking place from 1994 through 1999. That finding mirrors the findings about anonymous terrorist groups and "lone assailants" for the 1968 through 1993 period presented in *Serenade of Suffering*. For the period between 1994 and 1999, unclaimed terrorist assaults accounted for 140 out of 615 acts or 22.8 percent of the total amount (see figure 6.2).

Compounding the matter even more, unclaimed terrorist assaults during the 1994-99 period were more focused against government targets with a rate of 30.4 percent, which is the second highest measure overall when uncompleted and unclaimed acts are include in the analysis. At the same time, increased attention devoted to government targets did correspond with a decrease in rates of deaths for anonymous terrorist assaults. The data show only 5.1 percent of unclaimed acts *killed* between one and fifty persons while a full 94.9 percent, the highest level recorded, were nonlethal terrorist assaults.[302]

With respect to property damage, rates for unclaimed terrorist assaults were on the high side, with 33.1 percent of unclaimed acts that resulted in "slight" property damage and 2.3 percent that resulted in "moderate" and "high" property damage. It is beyond the scope of this study to determine why a rather high rate of property damage accompanies relatively low rates of death and injury, but those findings are consistent with two underlying themes presented in *Serenade of Suffering*. First is the idea that unclaimed actions serve to generate and sustain pressure for change if the issues of political contention and the goals both sides pursue are relatively clear-cut and well understood by protagonists and the populace in the political fray. Second is the notion that if the foregoing condition is the emergent reality, it may be in the interest of terrorist groups to engage in some degree of anonymous activity for cost-effectiveness and to reduce the risk of capture or death for terrorist group activists.[303]

Reflections

At first blush, what seems significant here is the generally recognizable downward trend in the amount of Israeli-Palestinian-Arab terrorism from 1994 through 1999, a time period that coincides with the implementation of the Oslo peace process interim agreements. While it is possible this downward trend could represent a trough phase of an especially long cycle, that, in my judgment, is unlikely given the time duration of that downturn and the cyclical activity found in my prior work. It would seem that part of that shift is a function of the enormous reduction in ethnocentric terrorist assaults between the 1968 through 1993 and the 1994 through 1999 time periods. To be more specific, ethnocentric terrorist assaults declined from 18.1 percent of the total to a mere 3.3 percent of the total, and that represents roughly a five-fold percentage drop in ethnocentric terrorist assault activity.[304] Seen from that vantage, it follows that one set of conclusions is that the "peace process" ought to continue if only to reduce the overall amount of terrorism and, equally important, to reduce the numbers and types of terrorist groups that practice Israeli-Palestinian-Arab terrorism.

Notwithstanding that, those results about Israeli-Palestinian-Arab terrorism only provide a partial picture of the dynamics at the heart of the matter. While there has been a general decline in terrorism amounts by year, when those data are disaggregated by location, it is observed the percentage rates of terrorist assaults that happen in Israel and the Occupied Territories are very similar in terms of relative percentages for the 1968 through 1993 period covered in my prior work and the 1994 through 1999 period that is analyzed in this research.[305]

Those findings about Israeli-Palestinian-Arab terrorist assault rates in Israel and the Occupied Territories have implications that are twofold. First, there has been an enormous drop in the percentage of Middle East and Israeli-Palestinian-Arab terrorist assaults that happen in Europe, from 12.6 percent between 1968 and 1993, to 2.7 percent between 1994 and 1999.[306] Those results are mirrored by a sizable drop in the rate of Middle East and Israeli-Palestinian-Arab terrorism in the United States that dropped from 4.8 percent during the 1968 through 1993 period to 2.4 percent during the 1994 through 1999 period (see figure 6.4). It follows there might be a variation in pressure to sustain the "peace process" elicited by the ruling elite in European states and the United States as compared to pressure evoked by persons in Israel and the Occupied Territories who have experienced precious little in the way of change in the amount of terrorism carried out at those primary venues of the Israeli-Palestinian-Arab conflict. I have no evidence to suggest that is a purposeful stratagem employed by the Palestinians to increase European and American pressure on Israel to make concessions but, in my judgment, those pressures help to do just that. Those differences in terms of American and European perceptions of results and the emergent reality for persons in Israel and the Occupied Territories need to be articulated to confront the isolation that the Israeli ruling elite and the populace experience. If the "peace process" hopes to generate and sustain increasing support, there needs to be stronger inducements, both positive and negative, as Baldwin might put it, that serve as a deterrent to terrorist assaults that happen at those venues.

Another important finding that presupposes and derives from the qualitative analysis concerns the harsh counter-terrorism actions elicited by the Israelis. For example, the killing of Shaykh Abbas al-Musawi of Hezbollah, who was known as a "pragmatist," removed a player from the political fray who might have become valuable given that Hezbollah was able to wrest southern Lebanon away from the Israelis and SLA, and that both Syria and Iran, perhaps to a lesser extent, want to strengthen interconnections with the United States. In a broader sense, what has been termed "collective punishment" elicited against Palestinians by the Israelis that includes, but is not limited to, the bulldozing of family homes of suspected terrorists, sealing off homes or parts of homes, and the curtailment of commerce has not eliminated generally recognizable anger and protest, but has exacerbated each. As Beres tells us, "negative physical sanctions unless they are devastating enough to ensure destruction of the group itself, are bound to be ineffective. Such sanctions might even have the effect of a stimulus."[307]

The findings about "proactive" and "reactive" terrorism suggest that when terrorism is inextricably bound up to political events, as I have defined them, care must be taken to implement counterterrorism actions that do not exacerbate nationalist or religious sentiments and other similar feelings. The use of counter-terrorism measures that evoke terrorist assaults with more or less focus against civilian targets can be manipulated with time frameworks for action in pursuit of political goals with less costly results. As a concomitant to those counter-terrorism techniques, counter-terrorism planners ought to consider a host of what Baldwin calls "positive sanctions" to augment "negative sanctions" with the aim of helping to induce terrorist group splitting or group cohesion based on the interests of counterterrorism specialists and policy makers. In chapter 7, a more in-depth discussion of possible counterterrorism measures within the context of a counterterrorism intervention taxonomy is offered.

Notes

1. *Middle East International.*

2. Butenschon 1998, 17, 24, 33.

3. Ben Gurion 1971, 843-845; St. John 1971, 354; Pearlman 1970; Butenschon 1998, 34-37; Parker 1999, 77.

4. Rubin 1999, 10-11, 141; Butenschon 1998, 20.

5. Lasswell 1950, xi, 42.

6. Sayigh 1979, 10, as found in Rothman 1992, 19.

7. Rothman 1992, 17; Goldberg, Sander, and Rogers, 1992.

8. Sprinzak 1999, 225; Hilal 1998, 122; Cubert 1997, 161, 177 n20; Hassassian 1997, 80; Parker 1999, 77; Butenschon 1998, 29-30. Butenschon suggests that the idea of a "two state-solution" was first articulated in official terms at the twelfth

Palestine National Council (PNC) Congress held in Cairo in 1974. Alternatively, Cubert tells us that the data is incorrect (Cubert 1997, 72).

9. Butenschon 1998, 17; Cubert 1997, 65; Hassassian 1997, 80.

10. Reich 1995, 230; Butenschon 1998, 32; Cubert 1997, 74; Winslow 1996, 283.

11. Reich 1995, 230-231; Rubin 1999, 11; Butenschon 1998, 20; Parker 1999, 88; Cubert 1997, 80 n33, quoting Dr. George Habash. Parker points out that the Palestinian "right to self determination" is not mentioned in any of the interim agreements or Declaration of Principles (DOP), while Butenschon (1998, 18, 25) and Parker (1999, 88) tell us that UN Security Council Resolutions 242 and 338 do not mention Palestinian rights.

12. Butenschon 1998, 19.

13. Declaration of Principles; Reich 1995, 230-231; Butenschon 1998, 18-24.

14. Declaration of Principles; Reich 1995, 232, 241; Butenschon 1998, 18-24, 40; *Middle East International.*

15. Declaration of Principles; Reich 1995, 233; Butenschon 1998, 18-24, 40.

16. Declaration of Principles; Reich 1995, 233; Butenschon 1998, 18-24.

17. The Oslo I Agreement is otherwise known as the Cairo Agreement or the Gaza-Jericho Autonomy Agreement. *Middle East International*; Cubert 1997, 170; Frisch 1997, 57.

18. Butenschon 1998; Hilal 1998; Reich 1995, 240-249.

19. The Cairo Agreement; Reich 1995, 241.

20. The Cairo Agreement; Reich 1995, 233, 246.

21. For example, see Oslo Agreement "Article XV Resolution of Disputes," Declaration of Principles; Reich 1995, 234.

22. The Cairo Agreement; Reich 1995, 264.

23. The Cairo Agreement; Reich 1995, 243. See Declaration of Principles (DOP), Article VII, Article IX, Article VI; Reich 1995, 232-233; Hilal 1998, 125; Cubert 1997, 162, 166-167; Parker 1999, 66, 71. Hilal tells us that Arafat is chairman of the Palestinian National Council Executive Committee.

24. Parker 1999, 66, 71; The Cairo Agreement; Reich 1995, 243. Under Article VI section 2a, the type of representative offices listed include "embassies, consulates or other types of foreign missions and posts . . . the appointment of or admission of diplomatic and consular staff, and the exercise of diplomatic functions."

25. The Cairo Agreement; Reich 1995, 243-244; Cubert 1997, 176 n18.

26. Reich 1995, 245.

27. The Cairo Agreement; Reich 1995, 247.

28. The Cairo Agreement; Reich 1995, 248; Butenschon 1998, 21. Seemingly, there is an oblique reference to Jerusalem and Israeli settlements in Oslo I under Article XXIII "Final Clauses," section 6, that stipulates "The two Parties view the West Bank and the Gaza Strip as a single territorial unit, the integrity of which will be preserved during the interim agreement." See Declaration of Principles (DOP), Article V; Reich 1995, 232; Parker 1999, 71.

29. Butenschon 1998, 23; Cubert 1997, 169; Parker 1999, 86; Winslow 1996, 287; Hopmann 1986, 12.

30. The Oslo II Agreement is otherwise known as the Taba Agreement or the Israeli-Palestinian Interim Agreement on the West Bank and the Gaza Strip. *Middle East International.*

31. Article XXXI, section 2, "Final Clauses" of the Oslo II Agreement; "The Israeli-Palestinian Interim Agreement on the West Bank and the Gaza Strip." *Jewish Virtual Library,* 27; Frisch 1997, 57.

32. Article XXXI, section 2, "Final Clauses" of the Oslo II Agreement; "The Israeli-Palestinian Interim Agreement on the West Bank and the Gaza Strip." *Jewish Virtual Library,* 27; Frisch 1997, 57.

33. Article XXXI, section 2, "Final Clauses" of the Oslo II Agreement; "The Israeli-Palestinian Interim Agreement on the West Bank and the Gaza Strip." *Jewish Virtual Library,* 27; Frisch 1997, 57.

34. Hilal describes *al-Ra'ees* as "the head of the PNA." Hilal 1998, 19; Article XVIII (3) of Oslo II, "The Israeli-Palestinian Interim Agreement on the West Bank and the Gaza Strip" *Jewish Virtual Library,* 19-20; Reich 1995, 232-233, 242-243. By contrast, under the Declaration of Principles (DOP), Article 7 states: "1. The Israeli and Palestinian delegations will negotiate an agreement on the interim period (the "Interim Agreement"). 2. The Interim Agreement shall specify, among other things, the structure of the Council, the number of its members, and the transfer of powers and responsibilities from the Israeli military government and its Civil Administration to the Council. The Interim Agreement shall also specify the Council's executive authority, legislative authority in accordance with Article IX below." Under Oslo I, the term "Palestinian Authority" is used instead, in Article IV "Structure and Composition of the Palestinian Authority" and Article VII "Legislative Powers of the Palestinian Authority."

35. Article XXII (2) of the Oslo II Agreement; "The Israeli-Palestinian Interim Agreement on the West Bank and the Gaza Strip." *Jewish Virtual Library,* 23-24. By contrast, Article XXII (1) and (3) of Oslo II are also found in Oslo I, Article XII; Reich 1995, 245.

36. Article XXVI (5) of the Oslo II Agreement; "The Israeli-Palestinian Interim Agreement on the West Bank and the Gaza Strip." *Jewish Virtual Library,* 24-25.

37. Butenschon 1998, 21-22, 24; Article XXXI (9) of the Oslo II Agreement; "The Israeli-Palestinian Interim Agreement on the West Bank and the Gaza Strip." *Jewish Virtual Library,* 28; Butenschon tells us that prior to the Oslo Agreement Prime Minister Rabin and PLO Chairman Arafat swapped letters that pertained to those PLO Charter changes.

38. National Congress of the Palestine Liberation Organization 1968, The Palestinian National Charter 1968, 1-17 July; Weston, Falk and D'Amato 1990, 89. Other Articles that are antithetical to the survival of the State of Israel include Articles 15, 21, 22, and 8; Hilal 1998, 135. Hilal tells us that twenty-four out of eighty-eight Palestinian Legislative Council members opposed revision of the Palestinian National Charter.

39. Article XXVIII (2) -"Missing Persons." *Jewish Virtual Library.*

40. *Jewish Virtual Library,* Article XIII "Security" (2) (a); Article VIII of the Declaration of Principles; Reich 1995, 234.

41. Oslo II Agreement Article XV, *Jewish Virtual Library.*

Chapter Six

42. Makovsky 1995c, 3; Makovsky 1995a, 1, 3; Makovsky 1995b, 1, 2: *Jerusalem Post* 1995l, 3; *Middle East International,* 1-2; "The Israeli-Palestinian Interim Agreement on the West Bank and the Gaza Strip," *Jewish Virtual Library*; Annex 3, 11; Parker 1999, 89.

43. Makovsky 1995c, 3; Makovsky 1995a, 1, 3; Makovsky 1995b, 1, 2: *Jerusalem Post* 1995l, 3; *Middle East International,* 1-2; "The Israeli-Palestinian Interim Agreement on the West Bank and the Gaza Strip," *Jewish Virtual Library*; Annex 3, p.11; Parker 1999, 89.

44. "Protocol Concerning the Redeployment in Hebron", section 3 "Agreed Security Arrangements", section 4 "Joint Security Measures," section 5 "The Palestinian Police,"; "Oslo Peace Process" (internet), section 2 "Security Powers and Responsibilities." *Israel Ministry of Foreign Affairs.*

45. "Protocol Concerning the Redeployment in Hebron," "Maps of the Hebron Redeployment" (Graphics by Consulate General of Israel- Chicago). For example, see Section 11, "Planning, Zoning and Building" and Section 12, "Infrastructure." Israel Ministry of Foreign Affairs 1997.

46. "Oslo Peace Process" (internet), 2.

47. "Oslo Peace Process" (internet), 2.

48. "Wye River Memorandum," *Agence Europe: agence internationale d'information depuis* 1953, 1, 2.

49. "Wye River Memorandum," *Agence Europe: agence internationale d'information depuis* 1953, "I. Further Redeployments: A. Phase One and Two Further Redeployments," 3.

50. "Wye River Memorandum," *Agence Europe: agence internationale d'information depuis* 1953, "I. Further Redeployments: A. Phase One and Two Further Redeployments," 3.

51. "Wye River Memorandum," *Agence Europe: agence internationale d'information depuis* 1953, "A. Security Actions 1. Outlawing and Combatting Terrorist Organizations section (c)," 4.

52. "Wye River Memorandum," *Agence Europe: agence internationale d'information depuis* 1953, "B. Security Cooperation 3. Trilateral Committee," 5.

53. "Wye River Memorandum," *Agence Europe: agence internationale d'information depuis* 1953, "B. Security Cooperation 3. Trilateral Committee," 5-6.

54. "Wye River Memorandum" (internet); "Oslo Peace Process" (internet).

55. "Wye River Memorandum" (internet); "Oslo Peace Process" (internet).

56. "Wye River Memorandum" (internet); "Oslo Peace Process" (internet).

57. "Wye River Memorandum" (internet); "Oslo Peace Process" (internet), 2.

58. "Wye River Memorandum" (internet); "Oslo Peace Process (internet).

59. "Wye River Memorandum" (internet); "Oslo Peace Process (internet).

60. "Oslo Peace Process" (internet), 3.

61. USDOS 2000i.

62. Engelberg 2001, 12.

63. USDOS 2000i; Engelberg 2001, 12; USDOS 2001.

64. USDOS 2000i; Engleberg 2001, 12; Miller 2001, A-1, A-7.

65. Zanini 1999, 247-248; Ranstorp 1998, 321.

66. Reiss and Roth 1993.

67. Allen, 1974; Hourani 1993, 316-319, 334; Anderson, Seibert, and Wagner 1998, 68-71.

68. Allen, 1994; Anderson, Seibert, and Wagner 1998, 79-80, 163-164, 272-273, 308.

69. Ranstorp 1998, 325.

70. Hourani 1991, 84, 125, 187, 300; Baker 1994; Ranstorp 1998, 325. As Hourani tells us, it was Salah al-Din himself, a person of Kurdish descent, who spawned the Egyptian Ayyubid Dynasty (1169-1252) that also controlled a western portion of Arabia until 1229 and Syria until 1260 (Hourani 1991, 84).

71. Lewis 1979.

72. Ranstorp 1998, 323-324; *FBIS* 1996f.

73. Engelberg 2001, 12-13; Ranstorp 1998, 321.

74. Engelberg 2001, 12-13; MacLeod 1996, 51-52.

75. Reiss and Roth 1993, Engelberg 2001, 1, 12; MacLeod, 1996, 52.

76. al-Shafi, *FBIS* 1999.

77. Engleberg 2001, 12, 13; Zanini 1999, 250.

78. *FBIS* 1998f.

79. Lasswell, 1935, 37, 107, 110, 252, 253; Lasswell 1978, 261-263; Long 1990, 24; Crozier 1960, 127; Flemming 1992, 231; Chasdi 1999, 173, 204 n65.

80. Ranstorp, 1997, 105-107, 109, 187, 190; Harris, 1997, 303; Winslow 1996; Wege 1994, 158.

81. Reiss and Roth 1993, 297-299.

82. USDOD 1988, 15; Taheri 1987, 89; Ranstorp 1997, 65, 79; Wege 1994, 54; Chasdi 1999, 96, 128; Jaber 1997, 52. Wege tells us that Islamic Amal was a Hezbollah branch crafted in 1982 under the aegis of Hussein Musawi, the cousin of Shaykh Abbas al-Musawi.

83. USDOS 2000d; Harris 1997, 315; Jaber 1997.

84. Harris 1997, 315.

85. Wege 1994, 155; Chasdi 1999; Chasdi 1997; Chasdi 1995.

86. Ranstorp 1997, 76-77, 104, 107, 184.

87. Ranstorp 1997, 79; Wege 1994, 154-155; Jaber 1997.

88. Wege 1994, 156; Ranstorp 1997, 183-184, 73. Ranstorp tells us that an array of "regional" Majlis al-Shura councils also exist.

89. Ranstorp 1997, 184-185; Winslow 1996, 286-287; Wege 1994, 156.

90. Wege 1994, 151; Harris 1997, 307.

91. Wege 1994, 151; Harris 1997, 323-324; Parker 1999, 86; Jaber 1997, 48, 64.

92. Winslow 1996, 276-278, 280; Harris 1997, 280, 283, 298, 313. Winslow tells us Dr. Samir Ja'Ja controlled the Lebanese Forces, once under the aegis of Bashir Gemayal.

93. Ranstorp 1997, Winslow 1996, 284, 280, 287-288, 291; Harris 1997, 292-295, 279-280, 300; Jaber 1997, 48-64.

94. Winslow 1996, 287, 280; Harris 1997, 306, 280-281, 305.

95. Ranstorp 1997, 76, 187-190; Harris 1997, 282, 321; Winslow 1996, 287-288.

96. Winslow 1996, 288; Harris 1997, 307.

97. Harris 1997, 324, 307, 282, 291.

98. Ranstorp 1997, 58, 72, 78-79, 109, 180, 183.

99. Ranstorp 1997, 77-78.

100. Ranstorp 1999, 158, 59; Wege 1994, 157-158; Taheri, *FBIS* 1994.

101. Ranstorp 1997, 183-186, 109, 78, 180, 58-59, 72.

102. Ranstorp 1997, 198, 188-189, 130, 133, 159, 198, 185, 72; Winslow 1996, 280; Harris 1997, 307. Ranstorp tells us that Lebanon's old system of "confessional politics" passed in eclipse with the Taif Accord of 1989 and with its implementation at the start of 1991 (Ranstorp 1997, 158-159).

103. Ranstorp 1997, 130-131, 189, 191-193, 72.

104. Winslow 1996, 285.

105. Ranstorp 1997, 192-193, 72, 104-105, 132, 159, 181, 189; Wege 1994, 153-154; Winslow 1996, 284.

106. Ranstorp 1997, 194, 106, 108, 191; Harris 1997, 284, 311, 314.

107. Winslow 1996, 285; Ranstorp 1997, 130.

108. Harris 1997, 301-303, 321; Wege 1994, 155, 158; Ranstorp 1997. Both Harris and Wege tell us that Iranian financial assistance to Hezbollah amounted to about $100 million per year.

109. *Jerusalem Post* 1996e, 2; Jaber 1997.

110. Jaber 1997, 47; Wege 1994, 154; Ranstorp 1997, 75.

111. Ranstorp 1997, 59, 22, 58, 76, 182; *Jerusalem Post* 1994o, 5; Rudge 1997b, 18.

112. Ranstorp 1997, 79, 73-74, 107.

113. Reiss and Roth 1993; Ranstorp 1997, 73, 181.

114. Reiss and Roth 1993; Ranstorp 1997, 73, 181.

115. Wallerstein 1974.

116. Reiss and Roth 1993; Huntington 1996.

117. Ranstorp 1997, 74, 159; Rudge 1997a, 2; Harris 1997, 302-303.

118. Winslow 1996, 279; Ranstorp 1997, 191; Reiss and Roth 1993, 299-300.

119. Ranstorp 1997, 178; Harris 1997, 325-326; Winslow 1996, 281-282, 286; Cubert 1997, 66; Rubin 1999, 10-11, 141.

120. Ranstorp 1997, 178; Harris 1997, 325-326; Winslow 1996, 281-282, 286; Cubert 1997, 66; Rubin 1999, 10-11, 141.

121. Ranstorp 1997, 106-107, 104-105; O'Sullivan 1996, 1, 2; Harris 1997, 316; Wege 1994, 156.

122. Ranstorp 1997, 74.

123. *Jerusalem Post* 1996e.

124. Harris 1997, 281-282; Jaber 1997, 72; Ranstorp 1997, 23, 58, 73-74, 76, 108, 183. Ranstorp reports that twelve out of one hundred twenty-eight seats in the National Assembly were garnered by Hezbollah in 1992.

125. Ranstorp 1997, 75-76, 77.

126. Ranstorp 1997, 76-77.

127. Wege 1994, 158; Ranstorp 1997, 75.

128. Ranstorp 1997, 130, Harris 1997, 282.

129. Harris 1997, 282; *Jerusalem Post* 1996f, 2.

130. Harris 1997, 322

131. Harris 1997, 282; *Jerusalem Post* 1996f, 2.

132. Ranstorp 1997, 76, 72-73, 58-59. For Ranstorp, Ayatollah Fadlallah sided with Shaykh Nasserallah on that important matter. Rudge 1997b, 18; Wege 1994, 157; Jaber 1997. Seen from a slightly different angle, Rudge tells us of Shaykh Tufeili's singular focus for Hezbollah insofar as he wants to "liberate south Lebanon as a prelude to freeing Jerusalem."

133. Hassassian 1997, 84; Parker 1999, 70.

134. Parker 1999, 66-67; The Cairo Agreement; Reich 1995, 264.

135. Parker 1999, 66; The Cairo Agreement; Reich 1995, 264.

136. Hilal 1998, 122-123, 125, 127, 131; Hassassian 1997, Parker 1999, 62, 72.

137. Jad, *FBIS* 1997.

138. Hilal 1998, 122, 127, 125, 131, 123; Hassassian 1997, 76, 78; Butenschon 1998, 31; Frisch 1997, 61.

139. Jad, *FBIS* 1997, 2, 3; Butenschon 1998; Parker 1999, 77. Jad suggests Mahmud 'Abbas, otherwise known as Abu Mazin, as a leading contender to succeed Yasser Arafat. One scripted account in 1998 informs us that, according to *Foreign Report,* Yasser Arafat told President William Jefferson Clinton about his preference for Mahmoud 'Abbas with respect to succession. See Davis 1998, 1. Butenschon and Parker both recount that Abu Jihad, otherwise known as Walid Khazir, was killed by the Israelis in 1988 precisely because of the reason he was, as leader of the PLO Unified National Command for the Uprising, in charge of events in the Occupied Territories.

140. Jad 1997, 3; Hilal 1998, 126.

141. Hilal 1998, 135, 129; Parker 1999, 63-64; Frisch 1997, 61-62.

142. Lindholm Schultz as found in Parker 1999, 65, 64; Hilal 1998, 140-141, 135; Hassassian 1997, 87-89.

143. Lindholm Schultz as found in Parker 1997, 65, 192; Parker 91, 189, 192.

144. Parker 1999, 70, 74, 92-93; Cubert 1997; Frisch 1997, 65.

145. Frisch 1997, 56, 61 Parker 1999, 72, 198 Hilal, 1998, 133-134, 141; Butenschon 1998.

146. Frisch 1997, 61-62.

147. Frisch 1997, 63.

148. Frisch 1997, 63, 61, 56, 58-60; Hilal 1998, 121, 142, 148; Parker 1999, 91. Frisch tells us the term "neopatriarchal state" is Hisham Sharabi's phrase (Frisch 1997, 55).

149. *FBIS* 1997i.

150. Frisch 1997, 61-62; Hilal 1998, 125; Parker 1999, 68, 79.

151. Reiss and Roth 1993, 297-299; Butenschon 1998.

152. Butenschon 1998, 20; Hassassian 1997, 75; Parker 1999, 75-76.

153. Nassar 1991, 53-54; Livingstone and Halevy 1990, 68-69; Cobban 1984, 30-33, 140-153, 142; Anderson, Seibert, and Wagner 1996; Smith 1996; Butenschon 1999, 20; Parker 1999, 75-76; Gresch 1983, 32; Chasdi 1999, 102-103, 105, 100, 129-130.

154. Seale 1992, 94; Gresch 1988, 133-136; Butenschon 1998, 29; Cubert 1997, 165; Chasdi 1999, 102-103, 130.

155. Reiss and Roth 1993, 297-299; Butenschon 1998, 24, 28-29, 33.

156. Butenschon 1998, 26-28; Hassassian 1997, 74, 80-81; Cubert 1997, 169.

157. Butenschon 1998, 26-28; Hassassian 1997, 74, 80-81; Cubert 1997, 169; Esposito 1992, 94.

158. Parker 1999, 79-80; Butenschon 1998, 26-28; Cubert 1997, 65, 75 n10; Hassassian 1997, 74, 81, 83.

159. Parker 1999, 78-80; Cubert 1997, 63.

160. Parker 1999, 79-80, 63; Cubert 1997, 63; Butenschon 1998, 32; Hilal 1998, 129, 137; Hassassian 1997, 74, 78.

161. Cubert 1997, 64.

162. Butenschon 1998, 20, 38; Cubert 1997, 66-67, 69; Hilal 1998, 122; Reiss and Roth 1993, 297-299.

163. Hilal 1998, 122; Cubert 1997, 67-68, 66; Harris 1997.

164. Hilal 1998, 122; Cubert 1997, 67-68, 66, 176 n18, 74; Parker 1999, 81-82, 85.

165. Cubert 1997, 68.

166. Cubert 1997, 68, 70, 161, 165, 177 n22, 76 n15; Hassassian 1997, 79; Parker 1999, 88-89; *FBIS* 1998n; *FBIS* 1998m.

167. *FBIS* 1998n.

168. Butenschon 1998, 33; Hilal 1998, 124, 125, 137; Parker 1999, 66-69; Frisch 1997, 65.

169. *FBIS* 1998n; Hilal 1998, 137; Cubert 1997, 63, 169.

170. Cubert 1997, 69-70, 67.

171. Cubert 1997, 69-71, 76, 168.

172. Parker 1999, 88-89; Cubert 1997, 169, 177 n22.

173. Hilal 1998, 137; Parker 1999, 88-89, 194; Riyadh Milaki as found in Cubert 1997, 174.

174. Hilal 1998, 134-135, 127-128, 131.

175. Hilal 1998, 134-135, 127-128, 131; Cubert 1997, 161; Frisch 1997, 66. In Oslo II, Article IV stipulates that the Ra'ees of the Executive Authority and eighty-two members will comprise an elected Palestinian Legislative Council (PLC).

176. Hilal 1998, 130, 132-133; Parker 1999, 83; Frisch 1997, 63, 66.

177. Parker 1999, 195; Cubert 1997, 30; Hilal 1998, 126, 141, 181 n64; Hassassian 1997, 85.

178. Reiss and Roth 1993,

179. Chasdi 1999, 167. In the case of terrorist assaults that caused deaths, the percentage rate for Jewish theocentric and Jewish theocentric charismatic groups remained virtually same for the 1968-93 and 1994-99 time periods. In the case of terrorist assaults that caused injuries, the percentage rate for Jewish theocentric groups remained virtually the same for the 1968-93 time period, but the rate for Jewish theocentric charismatic groups almost doubled from 6.8 percent to 12.0 percent.

180. Sprinzak 1991, 245, 5, 211, 305; Sprinzak 1999, 215; Chasdi 119, 135.

181. Cochrane 1929, 79, 132, 135-137; Edmonds 1975, 82-83; Orwin 1988; Garst 1989; Livingstone 1946; Strauss 1964, 156.

182. Sprinzak 1999, 223; Sprinzak 1991, 96-98, 156.

183. Sprinzak 1999, 223, 146, 211, 178, 217.

184. Sprinzak 1999, 217-219, 223.

185. Sprinzak 1999, 219-220.

186. Sprinzak 1999, 219-220; Sprinzak 1991, 298; Don-Yehiya 1994, 266-267; Chasdi 1999, 113, 133.

187. Sprinzak 1994, 219.

188. Reiss and Roth 1993, 297-299.

189. Schlein 1991; Sprinzak 1999, 234; Chasdi 1999, 121, 135.

190. Reiss and Roth 1993, 297-299; Sprinzak 1999, 178.

191. Sprinzak 1999.

192. Reiss and Roth 1993; Allport 1954; Coser 1956.

193. Keinon and Hutman 1994, 2.

194. Hutman 1994b, 2; Kifner 1988, A-3.

195. Sprinzak 1999, 220-221.

196. Reiss and Roth 1993, Dollard et al. 1939.

197. Sprinzak 1999, 211.

198. Gordon 1994, 2.

199. Keinon and Hutman, 1994, 2.

200. Keinon 1996b, 18.

201. Sprinzak 1999, 265-266; *Jerusalem Post* 1999c, A-9.

202. *Jerusalem Post* 1999c, A-9; *Jerusalem Post* 1994j, 2; Hutman 1994c, 12; Hutman 1994d, A-12.

203. Sprinzak 1999, 266, 265.

204. Sprinzak 1999, 266, 265, 259, 274, 295; *Jerusalem Post* 1999d, 2. After the assassination of Prime Minister Rabin, Avishai Raviv was isolated, identified as a General Security Services (GSS) "informant," and was placed on trial for his decision not to report Yigal Amir's interest in killing Rabin.

205. *FBIS* 1996b; Sprinzak 1999, 266, 265, 259, 279-280, 283.

206. Sprinzak 1999, 211, 216, 236-238.

207. Sprinzak 1999, 235-236.

208. Pinkas 1994a, 1.

209. Sprinzak 1999, 224.

210. Sprinzak 1999, 234, 223-225, 295, 145; Demant 1994, 6; Helmreich 1996, 8, as found in Rapaport 1996; Sprinzak 1988, 194-216, 156, 96-98; Wilkinson 1986, 204-205; Lustick 1988, 67; Merkel 1986, 25; Peri 1983, 98-99, 268-272; Smooha 1978, 231-237, 406; Chasdi 1999, 114-116, 133.

211. Klein 1998, 2.

212. Sprinzak 1999, 268-274, 279, 312.

213. Sprinzak 1999, 269-270, 268-269.

214. Sprinzak 1999, 269-270, 268-269.

215. Sprinzak 1999, 274.

216. Hutman 1995, 1.

217. *Jerusalem Post* 1995r, 1, 2.

218. Milibank, 1976, 11-17; Elliott 1977, 7, 10; Mickolus 1980; Flemming 1992, 2, 4; Chasdi 1999, 59, 4, 17.

219. Pinkas 1994b, 1; Immanuel and Makovsky 1995, 1; Shapiro 1995, 1, 22; Collins 1997, 1, 2.

220. Chasdi 1999; Chasdi 1997; Chasdi 1995.

221. Enders, Parise, and Sandler 1992, 305-306; Flemming 1992, 133 n2; Jenkins 1988, 252, 246-266; Johnson 1978, 270; Ross and Gurr 1989, 410; Mickolus 1980, xviii; National Security Assessment Center 1979, iv; Elliot 1977, 4; Milibank 1977, 11 as found in Elliot; FBI sources found in Smith 1994, 18-21; Chasdi 1999, 148, 202 n33.

222. Demant 1994, 1; Don-Yehiya 1994, 272, 264; Sprinzak 1991. To be sure, "Jewish extremists" in the State of Israel and the geographical sites of "Judea and Samaria" comprise a rather freewheeling group rather than a monolithic one. As both Demant and Don-Yehiya suggest, there are "religious Zionists" as well as "anti-Zionists." Compounding the matter even more, Sprinzak points out that "settler types" range from hard-core ideologues to more pragmatic persons that are motivated more by economic factors (Sprinzak 1991, 160, 132; Chasdi 1999, 216, 220).

223. Theocentric groups (19.3 percent) + theocentric charismatic groups (15.8 percent) + anonymous groups (22.8 percent) + "lone assailants" (13.0 percent) + uncompleted assaults (12.8 percent) = 83.7 percent.

224. Chasdi 1999; Chasdi 1997; Chasdi 1995.

225. Chasdi 1999, 148, 150, 151; Chasdi 1997, 80-81; Chasdi 1995, 147-148. In essence, there are two caveats at work here with respect to data comparisons between *Serenade of Suffering* and this work. In *Serenade of Suffering,* the terrorist assault data are amalgamated data, while in *Tapestry of Terror* the data are more finely sorted out according to particular "systems" of Algerian, Egyptian, Turkish, and Israeli-Palestinian-Arab terrorism. Moreover, precisely because of the reason that data in *Serenade of Suffering* presuppose and derive from *Jerusalem Post* accounts and Mickolus's data base primarily, it follows that comparisons between findings from *Serenade of Suffering* and *Tapestry of Terror* cannot be exact due to methodological differences between the works.

226. Chasdi 1999, 148, 151; Chasdi 1997, 80-81; Chasdi 1995, 147-148.

227. Chasdi 1999, 148, 151; Chasdi 1997, 80-81; Chasdi 1995, 147-148.

228. al-Fatah (.9 percent) + PFLP (1.2 percent) + PFLP-GC (.2 percent) + DFLP (.9 percent) + Kach (3.0 percent) + Kahane Chai (.5 percent) + Ansarallah (.2 percent) + Believers Resistance (.2 percent) + Organization for Oppressed on Earth (.2 percent) + al-Qaida (.7 percent) = 8.0 percent + multiple terrorist events = 1.4 percent; + 3.5 percent = 12.9 percent. I did not include the Ressam incident or the Garafolo incident in the data base because of the possibility there was an exaggeration of charges, and that tactics/targets remained unclear.

229. Committee for Road Safety (.5 percent) + Repression of the Traitors (.2 percent) + Eyal (.3 percent) + Sword of David (.5 percent) + Jewish Group of Vengeance (.2 percent) + Hagai (.2 percent) + United Command for the Global Uprising (.2 percent) + Ayin (Jewish Agency Organization) (.2 percent) + Students of Musa Abu Marzouq (.2 percent) + Islamic Revolutionary Army (.2 percent) + Palestine Resistance Jafa (.3 percent) = 3.5 percent. I do not include Zo Artzenu in this calculation.

230. For this analysis, the category "Western Europe" consists of collapsed categories of European states that include France (category no. 43), Great Britain (category no. 44), Germany (category no. 45), Belgium (category no. 46), Switzerland (category no. 59), Austria (category no. 60), Greece (category no. 61), and Sweden (category no. 65).

231. Chasdi 1999, 150, 154, 202; Chasdi 1997, 83; Chasdi 1995, 149, 152.

232. Chasdi 1999, 150, 154, 202; Chasdi 1997, 83; Chasdi 1995, 149, 152.

233. Chasdi 1999, 150, 154, 202; Chasdi 1997, 83; Chasdi 1995, 149, 152.

234. Chasdi 1999, 150, 154, 202; Chasdi 1997, 83; Chasdi 1995, 149, 152.

235. Henry 1998, 1; O'Sullivan 1998c, 1, 2; *Jerusalem Post* 1998e, 1; O'Callaghan 1998, 1, 2; *FBIS* 1998g; Perlez 1998, 10.

236. Chasdi 1999, 150, 155-156, 202.

237. Chasdi 1999, 150, 155-156, 202.

238. Chasdi 1999, 155; Chasdi 1997, 86, Chasdi 1995, 156-157, 159, 336, 341.

239. Dahl 1957, 202-203; Jenkins 1998, 230; Drake 1988, 181.

240. Chasdi 1999, 155, 158; Chasdi 1997, 86; Chasdi 1995, 182-187.

241. Chasdi, 1999, 155, 159; Chasdi 1997, 86- 87, Chasdi 1995, 156, 158-159.

242. Chasdi 1999, 213, 182; Chasdi 1997, 100, 111 n54; Chasdi 1995; Drake 1988, 22-23.

243. Chasdi 1999, 186; Chasdi 1997, 103, 111 n59.

244. When bivariate testing was performed with only terrorist groups included in the analysis, the Chi Square statistic is 16.609 with a "p-value" of .005 at five degrees of freedom (5 d.f.). In terms of the strength of the association, a Goodman and Kruskal *tau* of .055 with a "p-value" of .005 is generated for "type of target" as the dependent variable. Still, 33.3 percent of the cells or four cells have an expected frequency of less than five. The data do not permit definitive conclusions to be drawn, but on the other hand one should not ignore findings that are suggestive or consistent with hypotheses I have been able to support in earlier work. To be sure, it is probably prudent to accept those findings for fear of making a "Type II" error. Hence, I ran a bivariate test and proffered results that included uncompleted and anonymous terrorist acts since those findings had only 12.5 percent of cells or two cells with an expected frequency of less than five. For that bivariate test, I collapsed the categories "lone assailants"(category no. 11) and "anonymous acts" (category no. 6) into "anonymous acts" (category no. 6). The "ethnocentric charismatic" (category no. 9) was deleted by a "SYSMIS" command (9=SYSMIS) to remove an empty cell from the analysis.

245. Chasdi 1999, 161-162, Chasdi 1997, 88-89: Chasdi 1995, 161-164.

246. Chasdi 1999, 161-162, Chasdi 1997, 88-89: Chasdi 1995, 161-164.

247. Infrastructure terrorist assaults account for 1.5 percent, and the multiple-target type "civilian-government" category accounts for .7 percent of the total.

248. Chasdi 1999, 162; Chasdi 1997, 89; Chasdi 1995, 163-164.

249. 1.5 percent (infrastructure) + .7 percent (civilian-government) = 2.2 percent.

250. Chasdi 1999, 182; Chasdi 1997, 102; Chasdi 1995.

251. In this case of bivariate testing, only terrorist group-types are included in the analysis.

252. As one might expect, uncompleted terrorist acts have the highest rate of nonlethal terrorist assaults with 98.7 percent or 76 out of 77 events.

253. Chasdi 1999, 164-165; Chasdi 1997, 91; Chasdi 1995, 169, 171.

254. Chasdi 1999, 164-165; Chasdi 1997, 91; Chasdi 1995, 169, 171.

255. Flemming 1992; Chasdi 1999, 168-170, 212; Chasdi 1997, 83.

256. Chasdi 1999, 169; Chasdi 1997, 93; Chasdi 1995, 182-187. For theocentric groups, 33.7 percent ("slight") + 4.7 percent ("moderate") + 4.7 percent ("high") +3.5 percent ("severe") = 46.6 percent. For ethnocentric groups, 29.4 percent ("slight") + 8.6 percent ("moderate") + 6.7 percent ("high") + 1.2 percent ("severe") = 45.9 percent.

257. Chasdi 1999, 169.

258. Chasdi 1999, 168-169, 143, 201; Chasdi 1997, 74, 107-108; Chasdi 1995.

259. In that bivariate test, the category "unclaimed acts" as well as six terrorist group-types are included. The category "ethnocentric charismatic" is removed by a SYSMIS=9 command to remove an empty cell from the analysis and the "lone assailant" category is collapsed into "unclaimed acts."

260. Wallerstein 1974; Chasdi 1999, 143; Chasdi 1997; Drake 1988, 22-23.

261. In this test, I include the ordinal categories for property damage "none," "slight," and "high" to generate meaningful summary statistics.

262. Long 1990, 24.

263. Karber and Mengel 1983, 23-39.

264. Flemming 1992, 231.

265. Chasdi 1999, 172-173, 183; Chasdi 1997.

266. Chasdi 1999, 173, 204; Lasswell 1935, 37, 107, 110, 252-253; Lasswell 1978, 261-263; Long 1990, 24, Crozier 1960, 127; Flemming 1992, 231.

267. Chasdi 1999, 173, 204; Lasswell 1935, 37, 107, 110, 252-253; Lasswell 1978, 261-263; Long 1990, 24, Crozier 1960, 127; Flemming 1992, 231.

268. Crenshaw 1983, 26 n12.

269. Russell, Banker, and Miller 1979, 34.

270. Smart 1987, 10.

271. Oots 1984, 63, 65, 88-105.

272. For that bivariate test, I collapsed the ordinal category "very small" (category no. 1) into the ordinal category "small" (category no. 2), and the ordinal category "very large" (category no. 5) into the ordinal category "large" (category no. 4). Commands: 1→2, 2→2; 4→4, 5→4.

273. Merari et al. 1985; Waugh 1982, 53, 56; Shultz 1978, 10; O'Neill 1978, 34, 40, 25; Osmond 1979, 115-118, 57-58, 101-102, 90-93, 142-143; Flemming 1992, 91.

274. Chasdi 1999, 173-175; Chasdi 1997, 94; Chasdi 1995, 194-199.

275. Chasdi 1999, 173-175; Chasdi 1997, 94; Chasdi 1995, 194-199.

276. In the case of this bivariate test, the location categories "Israel," "PA (Palestinian Authority)," and "the United States" were removed to generate summary statistics that are significant. The "other" category includes "all other values" inclusive of those outside of articulated location categories. As before, Europe is a category that consists of France (no. 43), Great Britain (no. 44), Germany (no. 45), Belgium (no. 46), Switzerland (no. 59), Austria (no. 60), Greece (no. 61).

277. *Jerusalem Post* 1994f, 1; *Jerusalem Post* 1994h, 1; Mickolus and Simmons 1997, 651-653, 878, 770, 601, 576; *Keesings* 1994b; *Jerusalem Post* 1994g, 2; *Jerusalem Post* 1996c, 2; *Jerusalem Post* 1998f, 1; *Jerusalem Post* 1998g, 1; Kuzmin, *FBIS* 1999; Bryson 1999, 7.

278. At first blush, those threats and clarion calls to violence seem especially pronounced for the "Operation Accountability" period of time.

279. Azar, Jureidini, and McLaurin 1978, 52-53. In the context of a communal conflict, in this case conflict in the Middle East, that way of thinking suggests, by extrapolation, that terrorist assaults ought to be highly dependent and serve as a counterweight to cooperative or perhaps benign political events. Here, Azar, Jureidini, and McLaurin's analysis seems to be the inverse of Axelrod's "Tit for Tat" approach to repetitive interactions with a potential adversary that presupposes and derives from "rational thinking" where "cooperative acts" are rewarded with cooperative acts and non-cooperative acts are, in turn, punished.

280. Brecher and James 1987, 9, 7-8.

281. When the category "no relation to political events" is removed, the analysis generates a Pearson Chi square statistic of 28.954 with a "p-value" of less than .001 at eight degrees of freedom (8 d.f.). A total of 33.3 percent or six cells have an expected frequency less than five. With respect to strength of the association, a Goodman and Kruskal's *tau* of .121 with a "p-value" of less than .001 when type of target is the dependent variable suggests a weak relationship, as do "Phi" and Cramer's V scores of .347 each with "p-values" of less than .001 for each. See Chasdi 1999, 175-177, 204 n69; Chasdi 1997, 95-96, 111 n51; Chasdi 1995, 212, 232 n37.

282. Chasdi 1999, 177-179; Chasdi 1997, 94-98; Chasdi 1995, 212-219.

283. The one deviant finding seems to be terrorist assaults carried out in reaction to terrorism with a rate of 71.1 percent, which is somewhat less than the expected findings.

284. Chasdi 1999; Chasdi 1997; Chasdi 1995; Drake 1998, 10-12.

285. Chasdi 1999, 175-179; Chasdi 1997, 94-98; Chasdi 1995, 213, 215.

286. To be sure, the overwhelming majority of "uncompleted" terrorist assaults caused no deaths, and hence "uncompleted" events are removed from the analysis so those terrorist assaults do not skew the results.

287. Frisch 1997, 57.

288. Parker 1999, 71; Hilal 1998, 134-135, 127-128, 131; Cubert 1997, 161; Frisch 1997, 66.

289. Chasdi 1999, 181, 162; Chasdi 1995, 313.

290. Chasdi 1999, 181, 162.

291. Reiss and Roth 1993.

292. Event deaths: $N=611$; minimum 0; maximum 247; mean 1.09; standard deviation 11.06. Event injuries: $N=606$; minimum 0; maximum 4,257; mean 10.28; standard deviation: 173.76.

293. Chasdi 1999, 186; Drake 1988, 22-23; Chasdi 1995, 239, 277 n20.

294. Chasdi 1999, 185-186, 205 n77, 193-196.

295. Mickolus and Simmons 1997, 748. This ANO terrorist assault involved death threats against Gian Federico Pedotti, the Swiss ambassador to Jordan in January 1995.

296. Chasdi 1999, 168-169.

297. Chasdi 1999, 183.

298. Chasdi 1999, 186-187; Chasdi 1997, 103-104, 111-112 n62, n63, n64; Chasdi 1995, 171, 228 n19.

299. For Jewish theocentric groups, the rate of terrorist assaults that caused the deaths of between one and fifty persons for the 1968 through 1993 period is 11.3 percent or 6 out of 53 acts, and for the 1994 through 1999 period, the rate for Jewish theocentric groups is 10.3 percent, or 4 out of 39 acts.

300. Goodman 1971, 116, 118, 32-33, 115-116, 118-119, 121-122; Chasdi 1995, 171-172.

301. Chasdi 1999, 169; Chasdi 1995, 182-187.

302. Chasdi 1999, 165; Chasdi 1995, 169-171. For the 1968 to 1993 period, 12.8 percent of unclaimed acts killed between one and fifty persons, while 87.2 percent were nonlethal terrorist assaults.

303. Duvall and Stohl 1983, 207-211; Stohl 1988, 161, 163; Im, Cauley, and Sandler 1987.

304. Chasdi 1999, 151; Chasdi 1997, 80; Chasdi 1995, 147-148.

305. Chasdi 1999, 176; Chasdi 1997, 95; Chasdi 1995, 197. For the 1968 through 1993 period, 35.3 percent of Middle East terrorism happened in Israel, while 29.9 percent happened in the Occupied Territories. For the 1994 through 1999 period, 34.1 percent happened in Israel, while 31.1 percent happened in the Occupied Territories.

306. Chasdi 1999, 154; Chasdi 1997, 83; Chasdi 1995, 152.

307. Beres 1991, 140; Stohl 1987, 163; Wilkinson 1984, 298; DiLaura 1987, 32; Falk 1983, 23-24.

Chapter Seven

Conclusions

Qualitative Analysis

All of the foregoing really distils down to the fundamental question of what new insights have been gleaned from this study. Seen from the vantage of qualitative analysis, a broader comparison of systems of Middle East terrorism provides a more complete picture of what factors generate and sustain terrorist group growth, terrorist group splintering, and terrorist "spin-off" group formation. In the broader sense, at the level of "predisposing-macrosocial" factors, there are common strands of economic malaise or economic backwater situations in countries that have spawned Middle East terrorism that are, in my judgment, antecedent conditions that may contribute to terrorist group formation.[1]

In the case of Algeria, President Chadli Benjadid's programs of "economic liberalization" compounded the structural problems associated with the "rentier state" framework even more to create enormous unemployment over time, especially among the young.[2] Likewise, there have been employment hardships for Algerians that are inextricably tied to the Islamic educational system.[3] Plainly, those endogenous problems were most probably exacerbated by very high and sustained birthrate trends in Algeria. As if those problems were not enough, exogenous factors such as the oil glut of the 1980s and the subsequent decrease in oil revenues made the prevailing economic condition in Algeria even more dire with the passage of time.

What seems significant here is that Nigeria is an example of another "rentier state" beset with political and economic problems that did not, however, experience generally recognizable, widespread terrorism even after the war in Biafra (1967-70). One way of thinking about why revolves around a more makeshift and never complete notion of national identity associated with Algerians, who continue to struggle with what Fuller calls "Arabophone" and "Francophone" dimensions to national identity, a condition that presupposes and derives in part from French "direct rule" that lasted for over one hundred years.[4]

In the case of Egypt, many writers suggest that the failed modernization programs of President Gamal Abdul Nasser and President Anwar el-Sadat served to stoke the burners of discontent among many Egyptians. As if that was not enough of a problem, economic backwater conditions in many parts of Egypt were in stark contrast to the affluence found by some Egyptians in the Gulf states. As both Gaffney and Esposito note, many of the potential recruits to both violent and nonviolent Islamic revivalist organizations are found at the margins of society.[5]

A similar set of antecedent economic conditions is found in Turkey where economic ills have continuously plagued the republic, and where the rise of the Turkish "political left" during the 1960s and 1970s and "leftist" oriented terrorist groups was found to presuppose and derive from economic problems that have fettered Turkey since the end of the Second World War. To make matters worse, systematic and government-sanctioned discrimination against the Kurds has thrived in effective and sustained ways, and includes a component of economic discrimination that lends itself to the dynamics of terrorism group formation previously described.

In the case of Israeli-Palestinian-Arab terrorism, there are also pervasive political and economic factors that contribute to terrorist group formation. Seen from a longitudinal vantage, the calamitous "al-Nakbah" ("the catastrophe") of Israel's war of independence in 1947-48 and the exodus of some seven hundred thousand Palestinians caused enormous economic challenges for Palestinians who lost their property, homes, and prized possessions. It is probably no exaggeration to say that many Americans fail to capture the horror and rage elicited by the sudden loss of property to a powerful victor with an enormous advantage in terms of power disparity. Perhaps one way of thinking about that is to imagine a situation where a beautiful old house that you have lived in all your life is suddenly lost to powerful individuals, who not only destroy the house but simultaneously the very essence of what that house represents as a part of a belle epoque period that has passed into eclipse, and what that house means to you.

At a substantive level, economic backwater conditions in the refugee camps, towns, and cities in the Occupied Territories that have been administered by the Israelis since 1967 are commonplace to note.[6] What is not at all clear is why the Israelis seemingly failed to recognize the radicalization process that in part presupposes and derives from the abject economic misery that so many Palestinians have faced.

What also seems significant with respect to Israeli-Palestinian-Arab terrorism are the economic hardships experienced by Shias in southern Lebanon that in part presuppose and derive from discrimination practiced by Sunnis in Lebanon against the Shia community. Compounding the problem for Shias in southern Lebanon even more are the Palestinians who have moved to Lebanon following the expulsion of the PLO from Jordan in 1970, and the political maneuvering of state-supported terrorist groups like Hezbollah and Amal, thereby in effect making Shia civilians, as well as terrorists, targets of Israeli counterterrorist actions.

In addition to the economic backwater conditions found that have been generated and sustained by endogenous and exogenous factors, another observation that stems from those case studies revolves around the presence or absence of effective political institutions. In some cases, political institutions exist but what Huntington would call "political decay" happens because those who staff political institutions are either unwilling or unable to respond to the political demands and aspirations of what really amounts to antecedent constituency groups for terrorist groups in the making.[7] At the same time, as Huntington suggests, socioeconomic development begets political mobilization, thereby in effect helping to compound the problem of responding to political demands and aspirations even more.

Seen from a slightly different angle from the foregoing discussion, what seems significant about the case of Algerian terrorism is the proposition that interconnections exist between terrorism in Algeria, even before 1991, to what Huntington might call incomplete "national identity" formation in Algeria. Huntington's notion revolves around the central idea that stable democracy in a country involves the successful resolution of a sequence of steps ranging from "national identity" through "institutionalization" and "modernization."[8] In this case, the proposition revolves around the central notion that the contradictions of Algerian "fractured identity" previously mentioned were never resolved, thereby in effect helping to contribute to full-blown brutalities that are a hallmark of the contemporary Algerian experience.

What makes that intriguing is that in Nigeria, by contrast, there does not seem to be the overarching "competing identity" problems among or within ethnic groups like Hausa-Fulanis, Yoruba, Ibo, Tiv, and Ijaw. That Algerians have been fettered with the basic crisis of what Fuller calls "competing identities" between "Francophone" and "Arabophone" components may, in turn, trace a curve to the "direct rule" style of the French and the enormous scope of French rule that did not end until 1962.[9] The notion that makeshift and never complete national identity helps to elicit long-haul political instability and social unrest in the guise of terrorism deserves the increased devotion of scholars in future empirical research about terrorism.

In the case of Egypt and Turkey, it is not so much the absence of political institutions as much, I think, as how those institutions work or do not work to include or exclude segments of the populace with relatively straightforward and clear-cut positions on political and economic reform. For Egypt, the problem seems to revolve around the central idea of the place of Islam in the political and social discourse. The powerful pull of Islamic revivalism on the populace, that in large part presupposes and derives from political, military, and economic failures of the past, might be acknowledged, for example, by the reinstitution of Islamic banking, more effective and sustained political representation, and attempts to build more "cross-cutting" economic and political institutions, if only to help defuse the enormous pressure of the latest terrorist war against the regime.

For Turkey, the problem is different insofar as that, from the start, the Turkish political and social discourse from the time of Mustapha Kemal onward has always been clear-cut about the predominant secularist political and social frameworks in place. At the same time, the systemic political and economic discrimination against the Kurds that thrives in effective and sustained ways seems counterproductive from a counterterrorist point of view, and, as many have suggested, certainly bodes ill for the health of Turkish "civil society."

To be sure, Turkish authorities are concerned about Turkish Islamic revivalist terrorist groups like Turkish-Hezbollah and the Islamic Federal State of Anatolia (AFID). However, what seems significant here is the indication that enormous change in the structure of the system of international politics with the end of the Cold War may make traditional Turkish Marxist-Leninist groups at war with the Turkish government, like the Kurdistan Workers' Party, more susceptible to appeals from Islamic revivalists as they seek to find a niche for themselves in what President George H. W. Bush termed "the new world order."[10] There is also additional pressure to confront the Turkish government because Turkey has also opened itself to influence from Europe, playing international politics with respect to admission to the European Union (EU) and oil pipeline construction that would benefit Western countries and the Turkish ruling elite. In turn, that condition in flux may present a real opportunity for a terrorist leader like Shaykh Osama bin Laden to expand the scope of his operations simultaneously against the U.S. and Turkish governments even further.

In the broader sense, "situational" factors can be more proximate causes for terrorist group coalescence, terrorist group splitting, or terrorist group "spin-off" formation. The analysis seems to underscore the enormous capacity of "situational factors" to exacerbate underlying strains and tensions associated with political-religious and social configurations of society, all of which probably fall in the realm of what Reiss and Roth might call "predisposing factors."

At one level, "situational factors" at the "macrosocial" level of analysis can be watershed political events with profound and lasting "transnational influence," like the Iranian revolution or the Soviet invasion of Afghanistan in 1979. At another level, "situational factors" can be internal events that include militant uprisings that serve as a guidepost for subsequent terrorist group activity or formation. Still another type of "situational" factor presupposes and derives from proactive government policy that works to amplify long-term or "predisposing" factor influences. It is to those types of "situational factors" the analysis now turns.

Perhaps the single most glaring event that could be viewed as either a proactive "situational factor" in the case of Armed Islamic Group (GIA) spin-off groups or an "activating factor" from the vantage of GIA, was the full-blown effort to thwart the 1991 Algerian national election by the military government, thereby in effect helping to bring to a head long-standing "national identity" issues and structural economic issues. Another example of proactive crafting of a "situational factor" leading to political destabilization and violence was the decision by Israeli Prime Minister Yitzhak Rabin to ban Kach and Kahane Chai completely, making them illegal organizations in the wake of the Hebron massacre in 1994.

Unequivocally, the effects of watershed political "situational factors" like the Iranian revolution of 1979 are over and beyond the control of contemporary counterterrorism policy makers. By extrapolation, the analysis suggests that certain aspects of proactive types of "situational factors" may be manipulated or their effects somehow modified to militate against their capacity to amplify manifestations of long-standing strains and tensions or unresolved conflict dynamics in a particular political social system.

For example, one "predisposing factor" previously mentioned is the fundamental and unresolved matter of what the role of Islam in the Egyptian political and social discourse is all about. Keeping that in mind, it may be possible, nay necessary, to frame simultaneously "situational" election results that empower the Mubarak regime in Egypt with government mechanisms or initiatives that provide some type of support to Islamic revivalist constituents, such as support for certain Islamic political or economic institutions like Islamic banking. In addition to releasing enormous political pressures, those actions might have the effect of helping to break up further potentially more monolithic terrorist organization constituency groups.

In a similar vein, within the context of the Israeli Labor party victory over Likud in 1992, the consequences of the Rabin cabinet's decision to ban Kach and Kahane Chai in 1994 were twofold. First, the ban on Kach and Kahane Chai removed any legitimate "opportunity structures" for nonviolent political expression, thereby in effect helping to reinforce the belief among some Jewish revivalists that the Declaration of Principles and Oslo Agreement of 1993 not only signaled an irrevocable change in Israeli policy direction, but that it represented a zero-sum game with no room for Jewish revivalism or Jewish revivalist political players, seemingly at odds with a government ready and able to sanction curtailment of freedom of assembly and political expression.

In my judgment, within the context of the Israeli national elections of 1992 and the Oslo Agreement of 1993, there is a critical link between the action by the Rabin cabinet to ban Kach and Kahane Chai and an increase in the volatility of the continuously evolving Israeli political fray that culminated in the assassination of Prime Minister Yitzhak Rabin on 4 November 1995. In the broader sense, that horrific empirical example signifies the importance of efforts to offset "situational" events with potential radicalization effects with government initiatives or mechanisms with the potential to facilitate dialogue in the hope of consensus on some smaller issues, with the aim of consensus on some larger issues with the passage of time.[11]

The analysis suggests that "activating" factors for the genesis of particular terrorist groups or "splinter" groups can include personal experiences, or the unpleasant experiences at the hands of government authorities of family members of those who become terrorist leaders. That is found to be case for the Hattab brothers in Algeria. In the case of Lieutenant Khalid al-Islambouli, who killed President Anwar el-Sadat on 6 October 1981, his brother Mohammad al-Islambouli was arrested in September 1981 by Sadat's police with over fifteen hundred others, and Kepel reports he was taken out of the Islambouli household clad only in his pajamas.[12] In a similar vein, Abdullah Öcalan, who would become the leader of the Kurdistan Workers' Party (PKK), was imprisoned in Turkey.[13] Other "activating factors" can include internal events like the 1988 riots in Algeria in the case of the Islamic Salvation Front (FIS), or the aborted 1991 Algerian national election in the case of the Armed Islamic Group (GIA).

Clearly, it is not possible to anticipate the broader political actions previously mentioned as specific "activating" factors, but when potential "activating" events, as Reiss and Roth might put it, like the latter happen, those events need to be constrained and suppressed in ways that take into account the long-haul deleterious effects of heavy-handed suppression.[14] Put another way, one observation that seems to stand with respect to all four case studies is that heavy-handed repressive techniques, or suppression that is so broad in scope that it creates a condition of simmering hatred that more than offsets any political or military gains made in the short run, ought to be avoided.

To be more specific, the foregoing may mean that the utility of counter-terrorism operations in Algeria, and Turkish operations in Iraqi Kurdistan that do not seem to net many prisoners when such events are chronicled, needs to be rethought within the context of what Baldwin calls "positive sanctions," or proactive incentives to induce change among constituent group support, thereby in effect helping to modify terrorist group actions.[15] In a similar vein, the Israeli practice of bulldozing or sealing homes of suspected Palestinian terrorists and their families as a form of "collective punishment" is not only ineffective and morally reprehensible, but it generates and sustains the kind of rage and bitterness that can only contribute to terrorist group coalescence, splintering, or the terrorist group "spin-off" process.

Quantitative Analysis

What follows is a basic discussion and summary of the major trends in the data for the four systems of Middle East terrorism under consideration. The framework of analysis involves: the comparison of findings from one terrorism system to findings for other systems of Middle East terrorism; efforts to tie together those findings in ways that shed light on the parameters of different types of Middle East terrorism; and counterterrorism policy alternatives.

At the single most fundamental level of analysis, Algerian, Egyptian, and Turkish terrorism are characterized by cyclical activity complete with peaks and troughs. For Im, Cauley, and Sandler those peaks and troughs may presuppose and derive from changes in both counterterrorism measure enhancement and the type and range of terrorist assaults.[16] The data findings that discern cycles in those data are consistent with other research on terrorism.[17]

Alternatively, it is found that relative frequencies of Israeli-Palestinian-Arab terrorism by year decline during the 1994 through 1999 time period. Even though a correlation exists between a decline in Israeli-Palestinian-Arab terrorism and the passage of time that corresponds with the unfolding "peace process," the causal factors for that unusual pattern in the data remain unknown. It follows that one tantalizing matter to explore is whether or not the PLO-PNA was actually more effective in policing than has been portrayed in the media and by the U.S. and Israeli governments. The year with the largest amount of Algerian terrorism recorded is 1997, while the year with the greatest amount of Egyptian, Turkish, and Israeli-Palestinian Arab terrorism is 1994.

When the data are broken down by terrorist group-type, it is found that theocentric terrorist groups are the most prolific type in the case of Algerian, Egyptian, and Israeli-Palestinian-Arab terrorism. Conversely, in the case of Turkish terrorism, ideo-ethnocentric charismatic groups are found to be the most active, and that probably reflects the predominant role of Kurdistan Workers' Party (PKK) terrorist activity between 1994 and 1999. Those findings suggest that Islamic revivalist terrorist groups, at least from a quantitative angle, are the most significant source of contemporary Middle East terrorist assaults.

When the analysis focuses special attention on particular Middle East terrorist groups, it is found that the Armed Islamic Group (GIA) is the most prolific among identifiable terrorist groups in the Algerian system of terrorism, while al-Jama'a al-Islamiya (the Islamic Group) is the most active group in the case of Egyptian terrorism. In turn, the Kurdistan Workers' Party or PKK has been most active in the system of Turkish terrorism while Hezbollah, followed very closely by Hamas, has been most active in the case of Israeli-Palestinian-Arab terrorism.

Analysis by location reveals some significant differences with respect to the seepage of different systems of Middle East terrorism outside the primary venue of conflict. At the low extreme, only 8.1 percent of Algerian terrorism is found to take place outside of Algeria, while 20.3 percent of Israeli-Palestinian-Arab terrorism occurred outside of Israel, the Occupied Territories, and the jurisdiction of the Palestinian National Authority (PNA). It is found that 21.0 percent of Egyptian terrorism happened outside Egypt as compared to a full 27.5 percent of Turkish terrorism that happened outside of Turkey, primarily in Western Europe with 20.8 percent. With respect to Middle East terrorist assaults carried out in the United States, it is found there were no completed Algerian terrorist assaults or Turkish terrorist assaults chronicled, while 7.0 percent of Egyptian terrorism or ten events happened in the United States. In the case of Israeli-Palestinian-Arab terrorism, 2.4 percent or fourteen events happened at that locale.

The reasons for those variations in terrorist assault rates at "non-primary locales" remain unclear. In the broader sense, those findings may or may not reflect qualitative distinctions in counterterrorist measures that result in lesser or greater degrees of effective suppression of terrorist groups by governments. At the same time, while relatively high rates of Turkish and Egyptian terrorism outside of Turkey and Egypt may reflect more effective counterterrorism practices in those countries, those findings may also stem from the presence of constituent group support in Europe, or perhaps as a result of both factors working in tandem.

With respect to terrorist assaults that *killed* fifty-one or more persons, a breakdown of the data shows that 3.6 percent of Algerian terrorism, 0.5 percent of Turkish terrorism, 0.4 percent of Israeli-Palestinian-Arab terrorism, and 0 percent of Egyptian terrorism fall into that ordinal category. In the case of terrorist assaults that *injured* fifty-one or more persons, the data reveal that 5.0 percent of Algerian terrorism, 1.7 percent of Israeli-Palestinian-Arab terrorism, 0.7 percent of Egyptian terrorism, and 0.6 percent of Turkish terrorism fall into that category. Those results are one of a set of statistics that showcase the greater lethality and injury rates for Algerian terrorism assaults.

Another set of findings demonstrates that terrorist group chieftains or tacticians favor terrorist assaults against civilian targets over government targets by a significant amount, except in the case of Egyptian terrorism. In the case of Algerian terrorism, the ratio of civilian targets to government targets is roughly 8:1, while the ratio of civilian to government targets is only .81:1 in the case of Egyptian terrorism. The ratios for Turkish and Israeli-Palestinian-Arab terrorism fall in between, with about a 2.4:1 ratio in the case of the former and about a 3.8:1 ratio in the case of the latter. In the case of the unusually high rate of 8:1 for Algerian terrorism, one issue that deserves the increased devotion of scholars is whether or not that rate is related to the condition of "civil war," to use Dunn's term, that has evolved in Algeria. It may be the case that this high rate of civilian target terrorist assaults presupposes and derives from a lower repressive potential by the Algerian government that itself derives from diminished central control of government due to those "civil war" conditions.

It should be noted that an overwhelming amount of terrorist assaults in all four systems of Middle East terrorism were directed either at civilian targets or government targets. Terrorist assaults against "multiple-type" targets, namely targets with both civilian and government attributes associated with them, are extremely rare, as are terrorist assaults that involve more than one target. It is found that multiple claimant terrorist assaults are found in the case of Egyptian and Israeli-Palestinian-Arab terrorism, but they too are very infrequent events.

One way that *Tapestry of Terror* moves beyond *Serenade of Suffering* is that analysis is performed to determine whether or not a statistically significant relationship exists between type of target and the nationality of victims for "discriminate" terrorist assaults. Meaningful findings would have predictive value insofar as discernable trends would help gauge the degree of terrorist assault violence perpetrated against foreign nationals and under what circumstances. In the case of Algerian terrorism, the data testing reveals that under one-quarter of civilian target terrorist attacks involve foreign nationals (30 out of 144), while over three-quarters of civilian target attacks (114 out of 144) involve Algerian nationals. Conversely, 60.0 percent of all government targets (15 out of 25) involve Algerian nationals, while 40.0 percent (10 out of 25) involve foreign nationals.

In comparison, in the case of Egyptian terrorism, it is found that nearly two-thirds of civilian target attacks (34 out of 53) involve foreign nationals, while barely over two-thirds of civilian target attacks (19 out of 53) involve Egyptian nationals. Seen from a different angle, 81.6 percent of all government attacks (40 out of 49) involve Egyptian nationals and only 18.4 percent (9 out of 49) involve foreign nationals. Those findings suggest that even though much is written about terrorist assaults directed against civilian targets in both Algeria and Egypt, there is a substantial difference in risk for civilians, either tourists or expatriates, who are vulnerable to the lurking calamity of Egyptian and Algerian terrorism. While the reasons for this difference may reflect the greater tourism in Egypt and/or greater opportunity, it is unclear why there is such an overwhelming difference in foreign national civilian target assault rates. In the cases of Turkish terrorism and Israeli-Palestinian-Arab terrorism, it is found that no statistically significant association exists between the variables "target type" and "victim nationality" for "discriminate" terrorist assaults.

Turning to the relationship between Middle East terrorism and political events, in each case study it is found that terrorism remains a highly proactive rather than reactive process. In the case of Algerian terrorism, the findings show that 57.4 percent is proactive terrorism, while 42.7 percent is reactive terrorism, namely terrorism that is interconnected to political events as I have defined them. In the case of Turkish and Egyptian terrorism, there is no statistically significant association between the variables "target type" and "political events," and hence there is no meaningful distribution of data to report. In the case of Israeli-Palestinian-Arab terrorism, the data reveal that 54.5 percent of all terrorist assaults are independent events as compared to 45.5 percent that are reactive or "dependent" events.

Perhaps the single, most dominant theme with respect to the relationship between "target type" and "political event" revolves around the central idea that in the case of "reactive" terrorism, terrorist assaults elicited by political events share a similar thematic emphasis with those political events. To be more specific, what Drake would call "symbolic" terrorism, with more emphasis on government targets, is found to be associated with "symbolic" political enterprises such as major diplomatic events and government policy, while political events with a more profound and lasting personal or even "intimate" effect, such as the commemoration of religious holidays, air strikes, and ground assaults, are matched in kind by terrorist assaults with a sharper focus against civilian targets.[18]

Those trends are found in Israeli-Palestinian-Arab terrorism and with somewhat less strength in the case of Algerian terrorism, where terrorist assaults in reaction to major diplomatic events and the commemoration of landmark events are unexpectedly found to have the sharpest focus against civilian targets. Although no definitive interpretation is available as to why that is the case, those findings may be somehow related to the symbolic value of the Algerian war of independence against the French that Martinez and other writers suggest is especially relevant for more contemporary terrorist activists.[19] In the cases of Egyptian and Turkish terrorism, there is found to be no statistically significant association between the variables "target type" and "political event."

Another way that *Tapestry of Terror* pushes beyond *Serenade of Suffering* revolves around the use of independent sample "T-Tests" to determine whether or not there are statistically significant differences in the mean number of deaths in terrorist assaults that precede different types of political events by a one-month period. In the case of Algerian terrorism, the data testing reveals a statistically significant difference in the mean number of deaths for terrorist assaults that precede the "commemoration of landmark events" by one month, and the mean number of deaths for terrorist assaults that precede "minor" or internal political events by one month. In the case of Israeli-Palestinian-Arab terrorism, the tests performed reveal a statistically significant difference in the mean number of deaths in terrorist assaults that precede major political-diplomatic events by one month, and the mean number of deaths in terrorist assaults that precede "minor" or internal political events by one month. Mean differentials should alert counterterrorism planners to expect more lethal terrorist assaults to happen sometime prior to particular kinds of political events.

Turning to the matter of the underlying theory that drives this work, when the Turkish and Israeli-Palestinian-Arab data are overlaid against the "structuralist-non-structuralist" framework of the continuum there is a good fit between those data and that construct. It is crucial to recall that it is only with respect to the Turkish and Israeli-Palestinian-Arab data that sufficient types of terrorist groups are found to be operative, thereby in effect making it possible to test the theory by means of a series of theoretical propositions.

In the case of Turkish terrorism, it is found that ideo-ethnocentric groups fall towards the "structuralist" axis, as expected, while theocentric groups, conceived to be "hybrid types," fall toward the middle of the continuum, also as expected (see figure 7.1). The proposition that ideo-ethnocentric terrorist groups led by a charismatic leader will favor civilian targeting is borne out, as Turkish ideo-ethnocentric charismatic groups fall to the right of ideo-ethnocentric groups, as expected. The one "deviant finding" concerns ethnocentric groups that fall near the "structuralist" axis, probably because of the reason that the bulk of recorded ethnocentric terrorist assaults were context specific attacks, aimed at government targets in the wake of the capture of PKK leader Abdullah Öcalan.

In the case of Israeli-Palestinian-Arab terrorism, those data are overlaid against the analytical construct of the "structuralist-nonstructuralist" continuum with a close fit as well (see figure 7.2). Moving from left to right along the

"Structuralist"			"Nonstructuralist"
	Ethnocentric*	Ideo-ethnocentric	Ideo-ethnocentric charismatic	Theocentric
Civilian targets	25.0% (3/12)*	56.3% (9/16)	72.9% (70/96)	84.6% (11/13)
Government targets	58.3% (7/12)*	43.8% (7/16)	19.8% (10/96)	15.4% (2/13)

Figure 7.1: Continuum of "Structuralist" and "Nonstructuralist" Turkish Terrorist Group-Types and Target (Jewish Fundamentalist Terrorist Group-Types Excluded)

continuum within the "civilian target" band, it is observed that placement of groups ranges from the ideo-ethnocentric group category that falls at the "structuralist" axis, to ethnocentric charismatic groups and the so-called "hybrid type" theocentric groups. In turn, theocentric groups are followed by ethnocentric groups, theocentric charismatic groups, and ideo-ethnocentric charismatic groups that fall toward the "nonstructuralist" axis of the continuum. While the placement of theocentric charismatic terrorist groups to the right of ethnocentric terrorist groups is an unexpected result, the findings for theocentric charismatic groups are consistent with the idea that theocentric groups, both with and without charismatic leaders, are "hybrid types" with both "structuralist" and "nonstructuralist" attributes associated with them. With respect to Jewish theocentric and Jewish theocentric charismatic groups, the data testing reveals high percentage rates for government-target terrorist assaults, and that conforms to the expected findings precisely because of the reason that Jewish revivalist terrorist groups operate predominantly in so-called "friendly" areas that include Israel and the Occupied Territories.[20]

Implications for Counterterrorism Planners

Turning to the matter of policy and counterterrorism stratagems, the underlying aim of this section is to present research findings to counterterrorism policy makers and planners in the larger world of action in ways that will be most fruitful. An underlying theme of my approach to thinking about counter-

"Structuralist"					"Nonstructuralist"
	Ideo-ethnocentric	Ethnocentric charismatic	Theo-centric	Ethno-centric	Theocentric charismatic	Ideo-ethnocentric charismatic
Civilian targets	0.0%	84.7% (100/118)	90.0% (18/20)	92.6% (88/95)	92.9% (13/14)
Government targets	100.0% (1/1)	11.9% (14/118)	10.0% (2/20)	6.3% (6/95)	7.1% (1/14)

Figure 7.2: Continuum of "Structuralist" and "Non-Structuralist" Israeli-Palestinian-Arab Terrorist Group-Types and Target (Jewish Fundamentalist Terrorist Group-Types Excluded)

terrorism draws from Reiss and Roth's notion of a multilevel, multivariate interventions scheme to respond to common criminal activity.[21] At the most basic level, the qualitative analysis delved into previously suggests that "situational" factors can amplify strains and tensions that presuppose and derive from social-political relationships, demographics, and other structural components of the lay of the land.

That qualitative analysis suggests that counterterrorism planners ought to take into account with more rigor the prospect that government reaction to political and economic conditions fraught with danger have an enormous capacity to transform those events into seminal "situational factors" that define and frame events to come, both internal and external to the dynamics of terrorist groups. To be sure, those events alone or in combination with others can serve as "activating" factors that release enormous pressures built up by the effects of "situational factors." What seems significant here is the capacity, albeit limited perhaps, for counterterrorist planners to help influence policy makers about how matters that oftentimes fall in the realm of "civil disobedience" or spontaneous political expression, rather than outright terrorism, ought to be handled.

Having said that, one way of thinking about a more proximate role for counterterrorist policy makers and planners revolves around findings about political events and terrorism. The approach here revolves around the central idea that the time frame for counterterrorism events, and the type of counter-terrorism actions selected, can be manipulated to reduce terrorist actions elicited by political events. For example, if counterterrorist actions must happen during emotionally-laden political periods, such as before key holidays, they can be tailor-made with respect to their capacity to offset political events that pull at the heartstrings of emotion. Conversely, if it is necessary to employ counter-terrorism measures that this research suggests evoke terrorist attacks with sharp focus against civilian targets, those counterterrorist operations should be carried out at a time far removed from political events that have profound and lasting emotional effects.

Extending the analysis further, the findings suggest that terrorist group cohesion, terrorist group splitting, or terrorist group "spin-off" formation may be affected by the manner with which government officials respond to political events in the making, and how government officials frame other national initiatives that include, but are not necessarily limited to, counterterrorism actions. To be sure, those actions are set against a host of long-haul factors and subsequent pressures, and the choice by governments to help alleviate those pressures or let them remain as they are, would most probably influence the effect of "situational" or middle-run factors or events. Bearing that in mind, there are several tools in the process of development here that focus on more "proactive" measures that in part use those government responses as a way to facilitate desirable outcomes for policy makers with respect to terrorist group configuration.

Until now, the central idea has revolved around making certain that "situational" events are not matched by government reactions that increase the radicalization process, or government reactions which put into question whether or not existing terrorist groups act in effective and sustained ways, thereby in effect helping to generate group splitting. Notwithstanding that, what seems significant here is that if counterterrorist planners deem it to be in the national interest to foment group splitting or greater group cohesion, political events that include counterterrorism strikes and government responses to political events can be manipulated with those aims in mind.

For example, in the case of Israeli-Palestinian terrorism, the findings about terrorist group size and target selection suggest that "large" and "very large" terrorist groups focus on civilian targets at a greater rate than do smaller groups and at a much greater rate than do middle-sized terrorist groups. Hence, it might be prudent under certain conditions to encourage terrorist group splitting, perhaps by providing negative sanctions coupled with certain selective inducements—to put space between "hard-liners" and pragmatists during a particularly sensitive political period for domestic politicians, in the hope those efforts help to reduce the number of terrorist assaults against civilian targets. In addition, there is the potential to use harder or softer "situational factor" responses to promote splitting or to modify the effects of the foregoing splintering stratagems. As previously mentioned, long-haul factor pressures need to be addressed to some degree in tandem to promote the process of group splintering, if that is deemed desirable.[22]

Conversely, if the goal is to promote terrorist group cohesion, perhaps to reduce the number of uncontrollable splinter-group progeny, efforts can be made to use counterterrorism measures that do not involve an especially sharp focus against civilians, but that are done during political event time frames to evoke group solidarity in the face of "the enemy." Certain situations where such comparatively "benign" tactics may be effective include, but are not limited to, sustained and concerted negotiations, clandestine contacts over issues like prisoner exchanges or broader issues concerning regional stability and interests, and efforts to promote a faction within the terrorist group that may be induced to alter the behavior of the terrorist group over time. It follows that softer or harder "situational factor" responses are available to encourage or dampen effects associated with the foregoing. To be sure, long-haul considerations and scenarios about the continuously evolving environment must be considered in light of the very troublesome experience where Israel helped to support Hamas in its fledgling stages as a counterweight to the PLO.[23]

The aforementioned efforts revolve around proximate responses to the behavior of terrorist group chieftains or tacticians. Another level of counter-terrorism initiatives concerns more direct efforts against constituent groups with the aim of creating fissures among terrorist constituency groups. As I relate in

Serenade of Suffering, one way of thinking about helping to generate and sustain different constituent group member viewpoints about "the enemy" is to employ what Baldwin calls "positive sanctions" that, in this application to counter-terrorism measures, range from generally recognizable prisoner exchanges, manipulation of prisoner rights like visitations, and the provision of nonlethal technologies such as medical equipment and medicines.[24]

One avenue of approach to counterterrorism is to build on the counter-terrorism intervention taxonomy presented in *Serenade of Suffering* (see figure 7.3).[25] First, efforts to integrate the foregoing analysis with counterterrorism initiatives in this taxonomy sorted out by "tactical crisis management," "positive strategic interactions," and "negative strategic interactions" deserve the increased devotion of counterterrorism specialists. Second, aspects of the

	Long haul	Middle run	Short term
Tactical crisis management	• Third party interconnections • Protracted contact with groups	• Constituent group contact • Prisoner's family contact	• Acts of prisoner exchange • Acts of communications with terrorist groups
Positive strategic interactions	• Promotion of participatory democracy • Economic support for refugee camps and other economic backwater areas	• Support for infrastructure of constituency groups (e.g., Schools, non-lethal technologies, hospitals)	• Acts of medicine transportation and disbursement • Acts of assistance for humanitarian reasons (e.g., earthquakes, floods)
Negative strategic interactions	• Appraisal of threat, region by region • Support various chieftains in ways that support group splitting (e.g., funneling monies)	• INTERPOL • Coordination with allies in military terms • Effective counterterrorism legislation	• Counter terrorism assassination • Other counterterrorism meausres • Disinformation campaigns

Figure 7.3: Counterterrorism Intervention Taxonomy

qualitative analysis in this work can work to augment the taxonomy as it now stands.

For example, in the sphere of "long-haul negative strategic interactions," matrixes that posit specific relationships between particular types of "political events" and different counterterrorism actions that elicit terrorist assaults with greater or lesser focus against civilian targets ought to be crafted within the context of further empirical research. In the realm of "middle-run tactical crisis management," the efficacy of counterterrorism programs such as the "post-release care" policy of the Egyptian Interior Ministry that provides financial assistance and social services to "repentant" terrorists (i.e., to address their "moral problems") needs to be studied with efforts to improve shortcomings at a functional level.[26] At the same time, political efforts to promote the underlying theme behind what seemingly amounts to a concrete example of Baldwin's "positive sanctions," as a way of thinking about the terrorism, need to be made in effective and sustained ways.

At a "short-run tactical crisis management" level, it might be fruitful to consider a set of interconnections between prison sentence manipulations and "acts of prisoner exchange" to assist in efforts to promote terrorist group cohesion or terrorist group splintering at the "long-haul negative strategic interactions" level. For example, one scripted account tells us of an Israeli death sentence against a Hamas activist overturned by an Israel Defense Force (IDF) appeals court in 1995, and such activities might be coordinated to some degree with some of the counterterrorism measures to splinter or help unify terrorist groups previously mentioned.[27] In a similar vein, it might be fruitful to consider a possible "feedback loop" between "acts of prisoner exchange" at the "short-term tactical crisis management level" with "support of various chieftains in ways that promote group splitting," or, may I add, group cohesion. For example, "acts of prisoner exchange" might facilitate support of terrorist chieftains, while support from certain terrorist chieftains within a terrorist organization might facilitate acts of prisoner exchange and in the process generate and sustain new opportunities for interaction.

Another dimension of the problem, that falls in the sphere of "long-haul level" factors, taps at the sources and origins of terrorism and efforts to create frameworks that militate against the effects of what is known in the field of comparative politics as "coincidental cleavage" effects, where "fissures" in society, that include rents by region, religion, ethnic group, and socioeconomic development, line up or "coincide" to increase the likelihood of violence.[28] One way of thinking about that matter is to ensure that particular ethnic and religious groups are not found at the economic margins of society, precisely because of the reason that when ethnic and religious lines coincide with an economic backwater condition, the chances of effective and sustained conflict increase.

In turn, political pressure that presupposes and derives from political demands and aspirations increases even more if those groups already defined along ethnic, religious, and socioeconomic lines are also defined by regional boundaries.[29] One underlying theme is to promote the development of cross-cutting institutions that include economic and social associations as well as political parties as concomitants to augment infusions of monies into economic backwater areas.[30] In regard to the development of cross-cutting institutions, circumstances conducive to crafting organizations might follow from efforts at "peace building," where specific teams of persons with specialized training work at specific levels of the "peace-building" process.[31] Seen from the vantage of Lederach, the central idea behind effective and sustained "peace-building" revolves around movement away from emphasis on boilerplate-type solutions for particular issues and towards a "reconciliation" process that places special focus on relationships between persons and groups. For Lederach, "in dealing with the challenge of contemporary conflict an important meeting point between realism and innovation is the idea of *reconciliation*."[32] With respect to capital, "neo-realist" approaches that place emphasis on financial institution involvement may serve as a springboard for action.[33]

At the same "long-haul" vantage, the qualitative analysis, and the quantitative analysis that breaks down terrorist assault frequencies by year, suggest that sustained hard-line counterterrorism stances without the prospect of meaningful negotiation help to radicalize terrorist groups, thereby in effect making it more difficult to suppress or even constrain their actions. Although there are many possible interpretations of the data, it is difficult to ignore the correlation between the overall decline in Israeli-Palestinian-Arab terrorist assaults for the 1994-99 period that really marks the start of the "peace process." It follows, as Ranstorp really suggests, that at a "positive strategic interactions" level in the taxonomy presented, it might be necessary to generate and sustain some distance from the "no negotiations" policy toward terrorists that has been a hallmark of official British, Israeli, and American counter-terrorism policy in stark contrast to French policy.[34] By extrapolation, it follows that terrorist groups, as rational actors, have what might be thought of as "group interests" rather than "national interests" and, as distasteful as it might be, it will be necessary at least to acknowledge that fact in the world of praxis and devise ways to exploit those interests. While negotiations with bin Laden or other extreme "hard-liners" may not be possible, negotiations might help to cause strains and tensions between some "hard-liners" and pragmatists.

It is my hope that this analysis of four Middle East terrorism systems has helped to shed more light on a type of political violence that still remains largely untouched by empirical investigation. Terrorism, in my judgment, will become an increasingly important mode of political expression in the wake of the Cold War in part because of its attachment to protracted communal conflicts and because it remains, as Crozier tells us, "a weapon of the weak."[35] Further empirical investigation needs to be conducted on terrorism in general, on theoretical propositions presented in *Tapestry of Terror* and on issues raised in the process of examining those theoretical propositions for validity, to develop what Zinnes calls the "cumulative integration" of scholarly work.[36] Terrorism studies deserve the increased devotion of scholars and policy makers alike, and if that is done, terrorism studies and counterterrorism measures development can move forward in fruitful ways.

Notes

1. Reiss and Roth 1993.
2. Vandewalle 1997, 34-35, 37-39; Zoubir 1993; Entelis and Arone 1992, 24; Entilis 1986, 49; Willis 1996.
3. Zoubir 1993, 87-88, 94; Fuller 1996; Ciment 1997, 86; Hume and Quandt 1999, 149; Willis 1996.
4. Fuller 1996, 12, 17-19; Crenshaw-Hutchinson 1978, 1-8; Mortimer 1991, 575-577; Huntington 1968; Theen and Wilson 1986, 512-583; Theen and Wilson 1992, 546-613; Theen and Wilson 1996, 533; Piscatori 1994, 361; Coleman 1971, 410.
5. Gaffney 1997, 263-264; Esposito 1992, 99; Guenena 1997, 130; Piscatori 1994, 366; Azzam 1996, 112, 116-118; Sonbol 1988, 25-27; Hatina 2000, 42, 62; Chasdi 1999, 92, 122-123.
6. Hilal 1998, 135, 129; Parker 1999, 63-64; Frisch 1997, 61-62.
7. Huntington 1968, 43, 84, 12-14, 78-79, 34-36.
8. Huntington 1968, 348.
9. Fuller 1996; Crenshaw-Hutchinson 1978; Vanderwalle 1997; Ciment 1997.
10. Brown 1994, 561-578.
11. Goldberg, Sanders and Rogers 1992, 335-358; Hopmann 1986, 12.
12. Kepel 1985, 210, 205. Kepel compares those dynamics to the arrest of V. I. Lenin's brother by the Russian czar's security apparatus.
13. Gunter 1997, 28.
14. Reiss and Roth 1993.
15. Baldwin 1985; Baldwin 1971; Beres 1988a; Beres 1988b; Beres 1990; Chasdi 1999; Chasdi 1997; Chasdi 1995; Chasdi 1994.
16. Im, Cauley, and Sandler 1987, 240-242.
17. Enders, Parise, and Sandler 1992, 305-306; Jenkins 1988, 252, 246, 266; Johnson 1978, 270; Milibank 1976, 11 as found in Elliot 1977, 4; FBI sources found in Smith 1994, 18-21; Ross and Gurr 1989, 410; Chasdi 1999, 148, 202 n33; Chasdi 1997, 78, 109 n21; Chasdi 1995, 145.
18. Drake 1998, 10-11; Chasdi 1999, 175-180,187; Chasdi 1997, 94-98, 104; Chasdi 1995, 211-219, 232 n36, n37, 229-230.
19. Martinez 2000, 10-11, 64-65.

20. Hoffman 1984, 10-15; Goodman 1971, 116, 118-119, 122; Lasswell 1978, 258; Pfaltzgraf 1986, 292; Lustick 1988, 67-71; Sprinzak 1988, 194-216; Merkel 1986, 25; Wilkinson 1986, 204-205; Chasdi 1999, 143, 201.

21. Reiss and Roth 1993, 311-319.

22. Nye 1993.

23. Fuller 1996, 30 n3.

24. Baldwin 1985; Baldwin 1971; Beres 1988a; Beres 1988b; Beres 1990; Chasdi 1999, 189-190, 214, 216; Chasdi 1997, 106, 112 n69, n70; Chasdi 1994, 82-86.

25. Reiss and Roth 1993, 297, 311-319; Nye 1993. I am indebted to Professor Frederic S. Pearson of Wayne State University for his help with respect to conceptualization of this counterterrorism taxonomy.

26. *FBIS* 1994a.

27. Pinkas 1995, 3.

28. Horowitz 1985; Diamond 1990, 360-361, 366-368, 378-380, 387; Diamond, Linz, and Lipset 1990; Melson and Wolpe 1971, 9-10, 19; Coleman 1971, 319, 330-331, 413; Nordlinger 1968, 502.

29. Horowitz 1985; Diamond 1990, 360-361, 366-368, 378-380, 387; Diamond, Linz, and Lipset 1990; Melson and Wolpe 1971, 9-10, 19; Coleman 1971, 319, 330-331, 413; Nordlinger 1968, 502.

30. Huntington 1968; Diamond 1990.

31. Lederach 1997; Sisk 1996.

32. Lederach 1997, 24-25.

33. Kolodziej 1996.

34. Ranstorp 1997.

35. Crozier 1960, 158; Jenkins 1998, 245.

36. Zinnes 1976a, 1976b; Chasdi 1999, 219-220.

Bibliography

Abu-Amr, Ziad. 1992. "Palestinian-Israeli Negotiations: A Palestinian Perspective." In *The Arab-Israeli Search For Peace*. ed. Steven L. Spiegel. Boulder, Colo.: Lynne Rienner Publishers.

———. 1997. "Shaykh Ahmad Yasin and the Origins of Hamas." In *Spokesmen of the Despised; Fundamentalist Leaders of the Middle East*, ed. R. Scott Appleby. Chicago: University of Chicago Press.

Abdelnasser, Walid Mahmoud. 1994. *The Islamic Movement in Egypt: Perceptions of International Relations, 1967-81*. London: Keegan Paul.

AbuKhalil, As'ad. 1991. "Ideology and Practice of Hizballah in Lebanon: Islamization of Leninist Organizational Principles." *Middle Eastern Studies* 27 (3): 390-403.

———. 1994. "Lebanon." In *Political Parties of the Middle East and North Africa*, ed. Frank Tachau. Westport, Conn.: Greenwood Press.

Abu-Stit, Nabil. 1999 (internet). "Egyptian Islamic Group Names New Military Leader." ("New Military Leadership for the Islamic Group in Egypt.") *FBIS-NES-1999-1025*. Publish Date: 10/14/1999; City source: London Al-Sharq al-Awsat, Document Id: 0fk874g0212ycv.

Abu-Sutayt, Nabil. 1999 (internet). "Egypt: Islamic Groups' War of Faxes Viewed." ("Egypt's Security Services View War of Faxes as Evidence of the Isolation of the Fundamentalist Leaders Abroad. Al-Zawahiri Attracted al-Islambouli to his Side and Rifa'i Acts as the Islamic Group's Leader.") *FBIS-NES-1999-1206*, Publish Date: 12/04/1999; City source: London Al-Sharq al-Awsat, Document Id: 0fmdh4e015thee.

Adams, James. 1986. *The Financing of Terror*. Kent, England: New English Library.

Agence Europe agence internationale d'information depuis 1953. 1998. "Wye River Memorandum." (internet) http://www.medea.be/en/index340.htm

Ahmad, Feroz. 1982. "Unionist Relations with Greek, Armenian, and Jewish Communities of the Ottoman Empire, 1908-1914." In *The Central Lands*. Vol. 1 of *Christians and Jews in the Ottoman Empire: The Functioning of a Plural Society*, eds. Benjamin Braude and Bernard Lewis. New York: Holmes & Meier.

Aldrich, John H., and Forrest D. Nelson. 1984. *Linear Probability, Logit and Probit Models*. Newburg Park, Calif.: Sage.

Alexander, Yonah. 1983. "Terrorism and High-Technology Weapons." In *Perspectives on Terrorism*, eds. Lawrence Zelic Freedman and Yonah Alexander. Wilmington, Del.: Scholarly Resources.

———. 1999. "Computer terror can't be ignored." *Jerusalem Post*. 14 June, 8.

Alexander, Yonah, and John Gleason, eds. 1981. *Behavioral and Quantitative Perspectives on Terrorism*. New York: Pergamon.

Alexander, Yonah, and Robert A. Kilmarx. 1979. *Political Terrorism and Business: The Threat and Response*. New York: Praeger.

Alexander, Yonah, and Robert A. Kilmarx, eds. 1979. "International Networks of Terrorist Movements." In *Political Terrorism and Business: The Threat and Response*. New York: Praeger.

Alexander, Yonah, and Joshua Sinai. 1989. *Terrorism: The PLO Connection*. New York: Taylor & Francis.

"Algeria." 1998. In *Countries of the World and Their Leaders Yearbook 1998*. Vol. 1. Detroit, Mich.: Gale Research.

Ali, Othman. 1997. "The Kurds and the Lausanne Peace Negotiations, 1922-23." *Middle Eastern Studies* 33 (3): 521-534.

Allen, Richard. 1974. *Imperialism and Nationalism in the Fertile Crescent: Sources and Prospects of the Arab-Israeli Conflict*. London: Oxford University Press.

Allport, Gordon W. 1954. *The Nature of Prejudice*. Cambridge, Mass.: Addison-Wesley.

Amon, Moshe. 1982. "The Unraveling of the Myth of Progress." In *The Morality of Terrorism: Religious and Secular Justifications*, eds. David C. Rapoport and Yonah Alexander. New York: Pergamon.

Anderson, Ray R., Robert F. Siebert, and Jon Wagner. 1998. *Politics and Change in the Middle East: Sources of Conflict and Accommodation*. 5th ed. Upper Saddle River, N.J.: Prentice Hall.

Anderson, Sean K. 1998. "Warnings versus Alarms: Terrorist Threat Analysis Applied to the Iranian State-Run Media." *Studies in Conflict and Terrorism* 21 (3): 277-303.

Arab News. 1993. "8 Austrian tourists hurt in Cairo bus attack," 28 December.
——. 1994. "Egypt thwarts attack plans," 1 January.
——. 1994. "60 Egyptians held in anti-violence crackdown," 20 January.
——. 1994. "38 arrested in south Egypt crackdown," 24 January.
——. 1994. "Two policemen killed in Egypt attack," 29 January.
Aras, Bulent. 1998. *Palestinian Israeli Peace Process and Turkey.* Commack, N.Y.: Nova Science.
Arquilla, John, and David Ronfeldt. 1999. "The Advent of Netwar: Analytic Background." *Studies in Conflict & Terrorism* 22: 193-201.
Art, Robert J. 1973. "Bureaucratic Politics and American Foreign Policy: A Critique." *Policy Sciences* 4 (4): 467-490.
Asher, Herbert B. 1983. *Causal Modeling.* 2nd ed., Beverly Hills, Calif.: Sage.
Aston, Clive C. 1980. "Restrictions Encountered in Responding to Terrorist Sieges: An Analysis." In *Responding to the Terrorist Threat: Security and Crisis Management,* eds. Richard H. Shultz and Stephen Sloan. New York: Pergamon.
Auda, Gehad. 1991. "An Uncertain Response: The Islamic Movement in Egypt." In *Islamic Fundamentalisms and the Gulf Crisis,* ed. James Piscatori. Chicago: American Academy of Arts and Sciences.
——. 1994. "The 'Normalization' of the Islamic Movement in Egypt from the 1970's to the early 1990's." In *Accounting for Fundamentalisms: The Dynamic Character of Movements,* eds. Martin E. Marty and R. Scott Appleby. Chicago: University of Chicago Press.
Avenarius, Tomas. 1998. (internet). "Germany: Daily Views Background to New Muslim Extremist Terrorism." ("God's Warriors as Scourge for the World.") *FBIS-WEU-98-226.* Publish Date: 08/14/1998, City source: Munich Sueddeutsche Zeitung, Document Id: 0exudm403zng6v.
Axelrod, Robert. 1984. *The Evolution of Cooperation.* New York: Basic Books.
Ayalon, Ami. 1989. "Regime Opposition and Terrorism in Egypt." In *Terror as a State and Revolutionary Strategy,* ed. Barry Rubin. Lanham, Md.: University Press of America.
Aykan, Mahmut Bali. 1996. "Turkey's Policy in Northern Iraq, 1991-95." *Middle Eastern Studies* 32 (4): 343-366.
Ayoade, John A. A. 1986. "Ethnic Politics in Nigeria: A Conceptual Reformulation." In *Ethnicity, Politics and Development,* eds. Dennis L. Thompson and Dov Ronen. Boulder, Colo.: Lynne Rienner.
Ayoob, Mohammed. 1996. "Subnational and Transnational Actors." In *Coping with Conflict after the Cold War,* eds. Edward A. Kolodziej and Roger E. Kanet. Baltimore: Johns Hopkins University Press.
Azar, Edward E., Paul Jureidini, and Ronald McLaurin. 1978. "Protracted Social Conflict Theory and Practice in the Middle East." *Journal of Palestine Studies* 8 (1): 41-60.

Azzam, Maha. 1996. "Egypt: The Islamists and the State Under Mubarak." In *Islamic Fundamentalism*, eds. Abdel Salam Sidahmed and Anoushiravan Ehteshami. Boulder, Colo.: Westview.

Baali, Fuad, and Ali Wardi. 1981. *Ibn Khaldun and Islamic Thought-Styles: A Social Perspective.* Boston: G. K. Hall.

Bahgat, Gawdat. 1999. "Iran and Terrorism: The Transatlantic Responses." *Studies in Conflict & Terrorism* 22: 141-152.

Bahn, Sushella, Ramanand Malaviya, Chand Mohan, Sudhir Mattoo, and C. Rayalakshmi. 1989. *Terrorism: An Annotated Bibliography.* New Delhi: Concept.

Bahry, Louay. 1997. "The Opposition in Bahrain: A Bellwether for the Gulf?" *Middle East Policy* V (2): 42-57.

Baker, Raymond William. 1997. "Invidious Comparisons: Realism, Postmodern Globalism, and Centrist Islamic Movements in Egypt." In *Political Islam: Revolution, Radicalism, or Reform?* ed. John L. Esposito. Boulder, Colo.: Lynne Rienner.

Baldwin, David. 1971. "The Power of Positive Sanctions." *World Politics* 24 (1).

———. 1985. *Economic Statecraft.* Princeton, N.J.: Princeton University Press.

Baligh, Dalia. 1995. "Mubarak: Sudanese behind assassination attempt." *Jerusalem Post,* 28 June, 4.

Ball, Nicole. 1996. "International Economic Actors." In *Coping with Conflict after the Cold War,* eds. Edward A. Kolodziej and Roger E. Kanet. Baltimore: Johns Hopkins University Press.

Bardakjian, Kevork B. 1982. "The Rise of the Armenian Patriarchate of Constantinople." In *The Central Lands.* Vol. 1 of *Christians and Jews in the Ottoman Empire: The Functioning of a Plural Society,* eds. Benjamin Braude and Bernard Lewis. New York: Holmes & Meier.

Barkey, Henri. 1996. "Turkey, Islamic politics, and the Kurdish question." *World Policy Journal.* Spring 13 (1) (internet: http://proquest.umi.com/ pdqweb?TS=970614 . . . &Fmt=3&Sid=22&Idx=2&Deli=1&RQT= 309&Dtp=), 1-10.

Barsoumian, Hagop. 1982. "The Dual Role of the *Amira* Class within the Ottoman Government and the Armenian *Millet* (1750-1850)." In *The Central Lands.* Vol. 1 of *Christians and Jews in the Ottoman Empire: The Functioning of a Plural Society,* eds. Benjamin Braude and Bernard Lewis. New York: Holmes & Meier.

Bassiouni, M. Cherif. 1974, 1975. *International Terrorism and Political Crimes.* Springfield, Ill.: Charles C. Thomas.

———. 1978. "Criminological Policy." In *Legal Aspects of International Terrorism,* eds. Alona E. Evans and John F. Murphy. Lexington, Mass.: Lexington Books.

———. 1986. *Crimes*. Vol. 1 of *International Criminal Law*. New York: Transnational.

Becker, Elizabeth. 2000. "U.S. Military Placed on Highest Alert in Several Hot Spots." *New York Times,* 24 October, A-12.

Bell, Alistar. 1999. "Kurd Rebel Öcalan inspires loyalty, hate." *Jerusalem Post,* 17 February, 2.

Bell, Bowyer J. 1975. *Transnational Terror*. Washington, D.C.: American Enterprise Institute for Public Policy Research.

Benac, Nancy. 1998. "Clinton orders strikes on Afghan, Sudanese Terrorist Sites." *Associated Press,* APTV-08-20-98 1614 EDT 20 August.

Ben Gurion, David. 1971. *Israel: A Personal History*. Translated by Nechemia Meyers and Uzy Nystar. Tel-Aviv: American Israel Publishing.

Beres, Louis Rene. 1987. *America Outside the World: The Collapse of U.S. Foreign Policy*. Lexington, Mass.: D.C. Heath.

———. 1988. "Terrorism and International Law." *Florida International Law Journal* 3 (3): 291-306.

———. 1988. "Genocide, Law and Power Politics." *Whittier Law Review* 10 (2): 329-351.

———. 1990. "Confronting Nuclear Terrorism." *Hastings International and Comparative Law Review* 14 (1): 129-154.

———. 1998. "Israel, the 'Peace Process' and Nuclear Terrorism: Recognizing the Linkages." *Studies in Conflict and Terrorism* 21 (1): 59-73.

———. 1999. "Should Terrorists Be Assassinated?" 6 July. (Internet: http://www.gamla.org.il/english/beres/31.htm).

———. 1999. "Letter from Professor Beres to Prime Minister Ehud Barak," 17 September. (Internet: http://www.gamla.org.il/english/beres/35.htm).

———. 1999. "Arafat Back in Washington, Again," 28 September. (Internet: http://www.gamla.org.il/english/beres/36.htm).

———. 1999. "Israel's Worst Case: A 'Successful' Agreement with the PLO," 5 December. (Internet: http://www.gamla.org.il/english/beres/48.htm).

———. 2000. "The Beres-Gazit Debate Revisited," 26 January. (Internet: http://www.gamla.org.il/english/beres/52.htm).

———. 2000. "Hating the Israelis as Jews: Why Territorial Surrenders Can Never Bring Peace to Israel," 8 February. (Internet: http://www.gamla.org.il/english/beres/54.htm).

Besikci, Ismail. 1986. *M Kemal Ataturk, UNESCO & Destruction of Kurdish Identity In Turkey*. Croydon Park, Australia: Committee for Decolonization of Kurdistan. (Oct 1986).

Binder, Leonard. 1997. "Strategic Reciprocity: The PLO and Israel." In *The PLO and Israel: From Armed Conflict to Political Solution, 1964-1994,* eds. Avraham Sela and Moshe Maoz. New York: St. Martin's Press.

Binyon, Michael. 1994. "Israel 'has developed 200 nuclear weapons.'" *Times* (London), 15 November, 13.

Blainey, Geoffrey. 1988. *The Causes of War.* 3rd ed. New York: Free Press.

Blakesley, Christopher L. 1992. *Terrorism, Drugs, International Law and the Protection of Human Liberty: A Comparative Study of International Law, Its Nature, Rule and Impact in Matters of Terrorism, Drug Trafficking, War and Extradition.* New York: Transnational.

Blakesley, Christopher L., and Otto Lagodny. 1991. "Finding Harmony Amidst Disagreement Over Extradition, Jurisdiction, the Role of Human Rights, and Issues of Extraterritoriality Under International Criminal Law." *Vanderbilt Journal of Transnational Law* 24 (1): 1-73.

Blitzer, Wolf. 1987. "U.S. weighing military strike to free hostages." *Jerusalem Post*, 26 January.

———. 1987. "Two more kidnapped in Beirut." *Jerusalem Post*, 27 January.

———. 1989. "'New York Times': Fatah hires killers to assassinate 'collaborators.'" *Jerusalem Post*, 25 October.

Bosworth, C. E. "The Concept of *Dhimma* in Early Islam." In *The Central Lands*. Vol. 1 of *Christians and Jews in the Ottoman Empire: The Functioning of a Plural Society*, eds. Benjamin Braude and Bernard Lewis. New York: Holmes & Meier.

Boyce, P. J. 1977. *Foreign Affairs for New States: Some Questions of Credentials.* New York: St. Martin's Press.

Bozeman, Adda B. 1971. *The Future of Law in a Multicultural World.* Princeton, N.J.: Princeton University Press.

Braude, Benjamin. 1982. "Foundation Myths of the *Millet* System." In *The Central Lands*. Vol. 1 of *Christians and Jews in the Ottoman Empire: The Functioning of a Plural Society*, eds. Benjamin Braude and Bernard Lewis. New York: Holmes & Meier.

Braude, Benjamin, and Bernard Lewis, eds. 1982. *The Central Lands*. Vol. 1 of *Christians and Jews in the Ottoman Empire: The Functioning of a Plural Society*. New York: Holmes & Meier.

———. 1982. *The Arabic-Speaking Lands*. Vol. 2 of *Christians and Jews in the Ottoman Empire: The Functioning of a Plural Society*. New York: Holmes & Meier.

Brecher, Michael, and Patrick James. 1987. "Crisis Management in the Arab-Israeli Conflict." In *Conflict Management in the Middle East*, eds. Gabriel Ben-Dor and David Dewitt. Lexington, Mass.: D.C. Heath.

Bremer, L. Paul III. 1987. *Practical Measures for Dealing with Terrorism.* Current Policy No. 913, 1-4. Washington, D.C.: U.S. Department of State.

———. 1987. *Counterterrorism: Strategy and Tactics.* Current Policy No. 1023, 1-4. Washington, D.C.: U.S. Department of State.

———. 1988. *Terrorism: Myths and Reality*. Current Policy No. 1047, 1-4. Washington, D.C.: U.S. Department of State.

———. 1989. "Continuing the Fight Against Terrorism." *Terrorism* 12 (2): 81-87.

Brierly, J. L. 1963. *The Law of Nations: An Introduction to the International Law of Peace*. 6th ed. Oxford: Oxford University Press.

Brilliant, Joshua. 1982. "New Jewish terror groups?" *Jerusalem Post*, 12 July.

———. 1982. "GSS probing possible links between Sicarii and Kach." *Jerusalem Post*, 2 August.

Broad, William J. 1998. "How Japan Germ Terror Altered World." *New York Times*, 26 May.

Brown, Richard Maxwell. 1989. "Historical Patterns of Violence." In *Protest, Rebellion, Reform*. Vol. 2 of *Violence in America*, ed. Ted Robert Gurr. Newbury Park, Calif.: Sage.

Brown, Seyom. 1994. *The Faces of Power*. 2nd ed. New York: Columbia University Press.

Bryson, Donna. 1999. "Four arrested in plot to bomb US embassy in India." *Jerusalem Post*, 21 January, 7.

Buckelew, Alvin H. 1985. "Fighting Terrorism: Does the United States need a new response structure?" *Security Management*, June: 36-42.

Burns, John F. 1989. "Afghans Disclose Deaths of 11,000." *New York Times*, 9 November, A-15.

Burns, John F., and Craig Pyes. 1999. "Radical Islamic Network May Have Come to U.S." *New York Times*, 31 December, A-16.

Burns, Robert. 1999. (internet) "FAA orders security tightened at US airports." *BostonGlobe*.(http://www.boston.com/news/packages/y2k/news/terrorism. htm). 21, December.

Burton, Anthony M. 1975. *Urban Terrorism: Theory, Practice and Response*. New York: Free Press.

Butenschon, Nils A. 1998. "The Oslo Agreement: From the White House to Jabal Abu Ghneim." In *After Oslo New Realities, Old Problems*, eds. George Giacaman and Dag Jorund Lonning. Chicago: Pluto Press.

Campbell, Donald T., and Julian C. Stanley. 1963. *Experimental and Quasi-Experimental Designs for Research*. Boston: Houghton Mifflin.

Carr, Maurice. 1958. "The Revolution of Despair." *Jerusalem Post*, 18 July.

———. 1962. "Salan Proud of Heading O.A.S.: Claims Government Responsible for Algerian Bloodshed." *Jerusalem Post*, 18 May.

Celmer, Marc A. 1987. *Terrorism, U.S. Strategy and Reagan Policies*. Westport, Conn.: Greenwood Press.

Central Intelligence Agency. *The World Factbook 1999—Algeria*. Washington DC: Central Intelligence Agency (internet) (http://www.odci.gov/cia/public-ations/factbook/aghtml).

Cevik, Inur, Hayri Birler, and Sinan Yilmaz. "PKK, Islamic, Left-Wing Terrorism Viewed." ("Turkey and Terrorism in 1994") *FBIS-WEU-95-018*, Publish Date: 01/19/1995, City source: Ankara TURKISH DAILY NEWS, Document Id: 0diamlr025eiql.

Charters, David A. 1994. "Conclusions: Security and Liberty in Balance— Countering Terrorism in the Democratic Context." In *The Deadly Sin of Terrorism: Its Effect on Democracy and Civil Liberty in Six Countries*, ed. David A. Charters. Westport, Conn.: Greenwood Press.

Chasdi, Richard J. 1994. "Terrorism: Stratagems for Remediation from an International Law Perspective." *Shofar: An Interdisciplinary Journal of Jewish Studies* 12 (4): 59-86.

———. 1995. "The Dynamics of Middle East Terrorism, 1968-1993: A Functional Typology of Terrorist Group-Types." Ph.D. diss., Purdue University.

———. 1997. "Middle East Terrorism 1968-1993: An Empirical Analysis of Terrorist Group-Type Behavior." *The Journal of Conflict Studies*, 17 (2): 73-114.

———. 1999. *Serenade of Suffering: A Portrait of Middle East Terrorism, 1968-1993*. Lanham, Md.: Lexington Books.

Chase's Annual Events: The Day to Day Directory to 1994. 1993. Chicago: Contemporary Books.

Chase's 1995 Calendar of Events. 1994. Chicago: Contemporary Books.

Chase's 1996 Calendar of Events. 1995. Chicago: Contemporary Books.

Chase's 1997 Calendar of Events. 1996. Chicago: NTC/Contemporary Publishing Company.

Chase's 1998 Calendar of Events. 1997. Chicago: NTC/Contemporary Publishing Company.

Chomsky, Noam. 1991. "International Terrorism: Image and Reality." In *Western State Terrorism*. ed. Alexander George. New York: Routledge, Chapman & Hall, Inc.

Ciment, James. 1997. *Algeria: The Fundamentalist Challenge*. New York: Facts on File.

Clark, Wesley K. 2000. "How to Fight an Asymmetric War. *Time*. 23 October, 40.

Clarity, James F. 1998. "The Day After In Ulster Town: Now 'Its Back.'" *New York Times,* 17 August.

Clogg, Richard. 1982. "The Greek *Millet* in the Ottoman Empire." In *The Central Lands*. Vol. 1 of *Christians and Jews in the Ottoman Empire: The Functioning of a Plural Society*, eds. Benjamin Braude and Bernard Lewis. New York: Holmes & Meier.

Cobban, Helena. 1984. *The Palestinian Liberation Organization: People, Power and Politics*. Cambridge, England: Cambridge University Press.

Cochrane, Charles Norris. 1929. *Thucydides and the Science of History*. London: Oxford University Press.

Cohen, Amnon. 1982. "On the Realities of the *Millet* System: Jerusalem in the Sixteenth Century." In *The Central Lands*. Vol. 1 of *Christians and Jews in the Ottoman Empire: The Functioning of a Plural Society*, eds. Benjamin Braude and Bernard Lewis. New York: Holmes & Meier.

Cohen, Benjamin J. 1973. *A Question of Imperialism: The Political Economy of Dominance and Dependence*. New York: Basic Books.

Coleman, James S. 1971. *Nigeria: Background to Nationalism*. Los Angeles: University of California Press.

Collins, Liat. 1997. "Knesset OK's Hebron pact." *Jerusalem Post*, 17 January, 1, 2.

Conde-Nast. 1992. "The new face of terrorism," May, 156-178.

Cook, Thomas D., and Donald T. Campbell. 1979. *Quasi Experimentation: Design and Analysis Issues for Field Settings*. Boston: Houghton Mifflin.

Cooley, John K. 2000. *Unholy Wars: Afghanistan, America and International Terrorism*. New Edition. London: Pluto Press.

Corbett, Michael. 1993. *Research Methods in Political Science: An Introduction Using Microcase*. Bellevue, Wash.: Microcase.

Corrado, Raymond R. 1981. "A Critique of the Mental Disorder Perspective of Political Terrorism." *International Journal of Law and Psychiatry* 4: 293-309.

Coser, Lewis A. 1956. *The Functions of Social Conflict*. New York: Free Press.

Cowell, Alan. 1990. "Egypt's Parliament Speaker Is Assassinated by Gunmen." *New York Times*, 13 October, 6.

Crawford, James. 1979. *The Creation of States in International Law*. Oxford, England: Clarendon Press.

Crenhaw-Hutchinson, Martha. 1972. "The Concept of Revolutionary Terrorism." *The Journal of Conflict Resolution* 16 (3): 383-396.

———. 1978. *Revolutionary Terrorism: The FLN in Algeria, 1954-1962*. Stanford, Calif.: Hoover Institution Press.

Crenshaw, Martha, ed. 1983. *Terrorism, Legitimacy and Power: The Consequences of Political Violence*. Middleton, Conn.: Wesleyan University Press.

———. 1995. *Terrorism in Context*. University Park: Pennsylvania State University Press.

Criss, Bilge. 1991. "Mercenaries of Ideology: Turkey's Terrorism War." In *Terrorism and Politics*, ed. Barry Rubin. New York: St. Martin's Press.

Criss, Nur Bilge. 1995. "The Nature of PKK Terrorism in Turkey." *Studies in Conflict and Terrorism* 18: 17-37.

Crozier, Brian. 1960. *The Rebels: A Study of Post-War Insurrections*. Boston: Martinus Nijhoff.

Cubert, Harold M. 1998. *The PFLP's Changing Role in the Middle East.* Portland, Ore.: Frank Cass.

Dahl, Robert A. 1957. "The Concept of Power." *Behavioral Science* 2 (3): 201-215.

Danilenko, G. M. 1992. *Law Making in the International Community.* Boston: Martinus Nijhoff.

Darnton, John. 1995. "A Prophet Tests the Honor of His Own Country." *New York Times,* 14 March, A-4.

Davis, Douglas. 1998. "Arafat names Abbas as his successor." *Jerusalem Post,* 5 February, 1.

Davison, Roderic H. 1982. "The Millets as Agents of Change in the Nineteenth-Century Ottoman Empire." In *The Central Lands.* Vol. 1 of *Christians and Jews in the Ottoman Empire: The Functioning of a Plural Society,* eds. Benjamin Braude and Bernard Lewis. New York: Holmes & Meier.

Dawisha, Adeed. 1986. *The Arab Radicals.* New York: Council on Foreign Relations.

DeAndres, Francisca. 1998. (internet). "Algeria: Algeria's Ataf Accuses UK of Harboring Islamic Terrorists." *FBIS-NES-98-058,* Publish Date: 02/27/1998, City source: Madrid ABC (internet version), Document Id:0epb93802olsg5.

Defense Mapping Agency Topographic Center. 1972. *Algeria: Official Standard Names Approved by the United States Board on Geographic Names.* Washington, D.C.: Defense Mapping Agency Topographic Center. Microfiche.

Demant, Peter. 1994. *Jewish Fundamentalism in Israel: Implications for the Mideast Conflict.* Israel Palestine Center for Research and Information 3 (3):

DeMaris, Alfred. 1992. *Logit Modeling: Practical Applications.* Newbury Park, Calif.: Sage.

Department of Justice Terrorist Research and Analytical Center. 1983. *The FBI Analysis of Terrorist Incidents in the United States, 1983.* Washington, D.C.: Federal Bureau of Investigation.

———. 1985. "Terrorism at Home and Abroad: The U.S. Government View." In *The Politics of Terrorism.* 3rd ed., ed. Michael Stohl. New York: Marcel Dekker.

———. 1986. *FBI Analysis of Terrorist Incidents in the United States, 1986.* Washington, D.C.: Federal Bureau of Investigation.

Detter De Lupis, Ingrid. 1987. *The Law of War.* Cambridge, England: Cambridge University Press.

deVattel, Emerich. 1964. *The Law of Nations or the Principles of Natural Law: Applied to the Conduct and to the Affairs of Nations and Sovereigns,* ed. James Brown Scott. New York: Oceana.

Diamond, Larry. 1990. "Nigeria: Pluralism, Statism and the Struggle for Democracy." In *Politics in Developing Countries: Comparing Experiences with Democracy,* eds. Diamond, Juan L. Linz, and Seymour Martin Lipset. Boulder, Colo.: Lynne Rienner.

Diamond, Larry, Juan L. Linz, and Seymour Martin Lipset. 1990. *Politics in Developing Countries: Comparing Experiences with Democracy.* Boulder, Colo.: Lynne Rienner.

Diehl, Paul. 1996. "The United Nations and Peacekeeping." In *Coping with Conflict after the Cold War,* eds. Edward A. Kolodziej and Roger E. Kanet. Baltimore, Md.: Johns Hopkins University Press.

DiLaura, Arnold E. 1987. "Preventing Terrorism: An Analysis of National Strategy." *SAIS Review* 7: 27-38.

Dollard, John, et al. 1939. *Frustration and Aggression.* New Haven, Conn.: Yale University Press.

Don-Yehiya, Eliezer. 1994. "The Book and the Sword: The Nationalist Yeshivot and Political Radicalism in Israel." In *Accounting for Fundamentalism: The Dynamic Character of Movements,* eds. Martin E. Marty and R. Scott Appleby. Chicago: University of Chicago Press.

Drake, C. J. M. 1998. *Terrorists' Target Selection.* New York: St. Martin's.

Dror, Yehezkel. 1983. "Terrorism as a Challenge to the Democratic Capacity to Govern." In *Terrorism, Legitimacy and Power: The Consequences of Political Violence,* ed. Martha Crenshaw. Middleton, Conn.: Wesleyan University Press.

Dudkevitch, Margot. 1999. "NY rally calls for 'State of Judea' to rise again." *Jerusalem Post,* 29 June, 4.

Dunn, John F. 1981. "Recent Issues Honor Famous Personages." *New York Times,* 13 December, 110.

Dunn, Michael Collins. 1994. "Algeria's Agony: The Drama So Far, the Prospects for Peace." *Middle East Policy* 3 (3): 147-156.

———. 1995. "'The Kurdish 'Question': Is There an Answer? A Historical Overview." *Middle East Policy* 4 (1,2): 72-86.

———. 1998. "Usama bin Laden: The Nature of the Challenge." *Middle East Policy* 6 (2): 23-28.

Durkheim, Emile. [1933] 1984. *The Division of Labor in Society.* Translated by W. D. Halls. New York: Free Press.

Dutter, Lee F. 1987. "Ethno-Political Activity and the Psychology of Terrorism." *Terrorism* 10 (3): 145-164.

Duvall, Raymond D., and Michael Stohl. 1983. "Governance by Terror." In *The Politics of Terrorism,* 2nd ed., ed. Stohl. New York: Marcel Dekker.

Earle, Edward Mead, ed. 1944. *Makers of Modern Strategy: Military Thought from Machiavelli to Hitler.* Princeton, N.J.: Princeton University Press.

Edmonds, Lowell. 1975. "Thucydides' Ethics as Reflected in the Description of Stasis." *Harvard Studies in Classical Philology* 79.

Eisner, Michael. 1993. "Jerusalem: An Analysis of Legal Claims and Political Realities." *Wisconsin International Law Journal* 12 (2): 221-259.

Elifson, Kirk W, Richard P. Runyon, and Audrey Haber. 1982. *Fundamentals of Social Statistics*. New York: Random House.

Elliott, John D. 1977. "Transitions of Contemporary Terrorism." *Military Review* 57 (5): 3-15.

Eltahawy, Mona 1995. "Islamic Group Claims 20 October Bomb Attack, Wants Qasim Let Go." *FBIS-TOT-95-021-L*, Publish Date: 10/22/1995, City source: Nicosia CYPRUS MAIL, Document Id: 0dk00us046ayhp.

Enders, Walter, Gerald Parise, and Todd Sandler. 1992. "A Time Series Analysis of Transnational Terrorism: Trends and Cycles." *Defense Economics* 3: 305-320.

Engelberg, Stephen. 2001. "One Man and a Global Web of Violence—Holy Warriors. *New York Times,* 14 January, 1.

Enloe, Cynthia. 1972. *Ethnic Conflict and Political Development*. Boston: Little, Brown.

Entelis, John Pierre. 1986. *Algeria: The Revolution Institutionalized*. Boulder, Colo.: Westview Press.

Entelis, John P., and Lisa J. Arone. 1992. "Algeria in Turmoil: Islam, Democracy and the State." *Middle East Policy* Vol. 1: 23-35.

Eshel, David. 2000. "A Palestinian State and Israeli Security." *Jane's Intelligence Review*, 13 October. (Internet: wysiwyg://31/http://www.janes.com/region. . . middle_east/news/jir/jir/jir001013_3_n.shtml).

Esman, Milton J. *Ethnic Politics*. Ithaca, N.Y.: Cornell University Press.

Esposito, John. 1992. *The Islamic Threat: Myth or Reality?* New York: Oxford University Press.

European Treaty Statutes. 1968. Protocol (No. 4) to the European Convention for the Protection of Human Rights and Freedoms, 2 May. Europ. T.S. No. 46.

———. 1978. European Convention on the Suppression of Terrorism, 4 August. Europ. T.S. No. 90.

Evans, Ernest. 1982. "Toward a More Effective U.S. Policy on Terrorism." In *Political Terrorism and Energy: The Threat and Response*, eds. Yonah Alexander and Charles K. Ebinger. New York: Praeger.

Facts on File. 1982. "Palestinians Slain in Lebanese Refugee Camps; Storm over Israel's Role; Israel Bars Inquiry." Vol. 42, no. 2184 (24) September, 697.

———. 1982. "Egypt Arrests Announced in Plot." Vol. 42, no. 2184 (24) September, 711.

————. 1990. "Egypt: Assembly Elections Boycotted." Vol. 50, no. 2614 (31) December, 957, 987.

————. 1994. "Other World News: Algeria." Vol. 54, no. 2798 (14) July, 499.

————. 1995. "Key Provisions of the Pact on Expanded Palestinian Self-Rule." Vol. 56, no. 2861, 710.

Falk, Richard. 1983. "Rethinking Counter-Terrorism." *Scandinavian Journal of Development Alternatives* 6 (2/3): 19-36.

————. 1988. *Revolutionaries and Functionaries: The Dual Face of Terrorism.* New York: E. P. Dutton.

Falkenrath, Richard A., Robert D. Newman, and Bradley A. Thayer. 1998. *America's Achilles Heel: Nuclear, Biological, and Chemical Terrorism and Covert Attack.* Cambridge: MIT Press.

Falvey, Anne. 1986. "Legislative Responses to International Terrorism: International and National Efforts to Deter and Punish Terrorists." *Boston College International and Comparative Law Review* 9 (2): 323-359.

Farrell, Stephen, and Kathryn Knight. 1997. "Two wounded as letter bombers aim for London target." *Times* (London), 14 January, 4.

Farrell, William R. 1986. "Organized to Combat Terrorism." In *Fighting Back: Winning the War against Terrorism*, eds. Neil C. Livingstone and Terrell E. Arnold. Lexington, Mass.: D. C. Heath.

Fattah, Ezzat. A. 1981. "Terrorist Activities and Terrorist Targets: A Tentative Typology." In *Behavioral and Quantitative Perspectives on Terrorism*, eds. Yonah Alexander and John M. Gleason. New York: Pergamon.

Fenwick, Charles G. 1924. *International Law.* New York: Century.

Findley, Carter. V. 1982. "The Acid Test of Ottomanism: The Acceptance of Non-Muslims in the Late Ottoman Bureaucracy." In *The Central Lands.* Vol. 1 of *Christians and Jews in the Ottoman Empire: The Functioning of a Plural Society*, eds. Benjamin Braude and Bernard Lewis. New York: Holmes & Meier.

Fischbach, Michael R. 1994. "The Palestinians." In *Political Parties of the Middle East and Africa*, ed. Frank Tachau. Westport, Conn.: Greenwood Press.

Fishkoff, Sue. 1993. "Moslem Terror Plot Foiled in New York." *Jerusalem Post*, 25 June.

Flemming, Peter A., Michael Stohl, and Alex P. Schmid. 1988. "The Theoretical Utility of Typologies of Terrorism: Lessons an Opportunities." In *The Politics of Terrorism*. 3rd ed. Edited by Michael Stohl. New York: Marcel Dekker.

Flemming, Peter, and Michael Stohl. "Myths and Realities of Cyberterrorism," unpublished paper, presented at the International Conference on Countering Terrorism Through Enhanced International Cooperation, 22–24 September 2000, Courmayeur, Italy.

Flemming, Peter A. 1992. "Patterns of Transnational Terrorism in Western Europe, 1968-1997: A Quantitative Perspective." Ph.D. diss., Purdue University.

Fodor's Israel. 1993. New York: Fodor's Travel Publications.

Foreign Broadcast Information Service. 1998. (Internet.) "Kakh Leaders Profiled: Party's Death Predicted." *FBIS-NES-20-217.* 7 November, Publication date: 8 November 1990.

———. 1994. (Internet). "Spokesman Explains Release of 'Terrorists'." *FBIS-NES-94-123*; Publish Date: 06/24/1994; City source: Cairo MENA; Document Id: 0di0id7017ikk9.

———. 1995. (Internet). "Increased Violence Expected to Increase in Ramadan." *FBIS-NES-95-019*; Publish Date: 01/28/1995; City source: Paris AFP; Document Id: 0diamqmo1d2ju7.

———. 1995. (Internet). "Detention of HADEP Leaders Extended, 1 Killed." *FBIS-WEU-95-086,* Publish Date: 05/01/1995, City source: Ankara TURKISH DAILY NEWS, Document Id: 0dilu3v02n48i0.

———. 1995. (Internet). "Terrorist Briefs Prosecution on Addis Ababa Attempt." *FBIS-TOT-95-018-L*; Publish Date: 10/03/1995; City source: Cairo MENA; Document Id: 0diapZr00e98n5.

———. 1995. "Croat Envoy Comments on Islamic Group's Threat." *FBIS-TOT-95-021-L,* Publish Date: 10/22/1995, City source: Paris AFP, Document Id: odk00ug04bitxe.

———. 1995. (Internet). "Sources Say Islamic Militants Trained in Pakistan." *FBIS-TOT-95-022-L,* Publish Date: 10/30/1995, City source: Paris AFP; Document ID: 0dk7hm900ppcb3.

———. 1995. (Internet). "'Powerful Bomb' at Egyptian Embassy; "At Least" 12 Dead—Further Report; Responsibility Claim." *FBIS-TOT-96-001-L*; Publish Date: 11/19/1995; City source: Hong Kong AFP; Document Id: 0dljzpp02dkmav.

———. 1995. (Internet). "'Powerful Bomb' At Egyptian Embassy; 'At Least 12 Dead—Second Islamic Group Makes Claim." *FBIS-TOT-96-001-L*; Publish Date: 11/19/1995; City source Paris AFP; Document Id:0dljzpt02rpzhv.

———. 1995. (Internet). "'Powerful Bomb' at Egyptian Embassy; 'At Least' 12 Dead—Egyptian Envoy Details Blast Causalities." *FBIS-TOT-96-001-L*; Publish Date: 11/19/1995; City source: Cairo MENA; Document Id: ODLJZPRO1NWP9P.

———. 1995. (Internet). "'Powerful Bomb' at Egyptian Embassy; 'At Least' 12 Dead—Gulf Papers." *FBIS-TOT-96-001-L*; Publish Date: 11/20/1995; City source: Paris AFP; Document Id: Odljzpz014xon5.

———. 1995. (Internet). "Ministry Source Reports Threats to Embassy in Yemen." *FBIS-TOT-96-002-L*; Publish Date: 11/24/1995, City source: Cairo MENA, Document Id: odlpt1903nyxdm.

———. 1995. (Internet). "Sudan's SPLA Confirms Presence of Terrorist Training Camps." *FBIS-TOT-96-004-L*. Publish Date: 12/23/1995, City source: Cairo MENA, Document ID: 0dmhlvd00dfgbt.

———. 1996. (Internet). "Chechens Counter Turks on MIT, Islamist Ferry Hijack Role." *FBIS-TOT-96-007-L*, Publish Date: 01/23/1996, City source: Ankara TURKISH DAILY NEWS, Document Id:0dnvdnc02dlgrs.

———. 1996. (Internet). "Palestine: 'Arafat on Hamas, Libyan Expulsions, Taba Talks." *FBIS-TOT-96-017-L*; Publish Date: 05/23/1996; City source: Cairo MENA; Document Id: 0DTZL4Y003ZAN4.

———. 1996. (Internet). "Yemen: source suggests 'Separatist Elements' Behind Embassy Blast." *FBIS-TOT-96-020-L*, Publish Date: 07/13/1996; City source: Cairo MENA; Document Id: odw5fir01v17ny.

———. 1996. (Internet). "Algeria: New Armed Islamic Group Statement Declares 'Holy War.'" *FBIS-TOT-96-021-L*, Publish Date: 07/22/1996, City source: Paris AFP, Document Id: 0dwmchw02dkz52.

———. 1996. (Internet). "Egypt: Al-Alfi on Ethiopian Court Verdicts, Anti-terrorism Measures." *FBIS-TOT-96-025-L*, Publish Date: 09/21/1996; City source: Cairo MENA; Document Id: 0e0s5wb03zzlc9.

———. 1996. (Internet). "Afghanistan: Bin Ladin, 'Afghan Arabs' Disappear as Talebon Surges." *FBIS-TOT-96-025-L*. Publish Date: 09/25/1996; City source: London Al Sharq Al-Awsat; Document Id: 0e0s5w404a7erb.

———. 1996. (Internet). "Switzerland Official &mdash: Algerian Insurgent Arms Bought." *FBIS-TOT-97-005-L*, Publish Date: 12/15/1996; City source: Paris AFP; Document Id:0e7348o018mrzm.

———. 1997. (Internet). "FRANCE, BELGIUM: France, Belgium Denounce Algiers Bombings." *FBIS-TOT-97-014-L*. Publish Date: 01/22/1997. City source: Paris AFP, Document Id: 0e927lq00pe9p8.

———. 1997. (Internet). "Algeria: Details on Two Massacres Reported." *FBIS-TOT-97-015-L*, Publish Date: 01/24/1997, City source: Paris AFP; Document Id: 0e95xbt01x88e3.

———. 1997. (Internet). "Algeria: Islamists Killed in Algeria Linked to Benhamouda Murder." *FBIS-TOT-97-018-L*, Publish Date: 02/13/1997. City source: Paris AFP; Document Id: 0e9q9sg04efzpl.

———. 1997. (Internet). "Algeria: New Islamic Organization Supports Jailed FIS Leaders." *FBIS-TOT-97-020-L*, Publish Date: 02/15/1997, City source: Paris AFP, Document Id: 0e9xnge041033j.

———. 1997. (Internet). "Algeria: Security Forces Kill Leader of Islamist Splinter Group." *FBIS-TOT-97-021-L*, Publish Date: 02/23/1997. City source: Paris AFP, Document Id:0ea57jr0lzi81j.

———. 1997. (Internet). "Algeria: Infighting Among Proliferating 'wings' of Armed Groups." *FBIS-TOT-97-021-L*, Publish Date: 02/24/1997. City source: London Al-Sharq Al- Awsat; Document Id: 0ea57fo00uvz3o.

————. 1997. (Internet). "Government Legalizes Anti-Islamist Self Defense Groups." *FBIS-NES-97-071*, Publish Date: 03/12/1997, City source: Paris AFP; Document Id: 0e734lnulsaw1.

————. 1997. (Internet). "Algeria: slamic (sic) Society Movement's Nahnah on Election." *FBIS-NES-97-058*, Publish Date: 03/25/1997, City source: London Al-Sharq al-Awsat, Document Id: 0e7q5q2008zy8c.

————. 1997. (Internet). "WEST BANK, GAZA STRIP: Fatah's Ghunaym Assails U.S. Policies." *FBIS-NES-97-086*, Publish Date: 05/02/1997; City source: London Al-Sharq al-Awsat, Document Id: 0e9s3ii00c0ace.

————. 1997. (Internet). "Algeria: FIS Seeks 'Dialogue" with Regime To Obtain a 'Truce'." *FBIS-NES-97-148*; Publish Date: 05/28/1997; City source: Paris AFP; Document Id: 0eb2cni04livsu.

————. 1997. (Internet). "Algeria: New Armed Group Statement Declares 'Holy War.'" *FBIS-TOT-96-021-L*, Publish Date: 07/22/1997. City source: AFP Paris Document Id: 0dwmchwo2dkz52.

————. 1997. (Internet). "Egypt: Islamic Group Claims Responsibility for Egypt Attack." *FBIS-TOT-97-234*; Publish Date: 08/22/1997; City source: Paris AFP, Document Id: 0efhny401j8twp.

————. 1997. (Internet). "Algeria: Algerian Hamas Leader Calls For Coalition Against Terrorism." *FBIS-TOT-97-258*; Publish Date: 9/15/1997; City source: Paris AFP, Document Id: 0egmf9k03v28ev.

————. 1997. (Internet). "Egypt: Egyptian Terror Suspect on Islamic Group Policy." *FBIS-NES-97-338*; Publish Date: 12/04/1997; City source: Cairo MENA; Document Id: 0ekq9nt00hm80u.

————. 1997. (Internet). "Egypt's al-Jihad Group Indicts Mubarak, Musa, Others." *FBIS-TOT-97-362*; Publish Date: 12/28/1997; City source: Beirut al-Nahar; Document Id: 0em4cqo00u9ejd.

————. 1998. (Internet). "Algeria: Algerian Envoy in Spain Interviewed on Terrorism." *FBIS-TOT-98-007*; Publish Date: 01/07/1998; City source: Madrid RNE International; Document Id: 0emkx5m03puvn7.

————. 1998. (Internet). "United Kingdom: Reopener—Further on Plans for EU Mission to Algeria." *FBIS-WEU-98-008*; Publish Date: 01/08/1998; City source: London Press Association; Document Id: 0emoyzvolmo3po.

————. 1998. (Internet). "Austria Official: Algeria Trip Aimed at 'Comprehensive Dialogue." *FBIS-WEU-98-017*, Publish Date: 01/17/1998; City source: Vienna Die Presse; Document Id: 0en5pw403xu4u9.

————. 1998. (Internet). "Algeria: Algerian General Says Terrorism 'Militarily Defeated.'" *FBIS-TOT-98-126*, Publish Date: 05/06/1998, City source: Paris AFP (Domestic Service), Document Id: 0esnd15034ei6f.

————. 1998. "West Bank: Yassin Discusses Hamas 'Opposition' to PA." *FBIS-NES-98-114*. 24 May, Publish Date: 05-24-98. Article Id: Drnes 05241998000109.

——. 1998. (Internet). "Lebanon: Islamic Army Communiques on US Embassy Bombings." *FBIS-TOT-98-225*, Publish Date: 08/13/1998, City source: Beirut al-Safir, Document Id: 0exoqcp03bky7e.

——. 1998. (Internet). "Egypt: Group 'Like' Bin-Ladin's 'probably' Bombed Embassies." *FBIS-TOT-98-225*, Publish Date: 08/13/1998, City source: London Al-Sharq al Awsat in Arabic 13 Aug 98 p4, Document Id: 0exoqcj00y35lt.

——. 1998. (Internet). "Switzerland: Paper: Bin Laden's Right Hand Man Hiding in Switzerland." *FBIS-WEU-98-235*; Publish Date: 08/23/1998; City source: Paris AFP (North European Service); Document Id: 0eyaybc00tbfhp.

——. 1998. (Internet). "United Kingdom: Further on UK-Based Fundamentalist Threats." *FBIS-TOT-98-237*; Publish Date: 08/25/1998; City source: London Al-Sharq al-Awsat; Document Id: 0eyayht001juhc.

——. 1998. (Internet). "Turkey: PUK Ankara Envoy Denies Talabani Aims at Autonomous State." *FBIS-WEU-98-254*, Publish Date: 09/11/1998, City source: Ankara Anatolia, Document Id: 0ezafsz00odqtf.

——. 1998. (Internet). "Algeria: Hattab Faction Announces Split from GIA." *FBIS-TOT-98-260*, Publish Date: 9/17/1998, City source: London Al-Sharq al-Awsat, Document Id: 0ezhgdr02xv18z.

——. 1998. (Internet). "Algeria: Nahnaf: Terrorism Helps Politico-Financial Mafia." *FBIS-NES-98-268*, Publish Date: 09/25/1998, City source: Brussels La Libre Belgique, Document Id: 0f003v203327uq.

——. 1998. (Internet). "West Bank & Gaza Strip: Palestinian Opposition Warns of Violence After Accord." *FBIS-NES-98-296*, Publish Date: 10/23/1998, City source: Paris AFP (North European Service), Document Id: 0flg23r0098xb9.

——. 1998. (Internet). "Israel: Six Palestinian Groups Reject Wye Plantation Pact." *FBIS-NES-98-299*, Publish Date: 10/26/1998, City source: Cairo MENA, Document Id: 0flhwei03t931g.

——. 1998. (Internet). "Turkey: Germany Asked to Ban Activities by Metin Kaplan." *FBIS-WEU-98-317*, Publish Date: 11/13/1998, City source: Ankara Anatolia; Document Id: 0f2j3hf04bd7aa.

——. 1998. (Internet). "Egypt: Jailed Egyptian Islamists Propose New Initiative." *FBIS-TOT-98-324*; Publish Date: 11/20/1998, City source: London Al-Sharq al-Awsat, Document Id: 0f2vujw02a0350.

——. 1998. (Internet). "Turkey: Six Illegal Organization Members Captured in Istanbul." *FBIS-TOT-98-331*, Publish Date: 11/27/1998, City source: Ankara Anatolia, Document Id: 0f38w6803ag11z.

——. 1998 (Internet). "Turkey: Police Catch 10 Illegal Islamic Organization Members." *FBIS-TOT-98-344*, Publish Date: 12/10/1998, City source: Ankara Anatolia, Document Id: 0f3z6a700ukwv2.

———. 1998. (Internet). "Egypt: Egyptian Source Denies Deal with Islamic Group." *FBIS-NES-98-351*; Publish Date: 12/17/1998, City source: Cairo MENA, Document Id: 0f4c0u002ru0wy.

———. 1999. (Internet). "Turkey: Structure, Goals of Fundamentalist Organizations Detailed." *FBIS-WEU-99-001*, Publish Date: 01/01/1999; City source, Ankara, Anatolia, Document Id: 0f54b3z01p2ham

———. 1999. (Internet). "AFP- - Jailed Egyptian Islamist Warns of Anti-US Attacks." *FBIS-Transcribed Text*, Document Number N/A; Publish Date: 02/04/1999; City source: Paris AFP (North European Service); Document Id: 0f6pabz013mm15.

———. 1999. (Internet). "AA Reports Discord Between YAJK, Öcalan. *FBIS Transcribed Test*, Document Number N/A; Publish Date: 02/07/1999; City source: Ankara Anatolia, Document Id: 0f6vlw500osi2o.

———. 1999. (Internet). "Security Official Says Bin-Ladin Bankrolled Egypt's Jihad." *FBIS-EAS-1999-0215*; Publish Date: 02/15/1999; City source: Paris AFP (North European Service); Document Id: 0f79qkb024zf31.

———. 1999. (Internet). "Iraqi Kurds Demonstrate in Support of Öcalan." *FBIS-EAS-1999-0221*, Publish Date: 02/21/1999, City source: Paris AFP (North European Service), Document Id: 0f7kuob04cae5d.

———. 1999. (Internet). "Egypt's Jihad Says Asked by Bin-Ladin To Turn Guns on US." *FBIS-NES-1999-0224*; Publish Date: 02/24/1999; City source: Paris AFP (North European Service); Document Id: 0f7q3uy001wwe4.

———. 1999. (Internet). "Egypt Seeks Help in Capturing Fugitives." *FBIS-NES-1999-0322*; Publish Date: 03/22/1999, City source: London Al-Majallah; Document Id: 0f92hpg02ooflb.

———. 1999. Government Legalizes Anti-Islamist Self Defense Groups." *FBIS-NES-97-071*; Publish Date: 03/29/1999, City source: Paris AFP, Document Id: 0e734ln01saw17.

———. 1999. (Internet). "Jihad Threatens Attacks on US, EGYPT, ISRAEL." *FBIS-NES-1999*-0401; Publish Date: 04/01/1999; City source: Paris AFP (North European Services); Document Id: 0f911wm00fi0n7.

———. 1999. (Internet). "56 HADEP Members Arrested in Aydin." *FBIS-WEU-1999-0410*, Publish Date: 04/09/1999; City source: Ankara Anatolia, Document Id: 0fa8jjy02yg43b.

———. 1999. (Internet). "Islamists' Financial Sources Detailed." *FBIS-NES-1999-0426*; Publish Date: 04/18/1999; City source: London Al-Majallah; Document Id: 0fauujg011pm7o.

———. 1999. (Internet). "Abu-Hamzah: Scotland Yard Fears My Escape." *FBIS-WEU-1999-0425*; Publish Date: 04/25/1999; City source: London Al-Sharq al-Awsat (Internet Version); Document Id: 0fauux703mlkp6.

———. 1999. (Internet). "Changes Seen in Islamic Group's Thinking." *FBIS-NES-1999-0430*; Publish Date: 04/29/1999; City source: London Al-Sharq al-Awsat; Document Id: 0fb6d120lffcq3.

———. 1999. (Internet). "Egyptian Minister on Terrorism, Human Rights, Detainees." *FBIS-NES-1999-0509*; Publish Date: 05/09/1999; City source: Cairo MENA; Document Id: 0fbjegj03daxjv.

———. 1999. (Internet). "More Egyptian IG Members Go on Trial." *FBIS-NES-1999-0517*; Publish Date: 05/17/1999; City source: London Al-Sharq al-Awsat; Document Id: 0fbxvot03ru6er.

———. 1999. (Internet). "Egyptian Military Court To Try 22 in 'Vanguards' Case." *FBIS-NES-1999-0528*; Publish Date: 05/28/1999; City source: London Al-Sharq al-Awsat; Document Id: 0fc060x00yhdid.

———. 1999. (Internet). "US Seeks Information From Egypt About al-Zawahiri." *FBIS-NES-1999-0621*; Publish Date: 06/21/1999; City source: London Al-Sharq al-Awsat; Document Id: 0fdqjuz01zzypl.

———. 1999. (Internet). "Algeria: GIA Sends Conditions For Joining Truce." *FBIS-NES-1999-0701*, Publish Date: 07/01/1999, Document Id: 0fe9fjxola 2ehi.

———. 1999. (Internet). "10 Caught for Demonstrating Against Ocalan Sentence." *FBIS-WEU-1999-07-8*, Publish Date: 07/08/1999, City source: Ankara Anatolia, Document Id: 0femc4zooqulhm.

———. 1999. (Internet). "Islamists' Arrest Linked to US 'Onslaught.'" *FBIS-NES-1999-0713*; Publish Date: 07/13/1999; City source: London Al-Sharq al-Awsat; Document Id: 0fewva801k4mdl.

———. 1999. (Internet). "Report on Egyptian Fundamentalists." *FBIS-NES-1999-0721*; Publish Date: 07/18/1999; City source: London Al-Sharq al Awsat; Document Id: 0ffamjwookltxr.

———. 1999. (Internet). "Egyptian IG Leader Rejects Politicization." *FBIS-NES-1999-0817*; Publish Date: 08/14/1999; City source: London Al-Sharq al-Awsat; Document Id: 0fgny2f0loefnf.

———. 1999. (Internet). "IG Leader Reacts to Letter by Rifa'i Taha." *FBIS-NES-1999-0818;* Publish Date: 08/14/1999; City source: London Al-Sharq al-Awsat; Document Id: 0fgposu02fegiq.

———. 1999. (Internet). "DFLP's Hawatmah Interviewed." *FBIS-NES-1999-0827*; Publish Date: 08/27/1999; City source: Cairo Al-Musawwar; Document Id: 0fha5by00yk6zj.

———. 1999. (Internet). "Egyptian Police Kill Islamist Leader, 3 Others." *FBIS-NES-1999-0907*; Publish Date: 09/07/1999; Document Id: 0fhrgls043mkbj.

———. 1999. (Internet). "Egyptian Islamist Foresees Repeat of Luxor Massacre." *FBIS-NES-1999-1129*; Publish Date: 11/28/1999; City source: London Al-Sharq al-Awsat; Document Id: 0fm10ab01d8ptw.

———. 1999. (Internet). "Islamic Group Prisoners Released." *FBIS-NES-1999-1206*. Publish Date: 12/06/1999; City source: London Al-Sharq al-Awsat; Document Id: 0fmdhln033ntb2.

Franz, Douglas. 2000. "Fearing Terrorism, U.S. Keeps Consulates in Turkey Closed." *New York Times,* 15 December, A-5.

Freudenheim, Yehoshua. 1967. *Government in Israel.* New York: Oceana.

Fried, John H. E. 1985. "The Nuclear Collision Course: Can International Law Be of Help?" *Denver Journal of International Law and Policy* 14 (1): 97-119.

Friedland, Nehemia. 1992. "Becoming a Terrorist: Social and Individual Antecedents." In *Terrorism: Roots, Impact, Responses,* ed. Lawrence Howard. New York: Praeger.

Friedman, Robert I. 1987. "Terror on Sacred Ground: The Battle for the Temple Mount." *Mother Jones* August/September, 37-44.

———. 1988. "How Shamir Used JDL Terrorism: The Kahane Connection." *The Nation* (247), 31 October.

———. 1990. *The False Prophet: Rabbi Meir Kahane: From FBI Informant to Knesset Member.* Brooklyn, N.Y.: Lawrence Hill Books.

———. 1992. *Zealots for Zion: Inside Israel's West Bank Movement.* New York: Random House.

Friedman, Thomas L. 1993. "The Missiles' Message: Yes, Washington Wants to Punish Hussein, but It Wants All State Terrorists to Beware." *New York Times,* 28 June.

Frisch, Hillel. 1997. "From Palestine Liberation Organization to Palestinian Authority: the Territorialization of 'Neopatriarchy.'" In *The PLO and Israel: From Armed Conflict to Political Solution, 1964-1994,* eds. Avraham Sela and Moshe Maoz. New York: St. Martin's Press.

Fuller, Graham E. 1996. *Algeria: The Next Fundamentalist State?* Santa Monica, Calif.: RAND Corporation.

Gaffney, Patrick D. 1997. "Fundamentalist Preaching and Islamic Militancy in Upper Egypt." In *Speaking for the Despised: Fundamentalist Leaders of the Middle East,* ed. R. Scott Appleby. Chicago: University of Chicago Press.

Gal-Or, Noemi. 1985. *International Cooperation to Suppress Terrorism.* New York: St. Martin's Press.

———. 1991. *Tolerating Terrorism in the West: an International Survey.* London: Routledge.

Ganley, Elaine. 1997. "Strife-torn Algeria holds peaceful vote." *Jerusalem Post,* 6 June, 6.

Garst, Daniel. 1989. "Thucydides and Neo-realism." *International Studies Quarterly* 33 (1): 3-27.

Gates, John M. 2001. "Understanding Terrorism." Unpublished manuscript (http://www.wooster.edu/history/gates/book-ch10.html).

Gentili, Alberico. 1964. *De Iure Belli Libri Tres,* ed. James Brown Scott. New York: Oceana.

George, Darren, and Paul Mallery. 1995. *SPSS/PC+ Step By Step: A Simple*

Guide and Reference. Belmont, Calif.: Wadsworth Publishing.

Gerner, Deborah J. 1994. *One Land, Two Peoples: The Conflict over Palestine.* Boulder, Colo.: Westview Press.

Geyer, Georgie Anne. 1995 "Palestinian Islamics reject and threaten the peace process." *Chicago Tribune,* 3 February.

Gibb, Cecil A. 1947. "The Principles and Traits of Leadership." *The Journal of Abnormal and Social Psychology* 42 (3): 267-284.

Gilpin, Robert. 1981. *War and Change in World Politics.* Cambridge, England: Cambridge University Press.

Golan, Galia. 1992. "Arab-Israeli Peace Negotiations: An Israeli View." In *The Arab-Israeli Search For Peace,* ed. Steven L. Spiegel. Boulder, Colo.: Lynne Rienner.

Goldaber, Irving. 1979. "A Typology of Hostage Takers." *The Police Chief* 46 (6): 21-23.

Goldberg, Stephen B., Frank E. A. Sander, and Nancy Rogers. 1992. *Dispute Resolution: Negotiation, Mediation, and Other Processes* 2nd ed. Boston: Little, Brown.

Goodman, Walter. 1971. "Rabbi Kahane says: 'I'd love to see the JDL fold up. But—.'" *New York Times Magazine,* 21 November.

Gordon, David C. 1966. *The Passing of French Algeria.* London: Oxford University Press.

Gordon, Evelyn. 1994. "Outlawing of Kach, Kahane Chai draws criticism from right, left." *Jerusalem Post,* 16 March, 2.

Gordon, Michael R. 2000. "Superpower Suddenly Finds Itself Threatened by Sophisticated Terrorists." *New York Times,* 14 October, A-9.

Gordon, Milton M. 1964. *Assimilation in American Life: The Role of Race, Religion and National Origins.* New York: Oxford University Press.

Goyal, Archana. 1990. *Terrorism: Causes and Consequences.* Bikaner, India: Institute of Environment.

Graham, Hugh Davis. 1989. "Violence, Social Theory and the Historians: The Debate over Consensus and Culture in America." In *Protest, Rebellion, Reform.* Vol. 2 of *Violence in America,* ed. Ted Robert Gurr. Newbury Park, Calif.: Sage.

Greenberger, Robert S. 2001. "Tracking Terrorism's Reach." *Wall Street Journal,* 25 September, B-1.

Gresch, Alain. 1983. *The PLO: The Struggle Within: Towards an Independent Palestinian State.* London: Zed Books.

Grotius, Hugo. 1964. *De Iure Pradae Commentarious,* ed. James Brown Scott. New York: Oceana.

Guenena, Nemat. 1986. "The 'Jihad': An 'Islamic Alternative' in Egypt." *Cairo Papers in Social Sciences* 9 (Summer 1986) monograph 2: 52-80.

Guenena, NematAllah Adel. 1997. "Islamic Activism in Egypt, 1974-1996." In

Islam in a Changing World, eds. Anders Jerichow and Jorgen Baek Simonsen. Surrey, England: Curzon Press.

Gunter, Michael. 1986. "Contemporary Armenian Terrorism." *Terrorism: An International Journal* 8 (3): 213-252.

———. 1997. *The Kurds and the Future of Turkey.* New York: St. Martin's Press.

Gürbey, Gülistan. 1996. "The Kurdish Nationalist Movement in Turkey Since the 1980's." In *The Kurdish Nationalist Movement in the 1990's: Its Impact on Turkey and the Middle East,* ed. Robert Olson. Lexington: University Press of Kentucky, 9-37.

Gurr, Ted Robert. 1988. "Some Characteristics of Political Terrorism in the 1960's." In *Politics of Terrorism.* 3rd ed. Edited by Michael Stohl. New York: Marcel Dekker.

———. 1989. "Political Terrorism: Historical Antecedents and Contemporary Trends." In *Protest, Rebellion, Reform.* Vol. 2 of *Violence in America,* ed. Ted Robert Gurr. Newbury Park, Calif.: Sage.

———. 1989. "The History of Protest, Rebellion and Reform in America: An Overview." In *Protest, Rebellion, Reform.* Vol. 2 of *Violence in America,* ed. Ted Robert Gurr. Newbury Park, Calif.: Sage.

Gurr, Ted Robert, and Barbara Harff. 1994. *Ethnic Conflict in World Politics.* Boulder, Colo.: Westview Press.

Haberman, Clyde. 1994. "Shamir Memoirs Say He Ordered Killing in 1943." *New York Times,* 15 January, 4.

———. 1994. "Israel votes ban on Jewish groups linked to Kahane." *New York Times,* 14 March.

———. 2001. "Dennis Ross's Exit Interview." *New York Times Magazine,* 25 March, 36-39.

Hacker, Frederick J. 1976. *Crusaders, Criminals, Crazies: Terror and Terrorism in Our Time.* New York: W. W. Norton.

Hacker, Joseph. 1982. "Ottoman Policy towards the Jews and Jewish Attitude toward the Ottomans during the Fifteenth Century." In *The Central Lands.* Vol. 1 of *Christians and Jews in the Ottoman Empire: The Functioning of a Plural Society,* eds. Benjamin Braude and Bernard Lewis. New York: Holmes & Meier.

Halawi, Jailan. 1998. "Conflicting signals from the Gama'a." *Al-Ahram Weekly one group, many voices.* (Internet). No. 402 5-11 November (http://163.121.116.16/weekly/1998/402/eg6.htm).

Hammoud, Mirna. 1998. "Causes for Fundamentalist Popularity in Egypt." In *Islamic Fundamentalism Myths and Realities,* ed. Ahmad S. Moussalli. Reading, England: Garnet.

Han, Harry H. 1993. *Terrorism and Political Violence: Limits and Possibilities of Legal Control.* New York: Oceana.

Hanauer, Lawrence S. 1995. "The Path to Redemption: Fundamentalist Judaism, Territory and Jewish Settler Violence in the West Bank." *Studies in Conflict and Terrorism* 18 (4), 245-270.

Hannikainen, Lauri. 1988. *Peremptory Norms (Jus Cogens) in International Law: Historical Development, Criteria, Present Status.* Helsinki: Lakimiesliiton Kustannus Finnish Lawyers' Publishing Company.

Harkabi, Yehoshafat. 1974. *Palestinians and Israel.* New York: John Wiley & Sons.

Harris, Ben M. 1964. "Leadership Prediction as Related to Measures of Personal Characteristics." *Personnel Administration* 27 (4): 31-34.

Harris, Christina Phelps. 1964. *Nationalism and Revolution in Egypt: The Role of the Muslim Brotherhood.* London: Mouton.

Harris, Rosemary. 1989. "Anthropological Views on 'Violence' in Northern Ireland." In *Ireland's Terrorist Trauma*, eds. Yonah Alexander and Alan O'Day. New York: St. Martin's Press.

Harris, William W. 1997. *Faces of Lebanon: Sects, Wars, and Global Extensions.* Princeton, N.J.: Markus Wiener.

Hassassian, Manuel S. 1997. "Policy and Attitude Changes in the Palestine Liberation Organization, 1965-1994." In *The PLO and Israel: From Armed Conflict to Political Solution, 1964-1994*, eds. Avraham Sela and Moshe Ma'oz. New York; St. Martin's Press.

Hatina, Meir. 2000. "On the Margins of Consensus: The Call to Separate Religion and State in Modern Egypt." *Middle Eastern Studies* 36 (1): 35-67.

Henry, Marilyn. 1998. "Moslem terrorists blamed for attacks in Kenya, Tanzania." *Jerusalem Post*, 9 August, 1.

Heper, Metin. 1979-80. "Recent Instability in Turkish Politics: End of A Monocentrist Policy?" *International Journal of Turkish Studies* 1 (1): 102-113.

Hewitt, Christopher. 1988. "The Cost of Terrorism: A Cross-National Study of Six Countries." *Terrorism* 11 (3): 164-180.

Heyworth-Dunne, James. 1950. *Religious and Political Trends in Modern Egypt.* Washington, D.C.: McGregor & Werner.

Hilal, Jamil. 1998. "The Effect of the Oslo Agreement on the Palestinian Political System." In *After Oslo: New Realities, Old Problems*, eds. George Giacaman and Dag Jorund Lonning. Chicago: Pluto Press.

Hobsbawm, Eric J. 1987. *The Age of Empire, 1875-1914.* London: Weidenfeld and Nicolson.

Hocking, Jenny. 1986. "Terrorism and counter-terrorism: institutionalizing political order." *The Australian Quarterly* 58 (3): 297-307.

Hoffman, Bruce. 1984. "The Jewish Defense League." *Terrorism, Violence Insurgency Journal* 5 (1): 10-15.

———. 1988. *Inside Terrorism.* London: Victor Gollancz.

——. 1993. "Terrorist Targeting: Tactics, Trends, and Potentialities." *Terrorism and Political Violence* 5 (2): 12-29.

Hoffman, Gil. 1998. "Carmon: No solid defense vs. terror." *Jerusalem Post,* 10 August, 2.

Hogg, Ian V. 1990. *Jane's Infantry Weapons.* 16th ed. (1990-1991). Surrey, England: Jane's Information Group.

Holsti, Kalevi Jaakko. 1970. "National Role Conceptions in the Study of Foreign Policy." *International Studies Quarterly* 14 (3): 233-309.

——. 1985. *The Dividing Discipline: Hegemony and Diversity in International Theory.* Boston: Allen and Unwin.

Holton, Gerald. 1977. "Reflections on Modern Terrorism." *The Jerusalem Journal of International Relations* 3 (1): 96-104.

Holy Bible. 1952. Revised Standard Version Reference Ed.

Homer, Frederic D. 1983. "Terror in the United States: Three Perspectives." In *The Politics of Terrorism.* 2nd ed. Edited by Michael Stohl. New York: Marcel Dekker.

Hopmann, P. Terrence. 1986. "Arms Control on Cobia: A Simulation Exercise–Instructor's Manual." Providence, R.I.: Brown University.

Horowitz, Dan, and Moshe Lissak. 1978. *Origins of the Israeli Polity: Palestine under the Mandate.* Chicago: University of Chicago Press.

Horowitz, Donald L. 1985. *Ethnic Groups in Conflict.* Berkeley: University of California Press.

Hourani, Albert. 1991. *A History of the Arab Peoples.* New York: Warner Books.

Houston, Chris. 1997. "Islamic Solutions to the Kurdish Problem: Late Rendezvous or Illegitimate Shortcut?" *New Perspectives on Turkey* 16: 1-22.

Hubbard, David G. 1975. " A Glimmer of Hope: A Psychiatric Perspective." In *International Terrorism and Political Crimes,* ed. M. Cherif Bassiouni. Springfield, Ill.: Charles C. Thomas.

——. 1983. "The Psychodynamics of Terrorism." In *International Violence,* eds. Tunde Adeniran and Yonah Alexander. New York: Praeger.

Hume, Cameron R., and William B. Quandt. 1999. "Brookings-Sadat Forum: Algeria." *Middle East Policy* 6 (3): 141-149.

Humphrey, Michael. 2000. "Violence, Voice and Identity in Algeria." *Arab Studies Quarterly* 22 (1): 1-23.

Huntington, Samuel P. 1968. *Political Order in Changing Societies.* New Haven, Conn.: Yale University Press.

——. 1996. *The Clash of Civilizations and the Remaking of World Order.* New York: Simon and Schuster.

Husaini, Ishak Musa. 1956. *The Moslem Brethren: The Greatest of Modern Islamic Movements.* Beirut: Khayat's College Book Cooperative.

Hutman. Bill. 1994. "Journalist critical of Kahane attacked by Kahane-Hai members." *Jerusalem Post,* 11 January.

———. 1994. "Cabinet bans Kach, Kahane Chai." *Jerusalem Post,* 14 March, 1.

———. 1994. "Kach camp organizers go into hiding." *Jerusalem Post,* 1 August, 12.

———. 1994. "Police launch probe of Kach-affiliated paramilitary training camp." *Jerusalem Post,* 29 July, A-12.

———. 1994. "Haredim suspected of vandalizing Jerusalem community center." *Jerusalem Post,* 2 October, 12.

———. 1995. "Protesters attack Amit during Zo Artzenu demo near Knesset." *Jerusalem Post,* 25 August, 1.

———. 1996. "Police demolish home of 'Engineer No. 2.'" *Jerusalem Post,* 21 March, 2.

———. 1996. "Kahane Chai leader expected here to try to revive movement." *Jerusalem Post,* 8 September, 24.

Hutman, Bill, and Alon Pinkas. 1994. "Wave of riots after Hebron massacre: Kiryat Arba doctor slays 39; over 20 Palestinians die in aftermath." *Jerusalem Post,* 27 February, 1, 2.

Ibrahim, Saad Eddin. 1988. "Egypt's Islamic activism in the 1980's." *Third World Quarterly* 10 (2): 632-657.

Ibrahim, Youssef. 1996. "Hamas Chief Says He Can't Curb Terrorists." *New York Times,* 9 March.

Im, Eric Iksoon, Jon Cauley, and Todd Sandler. 1987. "Cycles and Substitutions in Terrorist Activities: A Spectral Approach." *Kyklos* 40: 238-255.

Immanuel, Jon. 1992. "Fatah gang linked to Jenin killings." *Jerusalem Post,* 27 January.

———. 1992. "Jewish terror group claims Freij attack." *Jerusalem Post,* 24 January.

———. 1995. "Jihad calls for revenge, appoints new leader." *Jerusalem Post,* 30 October, 1.

———. 1995. "Shkaki buried in Damascus; followers vow revenge." *Jerusalem Post,* 2 November, 2.

Immanuel, Jon, and David Makovsky. 1995. "Second stage agreement to be signed July 25." *Jerusalem Post,* 5 July, 1.

Inalcik, Haili. 1982. "Ottoman Archival Materials on *Millets.*" In *The Central Lands.* Vol. 1 of *Christians and Jews in the Ottoman Empire: The Functioning of a Plural Society,* eds. Benjamin Braude and Bernard Lewis. New York: Holmes & Meier.

Inbar, Efraim. 1991. "Israel's Small War: The Military Response to the *Intifada.*" *Armed Forces & Society* 18 (1): 29-50.

International Labor Organization. 1989. Convention (No. 169) Concerning

Indigenous and Tribal Peoples in Independent Countries, 27 June. Draft Report of the Committee Convention No. 107, App. I. C.C. 107/D. 303 (June 1989).

Intoccia, Gregory F. 1985. "International Legal and Policy Implications of an American Counter-Terrorist Strategy." *Denver Journal of International Law and Policy* 14 (1): 121-146.

Israel Ministry of Foreign Affairs. 1997. "Protocol Concerning the Redeployment in Hebron." (Internet: ask@israel-info.gov.il).

———. 1997. "Further Redeployments (FRD): The Next Stage of the Israeli-Palestinian Interim Agreement: Legal Aspects." 19 January.

Israeli, Raphael, ed. 1983. *PLO in Lebanon: Selected Documents.* London: Weidenfeld and Nicolson.

Issawi, Charles. 1982. "The Transformation of the Economic Position of the *Millets* in the Nineteenth Century." In *The Central Lands.* Vol. 1 of *Christians and Jews in the Ottoman Empire: The Functioning of a Plural Society,* eds. Benjamin Braude and Bernard Lewis. New York: Holmes & Meier.

Iviansky, Ze'ev. 1977. "Individual Terror: Concept and Typology." *Journal of Contemporary History* 12 (1): 43-63.

Jaber, Hala. 1997. *Hezbollah: Born with a Vengeance.* New York: Columbia University Press.

Jad, 'Imad. 1997. "West Bank: Report Speculates on 'Succession' to Arafat." *FBIS-NES-97-341.* Publish Date: 12/07/1997, City source: London al-Majallah, Document Id: 0ekxsrf02w99il.

Jamil, Salah. 1998. (Internet). "Algeria: Algerian Ennahda Movement Leader Interviewed." *FBIS-NES-98-058,* Publish Date: 02/27/1998, City source: London Al-Sharq al-Awsat, Document Id: 0epb92w04e0Sa9.

Janis, Irving L. 1972. *Victims of Groupthink: a Psychological Study of Foreign-Policy Decisions and Fiascoes.* Boston: Houghton Mifflin.

Jansen, Johannes, J.G. 1986. *The Neglected Duty: The Creed of Sadat's Assassins and Islamic Resurgence in the Middle East.* New York: Macmillan.

Jehl, Douglas. 1997. "For Palestinians, New Sense of Order." *New York Times,* 16 January, A-8.

———. 2001. "Arab Allies Not Jumping to Join U.S. Side." *New York Times,* 27 September, B-3.

Jenkins, Brian. 1981 "A U.S. Strategy for Combatting Terrorism." *Conflict* 3 (2/3): 167-176.

———. 1998. "Will Terrorists Go Nuclear? A Reappraisal." In *The Future of Terrorism: Violence in the New Millennium,* ed. Harvey W. Kushner. Thousand Oaks, Calif.: Sage.

Jenkins, Brian M. 1988. "Future Trends in International Terrorism." In *Current*

Perspectives on International Terrorism, eds. Robert O. Slater and Michael Stohl, 246-266. Basingstoke, England: Macmillan.

Jenkins, Philip. 1988. "Under Two Flags: Provocation and Deception in European Terrorism." *Terrorism* 11 (4): 275-287.

Jenkins, William O. 1947. "A Review of Leadership Studies with Particular Reference to Military Problems." *Psychological Bulletin* 44 (1): 54-79.

Jervis, Robert. 1976. *Perception and Misperception in International Politics.* Princeton, N.J.: Princeton University Press.

Jerusalem Post. 1970. "El Al crew foils hijackers but 3 other planes seized." 7 September.

———. 1970. "BOAC airliner at desert strip." 10 September.

———. 1970. "UN Security Council meets as British plane hijacked." 10 September.

———. 1970. "Terrorists blow up 3 airliners, say they'll free all but 40 hostages." 13 September.

———. 1970 "Freed hostages tell of chaos in Amman, terror in desert." 13 September.

———. 1974. "New terror group acts in Syria." 16 August.

———. 1984. "Lifta suspect sent to mental hospital." 15 June.

———. 1984. "The Accused: Brief biographies of the suspects in the alleged Jewish terror underground, publication of whose identities was banned until yesterday's court decision." 19 June.

———. 1987. "Second German abducted in Beirut." 22 January.

———. 1987. "Fears grow Waite now kidnap victim." 1 February.

———. 1988. "The Algerian equation." 11 March.

———. 1989. "Jewish Intifada." 31 July.

———. 1989. "Hizbullah reportedly operating terror network in West Africa." 28 November.

———. 1991. "Turkish Islamic Jihad claims responsibility for Ankara attacks on American, Egyptian." 29 October.

———. 1992. "Grenade kills one in Old City: Kahane Hai takes responsibility for attack in Moslem Quarter." 17 November.

———. 1993. "Police suspect terrorists behind bombing of World Trade Center." 28 February.

———. 1994. "Five die in Turkish blast." 13 February, 3.

———. 1994. "Katzover's car vandalized by extremist." 31 March, 2.

———. 1994. "Rabin warned of assassination threat." 20 June, 2.

———. 1994. "Blasts wound 56 in Algerian march for democracy." 30 June, 4.

———. 1994. "Turkish diplomat slain in Athens." 5 July, 5.

———. 1994. "Panama Jews fear sabotage in crash." 21 July, 1.

———. 1994. "Embassy in Chile emptied by bomb scare." 31 July, 2.

———. 1994. "Islamic group claims responsibility for Argentina, Panama bombings." 24 July, 1.

——. 1994. "Islamic group threatens France." 7 August, 4.

——. 1994. "Kach camps still in operation." 16 August, 2.

——. 1994. "Police arrest North Africans linked to Morocco tourist murder."
2 September, A-4.

——. 1994. "Newsline with Prof. Yonah Alexander." 20 October, 2.

——. 1994. "Algerian airliner hijacking ends peacefully." 14 November.

——. 1994. "Moslem militants attack Egyptian prisoner train." 14 December,
4.

——. 1994. "Iranian-Arab rift splits Hizbullah." 21 December, 5.

——. 1994. "Hijackers reportedly kill 7 in Algiers airport." 25 December, 1.

——. 1995. "Eighteen killed in Egyptian clashes." 29 January, 1.

——. 1995. "Algiers car bomb kills 38, wounds over 250." 31 January, 4.

——. 1995. "Car bomb in Zakho kills 54 Kurds." 28 February, 8.

——. 1995. "Chemical attack suspected at Washington B'nai B'rith." 25 April,
2.

——. 1995. "Sudan denies role in Mubarak attack; Mubarak: I was cool all the
time." 27 June, 1.

——. 1995. "Ethiopia kills three Mubarak hitmen." 2 July, 4.

——. 1995. "Moslem militants: "We'll keep trying to kill Mubarak." 5 July,
4.

——. 1995. "Algerian moderate cleric shot dead in French mosque." 13 July,
4.

——. 1995. "Car bomb kills five in Algeria." 26 July, 4.

——. 1995. "3 suspected Mubarak attackers arrested." 4 August, 6.

——. 1995. "Threats made against US targets in Egypt." 6 August, 2.

——. 1995. "Summary of Israel-PA agreement." 27 September, 3.

——. 1995. "Paris bomb injures 13." 8 October, 3.

——. 1995. "29 commuters wounded in Paris train bombing." 18 October, 1.

——. 1995. "Algerian troops deploy to curb Moslem riots ahead of poll." 13
November, 4.

——. 1995. "Algeria's Zeroual wins poll, not war." 19 November, 3.

——. 1995. "Suicide truck bomber blasts Egyptian Embassy in Islamabad." 20
November, 1.

——. 1995. "Indictments against 3 Zo Artzenu leaders for sedition." 3
December, 1, 2.

——. 1996. "Algeria denies report on Islamist leader release." 7 February, 5.

——. 1996. "Islamic extremists urge army to topple Mubarak." 21 February,
5.

——. 1996. "Report: Hizbullah men stopped in South America." 29 April, 2.

——. 1996. "Shekel drops .03% against dollar." 3 May, 1.

——. 1996. "Hizbullah renews offer of prisoner, body swap." 11 July, 2.

——. 1996. "Hizbullah makes comeback in Lebanon election." 10 September,
2.

———. 1996. "Police investigate Kach leader for incitement." 17 November, 12.

———. 1996. "Two killed, 80 wounded in Paris subway bombing." 4 December, 1.

———. 1996. "Algerian rebel group names former Bosnian fighter as new leader." 9 December, 4.

———. 1997. "Report: Two bombs wound 18 in Algeria." 1 January, 5.

———. 1997. "Report: Extremist group threatens PM." 21 January, 2.

———. 1997. "Chemical attack suspected at Washington B'nai B'rith." 25 April, 2.

———. 1997. "Turkish journalists protest threats." 14 May, 5.

———. 1997. "IAF helps put out fire at Turkish munitions factory." 6 July, 12.

———. 1997. "Algerian massacres claim 50." 1 October, 6.

———. 1997. "Gunmen kill 29 in Southwest Algeria." 2 November, 7.

———. 1997. "Algerian gov't behind '95 bombs, paper." 10 November, 6.

———. 1998. "55 more killed in Algeria." 11 January, 1.

———. 1998. "EU to send ministers to Algeria." 16 January, 6.

———. 1998. "US: Jobs, housing will save Algeria." 10 February, 7.

———. 1998. "Algeria imposes Arabic as official language." 5 July, 5.

———. 1998. "Investigators suspect Semtex used in attacks." 12 August, 1.

———. 1998. "SA bomb kills 2 in revenge for US attacks." 26 August, 1.

———. 1998. "S. African police detain 3 in Planet Hollywood bombing." 28 August, 1.

———. 1998. Ecevit asked to form new Turkish gov't." 3 December, 7.

———. 1999. "Bomb blast kills one, injures eight in Istanbul." 11 March, 7.

———. 1999. "Algerian leader approves plan to end war." 13 June, 5.

———. 1999. "Kahanist youth convicted of terror activities." 17 September, A-9.

———. 1999. "Raviv trial begins." 4 October, 2.

———. 1999. "Jihad calls for revenge, appoints new leader." 30 October, 1.

Johnson, Chalmers. 1978. "Perspectives on Terrorism." In *The Terrorism Reader: A Historical Anthology*, ed. Walter Laqueur. New York: New American Library.

———. 1982. *Revolutionary Change*. 2nd ed. Stanford, Calif.: Stanford University Press.

Johnston, David. 1999. "Few Answers About Man Being Held in Bomb Case." *New York Times*, 21 December, A-24.

Joint Publications Research Service. 1994. (internet). "PKK Said Developing Strategy for Assassinations." *JPRS-TOT-94-025-L*, Publish Date: 06/14/1994. City source: Ankara Turkish Daily News; Document Id: 0dhyoih00qh90z.

———. 1994. "Turkey, Iran Improve Counterterrorism Relations." *JPRS-TOT-94-026-L*, Publish date: 06/16/1994, City source: Ankara TURKISH DAILY NEWS, Document Id: 0dhyiqq043hzfx.

———. 1994. (Internet.) "Egypt Considered Bombing Khartoum 'Terrorist' Sites." *JPRS-TOT-94-036-L*, Publish Date: 08/20/1994, City source: Beirut AL-SAFIR, Document Id: 0dhy84i02jelte.

———. 1994. (Internet.) "National Transition Council Member Assassinated— Shot At Home." *JPRS-TOT-94-036-L*, Publish Date: 08/25/1994, City source: Paris AFP, Document id: odhy84j00px1x3.

———. 1994. (Internet.) "Dev-Sol Leader Captured in France; Extradition Underway—Interrogated by French Police." *JPRS-TOT-94-039-L*, Publish Date: 09/12/1994, City source: Paris AFP, Document Id: 0dhxw8bo2tduq4.

———. 1994. (Internet.) "Dev-Sol Leader Captured in France; Extradition Underway—Charged With 'Terrorist' Offenses." *JPRS-TOT-94-039-L*, Publish Date: 09/12/1994, City source: Paris AFP, Document Id: 0dhxwk600y23sx.

———. 1994 (Internet.) "New Group Kills Former Justice Minister in Ankara." *JPRS-TOT-94-041-L*, Publish Date: 09/29/1994; City source: Ankara ANATOLIA; Document Id: 0dhxoj902z5q15.

———. 1994. "German Police Raid on 76 PKK Front Organizations Detailed." *JPRS-TOT-94-049-L*, Publication Date: 12/10/1994, City source: Ankara Turkish Daily News: Document Id: Odiaszao2h6j10.

———.1995. (Internet.) "Armed Islamic Group Says Ready to Stop War." *JPRS-TOT-95-003-L*, Publish Date: 01/15/1995, City source: Paris AFP, Document Id: 0di9t9802bsj07.

———. 1995. (Internet.) "Paroled Turkish Dev-Sol Leader Vanishes in France— Not Seen Since Releleased (sic) on Parole." *JPRS-TOT-95-005-L*, Publish Date: 02/07/1995 City source: Paris AFP, Document Id: 0di2hed02dvnyb.

Joyner, Christopher C. 1988. "In Search for an Anti-Terrorism Policy: Lessons from the Reagan Era." *Terrorism* 11 (1): 29-42.

Juckes, Jim J. 1995. *Opposition in South Africa: The Leadership of Z. K. Mathews, Nelson Mandela, and Stephen Biko.* Westport, Conn.: Praeger.

Jung, Carl G. 1933. *Modern Man in Search of a Soul.* Translated by W. S. Dell and Cary F. Baynes. New York: Harcourt Brace Jovanovich.

Kapil, Arun. 1998. "The Algerian Civil War: A Review Essay." *Middle East Studies Association Bulletin* 32 (2): 155-160.

Kaplan, Abraham. 1978. "The Psychodynamics of Terrorism." *Terrorism: An International Journal* 1 (3/4): 237-254.

Karber, Phillip A., and R. William Mengel. 1983. "Political and Economic Forces Affecting Terrorism" In *Managing Terrorism: Strategies for the Corporate Executive,* eds. Patrick J. Montana and George S. Roukis. Westport, Conn.: Quorum Books.

Karpat, Kemal H., ed. 1968. *Political and Social Thought in the Contemporary Middle East.* New York: Praeger.

Karpat, Kemal H. 1981. "Turkish Democracy at Impasse: Ideology, Party Politics and the Third Military Intervention." *International Journal of Turkish Studies* 2 (1): 1-43.

———. 1982. "Millets and Nationality: The Roots of the Incongruity of Nation and State in the Post Ottoman Era." In *The Arabic-Speaking Lands*. Vol. 2 of *Christians and Jews in the Ottoman Empire: The Functioning of a Plural Society*, eds. Benjamin Braude and Bernard Lewis. New York: Holmes & Meier.

Kash, Douglas A. 1998. "An International Legislative Approach to 21st-Century Terrorism." In *The Future of Terrorism: Violence in the New Millennium*, ed. Harvey W. Kushner. Thousand Oaks, Calif.: Sage.

Katz, Samuel. 1968. *Days of Fire*. Garden City, N.Y.: Doubleday.

Kedourie, Elie. 1992. *Politics in the Middle East*. Oxford University Press.

Keinon, Herb. 1993. "Kahane Hai calls arrests 'provocation'." *Jerusalem Post*, 14 July.

———. 1994. "Ariel mother slain by terrorists: husband, daughters survive midnight ambush on Samaria road." *Jerusalem Post*, 20 February, 1.

———. 1995. "Police ordered to investigate Zo Artzenu for inciting rebellion." *Jerusalem Post*, 29 August, 1.

———. 1995. "IDF pulls out of Ramallah today." *Jerusalem Post*, 27 December, 1, 4.

———. 1996. "Ideological Front seeks permit to stage protest against Oslo Accords at Rabin's grave." *Jerusalem Post*, 20 December, 2.

———. 1996. "New group formed to promote teachings of Meir Kahane." *Jerusalem Post*, 1 November, 18.

———. 1997. "Zo Artzenu leaders guilty of sedition." *Jerusalem Post*, 3 September, 3.

———. 1998. "Yassin: Is the sheikh a real threat?" *Jerusalem Post*, 12 June, 13.

Keinon, Herb, and Bill Hutman. 1994. "Kach, Kahane Chai vow to continue in new guise." *Jerusalem Post*, 14 March, 2.

Kellet, Anthony, Bruce Beanlands, and James Deacon. 1991. *Terrorism in Canada, 1960-1989*. Ottawa: Solicitor General, Canada Ministry Secretariat.

Kepel, Gilles. 1985. *Muslim Extremism in Egypt: The Prophet and Pharaoh*. Translated by Jon Rothschild. Los Angeles: University of California Press.

Keesings Worldwide. 1994. (Internet). Vol. 40 (June 1994), Turkey. "Bomb attacks on turkish resorts" (wysiwyg://doc.3/http://keesings.gvpi.net/ . . . ntry%3ATurkey%5D%20%7C%20)&x=Advanced&2.0).

———. 1994. (Internet). Vol. 40 (July 1994), Israel. "Bomb attacks on Israeli targets" (wysiwyg://doc.45/http://keesings.gvpi.net. . .20year%3A1989% 5D%20%7C%20)&x=Advanced&2.0).

———. 1994. (Internet). Vol. 40 (September 1994), Turkey. "Arrest of Dev-Sol Leader" (wysiwyg://doc.3/http://keesings.gvpi.net/ . . . ntry%3ATurkey%5D%20%7C%20)&x=Advanced&2.0).

———. 1994. (Internet). Vol. 40 (November 1994), Algeria. "Hijack" (wysiwyg://doc.8/http://keesings.gvpi.net/ . . . try%3AAlgeria% 5D%20%7C%20)&x=Advanced&2.0.

———. 1995. (Internet). Vol. 44 (January 1995), Turkey. "German Ruling on PKK-failed attack on airbase" (wysiwyg://doc.3/http://keesings.gvpi.net/ . . . ntry%3ATurkey%5D%20%7c%20)&x=Advanced&2.0).

———. 1995. (Internet). Vol. 41 (March 1995), Turkey. "Alawite allegations against security forces—Further riots" (wysiwyg://doc.3/http://keesings.gvpi.net/ . . . ntry%3ATurkey%5D%20%7C%20)&x=Advanced&2.0).

———. 1995. (Internet). Vol. 41 (November 1995) Egypt. (wysiwyg://doc. 45/http://keesings.gvpi.net . . . 20year%3A1989%5D%20%7C%20)&x= Advanced&2.0).

———. 1996. (Internet). Vol. 42 (January 1996) Turkey. "Killing of businessmen" (wysiwyg://doc.3/http://keesings.gvpi.net/ . . . ntry%3ATurkey%5D%20%7C%20)&x=Advanced&2.0).

———. 1998. (Internet). "Hijacking of Airliner" (wysiwyg://doc.3/http://keesings.gvpi.net/ . . . ntry%3ATurkey%5D%20%7C%20)&x=Advanced &2.0).

———. 1999. (Internet). Vol. 45 (May). "New leader for Islamic extremist group" (wysiwyg://doc.4/http://keesings.gvpi.net/ . . . try%3AAlgeria%5D%20%7C%20)&x=Advanced&2.0).

Khalaf, Samir. 1982. "Communal Conflict in Nineteenth-Century Lebanon." In *The Arabic-Speaking Lands*. Vol. 2 of *Christians and Jews in the Ottoman Empire: The Functioning of a Plural Society,* eds. Benjamin Braude and Bernard Lewis. New York: Holmes & Meier.

Khashan, Hilal. 1997. "The new Arab cold war." *World Affairs*, Spring 159 (4): 1-13 (Internet: http://proquest.umi.com/pqdweb?TS=970615 . . . = 1&Dtp=1&Did=000000011654290&Mtd=1&Fmt=).

Khatib, al-Majid. 1999. "German Intelligence: Fundamentalists Are Preparing New Terror Campaign in the West." (Internet). "Germany's BND Warns of New Terror Campaign in the West." *FBIS-WEU-1999-0601*. Publish Date: 05/31/1999, City source: London Al-Sharq al-Awsat, Document Id: 0fcpucr02sduoa.

Khiari, Rachid. 1994. "Algeria launches anti-Islamist offensive." *Jerusalem Post,* 7 November, 4.

Khouri, Fred J. 1976. *The Arab-Israeli Dilemma Second Edition*. Syracuse, N.Y.: Syracuse University Press.

Kibble, David G. 1996. "The Threat of Militant Islam: A Fundamental Reappraisal." *Studies in Conflict & Terrorism* 19: 353-364.

Kifner, John. 1988. "2 Recount '48 Killing in Israel." *New York Times*, 12 September, A-3.

———. 1990. "Kahane Suspect Is a Muslim with a Series of Addresses." *New York Times*, 7 November.

———. 1990. "Kahane Suspect Said to Have Arms Cache." *New York Times*, 11 December, B-1.

———. 1999. "Terrorists Said to Hide in Canada's Melting Pot." *New York Times*, 24 December, A-8.

Kifner, John, and William K. Rashbaum. 1999. "Brooklyn Man Is Charged with Aiding in Bomb Plot." *New York Times*, 31 December, 1.

King, Neil, Jr. 1999. "Instead of Big Strikes, U.S.'s Terrorism Battle Focuses on Harassing Would-Be Troublemakers." *Wall Street Journal*, 4 August, 1.

Kissinger, Henry A. 1999. "New World Disorder." *Newsweek*, 31 May, 41-43.

Klan Watch Intelligence Report. 1996. "Terrorists in the Name of God and Race: Phineas Priests Use Religious Arguments to Justify Their Violent Crimes." No. 83 (August), 1, 3.

———. 1996. "Three Suspected Phineas Priests Charged in Spokane Bombings: Idaho Militants Linked to Prominent Identity Minister and Publication." No. 24 (November), 1, 4.

Klein, Amy. 1998. "Hai Vikayam members acquitted." *Jerusalem Post*, 14 September, 2.

Kolko, Gabriel. 1988. *The Politics of War: The World and United States Foreign Policy, 1943-1945.* New York: Random House.

Kolodziej, Edward A. 1996. "Thinking about Coping: Actors, Resources, Roles, and Strategies." In *Coping with Conflict after the Cold War*, eds. Edward Kolodziej and Roger E. Kanet. Baltimore, Md.: Johns Hopkins University Press.

Kolodziej, Edward A., and I. William Zartman. 1996. "Introduction: Coping with Conflict: A Global Approach." In *Coping with Conflict after the Cold War*, eds. Kolodziej and Roger Kanet. Baltimore, Md.: Johns Hopkins University Press.

Kramer, Martin. 1997. "The Oracle of Hizbullah: Sayyid Muhammad Husayn Fadlallah." In *Spokesmen of the Despised: Fundamentalist Leaders of the Middle East*, ed. R. Scott Appleby. Chicago: University of Chicago Press.

Kuhn, Thomas S. 1970. *The Structure of Scientific Revolutions.* Chicago: University of Chicago Press.

Kupperman, Robert H., and Robert A. Friedlander. 1979. "Terrorism and Social Control: Challenge and Response." *Ohio Northern University Law Review* 6 (1): 52-59.

Kushner, Harvey W. 1998. "The New Terrorism." In *The Future of Terrorism; Violence in the New Millennium.* Thousand Oaks, Calif.: Sage.

Kuttler, Hillel. 1998. "Egypt, US to discuss cutting aid." *Jerusalem Post,* 21 June, 3.

Kuzmin, Oleg. 1999. (Internet). "Karimov Blames Hezbollah for Tashkent Bombs." *FBIS-NES-1999-0218,* Publish Date: 02/18/1999; City source: Moscow ITAR-TASS World Service, Document Id: 0fhsrpn00ilnuw.

Labaton, Stephen. 1999. "National Security Adviser Warns of Risk of Terrorism." *New York Times,* 20 December, A-30.

Lahoud, Lamia. 1992. "Inside the Black Panthers' den in the mountains of Jenin." *Jerusalem Post,* 3 July.

Lakos, Amos. 1991. *Terrorism 1980-1990: A Bibliography.* Boulder, Colo.: Westview Press.

Lancaster, John. 1999. (Internet). "U.S. Moves toward Better Ties to Libya." *Washington Post.* (wysiwyg://23/http://www.washington...enews/terror/A31290-1999Dec24.html). 24 December.

Laqueur, Walter. 1987. "Reflections on Terrorism." In *The Terrorism Reader: A Historical Anthology,* eds. Laqueur and Yonah Alexander. New York: New American Library.

———. 1999. *The New Terrorism: Fanaticism and the Arms of Mass Destruction.* New York: Oxford University Press.

Laqueur, Walter, and Yonah Alexander, eds. 1987. *The Terrorism Reader: A Historical Anthology.* New York: New American Library.

Lasswell, Harold D. 1935. *World Politics and Personal Insecurity.* New York: Whittlesey House, McGraw Hill.

———. 1950. *National Security and Individual Freedom.* New York: McGraw-Hill.

———. 1978. "Terrorism and the Political Process." *Terrorism: An International Journal* 1 (3/4): 255-263.

Laurance, Edward J. 1996. "The Role of Arms Control in Coping with Conflict after the Cold War." In *Coping with Conflict after the Cold War,* eds. Edward A. Kolodziej and Roger Kanet. Baltimore, Md.: Johns Hopkins University Press.

Lederach, John Paul. 1997. *Building Peace: Sustainable Reconciliation in Divided Societies.* Washington, D.C.: United States Institute of Peace Press.

Leedy, Paul D. 1993. *Practical Research Planning and Design.* 5th ed. New York: Macmillan.

Legrain, Jean-Francois. 1994. "Palestinian Islamisms: Patriotism as a Condition of Their Expansion." In *Accounting for Fundamentalisms: The Dynamic Character of Movements,* eds. Martin E. Marty and R. Scott Appleby. Chicago: University of Chicago Press.

———. 1997. "HAMAS: Legitimate Heir of Palestinian Nationalism?" In *Political Islam: Revolution, Radicalism, or Reform?* ed. John L. Esposito. Boulder, Colo.: Lynne Rienner.

Lehn, Walter. 1988. *The Jewish National Fund*. New York: Kegan Paul International.

Lenczowski, George. 1980. *The Middle East in World Affairs*. 4th ed. Ithaca, N.Y.: Cornell University Press.

Lewis, Bernard. 1960. *The Arabs in History*. London: Hutchinson.

———. 1979. *The Emergence of Modern Turkey*. 2nd ed. London: Oxford University Press.

———. 1993. *The Arabs in History*. London: Oxford University Press.

Lifton, Robert Jay. 1986. *The Nazi Doctors; Medical Killing and the Psychology of Genocide*. New York: Basic Books.

Lindblom, Charles. 1980. *The Policy-Making Process*. 2nd ed. Englewood Cliffs, N.J.: Prentice Hall.

Linowes, David F. 1996. "Privatization." In *Coping with Conflict after the Cold War*, eds. Edward A. Kolodziej and Roger E. Kanet. Baltimore, Md.: Johns Hopkins University Press.

Livingstone Neil C., and Terrell E. Arnold. 1986. "Democracy Under Attack." In *Fighting Back and Winning the War against Terrorism*, eds. Neil C. Livingstone and Terrell E. Arnold. Lexington, Mass.: D. C. Heath.

Livingstone, Neil C., and David Halevy. 1990. *Inside the PLO: Covert Units, Secret Funds and the War Against Israel and the United States*. New York: William Morrow.

Livingstone, Richard Winn, ed. 1946. *The History of the Peloponnesian War*. London: H. Milford, Oxford University Press.

Long, David E. 1990. *The Anatomy of Terrorism*. New York: Free Press.

Lopez, George A. 1986. "National Security Ideology as an Impetus to State Violence and State Terror." In *Government, Violence and Repression: An Agenda for Research*, eds. Michael Stohl and George Lopez. Westport, Conn.: Greenwood Press.

Luckabaugh, Robert H., Edward Fuqua, Joseph P. Cangemi, and Casimir J. Kowalski. 1997. "Terrorist Behavior and United States Foreign Policy: Who Is the Enemy? Some Psychological and Political Perspectives." *Psychology: A Journal of Human Behavior* 34 (2): 1-16.

Lustick, Ian S. 1980. *Arabs in the Jewish State: Israel's Control of a National Minority*. Austin: University of Texas Press.

———. 1988. *For the Land and the Lord: Jewish Fundamentalism in Israel*. New York: Council on Foreign Relations.

———. 1993. *Unsettled States, Disputed Lands: Britain and Ireland, France and Algeria, Israel and the West Bank*. Ithaca, N.Y.: Cornell University Press.

MacLeod, Scott. 1996. "The Paladin of Jihad." *Time*, 6 May, 51-52.

Makovsky, David. 1994. "Israel targets in US threatened: missions on alert after second bomb explodes in London." *Jerusalem Post*, 28 July, 1.

——. 1994. "Cabinet bans Kach, Kahane Chai." *Jerusalem Post,* 14 March, 1, 2.

——. 1995. "Israel, PA on verge of closing Oslo 2 deal." *Jerusalem Post,* 24 September, 1.

——. 1995. "Cabinet to approve Oslo 2 pact today." *Jerusalem Post,* 27 September, 1.

——. 1995. "Inside look at what Oslo says." *Jerusalem Post,* 8 October, 3.

Makram-Ebid, Mona. 1996. "Egypt's 1995 Elections: One Step Forward, Two Steps Back?" *Middle East Policy* 4 (3): 119-136.

Mango, Andrew. 1994. *Turkey: the Challenge of a New Role—the Washington Papers/163.* Washington, D.C.: Center for Strategic and International Studies.

——. 1995. "Turkey in Winter." *Middle Eastern Studies,* July 31 (3): 1-23. (Internet: http://proquest.umi.com/pqdweb?TS=970614 . . . &Fmt= 3&Sid=22&Idx=4Deli=1&RQT=309&Dtp=).

Maoz, Moshe. 1968. *Ottoman Reform in Syria and Palestine 1840-1861: The Impact of the Tanzimat on Politics and Society.* London: Oxford University Press.

——. 1982. "Communal Conflict in Ottoman Syria during the Reform Era: The Role of Political and Economic Factors." In *The Arabic-Speaking Lands.* Vol. 2 of *Christians and Jews in the Ottoman Empire: The Functioning of a Plural Society,* eds. Benjamin Braude and Bernard Lewis. New York: Holmes & Meier.

Marcus, Raine. 1994. "Khan Yunis youths admit attempted murder after being arrested for other offenses." *Jerusalem Post,* 29 June, 2.

Markham, James M. 1987. "Hijacking Suspect Arrested by Bonn." *New York Times,* 16 January , A-1.

——. 1987. "Bonn May Balk at Extraditing Terror Suspect." *New York Times,* 17 January, 6.

——. 1987. "Beirut Abductors Linked to Suspect." *New York Times,* 24 January, 5.

Matbaacilik, Feryal. 1983. *State of Anarchy and Terror in Turkey.*

Martin, Marty E., and R. Scott Appleby, eds. 1991. *Fundamentalisms Observed.* Chicago: University of Chicago Press.

Martin, R. C. 1987. "Religious Violence in Islam: Towards an Understanding of the Discourse on Jihad in Modern Egypt." In *Contemporary Research on Terrorism,* eds. Paul Wilkinson and Alasdair M. Stewart. Great Britain: Aberdeen University Press.

Martinez, Dolores. 1996. (Internet). "Spain/Algeria: Police Dismantle GIA Infrastructure in Spain." *FBIS-TOT-96-019-L,* Publish Date: 06/15/1996, City source: Madrid ABC; Document Id: 0dvj53101nwvk4.

Martinez, Luis. 2000. *The Algerian Civil War, 1990-1998,* Jonathan Derrick trans. New York: Columbia University Press.

McEwen, Michael T., and Stephen Sloan. 1980. "Terrorism Preparedness on the State and Local Level: An Oklahoma Perspective." In *Clandestine Tactics and Technology: A Technical and Background Information Service.* Gaithersburg, Md.: International Association of Police Chiefs.

McKinley, James C., Jr. 1990. "Suspect in Kahane Slaying Kept List of Prominent Jews." *New York Times,* 1 December.

———. 1998. "Bombs Rip Apart 2 U.S. Embassies in Africa: Scores Killed; No Firm Motives or Suspects." *New York Times,* 8 August.

———. 1998. "Toll Rises as Rescue Effort Goes on in Kenya." *New York Times,* 9 August.

McKnight, Gerald. 1974. *The Terrorist Mind.* Indianapolis: Bobbs-Merrill.

Medd, Roger, and Frank Goldstein. 1997. "International Terrorism on the Eve of a New Millennium." *Studies in Conflict and Terrorism* 20: 281-316.

Melman, Yossi. 1986. *The Master Terrorist: The True Story Behind Abu Nidal.* New York: Adama Books.

Melson, Robert, and Howard Wolpe. 1971. "Modernization and the Politics of Communalism." In *Nigeria: Modernization and the Politics of Communication,* eds. Melson and Howard Wolpe. East Lansing: Michigan State University Press.

Merari, Ariel. 1978. "A Classification of Terrorist Groups." *Terrorism: An International Journal* 1(3/4): 331-346.

Merari, Ariel, and Yosifa (Daiksel) Braunstein. 1984. "Shi'ite Terrorism: Operational Capabilities and the Suicide Factor." *Terrorism, Violence, Insurgency Journal* 5 (2): 7-10.

Merari, Ariel, Tamar Prat, Sophia Kotzer, Anat Kurz, and Yoram Schweitzer. 1986. *Inter 85: A Review of International Terrorism in 1985.* TelAviv: Jaffee Center for Strategic Studies.

Meri-Lichter, S. 1984. "There Is More Than One T.N.T. Group (*al-Ha'mishmar*)." *Israeli Mirror,* No. 680/8.3.1984.

Mergui, Raphael, and Phillippe Simonnot. 1987. *Israel's Ayatollah's: Meir Kahane and the Far Right in Israel.* London: Saqi Books.

Merkel, Peter H. 1986. "Approaches to the Study of Political Violence." In *Political Violence and Terror: Motifs and Motivations,* ed. Merkel. Berkeley: University of California Press.

Messaoudi, Khalida. 1995. *Unbowed: An Algerian Woman Confronts Islamic Fundamentalism—Interviews with Elisabeth Schemia.* Philadelphia: University of Pennsylvania Press.

Metz, Helen Chapin, ed. 1994. *Algeria: A Country Study.* 5th ed. Washington, D.C.: Library of Congress.

Mickolus, Edward F. 1976. "Negotiating for Hostages: A Policy Dilemma." *Orbis: A Journal of World Affairs* 19 (4): 1309-1325.

———. 1980. *Transnational Terrorism: A Chronology of Events, 1968-1979.* Westport, Conn.: Greenwood.

———. 1989. *International Terrorism in the 1980's: A Chronology of Events.* Vol. 2 (1984-1987). Ames: Iowa State University Press.

———. 1993. *Terrorism, 1988-1991: A Chronology of Events and a Selectively Annotated Bibliography.* Westport, Conn.: Greenwood.

Mickolus, Edward, F., Todd Sandler, and Jean M. Murdock. 1989. *International Terrorism in the 1980's: A Chronology of Events.* Vol. 1 (1980-1983). Ames: Iowa State University Press.

Mickolus Edward F., with Susan L. Simmons. 1997. *Terrorism, 1992-1995: A Chronology of Events and a Selectively Annotated Bibliography.* Westport, Conn.: Greenwood.

Middle East International. "Oslo Peace Process." (Internet http:www.medea.be/en/index133.htm.)

Miller, Charles. 1997. "Rifkind Pledges Tough Line Against Muslim Extremists." *FBIS-TOT-95-022-L,* Publish Date: 01/18//1997: City source: London Press Association, Document Id: 0dk7hmdoifs6no.

Miller, Judith. 2000. "Suspect in New Year's Terror Plot Is Arrested in Algeria." *New York Times,* 7 December, A-3.

———. 2001. "Dissecting a Terror Plot from Boston to Amman—Holy Warriors: The Jordanian Connection." *New York Times,* 15 January. A-1.

Miller, Rubin. 1986. "Acts of International Terrorism: Governments' Responses and Policies." *Comparative Political Studies* 19 (3): 385-413.

Mitchell, Richard P. 1969. *The Society of the Muslim Brothers.* London: Oxford University Press.

Modelski, George. 1978. "The Long Cycle of Global Politics and the Nation State." *Comparative Studies in Society and History* 20 (2): 214-235.

Mohindra, S. 1993. *Terrorist Games Nations Play.* New Delhi, India: Lancer.

Molander, Roger C., Andrew S. Riddile, and Peter A. Wilson. 1996. *Strategic Information Warfare: a New Face of War.* Santa Monica, Calif.: National Defense Research Institute, RAND.

Mortimer, Robert 1991. "Islam and Multiparty Politics in Algeria." *The Middle East Journal* 45 (4): 575-593.

Moore, John V., and Robert G. Smith Jr. 1953. "Some Aspects of Noncommissioned Officer Leadership." *Personal Psychology* 6: 427-443.

Moxon-Browne, Edward. 1981. "Terrorism in Northern Ireland: The Case of the Provisional IRA." In *Terrorism: A Challenge to the State,* ed. Juliet Lodge. New York: St. Martin's Press.

Mulholland, David. 1999. "U.S. Funding Boost Counters Mass Destruction Weapons." *Defense News,* 16 August.

Muller, Mark. 1996. "Nationalism and the Rule of Law in Turkey: The Elimination of Kurdish Representation During the 1990's." In *The Kurdish Nationalist Movement in the 1990's: Its Impact on Turkey and the Middle East,* ed. Robert W. Olson. Lexington: The University Press of Kentucky.

Murphy, John F. 1974, 1975. "United Nations Proposals on the Central and Repression of Terrorism." In *International Terrorism and Political Crimes,* eds. M. Cherif Bassiouni. Springfield, Ill.: Charles C. Thomas.

———. 1978. "Protected Persons and Diplomatic Facilities." In *Legal Aspects of International Terrorism,* eds. Alona E. Evans and John F. Murphy. Lexington, Mass.: Lexington Books.

Myers, Steven Lee, Barbara Crossette, Judith Miller, and Tim Weiner. 1998. "U.S. Says Iraq Aided Production of Chemical Weapons in Sudan." *New York Times,* 25 August, A-1.

Myers, Steven Lee. 2000. "Destroyer Damaged: 6 Dead, 11 Missing—U.S. Sees Terrorism and Vows Response." *New York Times,* 13 October, A-1.

———. 2000. "U.S. Officials Tell of Getting Warning Last Month, but Say It Was Too Vague." *New York Times,* 14 October, A-10.

Nasr, Kameel B. 1997. *Arab and Israeli Terrorism: The Causes and Effects of Political Violence, 1936-1993.* Jefferson, N.C.: McFarland.

Nasser, Jamal R. 1991. *The Palestine Liberation Organization: From Armed Struggle to the Declaration of Independence.* New York: Praeger.

National Congress of the Palestine Liberation Organization. *The Palestinian National Charter* of 1968 *reproduced in* 3 The Arab-Israeli Conflict 706 (J.N. Moore ed. 1974).

National Foreign Assessment Center. 1980. *International Terrorism in 1979.* Washington, D.C.: Central Intelligence Agency.

National Geographic Atlas of the World. 1990. 6th ed. Washington, D.C.: National Geographic Society.

National Governor's Association Emergency Preparedness Project. 1979. *Domestic Terrorism.* Washington, D.C.: Center for Policy Research, National Governor's Association.

Nef, Jorge. 1978. "Some Thoughts on Contemporary Terrorism: Domestic and International Perspectives." *Terrorism in Theory and Practice: Proceedings of a Colloquium,* ed. John Carson. Toronto: Atlantic Council of Canada.

Nelan, Bruce W. 1994. "Raging against peace: Still furious over the Hebron massacre, palestinians insist Rabin's concessions are not enough." *Time,* March.

Netanyahu, Benjamin. 1986. "Terrorism: How the West Can Win." In *Terrorism: How the West Can Win,* ed. Benjamin Netanyahu. New York: Farrar, Straus and Giroux.

New York Times. 1999. "Jordan Seizes 13 and Links Them to Afghan Explosives Training." 16 December, A-13.

Nigogosian, Aram. 1996. "Turkey's Kurdish Problem: Recent Trends." In *The Kurdish Nationalist Movement in the 1990's: Its Impact on Turkey and the Middle East,* ed. Robert W. Olson. Lexington: University Press of Kentucky.

Nordlinger, Eric A. 1968. "Political Development: Time Sequences and Rates of Change." *World Politics: A Quarterly Journal of International Relations* 20 (October 1967-July 1968): 494-520.

Norton, Augustus R. 1987. *Amal and the Shi'a: Struggle for the Soul of Lebanon.* Austin: University of Texas Press.

——. 1988. "Terrorism in the Middle East." In *Terrorist Dynamics,* ed. Vittorfranco S. Pisano. Arlington, Va.: International Association of Chiefs of Police.

Norusis, Marija J. 1990. *SPSS/PC+ Advanced Statistics 4.0 for the IBM PC/XT and PS/2.* Chicago: SPSS.

——. 1991. *The SPSS Guide to Data Analysis.* 2nd ed. Chicago: SPSS.

Nutting, Ruth L. 1923. "Some Characteristics of Leadership." *School and Society* 18 (457): 387-390.

Nye, Joseph S., Jr. 1993. *Understanding International Conflicts: An Introduction to Theory and History.* New York: HarperCollins College Publishers.

——. 1997. *Understanding International Conflicts: An Introduction to Theory and History.* 2nd ed. New York: Longman.

O'Ballance, Edgar. 1997. *Islamic Fundamentalist Terrorism, 1979-95; The Iranian Connection.* New York: New York University Press.

——. 1998. *The Palestinian Intifada.* New York: St. Martin's Press.

O'Brian, William V. 1985. "Counterterrorism: Lessons from Israel." *Strategic Review* 13 (4): 32-44.

O'Callaghan, John. 1998. "Kenya arrests suspects in embassy bombing: IDF rescue team due home." *Jerusalem Post,* 13 August, 1.

O'Day, Alan. 1994. *Dimensions of Irish Terrorism.* New York: G. K. Hall.

Olson, Robert W. 1989. *The Emergence of Kurdish Nationalism and the Sheikh Said Rebellion, 1880-1925.* Austin: University of Texas Press.

Olson, Robert. 1990-91. "The Churchill-Cox Correspondence Regarding The Creation of The State of Iraq: Consequences For British Policy Towards The Nationalist Turkish Government, 1921-1923." *International Journal of Turkish Studies* 5 (1/2): 121-136.

——. 1997. "Turkey-Syria relations since the Gulf War: Kurds and water." *Middle East Policy* May 1997, 5-21. (Internet: http://proquest. umi.com/pqdweb?TS=970613 ... =1&Dtp=1&Did=0000000 194119897&Mtd=1&Fmt=.)

Omoruyi, Omo. 1986. "State Creation and Ethnicity in a Federal (Plural) System: Nigeria's Search for Parity." In *Ethnicity, Politics and Develop-*

ment, eds. Dennis L. Thompson and Dov Ronen. Boulder, Colo.: Lynne Rienner.

O'Neill, Bard E. 1978. "Towards a Typology of Political Terrorism: The Palestinian Resistance Movement." *Journal of International Affairs* 32 (1): 17-42.

Oots, Kent Layne. 1984. "Transnational Terrorism: A Political Organization Approach." Ph.D. diss., Northern Illinois University.

———. 1989. "Organizational Perspectives on the Formation and Disintegration of Terrorist Groups." *Terrorism* 12: 139-152.

Oppenheim, L. 1948. *International Law: A Treatise.* Vol 1. Edited by H. Lauterpacht. London: Longmans, Green.

Orwin, Clifford. 1988. "Stasis and Plague: Thucydides on the Dissolution of Society." *Journal of Politics* 50 (4): 831-847.

Osmond, Russell Lowell. 1979. "Transnational Terrorism 1968-1974: A Quantitative Analysis." Ph.D. diss., Syracuse University.

O'Sullivan, Arieh. 1996. "Hizbullah promises to help find Arad." *Jerusalem Post,* 23 July, 1, 2.

———. 1998. "The problems of 'cyber-terrorism.'" *Jerusalem Post,* 18 March, 4.

———. 1998. "Virtual terror: Threat of a new world disorder." *Jerusalem Post,* 27 March, 15.

———. 1998. "IDF team rescues survivor from Nairobi bomb rubble." *Jerusalem Post,* 9 August, 1.

Oufella, Murad. 1999. "Death fuels the demand for legitimacy." *Jerusalem Post,* 7 December, 9.

Özbudun, Ergun. 1990. "Turkey: Crises, Integrations and Reequilibriums." In *Politics in Developing Countries: Comparing Experiences with Democracy.* Boulder, Colo.: Lynne Rienner.

Pacal, Jan. 1998. "Turkey: Islamist IBDA-C Structure, Links Examined." *FBIS-TOT-96-021-L,* Publish Date: 09/06/1998, City source: Ankara TURKISH DAILY NEWS, Document Id: 0dwmcj9036qrn2.

Parker, Christopher. 1999. *Resignation or Revolt? Sociopolitical Development and the Challenges of Peace in Palestine.* New York: I. B. Tauris.

Parry, Albert. 1976. *Terrorism from Robespierre to Arafat.* New York: Vanguard Press.

Parsons, Talcott. 1964. *Max Weber: The Theory of Social and Economic Organization.* New York: Free Press.

Pearlman, Moshe. 1970. *Ben Gurion Looks Back in Talks with Moshe Pearlman.* New York: Schocken Books.

Pearson, Frederic S. 1974. "Geographic Proximity and Foreign Military Intervention." *The Journal of Conflict Resolution* 18 (3): 432-460.

Pearson, Frederic S., and J. Martin Rochester. 1998. *International Relations: The Global Condition in the Twenty-First Century.* Boston: McGraw-Hill.

Peleg, Ilan. 1988. "Terrorism in the Middle East: The Case of the Arab-Israeli Conflict." In *The Politics of Terrorism.* 3rd ed., ed. Michael S. Stohl. New York: Marcel Dekker.

Perdue, William D. 1989. *Terrorism and the State: A Critique of Domination through Fear.* New York: Praeger.

Peri, Yoram. 1983. *Between Battles and Ballots: Israeli Military in Politics.* Cambridge, England: Cambridge University Press.

Perlmutter, Amos. 1969. *Military and Politics in Israel: Nation-Building and Role Expansion.* New York: Praeger.

Perlez, Jane. 1998. "U.S. Experts Arrive to Study Clues in Blast That Killed 9." *New York Times,* 9 August, 10.

———. 2000. "Arafat's Task: Negotiating Sacred Ground." *New York Times,* 12 September, A-10.

———. 2001. "U.S. Scolds Russia for Plans to Resume Arms Sales to Iran." *New York Times,* 15 March, A-15.

Pfaltzgraf, Robert L., Jr. 1986. "Implications for American Policy." In *Hydra of Carnage: The International Linkages of Terrorism and Other Low-Intensity Operations,* eds. Uri Ra'anan, Robert L. Pfaltzgraf Jr., Richard H. Shultz, Ernest Halperin, and Igor Lukes. Lexington, Mass.: D. C. Heath.

Philipp, Thomas. 1982. "Image and Self-Image of the Syrians in Egypt: From the Early Eighteenth Century to the Reign of Muhammad Ali." In *The Arabic Speaking Lands.* Vol. 1 of *Christians and Jews in the Ottoman Empire: The Functioning of a Plural Society,* eds. Benjamin Braude and Bernard Lewis. New York: Holmes & Meier.

Pinkas, Alon. 1994. "IDF kills Fatah Hawk in Gaza clash." *Jerusalem Post,* 4 February, 1.

———. 1994. "Anatomy of the autonomy." *Jerusalem Post,* 4 May, 1.

———. 1994. "Jaffe Center head suggests modifying Oslo agreement." *Jerusalem Post,* 16 November, 1.

———. 1995. "Appeals court overturns terrorist's death sentence." *Jerusalem Post,* 2 June, 3.

Pinkas, Alon, and John Immanuel. 1995. "Mossad reportedly kills Jihad leader Shkaki." *Jerusalem Post,* 29 October, 1.

Pion-Berlin, David, and George A. Lopez. 1991. "Of Victims and Executioners: Argentine State Terror, 1975-1979." *International Studies Quarterly* 35: 87-108.

Pisano, Vittorfranco S., ed. *Terrorist Dynamics.* Arlington, Va.: International Association of Police Chiefs.

Piscatori, James. 1994. "Accounting for Islamic Fundamentalisms." In *Accounting for Fundamentalisms: The Dynamic Character of Movements,* eds. Martin E. Marty and R. Scott Appleby. Chicago: University of Chicago Press.

Pluchinsky, Dennis. 1981. "Political Terrorism in Western Europe: Some Themes and Variations." In *Terrorism in Europe,* eds. Yonah Alexander and Kenneth A. Meyers. New York: St. Martin's Press.

Post, Jerrold M. 1984. "Notes on a Psychodynamic Theory of Terrorist Behavior." *Terrorism: An International Journal* 7 (3): 241-256.

Pyes, Craig, John Kifner, Sam Howe Verhovek, and John F. Burns. 1999. "Arrest at U.S. Border Reverberates in France." *New York Times,* 22, December, 1.

Quandt, William B. 1977. *Decade of Decisions: American Policy toward the Arab-Israeli Conflict, 1967-1976.* Berkeley: University of California Press.

Quester, George H. 1988. "Some Explanations for State-Supported Terrorism in the Middle East." In *Terrible Beyond Endurance? The Foreign Policy of State Terrorism,* eds. Michael S. Stohl and Gary A. Lopez. Westport, Conn.: Greenwood Press.

Rabi, Muhammad Mahmoud. 1967. *The Political Theory of Ibn Khaldun.* Leiden, Netherlands: E. J. Brill.

Raitberger, Francois. 1997. "Algeria to accept revel cease-fire." *Jerusalem Post,* 25 September, 5.

Ranstorp, Magnus. 1996. "Terrorism in the Name of Religion." *Journal of International Affairs* 50 (1): 41-62.

———. 1997. *Hizb'allah in Lebanon: The Politics of the Western Hostage Crisis.* London: Macmillan.

———. 1998. "Interpreting the Broader Context and Meaning of Bin-Laden's Fatwa." *Studies in Conflict & Terrorism* 21: 321-330.

Rapaport, David C. 1984. "Fear and Trembling: Terrorism in Three Religious Traditions." *American Political Science Review* 78: 658-675.

Rapoport, D. C. 1987. "Why Does Religious Messianism Produce Terror?" In *Contemporary Research on Terrorism,* eds. Paul Wilkinson and Alasdair M. Stewart. Great Britain: Aberdeen University Press.

Rapaport, Era. 1996. *Letters from Tel Mond Prison: An Israeli Settler Defends His Act of Terror.* New York: Free Press.

Reich, Bernard, ed. 1995. *Arab-Israeli Conflict and Conciliation, a Documentary History.* Westport, Conn.: Greenwood Press.

Reiss, Albert J., Jr., and Jeffrey A. Roth, eds. 1993. *Understanding and Preventing Violence.* Washington, D.C.: National Academy Press.

Ring, Wilson. 1999. "Border Suspect Tied to Terror Group." (washingtonpost.com) 23 December (wyswyg://12/http://www.washington. . . dyn/articles/A29335-1999Dec23.html).

Roberts, Hugh. 1991. "A Trial of Strength: Algerian Islamism." In *Islamic Fundamentalisms and the Gulf Crisis,* ed. James Piscatori. Chicago: American Academy of Arts and Sciences.

———. 1994. "From Radical Mission to Equivocal Ambition: The Expansion and Manipulation of Algerian Islamism, 1979-1992." In *Accounting for Fundamentalisms: The Dynamic Character of Movements,* eds. Martin E. Marty and R. Scott Appleby. Chicago: University of Chicago Press.

———. 1995. "Algeria's ruinous impasse and the honorable way out." *International Affairs* 71 (2): 247-267.

Rohde, David. 2001. "Afghan Rebels Courted by U.S. and Russia to Defy Taliban." *New York Times,* 25 September, B1.

Roncek, Dennis W. 1991. "Using Logit Coefficients to Obtain the Effects of Independent Variables on Changes in Probabilities." *Social Forces* 70 (2): 509-518.

Ronchey, Alberto. 1978. "Terror in Italy, Between Red and Black." *Dissent* 25 (2): 150-156.

Ronen,. Dov. 1986. "Ethnicity, Politics, and Development: An Introduction." In *Ethnicity, Politics and Development,* eds. Dennis L. Thompson and Dov Ronen. Boulder, Colo.: Lynne Rienner.

Rosenberg, Robert. 1983. "Security forces probing West Bank vigilantes." *Jerusalem Post,* 16 May.

———. 1984. "Major anti-Arab terror cases cracked by security services." *Jerusalem Post,* 3 May.

———. 1984. "Suspects show pride in Jewish terror action." *Jerusalem Post,* 4 May.

———. 1984. "Seven more Jewish terror arrests." *Jerusalem Post,* 8 May.

———. 1984. Gush Emunim leader claims political, military chiefs 'urged settlers to act.'" *Jerusalem Post,* 19 June.

Ross, Jeffrey Ian. 1993. "Structural Causes of Oppositional Political Terrorism: Towards a Causal Model." *Journal of Peace Research* 30 (3): 317-329.

Ross, Jeffrey Ian, ed. 1995. *Violence in Canada: Sociopolitical Perspectives.* Toronto: Oxford University Press.

Ross, Jeffrey Ian, and R. Reuben Miller. 1997. "The Effects of Oppositional Political Terrorism: Five Actor-Based Models." *Low Intensity Conflict and Law Enforcement* 6 (3) (winter): 76-107.

Ross, Jeffery Ian, and Ted Robert Gurr. 1989. "Why Terrorism Subsides: A Comparative Study of Canada and the United States." *Comparative Politics* 21 (4): 405-426.

Rothman, Jay. 1992. *From Confrontation to Cooperation: Resolving Ethnic and Regional Conflict.* Newbury Park, Calif.: Sage.

Rowe, Dennis. 1988. *Considered Responses To Contemporary Terrorism in Democratic Societies.* Chicago: University of Illinois at Chicago.

Rubenstein, Richard E. 1987. *Alchemists of Revolution: Terrorism in the Modern World*. New York: Basic Books.

———. 1987. "Rebellion in America: The Fire Next Time?" In *Protest, Rebellion, Reform*. Vol. 2 of *Violence in America*, ed. Ted Robert Gurr. Newbury, Calif.: Sage.

Rubin, Barry. 1993. "Hizbullah's goal: Islamic statehood." *Jerusalem Post*, 30 July.

———. 1999. *The Transformation of Palestinian Politics: From Revolution to State-Building*. Cambridge, Mass.: Harvard University Press.

Rudge, David. 1991. "New terror group appears in Lebanon." *Jerusalem Post*, 13 October.

———. 1997. "SLA soldier wounded." *Jerusalem Post*, 29 May, 2.

———. 1997. "Hizbullah power struggle may have sparked attacks." *Jerusalem Post*, 23 May, 18.

———. 1997." 'Algeria gov't still in control." *Jerusalem Post*, 1 September, 12.

———. 1999. "Expert: Syria slowly becoming less totalitarian." *Jerusalem Post*, 3 June, 2.

Rudge, David, and Jay Bushinsky. 1998. "UN Chief discusses Lebanon pullout in Beirut, Damascus." *Jerusalem Post*, 22 March, 1.

Ruedy, John, 1992. *Modern Algeria: The Origins and Development of a Nation*. Indianapolis: Indiana University Press.

Russell, Charles A., Leon J. Banker, and Bowman H. Miller. 1979. "Out-Inventing the Terrorist." In *Terrorism: Theory and Practice*, eds. Yonah Alexander, David Carlton, and Paul Wilkinson. Boulder, Colo.: Westview Press.

Sacher, Howard M. 1976. *A History of Israel: From the Rise of Zionism to Our Time*. New York: Alfred A. Knopf.

Sachs, Susan. 2000. Germans Seeking to Mediate Israel-Lebanon Prisoner Trade." *New York Times*, 13 December, A-10.

Safran, Nadav. 1969. *From War to War: The Arab-Israeli Confrontation, 1948-1967: A Study of the Conflict from the Perspective of Coercion in the Context of Inter-Arab and Big Power Relations*. New York: Western Publishing.

———. 1978. *Israel: The Embattled Ally*. Cambridge, Mass.: Harvard University Press.

St. John, Robert. 1971. *Ben Gurion: A Biography*. Garden City, N.Y.: Doubleday.

Sanger, David E. 2000. "Clinton Warns UN of a New Age of Civil Wars." *New York Times*, 7 September. A-1.

Schachter, Jonathan, and Michael Rotem. 1990. "Security forces on alert for Kahane's funeral." *Jerusalem Post*, 7 November.

Scherer, John L. 1982. *Terrorism: An Annual Survey.* Vol. 1. Minneapolis: J. L. Scherer.

Schiller, David T. 1988. "A Battlegroup Divided: The Palestinian Fedayeen." In *Inside Terrorist Organizations,* ed. David C. Rapaport. New York: Columbia University Press.

Schlagheck, Donna M. 1988. *International Terrorism: An Introduction to the Concepts and Actors.* Lexington, Mass.: Lexington Books.

Schlein, Hanan. 1991. "NEAR EAST: Settlement, Leadership Plans in Kakh Discussed." *JPRS-NEA-91-011* 5 February page 5. ("91P40117A Tel-Aviv MA'ARIV in Hebrew 9 Jan 91 p. 8").

Schmemann, Serge. 1995. "Lives Are at Stake; So Are Postal Services and Gas Tanks." *New York Times,* 29 September, A-13.

———. 1996. "Israeli Forces Seal Off Big Parts of West Bank." *New York Times,* 6 March, A-1.

———. 1997. "Accord on Hebron Gets Endorsement of Israeli Cabinet." *New York Times,* 16 January, A-1.

Schmid, Alex P. 1983. *Political Terrorism: A Research Guide to Concepts, Theories, Data Bases and Literature.* Amsterdam: Transaction Books.

Schmid, Alex P., and Albert J. Jongman. 1988. *Political Terrorism: A New Guide to Actors, Authors, Concepts, Data Bases, Theories and Literature.* Amsterdam: North Holland Publishing.

Schmitt, Eric. 2000. "House Vote Averted on Turks' 'Genocide.'" *New York Times,* 20 October, A-15.

Sciolino, Elaine. 1988. "The Arm of American Law Turns Out to Be Not So Long." *New York Times,* 3 July, Section IV, 3.

———. 1995. "A Failed Plot to Overthrow Hussein is Reported in Iraq." *New York Times,* 14 March, A-6.

Seale, Patrick. 1992. *Abu Nidal: A Gun for Hire.* London: Hutchinson.

Segaller, Stephen. 1987. *Invisible Armies; Terrorism into the 1990's.* Orlando, Fla.: Harcourt Brace Jovanovich.

Seigel, Judy, and Raine Marcus. 1994. "Right wing arsonists suspected of destroying Bazek facility." *Jerusalem Post,* 19 October, 3.

Sela, Michal. 1989. "Sicarii threaten 'anyone who meet with PLO.'" *Jerusalem Post,* 31 March.

———.1989. "Sicarri intimidate women." *Jerusalem Post,* 12 April.

———. 1989. "Defense Ministry outlaws Islamic Movement Hamas." *Jerusalem Post,* 29 September.

Selth, Andrew. 1988. *Against Every Human Law: The Terrorist Threat to Diplomacy.* Rushcutters Bay, Australia: Australian National University Press.

Seriphas, Matthew. 1990. "Hamas Founder Freed from jail." *Jerusalem Post,* 6 September.

al-Shafi'i, Muhammad. 1998. Foreign Broadcast Information Service. (Internet). "Egypt: Egyptian 'Vanguards' Urge 'World Islamic Front' To Expand." ("Egyptian 'Armed Vanguards of Conquest' Calls on 'Islamic Front' To Expand Membership") *FBIS-TOT-98-057*; Publish Date: 02/26/1998; City source: London Al-Sharq al-Awsat; Document Id: 0ep96zh024dnek.

———. 1999. Foreign Broadcast Information Service. (Internet). "Islamists' Arrest Linked to US 'Onslaught'." *FBIS-NES-1999-0713*; Publish Date: 07/13/1999; City source: London Al-Sharq al-Awsat; Document Id: 0fewva801k4mdl.

———. 1999. Foreign Broadcast Information Service. (Internet). "Egyptian 'Fundamentalist' on Asylum." *FBIS-NES-1999-1013*; Publish Date: 10/12/1999; City source: London Al-Sharq al-Awsat; Document Id: 0fjm71602p6vh6.

Shapiro, Haim. 1995. "Bethlehem celebrates as PA takes control." *Jerusalem Post,* 22 December, 1, 22.

———. 1996. "'Religious fervor isn't main motivation of bombers.'" *Jerusalem Post,* 20 March, 3.

Sharaf-al-Din, Khalid. 1999. Foreign Broadcast Information Service. (Internet). "More on Islamic Jihad Trials." *FBIS-NES-1999-0309*; Publish Date: 03/07/1999; City source: London Al-Sharq al-Awsat; Document Id: 0f8egge03tp8yr.

Shenon, Philip. 1987. "US Might Seek Consecutive terms in Hijacking." *New York Times,* 20 January, A-7.

———. 1996. "US to Transfer Most of Its Force in Saudi Arabia." *New York Times,* 18 July.

———. 1998. "Now, a Push To Shore Up Ramparts At Embassies." *New York Times,* 10 August, A-6.

Shimko, Keith L. 1991. *Images and Arms Control: Perceptions of the Soviet Union in the Reagan Administration.* Ann Arbor: University of Michigan Press.

Shultz, Richard. 1978. "Conceptualizing Political Terrorism: A Typology." *Journal of International Affairs* 32 (1): 7-15.

Shultz, Richard H. 1986. "Can Democratic Governments Use Military Force in the War Against Terrorism?" *World Affairs* 148 (4): 205-215.

Silber, Laura, and Allan Little. 1997. *Yugoslavia: Death of a Nation.* New York: Penguin Books.

Silke, Andrew. 2001. "Chasing Ghosts: Offender Profiling and Terrorism." In *Sex and Violence: The Psychology of Crime and Role Assessment,* eds. D. Farrington, C. Hollin, and M. McMurran. London: Harwood.

Simpson, Howard R. 1982. "Organizing for Counter-Terrorism." *Strategic Review* 10 (1): 28-33.

Sirkin, R. Mark. 1999. *Statistics for the Social Sciences*. 2nd ed. Thousand Oaks, Calif.: Sage.

Sisk, Timothy D. 1996. *Power Sharing and International Mediation in Ethnic Conflicts*. Washington, D.C.: Institute of Peace Press.

Skendi, Stavro. 1982. "The *Millet* System and its Contribution to the Blurring of Orthodox National Identity in Albania." In *The Central Lands*. Vol. 1 of *Christians and Jews in the Ottoman Empire: The Functioning of a Plural Society*, eds. Benjamin Braude and Bernard Lewis. New York: Holmes & Meier.

Sklar, Richard L. "The Ordeal of Chief Awolowo." In *Politics in Africa*, ed. Gwendolen M. Carter. New York: Harcourt, Brace & World.

Skocpol, Theda. 1979. *States and Social Revolutions: A Comparative Analysis of France, Russia and China*. New York: Cambridge University Press.

Slavin, Barbara. 1999. (Internet). "U.S. Deals With a New Facet of Terrorism." *USA Today* 4 August. (http://ebird.dtic.mil/Aug1999/e19990804deals.htm).

Smart, Jan. 1987. "International Terrorism." *Behind the Headlines* 44 (3): 1-19.

Smith, Brent. 1994. *Terrorism in America: Pipe Bombs and Pipe Dreams*. Albany: State University of New York Press.

Smith, Charles D. 1996. *Palestine and the Arab-Israeli Conflict*. 3rd ed. New York: St. Martin's Press.

Smooha, Sammy. 1978. *Israel: Pluralism and Conflict*. Berkeley: University of California Press.

Snyder, Jack. 1996. "Military Force and Regional Order." In *Coping with Conflict after the Cold War*, eds. Edward A. Kolodziej and Roger E. Kanet. Baltimore, Md.: Johns Hopkins University Press.

Sobel, Lester A. 1975. *Political Terrorism*. New York: Facts on File.

Sonbol, Amira El-Azhary. 1988. "Egypt." In *The Politics of Islamic Revivalism Diversity and Unity*, ed. Shireen T. Hunter. Bloomington: Indiana University Press.

Spencer, Claire. 1996. "The Roots and Future of Islamism in Algeria." In *Islamic Fundamentalism*, eds. Abdel Salam Sidahmed and Anoushiravan Ehteshami. Boulder, Colo.: Westview Press.

Sprinzak, Ehud. 1988. "From Messianic Pioneering to Vigilante Terrorism: The Case of the Gush Emunim Underground." In *Inside Terrorist Organizations*, ed. David C. Rapaport. New York: Columbia University Press.

———. 1991. *The Ascendance of Israel's Radical Right*. New York: Oxford University Press.

———. 1999. *Brother Against Brother: Violence and Extremism in Israeli Politics from Altalena to the Rabin Assassination*. New York: Free Press.

SPSS Base 10.0 User's Guide. 1999. Chicago: SPSS.

SPSS Interactive Graphics 10.0. 1999. Chicago: SPSS.

Starr, Harvey, and Benjamin Most. 1976. "The Substance and Study of Borders in International Relations Research." *International Studies Quarterly* 20 (4): 581-620.

———. 1983. "Contagion and Border Effects on Contemporary African Conflict." *Comparative Political Studies* 16 (1): 92-117.

———. 1985. "Patterns of Conflict: Quantitative Analysis and the Comparative Lessons of Third World Wars." In *Approaches and Case Studies.* Vol. 1 of *The Lessons of Recent Wars in the Third World,* eds. Robert E. Harkavy and Stephanie G. Neumann. Lexington, Mass.: D. C. Heath.

Stata Reference Manual Release 6. 1999. Vol. 4. College Station, Tex.: Stata Press.

Stein, Janice Gross. 1996. "Communications, Signaling, and Intelligence." In *Coping with Conflict after the Cold War,* eds. Edward A. Kolodziej and Roger Kanet. Baltimore, Md.: Johns Hopkins University Press.

Stephenson, T. E. 1954, "The Leader-Follower Relationship." *The Sociological Review* 7: 179-195.

Stogdill, Ralph M. 1974. *Handbook of Leadership: A Survey of Theory and Research.* New York: Free Press.

Stohl, Michael S. 1987. "Terrorism, States and State Terrorism: The Reagan Administration in the Middle East." *Arab Studies Quarterly* 9 (2): 162-172.

———. 1988. "States, Terrorism and State Terrorism: The Role of the Superpowers." In *Current Perspectives on International Terrorism,* eds. Robert O. Slater and Stohl. Basingstoke, England: Macmillan.

Stohl, Michael, and George A. Lopez. 1984. "Introduction." In *The State as Terrorist: The Dynamics of Governmental Repression and Violence.* Westport, Conn.: Greenwood Press.

Stone, Martin. 1997. *The Agony of Algeria.* New York: Columbia University Press.

Stout, David, and Elizabeth Olson. 1999. "U.S. Linking Jailed Couple to Terrorists from Algeria." *New York Times,* 24 December, A-8.

Strauss, Leo. 1964. *The City of Man.* Chicago: Rand McNally.

Struminski, Wladimir. 1987. "4 Americans also abducted in Beirut." *Jerusalem Post,* 22 January.

Taheri, Amir. 1987. *Holy Terror: Inside the World of Islamic Terrorism.* Bethesda, Md.: Adler & Adler.

———. 1994. "Iran Lacks 'Absolute Control' Over Foreign Cells Groups." ("Despite Financial Support and Ideological Sympathy, Iran Does not Exercise Absolute Control Over Extremist Organizations; Priorities of Both Parties Vary According to the Influence of Political Factors."), *JPRS-TOT-94-033-L,* Publish Date: 07/30/1994, City source: London AL-SHARQ AL-AWSAT, Document Id: 0di0j7f01swbgc.

———. 1997. "Despite Financial Support and Ideological Sympathy, Iran Does Not Exercise Absolute Control Over Extremist Organizations; Priorities of Both Parties May Vary According to the Influence of Political Factors." (internet), "Iran Lacks 'Absolute Control" Over Foreign Cells, Groups." *JPRS-TOT-94-033-L* Publish Date: 07/30/1994. City source: London Al-Sharq Al-Awsat, Document id: 0di0j7f01swbgc.

Terrorism Violence and Insurgency Journal. 1985. "A Chronology of Significant Attacks on Israel and Israeli Reprisals Operations." 5 (4): 26-31.

———. 1989. "TVI Report Profile: Al Fatah." 8 (3): 1-3.

———. 1989. "TVI Report Profile: Popular Front for the Liberation of Palestine (PFLP)." 8 (3): 9-11.

———. 1989. "TVI Report Profile: Popular Front for the Liberation of Palestine–General Command (PFLP-GC)." 8 (3): 13-14.

———. 1990. "TVI Report Profile: Hizbollah (Party of God)." 8 (3): 1-6.

Theen, Rolf, and Frank L. Wilson. 1986. *Comparative Politics: An Introduction to Six Countries.* Englewood Cliffs, N.J.: Prentice Hall.

———. 1992. *Comparative Politics: an Introduction to Seven Countries.* 2nd ed. Englewood Cliffs, N.J.: Prentice Hall.

———. 1996. *Comparative Politics: An Introduction to Seven Countries.* 3rd ed. Upper Saddle River, N.J.: Prentice Hall.

"The Israeli-Palestinian Interim Agreement on the West Bank and the Gaza Strip." *Jewish Virtual Library—A division of the American-Israeli Cooperative Enterprise.* (Internet.) Washington D.C. (September 28, 1995). (http://www.jsource.org/jsource/Peace/interim.html).

The Middle East and North Africa 2000. 46th ed. 1999. London: Europa Publications.

The Times Atlas of the World. 1999. 10th ed. New York: Times Books.

The University Atlas. 1983. 22nd ed. London: George Philip & Son.

Tibi, Bassam. 1993. *Conflict and War in the Middle East, 1967-91.* New York: St. Martin's Press.

Tilbury, Neil. 1992. *Israel—A Travel Survival Kit.* Hawthorn, Vic., Australia: Lonely Planet Publications.

Time. 2000. "Notebook Verbatim," 23 October, 23.

Times London. 1994. "Algerian hijackers surrender in Majorca," 14 November, 12.

———. 1997. "Algerian teachers murdered," 30 September, 13.

———. 1997. "Baby beheaded in Algerian massacre," 1 October, 11.

Tizghart, 'Uthman. 1999. (Internet.) "Report on History of Terrorism in Algeria." *FBIS-NES-1999-0627*, Publish Date: 06/20/1999, City source: London Al-Majallah, Document Id: 0felvz2048nxfq.

Toy, Eckard V. 1989. "Right Wing Extremism from the Ku Klux Klan to the Order, 1915-1988." In *Politics, Rebellion, Reform.* Vol. 2 of *Violence in*

America, ed. Ted Robert Gurr. Newbury Park, Calif.: Sage.

Trent, Darrell M. 1979. "A National Policy To Combat Terrorism." *Policy Review* 9: 41-54.

Tsur, Batsheva. 1998. "Court leaves shut Kach offshoot office." *Jerusalem Post,* 1 January. 3.

Turgay, Uner A. 1982. "Trade and Merchants in Nineteenth-Century Trabzon: Elements of Ethnic Conflict." In *The Central Lands.* Vol. 1 of *Christians and Jews in the Ottoman Empire: The Functioning of a Plural Society,* eds. Benjamin Braude and Bernard Lewis. New York: Holmes & Meier.

Turki, Fawaz 1974. *The Disinherited: Journal of a Palestinian Exile with an Epilogue.* New York: Monthly Review Press.

United Nations. 1945. Charter of the United Nations, 24 October. T.S. no. 993, 59 Stat 1031.

———. 1945. Statute of the International Court of Justice, 24 October. T.S. no. 993, 59 Stat 1031.

———. 1945. Agreement for the Prosecution and Punishment of the Major War Criminals of the European Axis Powers and Charter of the International Military Tribunal, 8 August. 59 Stat. 1544, 82 U.N.T.S. 279.

———. 1950. Convention for the Amelioration of the Condition of the Wounded and Sick in Armed Forces in the Field, 21 October. T.I.A.S. no. 3362, 75 U.N.T.S. 31.

———. 1950. Convention for the Amelioration of the Condition of the Wounded and Sick and Shipwrecked Members of Armed Forces at Sea, 21 October T.I.A.S. no. 3363, 75 U.N.T.S. 85.

———. 1950. Convention Relative to the Treatment of Prisoners of War, 21 October. T.I.A.S. no. 3364, 75 U.N.T.S. 135.

———. 1950. Convention Relative to the Protection of Civilian Persons in Time of War, 21 October. T.I.A.S. no. 3363, 75 U.N.T.S. 287.

———. 1951. Convention on the Prevention and Punishment of the Crime of Genocide, 12 January 78 U.N.T.S. 277.

———. 1963. Convention on Offenses and Certain Other Acts Committed on Board Aircraft, 14 September. T.I.A.S. no. 6768, 704 U.N.T.S. 219.

———. 1965. Declaration on the Inadmissibility of Intervention in the Domestic Affairs of the States and the Protection of Their Independence and Sovereignty, 21 December. UN G.A. Res. 2131 (XX).

———. 1969. International Convention on the Elimination of All Forms of Racial Discrimination, 4 January. 660 U.N.T.S. 195.

———. 1970. Procedure for Dealing with Communications Relating to Violations of Human Rights and Fundamental Freedoms, 27 May. UN Doc. E/4832/Add. 1 (1970).

———. 1971. Convention for the Suppression of Unlawful Seizure of Aircraft, 14 October. T.I.A.S. 7192, 860 U.N.T.S. 105.

——. 1973. Convention for the Suppression of Unlawful Acts Against the Safety of Civil Aviation, 26 January. T.I.A.S. 7570, 1971 UN JURID Y.B. 143.

——. 1974. Universal Declaration on the Eradication of Hunger and Malnutrition, 16 November. UN Doc. E/Conf. 65/20, Chap. 4 (1974).

——. 1974. Resolution on the Definition of Aggression, 14 December. U.N.G.A. Res. 3314 (XXIX), UN Doc. A/9631 (1975).

——. 1976. International Convention on the Suppression and Punishment of the Crime of "Apartheid," 18 July U.N.G.A. Res. 3068 (XXVIII), UN Doc. A/9030 (1974).

——. 1977. Convention on the Prevention and Punishment of Crimes Against Internationally Protected Persons, Including Diplomatic Agents, 20 February. T.I.A.S. no. 8532.

——. 1978. Protocol Additional to the Geneva Conventions of 12 August 1949 and Relating to the Protection of Victims of International Armed Conflicts, 7 December. 1977 U.N. J.U.R.I.D. Y.B. 95.

——. 1978. Protocol Additional to the Geneva Conventions of 12 August 1949, and Relating to the Protection of Victims of Non-International Armed Conflicts, 7 December. 1977 U.N. J.U.R.I.D. 135.

——. 1978. Resolution on Disappeared Persons, 20 December. U.N.G.A. Res. 33/173, UN Doc. A/33/509 (1978).

——. 1980. Vienna Convention on Laws of Treaties, 27 January. UN Doc. A/CONF.39/27 at 289 (1969), 1155 U.N.T.S. 331.

——. 1981. Declaration on the Elimination of All Forms of Intolerance and of Discrimination Based on Religion or Belief, 25 November.

——. 1983. International Convention Against the Taking of Hostages, 4 June. U.N.G.A. Res. 34/146 (XXXIV), UN Doc. A/34/786 (1979).

——. 1985. Resolution on Measures to Prevent International Terrorism, 9 December. U.N.G.A. Res. 40/61, UN Doc. A/40/1003 (1985).

——. 1985. Security Council Resolution Condemning Hostage Taking, 18 December, U.N.S.C., Res. 579, UN Doc. S/Res/579 (1985).

——. 1987. Convention Against Torture and Other Cruel Inhuman or Degrading treatment or Punishment, 26 June. U.N.G.A. Res. 39/46 Annex, UN Doc. E/CN.4/1984/72.

——. 1990. Convention on the Rights of the Child, 26 January. U.N.G.A. Res. 25 (XLIV), UN Doc. A/Res/44/25 (1989).

United States. 1998. "Memorandum Report 98-CG-014, Survey of US Information Agency, Freedom Support Act Funding to the New Independent States," Office of Audits, June, 1-5.

United States Congress. 1991. Senate Governmental Affairs Committee *Terrorism After the Gulf War*. 102 Cong., 15 July. C-SPAN video #91-07-16-02-2.

U.S. Department of Defense. 1988. *Terrorist Group Profiles*. Washington, D.C.: GPO.

——. "Responding to Terrorism Part II Pursuing Defense Initiatives." Washington, D.C., 76-79.

U.S. Department of State. 1910. Convention (No. IV) Respecting the Laws and Customs of War on Land, with Annex of Regulations, 26 January TS no. 539.

——. 1972. Treaty between the United States of America and the Union of Soviet Socialist Republics on the Limitation of Anti-Ballistic Missile Systems. TIAS No. 7503. Reprinted in 11 I.L.M. 784 (1972).

——. 1974. Antihijacking Act of 1974. 49 USCA 1301, 1472, 1514 (Supp. 1989).

——. 1994. (Internet). *Patterns of Global Terrorism 1993* (Publication 10136). Office of the Coordinator for Counterterrorism. Released April 1994.

——. 1995. (Internet). *Patterns of Global Terrorism 1994*. Office of the Coordinator of Terrorism.

——. 1995. (Internet). "Algeria." *Patterns of Global Terrorism*, 1996, (http://www.state.gov/www/global/terrorism/1996Report/middle.html), 2.

——. 1996. (Internet). *1995 Patterns of Global Terrorism*. Office of the Coordinator for Counterterrorism, Release date: April 1996, (gopher://dosfan.lib.uic.edu:70/00ftp%ADO . . . 0Global%20Terrorism%3A1995%20PGT%20Report).

——. 1997 (Internet). "Jihad Group." *Patterns of Global Terrorism, 1998*. April. (http://web.nps.navy.mil/ ~ library/tgp/jihad.htm).

——. 1997. (Internet). "Middle East Overview." *Patterns of Global Terrorism*. (http://www.state.gov/www/global terrorism/1997Report/mideast.html).

——. 1998 (internet). "Middle East Overview." *Patterns of Global Terrorism: 1998*. (http://www.state.gov/www/global/terrorism/1998Report/mideast.html).

——. 1998. (Internet). "Revolutionary People's Liberation Party/Front (DHKP/C). "*Patterns of Global Terrorism, 1998*. Dudley Knox Library, Terrorist Group Profiles, Naval Postgraduate School (http://web.nps.navy.mil/ ~ library/tgp/devrimi.htm), April 1999.

——. 1999. (Internet). "Abu Nidal Organization." *Patterns of Global Terrorism, 1998*, Terrorist Group Profiles, Dudley Knox Library, Naval Postgraduate School, (http://web.nps.navy.mil/ ~ library tgp/abu.htm).

——. 1999. (Internet). "Algerian Terrorism." *Patterns of Global Terrorism Publication 10321*. (http://web.nps.navy.mil/ ~ library/tgp/algerian.htm).

——. 1999. (Internet). "Armenian Secret Army for the Liberation of Armenia (ASALA)." *Patterns of Global Terrorism Publication 10321*. Terrorist Group Profiles, Dudley Knox Library, Naval Postgraduate School (http://web.nps.navy.mil/ ~ library/tgp/armenian.htm).

———. 1999. (Internet). "Background Information on Foreign Terrorist Organizations: Released by the Office of Counterterrorism, October 8, 1999." (http//www/state.gov/www/global/terrorism/fto_info_1999.html).

———. 1999. (Internet). "Al-Fatah." *Patterns of Global Terrorism Publication 10321*. Terrorist Group Profiles, Dudley Knox Library, Naval Postgraduate School, (http://web.nps.navy.mil/~library/tgp/alfatah.htm).

———. 1999. (Internet). "Force 17." *Patterns of Global Terrorism Publication 10321*. Terrorist Group Profiles, Dudley Knox Library, Naval Postgraduate School, (http://web.nps.navy.mil/~library/tgp/force17.htm).

———. 1999. (Internet). "Hizballah (Party of God)." *Patterns of Global Terrorism, 1998*. Terrorist Group Profiles, Dudley Knox Library, Naval Postgraduate School, (http://web.nps.navy.mil/~library/tgp/hizbalah.htm). April, 1999.

———. 1999. (Internet). "Kach and Kahane Chai." *Patterns of Global Terrorism, 1998*. Terrorist Group Profiles, Dudley Knox Library, Naval Postgraduate School, (http://web.nps.navy.mil/~library/tgp/kach.htm).

———. 1999. (Internet). "Jihad Group." *Patterns of Global Terrorism, 1998*. Terrorist Group Profiles, Dudley Knox Library, Naval Postgraduate School, (http://web.nps.navy.mil/~library/tgp/jihad.htm).

———. 1999. (Internet). "al-Jihad a.k.a. Egyptian al-Jihad, New Jihad, Egyptian Islamic Jihad, Jihad Group." *10/8/99: Foreign Policy Terrorist Organizations*. (http://www.state.gov/www/global/terrorism/fto_info_1999.html).

———. 1999. (Internet). "Kurdistan Workers Party (PKK)." *Patterns of Global Terrorism, 1998,* Terrorist Group Profiles, Dudley Knox Library, Naval Postgraduate School, (http://web.nps.navy.mil/~library tgp/kurds.htm). April.

———. 1999. (Internet). "Middle East Overview." *Patterns of Global Terrorism 1999*. (http://www.state.gov/www/global/terrorism/1999report/mideast.html).

———. 1999. (Internet). "Palestine Islamic Jihad-Shaqaqi Faction a.k.a. PIJ-Shaqaqi Faction, PIJ-Shallah Faction, Palestinian Islamic Jihad (PIJ), Islamic Jihad of Palestine, Islamic Jihad in Palestine, Abu Ghunaym Squad of the Hizballah Bayt Al-Maqdis." *10/9/99 Foreign Terrorist Organizations*. (http://www.state.gov/www/global/terrorism/fto_info_1999.html).

———. 1999. (Internet). "Palestinian Islamic Jihad (PIJ)." *Patterns of Global Terrorism, 1998*. Terrorist Group Profiles, Dudley Knox Library, Naval Postgraduate School, (http://web.nps.navy.mil/~library/tgp/pij.htm).April 1999.

———. 1999. (Internet). "Palestine Liberation Organization." *Patterns of Global Terrorism Publication 10321*. Terrorist Group Profiles, Dudley Knox Library, Naval Postgraduate School, (http://web.nps.navy.mil/~library/tgp/plo.htm).

———. 1999. (Internet). "Popular Front for the Liberation of Palestine-Special Command (PFLP-SC)." *Terrorist Group Profiles*, Dudley Knox Library, Naval Postgraduate School, (http://web.nps.navy.mil/~library/tgp/pflpsc.htm).

———. 1999. (Internet). "Al-Qaida." *Patterns of Global Terrorism, 1998.* Terrorist Group Profiles, Dudley Knox Library, Naval Postgraduate School, (http://web.nps.navy.mil/~library/tgp/qaida.htm), April.

———. 2000. (Internet). "Abu Nidal Organization." *Patterns of Global Terrorism, 1999,* Terrorist Group Profiles, Dudley Knox Library, Naval Postgraduate School, (http://web. nps.navy.mil/~library/tgp/abu.htm), April.

———. 2000 (Internet). "Armed Islamic Group (GIA)." *Patterns of Global Terrorism, 1999,* Terrorist Group Profiles, Dudley Knox Library, Naval Postgraduate School, (http://web.nps.navy.mil/~library/tgp/gia.htm)

———. 2000. (Internet). "HAMAS (Islamic Resistance Movement)." *Patterns of Global Terrorism, 1999.* Terrorist Group Profiles, Dudley Knox Library, Naval Postgraduate School, (http://web.nps.navy.mil/~library/tgp/hamas.htm), April.

———. 2000. (Internet). "Hizballah (Party of God)." *Patterns of Global Terrorism.* Terrorist Group Profiles, Dudley Knox Library, Naval Postgraduate School, (http://web.nps.navy.mil/~library/tgp/hizbalah.htm).

———. 2000. (Internet). "al-Jihad." *Patterns of Global Terrorism, 1999.* Terrorist Group Profiles, Dudley Know Library, Naval Postgraduate School, (http://web.nps.navy.mil/~libary/tgp/jihad.htm), April.

———. 2000. (Internet). "Mujahedin-e Khalq Organization (MEK or MKO)." *Patterns of Global Terrorism, 1999.* Terrorist Group Profiles, Dudley Knox Library, Naval Postgraduate School, (http://web.nps.navy.mil/~library/tgp/mek.htm).

———. 2000. (Internet). "Popular Front for the Liberation of Palestine (PFLP)." *Patterns of Global Terrorism, 1999.* Dudley Knox Library, Naval Postgraduate School, (http://web.nps.navy.mil/~library/tgp/pflp.htm), April.

———. 2000. (Internet). "Popular Front for the Liberation of Palestine-General Command (PFLP-GC)." *Patterns of Global Terrorism, 1999.* Terrorist Group Profiles, Dudley Knox Library, Naval Postgraduate School, (http://web.nps.navy.mil/~library/tgp/pflpgc.htm), April.

———. 2000. (Internet). "Al-Qaida." *Patterns of Global Terrorism 1999.* April. Terrorist Group Profiles, Dudley Knox Library, Naval Postgraduate School, (http://web.nps.navy.mil/~library/tgp/qaida.htm).

———. 2000. (Internet). "Revolutionary People's Liberation Party/Front (DHKP/C)." *Patterns of Global Terrorism, 1999,* Terrorist Group Profiles,

Dudley Knox Library, Naval Postgraduate School, (http://web.nps.na-vy.mil/~library/tgp/devrimi.htm), April.

———. 2001. (Internet) "The Harakat ul-Mujahidin." *Patterns of Global Terrorism, 2000,* Terrorist Group Profiles, Dudley Knox Library, Naval Postgraduate School, (http://web.nps.navy.mil/~libray/tgp/hua/htm).

U.S. Directorate of Intelligence. 1992. *Palestinian Organizations.* LDA 92-12531. Washington, D.C.: Central Intelligence Agency.

U.S. National Security Council. 1999. "Protecting America's Cyberspace Version 1.0 of the National Plan, Richard A. Clarke, National Coordinator for Security, Infrastructure Protection and Counter-Terrorism, National Security Council, July 22, 1999, CIAO.0206–June," 1-14.

Vandewalle, Dirk. 1997. "Islam in Algeria: Religion, Culture, and Opposition in a Rentier State." In *Political Islam Revolution, Radicalism or Reform,* ed. John L. Esposito. Boulder, Colo.: Lynne Rienner.

Voll, John O. 1991. "Fundamentalism in the Sunni Arab World: Egypt and the Sudan." In *Fundamentalisms Observed,* eds. Martin E. Marty and R. Scott Appleby. Chicago: University of Chicago Press.

von der Mehden, Fred R. 1973. *Comparative Political Violence.* Englewood Cliffs, N.J.: Prentice Hall.

von Pufendorf, Samuel. 1964. *De Officio Hominis et Civis Juxta Legem Naturalem Libri Duo,* ed. James Brown Scott. New York: Oceana Publications.

Walker, Christopher. 1994. "Mubarak warns of Islamic threat to Europe." *Times* (London), 18 November, 11.

———. 1997. "Israel frees ailing founder of Hamas." *Times* (London), 2 October, 17.

———. 1998. "Netanyahu defies assassination alert." *Times* (London), 29 October, 16

———. 1998. "Muslim extremists threaten Arafat." *Times* (London), 2 November, 12.

Walker, Christopher, and Ben Macintyre. 1997. "Netanyahu defeats hardliners to seal withdrawal pact." *Times* (London), 16 January, 11.

Wallerstein, Immanuel M. 1974. *The Modern World System: Capitalist Agriculture and the Origin of the European World Economy in the Sixteenth Century.* New York: Academic Press.

Walsh, Anthony. 1987. "Teaching Understanding and Interpretation of Logit Regression." *Teaching Sociology* 15 (2): 178-183.

Waltz, Kenneth N. 1959. *Man, the State and War: a Theoretical Analysis.* New York: Columbia University Press.

Wardlaw, Grant. 1982. *Political Terrorism: Theory, Tactics, and Countermeasures.* Cambridge, England: Cambridge University Press.

———. 1986. "Policy Dilemmas in Responding to International Terrorism." *The Australian Quarterly* 58 (3): 278-285.

———. 1988. "State Response to International Terrorism: Some Cautionary Comments." In *Current Perspectives on International Terrorism*, eds. Robert O. Slater and Michael Stohl. Basingstoke, England: Macmillan.

Washington Post. 1999. (Internet.) "French Link Algerian to Islamic Radicals." 22 December. (wysiwyg://15/http://www.washington . . . ecials/inthenews/terror/index.html).

Waugh, William L. 1982. *International Terrorism: How Nations Respond to Terrorists.* Salisbury, N.C.: Documentary Publications.

Webster's New Collegiate Dictionary. 1977. Springfield, Mass.: G. R. C. Merriam.

Wege, Carl Anthony. 1994. "Hizbollah Organization." *Studies in Conflict and Terrorism* 17: 151-164.

Weimann, Gabriel, and Conrad Winn. 1994. *The Theater of Terror: Mass Media and International Terrorism.* White Plains, N.Y.: Longman.

Weinberg, Leonard, and William Lee Eubank. 1988. "Neo-Fascist and Far Left Terrorist in Italy: Some Biographical Observations." *British Journal of Political Science* 18 (4): 531-553.

Weisburd, David. 1989. *Jewish Settler Violence: Deviance as Social Reaction.* University Park: Pennsylvania State University Press.

Weston, Burns H., Richard A. Falk, and Anthony D'Amato. 1980. *International Law and World Order: A Problem-Oriented Coursebook.* St. Paul, Minn.: West Publishing.

Weston, Burns H., Richard A. Falk, and Anthony D'Amato, eds. 1990. *Basic Documents in International Law and World Order.* St. Paul, Minn.: West Publishing.

White, Jonathan Randall. 1998. *Terrorism: An Introduction.* 2nd 3d. Belmont, Calif.: Wadsworth.

White, Louis G. 1990. *Political Analysis: Technique and Practice.* 2nd ed. Pacific Grove, Calif.: Brooks/Cole Publishing.

Williams, William A. 1972. *The Tragedy of American Diplomacy.* New York: W. W. Norton.

Wilkinson, Paul. 1974. *Political Terrorism.* New York: John Wiley & Sons.

———. 1979. "Terrorist Movements." In *Terrorism: Theory and Practice*, eds. Yonah Alexander, David Carlton, and Paul Wilkinson. Boulder, Colo.: Westview.

———. 1984. "State-Sponsored International Terrorism: the Problems of Response." *The World Today* 40 (7): 292-298.

———. 1986. *Terrorism and the Liberal State.* 2nd rev. ed. London: Macmillan.

Willis, Michael. 1996. *The Islamist Challenge in Algeria: A Political History.* Berkshire, England: Ithaca Press.

Wines, Michael. 2001. "Aligning with the US: One Goal for Moscow is Ending the Region's Islamic Militance." *New York Times,* 25 September, A-1.

———. 2001. "An Act of Terror Reshapes The Globe." *New York Times,* 30 September, section 4, 1, 2.

Winslow, Charles. 1996. *Lebanon: War and Politics in a Fragmented Society.* New York: Routledge.

Wonnacott, Thomas H., and Ronald J. Wonnacott. 1990. *Introductory Statistics for Business and Economics.* 4th ed. New York: John Wiley and Sons.

Yaari, Ehud. 1970. *Strike Terror: The Story of Fatah.* New York: Sabra Books.

———. 1993. "Middle East Peace Talks." Speech at Washington Institute for Near East Studies, Washington D.C., C-SPAN videocassette no. 93-02-10-18-2.

Yanai, Nathan. 1994. "Israel." In *Political Parties of the Middle East and North Africa,* ed. Frank Tachau. Westport, Conn.: Greenwood Press.

Yegen, Mesut. 1996. "The Turkish State Discourse and the Exclusion of Kurdish Identity." *Middle Eastern Studies* 32 (2): 216-229.

Yerushalmi, Mordechai. 1987. "A 'Control Code' Model of Terrorism." In *International Terrorism: The Domestic Response,* eds. Richard H. Ward and Harold E. Smith. Chicago: The University of Illinois at Chicago.

Yudelman, Michal. 1984. "Lifta suspect nabbed at cafe in Netanya." *Jerusalem Post,* 25 June.

Zagaris, Bruce. 1993. "Championing Moralism and the Rule of Law in Combating International Terrorism and Drug Trafficking." *Criminal Law Forum* 4 (1): 189.

Zanini, Michele. 1999. "Middle Eastern Terrorism and Netwar." *Studies in Conflict & Terrorism* 22: 247-256.

Zariski, Raphael. 1989. "Ethnic Extremism among Ethnoterritorial Minorities in Western Europe: Dimensions, Causes and Institutional Responses." *Comparative Politics* 21 (3): 253-272.

Zartman, I. William. 1992. "The Negotiation Process in the Middle East." In *The Arab-Israeli Search For Peace,* ed. Steven L. Spiegel. Boulder, Colo.: Lynne Rienner.

———. 1996. "Bargaining and Conflict Resolution." In *Coping with Conflict after the Cold War,* eds. Edward A. Kolodziej and Roger E. Kanet. Baltimore, Md.: Johns Hopkins University Press.

Zeleney, Leslie Day. 1939. "Characteristics of Group Leaders." *Sociology and Social Research* 24: 140-149.

Zinnes, Dina A. 1976. "The Problem of Cumulation." In *Search of Global Patterns,* ed. James Rosenau. New York: Free Press.

———. 1976. *Contemporary Research in International Relations: A Perspective and a Critical Appraisal.* New York: Free Press.

Zoubir, Yahia H. 1993. "The Painful Transition from Authoritarianism in Algeria." *Arab Studies Quarterly* 15 (3): 83-110.

Author Index

Subject Index

About the Author

Dr. Richard J. Chasdi is a visiting assistant professor in the department of political science at the College of Wooster. He has been a news consultant on Middle East terrorism and Middle East political affairs for several television networks in the greater Detroit metropolitan area. He was born in Boston, Massachusetts, and received a B.A. in Politics from Brandeis University in 1981 and an M.A. in Political Science from Boston College in 1985. Dr. Chasdi received his Ph.D. in Political Science from Purdue University in 1995. His first book, *Serenade of Suffering: A Portrait of Middle East Terrorism, 1968–1993,* received *Choice* magazine's Outstanding Academic Title Award for 2000. He is also a coauthor of an international relations textbook teaching manual and has published his articles, "Terrorism: Stratagems for Remediation from an International Law Perspective," in *Shofar: An Interdisciplinary Journal of Jewish Studies,* and "Middle East Terrorism 1968-1993: An Empirical Analysis of Terrorist Group-Type Behavior" in the *Journal of Conflict Studies.*